OXI

THE O)

Gene. ..cns

The Oxford Shakespeare offers new and authoritative editions of Shakespeare's plays in which the early printings have been scrupulously re-examined and interpreted. An introductory essay provides all relevant background information together with an appraisal of critical views and of the play's effects in performance. The detailed commentaries pay particular attention to language and staging. Reprints of sources, music for songs, genealogical tables, maps, etc. are included where necessary; many of the volumes are illustrated, and all contain an index.

RANDALL MARTIN, the editor of *Henry VI, Part Three* in the Oxford Shakespeare, is Associate Professor of English at the University of New Brunswick.

THE OXFORD SHAKESPEARE

Currently available in paperback

The rest of the plays and poems are forthcoming

OXFORD WORLD'S CLASSICS

WILLIAM SHAKESPEARE

Henry VI, Part Three

Edited by
RANDALL MARTIN

OXFORD
UNIVERSITY PRESS

Great Clarendon Street, Oxford OX2 6DP

Oxford University Press is a department of the University of Oxford.
It furthers the University's objective of excellence in research, scholarship,
and education by publishing worldwide in

Oxford New York

Athens Auckland Bangkok Bogotá Buenos Aires Cape Town
Chennai Dar es Salaam Delhi Florence Hong Kong Istanbul Karachi
Kolkata Kuala Lumpur Madrid Melbourne Mexico City Mumbai Nairobi
Paris São Paulo Shanghai Singapore Taipei Tokyo Toronto Warsaw

with associated companies in Berlin Ibadan

Oxford is a registered trade mark of Oxford University Press
in the UK and in certain other countries

Published in the United States
by Oxford University Press Inc., New York

British Library Cataloguing in Publication Data

Data available

Library of Congress Cataloging in Publication Data
Shakespeare, William, 1564–1616.
Henry VI. Part Three / edited by Randall Martin.
p. cm.—(The Oxford Shakespeare)
Includes index.
1. Henry VI, King of England, 1421–1471—Drama. 2. Great Britain—
History—Henry VI, 1422–1461—Drama. I. Title: Henry the Sixth, Part Three.
II. Martin, Randall. III. Title.
PR2816.A2M37 2001 822.3′3—dc21 2001021558
ISBN 0–19–812365–5 (hbk.)
ISBN 0–19–283141–0 (pbk.)

1 3 5 7 9 10 8 6 4 2

Typeset in Photina MT
by Best-set Typesetter Ltd., Hong Kong
Printed in Spain by
Book Print S.L., Barcelona

ACKNOWLEDGEMENTS

LIKE any Shakespeare edition, this one has depended at many points on the research of recent scholars, even when it sometimes disagrees with their conclusions: the work of Andrew S. Cairncross, Michael Hattaway, and William Montgomery, editor of *Richard Duke of York* in the Oxford *Complete Works*, has informed my present task and made it considerably easier. Many colleagues have also liberally shared information on particular historical and theatrical matters: Edward Berry, David Bevington, Alan Dessen, Charles Edelman, Donna Hamilton, Robin Hamilton, Stuart Hampton-Reeves, S. J. Gunn, Russell Jackson, Katherine Duncan-Jones, Clarissa Hurley, Randall McLeod, M. J. Mills, Helen Ostovich, Patricia Parker, Peter Seary, Tiffany Stern, Steven Urkowitz, and Rachel Wifall.

I am indebted to the following people and institutions for aiding my research and granting me permission to consult their material: Kit Leary, Archivist of the Oregon Shakespeare Festival, Ashland; Niky Rathbone and the staff of the Shakespeare Library of the Birmingham Central Reference Library; the Bodleian Library; the British Library; Georgianna Ziegler and the librarians of the Folger Shakespeare Library; the Huntington Library; Sylvia Morris and the staff of Shakespeare Centre Library; the Robarts Library of the University of Toronto; the archives of the Washington Shakespeare Theatre; Andrew Kirk and the staff of the Theatre Museum, London; Jim Shaw and the Shakespeare Institute Library; and the University Library, Cambridge.

The Warden, Dr Jessica Rawson, and Fellows of Merton College awarded me a visiting research fellowship in 1999 which provided uninterrupted time for bringing the edition near to completion. The College's exceptionally generous hospitality also made for a memorable return to Oxford.

Research for this project began with the help of funding from the University of New Brunswick, and then was substantially supported by a three-year grant from the Social Sciences and Humanities Research Council of Canada.

I am very grateful to Linda McNutt for sharing her professional

theatre experience with me as we re-examined the casting and doubling requirements of the two original texts, the results of which
appear in Appendix C. My colleague John Ball read sections of the
introduction at an early stage and offered excellent suggestions.
Frances Whistler, the series editor at Oxford University Press, has
been steadily encouraging and helpful as the whole volume
approached completion. Kathleen Barnes patiently proof-read several sections and verified many details of preliminary drafts. Made-
line Bassnett prepared the index and proofread the entire volume
with a wonderfully discerning eye. Christine Buckley meticulously
copy-edited the typescript, offered enthusiastic research on local
and family histories, and saved me from several blunders. Any
which now remain are my responsibility. My office staff, Susan
Miller and Vera Zarowsky, helped with the production of several
drafts and have cheerfully assisted me from day to day.

I have especially benefited from stimulating exchanges with
Roger Warren, Oxford Shakespeare editor of *Henry VI Part Two*,
who kindly took the time to read through my entire typescript and
offered excellent suggestions, particularly on textual problems and
stage productions. The General Editor of this series, Stanley Wells,
has likewise commented expertly on the whole edition, and wisely
guided my presentational choices throughout.

Elizabeth Archibald, Jonathan and Henrietta Freeman-Attwood,
Patricia Parker, and Peter and Betsy Newell have sustained
my work with their friendship and hospitality on several research
trips.

Finally, my edition is dedicated to Jill Levenson, who enabled this
journey to begin, and to Andrea Sella, who enabled the last stages
to be completed.

RM
15 April 2000
Fredericton, New Brunswick

CONTENTS

Contents

LIST OF ILLUSTRATIONS

INTRODUCTION

Rediscovery and reception

Henry VI, Part Three powerfully depicts a country torn apart by civil war. Unlike Shakespeare's other plays about war's stirring and terrible effects, there is no foreign enemy to demonize, no epic hero to inspire patriotic sacrifice, and little evidence of the human kinship that, paradoxically, war seems sometimes to breed more readily than peace. Instead a nation turns on itself in epidemic savagery, dissolving its own social foundations. While Shakespeare writes about the fifteenth-century English conflict known as the Wars of the Roses, he universalizes its key events—revenge, betrayal, battle, lamentation, and death—within largely abstract spaces, using ritualized gestures and formally heightened language. The result is a historical portrait that leaves modern players and spectators imaginative room to make connections with the shattering effects of civil wars in other periods. The twentieth century's appalling devotion to such activity partly explains why the play has been rediscovered in the theatre during the past fifty years. So too do postwar tastes for black humour and sardonic comedy, which Shakespeare gratifies abundantly amid the atrocities and suffering.

Gleeful brutality and social reproof are not the only reasons for *3 Henry VI*'s modern stage appeal, however. Four of the play's five acts contain scenes of great emotional intensity which never fail to move audiences: Margaret's harrowing torment of York, Henry's moving lament for the victims of civil war, Richard's bravura soliloquy revealing his murderous ambitions, and the doomed confrontation between Henry and Richard in the Tower. The first of these encounters brought Shakespeare swift and controversial recognition in his own day when a rival playwright, Robert Greene, parodied one of its lines in a bitter outburst.[1] All of them remain the play's most powerfully expressive scenes in modern stage productions.

---

[1] 'Tiger's heart wrapped in a player's hide.' Greene's allusion is discussed in the section on the play's dates, below, pp. 124–5.

Yet none of the main characters—which include Edward and Warwick as well as those just mentioned—dominates the play absolutely.[1] Though they remain meaningfully networked in series of emotional surges and retributive responses, Shakespeare distributes dramatic interest equitably among multiple figures and rhetorically charged high points in each of the play's five acts. This articulated structure brilliantly underpins his dynamic representation of civil war as the fracturing of unifying political authority and family bonds.

Unfortunately this design has also often proved to be a challenge or even impediment to directors and critics. Many have misjudged the play's lack of a dominant through-narrative as randomness, and responded to the perceived fault by refocusing primary attention on just one or two of its main characters and their stories. Alternatively, directors have chopped up and rewritten the play within larger sequences of the *Henry VI* trilogy and *Richard III*. Some of these adaptations have been highly popular and admirable. But almost invariably they have diminished Shakespeare's script, and reinforced a perception that the play *needs* to be revised to be made comprehensible. And so *3 Henry VI* has rarely been performed with a full sense of its imaginative range. On the few occasions when it has, such as Douglas Seale's 1952–3 Birmingham Repertory Theatre productions, which launched the play's modern stage life, or Katie Mitchell's 1994 Royal Shakespeare Company production, the play's dramatic power has been unquestionably vindicated.

Dispersal as interpretation: dramatic titles, stories, and action. It will be useful right away to gain a broad sense of Shakespeare's overall design by considering the play's various titles—original, acquired, and implied by adaptation and performance. These identify its interweaving storylines and main characters as multiple dramatic focal points. They also reveal evolving critical interest in, and stage approaches to, each personalized history within the greater dramatic narrative.

The first version of the play to appear was published in 1595 under the title *The True Tragedy of Richard Duke of York, and the*

[1] Despite the fact that Edward has the greatest number of speeches in the play, while Warwick has the largest number of lines.

Death of Good King Henry the Sixth, with the Whole Contention Between the Two Houses, Lancaster and York (hereafter *True Tragedy*). The 'Contention' refers to the play's opposing forces led by York and, nominally, by King Henry. It also alludes to *True Tragedy*'s predecessor, *The First Part of the Contention Betwixt the Two Famous Houses of York and Lancaster, with the Death of the Good Duke Humphrey*, published in 1594. *True Tragedy* is therefore the second part of a two-part play telling the story of the closing events of Henry VI's reign. The beginning of his reign is dramatized in *1 Henry VI*, not published until 1623, but written earlier, though probably *after* both *The First Part of the Contention* and *True Tragedy*.[1] In terms of epitomizing the play's action, *True Tragedy*'s full title gives priority to York's story over Henry's, even though York dies by the end of the first act, while Henry appears throughout the play and is killed only in the penultimate scene. The wider implications of this title, as well as other aspects of this early edition—a shorter and substantially different text of the play, traditionally believed to be a corrupt, memorially derived version of the play offered here—are complicated, and will be discussed fully in later sections on the original texts, their relationship, and their dates of composition (pp. 96–132). There I shall argue that *True Tragedy*, probably written in 1591, represents Shakespeare's first version of the play, though still in an imperfect reported text. But for now it is enough to notice the way this title divides attention between historical subjects, in dramatic actions that unfold asymmetrically.

By contrast, Shakespeare's later and considerably longer version of the play, probably written sometime between 1594 and 1596, was published with the title *The Third Part of Henry the Sixth, with the Death of the Duke of York*. It appeared in the Folio of 1623, the collected volume of plays issued seven years after Shakespeare's death. The present edition is based on this text, with this title.[2] Shakespeare's fellow actors positioned the play in its proper historical sequence after the first and second parts of *Henry VI*, and

---

[1] This continues to be a matter of scholarly debate, and is considered more fully below, pp. 123–9.

[2] And not *Richard Duke of York*, which the Oxford editors of *The Complete Works* gave to this version, believing it to be the title under which the play was originally staged, even though their edition was based on the Folio text which they assumed was written first. Throughout this edition, quotations and references to other Shakespeare plays are taken from the Oxford *Complete Works*.

before *Richard III*, whose events Part Three anticipates. This arrangement has encouraged scholars and directors to situate the play within a larger narrative covering the reign of Henry VI. In this context, Part Three brings Lancastrian rule to an end, while York's death secondarily marks the failure of his political ambitions, which he plotted and fomented in the previous two plays.

His sons keep those ambitions alive, however. While the Folio title reverses the dramatic priority of the play's chief political rivals, the continued focus on both families, and the wider context of the Folio's multi-part chronological sequence, open up further narrative combinations involving other figures and events. The situation of a disputed succession between two kings, Henry VI and Edward IV, each with plausible claims to the throne, would have had strong topical resonances for Elizabethan spectators. Edward inherits the Yorkist title after the death of his father, and finally triumphs in battle over the Lancastrians at the end of Act 5. Modern performances and adaptations have sometimes recognized his emerging reign by renaming the play *Edward IV* when it is performed in a four-play cycle which includes *Richard III*. This reorients the play's action forward as a Yorkist political narrative, overtaking the Lancastrian dominance of *1* and *2 Henry VI*. And in this context, another possibility emerges: the striking rise of Richard of Gloucester. His personal history erupts at the exact midpoint of the play (3.2.124 ff.), in Shakespeare's longest soliloquy. If attention becomes centred on him, as it often does because of the role's star reputation and popularity with audiences, then *3 Henry VI* may become a kind of induction to *Richard III*. This dramatic anticipation is intrinsically part of Shakespeare's original conception, and has been exploited by performers of *Richard III* going back to the eighteenth century, and more recently in film versions such as Laurence Olivier's in 1955. These productions have been unable to resist splicing in substantial passages and even whole scenes from *3 Henry VI*. While this borrowing may be useful for clarifying historical references early in *Richard III*, it has also suppressed the need to perform *3 Henry VI*, and implicitly suggested it is not stageable in its own right.

One of *3 Henry VI*'s other centres of dramatic interest for stage companies and spectators is the battles. On the page, the cryptic directions '*Alarums and Excursions*' are easily glossed over. Not so in the theatre, where these moments loom large for actors and directors. Presenting battles successfully requires dedicated resources of imagination, skill, energy, and rehearsal time. For audiences, they are integral to dramatic language in the same way as spoken dialogue and poetic imagery, and are inescapably part of the sensory and emotional experience of watching the play. The *Henry VI* plays owed their early popularity partly to memorable combat scenes. Elizabethan playgoers could appreciate a good stage battle because of their familiarity with military drills and live combat in the wartime conditions of the early 1590s, all of which directly influenced performances in the theatre. Though relatively few modern spectators possess personal experience of war and soldiery, most know that the kinetic energy and balletic design of a well-executed 'virtual' battle, enlivened with the sonic and visual possibilities of modern stage technology, can be exhilarating. *3 Henry VI* is Shakespeare's most demanding play in this regard, since it contains four battles spread over five acts. Invariably, the most successful stage productions take these seriously, and try to vary each one in inventive ways (for example, a haunting snowstorm during the Battle of Tewkesbury in Peter Hall and John Barton's 1963–4 *Wars of the Roses* and in Jane Howell's 1983 BBC production).[1]

On the other hand, audiences know that the dissatisfying rattle of a poorly staged battle invites ridicule. In Shakespeare's own day, Ben Jonson jeered at the mimetic gap that can open when 'three rusty swords, | . . . Fight over York and Lancaster's long jars'.[2] Unfortunately, Jonson was mocking not just the shortcomings of a particular performance, but Elizabethans' supposedly crude tastes for noisy spectacle in general. His attitudes, based on a neoclassicizing agenda and a personally ambivalent relationship with the theatre, have inspired a long history of patronizing assumptions about the *Henry VI* plays. For too long Part Three's martial action has been misjudged to be repetitive and empty, raising doubts about the play's very purpose and identity. The situation parallels attitudes taken towards *Titus Andronicus*, probably written

---

[1] In his review of the latter, Stanley Wells attributed part of its success to brilliantly staged battle scenes by Howell and her fight director, Malcolm Ranson, 'sometimes with slow motion to convey the passage of time, sometimes with economical but thrilling images of rows of drummers, pikesmen and archers in action' (*Times Literary Supplement*, 4 February 1983, p. 105).

[2] *Every Man in His Humour*, Prologue 9–11.

immediately after *3 Henry VI*, which until recently was derided for indulging primitive tastes for gory violence.

Literary critics have also often viewed the play's shifting dramatic focus and discrete lines of action as signs that Shakespeare was not yet fully in control of his source material or his craft. While recognizing his astonishing ambition, unprecedented since classical times, in choosing to dramatize over three or four plays a period in English history which even today historians find complex and sometimes baffling, they nonetheless regret Part Three's alleged lack of narrative and dramatic unity. Dealing with the play's confluence of residual and emergent narratives has often tempted stage adapters and critics to emphasize one or two at the expense of the others to simplify the play.

Productions during the past fifty years, and more stage-oriented critics, have successfully challenged these negative attitudes by treating the play's decentralized structure and battle representations not as artistic lapses, but as diversified opportunities for creative dramaturgy and searching interpretations. The introduction which follows will explore the critical and stage interests evoked by each of the personal histories of York, Henry, Richard, Edward, and Margaret, as they successively become the focus of attention over the course of the play. *3 Henry VI*'s equitable distribution of imaginatively engaging roles has proved to be highly attractive to modern acting companies. Its most memorable performances tend to be strong ensemble productions, particularly those in which Henry, traditionally regarded by pre-twentieth-century commentators as the weak link of both history and the play, is performed with robust intelligence and prophetic insight. The play's ensemble affinities partly explain why it was all but ignored on the English stage (though not in Germany) during the eighteenth and nineteenth centuries, when productions favoured star characters in big scenes. Familiarity with modern dramatic modes—expressionism, anti-naturalism, and Brechtian 'epic' theatre—have further shown companies how to explore, and audiences how to appreciate, the play's stylized actions and ritualized emotion. Finally, a series of outstanding performances in the context of entire staged sequences of the *Henry VI* plays has reclaimed the role of Queen Margaret as one of Shakespeare's great tragic heroines.

Henry VI and the Wars of the Roses. Since neither the play nor its history is well known, an outline of the events Shakespeare chose to dramatize may be helpful.

In Elizabethan historical memory, three reigns typified crises of royal authority leading to civil war: those of Richard II, Edward II, and Henry VI.[1] Shakespeare later dramatized the deposition of Richard II, just as Christopher Marlowe, Elizabeth Cary, and others wrote about the sufferings of Edward II. But Shakespeare seized first on the most cataclysmic of these reigns when he chose to write about Henry VI and the Wars of the Roses, in three plays between 1590 and 1592, or perhaps several years earlier.

Henry was nine months old when he succeeded to the throne in 1422 upon the premature death of his father Henry V, who had reconquered substantial areas of France before his decisive victory at Agincourt (1415). These events were part of the Hundred Years War, which continued during the early part of Henry VI's reign with France fighting under Joan of Arc to win back much of the territory it had lost.

In *1 Henry VI* Shakespeare intertwines this action abroad with fragmenting national unity during Henry's minority, as personal quarrels break out between the Protector, Humphrey Duke of Gloucester, and his political enemies. Shakespeare presents the country's essential problem as a lack of effective governing power, which leads to political factionalism, social breakdown, and ultimately civil war. Henry's problems increase with his impolitic marriage to Margaret of Anjou in 1445, which Shakespeare represents at the end of Part One and beginning of Part Two.

The young French princess brings no dowry with her, and the terms of her marriage require England to return more French provinces. Henry's aversion to rule, and (historically, but not in Shakespeare) his temporary mental illness, lead Margaret to govern on his behalf, which deepens English resentment towards her as a foreign woman meddling in English politics. Shakespeare also dramatizes other events that destabilize the country and

---

[1] Among many citations see, e.g., the widely read *Copy of A Letter, written by a Master of Art of Cambridge,* later known as *Leicester's Commonwealth* (1584). Tragically framed stories of these three kings also appear in the equally well known *Mirror for Magistrates,* discussed at several points below. Shakespeare wrote about Richard II in 1595, while Marlowe's *Edward II* (*c.*1592) is almost certainly indebted to *Henry VI,* Parts Two and Three.

undermine Lancastrian rule. A plot by Margaret, her lover the Duke of Suffolk, the Bishop of Winchester, and the Duke of Somerset deprives Humphrey of his Protectorship, the commonwealth of its defender, and leads to his murder. Henry reacts decisively by exiling Suffolk and imprisoning Somerset, but faces other threats from rebellions in Ireland and at home. Though these fail, they serve the ambitions of Richard Duke of York, who voices wide frustration at Henry's inept rule and openly challenges his right to the throne. His claim is based on descent from Lionel Duke of Clarence, third son of Edward III (1312–77), through his great-grandmother, and from Edward's fifth son, Edmund Duke of York. Henry was descended from Edward III's fourth son John of Gaunt, Duke of Lancaster, whose son Henry Bolingbroke had deposed Richard II (1367–1400) and was commonly blamed for his murder. Bolingbroke became Henry IV (1367–1413) and established Lancastrian political dominance, which continued under Henry V (1387–1422). Shakespeare symbolically invents the origins of Lancastrian and Yorkist rivalry in *1 Henry VI* 2.4, in which York emblematically plucks a white rose to represent his side in a trivial after-dinner dispute, while his Lancastrian enemy the Duke of Somerset chooses a red rose. The growing enmity and bitterness between the parties break out in open conflict at the end of *2 Henry VI*, when York publicly declares his claim to the throne and the first Battle of St Albans (1455) leads to the first Yorkist victory of the Wars of the Roses.

 3 Henry VI opens by merging the political aftermath of the first Battle of St Albans with the legal settlement following the Yorkist victory at Northampton in July 1460. York forces Henry to declare him heir apparent and Protector, and to surrender the Lancastrian title to the Crown, though Henry is allowed nominally to reign for the remainder of his lifetime. This arrangement disinherits Henry's son Prince Edward. Historically these events took place within the framework of parliamentary debate and approval. But Shakespeare eliminates this context, referring only abstractly to the 'parliament house'. This concentrates attention on a clash of feuding personalities and armed coercion. Henry's actions galvanize Queen Margaret into defending her son's rights and becoming de facto leader of the Lancastrian forces at Wakefield (30 December 1460), the first of the play's four main battles (1.3–4), in which Clifford murders York's young son Rutland in revenge for the death of

his father at the first Battle of St Albans. York himself is also captured, tormented, and killed by Margaret, Clifford, and other
vengeful Lancastrian lords, who regain the upper hand in the war.
A further Yorkist reverse at the second Battle of St Albans (17
February 1461) is reported by the Earl of Warwick in 2.1. Both
sides, seeking revenge, regroup for the play's second major
encounter at Towton. The Yorkists prevail, Clifford and other Lancastrian lords are killed, Henry and Margaret flee to Scotland, and
York's eldest son becomes Edward IV. His brothers George and
Richard become Dukes of Clarence and Gloucester respectively.

In the third act Henry is captured while re-entering England
and is sent to the Tower (July 1465). Edward makes an impulsively
self-indulgent marriage to Elizabeth, Lady Grey (1 May 1464).
This infuriates his envoy Warwick, who has been sent to France to
negotiate the hand of Lady Bona, sister-in-law of Lewis (King Louis
XI). When Warwick hears of Edward's decision, he switches loyalties to the Lancastrians and Queen Margaret, who have come to
France with Prince Edward to seek aid. Warwick seals his new allegiance by offering to wed his daughter to Prince Edward. King
Edward's marriage to a commoner also alienates his brother
Gloucester, who reveals to us his own ambitions for the throne, and
Clarence, who repudiates Edward, joins the Lancastrians, and
marries another of Warwick's daughters (11 July 1469). Warwick
invades England, captures Edward, and restores Henry to the
throne, although Henry devolves the actual rule of government on
him and Clarence as joint protectors. He also prophesies the future
rule of young Henry Tudor, Earl of Richmond, who for safety is
sent to Brittany. The former Lady Grey, now Queen Elizabeth, takes
sanctuary to save the child she is carrying, the future Prince
Edward (b. 2/3 November 1470). But immediately before this,
though unknown to her, Edward is rescued by his brother Gloucester. He travels to Flanders to seek help from his sister the Duchess of
Burgundy and re-enters England with his forces at Ravenspur
(where Henry Bolingbroke landed to challenge Richard II). Edward
marches via York to recapture and re-imprison Henry (1470) and
to confront Warwick and the Lancastrians at Coventry at the
beginning of Act 5, where Clarence switches loyalties back to his
brother and the Yorkists (1471).

In the play's final sequence, Warwick is killed and the Lancastrians are defeated at Barnet (14 April 1460), the play's third major

battle (5.2–3). Margaret returns from France and vigorously assumes command, but Yorkists again defeat the Lancastrians, this time decisively, at the fourth and last Battle, of Tewkesbury (4 May 1471). Margaret and Prince Edward are captured, and Edward, Clarence, and Gloucester impetuously murder her son before her eyes. Gloucester immediately leaves for London where he kills Henry in the Tower after the latter prophesies the continuing civil bloodshed Richard's pursuit of power will cause. Richard himself tells us of his policy to eliminate everybody who stands in his way to the throne. The final scene depicts Edward celebrating the Yorkist ascendancy over the Lancastrians as well as the birth of his son and heir Prince Edward, but with Richard of Gloucester threatening to destroy this newborn stability.

Shakespeare's interest in the Wars of the Roses reflects his professional awareness of the popularity of dramatized history among Elizabethan audiences. But it may have also begun as something personal and local. As a boy growing up in Stratford-upon-Avon, he would have known older people who could just remember the reign of Richard III and the Battle of Bosworth, which marked the end of the long-term conflict and the beginning of Tudor rule. Many of the Wars' main events took place in and around Warwickshire, some close to Stratford. Shakespeare seems to acknowledge these local connections at the beginning of 5.1, which takes place before the gates of Coventry, in an unusual cluster of place-names. The moment is entirely fictional, and appears to function as a memory site, creating a kind of personalized dramatic signature (discussed further below, pp. 75–7). If Shakespeare also spent some time between leaving Stratford and arriving in London in the service of the Lancashire-based Earls of Derby, as E. A. J. Honigmann and others have argued,[1] it may explain the prominence he gives to several members of the Stanley family in his early history plays, including both versions of *3 Henry VI*, and *Richard III*. We know they later became his patrons when he joined the Chamberlain's Men in 1594, and before that as a member of Strange's and probably Pembroke's Men. The last of these was the company for which he wrote the first version of the play underly-

[1] *Shakespeare: the 'lost years'* (1985; 2nd edn Manchester, 1998). Richard Wilson, 'Shakespeare and the Jesuits', *Times Literary Supplement*, 19 December 1997, pp. 11–13.

ing the printed text of *True Tragedy*. He may have done so with an eye to gratifying them as his patrons.[1]

The Duke of York's 'true tragedy'. The first and presumably original title, *The True Tragedy of Richard Duke of York*, directs attention to a story that goes back to Part Two[2] and which culminates in York's agonizing death in 1.4. York's 'tragedy' of failed dynastic ambition was known to contemporary readers from William Baldwin's *The Mirror for Magistrates* (1559), which presents moralized verse-histories relating the worldly falls of princes and nobles.[3] Shakespeare certainly knew Baldwin's collection, but, as with all his characters in the two versions of *3 Henry VI*, he derived most historical details from two main chronicle sources, Edward Hall's *Union of the Two Noble and Illustre Families of Lancaster and York* (1548), and the editorial compilation we know as Raphael Holinshed's *Chronicles of England, Scotland, and Ireland*, second edition (1587).

In *2 Henry VI* York emerges as a shrewd challenger to Lancastrian rule, his abilities as a military leader setting up obvious contrasts with King Henry's diffidence and piety. Rhetorically, he occasionally recalls both the lofty aspirations of Christopher Marlowe's *Tamburlaine* (*c.*1587) and the political opportunism of Fergus in Thomas Sackville and Thomas Norton's *Gorboduc* (1561). Early nineteenth-century critics admired York's combination of charismatic leadership and daring ambition, while deploring Henry's lack of muscular authority. They also found little sentimentality in the latter's death, or indeed in the play generally. Seeking a 'principal and striking personage' to remedy these perceived weaknesses, J. H. Merivale adapted *2* and *3 Henry VI* to turn York's part into a star role for Edmund Kean as *Richard Duke of York*

---

[1] Peter Thomson, *Shakespeare's Professional Career* (Cambridge, 1992), pp. 27–48. Andrew Gurr also notes the striking 'recurrence of references to the Stanleys . . . through the first Henriad and into *Richard III*. . . . This appears to suggest that their author was invoking his patron's name throughout the course of their composition, despite the fact that *2* and *3 Henry VI* became Pembroke [Men's] plays' (Gurr, *Companies*, p. 262).

[2] And Part One, if (as some scholars argue) it came first. The original title of Part Two refers to '*the Duke of York's first claim unto the Crown*'.

[3] Richard Plantagenet's story is the thirteenth of these, nearly half of which portray figures from the Wars of the Roses.

(1817).[1] Merivale cut out more or less everything not directly involving York, and rewrote his story as a determined but increasingly isolated and doomed hero. Despite Kean's best efforts, the play was not well received.[2]

Whereas Merivale refashioned York as a Romantic figure, Shakespeare's character develops in more multidimensional ways. Beyond 'scenical strutting, and furious vociferation',[3] his theatrical power in Part Two derives from the double role he plays both within and outside the dramatic action. When he lingers at the end of scenes 1.1 and 3.1 to impart his plans in soliloquy, his confidential tone leads us to feel we are overhearing somebody with an independent and pragmatic political consciousness. In formal terms, his privileged relationship with the audience recalls the civic-pageant tradition of presenter–narrators who expound the meaning of what was just seen for observers.[4] These are features York's son Richard will inherit in *True Tragedy* and *3 Henry VI*, and take in new directions by disclosing psychological motives which differentiate his private and public identities. In Part Two, on the other hand, York's wilfulness remains largely defined by traditional Luciferian qualities of transgressive pride and love of dominance inherited from the mystery-play and interlude traditions.

In both versions of *3 Henry VI*, Shakespeare personalizes York's story. His death scene, in particular, redefines his characterization from that of a political overreacher struck down by capricious fortune (the way *Mirror for Magistrates* and Merivale present him) to someone who belatedly develops a near-heroic capacity for suffer-

---

[1] With additional passages from Chapman and others, performed at Drury Lane. Reprinted in the Cornmarket facsimile series (1971). Norman J. Myers, 'Finding "a Heap of Jewels" in "Lesser" Shakespeare: *The Wars of the Roses* and *Richard Duke of York*', *New England Theatre Journal*, 7 (1996), 95–107. George C. D. Odell, *Shakespeare from Betterton to Irving*, 2 vols. (New York, 1920), ii. 128–30.

[2] Reviews were mixed. The *European Magazine* reported it played to packed houses and was well acted. It thought Kean was 'unusually great' in many scenes, and that Henry was performed with moving pathos (Gāmini Salgādo, *Eyewitnesses of Shakespeare* (1975), pp. 86–7). Leigh Hunt, on the other hand, wrote that while audiences enjoyed certain passages, he himself found the play disappointing because York's story lacked a substantially defining context and enough interest for its own sake. He also thought Kean's performance was weak and over-declamatory (*Leigh Hunt's Dramatic Criticism*, ed. L. H. and C. W. Houtchens (New York, 1949), pp. 180–2).

[3] David Riggs, *Shakespeare's Heroical Histories* (Cambridge, Mass., 1971), pp. 23, 131–8.

[4] See below, pp. 28–9.

1. The House of York seizes power. Clockwise from top right: York
(Bernard Hill, seated), George (Paul Jesson), Richard (Ron Cook),
Edward (Brian Protheroe), Warwick (Mark Wing-Davey), and Norfolk
(Peter Wyatt) in Jane Howell's BBC television production, 1983.
Copyright © BBC.

ing. The power of this ending was implicitly recognized by another
adaptation of Part Three, Richard Valpy's *The Roses* (1795), which
avoided beginning its action until after York's death.[1]

Shakespeare anticipates this transformation by dignifying York
with new dimensions of maturity and vulnerable humanity.[2] He is
less splenetic and impulsive. And as he prepares himself to seize the
throne in the opening scene, he appears somewhat dependent on
others, emotionally as well as materially:

> Assist me then, sweet Warwick, and I will . . .
> Stay by me my lords,

[1] Discussed below, pp. 83–4.
[2] When *3 Henry VI* is performed as part of a wider dramatic cycle, modern productions sometimes briefly carry over York's more energetic qualities to the beginning of the play by showing him in an opening tableau, fighting in the Battle of Northampton, prior to the dialogue; e.g. Ashland, Oregon, productions in 1966, 1977, and 1992.

> And soldiers stay and lodge by me this night . . .
> Then leave me not. My lords . . .
>
> (1.1.28, 31–2, 43)

He may even hesitate momentarily from seizing power when the opportunity finally comes within his grasp, as Stephen Simms did in Katie Mitchell's 1994 RSC production. If he does so, the hint of personal diffidence realigns him very slightly with Henry. Other modern performers, such as Bernard Hill in the 1983 BBC production, play this scene with confident, even arrogant, aggression, so that York's calls for support sound like courtesies extended by someone who can afford to appear magnanimous because he is triumphantly in charge. Nonetheless, after Warwick threatens Henry with armed force to compel him to entail the crown, York is satisfied to forgo reigning himself, and his apparent contentment is confirmed early in the next scene (1.2.9–10) in conversation with Edward and Richard. These actions are more compromising, even public-spirited, than the York of Part Two leads us to expect. Historically, the arrangement in 1.1 came about because Parliament was unwilling to recognize York's dynastic claims above Henry's long-established rule. But Shakespeare chose to ignore this rationale, so that York seems to sacrifice personal glory for the sake of national peace—and of course the future of his heirs.

Shakespeare's new emphasis on York's family piety continues in the almost domestic atmosphere of 1.2, in which York appears as an indulgent—or perhaps indulgently cynical—father figure, persuaded by emotion rather than logic into breaking his oath.[1] *True Tragedy* imparts a distinctly sentimental edge to this mood by having 'the young *Earl of Rutland*' appear with York's other sons in the opening scene, while York himself addresses Richard affectionately as 'boy' and 'Dick' in 1.2. One effect of these details is to recreate a dramatic aesthetic closer to popular Elizabethan plays such as Thomas Preston's *Cambises* (1569) which juxtapose moments of maudlin emotion with raw violence. John Crowne's adaptation of *2* and *3 Henry VI, The Misery of Civil-War* (1680), tried to pull hard

---

[1] Edward I. Berry, *Patterns of Decay: Shakespeare's Early Histories* (Charlottesville, 1975), pp. 57–8. Montague, as Warwick's brother, is York's 'cousin' in *True Tragedy* (a term suggesting familiar affection as well as kinship), but Warwick's elder brother (or father) in *3 Henry VI*. Shakespeare complicates the dynamics of moral responsibility by having the news of Margaret's army—and Lancastrian oath-breaking—immediately follow York's decision.

at spectators' heartstrings by inventing a silent farewell between York and Rutland between 1.2 and 1.3. This moment was repeated in Theophilus Cibber's adaptation of Parts Two and Three in 1723, *King Henry VI: A Tragedy*, and in Merivale's *Richard Duke of York*,[1] and has occasionally been recalled in abbreviated form by modern productions. The emotional contrast between 1.2 and the murder of Rutland is also often sharpened by stressing the close-knit relationship of the York family. Peter Hall and John Barton's 1963–4 *The Wars of the Roses* had them all playfully rough-housing before Donald Sinden's patriarchal York entered. The 1992 Ashland, Oregon, production had all the Yorkists tightly grouped around the throne in the opening scene to create a family portrait, with Rutland seated on York's knee. In 1.2 George as well as an invented Duchess of York were included, the latter's mute presence drawing attention to the real absence of female voices in the York household. Besides heightening the pity of Rutland's and York's deaths, these readings and adaptations stress the personal losses underlying York's political 'tragedy', while magnifying the play's wider theme of civil war's destruction of family relationships.

In an irony typical of Shakespeare's view of history and politics, York gains his greatest dramatic power at the very moment his worldly power is swept away. The playwright recalled an archetype of that paradox in the mystery cycles' depiction of the suffering Christ, which it is possible he saw locally, perhaps at nearby Coventry. The jeering humiliation endured by an initially silent York resembles the Townley cycle's *Buffeting and Scourging of Christ* as well as the York cycle's *Second Trial Before Pilate* and the *Judgement of Jesus*.[2] His depiction as man of sorrows forges an associative link with Rutland's murder in the previous scene by echoing another well known cycle play, the *Slaughter of the Innocents*. Holinshed related York's torment in terms recalling the Passion, from which Shakespeare derived emblematic details such as the molehill York is forced to stand upon, his mock crown, and the soldiers bowing before him (see 1.4.67 ff.).[3] Jane Howell's 1983 BBC production

---

[1] Leigh Hunt thought this was the best scene in Merivale's play, 'very deep, natural, and quiet' (*Dramatic Criticism*, p. 180).

[2] S. Schoenbaum, *William Shakespeare: A Documentary Life* (Oxford, 1975), pp. 48, 88; Jones, pp. 53–5.

[3] The 1966 Ashland production introduced an image of martyrdom by having the molehill piled up with faggots.

2. 'Ay, marry sir, now looks he like a king': Margaret (Mimi Carr)
jubilantly deriding York (Joseph DeSalvio) in Pat Patton's 1977
Oregon Shakespeare Festival production, Ashland, Oregon.

amplified these ritual gestures by having the soldiers cry 'all hail' as
they knelt (another detail noted by Holinshed), while Ashland productions in 1977, 1988, and 1992 recreated a crucifixion image by
having York stand with his arms lashed lengthwise on a staff.

Shakespeare has Margaret crown York's brows with paper,
rather than Holinshed's crown of 'sedges and bulrushes'. She does
so before he is beheaded, thereby adding a symbolic dimension of
festive derision associated with medieval and early modern mock-
king ceremonies. These were part of an iconography of protest in
sixteenth-century civil rebellions, midsummer games and other
holiday shows. The conflict between real and carnival kings
appears most prominently in the Cade rebellion scenes of *2 Henry
VI*, but is also distantly present in *True Tragedy* and *3 Henry VI* when
York provocatively seats himself in Henry's throne and the rival

kings wrangle over their legitimacy.[1] More immediately felt by modern spectators are this scene's echoes of blood sports and children's games. When an isolated, battle-weary York initially taunts his multiple opponents but then is captured, bound, and tormented by Margaret's exultant supporters, the action becomes reminiscent of Elizabethan bear-baiting, king-of-the-castle, or cat-and-mouse games.[2] The presence of such darkly carnivalized violence is first established by the grotesque little game of show-and-tell in the play's opening scene, where York's sons competitively display their bloody tokens of battle, and abuse Somerset's severed head. (The 1987 ESC production carried this frolicsome savagery further by turning the head into a stage football.)

Margaret overrules Clifford's impulse to kill York immediately after he is captured, and some productions draw additional attention to her personal dominance by having her enter to restrain Clifford just before he is about to stab him (1.4.51).[3] She also theatricalizes the situation by turning York into her spectacle, contrasting his pretensions to kingship with his present powerlessness, and humiliating him as a mere 'shadow' or player king.[4] Her long taunting speech also attacks him personally in his role as a loving parent. This follows from Shakespeare's emphasis on York as a father figure in the previous scenes, and on his pride in his sons, which he expresses a final time in his opening speech of the scene (1.4.6–17). Margaret belittles each son in turn, her sarcastic colloquialisms and affected tone of concern effectively 'invad[ing] his home privacy in order to desecrate it'.[5] Her cruelty reaches an

[1] '[A] classic mock king image', Sandra Billington, *Mock Kings in Medieval Society and Renaissance Drama* (Oxford, 1991), p. 145.

[2] Naomi Conn Liebler, 'King of the Hill: Ritual and Play in the Shaping of 3 *Henry VI*', in *Shakespeare's English Histories: A Quest for Form and Genre*, ed. John W. Velz (Binghamton, NY, 1996), pp. 31–54.

[3] Such as the BBC production, in which Margaret also gives the signal to bind York. This stage business goes back to Crowne's *Misery of Civil-War*. In other productions, such as Ashland 1992, Northumberland signals after his speech at ll. 54–60. His initial forwardness heightens the reversal in sympathies he experiences later in the scene.

[4] Jones, pp. 278–82, traces this favourite Shakespearian topos to Erasmus's 'Tragicus Rex' and numerous theatrical metaphors in More's *Utopia* and *History of Richard III*, the second of which Hall and Holinshed incorporated into their chronicles and Shakespeare drew on in this play as well as *Richard III*.

[5] Jones, p. 185.

3. Margaret (Peggy Ashcroft) wipes York's face (Donald Sinden) with the blood of his murdered son Rutland, in *Edward IV*, directed by Peter Hall and John Barton for the RSC, the second part of their cycle *The Wars of the Roses*, 1963–4.

obscene climax when she hands or throws him a napkin dipped in Rutland's blood. In Hall and Barton's *The Wars of the Roses*, Peggy Ashcroft viciously smeared York's face.[1]

But these violations of human decency recoil on the aggressors. Margaret's successful mastery of the scene depends upon sustaining the sympathy of her on- and off-stage audiences, as she awaits the furious response that might otherwise confirm the criminal status she projects on to York. But as their confrontation continues, he repositions himself as the victim of her flamboyant brutality. Rhetorically his long speech, matching her own in length, is modelled on classical orations of praise. Shakespeare keeps the form but

---

[1] So too Penny Downie in Adrian Noble's 1988 *The Plantagenets*. In Crowne's *Misery of Civil-War* and Cibber's 1723 adaptation, Rutland's body is also brought before York to increase his torment. It became a red rose in Margaret's bloody napkin in the 1977 Ashland production.

inverts its content by having York attack her foreign background, family poverty, and unnatural transgressions of traditional female virtues.[1] Emrys James's performance in the 1977 RSC production was typical of many actors' handling of this moment. After suffering Margaret's torment with stoical dignity, he began his response quietly, focusing intensely on Margaret's impassive face. Growing more passionate, he turned his attention to the surrounding figures, his speech becoming punctuated by a series of spasmodic sobs.[2] Towards the end he tried desperately to wipe Rutland's blood off the napkin—a gesture some reviewers found particularly disturbing—before finally collapsing, physically spent. Clifford's and Margaret's furious stabbing which follows confirms the rebounding of moral odium on to themselves, as well as Margaret's personal defeat in the contest for audience sympathy. Shakespeare earlier signals control slipping from her when Northumberland weeps openly at York's plight (ll. 150–1).[3] As Peter Hall observed to Peggy Ashcroft, who unforgettably brought to life this scene's emotional complexities, 'the thing to remember is that Margaret is the weak one and that York is the power. . . . He has the strength of endurance and she does what she does out of hysteria, hatred and violence.'[4]

'The Third Part of Henry the Sixth, with the Death of the Duke of York'

The Folio title, plain and probably non-authorial as it is,[5] announces a new narrative giving priority to Henry's reign, yet it neither mentions his death nor offers any appraisal of his life. Whereas *True Tragedy*'s 'death of good King Henry' raises expectations of a redemptive ending, Part Three's title forestalls moral

---

[1] Jones, p. 186. The gendered nature of their confrontation was accentuated by Helen Mirren's Margaret in 1977, who taunted York with 'sexual relish'.

[2] Some observers, however, felt these vocal mannerisms were carried too far and detracted from the human intensity of the scene (e.g. Roger Warren, 'Comedies and Histories at Two Stratfords, 1977', *Shakespeare Survey 31* (1978), p. 150).

[3] A moment of conscience he shares with Exeter at 1.1.146–51, and with Henry throughout the play. The 1977 Ashland production extended Northumberland's recognition by having him pause near the end of the scene to pick up the paper crown which had fallen from York's head.

[4] Quoted in Michael Billington, *Peggy Ashcroft* (1998), pp. 201–2.

[5] It was probably invented by the editors of the Folio volume.

judgement, leaving Henry's character to be revealed by the coming action, just as it avoids the *contemptus mundi* associations hinted at by York's 'true tragedy'. However fortuitous the Folio's renaming of the play may be, it anticipates certain important revisions in the longer Folio text, as well as new thematic perspectives on the Wars of the Roses.

Among the most notable differences between *True Tragedy* and *3 Henry VI* is the latter's deepened characterization of Henry. He is no longer merely naïve and dependent as he was in Part Two, and largely remains in *True Tragedy*. Instead we see him grow into a more self-possessed, questioning, and prophetic figure. He credibly focuses Part Three's more forceful anti-war perspective, and may—depending on the performer—become its pacifist anti-hero. These elements come together intensively at another of Part Three's dramatic high points, 2.5, in which Henry grieves for the plight of ordinary people caught up in the protracted and increasingly pointless Lancastrian and Yorkist feud.

In many modern productions, this scene becomes the emotional and philosophical core of the play. Its poignant stillness depends on the contrasting clamour that surrounds it, depicting the Battle of Towton. Elizabethans remembered this as the bloodiest conflict of the Wars of the Roses because no quarter was declared and the fighting dragged on indecisively for hours before ending in a Yorkist victory. In historical memory it came to epitomize the Wars' bleakest horrors. These battle scenes thus share with 2.5—in total much of Act 2—a claim to be regarded as the extended thematic centre of *3 Henry VI* as a civil-war play.

If that is the case, we must distinguish the emotional effects of these scenes, since stage combat moves audiences in different ways from formal meditation and lament. Given Towton's historical reputation, it is reasonable to assume it was the 'biggest' of Part Three's battles (as it is normally in modern productions). For Elizabethan acting companies this made it potentially the most demanding in terms of re-creating martial action through theatrical art. And for both players and audiences these scenes connected most obviously with their own wartime conditions in the early 1590s and their related political contexts. Act 2 thus focuses *3 Henry VI*'s complex responses towards civil war as understood historical memory and re-created theatrical event.

An Elizabethan civil war play. *3 Henry VI* is closely related to a body of political tragedies from the 1580s and preceding decades that explore themes of divided state rule, and the breakdown of civil law into social disorder and armed conflict.[1] Because the events of Henry VI's reign had occurred less than a century before, they seemed to Elizabethans ominously to mirror threats to their own monarch's authority, which remained active throughout the late 1580s and early 1590s. The recently solved challenge to Elizabeth's rule by Mary Queen of Scots was still fresh in people's minds. Since her arrival in England in 1568, Mary had underlined the instability caused by the presence of two monarchs in one kingdom, each with justifiable claims to the throne. She was also menacing as a foreign Catholic, connected by marriage to the detested French house of Guise. Following the Babington plot of 1586, which involved plans to assassinate Elizabeth and place Mary on the throne, government apologists called for Mary's execution, which ultimately took place the following year. This abated the immediate crisis but did not end uncertainty about Elizabeth's successor. At this point the Queen's ability to have children had passed, but she refused to name an heir. James VI of Scotland was the leading but by no means only contender. Although he eventually succeeded to the throne peacefully in 1603, this outcome was not clear or assured in the early 1590s.[2]

Sackville and Norton's *Gorboduc* was the first Elizabethan play to debate these issues. Although written and performed at the beginning of Elizabeth's reign, it was reprinted in 1590, the year before Shakespeare wrote the first version of *3 Henry VI*.[3] The legendary British king Gorboduc divides his kingdom between his two sons, who turn against each other and plunge the country into civil war.

[1] Thomas Sackville and Thomas Norton's *Gorboduc* (1561, printed 1565, 1570, repr. 1590), George Gascoigne and Francis Kinwelmarshe's *Jocasta* (1566, printed 1575, 1587), Thomas Hughes's *The Misfortunes of Arthur* (1587), and Thomas Lodge's *The Wounds of Civil War* (printed 1594, *c.*1580s). Although rather different in form and tone, Christopher Marlowe's *Massacre at Paris* (*c.*1589–92) is related to this group as well. See Jones, ch. 5, pp. 119–26.

[2] When it happened without bloodshed, contemporaries viewed James's accession as a virtual miracle.

[3] And probably the same year in which he wrote its companion, *The First Part of the Contention* or *2 Henry VI*. As Marie Axton observes, 'Gorboduc and his sons were familiar stage figures in the 1590s' (*The Queen's Two Bodies: Drama and the Elizabethan Succession* (1977), p. 90 n. 2).

Part Three alludes to Sackville and Norton's play in half a dozen places, concentrated in Act 2,[1] and overall it remained Shakespeare's most important—if artistically distant—model for exploring and representing the destruction of civil society by factional conflict.[2] Though it now reads drearily, with its long speeches, formal neo-Senecan conventions, and relentless didacticism, Elizabethans did not experience *Gorboduc* this way. It was staged for members of the Inns of Court, an educated elite audience, on 5 January 1561/2, and again several weeks later at the command of the Queen.[3] A recently discovered eyewitness account by Robert Beale, courtier and administrator, demonstrates that it was understood in performance as a direct commentary on potential marriage partners for Elizabeth, with political chaos the likely outcome if she failed to wed and produce an heir.[4] Beale's report reveals differences between the performed text and the printed version, the close relationship between drama and contemporary politics, and spectators' normal habit of reading topical significance into historical subjects. Moreover, the Inns of Court audience clearly found the play memorable because of its dumb shows, which Beale confirms were more elaborately staged than printed directions indicate.[5] The most spectacular of these, preceding the final act, represents the beginning of full-blown civil war:

[1] See commentary to 1.1.217–26, 1.2.16, 2.1.201–3, 2.5.54.1–3, 56–60, 116–17. *True Tragedy* also contains several unique allusions to *Gorboduc*'s theme of a disputed succession. In the opening scene, Henry tries to mollify York by pointing out that they are both members of the same family, 'both Plantagenets by birth, | And from two brothers lineally descent' (A4ʳ–A4ᵛ). This situation recalls the turmoil created by divided family rule in the opening act of Sackville and Norton's play. Act 2, Scene 5 begins with a prayer in which Henry's despair, 'O would my death might stay these civil jars!' (C2ᵛ) recalls the besieged Gorboduc, 'O ye gods, . . . wreak [destruction] on me | . . . not on this guiltless realm' (3.1.22–4).

[2] These verbal and thematic affinities were recaptured by Katie Mitchell's 1994 RSC script, which added anti-war passages from *Gorboduc*, as well as from *2 Henry VI*, *Richard II*, and *Richard III*. In Shakespeare's day, the Gorboduc story also appeared as part of *2 Seven Deadly Sins*. According to an extant theatrical plot of the play probably made for Strange's Men *c.*1590, Gorboduc was played by Richard Burbage, later associated with Pembroke's Men and the performance of the first version of *3 Henry VI*. The play's framing action represents Henry VI in the Tower and his release by Warwick in 1470, corresponding to *3 Henry VI* 4.6. See W. W. Greg, *Dramatic Documents from the Elizabethan Playhouses*, 2 vols. (Oxford, 1931), i. 105–22.

[3] Sackville was Elizabeth's cousin and later her Lord High Steward, while Norton, a member of the Inner Temple, was an MP and government legal counsellor.

[4] Henry James and Greg Walker, 'The Politics of *Gorboduc*', *English Historical Review*, 110, no. 435 (1995), 109–21.

[5] Discussed in detail by Dieter Mehl, *The Elizabethan Dumb Show* (1965), pp. 29–41.

First, the drums and flutes began to sound, during which there came forth upon the stage a company of harquebussiers [soldiers with harquebuses, an early form of large musket] and of armed men [with hand weapons], all in order of battle. These, after their pieces discharged, and that the armed men had three times marched about the stage, departed, and then the drums and flutes did cease. Hereby was signified tumults, rebellions, arms, and civil wars to follow as fell in the realm of Great Britain which, by the space of fifty years and more, continued in civil war between the nobility after the death of King Gorboduc and of his issues, for want of certain limitation in the succession of the crown. . . .[1]

If Beale's account of *Gorboduc*'s other shows is an indication, this scene was choreographed with energy and skill. The direction suggests there are two distinct groups of soldiers performing elaborate actions. The 'company of harquebussiers' 'sounds more professional' than the group performing marching movements, although the latter, co-ordinated by drums and fifes, was also a central component of real military training.[2] If this 'company' were hired harquebussiers, as seems likely, this passage documents the common ground shared by the contemporary stage and the militia, and a crossover between drill as theatrical rehearsal and combat as performance.[3] Such collaboration was usual for Inns-of-Court plays, which involved both amateur and professional poets, dramatists, and players.[4] Though past scholars have argued over whether the

[1] *Gorboduc or Ferrex and Porrex*, ed. Irby B. Cauthen Jr (Lincoln, Nebraska, 1970), dumb show 5.1–11.

[2] Nick de Somogyi, *Shakespeare's Theatre of War* (Aldershot, 1998), pp. 123, 128.

[3] Richard Southern has suggested that performances of the battle scenes in James Pickeryng's *Horestes* (1567), probably staged at Lincoln's Inn, might have drawn on members of the local militia (*The Staging of Plays before Shakespeare* (1973), p. 497): e.g. '*Go and make your lively battle, and let it be long ere you can win the city, and when you have won it, let Horestes bring out his mother* [Clytemnestra] *by the arm and let the drum cease playing and the trumpet also*' (after l. 725, in *Three Tudor Classical Interludes*, ed. Marie Axton (Cambridge, 1982).

[4] Adwin Wigfall Green, *The Inns of Court and Early English Drama* (New Haven, 1931), pp. 17–20. It is worth citing another pertinent example from *Jocasta*: 'Before the beginning of this fourth act, the trumpets, drums and fifes sounded, and a great peal of ordnance was shot off: in the which there entered upon the stage six knights armed at all points . . . accompanied with seven other armed men; and after they had marched twice or thrice about the stage, the one party menacing the other by their furious looks and gestures, the six knights caused their other attendants to stand by, and drawing their swords, fell to cruel and courageous combat . . . till two on the one side were slain. The third, perceiving that he only remained to withstand the force of three enemies, did politicly run aside: wherewith immediately one of the three followed after him, and when he had drawn his enemy thus from his company, he turned again and slew him. Then the second also ran after him, whom he

actions represented here are naturalistic or stylized,[1] they are clearly both, and therefore typical of most battle displays on the Elizabethan stage.

Gorboduc's relevance to *True Tragedy* and *3 Henry VI*, as well as other Shakespearian histories and tragedies (for instance *King Lear*), is therefore not just political and thematic, but spectacular as well. Its staging of martial action has been under-noticed, however, because standard accounts of the development of the history play tend to cite it and other neoclassical tragedies chiefly as models for formal rhetorical expression, topical allegory, and historical and moral themes.[2] While these connections are all valid, they have been discussed with little relation to the play's 'tumultuous' elements, which derive from popular heroic and civic drama (romance, farce, and combat scenes).[3] The appeal of well-staged martial spectacle was shared by all the dramatic traditions which inform *True Tragedy* and *3 Henry VI*, and the history play in general.

From the perspective of traditional literary history, a further difficulty has been that battle shows in Inns-of-Court tragedies appear to break neoclassical rules of decorum stipulating that violence could not be directly represented but only reported. These moments must therefore be discounted as defects and aberrations, as Philip Sidney does when otherwise praising *Gorboduc* in *An Apology for Poetry* (*c.*1579–80). Spectacular 'action' scenes contradict theoretical distinctions between 'serious' and 'popular' drama that

---

slew in like manner, and consequently the third, and then triumphantly marched about the stage with his sword in his hand . . .' (*Early English Classical Tragedies*, ed. John W. Cunliffe (Oxford, 1912), dumb show IV, 1–18, p. 125).

[1] '[A] short piece of realistically portrayed action' (Mehl, p. 39); 'the dumb shows were symbolic, not realistic' (*Gorboduc*, ed. Cauthen, p. 58).

[2] Irving Ribner, *The English History Play in the Age of Shakespeare* (1957; London, rev. edn 1965), pp. 12–51, E. M. W. Tillyard, *Shakespeare's History Plays* (1944), Lily B. Campbell, *Shakespeare's 'Histories': Mirrors of Elizabethan Policy* (San Marino, 1947), A. P. Rossiter, *English Drama from Early Times to the Elizabethans* (1950). E. Catherine Dunn's attempt to redress an overemphasis on the morality play and non-dramatic *de casibus* origins of the history play is welcome, even though another area of continuity she cites, between an older cosmic vision of history and a Protestant nationalistic one—both of which are generically comedic—seems to me contradicted by the non-eschatological and non-redemptive world of *3 Henry VI* ('The Medieval "Cycle" as History Play: An Approach to the Wakefield Plays', *Studies in the Renaissance*, 7 (1960), 76–89).

[3] E. W. Talbert, *Elizabethan Drama and Shakespeare's Early Plays* (Chapel Hill, NC, 1963), p. 223.

4. Battle as theatrical art: Adrian Noble's *The Rise of Edward IV*, the second part of *The Plantagenets*, Royal Shakespeare Theatre, 1988.

were beginning to be developed by classicizing treatises such as Sidney's, which mocked plays showing 'two armies fly[ing] in, represented with four swords and bucklers, and then what hard heart will not receive it for a pitched field?'[1] Ben Jonson, as we have seen, and certain university-educated playwrights, endorsed Sidney's agenda of separating 'low' from 'high' art, with staged combat being denigrated as sensational and unsophisticated.[2] As Jonson remarked, martial spectacle was 'for the vulgar, who are better delighted with that which pleaseth the eye, than contenteth the ear'.[3]

Such distinctions misrepresent Elizabethan drama, which freely mingles 'official' and popular cultures that only later became more widely separated.[4] They also misconstrue the productive the-

[1] *An Apology for Poetry*, ed. Geoffrey Shepherd (1965), p. 134.

[2] For example, George Peele in his *Old Wives Tale*, and Francis Beaumont in *The Knight of the Burning Pestle*, each of which burlesques audiences' devotion to military spectacle which became associated with the rowdy public theatres.

[3] Jonson, *The Masque of Blackness* (1605).

[4] Mikhail Bakhtin, *Rabelais and his World*, trans. Hélène Iswolsky (Cambridge, Mass., 1968).

atrical tension of plays such as *Gorboduc* and the two versions of *3 Henry VI* that juxtapose the stirring aesthetic appeal of martial action with discursive reflection on its political causes and social consequences.

Civic and royal pageantry. Shakespeare makes conspicuous use of various pageant forms and symbolic modes in *3 Henry VI*, and again there are revealing differences between this version and *True Tragedy*, which tends to exploit stage spectacle more lavishly. Some modern productions follow the latter's opening directions calling for the Yorkists and Lancastrians to wear white and red roses 'in their hats'. These were perhaps the most common visual emblems of Elizabethan royal pageants, reminders of Henry Tudor's endlessly praised political solution to the Wars of the Roses by his marriage to Elizabeth of York.[1] Visually, they usefully distinguish members of each faction, and they recall the kind of heraldic display that was a part of early modern military life. Part Three's opening direction, on the other hand, omits the roses (though they may be implied[2]). If they are not worn, dynastic allegiances may become blurred, thereby reinforcing their shifting and unstable nature. Their absence removes a marker of official Tudor ideology, and by extension its restricting historical perspective, which tended to mitigate the human casualties of civil war within a triumphalist narrative. Recent directors have often taken up Part Three's option of omitting the roses to underscore the play's focus on the painful confusion of war. Costumes that are less visually marked also allow spectators greater imaginative room for constructing parallels with other wars in later periods.

Pageant forms also provided Shakespeare with dramatic templates to express historically recurrent public ceremonies and ritu-

---

[1] Intertwined red and white roses signifying the uniting of the houses of York and Lancaster appear in royal entries from Elizabeth's 1559 coronation in London onwards. See *The Quenes Maiesties Passage through the Citie of London to Westminster the Day before her Coronacion*, ed. James M. Osborn (New Haven, 1960), B1ʳ, p. 33. A provincial occasion is reported in Thomas Churchyard, *The Joyful Receiving of the Queen's most excellent Majesty into her Highness' City of Norwich* (1578). The roses later become nostalgic emblems of Tudor national unity in Lord Mayors' shows of 1612, 1613, 1621, 1624, and 1628 (David M. Bergeron, 'Civic pageants and historical drama', *Journal of Medieval and Renaissance Studies*, 5 (1975), 89–105; pp. 104–5.

[2] Richard in *True Tragedy* 2.1 refers to 'this white rose', whereas in *3 Henry VI* 1.2.33 he speaks of 'the white rose that I wear', which could be notional. There are other instances of this sense of stage immediacy in *True Tragedy*. See pp. 35–7.

als, and to order often jumbled chronicle details as coherent dramatic action.[1] The public triumph, for example, was familiar to Elizabethan audiences from annual Lord Mayors' shows, royal entries to cities, and court progresses in the country.[2] Shakespeare employs this form, associated with heroic celebrations of official state power, at the beginning of 5.3, when Edward returns victorious from the field of Barnet. But on the whole *3 Henry VI* simulates this kind of civic spectacle less frequently than *True Tragedy*. A telling point of difference occurs when the latter calls twice for royal processions in Act 4. Having just been proclaimed king by his champion Sir John Montgomery—a moment that combines chivalric honour with public ritual—Edward is led out by the Mayor of York bearing the keys of the city at the end of 4.7 (*3 Henry VI* 4.6):[3]

> *Edward.* We thank you all, Lord Mayor lead on the way . . .
> We'll march to London to meet with Warwick,
> And pull false Henry from the regal throne.
>
> (D7ᵛ–D8ʳ)

Another formal procession immediately follows marking Henry's return to power in London: 'Enter Warwick and Clarence, with the crown, and then King Henry, and Oxford, and Somerset, [Montague] and the young Earl of Richmond.' The back-to-back ceremonies visually express the power struggle between two monarchs, each making publicly disputed claims to the throne. Henry's entry includes a formal display of the crown, a gesture which flatters the temporal monarch with associations of transcendent power. By contrast, *3 Henry VI*'s use of this common stage prop is less iconic and more dramatically integrated into the narrative action. Warwick explicitly uncrowns Edward after surprising him in his tent (4.3.48.1), assuming an authority above the king's. A line unique

[1] Bruce R. Smith, 'Pageants into Play: Shakespeare's Three Perspectives on Idea and Image', in *Pageantry in the Shakespearean Theater*, ed. David M. Bergeron (Athens, Ga., 1985), pp. 220–46; p. 224. Martin, *Pageantry*.

[2] For example, on 24 November 1588 Elizabeth travelled in a 'Roman' triumphal chariot with pillars and a canopy from Westminster to St Paul's Cathedral, where she greeted the Bishop and clergy of London at the west door (John Stow, *The Annals of England* (1592), p. 1282, sig. Pppp1ᵛ). See Gordon Kipling, 'Triumphal Drama: Form in English Civic Pageantry', *Renaissance Drama*, 8 (1977), 37–56.

[3] Another contemporary example: on 30 January 1589 Elizabeth returned from the City to Westminster in a torchlight procession led by the Lord Mayor and Aldermen (Stow, *Annals*, pp. 1282–3, sigs. Pppp1ᵛ–2ʳ).

to the Folio text also opens up a characteristically Shakespearian metadramatic perspective, when Warwick boasts of reducing Edward to a 'shadow' of his former self (l. 50). The word conveys a double sense of the king's image and the actual stage player, thereby suggesting they are one and the same. This is entirely appropriate in a section of the play where kings swap back and forth in a kind of schoolboy war game, and monarchy ceases to signify in any stable or transcendant way, but becomes purely contingent on material possession of the crown.[1]

Both versions of *3 Henry VI* also rely on Elizabethan audiences' recognition of civic pageantry's basic physical relationship of performer, presenter–mediator, and spectator, using it to create multiple interpretive perspectives on historical events. This scenic structure informs 3.1, when the two Gamekeepers observe Henry passing by from his captivity in Scotland, then comment on his appearance and speeches, before intervening to seize his attention and eventually his person. Shakespeare recycles this sequence of action in 4.5, when Richard, Hastings, and Stanley lie waiting for the captive Edward to pass by whilst hunting in the Archbishop of York's park. The identical visual arrangement to 3.1 may lead spectators to expect that the action will unfold in the same way. The BBC *3 Henry VI* underscored this anticipated repetition by having Richard and the others wait downstage (i.e. in a divided frame close-up) at the end of the same bower-corridor in which the Gamekeepers watched Henry. But here the action fails to unfold as before because Edward knows of Richard's plans beforehand and simply walks up to him upon entry.[2] Shakespeare defamiliarizes the pageant-derived model by staging a dramatically eccentric but historically real event. A gap opens as he makes his original scenic form redundant, alienating spectators' expectations of conventional public action. The stagy awkwardness of the moment draws attention to the limited usefulness of the pageant model, and perhaps the obsolescence of its idealizing ideology. History seems less able to be moulded into an existing dramatic matrix or

[1] J. P. Brockbank, 'The Frame of Disorder: *Henry VI*', in *Early Shakespeare*, ed. John Russell Brown and Bernard Harris (1961; New York, 1966), pp. 73–99; p. 93. Liebler, 'King of the Hill', p. 47.

[2] Joseph Candido compares these two scenes within a wider discussion of *Henry VI* as a 'network of captures and escapes': 'Getting Loose in the *Henry VI* Plays', *SQ* 35 (1984), 392–406; pp. 403–6.

narrative format, as the ceremonially derived forms mutate in random, unpredictable ways, suggesting local variations which cannot be contained or explained by conventional or generalizing interpretations.

Historical drama. Throughout the sixteenth century, 'warlike shows' were a popular element of local celebrations, holiday festivities, and civic drama, and had a close, indeed overlapping, relationship with real military life.[1] For Shakespeare, it was nearby Coventry that may have provided theatrical inspiration for the battle scenes which crowd his early histories, and *3 Henry VI* in particular.[2] During the Elizabethan period, Coventry regularly staged plays that adapted the forms and stagecraft of officially suppressed mystery cycles and folk rituals to historical subjects. In May 1591, the year the play underlying *True Tragedy* was written, the city corporation met to choose from among three previously performed plays: *The History of King Edward IV*, *The Conquest of the Danes*, and *The Destruction of Jerusalem*. All had in common historical verse narratives, heroic leaders, and spectacular battle scenes.[3]

Regrettably we do not know the exact events depicted in the anonymous *Edward IV*, which is potentially of greatest interest for *3 Henry VI*. Stephen K. Wright argues that they may have been similar to those dramatized by Thomas Heywood's *King Edward the Fourth*, printed in 1599 but written and performed earlier by

[1] A point distantly conveyed by the film *Shakespeare in Love*. When the playhouse owner Fenniman enters to find a fight taking place on stage, he initially assumes a rehearsal is in progress. Only later does he realize the fighting is real.

[2] He may have heard about war shows staged elsewhere too. In 1572, for instance, soldiers brought twelve mortar pieces from London to Warwick to stage a large mock-battle before the Queen with fireworks, assaults, and charges. Two years later a pageant representing 'civil broil' staged mock-battles for two days during a visit by the Queen to Bristol: Thomas Churchyard, *The First Part of Churchyard's Chips* (1575), Nvii^r–Ovi^v, reproduced in John Nichols, *The Progresses and Public Processions of Queen Elizabeth*, 3 vols. (1823), i. 319, 396–407. Similar mock-battles were staged at Whitehall in 1581 and Eltham in 1591: David M. Bergeron, *English Civic Pageantry 1558–1642* (1971), pp. 25–6, 45–6, 57–60.

[3] Benjamin Griffin, 'The Breaking of the Giants: Historical Drama in Coventry and London', *English Literary Renaissance*, 29 (1999), 3–21. Griffin demonstrates that all these plays were indeed real drama and not just mimed seasonal rituals, as C. L. Barber originally believed (*Shakespeare's Festive Comedy* (Princeton, 1959), p. 33). Griffin's arguments are partially anticipated by Talbert, *Elizabethan Drama*, p. 176, and Wright (see next note). Richard Axton also discusses evidence of formally stylized choreography in battle plays, common to both courtly and folk traditions, in *European Drama of the Early Middle Ages* (1974), pp. 33–46.

Lord Derby's Men.[1] (Further discussion of Heywood's play follows below, pp. 73–4). *The Conquest of the Danes* had also been performed previously, most notably for Elizabeth by 'Coventry men' at Kenilworth Castle in Warwickshire in 1575.[2] It was a Hock Tuesday play (i.e. intended for the second Tuesday after Easter Sunday), which traditionally consisted of a festive contest between the sexes. This was grafted on to commemoration of a historical event with local significance, the English victory over the Danes on St Brice's Day 1002, in which women intervened 'in actions and rhymes after their manner' to turn the tide of battle and lead the vanquished Danes in triumph.[3] The third play being considered for performance in 1591 was *The Destruction of Jerusalem*. It was apparently based on Josephus' *Antiquities* and had been performed earlier in 1584. Its *mise en scène* featured special stage effects such as thunder and a blizzard.[4] Earnings from this innovative genre of civic history plays, like its public theatre counterparts, could be high, a prospect which clearly attracted ambitious playwrights, including Shakespeare himself.[5]

---

[1] '"The Historie of King Edward the Fourth": A Chronicle Play on the Coventry Pageant Wagons', *Medieval and Renaissance Drama in England*, 3 (1986), 69–82. *Edward IV* borrows from several passages in *3 Henry VI* (see below pp. 73–4). It features the rebellion of Thomas Falconbridge, who tries unsuccessfully to restore Henry VI to the throne. Wright speculates that Heywood's play was itself related to the earlier anonymous *Siege of London* performed at the Rose Theatre on 26 December 1594 and dating from 1590 onwards (pp. 74–5).

[2] The Kenilworth entertainments were reported in several pamphlets, one of which Shakespeare is believed to have known: Robert Laneham, *A Letter wherein Part of the Entertainment unto the Queen's Majesty at Killingworth in Warwickshire . . . is Signified* (1575), ed. R. J. P. Kuin (Amsterdam, 1973). Only Laneham mentions the Coventry play. Also George Gascoigne, *The Princely Pleasures at the Court at Kenilworth* (1576).

[3] *Coventry*, Records of Early English Drama, ed. R. W. Ingram (Toronto, 1981), p. 233. Laneham reports that *The Conquest of the Danes* had been performed each year for some time as part of the city's civic festivities (*A Letter*, pp. 32–7). R. W. Ingram believes it dates from about 1416 ('Fifteen seventy-nine and the Decline of Civic Religious Drama in Coventry', in *The Elizabethan Theatre VIII*, ed. G. R. Hibbard (Port Credit, Ontario, 1982), pp. 114–28; p. 118 n. 10).

[4] Suggestive in terms of modern stagings of the Battle of Tewkesbury. See p. 5 above.

[5] John Smith earned a handsome £3 6s 8d for *The Destruction of Jerusalem*, while the *Siege of London* (see p. 74 n. 1 below) coined £3 3s for a single performance at the Rose (Wright, 'Historie', pp. 69, 75). In this context, the startling success of Shakespeare's 'harey the vi', which earned £3 16s 8d on 3 March 1592, looks a little less remarkable but still impressive, Shakespeare having graduated early into the high-earners bracket.

The adaptation of medieval stagecraft to chronicle history may explain both the Passion emblems which add a dimension of ritual drama to Margaret's baiting of York in 1.4, and the schematic presentation of the Father's and Son's laments in 2.5 (of which more below). As far as its battle scenes were concerned, Coventry's civic drama was deftly choreographed to represent different kinds of fighting. Like the action called for by *Gorboduc*'s directions, it must have combined stylized and naturalistic modes. Costumed soldiers moved in intricate formations to fifes and drums, creating strongly rhythmic patterns that were designed to differentiate 'hot skirmishes' from 'blazing battles'.[1] There was also skilful and realistic swordplay, just as there was on the professional stage.[2] Such action was co-articulate with the verbal narrative, expressing chronicle descriptions of battlefield encounters through a visual mimetic language, much as film-makers today try to translate Shakespeare's poetic imagery into meaningful screen effects. Moreover, as *The Conquest of the Danes* attests, battle scenes could include women warriors.[3] This anticipates Queen Margaret's appearance in battle-dress at Wakefield, Towton, and Tewkesbury, and suggests she could have participated in personal combats, as some modern productions have had her do.[4] It also indicates that her martial roles might not have been quite as unprecedented, or scandalous, on stage as some recent critics have claimed, and that spectators would not necessarily have associated her exclusively with Elizabeth's celebrated appearance in armour before her troops at Tilbury.[5]

'*Food for powder*'. *3 Henry VI*'s major concern with representing soldiers and war reflects the fact that Elizabethan public theatres

---

[1] R. Axton, p. 43; Laneham: 'the footmen . . . first marching in ranks: then war-like turning, then from ranks into squadrons, then into triangles, from that into rings, and so winding out again' (p. 37).

[2] Laneham refers to a local mason, who played the legendary hero Captain Cox, as being 'very cunning in fenc[ing]' (pp. 34, 36). Robert E. Morsberger, 'Of the Performance of Stage Fights', *Swordplay and the Elizabethan and Jacobean Stage* (Salzburg, 1974), ch. 6, pp. 80–95 and *passim*.

[3] As characters but not actors. Women probably did not perform in these plays, as Griffin observes (p. 8).

[4] See below, pp. 86–7.

[5] Indeed the performance at Kenilworth suggests the direction of influence was the other way round, with historical subjects celebrating heroic women being chosen because 'they thought it might move some mirth to her majesty the rather' (Laneham, p. 33).

were enthralled by the psychology, vocabulary, and habits of military culture, as stage battles became virtual demonstration sites for martial skill.[1] Military service became a ubiquitous but increasingly controversial part of everyday English life in the final decades of Elizabeth's reign. The defeat of the Armada in 1588 is the legendary event of these years, and the celebratory patriotism that preceded and followed it has traditionally been cited to explain Shakespeare's interest in developing the national history play. But as modern historians point out, this lucky victory did not end the war or the threat of invasion. During this time the country also became increasingly committed to supporting Henry IV in France and the Dutch against the Spanish, and in conquering Ireland. All these conflicts required unprecedented efforts at recruitment. The year 1585 marked a turning point in this regard when England officially entered the war with France against Spain, and mobilization increased rapidly.[2] Government conscription replaced the older and more limited feudal custom of local nobility and gentry raising troops from among their tenantry. *3 Henry VI* alludes to both practices—traditional and modern—when the Son who has killed his father states:

> From London by the King was I pressed forth.
> My father, being the Earl of Warwick's man,
> Came on the part of York, pressed by his master . . .
>
> (2.5.64–6)

The Son's complaint is also generationally and regionally marked. Political and social changes have forced him, like many young men in the sixteenth century (including Shakespeare), to leave his home and family in Warwickshire or elsewhere to take up an unfamiliar life in the capital. His provincial identity has been left behind, and his blind killing of his father is the extreme symptom of his broken connection with local history and his uncertain embrace of metropolitan culture. Civil war here becomes a conflict

---

[1] De Somogyi, *passim*.

[2] C. G. Cruickshank, *Elizabeth's Army* (1946; 3rd edn, London, Oxford, and New York, 1996), pp. 13–15. Recent research indicates that between this date and 1603, when peace was negotiated, 11 to 12 per cent of the eligible male population was recruited—or more often, impressed. In total over 75,000 soldiers were sent overseas, only about half of whom returned.

of the social self, as the son loses his regional ethnicity to deforming state imperatives.[1]

Though *True Tragedy* and *3 Henry VI* do not stage the evasion and corruption of recruitment practices dramatized in later histories such as *1* and *2 Henry IV*, both display an awareness of the regular training of militia soldiers at various sites around London, many of which were located close to the public playhouses. Infantry levies were far greater in London than any county, with over 10,000 men being conscripted out of a total population of 250,000.[2] As a Pembroke's Men play, *True Tragedy* was performed at The Theatre, which stood beside one of the most prominent muster grounds, Finsbury Fields. In its opening scene, Warwick refers to another well-known drilling area: 'Captain, conduct [the soldiers] into Tuttle Fields.' These were in Westminster, near the palace in which the events of the opening scene took place. Warwick later emphasizes that his mustered soldiers were 'very well appointed', despite their defeat at the second Battle of St Albans. He seems to take pride in a matter that Elizabethan spectators with militia experience would have appreciated.[3]

Material connections between military training and the staging of both versions of *3 Henry VI* would have been extensive. Unlike today, weapons were not simulated period props but actual contemporary equipment, and armour was real enough for bodily protection.[4] The sound of chambers being discharged, which *True*

---

[1] Stuart Hampton-Reeves, 'Alarums and Defeats: *Henry VI* on Tour', *Early Modern Literary Studies*, 5 (1999), 1.1–18 (URL: http://purl.oclc.org./emls/05-2hampalar.html). Hampton-Reeves reads this moment in the light of the Bogdanov and Pennington 1987 ESC production, which made frequent use of regional accents and popular cultural symbols as foils to national and imperial perspectives on Shakespearian history.

[2] John McGurk, *The Elizabethan Conquest of Ireland: The 1590s Crisis* (Manchester, 1997), pp. 52–6. Wallace T. MacCaffrey, *Elizabeth I: War and Politics 1558–1603* (Princeton, 1992), pp. 42–4.

[3] *True Tragedy*, B4ᵛ (2.1.113). This line may have been inadvertently omitted from *3 Henry VI*.

[4] Charles Edelman, *Brawl Ridiculous: Swordfighting in Shakespeare's Plays* (Manchester, 1992), pp. 32–3. Successful modern productions strive to enliven combat scenes with a variety of stage weapons of authentic appearance. The 1977 Ashland production, for example, began with broadswords in a prologue battle, and went on to include pikes, shields, great axes, hand axes, daggers, swords, and maces. Productions seeking to draw parallels with modern civil wars may also evolve their weaponry. In Michael Kahn's 1996 Washington Shakespeare Theatre production, medieval broadswords, mattocks, and axes gave way to pikes, daggers, swords, combat knives, pistols, rifles, bayonets, revolvers, shotguns, and machine guns.

Tragedy calls for to mark the Battle of Tewkesbury in Act 5 (see below), would have literally echoed artillery practice in neighbour-ing Finsbury Fields. The theatre manager Philip Henslowe records purchasing banners, shields, and lances for his company at the Rose.[1] Field tents were used on stage in Elizabethan history plays, and may have been used in *True Tragedy* 4.3 (although the equi-valent scene in *3 Henry VI* seems less likely[2]), when Warwick, Clarence, and their men surprise Edward's tent. Trumpets, drums, and flags were as essential for representing marching troops and combat scenes in the theatre as they were for strategic communica-tion and regimental display on the muster- or battlefield.[3] Militia drills and shows were 'a continual feature of London life' in the late 1580s and 1590s, which suggests that performances of Shake-speare's history plays would have had to live up to high expecta-tions of realism.[4] City authorities regularly complained that the noise of trumpets, drums, and battle scenes from the playhouses disturbed services in neighbourhood churches. Conversely, the overlap between stage and muster-ground could be pressed into service to defend the theatre against its puritan detractors:

[An acting company] playing late in the night, at a place called Perin in Cornwall, certain Spaniards were landed the same night, unsuspected and undiscovered, with intent to take in the town, spoil and burn it, when sud-denly, even upon their entrance, the players (ignorant as the townsmen of any such attempt), presenting a battle on the stage, with their drum and trumpets struck up a loud alarum; which the enemy hearing, and fearing they were discovered . . . in a hurly-burly, fled disorderly to their boats. (Thomas Heywood, *An Apology for Actors* (1612) G2ʳ)

Thomas Nashe and Heywood also commended the didactic benefits of history plays with battle scenes for teaching tactical strategies,

---

[1] *Henslowe's Diary*, pp. 215–17. At the well-received 1992 Ashland production, Alan C. Dessen noted director Pat Patton's 'mastery of banners on the large outdoor stage: to simulate battles and processions; to facilitate exits and entrances; and to conceal bodies or groups of upstage figures' ('Taming the Script: *Henry VI*, *Shrew*, and *All's Well* in Ashland and Stratford', *Shakespeare Bulletin* (Spring, 1993), p. 35).

[2] See further discussion below, pp. 68–9.

[3] Shirley, pp. 54–71.

[4] John Rigby Hale, 'Shakespeare and Warfare', in *William Shakespeare: His World, His Work, His Influence*, ed. John F. Andrews, 3 vols. (New York, 1985), i. 85–98; de Somogyi, p. 109.

as well as inspiring morale.[1] They both attest that captains and soldiers were a regular part of London playhouse audiences. For these theatregoers in particular, but also for the many citizens who turned out to watch drills and musters, stage battles would have closely resembled actual training or battle conditions, and a shared imaginative participation would have marked both experiences. Shakespeare would later explicitly invoke such collaboration in the urgings of the Chorus in *Henry V*, another, but very different, play about war.

Of Shakespeare's two versions, *True Tragedy* seems to gratify audiences' enjoyment of martial action more readily than Part Three. Just as its re-creation of pageant-derived spectacle is more celebratory, and arguably more ideologically conservative, its approach to stage combat is robust and realistic, whereas Part Three's is more restrained, stylized, and questioning. These changes may reflect changing public attitudes towards English involvement in colonial and Continental wars as the 1590s wore on, and are consistent with Part Three's heightened anti-war perspective. As recruitment demands increased and casualties mounted, resistance from citizens grew.[2] Writing around 1587, William Lambarde stated that the impressed soldier 'comes as willingly to serve as does the beggar to the stocks or the dog to hanging'.[3] And by 1600, the Privy Council complained that only 140 of 350 men called up in a recent London mobilization had turned up for embarkation.[4]

In the opening scene of *3 Henry VI*, Warwick 'stamps with his foot' at l. 170.1 and the soldiers 'show themselves', which suggests they have been partially hidden. The effect is unspectacular, but perhaps more subtly menacing. *True Tragedy* by contrast calls for a

---

[1] *Pierce Penniless*, 'In plays . . . all stratagems of war . . . are most lively anatomized', referring specifically to a performance of *1 Henry VI* in 1592 (Stanley Wells, ed., *Thomas Nashe: 'Pierce Penniless' . . . and Selected Writings* (London, 1964; Cambridge, Mass., 1965), p. 65). *An Apology for Actors*, referring to the staging of *Henry V*: 'What English Prince [or other spectator] . . . would not be suddenly inflamed with so royal a spectacle [as that presented by "our domestic histories"], being made apt and fit for the like achievement. So of *Henry* the Fifth' (B4ʳ). Heywood also claimed that 'so bewitching a thing is lively and well-spirited action, that it hath power to new-mould the hearts of the spectators, and fashion them to the shape of any noble and notable attempt'.

[2] Cruickshank, p. 16. McGurk, pp. 51, 63–4.

[3] Letter quoted in McGurk, p. 51. [4] McGurk, pp. 33–4.

full display of force meant to coerce Henry into submitting to Yorkist demands. *True Tragedy* also places a greater emphasis on pageant-like staging when it includes scripted battle shouts for Richard and Clifford in 2.4, where they engage in single combat. Warwick then joins them to rescue Richard from Clifford, who appears to be gaining the upper hand. In *3 Henry VI* there are no shouts and the action is anticlimactic because the stand-off between Richard and Clifford is aborted by Warwick's arrival. In 2.6 the Folio text omits the graphic direction requiring Clifford to enter wounded 'with an arrow in his neck', a sensationalizing detail recalling Elizabethan potboilers such as Thomas Preston's *Cambises*. The dialogue and directions of *True Tragedy* 4.2–3 suggest that a brief skirmish takes place involving Gloucester and Hastings, who are with Edward in his tent and then flee when they are surprised by Warwick's soldiers. Part Three simply calls for them to 'flee over the stage', which means they would enter from the tiring house through one stage door and exit through another. The Folio's directions also suggest that Edward's tent was notion-ally represented by the tiring house wall, since Warwick's men chase the Watchmen in, who are armed with halberds, and then re-emerge with Edward as prisoner. Martial histrionics are re-presented directly in *True Tragedy* 5.1 when Clarence enters, a par-ley is sounded, he and Richard whisper together, 'and then Clarence takes his red rose out of his hat, and throws it at Warwick' (E2^r). Again, *3 Henry VI* downplays this moment as a sudden, unexpected anticlimax.[1] Finally, and most tellingly, *True Tra-gedy* follows the pattern of both festive and neoclassical plays by maximizing the spectacular impact of the play's final stage battle:

Alarms to the battle, York flies, then the chambers be discharged. Then enter the King, Clarence and Gloucester and the rest, and make a great shout, and cry 'For York, for York'; and then the Queen is taken, and the Prince and Oxford and Somerset, and then sound and enter all again. (E4^r)

Similarly placed scenes occur in *Horestes*, *The Famous Victories of Henry V*, *The Wounds of Civil War*, *The Battle of Alcazar*, and *Richardus Tertius*. *3 Henry VI*'s considerably more abstemious direc-tions at this point may be partly the result of printing-house editing or the manuscript-derived origin of the Folio text. But the fact that

---

[1] See also pp. 119–20.

it substantially alters the narrative action by having Prince Edward captured separately from Margaret, and substitutes Holinshed's version of events for Hall's, suggests that Shakespeare reconceived the action, toning down the sound and fury, and thereby altering the overall effect and meaning of Part Three as a play whose attitude towards war is more rueful.[1]

Clearly such passages do not amount to any sustained commentary on England's military involvement in Continental wars during the 1580s and 1590s. Shakespeare avoided writing too directly about contemporary or near-recent events because public discussion of state affairs was officially prohibited, and plays were subject to approval by the Master of the Revels, the government's censor. But such differences between the two versions of *3 Henry VI* seem to distance the later Folio version from official Elizabethan wartime and political contexts.

'What should be the meaning of all those foughten fields?' asks Holinshed towards the end of his chapter on Henry's reign.[2] His immediate explanation is that feuding nobles took advantage of Henry's weak sovereignty to promote their personal ambitions by 'sundry practices', including armed conflict. But his puzzled tone shows he is neither entirely convinced nor satisfied by this. His misdoubt goes unanswered, as he moves on to Edward's reign.

Part Three moves in the same direction. Shakespeare is more concerned with representing multiple causes and effects of the Wars of the Roses than arriving at totalizing explanations. One of the perspectives he develops in expanded passages of Acts 2 to 5 is Henry's greater awareness of the moral nullity of factional revenge. Significantly, he gives no hint of Henry's temporary insanity, which led to the devolving of royal authority first on to Margaret, and later York as Protector. The only signs of Henry's 'madness' lie in his otherworldliness, and his empathy for the subjected and dispossessed, traits which earned him his early Tudor

---

[1] Such distinctions are reinforced further by *True Tragedy*'s apparent endorsement of popular contemporary attitudes towards English military involvement on the Continent, alliances between England and France, and the threat of foreign invasion, most notably in 3.3, the only scene set outside England.

[2] Or more precisely one of Holinshed's contributors, the traditionally moralizing Abraham Fleming (Qqqv^r).

5. Buffeted weakling, saintly idealist, or pacifist visionary? Henry
(David Oyelowo) listens to Margaret's objections (Fiona Bell) after
disinheriting their son to stop the civil war, in Michael Boyd's production
of *Henry VI Part Three* ('The Chaos'), the seventh play in the RSC's cycle
This England, 2000–1.

reputation as 'holy Harry'.[1] In dramatic terms they anticipate the
more wrenching divestments and belated humanity of later tragic
figures such as Lear. Modern actors have conveyed this evolution of
conscience in various ways, but all have tried to show that Henry's
awareness of the futility of the Lancastrian and Yorkist feud, and
his corresponding embrace of pacifist values, are the result not of
weakness or cowardice but of growing emotional and intellectual
courage.

A representative spectrum of modern stage interpretations
could begin with David Warner's much admired performance in
Hall and Barton's 1963–4 *Wars of the Roses*. Warner created a
painfully shy, physically awkward, but ultimately saintly figure,

---

[1] Henry VII made overtures to the Pope to have Henry canonized. See *Richard III*
4.4.25.

who passed through agonies of doubt before reaching a Christ-like serenity. Warner characterized Henry above all through qualities of deep piety and lost innocence. Alan Howard's performance in the 1977 RSC production was based on a more rigorously intellectual and less sentimental journey, in which he stripped himself of complacent moral assumptions and false idealism to achieve a potentially revolutionary vision. And in the 1988 *Plantagenets*, Ralph Fiennes portrayed Henry as a militant pacifist, whose growing tragic insight was accompanied by powerful outbursts of rage and grief towards the incomprehension of those around him.

For these actors, 2.5 became the pivotal moment of their performances in Part Three, as Henry's yearning for a domain of integrated physical and spiritual being coincides with his exclusion from the fighting by Margaret and Clifford. His idealistic—or radical—repudiation of opportunistic power is the exemplary personal act which validates his compassion for the victims of war. Like Ralph Vaughan Williams's haunting evocation of the First World War in the first movement of his Pastoral Symphony, Henry's opening passage memorializes the devastation of battle within a tranquil lyrical space. It also unfolds a traditional contrast between the measured simplicity of a shepherd's life and the restless burdens and meretricious glamour of kingship.[1] In doing so Henry achieves a limited but authentic spiritual authority which eludes York during his performance as a man of sorrows in 1.4. His molehill may be the same spot on which York was made to stand, in which case it reminds us that Henry, like York, is another *roi manqué*. Even *in extremis*, however, York never renounces his personal ambitions for power and vengeance, and there is no thought for the welfare, let alone forgiveness, of others.

The accidental killing by fathers and sons of their own sons and fathers was a conventional civil-war topos which Shakespeare found in both Hall and *Gorboduc*, but typically he did not adopt it

---

[1] Harold C. Goddard, writing in the shadow of the Second World War, first suggested that Shakespeare revised Henry's characterization in this scene to create companion pieces to his grandfather's speech on sleep in *2 Henry IV* and his father's on ceremony in *Henry V*: see *The Meaning of Shakespeare* (Chicago, 1951), p. 30. While this kind of programmatic rewriting now seems unlikely, lines 21–54 do look like new material inserted after the earlier, very different, brief speech by Henry in *True Tragedy*.

unquestioningly.[1] Reflecting the political instability of the early years of Elizabeth's reign, Sackville and Norton took a didactic approach to expounding the errors of political division and civil war in order to promote obedience to hierarchical authority and unified rule. In the late seventeenth century, in the heated factional atmosphere of the Exclusion Crisis, this message was resuscitated in John Crowne's fanatically royalist adaptation of *2 and 3 Henry VI, The Misery of Civil-War* (1680). Crowne makes the Battle of Towton the heart of his play, which begins with Lancastrian soldiers terrorizing several old countrymen, robbing them of their gold, and raping their daughters.[2] The scene culminates in a sensational tableau of 'Houses and Towns burning, Men and Women hang'd upon Trees, and Children on the tops of Pikes' (p. 36). Shakespeare, by contrast, avoids such caricature, refusing to falsify the human misery of civil strife with a dramatized homily on the evils of rebellion and the joys of absolutism.

Henry's attempt to transcend the reflex of compulsive revenge by embracing radical non-aggression is tested by inner conflict, and by the irreducibility of partisan ties, as his later encounter with the two Gamekeepers in 3.1 reveals. The First Gamekeeper is older, kindly, and concerned to pass on his experience; he may be played as father to the Second Gamekeeper. Unlike the fathers and sons of 2.5, however, their initial disagreement and potential separation is mutually redirected in a way that binds their self-interest. They confront Henry's pastoral escapism with rural pragmatism and material responsibilities. He enters undisguised but carrying a prayer book,[3] a non-historical detail in keeping with Part Three's greater emphasis on Henry's stoicism and Christian patience (e.g.

---

[1] For Hall, see note to 2.5.54.1–3. Katie Mitchell's 1994 RSC production took this further by actually inserting several speeches from *Gorboduc* into her script. D. J. Womersley traces the topos back to Tacitus: '3 *Henry VI*: Shakespeare, Tacitus, and Parricide', *N&Q* 32 (230) (1985), 468–73.

[2] See Joyce Green MacDonald, '"Hay for the Daughters!" Gender and Patriarchy in *The Miseries of Civil War* and *Henry VI*', *Comparative Drama*, 24 (1990), 193–216.

[3] In *True Tragedy* Henry enters disguised, a detail suggested by the chronicles. Dramatically, it also recalls conventional Elizabethan romance scenarios in which kings seek self-assurance by meeting their subjects temporarily as social equals, to try to convince themselves that their mutual interests are really the same. But such ruses were not merely the fanciful stuff of romance or drama, since contemporary military manuals commended disguises as useful strategy for deceiving enemy soldiers, and supplied classical and modern examples (de Somogyi, pp. 95–6).

'Let me embrace the sour adversities'). Yet Henry remains haunted by the loss of his royal identity. His imagined scenario of Margaret and Warwick pleading for support from King Lewis demonstrates that his political insight has not matured in the same way as his moral vision. While Henry foresees Warwick's rhetorical victory over Margaret, when the event actually takes place in 3.3, neither Margaret nor Warwick speaks or acts in the stilted manner Henry imagines, nor can he foresee the news of Edward's surprise marriage to Lady Grey. The difference in staging and outcome between these imagined and 'real' scenic moments discredits Henry's tendency to interpret political events as repeatable occurrences of older dramatic forms implying eternal metaphysical principles. Moreover, whereas Henry just a few scenes earlier was anxious to renounce his royal authority to embrace pastoral simplicity, when he actually confronts a real version of it, he finds it impossible to shift his former self-image:

> Ah simple men you know not what you swear.
> Look as I blow this feather from my face
> And as the air blows it to me again,
> Obeying with my wind when I do blow
> And yielding to another when it blows,
> Commanded always by the greater gust:
> Such is the lightness of you, common men.
>
> (3.1.82-8)

Yet Henry is equally aware that the solution does not lie in choosing between absolutes of goodness and evil, natural and unnatural motives. When he earlier describes the Battle of Towton at the beginning of 2.5, he compares it to the everyday ebb and flow of elemental forces:

> Now sways it this way like a mighty sea
> Forced by the tide to combat with the wind,
> Now sways it that way like the selfsame sea
> Forced to retire by fury of the wind.
> Sometime the flood prevails and then the wind,
> Now one the better then another best,
> Both tugging to be victors, breast to breast . . .
> So is the equal poise of this fell war. (5–11, 13)

This contention balances preservation and destruction in a morally neutral condition of raw creative strife. Henry's perspective becomes all the more fascinating when one compares Shakespeare's two versions of the play. For this class of metaphors is almost completely absent in *True Tragedy*,[1] even though it shares with Part Three a relatively equal proportion of all the other images common to the *Henry VI* plays (for instance, family dynasties as trees with roots and branches, war as slaughterhouse butchery, and revengers as beasts of prey[2]). The introduction of wind, sea, and tide imagery not only suggests Shakespeare revised the play reported by *True Tragedy*, but also sheds light on his evolved historical interpretation of the Wars of the Roses. Henry reads combat and shifting dynastic allegiances as inherent conditions of creation, rather than the material symptoms of sinful human behaviour.[3] Although war may represent the terminal breakdown of human rationality and the confounding of kinship relations, Shakespeare does not represent it as utter depletion or negation, the physical correlative of an ontological lapse into non-being or chaos.[4] Though English society tears itself apart, human bonds are never entirely extinguished.[5] Though blood-revenge extinguishes dynastic right, comradery and chivalry do not disappear entirely from the battlefield. Though ceremonies are interrupted, inverted,

---

[1] Henry's opening speech in *True Tragedy* compares the battle to 'a mastless ship upon the seas . . . | Now leaning this way, now to that side drive[n]' (C2ᵛ). If the Folio text represents his revision, then Shakespeare transferred this image to Queen Margaret's speech to her troops in 5.4, greatly expanding it with the help of Arthur Brooke's *Romeus and Juliet*, which he may have recently reread. See Appendix D.

[2] Kernan, pp. 431–42. Caroline F. E. Spurgeon, *Shakespeare's Imagery and What It Tells Us* (Cambridge, 1935), pp. 217–31. The play's natural imagery was vividly conveyed through recorded sounds—of birds, animals, weather conditions—in Katie Mitchell's 1994 RSC production. As Peter Holland observed, their presence had an estranging effect, as familiar phenomena appeared to be desecrated by human acts of brutality (*English Shakespeares: Shakespeare on the English Stage in the 1990s* (Cambridge, 1997), pp. 199–200).

[3] Nor is it the heroic game of traditional epic, in which humans are the unwitting subjects and agents of fate or providence. See George's references to his men as Olympians in 2.3 and discussion below, Appendix A, 2.3.49–53.

[4] There is nothing to match the apocalyptic hyberbole of Clifford's vow to revenge his father's death during the first Battle of St Albans at the end of *2 Henry VI*. As T. McAlindon has suggested, early modern cosmography admitted chaos, disorder, and death as part of the universal condition of contending elemental forces, which included their opposites, reason, order, and beauty (*Shakespeare's Tragic Cosmos* (Cambridge, 1991), pp. 4–8).

[5] This is otherwise a critical commonplace about the play; e.g. Carol McGinnis Kay, 'Traps, Slaughter, and Chaos: A Study of Shakespeare's *Henry VI* Plays', *Studies in the Literary Imagination*, 5 (1972), 1–26; Donald G. Watson, *Shakespeare's Early History Plays* (1990), pp. 80–4.

and travestied, vestiges of civilizing protocols linger. Though atrocities multiply, they continue to take comically macabre forms.[1] The fact that these traces of creative order and social discipline remain deepens the credibility of the play's anti-war vision. In terms of Henry's personal experience, though his family strife and mental sufferings profoundly transform his attitudes and behaviour, they never drive him mad.

Shakespeare's representation of civil war as natural fluctuations of wind, sea, and tide is indicative of *3 Henry VI*'s tendency to interpret historical causes phenomenologically. When these same images recur in the allegorical Father and Son tableaux which follow Henry's speeches,[2] their presence reinforces the idea that war, while undoubtedly the painful outcome of personal egotism and ambition, is a naturally recurring and therefore unavoidable condition. Henry becomes a pageant-like presenter of the two personal histories that unfold before him. His choric lamentations antiphonally match the Father's and Son's formally structured outpourings of grief, just as random moments of disinterested human empathy elsewhere in the play occasionally divert apparently endemic impulses towards communal destruction. The moment's visual austerity also throws dramatic emphasis on mourning the human waste of war, leaving its local origins and remedies to be assessed individually. Shakespeare resists co-opting these moments into an overreaching sectarian ideology, or a providential teleology.

Given how crucial Act 2, Scene 5 has become for modern productions, it is now somewhat surprising to read how difficult earlier directors found its allegorical mode. While rehearsing their 1952–3 Birmingham Repertory Theatre production, Sir Barry Jackson and Douglas Seale thought the stylized action and sudden change in mood from the surrounding battle scenes would seem comical, and therefore they planned initially to cut the scene. But eventually they recognized that its dramatic value derives from its formal dignity:

---

[1] Jones, pp. 183–92, Watson, p. 90.

[2] But not, as Kernan again observes ('A Comparison', p. 440), in *True Tragedy*'s version of the Father and Son speeches: 'Ill blows the wind that profits nobody' (*3 Henry VI* 2.5.55), 'See, see, what showers arise, | Blown with the windy tempest of my heart' (85–6), 'How will my wife for slaughter of my son | Shed seas of tears' (105–6).

The scene was retained, but treated as a static tableau: it shone out away and above the violent episodes with which it is surrounded and threw more light on the horror of civil war than all the scenes of wasteful bloodshed. The still figures of the father and son speaking quietly and unemotionally, as though voicing the thoughts that strike the saintly, sad King's conscience, presented a moment of calm and terrible reflection.[1]

While the Father and Son need not speak as 'unemotionally' as Jackson and Seale imagined, the latter became aware of the tableau's effective contrasts with the clashing movements before and the bitter grotesquerie after. In the same way, Shakespeare heightens the narrative impact of the Yorkist victory at the end of Act 2 by magnifying their losses and downplaying the Lancastrians' gains, prior to Towton.[2] Both kinds of experiences interweave in the theatre to create one of *3 Henry VI*'s memorable achievements: its ability to evoke contrary emotional and aesthetic responses towards representations of war. On the one hand audiences feel the wrenching anguish expressed by Henry, the Father, and the Son. On the other, what spectator is not affected and perhaps thrilled by the kinetic exuberance of artfully staged martial combat?

The (resistible?) rise of Richard of Gloucester

If some productions have chosen Henry's sorrowful insights into war as their guiding theme, many more have decided to centre the play on his emerging dramatic rival and ideological adversary, Richard of Gloucester, albeit for reasons that have more to do with the latter's stage life after this play. Until F. R. Benson's 1906 revival at the Shakespeare Memorial Theatre in Stratford-upon-Avon, *3 Henry VI* had been seen in England beyond the Elizabethan period only in adaptations by Theophilus Cibber, Crowne, Merivale, and Valpy. In Germany, however, the play was not neglected. Prior to 1914, over forty versions of *Henry VI* were performed, chiefly in

---

[1] 'On Producing *Henry VI*', *Shakespeare Survey* 6 (1953), 49–52; p. 51. Watson, pp. 83–4.

[2] In 2.1 a messenger reports York's death to Edward and Richard, and Warwick recounts another major Yorkist defeat at the second Battle of St Albans, and Lancastrian preparations for a further encounter. Shakespeare also virtually eliminates any mention of the Yorkist victory over Welsh Lancastrian forces at Mortimer's Cross. See Appendix A, 2.1.

Berlin and Weimar.[1] These began with Franz Dingelstedt's productions at the Weimar Court Theatre in 1857. Following A. W. Schlegel's discussions of Shakespeare's histories as national epics, Dingelstedt mounted both tetralogies over eight days.[2] The production was a landmark in the nineteenth-century German theatre and the pinnacle of Dingelstedt's long career.[3] Other distinguished productions were Jocza Savits's *2* and *3 Henry VI* and *Richard III* at the Munich Court Theatre in 1899–1906, performed on an enlarged 'Shakespeare stage' which extended the forestage over the pit.[4] The most famous festival at Saladin Schmitt's classical Municipal Theatre in Bochum was his June 1927 production of Shakespeare's histories. Schmitt was a pictorialist who created visually lavish productions in what was dubbed his 'heraldic' style. The focus of the first tetralogy was Richard of Gloucester: gestures, dress, and allusions in the preceding plays all looked forward to his performance as Richard III. Although Schmitt's reading was historically and culturally conservative, it was attacked by the Nazis for not being politically topical.[5]

Elsewhere, *Henry VI* was performed in seventeenth-century France before Louis XIII, who was reportedly struck by one of its scenes (which one is unknown).[6] More recently, the entire first tetralogy was staged in a twelve-hour adaptation directed by Denis Llorca in Carcassonne in 1978 and the following year in Créteil outside Paris.[7] Giorgio Strehler staged college productions of all three parts of *Henry VI* in 1973–5 at Vienna and Salzburg.[8] The first recorded production in America seems to have taken place in California, in a complete cycle of all ten Shakespeare history plays

[1] Wilhelm Hortmann, *Shakespeare on the German Stage: The Twentieth Century* (Cambridge, 1998), pp. 95–6. Ernst Leopold Stohl, *Shakespeare und das Deutsche Theater* (Stuttgart, 1947).

[2] They were revived in 1864 in Weimar and taken to Vienna's Burgtheater in 1873.

[3] Simon Williams, *Shakespeare on the German Stage, 1586–1914*, 2 vols. (Cambridge, 1990), i. 153–4.

[4] Williams, i. 185–8.

[5] Hortmann, pp. 94–8. Two more productions took place in 1926 and 1927 at Berlin and Weimar (Stohl).

[6] Christopher Smith, 'Shakespeare on French Stages in the Nineteenth Century', in *Shakespeare and the Victorian Stage*, ed. Richard Foulkes (Cambridge, 1986), 223–39; p. 230 n. 3.

[7] Hattaway, p. 47.

[8] Christian Jauslin, 'Das Spiel der Mächtigen: Giorgio Strehlers Einrichtung von *Henry VI*', *Deutsche Shakespeare-Gesellschaft West Jahrbuch*, 112 (1976), 15–22.

directed by Gilmor Brown at the Pasadena Community Playhouse, 25–7 July 1935. And to return to Germany, Peter Palitzsch staged a Brechtian version (*Der Rosenkriege*) in Berlin in 1967.[1]

Perhaps the main reason for the play's limited stage life in the English-speaking world during most of this period was that it had been partially absorbed into one of the most successful and enduring Shakespearian adaptations of all time: Colley Cibber's *The Tragical History of King Richard the Third. Containing The Distresses and Death of King Henry the Sixth* . . . (1700). Richard became the supreme star in Cibber's melodramatic offering of just over 2,000 lines, only about half of which were by Shakespeare. The play's first act derives largely from *3 Henry VI*: reports of the Battle of Tewkesbury, Henry's molehill lament on civil war and the burdens of kingship, and much of 5.6, in which Richard murders Henry in the Tower. A soliloquy by Richard in Act 2 borrows from his longer speech in *3 Henry VI* 3.2. And during his wooing of Lady Anne, Tressel and Stanley comment in the same manner as Clarence and Gloucester when Edward bluntly woos Lady Grey, though their ribald sarcasm is directed against Anne rather than Richard.

Cibber's play entirely displaced Shakespeare's *Richard III* between 1700 and 1821, when Macready briefly revived the original, and remained dominant until Henry Irving's productions of Shakespeare in 1877 and 1896–7.[2] Even after this, bits of Cibber, including passages derived from Part Three, continued to be interpolated into performances of *Richard III* well into the twentieth century. The best known example is Laurence Olivier's 1955 film version, which opens with Edward IV's coronation and borrows lines from Gloucester's two soliloquies in *3 Henry VI*. Before this, F. R. Benson's 1911 silent film version of *Richard III* began with the aftermath of Tewkesbury, and Gloucester's murder of Henry in the Tower.[3] Raiding Part Three is a temptation which modern produc-

---

[1] Anthony Vivis, 'Shakespeare without the shadows', *Gambit*, 3.10 (1965), 96–9.

[2] Odell, *Betterton to Irving*, i. 75, ii. 153–4, 310–11.

[3] Reproduced in the British Film Institute's video, *Silent Shakespeare* (1999). In Scene 1, a defeated Henry and Margaret are brought in among the Yorkist troops. Henry resigns his crown to Edward and is quietly escorted away, followed by a furious Margaret. The handcuffed and defiant Prince Edward is brought in, violently run through by Clarence and multiply stabbed by a jubilant Gloucester. In the extraordinary second scene, Henry sits reading as Gloucester enters and provokes him into righteous anger. Explosively, Gloucester stabs Henry, who falls on his back on the table. Gloucester then climbs up and, standing over Henry's still twitching body, stabs him deeply in the heart. He wipes his dagger several times on Henry's clothes,

tions of *Richard III* continue to find hard to resist, in order to provide greater background and depth to Richard's story. In America, Cibber's adaptation proved just as tenaciously popular. It was first performed in New York City by a company from Philadelphia in 1750, and then was staged very regularly until 1878.[1] As late as the 1920s, John Barrymore included much of Cibber in his productions of *Richard III*.[2]

Such assimilation is symptomatic of the tendency to view *3 Henry VI* as an induction to *Richard III*. This is understandable, of course, since Shakespeare wrote Part Three with his next history play in mind. The plans Gloucester lays out at the end of his soliloquy in 5.6, and his threatening asides in the final scene, both anticipate the coming action.[3] But critics have sometimes pitted the success of *Richard III* against the different fortunes of Part Three, speculating that Shakespeare was bored when writing it.[4] The stage equivalent is that Cibber's practice of borrowing passages from *3 Henry VI* has been reversed: the opening moments of *Richard III* are routinely appended to Part Three's final scene. This adaptation was introduced by Seale's 1952 production. Richard slowly approached the throne as the court left the stage, turned to the audience upon reaching it, and began his opening soliloquy from *Richard III*, 'Now is the winter of our discontent . . .'. He continued for thirty lines to 'I am determined to prove a villain' as the curtain fell and his voice faded.[5] When the production reappeared at the Old Vic in 1957, this relatively quiet alteration was taken even further:

sheathes it slowly, and with one foot on Henry's chest flourishes a triumphant wave, before stepping down to carry him out slung over his back.

[1] George C. D. Odell, *Annals of the New York Stage*, 15 vols. (New York, 1927–49), i. 32–4, x. 365.

[2] Hazelton Spencer, *The Art and Life of William Shakespeare* (New York and London, 1940), p. 164.

[3] Although Edward's command to 'waft' Margaret to France, which appears in both texts of the play, suggests that *Richard III* may have not followed directly after. Many commentators believe *Titus Andronicus* came in between. But if this is the case, Shakespeare must have decided to allow this discrepancy to remain when he revised *True Tragedy* as the Folio *3 Henry VI*, which almost certainly took place after writing *Richard III*.

[4] E. M. W. Tillyard, *Shakespeare's History Plays* (1944), p. 190. Robert Ornstein, *A Kingdom for a Stage* (Cambridge, Mass., 1972), p. 53. Victor Kiernan, *Shakespeare, Poet and Citizen* (London and New York, 1993), p. 44.

[5] Susan Margaret Kay, 'A Stage History of William Shakespeare's "Henry VI" Trilogy' (unpublished MA dissertation, Shakespeare Institute, University of Birmingham, 1980), pp. 82–3.

Richard of Gloucester limped towards the royal throne and, silhouetted against the spider's web of a backcloth, began hysterically to proclaim his first soliloquy [from *Richard III*]. . . . His voice was drowned by the shouts of jubilation off-stage [for Edward IV's coronation], but his lips continued to move and the effect on an audience . . . was tremendous.[1]

Critics were divided about this ending, some considering it effective and others unnecessary. Kenneth Tynan praised it as 'a magnificent stroke of textual audacity'.[2] While it undoubtedly intensified the irony of Part Three's festive closure and the hollowness of Edward's triumph, it weakened the play's overall dramatic integrity, and certainly changed its reading of history by decisively orienting events forward, towards Richard's 'evil' reign and the 'providential' Tudor victory at Bosworth. No production since then has adapted the final scene so elaborately, but many have continued to make some link with *Richard III*. In the 1987 ESC and 1988 RSC productions, for example, Gloucester moved downstage following King Edward's last speech and shouted 'Now!' and 'Now is the winter of our discontent', respectively, before the stage went black.

The impulse of these productions was the same as Cibber's: to foreground Richard's story to gratify the desires of actors and audiences for star parts, and to subordinate the play's multiple plotlines to a single dominant character and narrative. It also gave spectators the satisfaction of seeing a connection with the more familiar play. But linking *3 Henry VI* explicitly to *Richard III* also reflexively imparts a politicized reading of history to Part Three's events which they themselves suggest far less certainly.

Part Three and the Tudor Myth. While Shakespeare found his immediate subject and suggestions for his historical characters in Hall and Holinshed, his dramatization, as we have seen, reflects his audience's experience of wartime conditions in the 1580s and 1590s, and their interest in contemporary political issues. Anticipating these guided his thematic selection and artistic presentation of events, giving them a range of historical, contemporary, and universal significance. Shakespeare clarified the chronicles' often repetitive and confusing accounts into a fast-paced story by delet-

---

[1] Mary Clarke, *Shakespeare at the Old Vic* (1958), n.p.
[2] *Curtains* (1961), p. 182.

ing a great deal of circumstantial material. He also rearranged the historical sequence to sharpen the thematic relationship of events, and he fictionalized bare facts to make them poetically and visually memorable. By condensing events which took place spasmodically over many years, Shakespeare creates a sustained sense of national turmoil in Part Three.

Modern historians tell us that the impact of the Wars of the Roses was restricted largely to feuding nobles and their immediate retainers in private armies, leaving other sections of society relatively unaffected. Shakespeare broadens the scope of the Wars' impact, insisting on the destruction of community values at all levels of society. The Sons and Fathers of 2.5, the Gamekeepers in 3.1, the Huntsman in 4.5, and the civic officials in 4.7 all mimic the cynical self-interest of their social superiors. Unlike modern civil wars, whose political conflicts are usually ideological[1] or ethnic, the quarrels of *3 Henry VI* are largely interpersonal. Close ties of kinship intensify violations of human decency. Though both sides appeal to past events in the opening scene and sporadically throughout the play, on the whole key events represented in *2 Henry VI* (and Part One, if it was written first) seem distant and secondary. Part Three's faint sense of long-term causality also reflects the absence of institutional law and customary values which rely on written records for their enabling authority. Spectators who have seen Part Two might link this erasure of civil memory to the destruction of books and legal documents during Cade's rebellion. But there are no direct references to such episodes in Part Three. Nor is the apocalyptic conflagration memorably anticipated by Clifford at the end of Part Two (5.3.31 ff.) emblematically borne out in the sequel play. Rather there are groups of mostly alienated and aggressive political animals, defined in the most extreme way by Richard's declaration, 'I am myself alone' (5.6.83).

The relatively few markers of historical memory in Part Three, when it is seen or read as a single play, make the relationship between individual human activities and wider unifying patterns or explanations ambiguous. Perhaps more than anything else, this contingency makes Part Three a *history* play in a modern sense of

[1] Peter Saccio, *Shakespeare's English Kings: History, Chronicle and Drama* (London, Oxford, and New York, 1978), p. 12.

the term.[1] If he had wished, Shakespeare could have strengthened references to definitive moral explanations and cyclical designs, as his chronicle sources regularly did in the face of humanly inexplicable or underdetermined events, to give his overall story a familiar sense of emplotment and thematic rigour closer to comic or tragic forms.[2] (The absence of these features often leads critics to describe the play as 'episodic'.) Doing so would have imposed a guiding theory on political events, such as the official Tudor view that rebellion against the king violates metaphysical laws, resulting in divine retribution in the form of social upheaval. His final scenes could have contained reminders, despite Gloucester's threats, of the future unification of the houses of Lancaster and York, as Elizabethan chroniclers and pageant writers retrospectively emphasized continually. Part Three would then have felt more solidly part of an epic narrative. But its tentative and sardonic ending limits the controlling order implied by the experience of narrative closure.[3] While Shakespeare patterns events scenically and emotionally, he avoids stabilizing their future meaning as definitively catastrophic or redemptive.

One important exception occurs in 4.6, when Henry prophesies over the young Henry of Richmond, future Henry VII. This moment, and the Tudor 'myth' or patterned reading of the Wars of the Roses it hints at, gains greater prominence when *3 Henry VI* is staged as part of a larger dramatic cycle. In this context, the play becomes the anarchic low point in a national *commedia* which ultimately ends in the restoration of political order after the Battle of Bosworth at the end of *Richard III*. This story of the country's fall and recovery was understood by many Elizabethans as God's plan for his chosen nation, with the Wars of the Roses representing divine punishment being meted out for the original deposition of England's rightful heir and king, Richard II.[4] But if the play is per-

---

[1] Clayton Roberts, *The Logic of Historical Explanation* (University Park, Pennsylvania, 1996).

[2] G. K. Hunter, *English Drama 1586–1642: The Age of Shakespeare* (Oxford, 1997), pp. 158–60.

[3] David L. Frey, *The First Tetralogy: Shakespeare's Scrutiny of the Tudor Myth* (The Hague, 1976). David Scott Kastan, *Shakespeare and the Shapes of Time* (Hanover, NH, 1982), pp. 48–55.

[4] This Tudor perspective on the whole group of history plays was reconceptualized by the German Romantic critic A. W. Schlegel in *Lectures on Dramatic Art and Literature* (1815), and restated by Tillyard in his influential *Shakespeare's History Plays*.

formed on its own, this wider historical narrative recedes, since apart from Henry's prophecy in 4.6, Part Three does not support it. Given that Shakespeare did not originally conceive of all these plays as a grand cycle, the play becomes more what it probably was for contemporary spectators: a play about the dangers of political instability, the miseries of civil war, and the compensations of sporadic individual valour.[1]

Richard sans Bosworth. Gloucester's soliloquy in 3.2, the longest in the canon, occurs at the exact midpoint of the play. It characterizes him in a dazzlingly innovative way, marking his transition to a new historical role and creating an arresting emotional and imaginative focus for spectators. Dramatically, both this and his second soliloquy in 5.6 recall York's monologues in *2 Henry VI* (1.1, 3.1), in which he outlines his bid for the crown. Father and son are eventually united by their superior tactical cunning and political pragmatism, and by their privileged relationship with the theatre audience. During much of Acts 1 and 2 of Part Three, however, Richard's fierce pride in his paternal inheritance takes the form of proving his physical courage in battle, and avenging York's and Rutland's deaths, motives he shares with Edward:

> My sons God knows what hath bechancèd them,
> But this I know, they have demeaned themselves
> Like men born to renown by life or death.
>
> (1.4.6–8)

Revenging fathers and sons in fact changes the nature of the 'contention' between Parts Two and Three, from political wrangling over dynastic legitimacy to a savage blood-feud. Beyond the opening scene, historical rights and legal obligations fade into the

---

[1] Donald G. Watson argues that the play's subversive nihilism is countered by our knowledge of Richard's eventual fall and his damning reputation for evil (p. 99). But this can work the opposite way, since we know that Richard's defamation was the result of Tudor propaganda. Peter L. Rudnytsky shows that More's *History of King Richard III*, which both Hall and Holinshed absorbed and which is largely responsible for vilifying Richard, also criticizes Henry VIII by analogous reference to both Edward IV's sexual depravity and Richard's absolutism ('More's *History of King Richard III* as an Uncanny Text', in *Contending Kingdoms*, ed. Marie-Rose Logan and Peter L. Rudnytsky (Detroit, 1991), 149–72, pp. 165–7). I would argue, moreover, that *not* linking the plays in terms of a triumphalist teleology is a legitimate conceptual alternative allowed by the play, and is unquestionably a theatrical option.

background, with the exception of Margaret's defence of Prince Edward. Clifford and Richard in particular mimic each other's ferocious brutality. Their language often recalls the declamatory rhetoric of Elizabethan revenge tragedy, epitomized by Thomas Kyd's enormously popular *Spanish Tragedy*.[1] Kyd's play initially lends *3 Henry VI* certain other features of the revenge play, besides the basic emphasis on the violent rupturing of bonds between father and son.[2] Henry's first response to the sight of York sitting in his throne is to remind Clifford and Northumberland of their fathers' deaths:

> Earl of Northumberland, he slew thy father,
> And thine Lord Clifford, and you both have vowed revenge . . .
>
> (1.1.54–5)

Clifford's speeches before he slaughters Rutland parade the deranged fantasies of a psychotic revenger:

> . . . if I digged up thy forefathers' graves
> And hung their rotten coffins up in chains,
> It could not slake mine ire nor ease my heart.
>
> (1.3.28–30)

The bloody napkin with which Margaret taunts York in 1.4 would almost certainly have reminded Elizabethan spectators who had seen Kyd's play of the handkerchief Hieronimo carries as a memento of his murdered son Horatio.[3] Richard also inherits the brutally jocular language and gestures of revenge and morality-drama villains.[4] His abuse of Somerset's head in the play's opening

---

[1] *True Tragedy* seems closer to this tradition than *3 Henry VI* at several points such as 2.4, where Richard and Clifford confront each other in single combat:

> *Richard* A Clifford, a Clifford.
> *Clifford* A Richard, a Richard.
> *Richard* Now Clifford, for York and young Rutland's death,
> This thirsty sword that longs to drink thy blood
> Shall lop thy limbs and slice thy cursed heart,
> For to revenge the murders thou hast made.   (C2ʳ)

[2] Ronald S. Berman, 'Fathers and Sons in the *Henry VI* Plays', *SQ* 13 (1962), 487–97.
[3] John Kerrigan, *Revenge Tragedy: Aeschylus to Armageddon* (Oxford, 1996), pp. 174–81.
[4] Tom McAlindon, 'The Evil of Play and the Play of Evil: Richard, Iago and Edmund Contextualized', in *Shakespeare's Universe: Renaissance Ideas and Conventions*, ed. John M. Mucciolo (Aldershot, 1996), 148–54; p. 151. McAlindon argues that Richard's talents for role-playing and deception do not actually derive from the

6. Savage mockery: Edward (Alfred Lynch, above left), Richard (Anton Lesser) and George (Jack Klaff, right) taunt the dead or dying Clifford (Anthony Naylor) in Terry Hands's *Henry VI Part Three*, Royal Shakespeare Theatre, 1977.

moments is an instance of this; others are the grotesque treatment of Clifford's corpse in 2.6, the re-stabbing of Henry's body in 5.6, and his grimly comic 'remorse' for murdering Henry: 'See how my sword weeps for the poor king's death' (5.6.63). He displays the Vice's and/or devil's wily persuasiveness in 1.2 when he convinces York to break his agreement with Henry.[1]

Vice of the morality plays but from non-dramatic representations of the devil. The two types are not mutually exclusive, however; one is simply more closely identified with a dramatic heritage and the other with theological and literary ones.

[1] Variant passages in *True Tragedy* also reveal Shakespeare moving away from the morality tradition in *3 Henry VI*; e.g.

> *Richard.* Then thus my lord. An oath is of no moment
> Being not sworn before a lawful magistrate.
> Henry is none but doth usurp your right,
> And yet your grace stands bound to him by oath.
> Then noble father resolve your self,
> And once more claim the crown. (A6ᵛ–A7ʳ)

Despite its initial connections with revenge drama and the morality interlude, *3 Henry VI* ultimately subverts these genres.[1] If plays such as *The Spanish Tragedy* and *Hamlet* test their protagonists' ability to remember lost family members, as John Kerrigan has argued,[2] *3 Henry VI* conspicuously abandons this imperative. When the York brothers lash out against Prince Edward in 5.5, they are responding to his personal taunts, with no thoughts of avenging their murdered father or brother. It is Margaret's anguished curses that recall York's cries for revenge in 1.4,[3] and Henry in the next scene who connects his anticipated death with the loss of his son, in his comparisons to Daedalus and Icarus. While the deaths of Prince Edward and Henry in Act 5 structurally reprise the deaths of Rutland and York in Act 1, the symmetry is not inflected by any sense of moral rebalancing ordained by fate or providence.[4] That is the perspective of *Richard III*, when the ghosts of Prince Edward and Henry haunt Richard on the eve of Bosworth. Edward's obtusely smug roll-call of the Wars' aristocratic victims in the final scene brings home for the last time how the revenge ethic has been outstripped by expedient violence with no aim other than the seizure of power.

In the midst of the Wars' self-confounding degradation of civil customs, Richard seizes the opportunity to imprint his ambitions. Family piety towards York, sustained beyond his father's death in pursuing revenge, held Richard's personal aspirations in check.

Ambidextrous Vices often contradicted themselves to reach deliberately illogical, morally confounding, conclusions. The fourth line, unique to *True Tragedy*, creates a non sequitur which Richard simply overrides. See also notes to 1.2.22–34, 29–31.

[1] Here again *True Tragedy* is closer to earlier dramatic models. In 5.1, for example, when Clarence switches loyalties back to the Yorkists before the walls of Coventry,

> *Edw.* A parley sirra to George of Clarence.
> Sound a parley, and Richard and Clarence whispers together . . .
> (E1ᵛ–E2ʳ)

Gloucester's whisperings are a stock bit of mischief in the Vice's repertoire, and one could assume he prompts Clarence's histrionic flinging of his rose which follows. *3 Henry VI* follows Holinshed in eliminating Richard's intervention and in making Clarence independently motivated (see Appendix A, 5.1.80–2).

[2] Kerrigan, *Revenge Tragedy*, ch. 7, pp. 170–92.   [3] Compare 5.5 and 1.4.

[4] There is no enlightenment or conventional catharsis, 'only a furious recapitulation of crime, quite unlike the ultimate synthesis of crime and "justice" of some sort even in the denouement of the revenge play' (Berman, 'Fathers and Sons', p. 494).

Edward's succession as king, and the dynastic implications of his plans to marry, create new obstacles which Richard first implicitly acknowledges in his bawdy commentary on Edward's crude wooing of Lady Grey. In this scene Shakespeare travesties the rituals of romantic courtship by partially recycling the Yorkists' sardonic baiting of Clifford in 2.6.[1] The earlier pattern of rapid-fire colloquial spite here takes the form of stichomythic repartee and a battery of double entendres. These sexualize Lady Grey's body as the source rather than the object of destabilizing male desire. And where emotional tension was generated in the earlier scene by ambiguity about the moment of Clifford's death, here it arises from the shifting target of Richard's barbs. Most of his remarks are meant to amuse Clarence (and us), but some may be intended to be overheard by Edward. Others seem to preview the aspirations he will disclose fully when left alone on stage: for example, 'Ay, good leave have you, ⌐aside¬ for you will have leave | Till youth take leave and leave you to the crutch' (3.2.34–5).

The important interpretive question of whether his new role is prefigured by words or actions in his earlier scenes has divided critical opinion and stage practice. Some performers wish to make Shakespeare's characterization more consistent by drawing out Richard's implicit but unstated motives and aspirations before 3.2. Others prefer to capitalize on the dramatic revelation of Gloucester's inner motives and hidden ambitions.[2] To cite just one instance of the second approach, in Ashland's (adapted) production of Part Three in 1992, Michael Hume made Richard's murderous ambitions apparent from the beginning. His menacing gestures and growling voice suppressed opportunities for comedy in favour of chilling intimidation. He also carried a metal dagger which he would casually and menacingly twirl while speaking. Reviewers described it as a mechanized extension of his malevolent body.

When Richard is persuading York to break his oath and seize the throne by force in 1.2, an actor can simultaneously convey the impression that Richard is speaking for himself, expressing underlying fantasies which anticipate his disclosures in 3.2.

[1] Watson, pp. 93–5.
[2] For example, no hint before 3.2 (Wilson, p. xxxii) versus, 'From his first appearance in Part 2 Richard's potential self glints from behind its future-mask in puns, asides, and a glibly vigorous idiom' (John W. Blanpied, *Time and the Artist in Shakespeare's English Histories* (Newark, NJ, 1983), p. 70).

> And father do but think
> How sweet a thing it is to wear a crown,
> Within whose circuit is Elysium
> And all that poets feign of bliss and joy.
>   (1.2.28–31)[1]

Elsewhere Richard seems fleetingly to reveal his thoughts about his place in the order of succession and his dreams of gaining the throne:

> EDWARD   . . . henceforward will I bear
>   Upon my target three fair-shining suns.
> RICHARD
>   Nay, bear three daughters; by your leave I speak it,
>   You love the breeder better than the male.
>   (2.1.39–42)

Richard's wordplay on Edward's 'suns' betrays his buried fears, but 'bear three daughters' serves as his imagined escape clause. Realizing he may have given himself away, Richard deflects suspicion with a waggish jibe at his brother's womanizing. At Ashland in 1977, Michael Santo's Richard grimaced openly during Warwick's later speech at ll. 193–4 when he declares Edward Duke of York and heir apparent to the crown, while in the 1983 BBC production Ron Cook simply looked away, expressionless.

Richard's soliloquy in 3.2 is an artistic watershed in terms of Shakespeare's conceptual powers as a playwright. As we noted, the soliloquy form can be related to York's monologues in Part Two, in which his will to dominate was the conventional manifestation of his chivalric valour and dynastic pride. But these public objectives were not connected to, or set against, disclosed inner motives, and in effect we eavesdropped on York's plans. Shakespeare makes Richard's new identity as cynical dissembler dependent on persuading us of the authenticity of his private desires. While his feelings of physical and sexual conflict are part of common human experience, Shakespeare formulates them uniquely in terms of Richard's personal history.

---

[1] Compare York's lines in *2 Henry VI* at 3.1.351–4:

> And this fell tempest shall not cease to rage
> Until the golden circuit on my head
> Like to the glorious sun's transparent beams
> Do calm the fury of this mad-bred flaw.

Having witnessed his brother's impulsive barter of royal author-ity for lust, Richard vents his disgust at Edward's conquest, and his frustration at the suddenly greater difficulty of gaining the crown. The topographical simile of an unreachable shore (134–45) and the self-mocking fantasy of seducing women in the teeth of his deformities (146–62) brilliantly convey his psychic distress and humiliating sense of physical paralysis.[1] But out of these imagined debilities, Richard discovers a new sense of purpose. Denied normal opportunities to achieve sexual and worldly satisfaction, Richard sees himself as exceptionally burdened by fate. This exempts him, in his view, from the moral constraints which govern the behaviour of ordinary persons.[2] Richard therefore feels justified in compensating for his physical disadvantages:

> Then since this earth affords no joy to me
> But to command, to check, to o'erbear such
> As are of better person than myself,
> I'll make my heaven to dream upon the crown . . .
>
> (3.2.165–8)

As many commentators observe, however, the deformities Richard catalogues here and in his later soliloquy fail to correspond with the physically vigorous soldier who fights with conspicuous success in *2* and *3 Henry VI*. True, his opponents label him 'indigest and deformed lump' and 'crookback'. Their thinking is traditional, linking moral depravity with physical deformity. But even if their remarks are not merely exaggeration, nothing in Richard's own descriptions to this point suggests the grotesque cripple who mat-erializes here. In the theatre this discrepancy may be especially glaring, since modern performers often choose to play Richard as minimally disabled.[3] If this is the case, he is not simply a passive victim of psychological wounds who salvages some scrap of self-worth from his physical disadvantages. Rather, he defiantly

---

[1] Pearlman, pp. 419–20.

[2] Although Edward's treatment of Lady Grey has just illustrated his gross lack of self-discipline, he was obliged to accept her insistence on marriage. There are several hints elsewhere of Edward's suppressed moral conscience. See pp. 72–3.

[3] For example, Ian Holm's deformities in Hall and Barton's 1963–4 *Wars of the Roses* were much mental as physical. Reviewers continually resorted to psy-chological terms to describe his attitudes and behaviour: 'narcissistic', 'manic-depressive', 'schizophrenic', 'psychopathic'. Holm clearly wished to avoid comparison with Laurence Olivier's jokester–villain.

amplifies his deformities to galvanize his transgressive desires, and excuses himself from suppressing what would otherwise be avoided as antisocial behaviour on the grounds that he is specially privileged.[1] His process of self-justification was noted by Freud, who quoted the opening speech of *Richard III* to illustrate the pathology of 'exceptional' persons: 'They say that they have renounced enough and suffered enough, and have a claim to be spared any further demands; they will submit no longer to any disagreeable necessity, for they are *exceptions* and, moreover, intend to remain so'.[2]

Freud's analysis applies equally well to Gloucester's soliloquies in 3 *Henry VI*:

'Nature has done me a grievous wrong in denying me the beauty of form which wins human love. Life owes me reparation for this, and I will see that I get it. I have a right to be an exception, to disregard the scruples by which others let themselves be held back. I may do wrong myself, since wrong has been done to me.'[3]

From this point onward, Richard's self-fashioned peculiarity also takes the form of his physical apartness on stage. Certainly by the final scene, but also often at earlier points such as 4.1, performers usually position themselves away from the rest of the other characters. This makes it easier to maintain Gloucester's rapport with the audience beyond his soliloquies through quick glances or sly gestures. The BBC television production reinforced his detached perspective through technical means by sometimes dividing the camera shot, with Richard appearing in close-up on one side while the others—who looked mechanical during these moments—carried on in the distance. Freud also discussed this rapport with the theatre audience and why spectators confer on Richard such psychological credibility. People who convince themselves they are exceptions, he explained, are not in fact abnormal but simply larger than life versions of ourselves, since

---

[1] Marjorie Garber, *Shakespeare's Ghost Writers* (New York and London, 1987), pp. 30–42.
[2] 'The "Exceptions"', in 'Some character-types met with in psycho-analytic work' (1916), *The Standard Edition of the Complete Psychological Works of Sigmund Freud*, ed. James Strachey, 23 vols. (1957), xiv. 312.
[3] 'The "Exceptions"', pp. 314–15.

We all think we have reason to reproach Nature and our destiny for congenital and infantile disadvantages; we all demand reparation for early wounds to our narcissism, our self-love. Why did not Nature give us . . . the strength of Siegfried or the lofty brow of genius or the noble profile of aristocracy? (p. 315)

Richard's ambitions are therefore outsize, but his impulses are, in Freud's terms, essentially universal.

Midway through Richard's soliloquy Shakespeare deepens the paradoxical ordinariness of Richard's motives by creating a rhetorical correlative for the mental hurdles he is ostensibly striving to overcome. Briefly his speech lapses into self-doubt and passionate frustration using the 'thorny wood' simile of entrapment (172–81).[1] The brute force recalls his battlefield prowess in Acts 1 and 2. But since that role now contradicts his new psychically empowering deformity, Richard cannot go back. Recoiling from vaunting his limitations, he lights on performativity as his supreme enabling power. Like *The Taming of the Shrew*'s Petruccio in his famous 'politic' speech ('He that knows better how to tame a shrew, | Now let him speak'), Richard confident(ial)ly promises his audience a virtuoso performance in exchange for their moral amnesia.

Shakespeare seems to take up hints of Richard's theatricalizing tendencies supplied by More's *History of King Richard III*,[2] while a contemporary label updates Richard's characterization in terms of a new and controversial political ideology. Towards the end of his speech, Richard boasts:

> I'll play the orator as well as Nestor,
> Deceive more slyly than Ulysses could,
> And like a Sinon take another Troy.
> I can add colours to the chameleon,
> Change shapes with Proteus for advantages,
> And set the murd'rous Machiavel to school.
>
> (3.2.188–93)

---

[1] Both this simile and the preceding one of the far-off shore are absent from *True Tragedy*. They look as if they were inserted as part of Shakespeare's revision.

[2] Rudnytsky, *passim*. Pearlman, pp. 421–4. Arthur Noel Kincaid, 'The Dramatic Structure of Sir Thomas More's *History of King Richard III*', *Studies in English Literature*, 12 (1972), 223–42.

Protean versatility and verbal manipulation extend the dramatic heritage of the morality Vice, as do the conventional classical comparisons to Nestor, Ulysses, and Sinon.[1] But 'Machiavel' sensationalizes Richard, since the Italian philosopher's ideas had been notorious for decades. The English response to Machiavelli was complex and paradoxical, partly because his theories were often encountered second-hand in caricatured form. His sanctioning of evil means was deplored by both Catholic and Protestant commentators as atheistical advice of the devil.[2] Yet as a cultural discourse, Machiavellism gained an enormous hegemony from readers or spectators who interpreted contemporary events in terms of his actual or supposed precepts, or who identified stage Machiavels with real public figures.[3] Machiavelli was also widely (or grudgingly) admired for his shrewd political pragmatism, rhetorical brilliance, and historical analysis.[4]

Only a year or two before Shakespeare wrote the first version of *3 Henry VI*, Marlowe's *The Jew of Malta* (c.1589–90) had burlesqued these conflicting reputations in spectacularly exaggerated form.[5] The play's prologue is spoken by Machiavel himself, while his villain–disciple Barabas torments his victims in a zany parody of social and religious iconoclasm. Shakespeare's Richard shares the arrogant aloofness and jaunty cynicism of both figures, especially in his asides. Marlowe's model, and the apparent originator of the figure as a theatricalized type, may have been Anne Dowriche, whose *The French History* (1589) portrays Catherine de Medici as a ruthlessly partisan oppor-

---

[1] In *True Tragedy* the allusions to Nestor, Ulysses, and Sinon are missing, and the final line reads: 'And set the aspiring Catiline to school' (C8^v). The variant references to 'Catiline' and 'Machiavel' allude jointly to Bishop John Leslie's *A Treatise of Treasons Against Queen Elizabeth* (1572), in which they appear interchangeably as terms of abuse for two of Elizabeth's most powerful ministers, Sir Nicholas Bacon, Lord Keeper, and William Cecil, Lord Treasurer and later Lord Burghley. These connections are explored in R. Martin, 'Rehabilitating John Somerville in *3 Henry VI*', *SQ* 51 (2000), 332–40.

[2] Felix Raab, *The English Face of Machiavelli* (London and Toronto, 1964). Antonio D'Andrea, 'Studies on Machiavelli and his Reputation in the Sixteenth Century', *Mediaeval and Renaissance Studies*, 5 (1961), 214–40. D'Andrea, 'Some Elizabethan Allusions to Machiavelli', *English Miscellany*, 20 (1969), 52–74.

[3] For example, *1 Henry VI*: 'Alençon, that notorious Machiavel?' (5.6.74).

[4] Victoria Kahn, *Machiavellian Rhetoric: From the Counter-Reformation to Milton* (Princeton, 1994).

[5] N. W. Bawcutt, 'Machiavelli and Marlowe's *The Jew of Malta*', *Renaissance Drama*, NS 3 (1970), 3–49.

tunist.[1] Her status as a female Machiavel is ironic in the light of Machiavelli's rigidly gendered political ideology. This celebrates masculine willpower, self-reliance, and physical aggression while depreciating conciliation, trust, and compassion as feminine weaknesses.[2] Such distinctions, as well as Machiavelli's association of powerful older mothers with infantilizing and emasculating dangers, explain Richard's visceral hostility towards Margaret, and his displacement of physical deformities on to his mother and her birth-women:

> Why, love forswore me in my mother's womb,
> And for I should not deal in her soft laws,
> She did corrupt frail nature with some bribe
> To shrink mine arm up . . .
>
> (3.2.153–6)

> 'O Jesus bless us, he is born with teeth!'
>
> (5.6.75)

Richard thus fashions himself in terms of immaculately macho *virtù*, with no emotional or kinship attachments to impair his purely expedient pursuit of power.

Richard's manifest revulsion from female sexuality and women's bodies can thus be explained in terms of the gender binaries of Machiavellian ideology. Or it can be interpreted psychoanalytically from the perspective of fraternal jealousy and Oedipal conflict. Or perhaps both. More's *History of King Richard III* compares the two reigns of Edward and Richard largely in terms of sexual mores, the former's enslavement to 'fleshly wantonness' being contrasted with the latter's 'chastity'.[3] Both contexts illuminate Richard's (and others') scorn for 'weak' men like his brothers, whose political judgements are compromised by their undisciplined passion for women. The BBC's Ron Cook conveys this contempt very well by looking at the camera when Edward is platitudinizing (as he often does) in the background. His wry expression strips Edward's manliness of credibility.

Clarence expresses similar resentment towards Edward's

---

[1] R. Martin, 'Anne Dowriche's *The French History*, Christopher Marlowe, and Machiavellian Agency', *Studies in English Literature*, 39 (1999), 69–87.

[2] Hanna Fenichel Pitkin, *Fortune is a Woman: Gender and Politics in the Thought of Niccolò Machiavelli* (Berkeley, Los Angeles, and London, 1984).

[3] Rudnytsky, pp. 155 ff.

7. 'Down, down to hell, and say I sent thee thither': Richard Gloucester (Michael J. Hume) and Henry (Dennis Rees) in Pat Patton's 1992 Oregon Shakespeare Festival production, Ashland, Oregon.

sensuality, first after his brother announces his intention to marry Lady Grey in 3.2, then more forcefully in 4.1, when he perceives the new queen's relations have displaced him in the aristocratic marriage market. This mercenary attitude towards women makes him resemble Edward more than he realizes, and his petulant repudiation of brotherly loyalty for the prospect of gaining Warwick's second daughter mirrors Edward's own sexual impulsiveness. On the other hand, Clarence receives support from Somerset, and later Montague quietly joins both them and his brother Warwick in 4.6 and 4.8, perhaps after initially dissembling his loyalty to Edward at the end of 4.1. Montague's reaffirmation of family loyalty marks a simple contrast with widening Yorkist divisions. The chronicles report that he shifted allegiance several times between Edward and Warwick. But Shakespeare makes Montague conspicuously attached to Warwick from their first appearance together as brothers in 2.1. The strength of their bond is ultimately affirmed by their joint deaths at the Battle of Barnet (5.2).[1] Warwick himself of course deserts the Yorkists after Edward's betrayal of his mission to Lady Bona. But he also reveals that he has been personally insulted by Edward's attempt to rape his niece (3.3.188), so that he belatedly takes up revenge after it has largely ceased to matter to others.

Richard sees greater tactical advantages to dissembling his disgust ('I hear, yet say not much, but think the more' (4.1.84)). He actively rescues Edward from house arrest in 4.5 and helps him to regain the throne from Henry. The historical background to Edward's escape opens up possible further contemporary dimensions to Act 4's whirligig of shifting fraternal loyalties. The chronicles report that the Archbishop of York, Warwick's younger brother in whose custody Edward was placed, may have colluded with his escape because he owed his appointment to Edward. The implication is that the position of being a younger brother and the necessity of finding a living in the absence of any inheritance may have caused him to sacrifice family loyalty under the guise of what Warwick later blandly calls his 'carelessness' (4.6.86).

The Archbishop's underlying motive in fraternal discontent speaks to the common Elizabethan experience of younger brothers frustrated and disenfranchised by a national system of primogeniture. It was a common grievance that would have struck a sympathetic chord with some members of Shakespeare's audience.[2] Antagonism between older and younger brothers is a recurring feature in many of his plays, and in *3 Henry VI* it parallels the theme of disrupted father and son relationships that dominates the first three acts. It also becomes another social metaphor for the human casualties of civil war, mutating in Richard's case into militant nihilism. Yet ironically, it is also remedied by the partial restoration of fraternal bonds in the fifth act. Part Three, as we have seen,

[1] And in Warwick's delirious pangs for Montague in his dying moments at ll. 33–9, a speech which anticipates the melodramatic sensuality of York and Suffolk's deaths in *Henry V* 4.6.
[2] Pearlman, pp. 427–9.

makes Clarence rather than Richard responsible for reuniting the York family and genuinely affirming brotherly loyalty as a more powerful instinct than personal profit masquerading as political 'right'. Margaret unexpectedly if more distantly confirms this bond by way of the play's prominent sea and tide metaphors during her oration before Tewkesbury:

> And what is Edward but a ruthless sea?
> What Clarence but a quicksand of deceit?
> And Richard but a ragged fatal rock—
> . . . there's no hoped-for mercy with the brothers
> More than with ruthless waves, with sands, and rocks.
>
> (5.4.25–7, 35–6)

When Edward, Clarence, and Richard soon murder Prince Edward, it occurs, on the level of Margaret's reasoning, as the determined outcome of inescapable natural forces. From this scene, Richard rushes off to his 'bloody supper' in the Tower with Henry, who has become his doppelgänger in terms of a similarly radical detachment from conventional customs and thinking. Killer and victim are united in eerie intimacy, as Henry colludes with future history by enlarging the fantastical lore of Richard's monstrous birth, while Richard becomes a kind of surrogate son, dutifully extending Henry's catalogue of prodigious deformities. The two play out a macabre parody of the inheritance entanglements and family bonds that divide and reform, ebb and flow, throughout the play. This uncanny affinity was expressed physically in the 1963–4 Hall–Barton production, as the dying Henry embraced and kissed Richard's head. Some reviewers thought it was a gesture of forgiveness, some a kiss of peace, but others found it more ambiguous, 'an inexplicably moving invention'.[1] As Henry collapsed, Richard became ensnarled in David Warner's gangly body and had to struggle to extricate himself. He finally hurled Henry to the floor, his defiant 'I have no brother, I am like no brother' now irrevocably true and untrue.

'Edward IV'

However powerful and clarifying the destructive polarities represented by Henry and Richard may be, the history of *3 Henry VI*'s per-

---

[1] Irving Wardle, *The Times*, 18 July 1963.

formances and adaptations, and of differences between its two original texts, does not end with their individual stories, though traditional criticism has tended to suggest otherwise. Despite Richard's mid-play metamorphosis, Acts 3 and 4 are not mainly concerned with his growing power. Rather they 'trace Edward's rise and the ironic reversals of the crown: these more objective concerns take precedence over the narrowed point of view that central character development imposes'.[1] Verbally, the two longest roles in the play belong to Warwick and Edward.[2] Four major productions of *3 Henry VI* in the past forty years have been reshaped as 'Edward IV', beginning with John Barton and Peter Hall's 1963–4 *The Wars of the Roses*.[3] All took place in the theatrical context of condensing the *Henry VI* trilogy from three plays to two for performance with *Richard III*, or as part of a seven-play epic with the four history plays of the second tetralogy. Barton's basic approach was to join main events from the last two acts of *2 Henry VI*, beginning with Cade's rebellion, with an abbreviated version of Part Three. Michael Bogdanov and Michael Pennington adopted this design for 'The Rise of Edward IV', part of their 1987 English Shakespeare Company cycle *The Wars of the Roses*; so too did Adrian Noble and Charles Wood for the second of their three-play adaptation *The Plantagenets* staged in 1988.[4] In 1992 Pat Patton used this script at the Oregon Shakespeare Festival, although he renamed it 'The Conclusion of Henry VI'. These English-speaking productions were preceded by similar adaptations in nineteenth-century Germany. Franz Dingelstedt, mentioned in the previous section, reworked the *Henry VI* trilogy as two plays in 1864, the second of which, *Die Weisse Rose: Haus York*, combined passages from Parts One and Two with most of Part Three. Alfred von Walzogen followed Dingelstedt's model for his own *Edward IV* at Hanover in 1875.[5]

Barton's script was unique, however, in adding hundreds of lines of Shakespearian pastiche to sharpen character traits and

[1] Barbara Hodgdon, 'Shakespeare's Directorial Eye: A Look at the Early History Plays', in *Shakespeare's More than Words Can Witness: Essays on Visual and Nonverbal Enactment in the Plays*, ed. Sidney Homan (Lewisburg and London, 1980), 115–29; p. 125.

[2] Edward has 428 lines and 132 speeches, while Warwick has 436 lines and 99 speeches.

[3] John Barton and Peter Hall, *The Wars of the Roses* (1970).

[4] *The Plantagenets* (London and Boston, 1989).

[5] Stohl, pp. 397–402, 405.

clarify historical relationships. His rewriting started from the pre-miss that the *Henry VI* plays were 'not viable as they stand' and needed to be adapted in the interests of audience accessibility.[1] Structurally, Barton's *Edward IV* shared approaches with Restoration and eighteenth-century adaptations: for example Crowne's *Misery of Civil-War* also begins with Cade's rebellion and continues into Part Three. But whereas Crowne reduced the *Henry VI* plays to political caricature, Barton created a compelling dynastic saga about the houses of Lancaster and York, as one falls and the other triumphs—or appears to do so. This emphasis on family history over any single personal story was reinforced by the play's relationship to the wider cycle, which affiliated individual episodes to an epic structure and teleological interpretation of history.[2] Barton's positioning of the interval also schematized the crossed paths of family fortunes, while heightening the original change in tone that occurs between Acts 3 and 4. In productions of *3 Henry VI* which focus on Richard (and even most that do not), the break normally occurs after his soliloquy in 3.2. Spectators return to their seats expecting to see him fulfilling his plans to gain the crown. In *Edward IV*, however, the interval came between the defeat of the Lancastrians at Towton and the death of Clifford in 2.6, and the new regime under King Edward in Act 3, a shift Barton underlined by reversing scenes 3.1 and 3.2. Ending the play's first half with the Yorkist victory at Towton raises the prospect—however fleeting—of political regeneration and social stability under an energetic young king following the divisions of civil war. That is Hall's and Holinshed's mood as they begin the 22-year reign of Edward IV. In terms of dramatic genre, Barton's changes heighten *3 Henry VI*'s temporary shift into the preoccupations of comedy, without losing the play's distinct sardonic edge.[3]

[1] Hall and Barton, p. xv. See also Barbara Hodgdon, '*The Wars of the Roses*: Scholarship Speaks on the Stage', *Deutsche Shakespeare-Gesellschaft West Jahrbuch 1972*, 170–84; p. 170.

[2] Robert Shaughnessy, *Representing Shakespeare: England, History and the RSC* (New York and London, 1994), pp. 38, 79–81.

[3] Frank Cox expressed the opinion of many reviewers and critics that '*Edward IV*' was ' "the strongest of the three [plays of *The Wars of the Roses*] . . . a triumph of scholarship and theatrical awareness"; and that "by inspired weeding, contradiction, and even in places by brazen invention, he has created from a seldom revived mass of sword-rattling chronicles, a positive addition to the canon of popular works" ': quoted in Richard Pearson, *A Band of Arrogant and United Heroes: The Story of . . . The Wars of the Roses* (1990), p. 20.

Potential renewal is on offer during the middle acts of Part Three because they focus on dynastic marriages, as stern alarums give way to court meetings. The ESC's 'Rise of the House of York' evoked this change in tone by staging 3.2 (as well as the final scene, with greater irony) as an elegant cocktail party, with men and women in evening dress and mellow jazz playing. The atmosphere suggested relaxed self-congratulation. In 3.3 at the French Court, the 1996 New York Public Theatre production further lightened the emotional mood by having Lady Bona played by a male actor in drag, coyly veiled and preciously demure. Oddly enough, this bit of otherwise questionable campery drew attention to King Lewis's patronizing treatment of his sister-in-law as a diplomatic bargaining chip, and Warwick's patriarchal barter of his daughters to Prince Edward and Clarence. Meanwhile Margaret and later Lady Grey each find new purpose as mothers seeking wives for their sons. The family bonds between parent and child that were shattered by war become temporarily reconfigured in ostensibly life-affirming ways.

Yet these departures from the martial action of the first two and final acts have struck some critics and directors as an artistic blunder, lacking meaningful significance. F. R. Benson's and Douglas Seale's groundbreaking productions of 1906 and 1952–3 cut much of Act 4, Edward's triumph at Barnet in 5.3, and short passages emphasizing his competence as a leader.[1] As a result, prior to the final battle sequence at Tewkesbury, Edward's tenure as king became a hasty blur. Benson and Seale, as we observed, focused on the emergence of Gloucester's Machiavellian ambitions (and Margaret's tragic career, discussed in the next section). Given these verbal and directorial limitations, it was not surprising that both Edward's and Warwick's performances generated little interest among reviewers and failed to challenge the conventional opinions of literary critics. Since then, neither Barton's *Edward IV* and similar adaptations nor individual performances have managed to shift perceptions greatly. The BBC, for example, tried to connect Edward's peremptory behaviour as King with that of his descendant Henry VIII by dressing Edward in 3.2 and 4.1 to appear like Henry in Holbein's portrait, which Brian Protheroe further

---

[1] For example, 5.1.61–4, in which he shrewdly restrains Gloucester (see below, p. 70).

recalled by standing with his legs slightly apart and his hands on his hips, arms akimbo. One critic of the 1987 ESC's 'Rise of Edward IV' complained about the title on the grounds that the *obvious* 'rising' figure was Richard, not Edward, and by implication that the play's definitive emotional climax was Henry and Richard's final confrontation in the Tower. Warwick has suffered much the same critical reception, again despite some outstanding performances by Brewster Mason in 1963–4 and Derrick Lee Weeden at Ashland in 1992. Both roles continue to be regarded largely as unchallenging and one-dimensional.

Yet Shakespeare provides clear if often subtle scope for actors to develop Edward in complex ways beyond the lascivious wilfulness that emerges so destructively in 3.2 and 4.1. In the first scenes he is eager to make an impression by fighting, although he is less tough than Richard. The repetitions in his speech at the beginning of 2.1 may either signal anxiety about the safety of his father[1] or they may indicate his trying to master or reason away his concern, as the BBC's Brian Protheroe appeared to do. When the messenger arrives, he refuses initially to hear the news, while Richard is fiercely determined to bear whatever is coming (2.1.48–9). Edward is shattered by his father's death, sounding for a moment like his mournful counterpart in *The Mirror for Magistrates*, whereas Richard's rage strengthens his self-determination. Edward turns to Warwick as a surrogate father and political mentor. His dependency on Burgundy for aid, where historically his aunt and later his sister were the duchesses, obliquely presages his weakness for 'feeling fair damsels', which Shakespeare distils in his attempt to sexually blackmail Lady Grey. His precipitous marriage offer repeats Henry's blunder in *1 Henry VI*, in which passion blinds him to the dangers of a politically useless alliance and destroys hopes for national reconstruction. Warwick vows to revenge Edward's betrayal, and Clarence rebels at degraded marriage prospects, as the York–Warwick alliance degenerates into an inter-family feud, even more petty in its tit-for-tat predictability than York and Lancaster's squabbles.

Edward's personal fortunes collapse in 4.3, when he is captured in his tent at night by Warwick, Clarence, and their followers. The

---

[1] In *3 Henry VI*; in *True Tragedy* only Richard expresses concern, Edward merely asking: 'How doth my noble brother Richard fare?'

8. Warwick 'the kingmaker' (Mark Wing-Davey) uncrowns
Edward (Brian Protheroe) in Jane Howell's 1983 BBC television
production. Copyright © BBC.

Folio stage direction calling for him to be brought out '*in his*
⌈*night-*⌉*gown, sitting in a chair*' conventionally signals his tactical
unpreparedness. But in performance this is one of Act 4's topsy-
turvy moments, often given a ribald spin. In Hall and Barton's
Edward IV, a mattress was flung out and Edward and a whore were
thrust in naked.[1] But like Henry after he is marginalized on the battlefield by Margaret and Clifford, adversity brings out new
depth in Edward. When Warwick confiscates Edward's crown, he
remains stoically unperturbed:

EDWARD
> Edward will always bear himself as king;
> Though Fortune's malice overthrow my state,
> My mind exceeds the compass of her wheel.

WARWICK
> Then for his mind be Edward England's king.

(4.3.45–8)

SECOND GAMEKEEPER   . . . thou talk'st as if thou wert a king.
HENRY
> Why so I am in mind, and that's enough.

(3.1.59–60)

---

[1] The same bit of business—without the mattress or chair—was repeated in the
1987 ESC and 1992 Ashland productions.

It is as if Edward adopts Henry's (harder-won) strategy of detaching himself from worldly affairs to counter his own unstable authority. Another display of self-possession occurs in 5.1 when he remains stolidly silent in the face of Clarence's betrayal.[1] And earlier in the same scene Edward demonstrates his mature martial leadership by overruling Gloucester's impetuous urge to pursue Oxford's troops into Coventry:

> GLOUCESTER
> The gates are open, let us enter too.
> EDWARD
> So other foes may set upon our backs.
> Stand we in good array, for they no doubt
> Will issue out again and bid us battle.
> If not, the city being but of small defence,
> We'll quickly rouse the traitors in the same.
> (5.1.60–5)[2]

Reviewers of the 1992 Ashland production observed that these indications of independent-mindedness emerged strongly in Robert Lisell-Frank's performance, in which Edward rapidly gained self-confidence after recapturing Henry. Throughout Act 5, and especially during his oration before Tewkesbury in 5.4, he rallied his army with a commanding voice and large heroic gestures, so that his closing line, 'For here I hope begins our lasting joy' (5.7.46), for once seemed plausible rather than naïve.

Despite these indications of Edward's personal growth, Shakespeare darkens his much more positive historical image with spasmodic bouts of irresponsibility and self-serving passivity. Edward managed before and after Henry's temporary restoration to exercise the kind of robust but imaginative centralized power needed to pacify years of aristocratic division.[3] Hall titled his chapter 'The Prosperous Reign of King Edward the Fourth', and praised the

---

[1] By contrast, his response in *True Tragedy*, 'Et tu Brute? Wilt thou stab Caesar too?' (E2ʳ), is histrionic and perhaps self-pitying. Shakespeare may have decided to cut these lines to give Edward's military leadership a more resilient integrity.

[2] The situation is reversed in *True Tragedy*:

> *Edward* The gates are open, see they enter in,
> Let's follow them and bid them battle in the streets.
> *Gloucester* No, some other might set upon our backs,
> We'll stay . . . (E1ᵛ)

[3] Saccio, *Shakespeare's English Kings*, p. 11.

timely amnesty and law reforms that Edward introduced after defeating the Lancastrians at Towton. He also noted Parliament's willing approval of him as a vigorous leader and effective adminis- trator. But Shakespeare includes few references to Edward's 'good reign'.[1] Warwick accuses him of failing 'to study for the peo- ple's welfare' (4.3.39), and instead Henry—unhistorically—is credited with governing his subjects justly and compassionately (4.8.39–47, Folio only). Shakespeare merely hints at Edward's rejuvenating qualities through the poetic images of fertility and harvest he is fond of invoking.

Dramatically, Edward is also hampered by a lack of public oppor- tunities to display and assert his new power.[2] By the middle of *3 Henry VI*, virtually all royal ceremonies have been compromised. Henry's entailing of the crown in the opening scene prolongs the degradation of kingship begun in Parts One and Two, and breaks the transgenerational continuity that traditionally raises the crown into an abiding authoritative symbol. Reduced to mere property—in both legal and theatrical senses—it becomes subject to all physical and temporal vicissitudes.[3] The loss of transcen- dence partly explains why Edward's accession is not marked by a coronation ceremony, which in stage terms was a perennial oppor- tunity for spectacle and pageantry.[4] *3 Henry VI*'s relatively subdued use of ritual denies Edward the myth-making spectacles of kingship.[5]

Some critics have argued that Shakespeare could not represent Edward's reign positively because this would have contradicted the predominantly moral basis of his understanding of historical causality, evident in the play's shift from public atrocities to self- centred and impulsive behaviour in the second half.[6] If this is so, it

[1] A dramatic strategy later paralleled by Shakespeare's suppression of Holin- shed's account of Macbeth's years of good rule.

[2] Stephen Orgel, *The Illusion of Power: Political Theater in the English Renaissance* (Berkeley, Los Angeles, and London, 1975). Leonard Tennenhouse, 'Rituals of State: History and the Elizabethan strategies of power', *Power on Display: The Politics of Shakespeare's Genres* (New York and London, 1986), ch. 2, pp. 72–101.

[3] F. W. Brownlow, *Two Shakespearean Sequences: Henry VI to Richard II and Pericles to Timon of Athens* (1977), pp. 45–9. Hattaway, intro., p. 14.

[4] As evidenced by Laurence Olivier's 1955 film version of *Richard III*, which opens with the coronation of Edward IV.

[5] We have already noted that *3 Henry VI* eliminates the two processions *True Tragedy* calls for at the end and beginning of 4.7 and 4.6 (above, p. 27).

[6] For example, Brockbank, 'The Frame of Disorder', pp. 90–4.

may explain why Edward often betrays signs of a repressed or belated conscience. On a simple level this seems to be latent in his taste for religious oaths and proverbial sentiments, none of which are shared seriously by his brothers or Warwick. At several points Edward actually sounds like Henry on the battlefield:

> I throw my hands, mine eyes, my heart to thee
> Thou setter-up and plucker-down of kings,
> Beseeching thee, if with thy will it stands
> That to my foes this body must be prey,
> Yet that thy brazen gates of heaven may ope
> And give sweet passage to my sinful soul.
>
> (2.3.36–41)

Modern productions nearly always cut this prayer. If they retain it, they tend to send it up, with Richard and George rolling their eyes at what they assume is a spurious show of piety. But Edward reveals an instinct for clemency remarkably like Henry's several scenes later, when, upon hearing a dying soldier's groans, he says: 'And now the battle's ended, | If friend or foe, let him be gently used.' (2.6.43–4). In this context 'gently' suggests a chivalrous impulse, although it will be stamped out moments later in the pitiless assault on Clifford's body. Nevertheless, it is one of several glimpses of Edward's awareness of the consequences of his actions, and is revealing here because it contradicts the chronicles' reports that Edward ordered all Lancastrian prisoners to be killed. Later in 4.1, he is anxious about his brothers' resentment of his marriage to Lady Grey—however much he brazens it out—and he admits his culpability towards Lady Bona: 'I blame not her, she could say little less, | She had the wrong' (101–2). Again, moments after stabbing Prince Edward when Gloucester turns to Margaret, Edward recognizes the violation of an ethical boundary:

EDWARD
> Hold, Richard, hold, for we have done too much . . .
> *Margaret faints*
> What, doth she swoon? Use means for her recovery.
>
> (5.5.43, 45)

In the BBC production, Brian Protheroe here recoiled in horror at what he and his brothers had rashly done. But other actors have played these lines coolly, briskly reimposing normal discipline on a momentary loss of control. And when Clarence reports Richard's departure to 'make a bloody supper in the Tower', Edward certainly reacts with wilful complacency: 'He's sudden if a thing comes in his head' (85–6). Overall, therefore, Edward oscillates continually between moral blindness and irrepressible human empathy, impulses that catch him going both ways on fortune's wheel, to which he or others refer continually.[1] In Part Three's world of diminishing options, he could abjure worldly power, as Henry does ('that I may conquer fortune's spite | By living low where fortune cannot hurt me', 4.6.19–20), or adopt Richard's realpolitik and ridicule ' "love" which greybeards call divine' (5.6.81). But Edward is caught in between, insufficiently principled or unethical to embrace either position fully, which makes him at times seem puny and laughable.

Shakespeare's ambivalent and somewhat complex portrayal of Edward contrasts markedly with popular and heroic representations in other Elizabethan plays. Thomas Heywood's *1* and *2 King Edward IV*, printed in 1599,[2] show Edward successfully confronting the rebellion of Thomas Neville, Lord Falconbridge, cousin to Warwick and Montague and commander of the Lancastrian navy. Following the Battle of Tewkesbury in 1471, Falconbridge tried unsuccessfully to depose Edward and restore Henry to the throne by gathering forces in Kent and Essex and laying siege to London. They were defeated after several assaults by a citizen army of merchants and apprentices, and Falconbridge was captured and executed on 22 September. Heywood represents these events with spectacular battle scenes, huffing speeches, and assaults on the city walls with scaling ladders. His *2 King Edward IV* alludes twice to *3 Henry VI*,[3] which suggests Heywood saw a

---

[1] 4.3.46, 58; 4.4.3; 4.6.19–20; 4.7.2, 55; 4.8.27; 5.3.1–2.

[2] Facsimile reprint, ed. Seymour de Ricci (Philadelphia and New York, 1922). This is more reliable than the standard 1874 *Dramatic Works* edition ([ed. R. A. Shepherd], 6 vols., vol. i).

[3] Compare 1.1.228 ff. and 4.6.41–3 respectively:

> *Anselm* Why then didst thou affirm [by the letter G]
> That it was meant by George the Duke of Clarence . . .
> *Dr Shaw* I was enforced by the Duke of Gloucester.
> *Anselm* Enforced sayst thou? wouldst thou then be enforced,
> Being a man of thy profession,
> To sin so vilely, and with thine own mouth,
> To damn thy soul? No thou wast not enforced,
> But gain and hope of high promotion
> Hired thee thereto . . .   (U2ʳ)

performance of the Folio text sometime after 1594 and before 28 August 1599 when *Edward IV* was entered in the Stationers' Register. It is thought that Heywood based his episodes of Falconbridge's rebellion on the anonymous and popular *Siege of London*, which was performed at the Rose Theatre between December 1594 and July 1596, and may date from around 1590.[1] Both *True Tragedy* and *3 Henry VI* refer to a figure who merges this younger Falconbridge, 'appointed by the Earl of Warwick, to be Vice-admiral of the sea,' with his father a decade earlier.[2] Perhaps Shakespeare toyed with idea of introducing his rebellion at a later point, but abandoned it as his interest grew in other characters, including Edward.

Roads from Coventry. Both the *Siege of London* and *Edward IV* are also probably related to the earlier *History of King Edward IV* performed at Coventry prior to 1591 (above, p. 29).[3] The city had switched sides twice during the Wars of the Roses,[4] a legacy which corresponds to revolving Yorkist loyalties in *3 Henry VI*, above all to Clarence, who deserts Edward in Act 4 but performs a volte-face before the walls of Coventry in 5.1. The city's ultimate reconciliation with King Edward, again like Shakespeare's own scene, was celebrated annually by military pageants.[5] These dated back to

> *Richard* Being your lawful prince by true succession,
> I could have wished, with all my heart I could,
> This majesty had sitten on the brow
> Of any other, so much do I affect a private life,
> To spend my days in contemplation.   (Y4^v)

Neither of these passages is shared with *True Tragedy*.

[1] Eleven performances with receipts as high as £3 3s: *Henslowe's Diary*, pp. 26–8, 30–1, 34, 47. Wright, 'Historie', pp. 74–5.

[2] Falconbridge's dramatic reputation as a bold warrior, which Heywood follows, may explain Shakespeare's epithet 'stern', meaning fiercely brave or resolute in battle (*OED* 2 *obs.*).

[3] Wright observes that Lord Derby's Men, who staged Heywood's *Edward IV*, had been performing regularly at Coventry since 1574 ('Historie', pp. 76–7).

[4] The city abandoned the Lancastrians to support the Earl of March, as he was then, in 1460, donating money after the second Battle of St Albans and before Towton. After rejoining Warwick in 1469, Edward's father-in-law and brother-in-law Rivers and Woodville were executed on Gosford Green. Following Edward's crushing victory at Barnet, the city prudently informed him that Margaret and Prince Edward had taken refuge there, allowing them to be captured. He nonetheless deprived and fined the city until Clarence obtained a pardon on its behalf in 1472, when cordial relations with Edward were restored: Wright, 'Historie', p. 73.

[5] Wright, 'Historie', pp. 72–3.

1474, when lavish shows were staged to mark the King's visit and recent pardon.

In this context of local drama and pageantry, Shakespeare's invented episode in the opening moments of 5.1 invites further consideration from several perspectives. As Warwick awaits reinforcements prior to the Battle of Barnet, two messengers inform him that Oxford is marching from Dunsmore, south-east of Coventry, and that Montague is at Daintry (i.e. Daventry), further to the south-east. A figure *3 Henry VI* identifies only as 'Somerville' enters to report that Clarence is two hours away at Southam, also south and a little east of Coventry but closer to Stratford-upon-Avon. Warwick hears an off-stage drum and jumps to the conclusion that Clarence has arrived:

> WARWICK
>   Then Clarence is at hand, I hear his drum.
> SOMERVILLE
>   It is not his, my lord, here Southam lies.
>   The drum your honour hears marcheth from Warwick.
> WARWICK
>   Who should that be? Belike unlooked-for friends.
> SOMERVILLE
>   They are at hand, and you shall quickly know. (11–15)

It is not Clarence who enters, however, but King Edward and his supporters. Warwick's reliance on others for information, and his surprisingly muddled sense of local directions, foreshadow his misplaced confidence and imminent loss of command later in the scene. He compounds these misjudgements by deciding to leave the security of the city to meet Edward on the battlefield. This differs from the chronicle accounts stating that Warwick prudently remained within the walls of Coventry and refused to accept Edward's challenge until several months later at Barnet.

The whole moment's brief excursion into place-names around Coventry and Stratford-upon-Avon unmistakably bears Shakespeare's personal signature. He portrays Somerville in an unexpectedly positive light, boldly correcting the mildly confused Warwick, yet clearly loyal to the Lancastrian cause.[1] Given that Somerville plays no further role in this scene, is never referred

---

[1] For Shakespeare's connections with and sympathies to this house and county, see Richard Dutton, 'Shakespeare and Lancaster', *SQ* 49 (1998), 1–21.

to again, and for dramatic purposes does not need to be named, his underlying purpose may be to present a coded portrait that alludes to the Elizabethan government's unjust treatment of Shakespeare's recently disgraced Catholic relations.[1]

The topographic specificity of this passage is also notable. Given that the English histories describe events most closely tied to the national landscape, it is curious that Shakespeare's *Henry VI* plays do not draw on contemporary maps such as Ortelius's *Theatrum Orbis Terrarum* (1570), or Christopher Saxton's well known *Atlas of the Counties of England and Wales* (1579, reprinted 1580, 1585, 1590).[2] Nor does Shakespeare show the awareness of changes in early modern cartography that has been detected in his other plays, and which it has been argued illustrates the emergence of a new land-focused social identity.[3] He generally ignores topographic details related by Hall and Holinshed which encourage readers to visualize the role played by physical terrain in determining the logistical movements and outcomes of battles.[4] Less unusual in terms of his dramatic practice is that scenic locations normally remain unidentified. (This indeterminacy has become more 'visible' of late, as modern editions drop the older practice of supplying locales for readers in opening stage directions.) Shakespeare also sometimes delays identifying a site until after its action has passed. The sequence representing the Battle of Wakefield, for example, begins with the deaths of Rutland and York in 1.3 and 1.4, but the place is not named until well into 2.1, when Warwick mentions the 'bloody fray at Wakefield fought'. Shakespeare of course wants to maintain narrative integrity and avoid letting characters know where they are before

---

[1] See R. Martin, 'Rehabilitating John Somerville in *3 Henry VI*', *SQ* 51 (2000), 332–40.

[2] Cf. Marlowe's use of *Theatrum Orbis Terrarum* in *Tamburlaine* (to which Richard alludes at 1.2.29–31), with its packed invocations of exotic cities and intercontinental expanses that mark the progress of the protagonist's transgressive ambitions.

[3] Victor Morgan, 'The Cartographic Image of "The Country" in Early Modern England', *Transactions of the Royal Historical Society*, 5th series, 29 (1979), 129–54. Richard Helgerson, 'The Land Speaks', in *Forms of Nationhood: The Elizabethan Writing of England* (Chicago and London, 1992), pp. 105–47. John Gillies, *Shakespeare and the Geography of Difference* (Cambridge, 1994).

[4] For example the Cotswold topography surrounding Tewkesbury: 'Herewith [Edward] approached the enemy's camp, which was right hard to be assailed by reason of the deep ditches, hedges, trees, bushes, and cumbersome lanes, wherewith the same was fenced' (Holinshed Sssvi^r). This is reduced to 'yonder . . . thorny wood' (5.4.67).

they have arrived or 'recognized' their surroundings. But this kind of deferral seems to go beyond dramatic convention, and to be working towards an effect different from the retrospective construction of topographic meaning found in works such as Stow's *Survey of London*, in which natural spaces are inscribed with memorially recuperated actions.[1] York for instance states that he will depart for 'my castle' at the end of the first scene, and a Messenger reports Margaret's approach to 'your castle' at 1.2.50, but the place, 'Sandal', is not named until later at 1.2.63 after the arrival of the Mortimer brothers, whose names resonate with the dramatic origins of York's claims to the throne in *1 Henry VI*. In *True Tragedy*, on the other hand, York mentions departing for his castle in 'Wakefield' in the first scene, as does Henry. York also identifies himself 'here in Sandal castle' twice in the second scene.[2] Consistent with its tendency to downplay theatrical pageantry, *3 Henry VI* also represents topography abstemiously. But this can have imaginative advantages in theatre. In Katie Mitchell's 1994 RSC production, the relative vagueness of place, combined with an emphasis on emblematic ritual, allowed her to universalize the human agonies of civil war and its destruction of religious values and the natural environment:

[The production's] staging reduces the contest to its basic components and the kingdom to a plaything: an upstage door, a window for siege debates, a downstage throne. It is as diagrammatic as a board-game, with every fresh atrocity coming as casually as the throw of a dice.[3]

As many critics observed, this approach permitted the national killing fields of fifteenth-century England to be associated with modern human catastrophes taking place in Bosnia and Rwanda, without resort to overt and reductive contemporary parallels. Mitchell's production showed how Shakespeare's dramatic representation of sites and locales is largely abstract and symbolic, closer to medieval conceptions of geography in which the earth's

---

[1] Steven Mullaney, *The Place of the Stage: License, Play, and Power in Renaissance England* (Chicago and London, 1988), pp. vii–viii, 15–18. Garrett A. Sullivan Jr, *The Drama of Landscape* (Stanford, 1998), pp. 2–3.

[2] We have seen how this text refers more often to precise London sites with topical associations while also garbling other geographic references; e.g. 'Tygers of *Arcadia*' (Folio = 'Hyrcania'), B3^r, or York's confusion about being in either Wakefield or St Albans in 1.2 (A7^r). Both these instances are probably owing to faulty reporting.

[3] Irving Wardle, *Independent on Sunday*, 14 August 1994.

places correspond to a moral cosmological landscape.[1] York's and Henry's molehills in 1.4 and 2.5, for example, distantly reminiscent of mystery-cycle *loci*, are archetypal rather than historical or even physical sites.

Symbolic modes likewise govern the confrontations before, or on, city gates and walls. Theatregoers in London (or Coventry) would relate such sites to their own vestigial Roman or medieval walls, which denoted the city's physical integrity and social cohesion. The walls would also demarcate economic and political zones of civic authority, differentiating citizen interests from spaces associated with royal or aristocratic prerogatives. These boundaries emerge clearly in Heywood's *Edward IV*, and they likewise mark points of friction in *3 Henry VI* before the gates of York in 4.7. Like Henry Bolingbroke before him (*Richard II* 2.1.298), Edward returns from foreign exile to Ravenspur under the pretext of defending his dynastic inheritance, whereupon he 'fraudulently seduces' the Mayor and Aldermen into handing over the keys to the city. Traditionally this was a ceremony of mutual respect between the Crown and civic leaders. But the Mayor surrenders the keys with apparent reluctance ('What, fear not man') and then is not referred to again. His silence hints at the possibility of non-verbal resistance to Edward's trampling of civic freedoms. When 5.1 opens at Coventry, a similar displacement has already taken place. Warwick has garrisoned the city, thereby reducing it to feudal dependency. The Mayor no longer represents citizen independence by virtue of his opposition on the walls, but plays a subaltern role at Warwick's side. Coventry's thresholds are crossed by dynastic combatants on both sides, as competing aristocratic demands overrun the city.[2]

---

[1] Alexander Koyré, *From the Closed World to the Infinite Universe* (Baltimore, 1968). Michel Foucault, 'Of Other Spaces', *Diacritics*, (Spring, 1986), 22–7. Henri Lefebvre, *The Production of Space*, trans. Donald Nicholson-Smith (Oxford, 1991), ch. 4, pp. 229–91.

[2] Helgerson, p. 214. Sullivan discusses the analogous situation of Heywood's *King Edward IV*, in which traditional guild culture is challenged first by new suburbanite forces represented by Falconbridge's rebels, and then by Edward's abuse of royal power. He contrasts the citizens' 'customary landscape' with 'the landscape of sovereignty' in Shakespeare's *2 Henry VI*. Part Three is notably far less 'ritualistically inscribed' than Part Two, and this, I would argue, reflects Shakespeare's withdrawal of theatrical opportunities for Edward to re-establish his royal authority: 'The Beleaguered City: Guild Culture and Urban Space in Heywood's *1 Edward IV* and Shakespeare's *2 Henry VI*', ch. 6, pp. 197–229.

The Kingmaker undone. If Edward represents Shakespeare's demysti-
fying treatment of a popular dramatic folk-hero, his substantial but
strangely limited portrayal of Warwick in Part Three can be seen in
the light of court nostalgia for chivalric ideals and supposed feudal
harmony and hierarchical stability. Elizabethan literature and
pageantry often celebrated these values to implicitly defend royal
and aristocratic privileges, which were under increasing attack by
parliamentary opposition and religious nonconformity. In *3 Henry
VI* Shakespeare conspicuously avoids drawing on any of Hall's and
Holinshed's abundant evidence attesting to Warwick's reputation
for antique courtesy and liberal hospitality.[1] Both chronicles portray him as a man of impeccable integrity, whose 'witty and gentle
demeanour' was praised in ballads, plays, and triumphs during his
years of exile in France, and later mythologized in national folk-
lore. For Elizabethan writers, Warwick epitomized the mystique of
a nearly extinct warrior aristocracy. In *The Mirror for Magistrates*,
Clarence describes both him and his brother Montague as

> . . . the keys of chivalry.
> For never lived the matches of them twain,
> In manhood, power, and martial policy.
>
> (p. 225)

Shakespeare, however, chose to concentrate in Part Three almost
exclusively on Warwick's brokering activity as a 'setter-up and
plucker-down of kings' (2.3.37, 3.3.157), in which the attribution of
godlike power is increasingly undermined by mundane self-interest.
His lack of chivalric idealism contrasts with the brief appearance of
Sir John Montgomery in 4.7, who appears for the sole purpose of displaying his fealty to Edward as king. Warwick's personal motives
also are the most closed of any of the play's main characters. Unlike
Edward, we see no glimpses of moral recognition until his dying
speech at Tewkesbury. Prior to his humiliation at the French court,
Warwick's only self-seeking impulse is vengeance towards Clifford
for his brother's death at Towton (2.3). Shakespeare conflates his
anger at the failed marriage negotiations with Lady Bona in 1461
with his visit to Louis XI four years later, at which time he joined
forces with Margaret and the Lancastrians. Otherwise Warwick's
ambitions seem fully identified with the claims of York and Edward.
In this regard, Brewster Mason's performance in Hall and Barton's

[1] In contrast to Part Two, which does allude to this reputation; e.g. 1.1.189–91.

Edward IV was memorably representative. Despite major cuts to his part, Mason's imperious gestures and large physical stature created a figure of Olympian bearing. In both *Henry VI*[1] and the first half of *Edward IV*, reviewers spoke of his commanding self-confidence, especially in 1.1 where he ordered York and Henry about like an 'autocratic schoolmaster', or otherwise stood aloof watching the proceedings, leaning casually on his sword. Mason had no need to stamp his foot to summon his soldiers at l. 170.1; instead he scratched a decisive line on the ground with his broadsword. When Edward reacted with surprised disapproval at his proposal to marry Lady Bona (2.6.89), Warwick overruled him with a glance, before patiently giving his reasons. His reply to Richard's little joke about Gloucester's ominous dukedom, 'Tut, that's a foolish observation' (l. 107), was witheringly disdainful. And though Roy Dotrice played Edward as more self-possessed than have many actors, when he turned to lead his troops at the end of this scene, he paused in order to receive Warwick's curt nod to depart.

After Warwick joined Margaret and the Lancastrians in 3.3, however, he seemed to become unscrupulous and opportunistic. The pivotal moment—to which audiences usually react with sniggers or outright laughter—in this and other modern productions comes when Warwick publicly shifts his allegiance. In the 1992 Ashland production even the Lancastrians were startled by Derrick Lee Weeden's volte-face. Before announcing, 'I here renounce him and return to Henry' (194), Weeden paused to look silently at the audience, waiting for them to read his thoughts and relish his knowing hypocrisy. For his part, Brewster Mason did not even try to pretend to hide his disgust when Margaret forced him to kneel and kiss her hand. Yet despite the demeaning adoption of blatant expediency, both performers managed to redeem Warwick's earlier dignity in powerfully moving death speeches (5.2.5–28, 33–9, 48–9). Their exhausted surrender to worldly loss conveyed Warwick's tragic awareness that he had betrayed his own best interests by deserting the Yorkist cause. An even more physical catharsis characterized Oliver Neville's performance in Douglas Seale's 1957 Birmingham Rep production at the Old Vic. His speeches worked towards a climax in the lines 'this cold congealèd blood | That glues my lips and will not let me speak' (37–8). 'His

---

[1] Hall and Barton's condensed version of *1* and *2 Henry VI*.

mortal wound was at the side of his mouth, and the blood, mingling with saliva, gave his voice a sickening, glutinous texture.'[1]
These almost repellent stage effects brought a startlingly conclusive reality to the formal *de casibus* observations about transitory
fame and inescapable physical decay in Warwick's main speech.

On the other hand, without this involving degree of emotional
intensity, an audience may feel that Warwick deteriorates into
sadly inglorious delirium, as Mark Wing-Davey's BBC performance
and others have suggested, thereby inviting a more detached
response to Warwick's death. Dr Johnson thought that Warwick's
iteration of 'my parks, my walks, my manors' in his first speech,
'diminishe[d] the pathetic [i.e. moving, earnest] effect' of his
confrontation with universal human mortality. Warwick's recol-
lection of the imperious control he once exercised may sound like
regretful boasting rather than humble insight. This final impression of contradictory impulses follows from his unenlightened
pursuit of revenge throughout Act 4, after retaliation has become
less pressing for most of the other characters.[2] By Warwick's own
admission, ambushing Edward in the dark resembles the 'sleight
and manhood' of Ulysses and Diomede stealing the Thracian steeds
(4.2.19–21), figures Shakespeare would later satirize in *Troilus and
Cressida*. Edward's escape in 4.5, and the strategic errors at Coventry, further undermine Warwick's earlier high standards of judgement and honour. From this perspective, Shakespeare appears
gradually to hollow out a figure who was otherwise lionized by history and legend for these qualities. If this is the case, Part Three's
portrayal also runs contrary to the fashionable Elizabethan nostalgia for knightly romance, and instead leans in the direction of revisionist studies by Machiavelli, Francis Bacon, and other historians,
who rigorously separated chivalric idealism from the pragmatic
determining factors of real political power.[3]

---

[1] Mary Clarke, *Shakespeare at the Old Vic*, n.p.

[2] He is the last person to vow revenge, at 3.3.197 and 266.

[3] John D. Cox observes that such anti-idealizing analyses of political change had
been available before Machiavelli in Augustine's discussion of Roman power relations in *The City of God* (*Shakespeare and the Dramaturgy of Power* (Princeton, 1989),
p. 91). But Augustine's empirical scepticism is always contained by his providential
superstructure, a relationship that 3 *Henry VI* can genuinely be said to question. For
a later instance of Shakespeare's scepticism about the contemporary fashion for
chivalry, see Robin Headlam Wells, '*Henry V* and the Chivalric Revival', *Shakespeare
and History*, Shakespeare Yearbook, vol. 6 (Lewiston, NY, 1996), pp. 119–49.

Margaret's story: a 'new' play

In a discussion of *The Plantagenets*, director Adrian Noble described the role of Queen Margaret as 'A King Lear for women'.[1] Although his claim was not new, it was still sufficiently unconventional to be surprising, perhaps even eccentric. We recall that among the original and adapted titles of *3 Henry VI*, none mentions Margaret, even though she is Shakespeare's most enduring royal figure, appearing prominently over the course of all four plays of the first tetralogy. From a late twentieth-century perspective, such invisibility seems readily explained by historical gender distinctions: late medieval England is a man's world in which queen consorts are ultimately marginal to exercising power and fighting battles, even ones who actively defend patrilineal principles in default of husbands who refuse to do so.

But Noble's comparison to Lear is based on dramatic character, and as such points to both figures' shared central experience—culpable suffering—and its imaginative and emotional impact on theatre audiences. Where Margaret distinguishes herself is in the breadth of her social roles. From her more narrowly defined position in Part Two as aspiring and adulterous royal consort, she grows into an epic figure. Her custody of Prince Edward's personal safety gains her new legitimacy as an embattled mother. Her defence of the royal succession authorizes her political activism. Her success in battle validates her martial leadership. And her grotesque cruelty throws these daring gender challenges into sharp relief. Margaret's remarkable hybridity of motive and action may in fact be unsurpassed among any of Shakespeare's female characters. Her ability to stir spectators' feelings and imaginations may have been what Kenneth Tynan had in mind when, after watching Rosalind Boxall perform in Douglas Seale's 1952 Birmingham Rep production, he declared *3 Henry VI* to be 'better than *King Lear*'.[2]

It is certainly the theatre that has revealed Part Three's unwritten dimension as 'Margaret's tragedy'. But as with other perceptions about the play, this change has come about recently. Barbara Jefford's performance in Seale's 1957 Old Vic production was only

---

[1] Shaughnessy, *Representing Shakespeare*, p. 82, quoting Robert Gore Langdon, 'The Plantagenets', *Plays and Players* (October, 1988).

[2] *Evening Standard*, 17 July 1953, cited in Kay, 'A Stage History', p. 84.

the second occasion, after Boxall in 1952, on which her role was credibly staged. In both cases Margaret stood out partly because Seale compressed Act 4, where she does not appear. This meant she 'returned' relatively quickly before Tewkesbury following her new alliances with Lewis and Warwick in 3.3, so that Part Three became 'less a play about the reign of King Henry than about the struggles of his wife . . . on behalf of the house of Lancaster'.[1]

Evidence from Shakespeare's time suggests that *Henry VI*'s depiction of Margaret managed temporarily to alter views about her historical reputation and significance. While Robert Greene invoked the stereotype of a monstrous virago in order to defame Shakespeare, Thomas Heywood borrowed neutrally from Margaret's speeches in *1* and *2 Edward IV*.[2] He later endorsed Shakespeare's portrayal in his widely read *Exemplary Lives and Memorable Acts of Nine of the Most Worthy Women of the World* (published 1640). Heywood praised Margaret's 'brave and heroic spirit', regarding her assumption of political rule as a necessity in the face of Henry's virtual abdication. He approved of her robust maternal defence of Prince Edward's inheritance rights, and he celebrated Margaret's warrior magnanimity and courageous defiance of Edward IV as public virtues undifferentiated by gender. In doing so, Heywood recalled a classical concept of heroic action that transcends everyday moral and gender categories, thereby challenging prevailing early modern references to her as a cautionary example of female leadership.[3]

But this view soon receded. In seventeenth- and eighteenth-century stage adaptations, when women began to act the role rather than boys, Margaret appeared only in mangled parts. Crowne's *Misery of Civil-War* essentially reduced her to two scenes: the baiting of York and the death of Prince Edward. Cibber fashioned her as a revenging Amazon, assigning her Clifford's folkloric examples of 'instinctive' retaliation at the beginning of 2.2, and substituting Henry V's St Crispin's Day speech for her oration at Tewkesbury. In Merivale's tragedy, she functioned simply as York's nemesis, borrowing lines from *2 Henry VI* 4.1.1–4:

---

[1] Mary Clarke, *Shakespeare at the Old Vic*, n.p.   [2] See above, pp. 73–4.
[3] Eugene M. Waith, 'Heywood's Women Worthies', *Concepts of the Hero in the Middle Ages and the Renaissance* ed. Norman T. Burns and Christopher J. Reagan (Albany, 1975), pp. 222–38. Celeste Turner Wright, 'The Elizabethan Female Worthies', *Studies in Philology*, 43 (1946), 628–43.

> The gaudy, blabbing, and remorseful day
> Is crept into the bosom of the sea,
> And now loud howling wolves arouse the jades
> That drag the tragic melancholy night . . .
> *My blood is chill'd—yet never from her birth*
> *Hath Anjou's Margaret known the taste of fear.*
> (4.1; italics are Merivale's)

Valpy, adapting Part Three from Act 2 onwards, gave her only revised bits of the fifth act, while Cibber's version of *Richard III*—which, as we have seen, incorporated long passages from *3 Henry VI*—cut her altogether.[1]

In F. R. Benson's 1906 production her part was also heavily cut, but for the first time it was taken seriously and 'strikingly portrayed' with 'unflagging force and spirit' by Constance Benson.[2] Despite this theatrical breakthrough, the truncated role ensured that nothing should challenge the dominance of Benson himself in his role as Gloucester anticipating Richard III. Mrs Benson also could do little to dislodge literary and cultural prejudices: 'Margaret is one of the worst of the poet's creations. She revels in butchery and is mad for blood. Such a dark story can scarcely stimulate interest.'[3] Between 1906 and 1952, she appeared only once more, at the Old Vic in 1923, in a shortened version of all three *Henry VI* plays directed by Robert Atkins.

During this period, dramatic and literary critics defined Margaret almost exclusively in terms of personal ambition and

---

[1] In terms of critical visibility, between 1623 and 1801 Brian Vickers finds only three references to Margaret (*Shakespeare: The Critical Heritage*, 6 vols. (London and Boston, 1974–81). Tillyard's *Shakespeare's History Plays*, which had a wide impact in raising the critical profile of the histories as thematically coherent cycles, nonetheless reduced Margaret to a personally aggrandizing agent of disorder, mistakenly accepting Edward's assessment ('For what hath broached this tumult but thy pride? | Hadst thou been meek our title still had slept' (2.2.159–60)) as a disinterested judgement (pp. 154–5).

[2] *Birmingham Express*, 5 May 1906, *The Times*, 5 May 1906, cited in Robert Potter, 'The Rediscovery of Queen Margaret: "The Wars of the Roses", 1963', *New Theatre Quarterly*, 14 (1988), 105–19, p. 110. Other reviews, however, were less enthusiastic. Lady Benson (as she became) herself regretted that the entire performance of Part Three had been little more than a run-through because of limited rehearsal time (*Mainly Players: Bensonian Memories* (1926), p. 202). Nonetheless, her stage energy can be glimpsed in the first scene of Benson's 1911 silent film of *Richard III*, in which Margaret gestures defiantly at King Edward before being led out, vowing revenge (*Silent Shakespeare*).

[3] *Stratford Herald*, 11 May 1906.

cruelty.[1] Informed by nineteenth-century concepts of character, they based her motives on predetermined textual and morally constructed narratives. Her experiences of adultery and bereavement in Part Two were assumed by Part Three to have deformed into sadistic vengeance and lunacy. She was inevitably compared with Shakespeare's most 'intrinsically evil' and politically ambitious woman, Lady Macbeth, as was to a lesser degree the play's other queen, Elizabeth, Lady Grey.

Rosalind Boxall finally challenged this dehumanized reading in her revelatory 1952–3 performances in Birmingham and London. Audiences experienced these productions of *3 Henry VI* as startlingly 'new', in large part because Boxall portrayed Margaret credibly. As an aggrieved mother, for example, she towered in righteous indignation at Henry's disregard for her son's birthright at the end of I.I.[2] And because her part was played in full—only two lines were cut—so too for the first time was Prince Edward's, since they appear together in all their scenes. Their continual presence reminded spectators that Margaret's 'ambitions' were not merely selfish. Rather, she had been radicalized by Henry's threat to her maternal identity, which she recalls in powerful physical imagery:

> Hadst thou but loved him half so well as I,
> Or felt that pain which I did for him once,
> Or nourished him as I did with my blood,
> Thou wouldst have left thy dearest heart-blood there,
> Rather than have made that savage Duke thine heir
> And disinherited thine only son.

(I.I.221–6)

Because Part Three was preceded in Seale's theatrical cycle by *2 Henry VI*, audiences could also relate the significance of Henry's provocation to the public humiliation that first catalysed Margaret's political consciousness: Duke Humphrey's attempt to exclude her from participating in court affairs as a woman.[3] As Boxall demonstrated convincingly, and critics recognized afterwards, Margaret is not born a she-wolf, she becomes one.[4]

---

[1] For instance, reviewers of the 1955 Ashland production described Irene Baird's Margaret as an intense and sustained avenger.

[2] *Daily Telegraph*, 22 August 1952.

[3] 'These are no women's matters' (I.3. 120).

[4] For example, Irene G. Dash, *Wooing, Wedding, and Power: Women in Shakespeare's Plays* (New York, 1981), ch. 7, pp. 155–207.

9. Margaret (Rosalind Boxall) crowns York (John Arnott) in paper, in Douglas Seale's 1953 Birmingham Repertory Theatre production.

Although Jack May's performance as Henry was enormously powerful, particularly in the molehill lament of 2.5, Boxall nonetheless also discovered Margaret's capacity to express spectators' feelings of frustration with Henry's passivity. She was literally more active, often moving about restlessly while he remained sitting.[1] Reviewers were also impressed by her military courage, describing her in terms normally reserved for Shakespeare's heroic men. Seale's decision to have Margaret participate as a combatant in both 1952–3 and 1957 decisively ended traditional doubts about

[1] Kay, 'A Stage History', p. 65.

the propriety of a female warrior: as Mary Clarke observed of the later production, 'in her scenes of battle, [Barbara] Jefford was superb. Red hair falling loose to her shoulders, a breastplate over her scarlet gown and a sword in her hand'.[1] And although Jefford's torment of York in 1.4 was 'spine-chilling', her interpretation brought out new dimensions of vulnerability and humour. This underlined her increasing power and brutality in a way that paralleled her political and dramatic rival, Richard of Gloucester.[2] In the end, commentators were divided on whether the production was more triumphantly his or hers. But regardless, the play's total emotional effect and meaning were fundamentally changed by allowing Margaret's full story to be told.[3]

Boxall's and Jefford's revisionist performances laid the groundwork for Dame Peggy Ashcroft's legendary Queen Margaret in the 1963–4 *Wars of the Roses*. Because Hall and Barton's cycle was a watershed in the establishment of the Royal Shakespeare Company, and because it was eventually seen across the English-speaking world in a 1965 BBC television version, Seale's bold experiments with the *Henry VI* plays were somewhat overshadowed.[4] For all this, Ashcroft's performance genuinely marked a further opening-up of the role, and helped to stimulate a critical reappraisal of the play which has continued to the present day.[5]

Ashcroft's full-spectrum performance added to Boxall's and Jefford's interpretations by extending the dramatic boundaries of Margaret's public agency and personal emotions. This came about despite Hall and Barton's extensive condensing and rewriting of Shakespeare's original plays, but in part because of their emphasis

---

[1] *Shakespeare at the Old Vic* (1958), n.p.   [2] *Shakespeare at the Old Vic*, n.p.
[3] J. C. Trewin, *John o'London's Weekly*, 18 April 1952. John Dover Wilson had been preparing his Cambridge edition in the year of Seale's production; having seen it, he declared Margaret to be the 'most conspicuous person in the play' (Wilson, p. xxxi). Wilson also thought much of the play was by Robert Greene, and during the performance he became 'so excited when a [rare] scene that he believed to be Shakespeare's proved itself on the stage that he would scandalise our neighbours by crying out, in a voice whose loudness he was unable, being slightly deaf, to gauge, "There now! That's the Master! Isn't it? Isn't it?"' (Richard David, *Shakespeare in the Theatre* (Cambridge, 1978), p. 50).
[4] The outstanding success of Part Three was recalled in an obituary for Douglas Seale which appeared in *The Independent*, 22 June 1999. Also, J. C. Trewin, *The Birmingham Repertory Theatre 1913–1963* (1963), p. 150.
[5] Potter, 'The Rediscovery of Queen Margaret', pp. 105–9. Many critics described it as another 'revelation'.

on psychological detail and motivational complexity. Ashcroft convinced audiences of Margaret's human growth from passionate youth to self-possessed maturity. By the time she reached *Edward IV*, and until the moment of Prince Edward's death, she dominated the production's two main sites of power and conflict: the council-board, and the battlefield.[1] She also went further than Boxall and Jefford in asserting her independence from Henry, aggressively repudiating their domestic relationship, and in bringing out the full potential of her first speeches:

> But thou preferr'st thy life before thine honour,
> And seeing thou dost, I here divorce myself
> Both from thy table, Henry, and thy bed,
> Until that act of Parliament be repealed
> Whereby my son is disinherited.

> (1.1.247–51)

The non-Shakespearian passages Barton wrote for Margaret also had the effect of giving greater 'humanity and background to [her] scolding', by clarifying her sublimation of a failed marriage to a weak and sexually unsatisfying husband in her energetic leadership of the Lancastrian cause.[2] At the same time, Ashcroft strongly conveyed Part Three's new dimension of maternal solicitude, problematizing the Amazon stereotype to which her male opponents always seek to reduce her.[3]

Yet internally these conflicting roles gradually took their toll, as Ashcroft's Margaret deteriorated morally, mentally, and physically. It was this aspect of her performance, perhaps more than any other, which led reviewers to praise Ashcroft's rediscovery not just of a great Shakespearian character, but of a new tragic heroine. Her validation of Margaret's cruel suffering sprang from a realistic awareness that she is both free and constrained in her choices of action, rather than simply doomed by circumstances or social discourses beyond her control, or by a 'naturally' wicked

[1] Reviewers' comparisons were no longer to Lady Macbeth but to Mother Courage, owing to the perceived Brechtian epic effects of Hall and Barton's production.

[2] John Barton and Peter Hall, *The Wars of the Roses*, pp. xviii–xix. This was also psychic damage from her loss of Suffolk, which Part Two specifically emphasizes (3.2.357–60, 4.4.1–3) but Part Three does not.

[3] In 1966 at Ashland, Claudia Wilkins persuaded reviewers that she was fighting on behalf of Prince Edward, not for personal gain.

personality.¹ As Peter Hall remarked in the context of the wider production: 'it's not power that corrupts, but that you have to corrupt yourself to be politically powerful'.²

Like Margaret before her, the play's other queen consort, Lady Grey, is initially coerced, but she makes different choices, refusing to sacrifice her personal integrity in order to salvage her children's birthright when she is crudely propositioned by Edward in 3.2. While in some productions such as Hall and Barton's *The Wars of the Roses*, actors have played her flirtatiously to suggest that she 'knows the game' as well as Edward, this variation on the sexually manipulative gold-digger has become less common in recent years.³ Most performers, such as the BBC's Rowena Cooper, play her with defiant dignity until she is compelled into marriage by Edward. By surrendering to passion, he manifests the same weakness and lack of control that Henry did by marrying Margaret in Part Two. He thereby undermines his relationships with his brothers, Warwick, and foreign allies,⁴ and they in turn project their wrath and frustration on to Lady Grey, just as they have continually done with Margaret.⁵

Beyond her first scene, however, Lady Grey, now Queen Elizabeth, reinstates the traditional female role of domestic handmaid, which Margaret rejects in 1.1 (and in *2 Henry VI* before that). Though Elizabeth is well informed and politically astute in 4.4,⁶ her main goal is to save Edward's child. Her displacement of Margaret's changing combination of maternal, politically militant, and violent roles with a unified image of 'devoted female domesticity'

---

¹ Patricia-Ann Lee, 'Reflections of Power: Margaret of Anjou and the Dark Side of Queenship', *Renaissance Quarterly*, 39 (1986), 183–217; p. 215.

² Quoted in Richard Pearson, *A Band of Arrogant and United Heroes* (1990), p. 8.

³ Though historical criticism has shown that such a reading is partly authorized by More's *History of King Richard III*, in which 'Elizabeth shrewdly manipulates the king's lust to empower herself legitimately by making their sexual relations contingent upon wedlock' (Alan Clarke Sheperd, ' "Female Perversity," Male Entitlement: The Agency of Gender in More's *The History of Richard III'*, *The Sixteenth Century Journal*, 26 (1995), 311–28; p.316).

⁴ Marilyn L. Williamson, ' "When Men Are Rul'd by Women": Shakespeare's First Tetralogy', *Shakespeare Studies*, 19 (1987), 41–59; p. 53.

⁵ Sarah Lyons, 'Shakespeare's Margaret of Anjou: "Oure Queene Margarete to signifie" ' (unpublished MA dissertation, The Shakespeare Institute, University of Birmingham, 1990), p. 21.

⁶ In the Folio text. In *True Tragedy* she is significantly weaker and less independent.

seems complete in the state-family portrait of the final scene.[1] But the celebration of dynastic rebirth and reconciliation is marred by Gloucester's private agenda, while Edward's self-satisfied sentimentality parodies the restoration of strong patriarchal authority the nation has supposedly lacked for so long under Henry. The fact that Edward 'wafts' Margaret to France, just a bit too casually, confirms the underlying impression of Yorkist make-believe.

Since Boxall's and Ashcroft's performances, scholarly discussion of Margaret, as well as of other women who play unconventional roles in Shakespeare's early histories, has grown steadily. Feminist scholars have explored new perspectives on Shakespeare's depiction of women, the masculine codes of behaviour which define patriarchal culture, and female representation in traditional accounts of history.[2] But Margaret's prominence as a major Shakespearian character has been ambivalently confirmed. Recent productions have often tended to roll back the textual and performative gains made by Boxall, Jefford, and Ashcroft. For example Terry Hands's 1977 RSC production claimed to position itself against Barton's adaptations by promising to stage all three *Henry VI* plays in full scripts. Yet Hands cut 164 lines of Part Three, nearly half of which were originally assigned to, or about, Margaret. Their absence seemed to affect Helen Mirren's performance by diminishing Margaret's maternal bond with Prince Edward. It weakened the legitimacy of her political interest in her son's succession, grounded ideologically in legal precedent and tradition.[3] Moreover, in the eyes of many reviewers, Mirren simply failed to

[1] Leah S. Marcus, *Puzzling Shakespeare: Local Reading and its Discontents* (Berkeley, Los Angeles, and London, 1988), p. 94. Barbara Hodgdon, *The End Crowns All: Closure and Contradiction in Shakespeare's History* (Princeton, 1991), pp. 70 ff. Nina S. Levine, *Women's Matters: Politics, Gender, and Nation in Shakespeare's Early History Plays* (Newark, NJ, and London, 1998), pp. 95–6.

[2] Madonne M. Miner, ' "Neither mother, wife, nor England's queen": The Roles of Women in *Richard III*', in *The Woman's Part: Feminist Criticism of Shakespeare*, ed. C. R. S. Lenz *et al.* (Urbana, 1980), pp. 35–55; Dash, *Wooing*; Williamson, ' "When Men Are Rul'd by Women" '; Joyce Green MacDonald, ' "Hay for the Daughters!" '; Phyllis Rackin, *Stages of History: Shakespeare's English Chronicles* (Ithaca, 1990), and 'Foreign Country: The Place of Women and Sexuality in Shakespeare's Historical World', in *Enclosure Acts: Sexuality, Property, and Culture in Early Modern England*, ed. Richard Burt and John Michael Archer (Ithaca, 1994), pp. 68–95; Howard and Rackin, *passim*; Kathryn Schwarz, 'Fearful Simile: Stealing the Breech in Shakespeare's Chronicle Plays', *SQ* 49 (1998), 140–67.

[3] Levine, *Women's Matters*, p. 95.

develop personally in new directions beyond the *femme fatale* of Part Two.[1] Her military career was clearly therapy for sexual frustration.

Reductions of Margaret's role in other recent productions, however, have not simply marked a regression to earlier social models and theatrical practices, but also indicated its altered cultural value and reception in the light of modern political attitudes. The two major English stage productions of the 1980s both reverted to the abridged format of *The Wars of the Roses*, yet without Barton's compensating additions, and even in relative terms Margaret's role was textually reduced (e.g. large cuts to the oration before Tewkesbury,[2] as well as shorter passages attesting to Margaret's political acumen). Whether the meaning of her role was also imaginatively undercut by the imposition of contemporized readings depends on wider assumptions about the function and purpose of theatre. Performances by June Watson in the ESC's self-styled radical production of 1987 and to a lesser extent by Penny Downie in *The Plantagenets* in 1988 alluded to the manner, and in Watson's case the appearance, of England's modern 'Amazonian', Margaret Thatcher. Faced with the latter's open contempt for the performing arts and her government's funding cuts, these companies could not resist satirizing the she-warrior of the Falklands through Margaret of Anjou, and for some critics and spectators, this political analogy was justifiably timely and appropriate. On the other hand the textual interventions made by these productions, compounded by both actors' tendencies to vocal stridency, left little scope for nuances that humanize Shakespeare's Iron Lady of Naples. Though both Watson and Downie were confident and ferocious—sufficiently so to make Noble's comparison to Lear seem plausible on the level of searing emotion[3]—their Margarets

---

[1] Roger Warren, 'Comedies and Histories at Two Stratfords, 1977', *Shakespeare Survey 31* (1978), 141–53. David Daniell, 'Opening up the text: Shakespeare's *Henry VI* plays in performance', *Drama and Society* (Cambridge, 1979), 247–77; pp. 259–68.

[2] Rhetorically, the oration is traditionally an elite male genre, associated with the gravest questions of public policy, as well as battlefield addresses. Margaret's ability to use the form adeptly substantiates her request to be 'For once allowed the skilful pilot's charge' (i.e. Henry's authority).

[3] Shaughnessy, *Representing Shakespeare*, p. 83. See also R. Martin, '"A Woman's generall: what should we feare?": Queen Margaret Thatcherized in Recent Productions of *3 Henry VI*', in *Shakespeare and his Contemporaries in Performance*, ed. Edward J. Esche (Aldershot and Burlington, Vt., 2000), pp. 321–38.

10. Margaret (Julia Foster) grieves over the body of her murdered son in Jane Howell's 1983 BBC television production. Copyright © BBC.

ultimately lacked complexity, and seemed to act only out of hard domination and sadistic vengeance, throwbacks to a Lady Macbeth caricature.

An important exception to this trend was Jane Howell's 1983 BBC television production of *3 Henry VI*. It made minimal cuts and allowed Julia Foster's Margaret full textual scope, even if her grim tone sometimes tended to sound like scolding. Katie Mitchell's 1994 stand-alone RSC production likewise cut very little from Margaret's part, but it tamed her in other ways in pursuit of a broader humanitarian theme. Mitchell's decision to eliminate stage violence to suit her anti-war reading of the play deprived Ruth Mitchell's Margaret of opportunities to display her martial leadership and heroic courage in battle (the largest verbal cuts were to her Tewkesbury oration).[1] Visually she appeared nearly identical to the other drably costumed male soldiers, with whose gestures and movements she became dramatically assimilated.[2] On the other hand, an ill-advised and unconvincing French accent kept her isolated as a foreigner and disadvantaged rhetorically as a

---

[1] Mitchell's renaming of the play, *Henry VI: the Battle for the Throne*, was deliberately ironic, since the production virtually refused to present any fighting.

[2] Annika I. Johansson, 'Review of *Henry VI: the Battle for the Throne*', *Mason Croft Review: A Publication of the Shakespeare Institute*, 2 (1994), 25–6; p. 26.

serious protagonist.[1] It also seemed to reinforce her status as a victimized woman, despite occasional counterblasts of 'embattled ferocity'.[2] Her foreign accent also diminished her credibility in defending national interests under a unified Lancastrian rule.[3]

A similar narrowing of perspective characterized major productions at Ashland, Oregon, during this period, all in varying degrees haunted by the legacy of Vietnam, though in many other ways they were theatrically innovative. Mimi Carr struggled in 1977 to raise Margaret's credibility as a leader in the face of substantial verbal cuts, especially those bearing on her political knowledge.[4] Michelle Morain was more enthusiastically received in 1992 because of her energetic participation in combat (a first, apparently, at Ashland). During the Battle of Towton in 2.4, for instance, she conspicuously drove off Richard and then Warwick, and later, at the merged battles of Barnet and Tewkesbury, she fought with Edward and two other lords before losing her sword. But Morain's 'mannish' determination as 'a fighter', combined with interpretive choices that downplayed her maternal and political roles, tended to make her sound merely irascible when she was off the battlefield.[5] Moreover, a prologue inserted at the beginning of the play consisting of lines from Parts Two and Three dwelt solely on her grief for Suffolk, thereby framing her motives mainly in terms of personal revenge.[6] Margaret's triumphant 'Off with his head!' after York's death was Morain's dramatic high point.

---

[1] Peter Holland, 'In a world with no use for goodness', review of *Henry VI: the Battle for the Throne, Times Literary Supplement*, 26 August 1994; reproduced and revised in *English Shakespeares*, pp. 199–202. By contrast, Peggy Ashcroft had lost the light French accent she started with in *Henry VI* by the time she reached *Edward IV*.

[2] Particularly when she crawled and prostrated herself with outstretched arms before (her cousin) Lewis at the beginning of 3.3. Lady Grey adopted the same posture before Edward in the opening of the previous scene. See Michael Billington, *The Guardian*, 12 August 1994.

[3] Schwarz, 'Fearful Simile', p. 160. Levine, *Women's Matters*, pp. 82–6. Audiences were visibly reminded of the question of who represents England, symbolically as well as politically, by the large spotlit image of St George at the back of the stage. It also functioned as an icon for the verbal invocations of the saint by Yorkists and Lancastrians (e.g. 2.1.204, 2.2.80).

[4] Including her entire appearance with Prince Edward at the end of 2.5, and sizeable passages in 3.3.

[5] Dan Isaac, 'Henry VI', *Lithiagraph* (August, 1992), p. 15.

[6] Alan Armstrong, 'Oregon Shakespeare Festival', *Shakespeare Bulletin* (Fall, 1992), 25–6.

11. 'A woman's general, what should we fear?': Margaret (Michelle Morain) in combat with Edward (Robert Lisell-Frank), in Pat Patton's 1992 Oregon Shakespeare Festival production, Ashland, Oregon.

Contemporizing relevance notwithstanding, the overall effect of these recent productions was to blunt Margaret's jagged bravery and (inadvertently?) to rehabilitate patriarchal biases against an outspoken non-domestic woman. Given late twentieth-century changes in attitude towards women in positions of public authority, this comes as a bit of a surprise. Yet in revealing anxieties about a fully scripted performance which might reflect favourably on contentious modern politicians such as Mrs Thatcher, these productions also recall early modern debates about the legitimacy of female rulers. In England the most notorious and spectacularly ill-timed intervention was John Knox's *First Blast of the Trumpet Against the Monstrous Regiment of Women*. Knox wrote with Queen Mary and Mary Queen of Scots in mind, but published his treatise just months before Elizabeth came to the throne in 1558. In *3 Henry VI*, York echoes *The First Blast* when responding to Margaret's brutality in 1.4 (see note to l. 141). Knox's traditional assertions about female inferiority and sinfulness were refuted by various Elizabethan apologists, beginning with John Aylmer's *An Harbour for Faithful and True Subjects* (1559). Aylmer argued that preserving the royal succession and defending national interests as defined by Parliament validated the Queen's authority. Shakespeare represents these alternative views—excepting Parliament's role—in his portrayal of Margaret and in comments about her.[1] She adopts rhetorical strategies publicly demonstrated by Elizabeth on several occasions, such as deliberately drawing attention to her 'natural' female weakness or subservience in order to contrast her own exceptional courage and abilities (e.g. 1.1.244–6, 5.4).[2] Like Joan la Pucelle in *1 Henry VI*, Margaret's participation in armed combat roles may have reminded playgoers of what soon became Elizabeth's legendary pre-Armada address to her troops at Tilbury, where she astonished contemporaries by appearing dressed in armour.[3] The political reality of a reigning female monarch was probably responsible for Holinshed's revision of Hall's misogyny towards Queen Margaret, and his praise for her rational policy and courage. These were changes that Shakespeare, in the course of revising *True Tragedy* as *3 Henry VI*, successfully incorporated to create his tragically conflicted heroine,[4] and the last of his five main

[1] They also characterize Baldwin's *Mirror for Magistrates*: in Henry's complaint she is innocent of ambition, whereas in Duke Humphrey's she yearns to rule absolutely. See Lyons, 'Shakespeare's Margaret of Anjou', pp. 2–3, 25.

[2] 'I know I have but the body of a weak and feeble woman; but I have the heart of a king, and of a king of England too' (from a speech reportedly delivered to troops at Tilbury: John Nichols, *Progresses*, ii. 536); '. . . though I be a woman, yet I have as good a courage answerable to my place as ever my father had: I am your anointed Queen' (from a response to Parliament's petition urging Elizabeth to marry, cited by Allison Heisch in 'Queen Elizabeth I: Parliamentary Rhetoric and the Exercise of Power', *Signs*, 1 (1975), 31–55, p. 35).

[3] John Aske, *Elizabetha Triumphans, 1588*, in Nichols, *Progresses*, ii. 545–82. Susan Frye's 'The Myth of Elizabeth at Tilbury', *Sixteenth Century Journal*, 23 (1992), 95–114, is challenged by Janet M. Green, ' "I My Self" : Queen Elizabeth I's Oration at Tilbury Camp', *Sixteenth Century Journal*, 28 (1997), 421–45. Marcus, *Puzzling Shakespeare*, p. 94.

[4] Levine, *Women's Matters*, pp. 26–46, 75–96.

personal histories. Whether Margaret's story is indeed the most central of these remains an open question, tied to shifting cultural and political perspectives, and interpretive choices by individual directors. Its prominence has been positively affirmed by several outstanding modern performances, but at the same time continues to be productively challenged, as this introduction has tried to show, by theatrical and historical validations of the play's other main roles and narratives.

The Original Texts: their history and relationship

This edition is based upon the text printed in the First Folio (hereafter referred to as F), the collected volume edited in 1623, seven years after Shakespeare's death, by his fellow actors John Heminges and Henry Condell. The full title reads 'The third Part of Henry the Sixt, with the death of the Duke of YORKE'. Overall, F is a clear text and relatively free of problems. It provided the copy for three subsequent folios issued in 1632, 1663, and 1684 (F2, F3, F4). These later editions corrected F's occasional typographical errors (while also introducing new ones of their own). They also modernized spellings as seventeenth-century conventions became standardized, and regularized metrical rhythms. But because these changes were introduced by the printers, they are not authoritative, though they sometimes provide modern editors with alternative readings in places where F requires emendation.

The copy underlying F is generally agreed to be Shakespeare's manuscript.[1] Scholarly debate arises over its state, and the degree to which, if at all, other hands have annotated it in anticipation of use in the playhouse as a prompt book or script.

F bears signs of being a draft which Shakespeare was in the later stages of composing and/or revising, rather than being in either a definitive or 'final' state.[2] It contains what are conventionally

---

[1] I am assuming Shakespeare is the only author of Part Three, whose poetic tone and dramatic structure are the most consistent throughout, unlike Parts One and Two, and whose dialogue from at least 3.2 looks forward to *Richard III*. Past suggestions of possible co-authors, such as Robert Greene, lack any substantial basis of evidence.

[2] Greg, *Folio*, p. 183. But Greg also hedged: a 'fair copy, which still left something to be desired'. Cairncross believed the copy to be scribal, but his evidence (pp. xxiii–xxiv) is unpersuasive since 'the errors he cites . . . may be explained just as plausibly and more simply as compositorial in origin' (*Textual Companion*, 198).

regarded as 'pre-performance' stage directions which are indefinite or vague, leaving exact personnel or numbers to be determined later: e.g. '*Enter King Henry, Clifford, Northumberland, Westmorland, Exeter, and the rest*' (1.1.49.1-3), '*Enter Edward, Richard, and their power*' (2.1.0.1), '*Enter one blowing*' (2.1.42.1), '*Warwick and his company follows*' (5.1.113.2-3), '*Enter King Edward in triumph, with Richard, Clarence, and the rest*' (5.3.0.1-2)'.[1] Other stage directions are 'descriptive', in the sense that they seem to reveal the playwright narrating or explaining the stage action he has in mind for his actors, which is not directly implied by the surrounding dialogue: '[*Warwick*] *stamps with his foot, and the Soldiers show themselves*' (1.1.170.1-2), '*Enter Lewis the French King . . . Lewis sits, and riseth up again*' (3.3.0.1-4), '*Enter Warwick and Oxford in England, with French Soldiers*' (4.2.0.1-2), '*Enter three Watchmen to guard* [*King Edward's*] *tent*' (4.3.0.1), '*Enter Warwick* [*et al.*] . . . *silent all*' (4.3.22.1-2); '*Warwick and the rest cry all, "Warwick, Warwick!" and set upon the guard, who fly, crying "Arm, arm!", Warwick and the rest following them*' (4.3.27.1-3). A variation on this kind of descriptive direction occurs when Shakespeare specifies the stage blocking, as he does at the beginning of Act 4 when the two Yorkist factions confront each other: '*Enter King Edward* [*et al.*] . . . *four stand on one side, and four on the other*' (4.1.6.1-3).

F also contains various loose ends and inconsistencies indicative of a working draft. Foremost among these is the complicated multiple identity underlying Montague. The different historical figures represented by his single persona, and a possible connection with Falconbridge, unquestionably reveal Shakespeare revising the role(s) as he wrote.[2] Beyond the example of Montague, there are smaller suggestions of a draft in progress. An erroneous speech prefix at 2.2.89 assigning part of Edward's speech to Clarence points to Shakespeare's changing his mind and neglecting to correct the initial version, rather than a compositorial misreading.[3]

None of F's errors is of the type commonly associated with scribal transcription of surviving dramatic manuscripts, nor is there observable regularization of the kind scribes routinely imposed in the course of their work.

[1] Paul Werstine and William B. Long have also called attention, however, to the presence of this kind of stage direction in texts deriving from playhouse copy: '"Foul Papers" and "Prompt-Books": Printer's Copy for Shakespeare's *Comedy of Errors*', *Studies in Bibliography*, 41 (1988), 232–46; 'Stage-Directions: A Misinterpreted Factor in Determining Textual Provenance', *Text*, 2 (1985), 121–37.

[2] See above pp. 73–4.   [3] See note to 2.2.89–92.

Two speeches are misassigned, at 2.2.133 (Warwick instead of Richard), and 5.7.30 (Clarence instead of Elizabeth). Various exits and entrances are lacking, at 1.1.189.1, 210.1, 264.1, 2.5.113.1, 5.1.6.1, 65.1, and 5.6.6.1. The '*Exeunt*' at 4.8.32.1 does not provide for Henry remaining on stage (if, as seems likely, the remainder of the scene does not constitute a separate scene[1]). F omits an entry for Exeter at the same place, and fails to mention him in the otherwise explicit direction '*Exit with King Henry*' near the end of this scene. There may be an undeleted or duplicated direction (or a re-entry) for the Father who enters '*bearing of his son*' after 2.5.78.[2] In the direction at 2.6.29.3 '*Montague, and Clarence*' are named after the conventionally conclusive '*and Soldiers*'. However, Montague has no lines or implied presence in the scene, unlike Clarence who does. Whether he is here a mute or an addition, his position in the direction suggests a different stage of composition, or an annotation in the underlying copy. Changes in speech prefixes seem also to reveal subtle shifts in a character's function or status: e.g. '*Plant⟨agenet⟩*' varies with '*Yorke*' in 1.1, and Lady Grey is '*Wid⟨ow⟩*' in 3.2, '*Lady Grey*' in 4.1.[3] Margaret is '*Queene*' or some variant thereof throughout the play, except in 3.3 where she is '*Marg.*'[4]

More revealing is the presence of actors' names in F substituting for dramatic parts or characters. These show that Shakespeare had specific players in mind for smaller roles as he wrote.[5] At 1.2.47.1 '*Gabriel*' enters as a messenger and is similarly designated in the

---

[1] See note to 4.8.0.2

[2] See note to 2.5.54.1–2. For further signs of revision in this scene, see pp. 110–12 below.

[3] She should also be '*Queene*' in 5.7, as she is named in the direction, but her speech prefix at l. 30 was mistakenly set '*Cla<rence>*'.

[4] These changes do not seem to be owing to a temporary shortage of italic type, a problem that could sometimes lead compositors to alter authorial speech prefixes. See Richard F. Kennedy, 'Speech Prefixes in Some Shakespearean Quartos', *Papers of the Bibliographical Society of America*, 92 (1998), 177–209. Paul Werstine, 'Narratives About Printed Shakespeare Texts: "Foul Papers" and "Bad Quartos"', *SQ* 41 (1990), 65–86, p. 72, rightly cautions against taking such variants axiomatically as signs of authorial papers, since they also exist in scribal transcripts. But since F is not scribal, they here remain plausible evidence of Shakespeare's evolving attitudes towards his characters.

[5] The names are unlikely to derive from a prompter annotating the play, since this kind of annotation typically takes the form of extra information or duplicate directions in extant playhouse manuscripts of the period. See Greg, *Folio*, pp. 114–15.

speech prefix. '*Sinklo*' and '*Humfrey*' enter in 3.1.0.1, 'with cross-bows in their hands' to identify them as gamekeepers. Prefixes of their full names or abbreviations recur throughout the scene. The first of these is assumed to refer to Gabriel Spencer, the second to John Sincklo or Sincler, and the third to Humphrey Jeffes. All three were minor actors in the early to mid-1590s associated with Pembroke's Men.[1] Their names appear without accompanying character designations in the directions and prefixes and therefore probably do not originate with a prompter. Actors' names alone would also become pointless beyond the time of a first production when other players came to perform the roles.[2] On the other hand Greg asserts that because it is '[not] of the least consequence who took these minor parts', 'their assignment cannot possibly be attributed to the author'.[3] While this is true in the sense that none of these actors seems to have been chosen to exploit known physical or artistic traits, such as John Sincklo's well-attested thinness, it does not mean that Shakespeare did not have other reasons for casting these men with whom he worked closely, but which we now simply cannot know. Shakespeare undoubtedly often relied on the gestural and vocal habits of individual players to vivify minor occupational roles.[4] The gamekeepers in *3 Henry VI* 3.1, for example, are unquestionably, if subtly, differentiated by their degrees of experience, perception, and patience. It is highly unlikely, moreover, that a book-keeper 'would have replaced 1 Keeper and 2 Keeper . . . with actors' names eighteen times in one brief scene'. The book-keeper's typical practice was to let a single annotation stand for each role throughout.[5] The personal names which appear in extant dramatic manuscripts, or in original printed editions of Shakespeare's plays, are overwhelmingly hired men rather than sharers.[6] Greg's objection therefore has no empirical basis.

If these traces and anomalies point to F being Shakespeare's working papers, a related question is whether they were annotated

---

[1] Gurr, *Companies*, pp. 72 n. 36, 107, 280. For the further significance of these names in F, see pp. 130–1.

[2] R. B. McKerrow, 'The Elizabethan Printer and Dramatic Manuscripts', *The Library*, 4th ser., 12 (1931), 253–75, p. 274; Greg, *Folio*, pp. 114–15.

[3] Greg, *Folio*, p. 183.

[4] Allison Gaw, 'Actors' Names in Basic Shakespearean Texts', *PMLA*, 40 (1925), 530–50; 'John Sincklo as one of Shakespeare's Actors', *Anglia*, NS 37 (1926), 289–303; McKerrow, 'Dramatic Manuscripts', pp. 274–5.

[5] Gaw, 'John Sincklo', p. 297.   [6] Wilson, p. 120.

to any degree by a book-keeper in anticipation of performance. All recent editors follow Greg in believing F's copy was edited for the playhouse, however lightly. I am not persuaded of this, but the possibility cannot be ruled out entirely. Several recent studies have shown that extant theatrical manuscripts were often inconsistent, incomplete, and/or lacking in specificity in many of their theatrical details or assignments. The presence of loose ends therefore does not necessarily exclude potential use in the playhouse as an acceptable, 'finished' script.[1] On the other hand, as Wilson observed, F bears none of the conventional marks of a book-keeper's hand in surviving dramatic manuscripts.[2] It does contain a large number of directions for music, mainly entry and exit fanfares, for example, some of which may be non-authorial.[3] But these are hardly beyond the imagination of Shakespeare himself, who foresaw the technical resources of his theatre continually while writing. F's musical cues are also consistent with the evidence of other Folio plays believed to derive from his papers. One particular example often cited as evidence of theatrical annotation is the direction '*Flourish*' which occurs at the beginning of 1.2 rather than at the end of 1.1. It may have been misplaced by the compositor reading a marginal note. But even if this is the case, it reveals nothing about who wrote it. For although prompters' annotations normally occur in the margins, so do playwrights' revisions and additions, of which '*Montague and Clarence*' (cited above) may be an instance. Related to this is '*Flourish. Sound*' at 4.7.70.1. Recent editors argue that the first word is original and the second a 'marginal annotation, possibly of playhouse origin', and a duplication.[4] But the direction is not actually misplaced, and as Hattaway observes in his note, F's direction

[1] William B. Long, ' "A bed/for woodstock": A Warning for the Unwary', *Medieval and Renaissance Drama in England*, 2 (New York, 1985), 91–118. This work revises McKerrow's assumption that 'no copy but a good, orderly, and legible one could possibly serve as a prompt-copy' ('Dramatic Manuscripts', p. 264).

[2] McKerrow lists four categories: advance calls for players or properties; directions listing props to be used later in a scene; actors' names assigned to character roles; anticipatory entries ('Dramatic Manuscripts', pp. 270–2). See also Wilson, p. 119, and Greg, *Folio*, p. 142. The application of McKerrow's categories as absolute generalizations has recently been questioned by Paul Werstine ('Narratives About Printed Shakespeare Texts'), who cautions that each textual document needs to be assessed individually.

[3] Greg, *Folio*, p. 182. Stanley Wells, *Re-Editing Shakespeare for the Modern Reader* (Oxford, 1984), p. 82.

[4] *Textual Companion*, note to 4.8.70.1, p. 204; Wilson, p. 189, Cairncross, p. xix .

may very well indicate that trumpets were sounded twice, before and after the proclamation. If this is the case and both directions appeared in the margin, there was probably not enough intervening text to separate them distinctively. The direction that follows Warwick's death, '*Here they bear away his body*' (5.2.50.1), is conspicuous for being the only one of its kind in F, despite the fact that bodies need to be carried off at many points. This too suggests the direction is authorial.

In the end all the putative evidence of playhouse editing of F is equivocal, and little positively indicates the hand of anybody other than the playwright. While some directions may be theatrically derived, professionally this origin included Shakespeare himself. It is simpler and more consistent with what we know about contemporary practices to imagine that any fair-copy manuscript, if it ever existed, would have been submitted to the Master of the Revels for licensing and then retained by the players as their official prompt book, which in all events is now lost. The copy submitted to Blount and Jaggard for printing as F, on the other hand, was Shakespeare's draft papers. This shows him continuing to invent and expand roles, dialogue, and directions, anticipating a performance which would draw on contemporary material and human resources. The Oxford editors observe that certain stage directions in 3.3, '*Speaking to Bona*' (59) and '*Speaks to Warwick*' (131, 163), are uncharacteristic of Shakespeare;[1] if this is so, they may have been added by the Folio editors for readers to clarify the shifting or potentially ambiguous dialogue at these points, since other directions in the scene are unexceptional. Additional signs of F as a revised version of the play are discussed in the next section.

In regard to the printing of F, Charlton Hinman first established that *3 Henry VI* was set by two compositors, A and B, from typecases x and y respectively.[2] Like the rest of the Folio, copy was cast off and set by formes, not seriatim. Peter W. M. Blayney has recently confirmed this analysis but refined the setting order.[3] His

[1] *Textual Companion*, p. 112.

[2] *The Printing and Proof-Reading of the First Folio of Shakespeare*, 2 vols. (Oxford, 1963), ii. 107–17.

[3] Introduction to the Second Edition, Charlton Hinman, *The First Folio of Shakespeare*, The Norton Facsimile (New York and London, 1996), p. xxxvi. Blayney observes that most plays in F experienced gaps in printing while pages of other plays were being set and machined.

results follow below. The first number indicates the page of the Hinman facsimile, second edition (1996), the second the Folio signature, and the third the number of that page in the overall setting order. The fourth column indicates the compositor now believed to have set the page.

501	04	412	A
502	04v	414	A
503	05	416	A
504	05v	418	A
506	06v	420	A
505	06	422	A
512	p3v	487	B
513	p4	488	A
511	p3	489	B
514	p4v	490	A
510	p2v	491	B
515	p5	492	A
509	p2	493	B
516	p5v	494	B
508	p1v	495	B
517	p6	496	A
507	p1	497	B
518	p6v	498	A
524	q3v	499	A
525	q4	500	B
523	q3	501	A
526	q4v	502	B
522	q2v	503	A
521	q2	505	A
520	q1v	507	A
519	q1	509	B

Between quires o and p (i.e. 2.1.75 and 4.3.41) the setting was interrupted when A and B returned to work on the end of *Richard II* and on *1* and *2 Henry IV* after a dispute over copyright was resolved.[1] This explains why *3 Henry VI*'s running-titles vary slightly. Quire o reads '*The third Part of Henry the Sixt*'. Quires p and q change to '*The third Part of King Henry the Sixt*'. Proof-reading

---

[1] Hinman, *Printing and Proof-Reading*, ii. 523.

variants are minimal. The only detectable corrections are changes made after corrected copy had been printed, and during machining.[1] There are no proof-reading variants in quire o, three non-textual variants in p, and four on q4v, the final page of the play. The latter are all obvious and do not suggest that different copy was consulted.[2] The only minor anomaly detected by Hinman was q1, the last page of the play to be set (4.3.41-4.6.15). Spelling tests indicate it was set by B but not from his own type-case, y, but A's, case x. This discrepancy remains unexplained.[3]

The question of whether the Folio compositors consulted any printed edition to supplement or clarify readings in Shakespeare's manuscript needs further consideration, in the light of claims made by recent editors. But this matter can be resolved with greater certainty after discussing other early texts of the play.

'The True Tragedy of Richard Duke of York'. A different version of *3 Henry VI* was issued as an octavo (small-format book, hereafter referred to as O) in 1595. Its title-page reads:

The true Tragedie of Richard *Duke of Yorke, and the death of* good King Henrie the Sixt, *with the whole contention betweene* the two Houses Lancaster and Yorke, *as it was sundrie times acted by the Right Honourable the Earle of Pembrooke his seruants.*

The edition was printed 'at London by P[eter]. S[hort]. for Thomas Millington' and is recorded to have sold for 8d.[4] It had not been entered in the Stationers' Register, but this was not unusual or irregular,[5] and the publication in any event may have been covered by an entry on 12 March 1594 for *The First part of the Contention betwixt the two famous Houses of Yorke and Lancaster*, a quarto version of *2 Henry VI* also published by Millington.[6] He re-issued

---

[1] Although Blayney makes the debatable claim that all manuscript copy was subject to editing and typographical emendation *before* printing: Blayney, p. xxxi.

[2] Hinman, *Printing and Proof-Reading*, i. 275–6.

[3] Hinman, *Printing and Proof-Reading*, ii. 116.

[4] Francis R. Johnson, 'Notes on English Retail Book-prices, 1550–1640', *The Library*, 5th ser., 5 (1950–1), 83–112, p. 109.

[5] C. J. Sisson, 'The Laws of Elizabethan Copyright: the Stationers' View', *The Library*, 5th ser., 15 (1960), 8–20.

[6] Arber ii. 646. Chambers, *WS*, ii. 130. This may explain why O is styled somewhat misleadingly '*the whole contention*'. *Pace* Greg (*Folio*, p. 176), the *OED* does not authorize the definition 'conclusion of' for 'whole'. Nonetheless, the latter was possibly included to create a verbal link in titles to make good on Millington's implied

True Tragedy (as I shall refer to it) in 1600 in a quarto (Q2) based on O. On 19 April 1602 Millington transferred his rights to both *True Tragedy* and *The First Part of the Contention* to Thomas Pavier,[1] who published both plays in 1619 (Q3) under a single title: *The Whole Contention betweene the two famous Houses, Lancaster and Yorke*. This formed part of a collection of ten plays alleged to be by Shakespeare and printed by William Jaggard, who later printed the First Folio in 1623. Q3 is based on an edited copy of O, but only one altered passage may possibly be authoritative; the rest derive from the printing house.[2]

In general, O is about a thousand lines, or one third, shorter than F. It omits a few minor roles (e.g. the three Watchmen in 4.3, the Lieutenant of the Tower in 4.6 and 5.6), as well as verbal ornament, classical allusions, and metaphorical expressions. But there is no actual reduction in personnel: the number of players required to perform both plays is virtually the same.[3] O's selection of historical events and its narrative sequence are also largely the same as F's. At particular moments, on the other hand, O's dialogue and scenic choreography are unique, and its substantial changes in characterization create different meanings and emotional effects. Some modern directors have found O's dramatic alternatives preferable

joint entry in 1594. '*The whole contention*' refers to the dynastic conflict between York and Lancaster that strictly constitutes the Wars of the Roses. This began with the first Battle of St Albans in 1455 (represented at the end of *The First Part of the Contention/2 Henry VI*) and ended with the death of Henry VI in 1471 (5.6 in *True Tragedy/3 Henry VI*).

[1] Arber, iii. 204. Confusingly, the entry refers to 'The first and Second parte of Henry the VJ' [= 6th] ij bookes'. This is presumed to refer to *The Whole Contention* and *True Tragedy*, since *1 Henry VI* is not believed to have been written until after them in 1592 (see pp. 125–9 below). While the last of these was therefore in existence by 1602, the earlier two plays do not seem to have been known as *2* and *3 Henry VI* until all three plays were grouped together in chronological sequence in F (*pace* Hattaway, p. 201). Still confusingly, a collective Stationers' Register entry on 8 November 1623 for sixteen unpublished or unregistered Folio plays (Arber, iv. 107) included 'The thirde parte of Henry ye Sixt'. This apparently refers to the hitherto unissued *1 Henry VI* (Chambers, *WS*, i. 139–40, 156, who observes that these registrations contradict Heminges and Condell's statement in the Preface to F about 'stolne, and surreptitious copies' in regard to *The Whole Contention* and *True Tragedy*).

[2] *Textual Companion*, p. 198, and see discussion below, pp. 122–3.

[3] *Pace* Scott McMillin, 'Casting for Pembroke's Men: The *Henry VI* Quartos and *The Taming of A Shrew*', *SQ* 23 (1972), 141–59; Robert E. Burkhart, *Shakespeare's Bad Quartos: Deliberate Abridgments Designed for Performance by a Reduced Cast* (The Hague, 1975). See Appendix C.

to F's, while in a few places O seems to correct and/or clarify F. Yet O also presents clear indications of being a faulty text whose verbal anomalies cannot be materially ascribed to compositorial blunders or the process of revision alone.[1] It contains conspicuous passages of nonsense, and often severely fractures the verse (both versions are in verse throughout).

O and F are therefore clearly related, but the nature of their relationship is difficult to determine. Previous scholars have put forward two basic theories to resolve it. Edmond Malone argued in 'A Dissertation on the Three Parts of *King Henry VI*' (vi. 407 ff.) that *True Tragedy* was an earlier version of the play written by other playwrights which Shakespeare later revised as *3 Henry VI*. In the twentieth century, others argued that O is a report of F, reconstructed—for whatever reasons—from memory by actors who at one time originally performed it (and who were presumably associated at some point with Pembroke's Men, named on O's title-page). According to this second theory, while O reached print before F, it actually comes after in terms of transmission. It may be closer to the play original audiences knew on Elizabethan stages, whereas F, as we have seen, is based upon Shakespeare's working papers. All modern editors accept O's status as a report. But recently strong efforts have been made to limit or demolish the general theory of memorial reconstruction, to defend the legitimacy and theatrical viability of O, in addition to other reported texts, and to resuscitate the case for revision in F.

Thus at present there is less certainty about the historical relationship between O and F, and the integrity of O, than there has been since earlier in the century just past. Each text must be freshly assessed for evidence of both reporting and revision. Having done this, and having also compared variant O and F readings against divergent source passages in Hall and Holinshed, I have concluded that there is compelling evidence to support both theories. In what follows, I shall argue that *True Tragedy* is a memorially reported early version of the play that Shakespeare substantially revised as *3 Henry VI*. Seeing O as the product of both authorial and

---

[1] O does not seem to show any variant patterns in spelling or punctuation-spacing indicative of multiple compositors. There seem to be recurrent shortages of italic upper-case Gs, Is, and Ws, and of lower case ws, but these do not establish any clear divisions of labour.

non-authorial agencies is the only way of accounting satisfactorily for the diversity of its verbal and theatrical differences from F.[1]

'True Tragedy': a memorially reported text. O contains evidence beyond reasonable doubt of memorial agency. Its presence was demonstrated by Peter Alexander's *Shakespeare's Henry VI and Richard III* (Cambridge, 1929), a groundbreaking study which drew on the precepts of the New Bibliography to establish memorial reconstruction as an analytical methodology and editorial theory.[2] The nub of Alexander's identification of *True Tragedy* as a memorial report, as the Oxford editors observe, 'lies in his explanation of a single variant passage, 4.1.4[8]–5[8] | 1892–1902, in which Gloucester and Clarence reproach their brother, King Edward, with preferring his wife's relatives before themselves'.[3] The passage from *True Tragedy* (original spelling) appears thus:

> *Cla.* For this one speech the Lord *Hastings* wel deserues,
> To haue the daughter and heire of the Lord *Hungerford.*
> *Edw.* And what then? It was our will it should be so?
> *Cla.* I, and for such a thing too the Lord *Scales*
> Did well deserue at your hands, to haue the
> Daughter of the Lord *Bonfield*, and left your
> Brothers to go seeke elsewhere. . . .

$(D3^v–D4^r)$

The version in F *3 Henry VI* reads:

> *Clar.* For this one speech, Lord *Hastings* well deserues
> To haue the Heire of the Lord *Hungerford.*
> *King.* I, what of that? it was my will, and graunt,
> And for this once, my Will shall stand for Law.
> *Rich.* And yet me thinks, your Grace hath not done well,
> To giue the Heire and Daughter of Lord *Scales*
> Vnto the Brother of your louing Bride;
> Shee better would haue fitted me, or *Clarence:*

---

[1] I am aware that a potential danger in arguing for a combination of both these theories is that contentious or ambivalent evidence can be made to go either way, arbitrarily. But this seems to me a more acceptable risk than perpetuating an unhelpful dualism that falsifies O's textual totality, as well as its multiple originating causes, and that until now has failed to resolve the relationship between these plays conclusively. For a related discussion about the multiple provenance of printer's copy, see Werstine, 'Narratives About Printed Shakespeare Texts', p. 86.

[2] Laurie E. Maguire reassesses Alexander's study in *Shakespearean Suspect Texts* (Cambridge, 1996), p. 26.   [3] *Textual Companion*, p. 197.

> But in your Bride you burie Brotherhood.
> *Clar.* Or else you would not haue bestow'd the Heire
> Of the Lord *Bonuill* on your new Wiues Sonne,
> And leave your Brothers to goe speede elsewhere.
>
>   (TLN 2073–84)

Alexander argues that *True Tragedy*'s presentation of these historical relationships is nonsensical:

> The point of the matter was that it was the daughter of Lord Scales, not Lord Scales himself, who was involved, and that the male party to the bargain was nearly related to the Queen, and that Lord Bonvill's daughter was given to another of her relatives. (p. 64)

F's version of events is documented by Shakespear's two chronicle sources, Hall and Holinshed:

> [In 1465 at her coronation Queen Elizabeth's] brother lorde Anthony, was maried to ye sole heyre of Thomas lord Scales, & by her he was lord Scales. Syr Thomas Grey, sonne to syr Iohn Grey, the quenes fyrst husband, was created Marques Dorset, and maried to Cicilie, heyre to the lord Bonuile. (Hall Hhvi^r; Holinshed's wording (Rrrii^v) is virtually identical)

In Hall alone, a later first-person speech by Clarence also reads:

> This you knowe well enough, that the heire of the Lorde Scales he hath maried to his wifes brother, the heire also of the lorde Bonuile and Haryngton, he hath geuen to his wifes sonne, and theire of the lorde Hungerford, he hath graunted to the lorde Hastynges: thre mariages more meter for his twoo brethren and kynne, then for suche newe foundlynges. (Ii.iv^v)[1]

In contrast to these accounts, *True Tragedy* has Lord Scales marrying 'the daughter of a nobleman described as Lord Bonfield'.[2] While recognizing that this is strictly unhistorical, Steven Urkowitz has asked whether it is theatrically significant, or attributable to memorial agency. He argues that only readers or spectators with specialized knowledge would identify *True Tragedy*'s version of events as mistaken. *True Tragedy*'s variant is dramatically defensible because it still supports Clarence's complaint against Edward and motivates his ensuing defection to the

---

[1] In both chronicles the marriage of Bonville's daughter is mentioned again on fols. Ii.vi^r and Rrriv^v respectively.

[2] Alexander, p. 64.

Lancastrians. This change therefore 'gets across the *intent* of the chronicle history'.[1]

But none of these objections answers Alexander's overlooked point that 'Lord Bonfield' is a *fictional* name with no existence in the chronicles, whereas Lord Bonville is mentioned numerous times. As an invented character, however, 'Lord Bonfield' does have a stage life elsewhere, in the historical romance *George a Greene, the Pinner of Wakefield*, traditionally attributed to Robert Greene and dated to the late 1580s or early 1590s.[2] In this play Bonfield appears prominently as member of a party of rebels against Edward III, as well as in other guises. A quarto of *George a Greene* published in 1599 represents an abridged but probably not reported version of the original text.[3] The title-page states it was performed by Sussex's Men.[4] The company dissolved soon after this when its patron died in December 1593,[5] though not before a 'ne[w]' performance on 23 January 1594 of 'titus & ondronicus', whose 1594 title-page states it also belonged previously to Strange's Men and Pembroke's Men.[6] *Titus Andronicus* confirms performance and personnel liaisons among all three companies.[7]

---

[1] ' "If I Mistake in Those Foundations Which I build Upon": Peter Alexander's Textual Analysis of *Henry VI Parts 2 and 3*', *English Literary Renaissance*, 18 (1988), 230–56, pp. 240–1. While Urkowitz is right that Shakespeare often freely rewrote Hall and Holinshed to suit his dramatic purposes, I believe he underestimates the fascination shared by many educated Elizabethans for tracing such genealogical connections accurately. See also Urkowitz's related work, 'Two Versions of *Romeo and Juliet* 2.6 and *The Merry Wives of Windsor* 5.5.215–45: An Invitation to the Pleasures of Textual/Sexual Di(Perversity)', in R. B. Parker and Sheldon P. Zitner, eds., *Elizabethan Theatre: Essays in Honor of Samuel Schoenbaum* (Newark, NJ, 1996), pp. 222–38; 'Five Women Eleven Ways: Changing Images of Shakespearean Characters in the Earliest Texts', in Werner Habicht *et al.*, eds., *Images of Shakespeare* (Newark, NJ, 1988), pp. 292–304.

[2] Tudor Facsimile Texts, ed. J. S. Farmer (Edinburgh and London, 1913). Also *The Life and complete Works . . . of Robert Greene*, ed. Alexander B. Grosart (New York, 1964), vol. 14. In Greene's prose source he is called 'Lord Bouteil' (xiv. 183).

[3] Maguire, pp. 253–4.

[4] *Henslowe's Diary* records that *George a Greene* was performed at the Rose Theatre five times between 29 December 1593 and 22 January 1594 (p. 20). 'harey the 6' was being performed during the same run (16, 31 Jan. 1594 (pp. 19–20)).

[5] Gurr, *Companies*, p. 176.

[6] Performed again on 28 January and 6 February 1594. A 'titus' was performed 6, 15, 25 January 1594 (*Henslowe's Diary*, pp. 19–21).

[7] *True Tragedy*'s title-page states 'it was sundrie times acted' by Pembroke's, who were formed between 1591 and 1593 out of Strange's Men by Richard Burbage after he had quarrelled with their leader Edward Alleyn. Pembroke's personnel most likely included Shakespeare, at least during the time when *True Tragedy* and its

'Lord Bonfield' appears in both *George a Greene* and *True Tragedy*, but not in the chronicle accounts on which this scene and the rest of the latter play, as well as *3 Henry VI*, are based.[1] Its presence in two historically unrelated texts performed by companies who shared scripts and personnel indicates that the name is a non-authorial interpolation by players.[2] This evidence supports Alexander's claim that *True Tragedy* was memorially reconstructed, probably after the collapse of both Pembroke's and Sussex's in 1593 by players who had originally staged both plays but did not come to inherit the original prompt books.[3] Nothing underhanded is implied by their making of the report.

Another instance of non-authorial interpolation in *True Tragedy* involves a name related to the most notorious case of censorship in the canon:

companion *The First Part of the Contention* were being performed (Gurr, *Companies*, pp. 261–73). When Pembroke's dissolved suddenly in 1593, the result of financial collapse, costumes were sold in an attempt to raise cash, and within two years several of the plays they had performed came into print, including *True Tragedy* (the Chamberlain's Men responded similarly when faced with a similar crisis in 1597, selling off playbooks of *Romeo, Richard II, 1 Henry IV,* and *LLL* (Gurr, *Companies*, pp. 281–8)). Some of Pembroke's personnel and playbooks apparently passed to Sussex's, and thereafter to the Chamberlain's Men, formed in the following year. Other members of their company may either have continued travelling separately and/or have linked up temporarily with a downsized Strange's. The fact that *True Tragedy* does not identify Sussex's as well as Pembroke's on its title-page, as in the case of *Titus,* suggests that one of these last regroupings of Pembroke's and/or Sussex's made the report.

[1] Certain verbal and visual details of *True Tragedy* are in fact closer to Hall and Holinshed than their equivalents in *3 Henry VI*, and constitute compelling evidence of authorial agency. These are discussed below and in Appendix A.

[2] Such external insertions are among the few criteria Maguire's revisionist study of suspect texts admits as evidence of memorial reconstruction. See pp. 186, 228, 250–2, 274–6, 279–81, 308–10.

[3] This does not, however, support all of Alexander's claims about *True Tragedy* as a memorial report. His notion that written 'fragments' or 'supplementary parts' were used in those sections which are very close to F, for example, is, as both Chambers (*WS*, i. 283) and Greg (*Folio*, p. 177) observe, inherently implausible. Alexander also speculated that the main reporters of O were Warwick and Clifford, whose speeches closely match those in F. But if that were the case, we would expect their cue lines in passages by other speakers immediately before their own speeches also to be very close in O and F, yet they are not. The report must have been made by most if not all of the actors who at one time performed the play, but who remembered their different speeches and scenes with varying degrees of accuracy (e.g. O's Henry and Richard had trouble remembering some of their passages). For a discussion of Elizabethan stage rehearsal practices, see Tiffany Stern, *Rehearsal from Shakespeare to Sheridan* (Oxford, 2000), pp. 22–123.

Edward, rhou [*sic*] shalt to *Edmund Brooke* Lord *Cobham*,   (A7^r)

You *Edward* shall vnto my Lord *Cobham*   (1.2.40)

The title alone is invariably the way the chronicles refer to this person. Recent editors follow Cairncross in assuming that F's version reflects 'an instance of late censorship'. But since this passage is not comical or satirical, a motive for censorship is lacking. Nor would such a motive have existed at this date, since Shakespeare did not intentionally set out to ridicule the Cobham family in *1 Henry IV*, which dates from 1596.[1] Even if this were a case of later censorship, why was the name not simply removed or changed completely, as in the cases of Oldcastle/Falstaff and Brooke/Broome in *The Merry Wives of Windsor*? Moreover, O is incorrect: the historical figure was Sir Edward Brooke ('Edmund' is therefore not 'extra historical information' (*Textual Companion*)). Hattaway suggested it represented an inaccurate interpolation by a reporter,[2] perhaps intended as a contemporary allusion to Sir William Brooke, seventh Lord Cobham in Shakespeare's time, and Lord Chamberlain between August 1596 and March 1597. Since F corrects O but does not remove the name, the change almost certainly occurred before the Oldcastle/Brooke controversy, in which case Shakespeare may have revised O prior to 1596.[3] But the main point here is that O's version is much more likely to be a player's error than Shakespeare's.

One other important category of evidence indicative of actors interpolating their performance experiences is inadvertent anticipation of events in the verbal narrative, or an actor's projection of action which, in character, he cannot possibly foresee.[4] Various instances of this discrepancy occur in *True Tragedy*, but are com-

---

[1] Gary Taylor, 'William Shakespeare, Richard James and the House of Cobham', *RES*, NS 38 (1987), 334–54, p. 352.

[2] See his note to 1.1.40, p. 86.

[3] See discussion of dating below, pp. 123–32.

[4] This type of anomaly bears on Janette Dillon's observation that if a text is memorially reconstructed, 'then we must not fail to acknowledge the extent to which it may deviate from actual performance via the operations of memory. . . . [T]he text is necessarily distanced from the physicality of stage practice through the fact that it is "remembered" in primarily verbal terms' ('Is There a Performance in this Text?', *SQ* 45 (1994), 74–86, p. 81).

pletely absent in *3 Henry VI*. Here I shall mention just two examples.[1] One occurs near the end of 2.5:

> Alarmes and enter the *Queene.*
> *Queen.* Awaie my Lord to *Barwicke* presentlie,
> The daie is lost, our friends are murdered,
> No hope is left for vs, therefore awaie.
> Enter prince *Edward.*
> *Prince.* Oh father flie, our men haue left the field,
> Take horse sweet father, let vs saue our selues.
> Enter *Exeter.*
> *Exet.* Awaie my Lord for vengance comes along with him:
> Nay stand not to expostulate make hast,
> Or else come after, Ile awaie before. (C3ᵛ)

> *Alarums. Excursions. Enter the Queen, the*
> *Prince, and Exeter.*
> *Prin.* Fly Father, flye: for all your Friends are fled.
> And *Warwicke* rages like a chafed Bull:
> Away, for death doth hold vs in pursuite.
> *Qu.* Mount you my Lord, towards *Barwicke* post amaine:
> *Edward* and *Richard* like a brace of Grey-hounds,
> Hauing the fearfull flying Hare in sight,
> With fiery eyes, sparkling for very wrath,
> And bloody steele graspt in their yrefull hands
> Are at our backes, and therefore hence amaine.
> *Exet.* Away: for vengeance comes along with them.
> Nay, stay not to expostulate, make speed,
> Or else come after, Ile away before.
> (2.5.125–36; TLN 1263–77)

O puts Exeter in the position of saying 'Away . . . for vengeance comes along with him' without providing an antecedent for 'him'. In F, Exeter's 'vengeance comes along with them' is explained by Margaret's reference to Edward and Richard, and Prince Edward's to Warwick. In O his line can only be explained with reference to the passage in F. O's entry was apparently changed so that Prince Edward preceded Exeter on stage. The player reporting Exeter's lines remembered Prince Edward's original speech about Warwick and tried to adjust ('them' to 'him') to the new arrangement, and

---

[1] For more discussion see R. Martin, 'Reconsidering the Texts of *The True Tragedy of Richard Duke of York* and *3 Henry VI*', *RES* 53 (2002).

to what he remembered Prince Edward saying. But the same player, or another, omitted Prince Edward's reference to Warwick, making nonsense of Exeter's entry line. The assumption must be that this entire moment was at least partly altered in the course of reporting. The fact that F's direction lists the characters in a different order from which they speak (but fortuitously, their speaking order in O) does not reveal anything because F routinely lists characters according to social rank. If one were to suppose that F revises O, then one must explain Exeter's line, which either as 'them' or 'him' is meaningless in this context.

Another telling example of anticipation occurs in 5.1:

> E*dw.* The Gates are open, see they enter in,
> Lets follow them and bid them battaile in the streetes.
> *Glo.* No, so some other might set vpon our backes,
> Weele staie till all be entered, and then follow them.
> $$(E1^v)$$

> *Rich.* The Gates are open, let vs enter too.
> *Edw.* So other foes may set vpon our backs.
> Stand we in good array : for they no doubt
> Will issue out againe, and bid vs battaile;
> $$(5.1.60-3; TLN 2740-3)$$

In O, how does Richard know that any other ('all') parties are coming, who they are, and that they will follow Oxford's example immediately beforehand of entering the 'city gates'? Again this is a case of the reporting actor projecting action which only happens later—the arrival of Montague and Somerset—into the present moment. F, by contrast, keeps Edward's reference to 'other foes' strategically hypothetical.

Beyond external echoes and anticipation, one other textual sign of non-authorial agency in *True Tragedy* is worth observing. Scholars have long noted that O lacks most of F's classical allusions.[1] While this could be owing partly to Shakespeare's later efforts to revise F, O nevertheless remains anomalous in not displaying any of the grammar-school echoes of classical works which are a con-

---

[1] An apparent exception to this tendency is O's 'Et tu Brute, wilt thou stab *Caesar* too?' (E2ʳ). But according to the Oxford editor of *Julius Caesar*, 'Et tu Brute' had probably already become a popular tag by the time of *True Tragedy*, readily understood by English speakers just as it is today.

spicuous feature of Shakespeare's early plays.[1] In 1.3, for example, O omits a line in Latin from the *Heroides* by Ovid, Shakespeare's favourite classical author:[2]

> *Clif.* No cause? Thy Father slew my father, therefore Die.
> *Plantagenet* I come *Plantagenet*. . .   (A8ᵛ)

> *Clifford.* No cause? thy Father slew my Father: therefore dye.
> *Rutland. Dij faciant laudis summa sit ista tuae.*
> *Clifford.* Plantagenet, I come *Plantagenet*. . .

(1.3.47–9; TLN 450–3)

The fact that this variant occurs in a passage which is otherwise identical in both texts suggests omission by reporters unfamiliar with the language, rather than a process of revision.[3]

'True Tragedy' and '3 Henry VI': original and revised versions

All twentieth-century commentators agree that revision accounts for at least some of the variants between O and F, regardless of differing views about overall priority and transmission, and that in a few places F seems to draw on the printed text(s) of O. Moreover the total diversity of variants is such that O cannot be fully explained by either memorial reporting or first-draft-and-revision theory alone. Several kinds of causes and agencies must be posited to determine the whole relationship between O and F, in which case

---

[1] Chambers, *WS*, i. 224. Park Honan, *Shakespeare: A Life* (Oxford, 1998), pp. 117, 127. Alfred Hart, *Stolne and Surreptitious Copies* (Melbourne, 1942), p. 151 reckons that F contains twice as many classical allusions as O (29 v. 16), with even greater proportion of poetic similes and references to natural history (15 v. 45, 24 v. 40).

[2] Madeleine Doran, *Henry VI, Parts II and III: Their Relation to the 'Contention' and the 'True Tragedy'* (Madison, 1928), p. 76; Gurr, *Companies*, p. 73.

[3] The case for *True Tragedy* as a memorially constructed text has also traditionally been supported by various kinds of internal literary comparisons. But most of these are disqualified if it is assumed *True Tragedy* represents an early version of the play Shakespeare later revised. In the case of purely literary echoes, external recollections virtually cease to have any heuristic value because Shakespeare could be the borrower in either case (if it is assumed *True Tragedy* predates *3 Henry VI*). Scholars earlier in the twentieth century presented long lists of alleged interpolations in efforts to show that *True Tragedy*, among other so-called 'bad' texts, was memorially reported and/or non-Shakespearian. Today most of these do not bear scrutiny, either because the echoes are too brief, undistinctive, or vague, or because we are more aware of phrases and expressions that were commonplace, proverbial, or derived from third-party sources. There remain only a few certain recollections of earlier non-Shakespearian plays, such as *Gorboduc*, *The Spanish Tragedy* and *The Massacre at Paris*. These are noted in the main Commentary.

any investigation must begin by addressing two questions: what is the origin of O's differences from F (in both authorial and chronological terms), and what authority, if any, do they carry?

Prior to the twentieth century, O was usually believed to be either not by Shakespeare, or the product of theatrical piracy—one of the 'stolen and surreptitious copies' Heminges and Condell refer to in their First Folio preface. When later studies by Greg, Alexander, Doran and others began to put forward the now dominant theory of memorial reconstruction, they sought to establish a more functional motive to explain why the reports were made, in order to account for O's considerably shorter length. O was accordingly said to represent a deliberate abridgement, or 'acting version', of F, probably made for touring performances in the provinces when the plague closed the London theatres for most of 1592–4.[1] In 1975 Robert E. Burkhart appeared to strengthen this view by comparing O and F in terms of acting personnel. He argued that O's shorter length was designed to reduce the minimum required number of players (a result which also led him, however, to reject the view that *True Tragedy* was memorially reported).[2] Since then several casting studies have supported Burkhart's conclusions,[3] but with discrepancies amongst them: inconsistencies between roles included or excluded from the calculations, variations in the number and distribution of minor roles, and different estimates concerning the extent and assignment of doubling. Previous studies have also neglected the contemporary practice, documented by surviving playhouse documents, of having older boys double mute roles such as soldiers and flag-carriers.

Taking these factors into consideration, I have reassessed the casting for O and F using a method which isolates role and doubling assignments precisely in terms of time on and off stage, and

---

[1] Doran, p. 81.

[2] *Shakespeare's Bad Quartos*. Burkhart speculated that the purpose of O's rearrangement of scenes in Act 4 was to reduce by two the number of characters needed to play guards or soldiers. But since other actors were readily available to double these minor roles, this rationale is implausible. Other commentators who have viewed O as an adaptation and/or abridgement are Greg, *Folio*, p. 176; Hart, p. 122; Hattaway, p. 60; McMillin, p. 148; Kathleen O. Irace, *Reforming the 'Bad' Quartos* (Newark, 1994), p. 69.

[3] McMillin, 'Casting for Pembroke's Men'; T. J. King, *Casting Shakespeare's plays: London actors and their roles 1590–1642* (Cambridge, 1992); David Bradley, *From text to performance in the Elizabethan Theatre: Preparing the play for the stage* (Cambridge, 1992).

thus to exact exits and entrances within scenes, as well as general scene clearances. The results, given in Appendix C, show that, while *True Tragedy* and *3 Henry VI* vary in roles and numbers within particular scenes or sequences—most notably Acts 4 and 5—they require the same number of players overall: 13 men and 4 boys. The only exceptions are F 4.7, 5.1 and O 2.1–2 where two extra players are needed for minor non-speaking roles. Hired walk-ons would probably have been assigned to these roles and scenes alone.

In the light of these figures, it follows that O was not written for the purpose of employing fewer actors, and the prevailing rationale of abridgement disappears. An alternative could be that it was reconstructed simply to reduce the playing time. But in that case we would expect the differences between F and O to take the form of uncomplicated cuts, not the often complex rearrangement of scenes and lines that constitutes a very roundabout way of saving time. Moreover, given that O sometimes expands F in purposeful ways, with longer passages and more detailed, chronicle-derived stage directions at certain points (see below), O's brevity cannot be accounted for exclusively by memorial lapses. A further previously suggested possibility is that O was subject to heavy censorship. Yet this can only be argued speculatively by analogy with known examples of censored texts, since direct textual proof is lacking. The intervention of censors seems unlikely given that O and F retain the first scene in which Henry disinherits his son and disrupts the succession. If we go by the censored deposition scene in F *Richard II*, this presumably should have been cut if government disapproval was really a factor in the shortening of O.[1]

This leads us to reconsider the priority of O and F, and back to the alternative view that O represents, in part, an earlier version of the play which Shakespeare later revised as F. This theory was first presented by Edmond Malone in 1790.[2] Rejecting Dr Johnson's opinion that *True Tragedy*, like its companion *The First Part of the Contention*, was derived from memory or shorthand and too corrupt to represent a first draft, Malone argued that both these texts were 'elder dramas' which Shakespeare 'new-modelled and amplified' as *2* and *3 Henry VI*. Unfortunately Malone also believed that *True Tragedy* was based only on Holinshed but not Hall. Had he

[1] Janet Clare, '*Art made tongue-tied by authority*': *Elizabethan and Jacobean Dramatic Censorship* (Manchester and New York, 1990), pp. 24–43.

[2] 'A Dissertation on the Three Parts of *King Henry VI*', Malone, vi. 407.

compared O and F with both chronicle sources, he might have discovered more substantial support for his ideas. He also neglected to
take into account O's connections with Pembroke's Men, despite
O's title-page ascription, since at the time this company was not
believed to be associated with any of Shakespeare's uncontested
work. Yet this association, like the discrete and variant connections
with Hall and Holinshed, proves to be crucial.

Several modern scholars have revived Malone's idea that *True
Tragedy*, like other suspect texts, represents an early version of *3
Henry VI*. But until now they have largely done so analogously: by
extrapolating parallel conclusions from studies of other early
Shakespeare texts, especially *The First Part of the Contention*; by sit-
uating *True Tragedy* within wider post-structuralist critiques of the
'bad quarto' master narrative;[1] and by defending the theatrical
viability of its alternative stagings and characterizations.[2] All these
have usefully shown the limitations of memorial reporting (without being able to discredit its value entirely in the case of this particular text) and led to heightened appreciation for O's dramatic
merits. Nonetheless, they lack an appeal to independent documentary evidence showing that the differences between O and F represent theatrical choices being made over time among variant
historical accounts by Hall and Holinshed. In other words, comparisons which rely exclusively on O and F will always be based
largely on literary judgement, attempting to discriminate the aesthetic value of variant readings.[3] Widening the investigation to
include the two chronicles can potentially establish a more reliable

---

[1] See Gary Taylor, *Textual Companion*, pp. 23–8; Werstine, 'Narratives About
Printed Shakespeare Texts'; Maguire, *Shakespearean Suspect Texts*.

[2] C. A. Greer, 'The Quarto–Folio Relationship in 2 and 3 *Henry VI* Once Again',
Notes and Queries, NS 3 (1956), 420–1; Grace Ioppolo, *Revising Shakespeare*
(Cambridge, Mass., 1991); Leah S. Marcus, *Unediting the Renaissance* (London and
New York, 1996), pp. 17–33; Urkowitz, 'Five Women Eleven Ways'; Irace, *Reforming
the 'Bad' Quartos*.

[3] As Paul Werstine observes when discussing *Hamlet*, 'the only imaginable
grounds for privileging Q2 and F with unassailable integrity would be evidence that
each is independently linked to Shakespeare'. In the case of *Hamlet*, however—but
unlike *True Tragedy*, *3 Henry VI*, and the chronicles—there is 'no document to
link the variants to the playwright' ('The Textual Mystery of *Hamlet*', *SQ* 39 (1988),
1–26; p. 24). Juliet Alison Grieg arrives at similar conclusions about the subjective
nature of studies advocating either memorial reconstruction or revision in her
unpublished MA thesis, '*The First Part of the Contention* (1594) and *The True Tragedy*
. . . (1595): Limitations in the Theory of Memorial Reconstruction' (The Shakespeare Institute, University of Birmingham, 1994).

basis for comparative analysis, since some of the differences in staging and language between O and F derive from unique episodes or wording in Hall or Holinshed. O and F's individual preferences for a particular chronicle account can therefore be determined with some certainty, and with them a clearer rationale for the dramatic choices made by each version of the play.

In the analysis that follows I have selected three examples of passages that illustrate O and F choosing between individual chronicle accounts.[1] While establishing the temporal priority of these differences often remains inferential, the nature of the differences between O and F in terms of factual details, diction, and interpretive commentary by Hall and Holinshed reasonably suggests a direction of change, as well as the presence of an informed agency at work in revising the play reported by O.

Preferences for Hall or Holinshed differentiating O and F. Let us begin with a straightforward instance of each text's use of separate chronicle details. Between Wakefield and Towton in 2.1 Warwick gives an account of the competing strengths of Yorkist and Lancastrian forces, but his numbers differ in O and F:

> Their power *I* gesse them fifty thousand strong.
> Now if the helpe of *Norffolke* and my selfe,
> Can but amount to 48. thousand . . .
>
> > (B5^v)
>
> Their power (I thinke) is thirty thousand strong:
> Now, if the helpe of Norfolke, and my selfe . . .
> Will but amount to fiue and twenty thousand . . .
> > (2.1.177–8, 181; TLN 835–6, 839)

According to both Hall and Holinshed, 'The people on the Marches of Wales, which above measure favoured the lineage of the Lord Mortimer, more gladly offered [Edward] their aid and assistance than he it either instantly required, or heartily desired, so that he had a puissant army, to the number of 23,000 ready to go against the queen' (Hall Ggiii^v, Holinshed Qqqiv^v). Holinshed alone also reports Lancastrian numbers at 20,000 for the second Battle of St Albans (Qqqiv^v). Shakespeare in F seems to have kept to the

---

[1] Additional documentation and categories of evidence appears in 'Reconsidering the Texts of *The True Tragedy of Richard Duke of York* and *3 Henry VI*'.

numbers in this range rather than in that for Towton, which were 60,000 for the Lancastrians and 48,660 for the Yorkists (Hall Ggvi^v, Holinshed Qqqvi^v; the latter also records John Whetham-sted's variant opinion that 'Henry's power exceeded in number King Edward's by twenty thousand men'). O's numbers, however, are closer to those for Towton: 50,000 for Lancaster and 48,000 for York. Thus it seems that O, with its figures linked to Towton, followed Hall, whereas F followed Holinshed, perhaps after Shakespeare reread the latter, since Hall reports about Towton in a different section from Holinshed. His account occurs at the end of the chapter on Henry VI's reign, where it follows information about Mortimer's Cross and the second Battle of St Albans. Holinshed does not report the details of Towton until his new chapter on Edward IV. Its account is separated from the previous two battles by a long section at the end of his chapter on Henry VI discussing non-political persons and events.

An important instance of alternative stage directions based upon divergent chronicle accounts occurs between 5.4 and 5.5 during the Battle of Tewkesbury:

F   *Alarum, Retreat, Excursions. Exeunt.*   (5.4.82.1; TLN 2970)

Hall and Holinshed both report that the Yorkists made a tactical retreat in order to draw out and entrap the Lancastrians: 'the Duke of Gloucester for a very politic purpose, with all his men recoiled back' (Hall Nnii^r, Holinshed Sssvi^r). Somerset pursued from the woods, thinking he was being supported from behind by Lord Wenlock's forces. But Wenlock may have been colluding with the Yorkists and failed to follow, leaving Somerset exposed to attack. O's direction conveys these events more explicitly:

Alarmes to the battell, *Yorke* flies, then the chambers be discharged.
(E4^r)

Both chronicles continue: 'The Duke of Gloucester, taking the advantage that he adventured for, turned again face to face to the Duke of Somerset's battle [Holinshed adds "and with great violence put him and his people up towards the hill from whence they were descended"] . . . The Duke of Gloucester entered the trench and after him the King, where after no long conflict, the Queen's part went almost all to wreck' (Hall Nnii^r, Holinshed Sssvi^v). O's continuing direction again represents this more directly:

Then enter the king, *Cla & Glo*. & the rest, & make a great shout, and crie, for *Yorke*, for *Yorke*, and then the *Queene* is taken, & the prince, & *Oxf. & Sum.* (E4ʳ)

But at this point the chronicle details diverge. O follows Hall's account by having Margaret and Prince Edward captured together in the field with the other Lancastrians ('The Queen was found in her chariot almost dead for sorrow, the prince was apprehended and kept close by Sir Richard Croftes' (Nniiʳ)). F, however, follows Holinshed's report that Prince Edward was captured separately 'as he fled towards the town' (Sssviᵛ), when he is brought in later at 5.5.10. So too Margaret's unexpectedly pious lines at 7–8,

> So part we sadly in this troublous World,
> To meet with Ioy in sweet Ierusalem
>
> (TLN 2980–1)

may derive from Holinshed's unique report that after Margaret fled the battlefield she 'was found in a poor house of religion, not far from thence, into the which she was withdrawn for safeguard of herself' (Sssviᵛ, see also note to 5.5.7–8).

These passages suggest that Shakespeare's revision of *True Tragedy* was associated with an interpretive shift away from Hall towards Holinshed—a change that in wider terms accords with his evolving career as a playwright, and with the English history plays in particular.

Another substantial variation in stage scenarios, and my final example, occurs in 5.1, when Clarence switches loyalties back to the Yorkists. To begin with the background to this event, both chronicles state that in early 1470

there landed at Calais a damsel, belonging to the Duchess of Clarence . . . [who] persuaded the Duke of Clarence that it was neither natural nor honourable to him, either to condescend or take part against the house of York (of which he was lineally descended) and to set up again the house of Lancaster. . . . These reasons . . . so sank in the Duke's stomach, that he promised at his return not to be so an extreme enemy to his brother, as he was taken for. . . . With this answer the damsel departed into England, the Earl of Warwick thereof being clearly ignorant. (Hall Kkviʳ)

Later in April, Hall alone reports that when Edward's army met Warwick at Coventry and Clarence approached,

Richard Duke of Gloucester, brother to them both, as though he had been made arbiter between them, first rode to the duke, and with him commoned very secretly: from him he came to King Edward, and with like secretness so used him, that in conclusion no unnatural war, but a fraternal amity was concluded and proclaimed, and . . . both the brethren lovingly embraced, and familiarly commoned together. (Mmii^v)

This corresponds to O's unique version of events:

> *Cla.* Clarence, Clarence, for *Lancaster.*
> *Edw.* Et tu Brute, wilt thou stab *Caesar* too?
>   A parlie sirra to *George* of Clarence.
>   Sound a Parlie, and *Richard* and *Clarence* whispers
>   togither, and then Clarence takes his red Rose out of
>   his hat, and throwes it at *Warwike.*
> *War.* Com Clarence come, thou wilt if *Warwike* call.
> *Cla.* Father of *Warwike*, know you what this meanes?
>   I throw mine infamie at thee . . .   (EI^v–E2^r)

Hall reminds the reader, however, that this result was expected because of the earlier persuasions of the Duchess of Clarence's envoy (Mmii^v-iii^r). He thus emphasizes that the outcome of Richard's intervention was in fact partly determined by the prior agency of the 'damosell'. O invests Gloucester alone with this agency. Warwick's line thus *reacts to* their parley and Clarence's defiant gesture. His words may be a challenge or an appeal, while Clarence's speech becomes a rationalization for his completed thought and action.

Holinshed by contrast makes Clarence more inwardly and independently motivated. He alone mentions that the aforementioned 'damsel' 'persuaded [Clarence] so much to leave off the pursuit of his conceived displeasure towards his brother King Edward', and he includes the marginal note 'The promise of the Duke of Clarence' (Rrrvi^r). He also states in a lengthy passage that, while Edward was gathering support in Flanders,

the Duke of Clarence began to weigh with himself the great inconvenience into the which as well his brother King Edward, as himself and his younger brother the Duke of Gloucester were fallen, through the dissension betwixt them (which had been compassed and brought to pass by the politic working of the Earl of Warwick). (Sssiii^r)

Clarence is counselled by 'right wise and circumspect persons', but 'most specially the Duchess of Burgundy their sister also'. He therefore decides eventually to be reconciled with his brothers, but marches to Coventry for the time being as Warwick's ally, a deception Holinshed pointedly observes in a marginal note: 'The dissimulation of the Duke of Clarence'. This sequence corresponds to F's version:

> *War.* And loe, where *George* of Clarence sweepes along,
> Of force enough to bid his Brother Battaile:
> With whom, in vpright zeale to right, preuailes
> More then the nature of a Brothers Loue.
> Come *Clarence*, come: thou wilt, if *Warwicke* call.
>   *Clar.* Father of Warwick, know you what this meanes?
>
>   (5.1.76–81; TLN 2759–64)

In F Warwick's over-confident statements about Clarence's loyalty to him over his brothers give the latter's sudden reversal greater dramatic force—all the more so because there is no break in the action and the audience is given no forewarning of Clarence's change of mind. F, moreover, transfers to Warwick's speech as dramatic irony Holinshed's report that when Clarence encountered Edward's army, he met the King, 'his brother of Gloucester, the Lord Rivers, the Lord Hastings, and a few other . . . betwixt both the hosts, with so sweet salutations, loving demeanour, and good countenances, as better might not be devised' (Sssiii^r–v). Holinshed's emphasis on Edward and Clarence's reconciliation also corresponds with F's singular 'brother' at line 99, referring to King Edward:

the king withal brought the duke unto his army, whom he saluting in most courteous wise, welcomed them into the land, and they humbly thanking him, did to him such reverence as appertained to the honour of such a worthy personage. . . . And either part showing themselves glad thus to meet as friends . . . they went lovingly together.

>   (Holinshed only, Sssiii^v)

whereas O's 'brothers' reflects Hall's focus on Richard's intervention in reuniting all three. It seems Shakespeare began by dramatizing events more along the lines of Hall. He then revised the stage moment in the light of Holinshed's alternative interpretations (see also note to 5.1.81.1).

Having established that O is a memorial report of an earlier version of the play which Shakespeare revised as F, we can return briefly to the question of F's possibly selective use of O or its derivatives as printer's copy. This idea was first proposed by R. B. McKerrow in 1937.[1] He argued that the opening direction and first eighteen lines of 4.2 were set from O or Q3. Unfortunately, these claims are now unconvincing because none of the variants McKerrow cites is indubitably an error. One is based on a mistaken emendation by Theobald, and other instances of 'contamination' can be attributed to the printing house. Although he offered only this single and largely analogous piece of evidence from *3 Henry VI*, McKerrow's suggestion was taken up by Cairncross in his influential Arden edition, which expanded McKerrow's argument to claim that much of F was set from O. But in this case the reason for consulting manuscript copy at all becomes unclear. The Oxford editors properly rejected most of Cairncross's hypothesis and were sceptical of McKerrow but still maintained 'intermittent contamination' of F by Q3, which Hattaway's New Cambridge edition also endorses. I have not found any of their residual examples persuasive enough to emend F in those places where its reliance on O or Q3 has been suspected. All such variants can be plausibly related to simpler or more familiar causes: acceptable metrical variation, differing chronicle details, and rewriting.[2] To cite one prominent instance:

O   *George.* Since when he hath broke his oath.
    For as we heare you that are king
    Though he doe weare the Crowne,
    Haue causde him by new act of Parlement
    To blot our brother out, and put his owne son in.

               (B7$^\mathrm{v}$)

F   *Cla.* Since when, his Oath is broke: for as I heare,
    You that are King, though he do weare the Crowne,
    Haue caus'd him by new Act of Parliament,
    To blot out me, and put his owne Sonne in.

         (2.2.89–92; TLN 964–7)

F's mistaken assignment of this speech to Clarence rather than as a continuation of Edward's lines immediately preceding (identical in O and F),

    Ed. I am his King, and he should bow his knee:
    I was adopted Heire by his consent.

           (TLN 962–3)

[1] 'A note on the "Bad Quartos" of *2* and *3 Henry VI* and the Folio Text', *RES*, 13, 64–72. [2] See notes to 4.2.2, 12, 15, and 5.6.89–91.

has been cited as evidence that the F compositors were following Q3, since it and F seem to agree in certain accidentals ('Crowne', 'Parliament', and the division of the next speech by Clifford into two lines). It is worth observing, however, that in O/Q3 these lines lack the logical symmetry and rhetorical balance of F, in which Edward compares the position of sons in relation to fathers. 'His own son' reciprocates (emphatically with the possessive 'own') the sense of 'blot out me' (as son and heir of *my* father). In O/Q3, by contrast, the point of 'his own' is lost with 'our brother'. It is also odd that George uses 'we' and 'our', which sound—anomalously—like royal plurals. He is not speaking on behalf of himself and Richard. Moreover in O/Q3, Clifford immediately after draws attention to the speaker's identity, who appears here (earlier than in F) for the first time in the play: 'And reason *George*'. If the F compositor was following O/Q3 at this point, which he believed to be clearer than Shakespeare's manuscript, why did he substitute 'And reason too' if he thought the speech really *was* by George/ Clarence? The evidence suggests F is a revised version of O, whose minor verbal discrepancies are probably owing to faulty reporting. It also indicates that cancellation of the prefix may not have been clear in its manuscript copy, since the compositor routinely altered O's *George* to F's *Clarence*.

The Dates of 'True Tragedy' and '3 Henry VI': composition, staging, report, and revision

If we assume that *True Tragedy* represents an earlier and memorially reported version of *3 Henry VI*, there are three main dates to investigate: the original composition and staging, the report, and Shakespeare's revision, eventually printed in the 1623 First Folio. The first of these is bounded by the publication of the second edition of Holinshed's *Chronicles* in 1587, and by four pieces of external evidence from 1592:

(1) an entry in Henslowe's diary recording a 'ne' performance of 'harey the vj' on 3 March;[1]

---

[1] *Henslowe's Diary*, p. 16. It earned exceptionally high returns of £3 16s 8d, which suggests that 'ne' means 'newly written' and/or 'performed', rather than newly licensed or revised. E. A. J. Honigmann, concerned to challenge the conventional idea of a 'late-start' chronology, is sceptical but not entirely dismissive of 'ne'

(2) the closing of the theatres because of the plague on 23 June;[1]

(3) an allusion in August by Thomas Nashe to a performance of *1 Henry VI*;

(4) Robert Greene's allusion to a line from *True Tragedy / 3 Henry VI* in September.

The last item establishes a *terminus ad quem* for the writing and probably also the performance of *True Tragedy*. It relates to Greene's *Groatsworth of Wit . . . written before his death and published at his dying request*, a pamphlet entered in the Stationers' Register on 20 September.[2] Greene was a poet and playwright who was reported to be dying on 2 September.[3] In *Groatsworth of Wit*, he complains to his university educated colleagues about actors who have gained renown from their own writing:

> . . . those puppets . . . that spake from our mouths, those antics garnished in our colours. Is it not strange that I, to whom they all have been beholding, it is not like that you, to whom they all have been beholding, shall (were ye in that case as I am now) be both at once of them forsaken? Yes, trust them not, for there is an upstart crow, beautified with our feathers, that with his 'Tiger's heart wrapped in a player's hide' supposes he is as well able to bombast out a blank verse as the best of you, and being an absolute *Iohannes fac totum* [Jack of all trades], is in his own conceit the only Shake-scene in a country.[4]

---

meaning newly written or performed (*Shakespeare's Impact on his Contemporaries* (1982), pp. 76–7). But Hanspeter Born observes that the only exceptions to 'ne' not meaning 'new' occur in later periods of Henslowe's *Diary* ('The Date of *2, 3 Henry VI*', *SQ* 25 (1974), 323–34, p. 325). Hattaway tentatively suggests 'ne' may mean 'newly licensed', in response to the 1589 Privy Council Order requiring all plays to be vetted by the Archbishop of Canterbury, the Mayor of London, and the Master of the Revels or their representatives (Chambers, *ES*, iv. 306–7). But besides the gap in time, we have no certain idea to what extent this order was ever enforced. See Richard Dutton, *Mastering the Revels: The Regulation and Censorship of English Renaissance Drama* (Basingstoke, 1991), pp. 77–8.

[1] Chambers, *ES*, iv. 310–11, 347–8.　　[2] Arber, ii. 620.

[3] *The Repentance of Robert Greene* (1592), D2[r-v]; Harold Jenkins, 'On the Authenticity of Greene's *Groatsworth of Wit* and *The Repentance of Robert Greene*', *RES*, 11 (1935), 28–41.

[4] F1[r]. Scholars have long disputed whether Greene is accusing Shakespeare of arrogance in presuming, as a mere performer, to write plays, or specifically of plagiarizing Greene's work. The various contexts and positions are summarized by D. Allen Carroll, 'Greene's "Vpstart Crow" Passage: A Survey of Commentary', *Research Opportunities in Renaissance Drama*, 28 (1985), 111–27. Cairncross's discussion (pp. xli–xliii) is also valuable, and he concludes along with all recent commentators that a charge of plagiarism, which could imply Greene's authorship of *True Tragedy*, is not actually intended.

Greene's quotation parodies a line present in both *True Tragedy* and
3 Henry VI: 'O tiger's heart, wrapped in a woman's hide!' (B2^v /
1.4.137). His attack implies that Shakespeare's play had been performed by this date.[1]

How much earlier *True Tragedy* was written is less easy to determine. The Henslowe entry (1) may conceivably refer to any of the
three parts of *Henry VI*. But contextual evidence strongly suggests it
refers only to the play we know as Part One, not Parts Two or Three.[2]
Nashe's allusion (3) demonstrates that Part One must have been
written by the summer of 1592[3] (and in fact Nashe may be one of its
co-authors; see below). In that case, if *True Tragedy* follows Part One
in terms of composition, it would have to have been written and performed between March and June, after which the theatres closed virtually until 1594. But this seems too brief a period to permit the
writing and performance of *True Tragedy* as well as *The First Part of
the Contention*, which appears to have closely preceded it. It has been
suggested that Shakespeare worked on Parts Two and Three in this
period and possibly into the summer in expectation of an initially
anticipated reopening at Michaelmas. But this involves accepting
the unlikely speculation that Greene read the line in a script of the
play underlying *True Tragedy*.[4]

[1] Hattaway observes that Strange's Men (who may originally have performed one
or more parts of *Henry VI*) were performing Greene's *Looking Glass for London and
England* and *Friar Bacon and Friar Bungay* in the same run as 'harey the vj', which
might be related to his attack and indicates he knew *True Tragedy* / *3 Henry VI* from
performances, since it is 'unlikely that he would have quoted the ['tiger's heart']
line, given his satirical intent, if he knew it only from manuscript, or . . . from
rehearsal' (p. 56). Henry Chettle's response to Greene defending Shakespeare's
integrity (*Kind-Heart's Dream*, entered in the Stationers' Register 8 December 1592
(Arber, ii. 623)) unfortunately does not enlighten us about when he saw Shakespeare personally, or his plays being performed.

[2] *Henslowe's Diary* (pp. 16–19) records fourteen more performances until 19 June.
Roslyn L. Knutson demonstrates that Henslowe normally recorded only the first
part of multi-part plays by the main title ('Henslowe's Naming of Parts', *N&Q* 228
(1983), 157–60). Also Born, p. 331, and *Textual Companion*, p. 113.

[3] Nashe writes in *Pierce Penniless his Supplication to the Devil* (entered in the Stationers' Register 8 August 1592 (Arber, ii. 619)): 'How would it have joyed brave
Talbot, the terror of the French, to think that after he had lien two hundred years in
his tomb he should triumph again on the stage, and have his bones new-embalmed
with the tears of ten thousand spectators at least, at several times, who in the tragedian that represents his person imagine they behold him fresh bleeding!' (*Pierce Penniless . . . and Selected Writings*, ed. Wells, pp. 64–5).

[4] Born, p. 332. He also suggests Greene could have heard it in rehearsal. But
plays normally received only one full-company rehearsal just prior to performance,
so this is not a possibility.

The alternative, first proposed by Chambers and Wilson and restated by the Oxford editors, is that *True Tragedy* and *The First Part of the Contention* were written before *1 Henry VI*.[1] Nonetheless, this dating presents difficulties because it is bound up with the knotty questions of which companies originally performed each of the three plays, the authorship of Part One, and the internal dramatic, stylistic, and narrative relationships of the whole trilogy. Part One can be placed securely with Strange's Men led by Edward Alleyn, who were resident at Henslowe's Rose Theatre. *True Tragedy*'s title-page states it was performed by Pembroke's Men. While its own title-page lacks the same attribution, *The First Part of the Contention* was undoubtedly performed by them as well. Pembroke's was a notable but short-lived company whose origins and activities are regrettably obscure, partly because the movement of players during this period was exceptionally fluid as companies merged and divided. Chambers and Wilson believed that Pembroke's was formed for the purposes of travelling as a branch of the large combined company of Strange's and the Admiral's Men in response to the closure of the theatres (2).[2] But Andrew Gurr has demonstrated more conclusively that it came into being earlier as a new troupe under Richard Burbage at The Theatre following a serious quarrel with Strange's leader Edward Alleyn in May 1591.[3] The latter scenario better accounts for the fact that certain Pembroke plays (e.g. *Titus Andronicus*) passed into the hands of Sussex's Men before reaching the Chamberlain's Men—Shakespeare's company—in 1594. It also explains the absence of other Shakespearian titles from Henslowe's records during 1592–3 (with the exception of *1 Henry VI*, a fact probably explained by its multiple authorship, see below), as well as Pembroke's apparently independent status after

---

[1] Wilson, *The First Part of King Henry VI* (Cambridge, 1952), pp. xi–xiii.

[2] Chambers, *ES*, ii. 128–31, *WS*, i. 41–50. Wilson, *The Second Part of King Henry VI* (Cambridge, 1952), pp. xii–xiii.

[3] Andrew Gurr, 'The Chimera of Amalgamation', *Theatre Research International*, 18 (1993), 85–93. Gurr, *Companies*, pp. 71–5, 267–72, also shows that Pembroke had close associations with Burbage's old master the Earl of Leicester. Chambers, *ES*, ii. 307. Karl P. Wentersdorf varies this account by arguing that at least some of Pembroke's personnel came from the Queen's Men, including Shakespeare ('The origin and personnel of the Pembroke's Company', *Theatre Research International*, 5 (1979–80), 45–68). Connections with Queen's are supported by the will of Simon Jewel dated August 1591. He evidently acted in both companies, and his will mentions provision for horses, a waggon, and apparel (Mary Edmond, 'Pembroke's Men', *RES*, NS 25 (1974), 129–36, pp. 130–1). Also McMillin and MacLean, pp. 29–30.

the failure of their provincial tour forced them in August 1593 to pawn their apparel and playbooks.[1] Prior to June 1592, however, they had experienced rapid success, enjoying the lucrative honour of performing at court during Christmas 1592 and 1593, an invitation shared only with Strange's. The popularity of Shakespeare's plays in Pembroke's repertoire may partially explain their good fortune. We have already seen that the *True Tragedy*'s reported dramatization of chronicle and other details indicates that Shakespeare was very likely its author. Andrew Gurr notes that the ultimate transfer of the entire early body of Shakespeare's early plays to the Chamberlain's Men indicates that he retained ownership or control of them throughout this period, which implies some temporary association with Pembroke's as a playwright.[2]

This leads to the question of which group of actors constructed *True Tragedy* from memory, and when. It may have been Pembroke's Men themselves if Shakespeare decided not to accompany them on their provincial tour in 1592–3.[3] On the other hand after Pembroke's collapse in August 1593, ownership of their books and some of their personnel passed briefly to Sussex's (following the sequence identified on the title-page of *Titus Andronicus*: Strange's to Pembroke's to Sussex's).[4] Other members of their company who did not follow this path may either have continued travelling separately while the London theatres remained closed and/or have linked up temporarily with a downsized Strange's. The fact that *True Tragedy* does not identify Strange's or Sussex's on its title-page, as in the case of *Titus*, suggests that one of these terminal and financially strapped regroupings of Pembroke's and/or Sussex's made the report sometime after August 1593, which they subsequently published in early 1595, following the issue of *The First Part of the Contention* in 1594 (probably under similar circumstances, and in both cases after the formation of the Chamberlain's Men in the latter year, who retained ownership of the original playbooks).

---

[1] Cairncross, p. lxvii. Chambers, *WS*, ii. 314. See also p. 131 n.1 below.

[2] Gurr, *Companies*, pp. 72–3.

[3] Shakespeare is not mentioned in Simon Jewel's will; but then again neither are other players believed to have been members of Pembroke's (Edmond, p. 130).

[4] Including, as we saw earlier, *George a Greene*, performed by Sussex's at the Rose 1593–4, and which confirms *True Tragedy*'s status as a memorially reported text (see above, pp. 108–9).

Thus, a likely scenario for the dating and original performance is that the script underlying *True Tragedy* was first written by Shakespeare prior to the debut of *1 Henry VI* in March 1592, probably in the year before. It could have been performed by Pembroke's either before or after this date in London up until June 1592. If it was actually written prior to the formation of Pembroke's in May 1591, the most likely company association is Strange's.[1] Its performance by 1591 is suggested by several echoes in *The Troublesome Reign of John, King of England*, which was published in the same year. Its composition during that year is suggested by a passage in *True Tragedy* 2.1 echoing *The Faerie Queene*, published in 1590.[2]

The issue cannot be left there, however, because the idea that the three parts of *Henry VI* were composed out of sequence continues to generate controversy. Many critics feel that *1 Henry VI*'s less structured dramatic design, monochromatic characterization, and unevenness of style all point to Shakespeare at an earlier stage of his career. The First Folio's presentation of the trilogy in historical order has also focused critical attention on the plays' apparent

---

[1] A passage in *True Tragedy* 5.3 referring to Warwick's physical characteristics possibly connects that play with the actor Edward Alleyn and Strange's Men: '*Edw.* The bigboond traytor *Warwike* hath breathde his last' (E3ʳ). Warwick refers to himself just before as 'Hercules' whose 'manie wounds . . . | Hath robd my strong knit sinews of their strength' (E2ᵛ). The same lines without the classical allusion occur earlier at 2.3.3–5 in both O and F. (The later recurrence only in O suggests repetition by a reporter. In F the Messenger applies the Hercules comparison to York at 2.1.53.) The description 'big-boned' also occurs in *Titus* 4.3.47: 'No big-boned men framed of the Cyclops' size'. *Titus* was performed by Strange's and Pembroke's. If the line describing Warwick as 'big-boned' alludes to a contemporary actor, it may be to Alleyn, who was known for his large stature, and suggests that *True Tragedy*, like *Titus* a relatively large-cast play, was written originally for Alleyn and Strange's before the former quarrelled with Richard Burbage in May 1591. Burbage left Henslowe's Rose to create Pembroke's Men at The Theatre, perhaps taking Shakespeare with him. The line's absence in F also suggests Shakespeare cut it after the move.

[2] Although Shakespeare could have read it before this date when it circulated extensively in manuscript. Since F's imagery at this point appears partially in O, it was likely present in the original version but partly lost in the process of reporting. Honigmann (*Shakespeare: the 'lost years'*, pp. 73–6) argues that a reference to 'Our pleasant Willy' in Spenser's *Teares of the Muses* (written 1580–90, printed 1590) alludes to Shakespeare and thus pushes back the dating of his early plays by several years. But as Sidney Thomas observes, in an article that trenchantly challenges Honigmann's revisionist theory of an 'early start', Elizabethan pastoral poetry never alludes to contemporary persons directly by their real names ('On the Dating of Shakespeare's Early Plays', *SQ* 39 (1988), 187–94). Honigmann's earlier identification of 'Willy' as John Lyly, which he revised to bolster his 'early start' evidence, is much more likely.

evolution in technical range and verbal imagery. To cite several examples, Part Three contains a higher number of feminine endings than Parts One and Two, a sign of Shakespeare's increasing poetic confidence and flexibility. Its handling of stichomythia is arguably more skilful, and it displays a deepening interest in psychological motivation, which is a traditional hallmark of Shakespearian characterization.[1] To posit Shakespeare's writing of *1 Henry VI* after its historical sequels seems to require an unacceptable reversion to an inferior level of craftsmanship.

These perceptions and discrepancies are not easily dismissed, but they may be explained by the fact that *1 Henry VI* is the least likely of the three *Henry VI* plays to be wholly by Shakespeare. The single authorship of all three parts has been questioned in varying degrees since the eighteenth century, partly because of what was taken to be the plays' failure to meet (largely classically) defined standards of literary unity and dramatic decorum, and partly because of their shortcomings in terms of Shakespeare's later achievements. But modern scholarship and stage productions have gradually revised such comparisons in the light of Elizabethan values and practices as well as the realities of Shakespeare's professional career. Shakespeare no longer needs to be shielded from responsibility for occasional structural weaknesses and bad writing, or from the indignity of collaborating with his contemporaries. Having said this, it is mainly Part One that continues to be seen as not wholly by him, with recent assessments assigning co-authorship to Nashe, and possibly George Peele and others.[2] Multiple authorship helps explain Part One's variety of tones and styles and its poetic inconsistencies. It probably also accounts for the theatrical associations of 'harey the vj' with Strange's Men and Henslowe but not Pembroke's. This would parallel the situation of *Sir Thomas More*, another play of multiple authorship that perhaps includes Shakespeare, and which belonged to Strange's.[3]

---

[1] For *3 Henry VI* as Shakespeare's first genuinely realized experiment in psychologically motivated characterization, see Pearlman, *passim*. Also Born, pp. 328–30; Kernan, *passim*.

[2] *Textual Companion*, pp. 112–13, 217. Gary Taylor, 'Shakespeare and Others: The Authorship of *Henry the Sixth, Part One*', *Medieval and Renaissance Drama in England*, 7 (1995), 145–205.

[3] Scott McMillin, *The Elizabethan Theatre and The Book of Sir Thomas More* (Ithaca and London, 1987), pp. 53–73.

This brings us to the third of our main dates: Shakespeare's revision of *True Tragedy* as represented by the Folio text. Again there is both external and internal evidence to suggest a time-frame but not a precise date. Besides the revisions relating to Shakespeare's reworking of his chronicle sources discussed earlier, *2* and *3 Henry VI* each record the names of actors believed to be associated with particular companies during the 1590s: John Holland and George Bevis in Part Two, and (more certainly) Gabriel Spencer, John Sincklo (or Sincler), and Humphrey Jeffes in Part Three.[1] Bevis and Holland were possibly members of Pembroke's Men and may have been part of the group which reconstructed *True Tragedy*, since an apparent in-joke reference to 'Bevis of Southampton' occurs in *The First Part of the Contention*.[2] Spencer had the unfortunate distinction of being killed in a duel by Ben Jonson on 22 September 1598.[3] His death therefore establishes a last possible date for Shakespeare's manuscript underlying F. The year before, as members of a briefly revived Pembroke's company at the Swan, Spencer, Jeffes, and Jonson (as an author) were temporarily imprisoned for staging the politically inflammatory *Isle of Dogs*. Afterwards until his death, Spencer became a sharer in the Admiral's Men with Jeffes.[4] By the same date Jeffes had risen from being a hired man to a half-sharer, and by 1604 he had become a full sharer in the Admiral's/Prince's Men.[5] But since both men play minor roles in *3 Henry VI*, it suggests that Shakespeare wrote with them in mind at a rather earlier date. Holland and Sincklo are named in an actors' manuscript plot of *2 Seven Deadly Sins*, which was performed by Strange's Men at the Curtain around 1590, and certainly before 1592.[6] Sincklo acquired stage notoriety for his thinness. He is identified in the Induction to *The Taming of the Shrew*, and he seems to have played similarly typecast roles in *2 Henry IV*, *Henry V*, and perhaps *King John* and *Twelfth*

---

[1] Possibly two others, Nicholas Tooley and Alexander Cooke, in Part Two: A. Gurr, *The Shakespearean Stage 1574–1642*, 3rd edn (Cambridge, 1992), pp. 39–42.

[2] Q 1594, l. 879: Gurr, *Shakespearean Stage*, p. 40.

[3] *Memoirs of Edward Alleyn*, ed. J. P. Collier (1841), pp. 50–2.

[4] Gurr, *Companies*, pp. 98, 106–9.

[5] Gurr, *Companies*, pp. 98, 253. During 1592 he may also have spent some time performing abroad. See W. Schrickx, *Foreign Envoys and Travelling Players in the Age of Shakespeare and Jonson* (Wetteren, 1986), pp. 188–93.

[6] W. W. Greg, *Dramatic Documents*, i. 107–13. Gurr, *Companies*, p. 71. McMillin and MacLean, p. 93. In the plot, 'Sincler' plays 'A Keeper' and a 'warder' who attends Henry VI in the Tower during his first captivity in 1470 (*Dramatic Documents*, ii).

Night. But there is nothing explicit in his role as gamekeeper or in the dialogue of 3.1 to indicate Shakespeare wrote to exploit this particular trait. Gurr speculates that this could be a sign that he joined Pembroke's Men late, after its formation under Burbage in 1591. Thereafter he most likely followed the path suggested by *Titus* to Sussex's, and then to the new Chamberlain's company in 1594—which was also the destination of the Shakespeare corpus, accompanied by Burbage, John Holland, and perhaps the playwright himself.[1] Whatever their individual paths, all these persons certainly regrouped as Chamberlain's Men in 1594. This therefore becomes a secure point from which we can date Shakespeare's revision of O and his casting of Spencer, Sincklo, and probably Jeffes, in *3 Henry VI*.

A *terminus ad quem* is suggested by the uncensored references to Lord Cobham in both texts (A7^r / 1.2.40). Since F corrects O but does not remove the name (see above, pp. 109–10), the change most likely occurred before the Oldcastle–Falstaff controversy caused by *1 Henry IV*, which dates from 1596. In 1597 Shakespeare was compelled by Sir William Brooke, seventh Lord Cobham and Lord Chamberlain between August 1596 and March 1597, to change Oldcastle to Falstaff in *2 Henry IV*.[2] This makes it likely that Shakespeare corrected O's inaccurate name prior to this. The revision of *True Tragedy* as the Folio-text version of *3 Henry VI* therefore took place between 1594 and 1596.

Several pieces of circumstantial evidence seem to confirm this period. Some significant shared vocabulary in F, the story of a bitter feud between rival houses, and the personality changes of Montague, all suggest that *Romeo and Juliet* may not have been far from Shakespeare's mind when he revised *True Tragedy*. His considerable expansion of Margaret's oration in 5.4 draws on Arthur Brooke's *The Tragical History of Romeus and Juliet* (see Appendix D). Shakespeare had read Brooke earlier when writing *The Two Gentlemen of*

---

[1] Gurr, *Companies*, p. 72 n. 36, pp. 73, 280. Gurr also observes that members of Pembroke's Men must have retained their playing licence and a residual identity after the company broke up in 1593 and some of its members, such as Gabriel Spencer and Humphrey Jeffes, joined the Chamberlain's Men, since they reappeared as Pembroke's players in 1597 (pp. 272–3). Honigmann notes that the likelihood of Shakespeare's association with Pembroke's and Sussex's is strengthened if it can be assumed he revised *True Tragedy* (*Shakespeare: the 'lost years'*, p. 63).

[2] See above, p. 110.

Verona (1590–1). But F's extensive reworking of this scene (evidenced, for example, by Shakespeare's reduction of Prince Edward's role and dialogue, which are larger in O) suggests that Shakespeare may have rewritten *True Tragedy* at about the same time he reread Brooke to compose *Romeo* in 1595. One further indication of this period for F's revision relates to what may be an inserted addition to F's manuscript in 2.5 (a scene already bearing clear marks of revision in the Son/Father staging). The passage occurs during Henry's opening speech following a couplet at ll. 19–20, which seems to divide it into two sections:

> Would I were dead, if God's good will were so,
> For what is in this world but grief and woe?

The ensuing passage contains Henry's pastoral meditation on the shepherd's orderly tranquil life, a passage whose dignified tone and formal control is reminiscent of Shakespeare's lyrical plays of the mid-1590s. *Richard II* (1595) comes particularly to mind when Henry goes on to compare the shepherd's responsibilities with the burdens and perturbations of kingship.

EDITORIAL PROCEDURES

THIS edition is based on the First Folio text, which represents Shakespeare's expansion and revision of an earlier version of the play reported by O. Since the two early texts are historically distinct and often differ substantially in dialogue and stage action, I have followed F's readings of variant passages in all but a few cases of error, omission, or indispensable clarification, and not added or substituted variant stage directions from O. Significant instances of the latter have been recorded in the collation, however, as have all substantive departures from and additions to F.

Collation entries first record the reading adopted by the present text, and then, to the right of the square bracket, its first source, followed by the rejected reading in F, and sometimes by alternative emendations proposed by earlier editors; e.g. 4.6.55 be confiscate] MALONE; confiscate F1; confiscated F2. Capitalized names refer to sources and authorities entered in the list of Abbreviations and References. Rejected readings from F appear in original spelling, as do readings from O. The collation also identifies instances where this edition restores a substantive reading from F which most previous editors, following different principles, have emended on the authority of O and/or independently; e.g. 1.1.11 dangerous] F; dangerouslie O, THEOBALD (*subs.*). The abbreviation *subs.* indicates the substantive form of a reading as it appears in the original source, aside from minor differences in spelling, capitalization, etc. Another abbreviation, *conj.*, indicates a reading conjectured though not adopted by a previous editor (usually because sufficient textual warrant is lacking), but that still merits being recorded as a possible alternative, even if this edition also does not adopt it; e.g. 240 Falconbridge] F, O; Montague OXFORD *conj.* The collation does not aim to provide a complete history of textual variants between F and O (which are in any case too global), or of editorial interventions; only substantive, notable, or debatable changes are recorded. Rearrangements of F's printed verse are recorded in Appendix E.

The collation also lists all changes to stage directions and speech prefixes, including additions and regularizations of characters' names and titles; e.g. 211.1 *Queen . . . Edward*] *the Queene* F; *the Queene* and *the Prince* O, ROWE. Such changes appear without square brackets in the present edition. Following F's normal but not invariable practice, a character's full title (e.g. *Richard Planta-genet Duke of York*) appears in the stage direction at his or her first entry, or when the title changes (e.g. *Lady Grey* to *Queen Elizabeth*); thereafter she or he appears in this edition by name only (e.g. *York*), unless F continues to supply a fuller title, in which case it is included. When a direction is plausible but debatable or ambiguous, in terms of either the nature of the action or its placement in the dialogue, it appears in broken brackets and its provenance is recorded in the collation; e.g.:

> ⌐*aside*⌐ I know not what to say, my title's weak.—
> 135 ⌐*aside*⌐⌐ CAPELL (*subs*.); *not in* F

All *asides* in the present edition are editorial. When an added direction appears at the beginning or within a verse line, it appears in round brackets and is also recorded; e.g. 1.2.36 (*To Montague*)] OXFORD *following* RANN; *not in* F. The term *following* indicates that a later editor (here Oxford) derives the substantial form of an emendation from an earlier one, but does not reproduce the original emendation verbatim. The collation also occasionally records directions proposed by other editions that are of interest for indicating alternative readings of stage action, but which this edition has not felt persuaded to adopt; e.g. 1.1.18 But] F; (*To the head*) But OXFORD.

Following the principles established by Stanley Wells in 'Modernizing Shakespeare's Spelling',[1] the present edition's changes to F in spelling and punctuation have been made without annotation unless they significantly affect the meaning, in which case they are recorded in the collation. The same applies to speech prefixes, which are normalized silently unless the change is substantive. In addition, all original passages quoted from early modern editions, such as Hall and Holinshed in the Commentary and Appendix A, have been modernized in spelling and punctuation, unless there are bibliographical or textual issues under consideration that make retention of original spelling desirable.

---

[1] In *Modernizing Shakespeare's Spelling, with Three Studies in the Text of Henry V,* Stanley Wells and Gary Taylor (Oxford, 1979).

In places where a complete verse-line is clearly divided between two speakers, the second part of the line is indented. This convention does not appear in F. Otherwise part-lines appear separately. In verse-lines where the metre requires a final *èd* to be sounded, this edition indicates it as such; otherwise *ed* words are pronounced in the normal way. Contractions and elisions of syllables are indicated when called for by the normal rhythmic pattern of a line; e.g. 1.1.117, 'Good brother as thou lov'st and honour'st arms'.

Line references to other Shakespeare plays follow *The Complete Works*, ed. Stanley Wells, Gary Taylor *et al.* (Oxford, 1986). Because my understanding of the relationship and priority of O and F is different from that of the Oxford editors, and my sense is that the two versions should be treated fairly independently, I have—with some unwillingness—retained the Folio title of the play, rather than substituting that of the earlier version, *Richard Duke of York*.

Abbreviations and References

Throughout the volume, place of publication is London unless otherwise stated.

EDITIONS OF SHAKESPEARE

O	*The True Tragedy of Richard Duke of York* (1595)
F, F1	*Comedies, Histories, and Tragedies*, The First Folio (1623)
F2	The Second Folio (1632)
F3	The Third Folio (1663)
F4	The Fourth Folio (1685)
Brooke	Tucker Brooke, *The Third Part of King Henry the Sixth* (New Haven and London, 1923)
Cairncross	Andrew S. Cairncross, *The Third Part of King Henry VI* (1964)
Cambridge	W. G. Clark and W. A. Wright, *Works*, 9 vols. (Cambridge and London, 1863–6), vol. v
Capell	Edward Capell, *Comedies, Histories, and Tragedies*, 10 vols. (1767–8), vol. vi
Chambers	E. K. Chambers, *The Works of William Shakespeare*, 10 vols. (1904–8)

Collier	John Payne Collier, *Works*, 8 vols. (1842–3), vol. v
Collier 1853	John Payne Collier, *Plays*, 9 vols. (1853), vol. iv
Collier MS	Manuscript emendations in J. P. Collier's copy of F2 (the 'Perkins' Folio)
Dyce	Alexander Dyce, *Works*, 6 vols. (1857), vol. iv
Dyce 1864–7	Alexander Dyce, *Works*, 9 vols. (1864–7), vol. v
Hanmer	Thomas Hanmer, *Works*, 6 vols. (1743–4), vol. iv
Harrison	G. B. Harrison, *Henry the Sixth Parts One to Three* (Harmondsworth, 1959)
Hart	H. C. Hart, *The Third Part of King Henry the Sixth* (1910)
Hart 1925	H. C. Hart, *The Third Part of King Henry the Sixth*, 2nd edn (1925)
Hattaway	Michael Hattaway, *The Third Part of King Henry VI* (Cambridge, 1993)
Hudson	H. N. Hudson, *Works*, 11 vols. (Boston, 1851–6), vol. vi
Hudson 1880–1	H. N. Hudson, *Works*, 20 vols. (Boston, 1880–1)
Johnson	Samuel Johnson, *Plays*, 8 vols. (1765; repr. New York, 1968), vol. v
Keightley	Thomas Keightley, *Plays* (1864)
Knight	C. Knight, *Comedies, Histories, Tragedies, and Poems*, 12 vols. (1842–3), vol. vi
Malone	Edmond Malone, *Plays and Poems*, 10 vols. (1790), vol. vi
Munro	John Munro, *The London Shakespeare*, 6 vols. (1958), vol. iii
Oxford	William Montgomery, *Richard Duke of York* (3 *Henry VI*), in Stanley Wells and Gary Taylor (gen. eds.), *The Complete Works* (Oxford, 1986)
Pelican	Robert K. Turner Jr and George Walton Williams, *Henry VI Parts Two and Three* (Baltimore, 1967)

Pope	Alexander Pope, *Works*, 6 vols. (1723–5), vol. iv
Rann	Joseph Rann, *Dramatic Works*, 6 vols. (Oxford, 1786–94)
Riverside	G. B. Evans, textual ed., *The Riverside Shakespeare* (Boston, 1974)
Rowe	Nicholas Rowe, *Works*, 6 vols. (1709), vol. iv
Rowe 1709	Nicholas Rowe, *Works*, 2nd edn, 6 vols. (1709), vol. iv
Rowe 1714	Nicholas Rowe, *Works*, 8 vols. (1714), vol. iv
Singer 1842–3	Samuel W. Singer, *Dramatic Works*, 10 vols. (1842–3)
Singer 1856	Samuel W. Singer, *Dramatic Works*, 10 vols. (1856)
Sisson	C. J. Sisson, *Complete Works* (1954)
Steevens	George Steevens, *Plays*, 10 vols. (1773), vol. iii
Steevens–Reed	George Steevens and Isaac Reed, *Plays*, 2nd edn, 15 vols. (1793)
Theobald	Lewis Theobald, *Works*, 7 vols. (1733), vol. iv
Warburton	William Warburton, *Works*, 8 vols. (1747), vol. v
Wilson	John Dover Wilson, *The Third Part of King Henry VI* (Cambridge, 1952)
Wright, *Works*	William Aldis Wright, *Works*, 9 vols. (1891–3), vol. v

OTHER ABBREVIATIONS

Abbott	E. A. Abbott, *A Shakespearian Grammar*, 3rd edn (1870). Cited by paragraph.
Aelian	Claudius Aelian, *On the Characteristics of Animals*, trans. A. F. Scholfield, 3 vols. (Cambridge, Mass., 1958–9)
Arber	Edward Arber, *A Transcript of the Registers of the Company of Stationers of London 1554–1640*, 5 vols. (1875–94)
BCP	*Book of Common Prayer*
Bullough	Geoffrey Bullough, *Narrative and Dramatic Sources of Shakespeare*, 8 vols. (1957–75)

Cartwright	Robert Cartwright, *New Readings in Shakspere, or Proposed Emendations of the Text* (1866)
Cercignani	Fausto Cercignani, *Shakespeare's Works and Elizabethan Pronunciation* (Oxford, 1981)
Chambers, *ES*	E. K. Chambers, *The Elizabethan Stage*, 4 vols. (Oxford, 1923)
Chambers, *WS*	E. K. Chambers, *William Shakespeare: A Study of Facts and Problems*, 2 vols. (Oxford, 1930)
Dent	Robert W. Dent, *Shakespeare's Proverbial Language* (Berkeley, 1981)
Dessen, *Recovering*	Alan C. Dessen, *Recovering Shakespeare's Theatrical Vocabulary* (Cambridge, 1995)
Dyce, *Notes*	Alexander Dyce, *A Few Notes on Shakespeare; with occasional remarks on the emendations of the MS-Corrector in Mr Collier's copy of the Folio of 1632* (1853)
Dyce, *Remarks*	Alexander Dyce, *Remarks on Mr J. P. Collier's and Mr C. Knight's Editions of Shakespeare* (1844)
ESC	English Shakespeare Company
Görlach	Manfred Görlach, *Introduction to Early Modern English* (Cambridge, 1991)
Greg, *Folio*	W. W. Greg, *The Shakespeare First Folio: Its Bibliographical and Textual History* (Oxford, 1955)
Gurr, *Companies*	Andrew Gurr, *The Shakespearian Playing Companies* (Oxford, 1996)
French	George Russell French, *Shakspeareana Genealogica* (London and Cambridge, 1869)
Henslowe's Diary	Philip Henslowe, *Henslowe's Diary*, ed. R. A. Foakes and R. T. Rickert (Cambridge, 1961)
Howard and Rackin	Jean E. Howard and Phyllis Rackin, *Engendering a Nation* (London and New York, 1997)
Hulme	Hilda Hulme, *Explorations in Shakespeare's Language*, 2nd edn (New York, 1977)
Jones, *Origins*	Emrys Jones, *The Origins of Shakespeare* (Oxford, 1977)
Kernan	Alvin B. Kernan, 'A Comparison of the Imagery in *3 Henry VI* and *The True Tragedie*

	of *Richard Duke of York*', *Studies in Philology*, 51 (1954), 431–42
Martin, *Pageantry*	R. Martin, 'Elizabethan Pageantry in *Henry VI*', *University of Toronto Quarterly*, 60 (1990/1), 244–64
Mason	John Monck Mason, *Comments on the Last Edition of Shakespeare's Plays* (1785)
McMillin and MacLean	Scott McMillin and Sally-Beth MacLean, *The Queen's Men and their Plays* (Cambridge, 1998)
Mirror	*The Mirror for Magistrates*, ed. Lily B. Campbell (Cambridge, 1938)
Nares, *Glossary*	Robert Nares, *A Glossary*, ed. James O. Halliwell[-Phillipps] and Thomas Wright, 2 vols. (1859)
Nichols, *Progresses*	John Nichols, *The Progresses and Public Processions of Queen Elizabeth*, 3 vols. (1823)
OED	*Oxford English Dictionary*, 2nd edn (1989)
Pearlman	E. Pearlman, 'The Invention of Richard of Gloucester', *SQ* 43 (1992), 410–29
Players 3	*Players of Shakespeare 3*, ed. Russell Jackson and Robert Smallwood (Cambridge, 1993)
Rackin, 'Foreign Country'	Phyllis Rackin, 'Foreign Country: The Place of Women and Sexuality in Shakespeare's Historical World', in *Enclosure Acts: Sexuality, Property, and Culture in Early Modern England*, ed. Richard Burt and John Michael Archer (Ithaca, 1994), pp. 68–95
RES	*The Review of English Studies*
RSC	Royal Shakespeare Company
Shaheen	Naseeb Shaheen, *Biblical References in Shakespeare's History Plays* (Newark, NJ, London, and Toronto, 1989)
Shirley	Frances Ann Shirley, *Shakespeare's Use of Off-Stage Sounds* (Lincoln, Nebr., 1963)
Sisson, *NR*	C. J. Sisson, *New Readings in Shakespeare*, 2 vols. (Cambridge, 1956)
SQ	*Shakespeare Quarterly*
Textual Companion	Stanley Wells and Gary Taylor with John Jowett and William Montgomery, *William*

	Shakespeare: A Textual Companion (Oxford, 1987)
Thomson	W. H. Thomson, *Shakespeare's Characters: A Historical Dictionary* (Altrincham, 1951)
Tilley	Morris Palmer Tilley, *A Dictionary of Proverbs in England in the Sixteenth and Seventeenth Centuries* (Ann Arbor, 1950)
Tillyard	E. M. W. Tillyard, *Shakespeare's History Plays* (1944)
Vaughan	Henry Halford Vaughan, *New Readings and Renderings of Shakespeare's Tragedies*, 3 vols. (1878–86), vol. ii
Walker	W. S. Walker, *A Critical Examination of the Text of Shakespeare*, 3 vols. (1860), vol. iii
Whitney	Geoffrey Whitney, *A Choice of Emblems and Other Devices* (Leiden, 1586; repr. Amsterdam and New York, 1969)
Williams	Gordon Williams, *A Dictionary of Sexual Language and Imagery in Shakespearean and Stuart Literature*, 3 vols. (1994)
Wright	George T. Wright, *Shakespeare's Metrical Art* (Berkeley, Los Angeles, and London, 1988)
Wright, 'Historie'	Stephen K. Wright, '"The Historie of King Edward the Fourth": A Chronicle Play on the Coventry Pageant Wagons', *Medieval and Renaissance Drama in England*, 3 (1986), 69–82

Henry VI, Part Three

THE PERSONS OF THE PLAY

King HENRY VI

Queen MARGARET of Anjou, daughter of René, King of Naples and Sicily

PRINCE EDWARD, Prince of Wales, son of Henry and Margaret

Lord CLIFFORD

Duke of EXETER

Duke of SOMERSET

Earl of NORTHUMBERLAND

Earl of WESTMORLAND

Earl of OXFORD

Henry, Earl of Richmond, future King Henry VII

SOMERVILLE

Richard Plantagenet, Duke of YORK

EDWARD, York's eldest son, Earl of March, later Duke of York and King Edward IV

GEORGE, York's son, later Duke of CLARENCE

RICHARD, York's son, later Duke of GLOUCESTER

Edmund Plantagenet, Earl of RUTLAND, York's youngest son

TUTOR to Rutland

Duke of NORFOLK

Richard Neville, Earl of WARWICK

MONTAGUE

Earl of PEMBROKE

Lord STAFFORD

Lord HASTINGS

SIR JOHN Mortimer

Sir Hugh Mortimer

Sir William STANLEY

Sir John MONTGOMERY

Elizabeth, LADY GREY, widow of Sir John Grey, later wife of Edward IV and Queen ELIZABETH

Anthony Woodville, Lord RIVERS, brother of Lady Grey

Prince Edward, infant son of Edward and Elizabeth

Nurse to Prince Edward

A NOBLEMAN

King LEWIS XI of France

Lady BONA of Savoy, Lewis's sister-in-law

Lord Bourbon, Admiral of France

MAYOR of York

Two Aldermen of York

Mayor of Coventry

LIEUTENANT of the Tower of London

A SON that has killed his father in battle

A FATHER that has killed his son in battle

Two GAMEKEEPERS

Three WATCHMEN, soldiers who guard King Edward

A HUNTSMAN who guards King Edward

MESSENGERS

POSTS

Soldiers, Drummers, Trumpeters, Colours, Attendants

King **HENRY VI** (1421–71) succeeded his father Henry V (1387–1422) at the age of nine months and was crowned in 1429. He appears as a boy in *1 Henry VI* and a young man in Part Two. He became mentally ill temporarily in 1453, during which time York was Protector, but Shakespeare does not allude to his condition. He recovered before the first Battle of St Albans in 1455.

Queen **MARGARET** (1430–82) married Henry at Nancy in 1445 by proxy, with the Duke of Suffolk representing the King. In *2 Henry VI* Suffolk becomes her lover, but is later exiled and killed for his involvement in the murder of Humphrey Duke of Gloucester. Margaret's intervention in English politics in the face of Henry's temporary mental illness caused considerable resentment at court.

PRINCE EDWARD (1453–71), Henry and Margaret's only son, created Prince of Wales

after the second Battle of St Albans in 1461. He and his mother took refuge in France in 1462 after Edward IV was proclaimed king. He was betrothed to Warwick's younger daughter Anne, but was killed during or shortly after the Battle of Tewkesbury before the marriage could be consummated.

Lord **CLIFFORD** John, ninth Baron Clifford (1435–61), son of Old Clifford whose death at the first Battle of St Albans is reported at 1.1.7–9, and represented, at the hands of York, in *2 Henry VI* 5.3.

Duke of **EXETER** Henry Holland (?–1473), son of John, Earl of Huntingdon. He married Anne Plantagenet, daughter of the Duke of York, but supported the Lancastrians. Left for dead after the Battle of Barnet, he recovered, but was attainted by Edward IV and died in poverty.

Duke of **SOMERSET** represents two figures: (1) Henry Beaufort (1436–64), third Duke, son of the Somerset whose head Richard carries in in 1.1. He supported Edward IV briefly from 1462 (see 4.1) but rejoined Margaret's forces in 1464 at the Battle of Hexham (not dramatized by Shakespeare, prior to Barnet), after which he was executed by the victorious Yorkists; (2) Edmund (1438–71), Henry's brother, styled fourth Duke, and last male of the Beaufort line, commanded the Lancastrian archers at Barnet and their vanguard at Tewkesbury, where he was captured and ordered beheaded by Edward IV (see 5.5.3).

Earl of NORTHUMBERLAND Henry Percy, third Earl (1421–61), son of the earl reported killed at the first Battle of St Albans at 1.1.4–9, and grandson of Hotspur (*1 Henry IV*). He defeated and killed York at the Battle of Wakefield (see 1.4) and died leading the Lancastrian vanguard at Towton.

Earl of WESTMORLAND Ralph Neville, second Earl (?–1484). It was his brother John who fought for the Lancastrians, but Shakespeare follows Holinshed, who records the Earl's death at the Battle of Towton.

Earl of OXFORD John de Vere, thirteenth Earl (1443–1513). After his father and elder brother Aubrey were attainted and executed by the Yorkists in 1462 (see 3.3.102–5), he joined Warwick to restore Henry VI in 1470. He led the vanguard and defeated Hastings at Barnet, but fled to France after the Lancastrian loss. He eventually fought as Richmond's Captain-General at Bosworth (see next note).

Henry, Earl of Richmond (1457–1509), son of Edmund Tudor and Margaret Beaufort, the great-granddaughter of John of Gaunt, Duke of Lancaster (see 3.3.81 and *Richard II*). During Henry VI's brief restoration in 1470, he was presented to the King (see 4.6) by his uncle Jasper Tudor. He took refuge in France during Edward IV's reign, where he remained until 1485, when he landed at Milford Haven and defeated Richard III at Bosworth. By marrying Elizabeth of York, daughter of Edward IV, in 1486, he united the lines of Lancaster and York in the new Tudor dynasty.

SOMERVILLE Not given a first name in the Folio text, and does not appear in Hall or Holinshed. He may possibly represent Thomas Somerville of Warwickshire (d. 1516), or be an anachronistic allusion to John Somerville, a possible distant relation of Shakespeare, executed for plotting to assassinate Queen Elizabeth in 1583 (see Introduction, pp. 75–6).

Duke of YORK Richard Plantagenet, third Duke (1411–60), descended through his mother Anne Mortimer from Lionel, Duke of Clarence, third son of Edward III, and through his father Richard, Earl of Cambridge, from Edmund of Langley, fifth son of Edward III and first Duke of York. His father was executed for conspiring to murder Henry V (see *Henry V* 2.2) and his family attainted. But the title was restored to his son, Richard Plantagenet, by King Henry (see *1 Henry VI* 3.1).

EDWARD (1442–83), eldest son of York and his wife Cicely Neville. He became Earl of March and helped to defeat Henry VI's forces at Northampton in 1460 (see 1.1). Proclaimed king after defeating Margaret's forces at Mortimer's Cross (not represented by Shakespeare) and Towton in 1461, he was deposed by Warwick in 1469 and the year after sought aid from his sister Margaret, Duchess of Burgundy, and her husband. In 1471 he returned to England, took King Henry prisoner, and defeated the Lancastrians at the battles of Barnet and Tewkesbury to regain the throne. He dies in *Richard III* 2.2.

GEORGE York's third surviving son (1449–78), created Duke of Clarence on Edward IV's accession in 1461. He married Warwick's elder daughter Isabella in defiance of Edward's wishes, joined Warwick's invasion from France, and helped him capture Edward. He also aided Warwick in restoring Henry to the throne in 1470, and was made joint protector, but left Warwick at Coventry in 1471 to rejoin the Yorkists at the battles of Barnet and Tewkesbury. Act I of *Richard III* portrays his arrest and murder after Richard has raised King Edward's suspicions against him (see 5.6.90).

RICHARD York's fourth surviving son (1452–85), sent to France with his brother George after the Yorkist defeat at Wakefield, created Duke of Gloucester when he returned to England on Edward's accession in 1461. He fled with him to Flanders in 1470, and returned to command the vanguard at the battles of Barnet and Tewkesbury when he was still only nineteen. He was rumoured to have murdered Henry VI in the Tower. His nickname 'Crookback' derived from Sir Thomas

More's report that his left shoulder was higher than his right, but this, and his other deformities, are probably the inventions of More and other Tudor propagandists.

Earl of RUTLAND Edmund Plantagenet, historically York's second son (1443–60), murdered by Clifford at the Battle of Wakefield. But Hall terms him the 'youngest' son of York and says he was only twelve at the time of his death, which Shakespeare follows.

TUTOR to Rutland, and his chaplain, Robert Aspall of Norfolk.

Duke of NORFOLK John Mowbray, third Duke (1415–61), hereditary Earl Marshal of England. He was York's uncle by marriage but supported his claims to the throne ambivalently prior to the Battle of Northampton in 1460. He was defeated with Warwick at the second Battle of St Albans in 1461, but fought successfully for Edward IV at Towton.

Earl of WARWICK Richard Neville (1428–71), 'the Kingmaker', son of 'Old Salisbury' in *2 Henry VI*. He became Earl of Warwick by marrying the heiress Anne Beauchamp in 1449. After supporting York at the first Battle of St Albans and at Northampton, he helped negotiate his adoption as heir-presumptive. He likewise supported Edward IV's proclamation as king, and fought for him at Towton, but was betrayed while negotiating a proposed marriage with Lady Bona of Savoy. He was also offended at Edward's enrichment of Elizabeth Woodville's relations, and at his attempted sexual abuse of his niece or daughter. Warwick joined the Lancastrians, captured Edward IV, and restored Henry VI. He later fought with the liberated and re-empowered Edward at Barnet, where he was killed.

MONTAGUE represents two figures: (1) Richard Neville (1400–60), who became Earl of Salisbury by marrying the heiress Alice Montague. In *2 Henry VI* 'Old Salisbury' supports King Henry until just prior to the first Battle of St Albans, when he joins the Yorkists. He was taken prisoner after the Battle of Wakefield and beheaded at Pontefract ('Pomfret'); (2) John Neville (1428/35–1471) whose life was spared by the Lancastrians after they captured him at the second Battle of St Albans, and he defeated their forces, led by Somerset, at Hexham in 1464. He was created Marquis of Montague the following year. He later renounced Edward

with Warwick, but failed to challenge the former's return to England in 1471, although he eventually fought and died with his brother at Barnet. See Appendix B.

Earl of PEMBROKE William Herbert (?–1469), long-serving Yorkist, created Earl in 1468 after the attainder of Jasper Tudor, when he also became guardian of the young Earl of Richmond. He was captured and executed at Edgecote, near Banbury (not dramatized by Shakespeare) while suppressing a rebellion in support of Henry VI.

Lord STAFFORD Humphrey Stafford (1439–69), knighted by Edward IV at Towton and created Lord Stafford in 1464. After quarrelling with and deserting the Earl of Pembroke before Edgecote, he was arrested and executed.

Lord HASTINGS William Hastings (1430–83), loyal Yorkist and Sheriff of Leicestershire and Warwickshire. Ennobled by Edward IV in 1461, he helped to win Clarence back to his side and commanded the third division at Barnet.

SIR JOHN Mortimer, Sir Hugh Mortimer Holinshed calls them York's 'bastard uncles' (brothers of York's mother Anne Mortimer), and says they died at the Battle of Wakefield in 1460. Not certainly identified.

Sir William STANLEY (1435–95), brother of Thomas, first Earl of Derby (see *Richard III*), appointed Chamberlain of Chester by Edward in 1461, who also granted him Lord Clifford's estates after the latter's death at Towton. He and his brother later supported Richmond at Bosworth.

Sir John MONTGOMERY Historically Sir Thomas (?–1495) as recorded by Hall and Holinshed. Although he had been an Esquire of the Body to Henry VI, he joined Edward with a large force at Nottingham (which Shakespeare changes to York, 4.7), fought for him at Barnet, and later escorted Queen Margaret to France in 1475.

Elizabeth, LADY GREY, later Queen ELIZABETH (1431–92), daughter of Sir Richard Woodville, later Earl Rivers, and Jacquetta of Luxembourg, widow of John Duke of Bedford. She married Sir John Grey (whom Shakespeare mistakenly calls Richard), killed at the second Battle of St Albans on the Lancastrian side (*pace* 3.2.6–7). Deprived of her inheritance by the Yorkists, Lady Grey appealed personally to Edward IV when he was visiting her mother in Northamptonshire. They were secretly married in 1464 and Elizabeth crowned in 1465. The advancement of her relations was resented by many in Edward's court (see *Richard III* 1.3.75 ff.) and later in that of Richard III. She died at Bermondsey Abbey.

Lord RIVERS Anthony Woodville (1442–83), eldest brother of Lady Grey, created second Earl in 1469. He supported Edward IV at Barnet but was executed for treason at Pontefract ('Pomfret'), probably without trial, on the initiative of Richard Duke of Gloucester (*Richard III* 3.3).

Prince Edward (1470–83), eldest son of Edward IV and Queen Elizabeth, created Prince of Wales in 1471. He succeeded to the throne in 1483 for two months as Edward V before being murdered in the Tower with his brother (*Richard III* 4.3), allegedly on the orders of Richard of Gloucester.

King LEWIS XI (1423–83), son of Charles VII (the Dauphin in *1 Henry VI*) and Marie of Anjou, aunt of Queen Margaret. He suc-

ceeded to the throne in 1461. His second wife was Charlotte of Savoy.

Lady BONA (?–1485), third daughter of Louis, first Duke of Savoy; married the Duke of Milan in 1468.

Lord Bourbon Jean, Count of Roussillon, bastard son of Charles Duke of Bourbon.

MAYOR of York Thomas of Beverley, merchant of the Staple, in office for the second time in 1471.

Mayor of Coventry John Brett, deprived of his office before the Battle of Barnet by Edward IV for supporting Henry VI. The citizens had to pay a fine of 500 marks to recover their franchise, but were reconciled to Edward four years later at the festival of St George.

LIEUTENANT represents two historical figures: (1) in 4.6, John Tiptoft (1427–70), first Earl of Worcester, known as the 'butcher of England' for hanging and impaling twenty of Clarence's men in 1470, and executed after Edward IV's flight; (2) in 5.6, John Sutton (1401–87), sixth Baron Dudley, who served both Henry V and Edward IV.

These historical details derive largely from Thomson.

The Third Part of Henry the Sixth, with the Death of the Duke of York

1.1   *Alarum. Enter Richard Plantagenet Duke of York,*
           Edward Earl of March, Richard carrying a severed
           head, the Duke of Norfolk, Montague, Warwick, and
           Soldiers. A chair of state

WARWICK

  I wonder how the King escaped our hands?

YORK

  While we pursued the horsemen of the north

Title *The . . . York*] F (*The third Part of Henry the Sixt, with the death of the Duke of* YORKE (*title-page*); *The third Part of Henry the Sixt* (*running titles, sigs.* o4ʳ–o6ᵛ); *The third Part of King Henry the Sixt* (*running titles, sigs.* p1ʳ–q4ᵛ); *The Third part of King Henry the Sixt* (*contents page*)); The true Tragedie of Richard Duke *of Yorke, and the good King* Henry the Sixt o
  1.1] F (*Actus Primus. Scoena Prima.*)   0.1–4 *Enter . . . Soldiers*] Enter Plantagenet, Edward, Richard, Norfolke, Mountague, Warwicke, and Souldiers F   0.2 *Richard*] F; *Crookeback Richard,* and the yong *Earle of Rutland* o   0.2–3 *carrying a severed head*] HATTAWAY (*subs.*); *not in* F   0.3 *Montague*] F (*subs.*); Falconbridge CAIRNCROSS (*and throughout this scene*)   0.4 *Soldiers*] F (*subs.*); Souldiers, with white Roses in their hats o *and some editors*   0.4 *A chair of state*] WILSON (*subs.*); *not in* F   2 YORK] o, ROWE; Pl. F (*or* 'Plan.' *or* 'Plant.' [*for Plantagenet*], intermittently throughout this scene; 'Yorke' intermittently from l. 88)

1.1 Begins historically in May 1460 after the Battle of Northampton, which Shakespeare telescopes with the Yorkist victory at the first Battle of St Albans in May 1455, presented at the end of *2 Henry VI*. Following each battle a Parliament was called: in 1455 York was made Protector when Henry for a time became mentally incapacitated; in 1460 York publicly asserted his claim to the crown and was made heir apparent. Shakespeare omits the civilizing legalities of parliamentary debate, however, to create a more personal and rancorous confrontation.

0.1 *Alarum* Usually a drum or trumpet call to arms or attack, but here sounding the Yorkists' violent and noisy entry. See also note to l. 29.

0.3 *Montague* In this act personifies Warwick's father, Richard Neville, who inherited his title Earl of Salisbury from his wife Alice Montague. 'Old Salisbury' fights for the Yorkists at the first Battle of St Albans at the end of *2 Henry VI*. See notes to ll. 14 and 210 and Appendix B.

0.4 *chair of state* Imposing armchair or throne, raised on dais, with a sumptuous canopy, back and side hangings (*OED, state, sb.* 17b, citing 1.1.51). One of the play's central properties, emblematic of royal authority. The entering lords and soldiers may surround it as they enter. It usually faces the audience, but the 1994 RSC production positioned it downstage facing back, so the Yorkists' faces appeared full on as they approached it.

1 **wonder** cannot understand; am astounded

2 **horsemen . . . north** The Lancastrians traditionally drew their strength from the North of England.

149

He slyly stole away and left his men,
Whereat the great lord of Northumberland,
Whose warlike ears could never brook retreat,   5
Cheered up the drooping army; and himself,
Lord Clifford and Lord Stafford, all abreast,
Charged our main battle's front, and breaking in,
Were by the swords of common soldiers slain.

EDWARD
Lord Stafford's father, Duke of Buckingham,   10
Is either slain or wounded dangerous.
I cleft his beaver with a downright blow.
That this is true, father, behold his blood.

MONTAGUE
And brother here's the Earl of Wiltshire's blood,
Whom I encountered as the battles joined.   15

RICHARD
Speak thou for me, and tell them what I did.
        He throws down the Duke of Somerset's head

YORK
Richard hath best deserved of all my sons.
But is your grace dead, my lord of Somerset?

6 army; and himself,] HART 1925; Army, and himselfe. F, HARRISON; Army, and himself,
ROWE   11 dangerous] F; dangerouslie O, THEOBALD (*subs.*)   13, 14 blood.] F; blood. | *He
shows a bloody sword* CAPELL (*subs.*)   14 brother] F; cousin PELICAN *following* 0 *at* 1.2.1   16.1
He throws . . . head] THEOBALD (*subs.*); *not in* F   18 But] F; (*To the head*) But OXFORD

5 **brook retreat** tolerate the sound of a call
   to retreat
6 **Cheered up . . . drooping** rallied; encouraged . . . flagging; dispirited
7 **Lord Clifford** *2 Henry VI* portrays 'Old Clifford' being killed by York in single combat,
   as Henry states later in this scene (55–6),
   which provides his son with a motive for
   revenge (162–3). But York claims here he
   was killed 'by the swords of common
   soldiers' (9).
8 **battle's front . . . in** foremost army line or
   battalion . . . through
9 **swords . . . slain** i.e. shameful deaths.
   Chivalric honour demanded that one die
   fighting one's social equals.
11 **dangerous** dangerously. Early modern
   English regularly interchanged adjectives
   for adverbs (Abbott ¶1).
12 **cleft his beaver** split or shattered the face-
   guard or visor of his helmet
   downright straight-down; clean all-
   powerful

13–14 **behold . . . blood** Conventionally
   Edward and the others display their
   bloody swords. But they may instead
   show their blood-stained clothes, bodies,
   or other weapons.
14 **brother** Brother-in-law, if Montague represents the Earl of Salisbury, since York
   had married his sister Cicely Neville.
15 **battles joined** armies met together in
   conflict
16.1 *He . . . head* Richard may carry the head
   uncovered, or by the hair, or wrapped up.
   It may be weighted with sand to create a
   thump when it lands. After the 1977
   RSC's Richard tossed it down, the Yorkists
   began to play football with it, adding a
   touch of gangster humour to this grisly
   game of one-upmanship. Alternatively
   Richard may have dragged in Somerset's
   body, letting the head and upper body fall.
18 **But . . . Somerset?** Often interpreted as an
   ironic remark to Richard, or a mocking
   gibe to the head itself, anticipating the

NORFOLK

Such hope have all the line of John of Gaunt.

RICHARD

Thus do I hope to shake King Henry's head.   20

WARWICK

And so do I, victorious prince of York.
Before I see thee seated in that throne
Which now the house of Lancaster usurps,
I vow by heaven these eyes shall never close.
This is the palace of the fearful King   25
And this the regal seat: possess it York,
For this is thine and not King Henry's heirs'.

YORK

Assist me then, sweet Warwick, and I will,
For hither we have broken in by force.

NORFOLK

We'll all assist you. He that flies shall die.   30

---

19 hope] F; hap DYCE 1864–7 *and some editors*   27 heirs'] WARBURTON; Heires F; heir's HANMER

---

later grotesquely comic treatment of York's, Clifford's, and Henry's bodies. York may shake the head by the hair as he speaks, acting out Richard's comment at l. 20.

19 **hope** fate; (ironically) fulfilment of desired expectations
have come to (Abbott ¶364–5)
line . . . Gaunt Duke of Lancaster and fourth son of Edward III; Henry VI's great-grandfather and the dead Duke of Somerset's grandfather. York derived his ancestry from Edward III's third and fifth sons.

23 **house . . . usurps** John of Gaunt's son, Henry Bolingbroke, deposed Richard II to become Henry IV (see *Richard II*).

25 Many modern productions such as the 1983 BBC begin the play here, omitting the Yorkists' savage jesting in favour of a smash-and-grab focus on the throne. Although this may propel the action more energetically, what is lost is the sportive degradation of chivalric customs and human decencies, which will recur in later scenes and distinguish the career of Richard in particular. Such behaviour, first displayed by Cade's rebels in *2 Henry*

VI, marks Part Three's descent into a more bestial phase of civil warfare.

25–6 **palace . . . regal seat** of Westminster, and the parliament house. Hall reports that York 'took his lodging in the king's own palace' and 'with a bold countenance, entered into the chamber of peers, and sat down in the throne royal, under the cloth of estate' (Hall Ffv[r]). Holinshed uses the phrase 'regal seat' (Qqqii[r]). See Appendix A.

26 **possess** seize (as rightfully belonging to you). Appendix A, 1.1.26–32.1, and next note.

28 **Assist** accompany, attend. Alternatively 'support, help', signalling York's slight uncertainty (see also ll. 31, 43), matched later by Henry's diffidence. This may create room for the compromise they reach, and explain why each defers his direct lineal claim (see Edward I. Berry, *Patterns of Decay: Shakespeare's Early Histories* (Charlottesville, 1975), pp. 55–6).

29 **broken . . . force** The 1952–3 Birmingham Rep production opened with a loud crash of breaking timber, followed by silence. In the 1983 BBC version, the Yorkists hack the stage-set doors from behind with axes.

30 **flies** flees, deserts

YORK

Thanks, gentle Norfolk. Stay by me my lords,
And soldiers stay and lodge by me this night.

They go up to the raised chair of state. York is seated

WARWICK

And when the King comes, offer him no violence
Unless he seeks to thrust you out perforce.

YORK

The Queen this day here holds her parliament   35
But little thinks we shall be of her counsel.
By words or blows here let us win our right.

RICHARD

Armed as we are, let's stay within this house.

WARWICK

The bloody parliament shall this be called
Unless Plantagenet, Duke of York, be king,   40
And bashful Henry deposed, whose cowardice
Hath made us bywords to our enemies.

YORK

Then leave me not. My lords be resolute,
I mean to take possession of my right.

32.1 *to . . . state*] This edition *following* CHAMBERS; *not in* F   *York is seated*] This edition; *after l.* 49 JOHNSON *and some editors; not in* F   36 counsel] F3 (*subs.*), ROWE; counsaile FI; council POPE   43 not. My lords∧ be resolute,] This edition *following* HATTAWAY; not, . . . Lords∧ resolute, F; not∧ my Lords: O, CAPELL (*subs.*)

---

32 **lodge** encamp; sleep. York's prudence contrasts with Edward's overconfidence in 4.3.

32.1 **They . . . state** The dais, perhaps with several levels, may accommodate both the throne and people standing around it.

33 **offer . . . violence** Historically this forbearance may relate to the admiration Henry enjoyed for his gentleness and piety. Or it may be Warwick's way of maintaining personal control of the action, and/or respect for the Crown, even as they overthrow Henry. Compare Bolingbroke's threatening submission before Richard II at Flint Castle in *Richard II* 3.3.

34 **perforce** by violent means

35–6 Shakespeare again merges events of 1460 with those of 1455, when Queen Margaret held a 'great council' at Greenwich to try to discharge York of his recently granted Protectorship (Hall Eeiiiᵛ, Holinshed Pppiiiʳ).

36 **of her counsel** in agreement with her advice, in her confidence (spoken ironically); aware of her secret plans. F's original spelling could also signify 'council', in which case the phrase means 'her unexpected (and unwanted) councillors'. At the end of *2 Henry VI* York reports that Henry has called 'a present court of Parliament' (5.5.30), but here the initiative is Margaret's, signalling a change in dramatic and political emphasis.

37, 44 **right** legal title (of the house of York to the crown)

41 **bashful** demoralized; timid
Henry A strong caesura may supply an extra beat for the sake of the metre.

42 **bywords . . . enemies** objects of contempt . . . foreign enemies. Compare Psalm 44: 14: 'Thou makest us to be a byword among the nations' (*BCP*).

43 **not . . . resolute** F's full stop separating 'Leave me not' and 'My lords be resolute'

WARWICK

Neither the King nor he that loves him best,   45
The proudest he that holds up Lancaster,
Dares stir a wing if Warwick shake his bells.
I'll plant Plantagenet, root him up who dares.
Resolve thee, Richard, claim the English crown.
> *Flourish. Enter King Henry, Lord Clifford, the Earl of
> Northumberland, the Earl of Westmorland, the Duke of
> Exeter, and the rest*

HENRY

My lords, look where the sturdy rebel sits,   50
Even in the chair of state. Belike he means,
Backed by the power of Warwick, that false peer,
To aspire unto the crown and reign as king.
Earl of Northumberland, he slew thy father,
And thine Lord Clifford, and you both have vowed
    revenge
                                                               55
On him, his sons, his favourites and his friends.

49.1–3 *Henry . . . Exeter*] *Henry, Clifford, Northumberland, Westmorland, Exeter* F; *Henrie* the sixt,
with the Duke of *Excester*, The Earle of *Northumberland*, the Earle of *Westmerland* and *Clifford*,
the Earle of *Cumberland*, with red Roses in their hats o *and some editors*

arguably makes York sound more commanding and self-possessed. Editors since
Rowe, however, have made 'my lords'
parenthetical, changing York's rhetorical
emphasis. 'Leave me not, my lords' may
sound more like an appeal.

46 **he . . . holds up** person . . . supports (the
cause of)
47 **wing . . . bells** The image is of a falcon, to
whose feet hunters attached bells to terri-
fy their prey. Compare *Lucrece*: 'Harmless
Lucretia, marking what he tells | With
trembling fear, as fowl hear falcons' bells'
(510–11).
49 **Resolve thee** be determined; i.e. do not
flinch. York may seat himself here, perhaps after hearing the Lancastrians
approach, rather than at l. 32.1.
crown The first of over sixty occurrences
of the word.
49.1 *Flourish* Trumpet fanfare announcing
the arrival of high-ranking persons.
49.3 *the rest* A 'permissive' or open direction
in F, here probably indicating two or more
soldiers.

50 **look . . . sits** Henry's reaction often
indicates an actor's initial interpretation
of his role. In 1963 David Warner was
barely able to face the sight of York
sitting in his throne, turning away in
timidity and chagrin. The BBC's Peter
Benson was meekly astonished at
York's audacity. In 1988 the RSC's
Ralph Fiennes reacted in fury at York's
presumption.
sturdy rebellious, obstinate; surly; reck-
lessly destructive. 'Sturdy beggar' was the
Elizabethan term of abuse for 'an able-
bodied man begging without cause',
sometimes violently (*OED*, *beggar*, 1b).
They were often unemployed labourers,
displaced by economic depression and
rural enclosures, or disabled or demobi-
lized soldiers unable to find work.
51 **Belike** it seems
54–5 **Northumberland . . . Clifford** Like 'Old
Clifford', Henry Percy, 2nd Earl of
Northumberland, father of the present
Earl, was killed by Yorkist forces at the first
Battle of St Albans in 1455. See Appendix
A, 1.1.4–9.

NORTHUMBERLAND
If I be not, heavens be revenged on me.

CLIFFORD
The hope thereof makes Clifford mourn in steel.

WESTMORLAND
What, shall we suffer this? Let's pluck him down.
My heart for anger burns, I cannot brook it.   60

HENRY
Be patient gentle Earl of Westmorland.

CLIFFORD
Patience is for poltroons such as he.
He durst not sit there had your father lived.
My gracious lord, here in the parliament
Let us assail the family of York.   65

NORTHUMBERLAND
Well hast thou spoken, cousin be it so.

HENRY
Ah, know you not the city favours them,
And they have troops of soldiers at their beck?

WESTMORLAND
But when the Duke is slain, they'll quickly fly.

---

66 spoken, cousin‸] F; spoken‸ cosen, O, THEOBALD (*subs.*)   69 WESTMORLAND] F (*Westm.*);
Exeter O (*Exet.*), THEOBALD

58 **steel** armour and weapons, as opposed to
civilian mourning dress
59 **WESTMORLAND** The 2nd Earl, Ralph
Neville, did not participate in the Wars of
the Roses, though his brother John did
and was killed at Towton. See Appendix
A.
   suffer endure; tolerate
62 **poltroons** lazy cowards, worthless
wretches (*OED*, citing this passage)
63 **father** Henry V, celebrated for defeating
the French at the Battle of Agincourt
in 1415, as depicted in the anonymous
Famous Victories of Henry V (*c.*1587, performed by the Queen's Men, with whom
Shakespeare may have temporarily been
associated (McMillin and MacLean, pp.
160–6)).
65 **family** Yorkists may be tightly grouped
around the throne in the style of a family
portrait. Some productions follow O by
including Rutland in this scene, magnifying the impression of a dynasty.
66 **cousin‸** F's punctuation creates a more

forceful spoken emphasis than O's parenthetical 'Cousin,', followed by most editors since Theobald.
67–8 **city . . . soldiers** After St Albans in 1455
York and his army were received warmly
by the citizens of London, who supported
his claims to the throne. See below, ll.
92–3 and Appendix A.
68 **beck** command
69 **WESTMORLAND** Most editors since Theobald
have reassigned this line to Exeter, partly
following *True Tragedy* and partly l. 72.
But the latter marks a shift in address,
and the bellicose tone seems inconsistent
with the Exeter of F, who supports
Henry's preference for compromise.
Exeter is Henry's only confidant, on
whom he relies several times at moments
of crisis (e.g. 1.1.192, 2.5.137, 4.8.34 ff.).
He shares Henry's peaceful instincts
('And I, I hope, shall reconcile them all',
1.1.274, F only) and ultimately shares
his fate, being captured with him in 4.8
(F only).

HENRY

Far be the thought of this from Henry's heart,   70
To make a shambles of the parliament house.
Cousin of Exeter, frowns, words, and threats
Shall be the war that Henry means to use.
Thou factious Duke of York, descend my throne
And kneel for grace and mercy at my feet,   75
I am thy sovereign.

YORK I am thine.

EXETER

For shame come down, he made thee Duke of York.

YORK

It was my inheritance, as the earldom was.

EXETER

Thy father was a traitor to the crown.   80

WARWICK

Exeter thou art a traitor to the crown
In following this usurping Henry.

CLIFFORD

Whom should he follow but his natural king?

WARWICK

True, Clifford, that's Richard Duke of York.

84 that's] F1; that is F2, COLLIER; and that is O

---

71 **shambles** slaughterhouse. Images of slaughter and butchery increase in frequency in *3 Henry VI* from Parts One and Two, marking the increasing barbarity of the country's civil war; see Carol McGinnis Kay, 'Traps, Slaughter, and Chaos: A Study of Shakespeare's *Henry VI* Plays', *Studies in the Literary Imagination*, 5 (1972), 1–26.

72 **Cousin** Familiar form of address to a peer by a king. It need not imply a family relationship.

72–3 **frowns . . . use** May not imply weakness or timidity, but principled defiance which stops short of physical violence. In the 1983 BBC production, Peter Benson's gentle Henry momentarily steels himself to confront York.

74 **factious** promoter of dissension, seditious

78 **he . . . York** *1 Henry VI* 3.1.168–73, when the attainder on York's father, Richard

Earl of Cambridge, was lifted. See note to l. 80.

79 **earldom** i.e. of March, derived from his mother Anne Mortimer in right of her brother Edmund Earl of March (d. 1425). She was descended from Philippa, daughter of Lionel Duke of Clarence and third son of Edward III, through whom York partly claimed the crown. The fact that his line passed twice through female ancestors, rather than 'directly' through male heirs, weakened his claim in the eyes of some.

80 **father** Executed for treason by Henry V, depriving his heirs of inheritance rights. See *Henry V* 2.2, especially 151–3.

83 **natural** by virtue of being born (*OED a.* 10b, citing this passage), with an underlying sense of being innately right and fair

84 **that's** Editors traditionally emend following F2 or O to regularize the metre. But this ignores Shakespeare's more

HENRY

And shall I stand, and thou sit in my throne?   85

YORK

It must and shall be so, content thyself.

WARWICK

Be Duke of Lancaster, let him be king.

WESTMORLAND

He is both king and Duke of Lancaster,
And that the lord of Westmorland shall maintain.

WARWICK

And Warwick shall disprove it. You forget   90
That we are those which chased you from the field
And slew your fathers, and with colours spread
Marched through the city to the palace gates.

NORTHUMBERLAND

Yes Warwick, I remember it to my grief,
And by his soul, thou and thy house shall rue it.   95

WESTMORLAND

Plantagenet, of thee and these thy sons,
Thy kinsmen and thy friends, I'll have more lives
Than drops of blood were in my father's veins.

CLIFFORD

Urge it no more, lest that instead of words

flexible—and theatrically expressive—practice, even in plays as early in his career as *3 Henry VI*. In this 'headless' line, an unstressed syllable is omitted before the first stressed one. Such lines constitute acceptable pentameters in so far as they preserve five strong beats, despite the lack of regular iambic rhythm, and may produce a dramatic effect 'of abruptness, anger, or astonishment' (Wright, pp. 174–5, 177–8).

85 **stand . . . sit** i.e. as if in respect to a superior

88 **both . . . Lancaster** Because since the reign of Henry V, all monarchs of England have held the title Duke of Lancaster. See Richard Dutton, 'Shakespeare and Lancaster', *SQ* 49 (1998), 1–21, p. 2.

92 **fathers** Many editors emend to 'father' following O. But F's plural makes good sense because Clifford's and Northumberland's fathers were killed at St Albans in 1455 (see ll. 54–5), and because histori-

cally Westmorland's father was *not* killed there (*pace* l. 98, which is Shakespeare's invention). Since O is a report, O's Warwick may be *anticipating* Westmorland's 'my father's veins' (l. 98) when he changes his own line to 'father'. Neither chronicle mentions an earl of Westmorland until Towton, where Holinshed confuses him with his brother (see Appendix A, 1.1.59; Vaughan, ii. 430).

92 **colours** flags, insignia; i.e. openly without fear, recalling the phrase, 'to show one's true colours'

95, 101 **his** i.e. my father's

98 **my father's** While assuming that Westmorland is responding to Warwick's 'fathers' at l. 92, recent editors point out that historically his father did not die in battle (see l. 59 n. above). But Westmorland—whose presence is invented anyway—does not cite revenge as a motive, as do Northumberland and Clifford. See also Appendix A, 1.1.59.

I send thee, Warwick, such a messenger   100
As shall revenge his death before I stir.

WARWICK

Poor Clifford, how I scorn his worthless threats.

YORK

Will you we show our title to the crown?
If not, our swords shall plead it in the field.

HENRY

What title hast thou, traitor, to the crown?   105
Thy father was as thou art, Duke of York,
Thy grandfather Roger Mortimer, Earl of March.
I am the son of Henry the Fifth,
Who made the Dauphin and the French to stoop,
And seized upon their towns and provinces.   110

WARWICK

Talk not of France, sith thou hast lost it all.

HENRY

The Lord Protector lost it and not I.
When I was crowned I was but nine months old.

RICHARD

You are old enough now, and yet methinks you lose.
Father, tear the crown from the usurper's head.   115

106 Thy] O, ROWE; My F

100 **messenger** Hattaway suggests this means an angel (literally, 'God's messenger') of death, as in Hebrews 1: 7. But the underlying image may be of a basilisk, the mythical reptile whose mere looks could kill. See 3.2.187 and *2 Henry VI*: 'Thou baleful messenger, out of my sight! | Upon thy eyeballs murderous tyranny | Sits in grim majesty to fright the world. | Look not upon me, for thine eyes are wounding . . . basilisk' (3.2.48–52).

103 **show** produce legally for inspection; explain
   title legal claim

104 **plead** sue for; urge; allege

105–31 **Thy . . . his** Henry sounds more self-assured and forceful in F than in O, a difference which may reflect revision and/or varying chronicle reports of Henry's response to York's demands prior to the first Battle of St Albans. See Introduction, p. 20, and Appendix A.

107 **Roger Mortimer** Father of York's mother. See above, l. 79 n.

109 **Dauphin** Louis, son and heir apparent of Charles VI, died shortly after the Battle of Agincourt in 1415. He is the figure represented by the Dauphin at the beginning of *Henry V*. *1* and *2 Henry VI* portray the subsequent loss of English conquests in France.
   stoop submit humbly

111 **sith** since

112 **Lord Protector** Humphrey Duke of Gloucester, murdered by political enemies in *2 Henry VI*.

113 **crowned . . . old** Henry succeeded to the throne at nine months in 1422 but was not crowned until 1429 in Westminster and 1430 in Paris. See 3.1.76 and *1 Henry VI* 4.1.

114–15 Irregular but not untypical Shakespearian lines: the first has an extra syllable at midline ('now') with a contracted

EDWARD

Sweet father do so, set it on your head.

MONTAGUE

Good brother as thou lov'st and honour'st arms,

Let's fight it out and not stand cavilling thus.

RICHARD

Sound drums and trumpets, and the King will fly.

YORK Sons peace.   120

HENRY

Peace thou, and give King Henry leave to speak.

WARWICK

Plantagenet shall speak first. Hear him lords,

And be you silent and attentive too,

For he that interrupts him shall not live.

HENRY

Think'st thou that I will leave my kingly throne   125

Wherein my grandsire and my father sat?

No, first shall war unpeople this my realm.

Ay, and their colours often borne in France—

And now in England to our heart's great sorrow—

Shall be my winding-sheet. Why faint you lords?   130

My title's good, and better far than his.

WARWICK

Prove it Henry, and thou shalt be king.

HENRY

Henry the Fourth by conquest got the crown.

128–9 colours . . . sorrow—] ROWE (*subs.*); Colours∧ | . . . England, . . . sorrow, F; colours—
. . . France; | . . . England, . . . sorrow,— CAPELL   131 good,] F; good∧ POPE

'you are'; the second three trochaic feet
followed by a rush of weak beats ('from
the us-') (Wright, pp. 168–9, 198–9). The
sense of packed extra syllables suggests
Richard's impatience, while his under-
cutting remark has a characteristically
sardonic tone.

114 **yet** still

118 **cavilling** disputing over petty matters
121 **Peace . . . speak** Henry may be entreat-
ing or commanding, depending on how
forcefully the actor expresses his ensuing
argument.
128 **their** i.e. my grandsire's and father's
129 **And . . . sorrow** i.e. in civil wars, conventionally considered more unnatural,

bloody, and dishonourable than foreign
conflict
130 **winding-sheet** shroud for burial
130–1 **faint . . . his** In the 1963–4 Hall–Barton production a silence fell as no one
spoke up to defend Henry, who shrank
back sorrowfully until Warwick spoke the
next line with quiet authority.
130 **faint** lose courage, weaken fearfully
131 **good,** Pope's omitted comma, adopted by
most editors, shifts the rhetorical emphasis from the second half of the line, ending Henry's speech less forcefully.
133 **conquest** Implies that Henry IV legiti-
mated his authority by the traditional
means of success in war. But in the later
Richard II, which contains an interrupted

YORK

'Twas by rebellion against his king.

HENRY ⌈*aside*⌉

I know not what to say, my title's weak.—   135
Tell me, may not a king adopt an heir?

YORK What then?

HENRY

And if he may, then am I lawful king,
For Richard in the view of many lords
Resigned the crown to Henry the Fourth,   140
Whose heir my father was, and I am his.

YORK

He rose against him, being his sovereign,
And made him to resign his crown perforce.

WARWICK

Suppose, my lords, he did it unconstrained,
Think you 'twere prejudicial to his crown?   145

EXETER

No, for he could not so resign his crown,
But that the next heir should succeed and reign.

HENRY

Art thou against us Duke of Exeter?

EXETER

His is the right, and therefore pardon me.
    Some lords whisper together

135 ⌈*aside*⌉] CAPELL (*subs.*); *not in* F   149.1 *Some . . . together*] This edition; *not in* F

trial-by-combat and no battles, Richard abdicates his throne under armed pressure from Henry Bolingbroke, who becomes Henry IV. Henry VI is similarly 'enforced' (see below, ll. 230–1).

134 **his king** i.e. Richard II

135 **I . . . weak** Traditionally spoken by Henry to himself or the audience (or the camera, intensifying the sense of inner turmoil); but could be addressed publicly to Exeter or Henry's supporters, as in the 1994 RSC production.

138 **And if** if indeed (Abbott ¶105)

139–40 **Richard . . . Fourth** *Richard II* 4.1. 'Henry' pronounced with three syllables.

143 **perforce** under constraint (with the threat of armed force)

145 **prejudicial** detrimental; i.e. extinguish his (or his son's) birthrights. Warwick implies, as Exeter grasps, that these are non-transferable because divinely ordained.

146–7 **he . . . reign** He could not resign his crown in any way that could prevent his son from legally succeeding (Abbott ¶121), because the royal succession was part of the perpetual corporate entity of the nation—the body politic—and not in the king's personal gift. See Marie Axton, *The Queen's Two Bodies: Drama and the Elizabethan Succession* (1977).

148 **Art . . . Exeter** Henry may be dejected by Exeter's apparent betrayal, or angrily provoked.

149.1–150 *Some . . . not?* Exeter's unexpected support of Warwick (ll. 144–7)

YORK

   Why whisper you, my lords, and answer not?   150

EXETER

   My conscience tells me he is lawful king.

HENRY

   All will revolt from me, and turn to him.

NORTHUMBERLAND

   Plantagenet, for all the claim thou lay'st,

   Think not that Henry shall be so deposed.

WARWICK

   Deposed he shall be, in despite of all.   155

NORTHUMBERLAND

   Thou art deceived, 'tis not thy southern power

   Of Essex, Norfolk, Suffolk, nor of Kent

   Which makes thee thus presumptuous and proud,

   Can set the Duke up in despite of me.

CLIFFORD

   King Henry, be thy title right or wrong,   160

   Lord Clifford vows to fight in thy defence.

   May that ground gape and swallow me alive

   Where I shall kneel to him that slew my father.

HENRY

   O Clifford, how thy words revive my heart.

YORK

   Henry of Lancaster, resign thy crown.   165

   What mutter you, or what conspire you lords?

---

152 All] F; *Aside* All CAPELL (*subs.*)

causes a stir among Henry's lords, and
perhaps York's too. If York's 'lords'
includes Exeter, who speaks before and
after him, there may be a pause while
they confer. If Exeter is not being consulted, the dialogue and the whispering
may continue simultaneously. The same
action occurs at l. 166 after Clifford speaks
out defiantly for Henry.

151 **conscience** inward conviction, moral
sense; heart; rational understanding.
These qualms are Shakespeare's invention, though Holinshed notes (Rrriii^r) that
Exeter was Edward's brother-in-law and
therefore York's son-in-law.

152 **All . . . him** Editors traditionally mark
this line as an aside, i.e. Henry speaking
to himself or partially to others. But he
may speak fully aloud, in a plea or out of
frustration.

156 **deceived** mistaken; deluded

156-7 **southern power . . . Kent** from
where the Yorkists chiefly drew their
forces. Northumberland implies his
northern power base is greater.

159 **set . . . up** i.e. as king

162 **ground . . . alive** Compare Numbers
16: 32-3: 'And the earth opened her
mouth, and swallowed them up . . . So
they . . . went down alive' (Geneva
Bible). Also Dent GG2.

WARWICK

  Do right unto this princely Duke of York
  Or I will fill the house with armèd men,
  And o'er the chair of state where now he sits,
  Write up his title with usurping blood.   170

     He stamps with his foot, and the Soldiers show
     themselves

HENRY

  My lord of Warwick, hear but one word:
  Let me for this my lifetime reign as king.

YORK

  Confirm the crown to me and to mine heirs,
  And thou shalt reign in quiet while thou liv'st.

HENRY

  I am content. Richard Plantagenet   175
  Enjoy the kingdom after my decease.

CLIFFORD

  What wrong is this unto the prince your son!

---

169 o'er] F2 (*subs.*); ouer F1, O   171 hear] F1; hear me F3, O

---

167 **right** justice; what is reasonable and
fair (as opposed to what is determined
chiefly by force (*OED sb.* 3)).
   princely worthy of being king;
prince-like
170.1 **stamps . . . foot** Alternatively Warwick may signal with a smaller gesture of
the hand or head, as in the 1987 ESC
production.
170.1–2 **show themselves** Suggests the soldiers may appear partially visible in the
doorways and/or in the stage gallery,
perhaps accompanied by the sounds
of a larger force. This allows a company
to employ fewer players (minimum two,
see Appendix C). Most modern productions, however, have the soldiers
rush in holding pikes and 'ambushing'
Henry.
171 **hear** Perhaps two syllables (Cercignani,
p. 147). But it is more likely that this is
what Wright calls a broken-backed line,
which purposefully omits a syllable after
the midline pause to suggest agitation or
urgency (pp. 102–7, 176–7). The same
omission occurs at l. 260 below, another
moment of stress for Henry.

173 **to me** i.e. if you die before me. See
Appendix A, 1.1.172–6.
175–6 **I . . . decease** Some recent editions precede this with two lines from O: '*King.*
Conuey the souldiers hence, and then I
will. | *War.* Captaine conduct them into
Tuthill fieldes.' Cairncross argues they
were skipped because lines 175–6 were
'inserted' and 'taken as alternative rather
than complementary' (note to ll. 178–9).
Hattaway claims they represent a revision
by 'the author to show Henry refusing to
act under duress' (note to ll. 174–5). Both
suggestions are unlikely because O's stage
action is incompatible with F's, and F
revises O. Unless it is supposed that these
are different soldiers from the 'armèd men'
(168) and who 'show themselves' at 170.1
(which the acting complement of Elizabethan companies could probably not
accommodate; see note to lines 210.1–2),
they must remain on stage to exit with
Warwick after 208, 'And I'll keep London
with my soldiers'. In O, by contrast, Warwick apparently exits alone ('I cannot staie
to hear these Articles. *Exit*'), his soldiers
having left earlier with the 'Captaine'.

WARWICK

  What good is this to England and himself!

WESTMORLAND

  Base, fearful, and despairing Henry.

CLIFFORD

  How hast thou injured both thyself and us!   180

WESTMORLAND

  I cannot stay to hear these articles.

NORTHUMBERLAND Nor I.

CLIFFORD

  Come cousin, let us tell the Queen these news.

WESTMORLAND

  Farewell faint-hearted and degenerate king,

  In whose cold blood no spark of honour bides.   185

NORTHUMBERLAND

  Be thou a prey unto the house of York,

  And die in bands for this unmanly deed.

CLIFFORD

  In dreadful war mayst thou be overcome,

  Or live in peace abandoned and despised.

            Exeunt Westmorland, Northumberland,

                    Clifford and their Soldiers

WARWICK

  Turn this way, Henry, and regard them not.   190

EXETER

  They seek revenge and therefore will not yield.

HENRY

  Ah Exeter.

WARWICK   Why should you sigh my lord?

HENRY

  Not for myself, Lord Warwick, but my son,

189.1–2 *Exeunt . . . Soldiers*] ROWE (*subs.*); *not in* F; o *and some editors provide individual exits at ll.* 185, 187, *and* 189

181 **articles** Terms of agreement subsequently drawn up by Parliament to ratify the new succession. See Appendix A, I.I.181–202.

183 **news** A common plural.

185 **cold blood** An oxymoron, blood being one of the hot humours; hence: apathy, inaction. Because heat also defined mas-

culinity, 'cold blood' suggests Henry is unmanly. Margaret describes him as being 'cold in great affairs' in *2 Henry VI* (3.1.224). See also 2.1.122 below. See Rackin, 'Foreign Country', pp. 77–8.

187 **in bands** in fetters, shackled

188 **dreadful** terrifying, fearful

Whom I unnaturally shall disinherit.
But be it as it may. (*To York*) I here entail   195
The crown to thee and to thine heirs for ever,
Conditionally, that here thou take an oath
To cease this civil war, and whilst I live,
To honour me as thy king and sovereign,
And neither by treason nor hostility   200
To seek to put me down and reign thyself.

YORK

This oath I willingly take, and will perform.

WARWICK

Long live King Henry. Plantagenet embrace him.

HENRY

And long live thou and these thy forward sons.

> *Sennet. Here York and his followers come down, and
> York embraces Henry*

YORK

Now York and Lancaster are reconciled.   205

EXETER

Accursed be he that seeks to make them foes.

YORK

Farewell my gracious lord, I'll to my castle.

195 (*To York*)] COLLIER 1853 *following* RANN (—); *not in* F   200 neither] F1; nor OXFORD (*conj.*
Taylor); F2 *omits preceding* 'And'   204.1 *Sennet . . . down*] F (*subs.*), *after l.* 206   204.1 *York
. . . followers*] This edition *following* OXFORD; *they* F; *York* HATTAWAY, *after l.* 203   204.1–2 *and
. . . Henry*] OXFORD (*subs.*), *after l.* 203; *not in* F   207 castle.] F; castell. *Exit Yorke and his sonnes*
0, CAIRNCROSS (*subs.*)

194 **unnaturally** denying him his natural
birthright
195 **entail** confer as an inalienable or legally
untransferable possession (*OED v.*² 2, citing this passage)
197 **Conditionally** on condition. Emphasized
in the 1963–4 Hall–Barton and 1988 RSC
productions, indicating Henry was disinheriting his son to avoid civil war, not out
of cowardice.
  take an oath Usually performed on the
hilt of a raised sword. But in the 1988 RSC
production, Henry and York held the
crown between them, and York let it go
with slight unwillingness. The moment
was reminiscent of *Richard II* 4.1.181 ff.
when Richard and Bolingbroke face each
other holding the crown between them.
203 **Long . . . Henry** If the Yorkists are clus-
tered around the throne, they may move

away reluctantly. This line was followed
by awkward silence in the 1987 ESC production, until Warwick repeated the line
as a command to the York brothers, who
responded feebly.
204 **forward** eager, spirited; advanced for
their years, precocious (*OED* 7, citing this
passage); presumptuous, bold. Possibly
spoken sarcastically.
204.1 **Sennet** An elaborate musical flourish,
ostensibly honouring Henry's royal
action. See Shirley, pp. 71–3. But by playing as York exchanges embraces with
him, it suggests a transfer of rule has
taken place—politically, Henry is already
a 'lame duck'.
205 **York . . . reconciled** The soldiers may
sheath their drawn swords.
207 **castle** Sandal Castle near Wakefield,
named in 1.2.

WARWICK

And I'll keep London with my soldiers.

NORFOLK

And I to Norfolk with my followers.

MONTAGUE

And I unto the sea from whence I came.   210

> *Exeunt York, Edward, Richard, Warwick,*
> *Norfolk, Montague and their Soldiers*

HENRY

And I with grief and sorrow to the court.

> *Enter Queen Margaret and Prince Edward*

EXETER

Here comes the Queen, whose looks bewray her anger:

I'll steal away.

HENRY   Exeter, so will I.

MARGARET

Nay go not from me, I will follow thee.

HENRY

Be patient gentle Queen and I will stay.   215

---

208 soldiers.] F; souldiers. *Exit.* O; *~Exeunt* CAIRNCROSS   209 followers.] F; followers. *Exit.*
O; *~Exeunt* CAIRNCROSS   210.1–2 *Exeunt . . . Soldiers*] ROWE (*subs.*); *not in* F; *Exit.* O (*at l.* 210),
CAIRNCROSS   211.1 *Queen . . . Edward*] *the Queene* F; *the Queene and the Prince* O, ROWE   213 I.]
F; *I. Going* ROWE

---

208 **keep** remain in; guard, defend

210 **unto the sea** Historically, neither
Warwick's father nor brother had any
connection to the sea. A figure named
Falconbridge did, however, whom Shakespeare may have confused or replaced
with 'Montague'.

210.1–2 *Exeunt . . . Soldiers* Rowe first
provided a missing direction, presumably
on the analogy of moments such as
4.8.32.1, where F's *Exeunt* indicates a
comparable group exit, which is consistent with the practice of manuscript-
derived texts. O's staging, substituted by
recent editors, provides individual exits
for Warwick, Norfolk, and Montague
(following Westmorland, Clifford, and
Northumberland at 185–9). With only a
line each, however, in terms of stage time,
they leave virtually together, so the difference between F and O is more apparent
than real and nothing is gained by confla-
tion. Furthermore, Pelican and later editors add 'with men' or 'with soldiers' for
each *Exit*. With a minimum of two men

for each direction, this totals 20 players,
with two more, Margaret and Prince
Edward, waiting to come on. This number
was probably beyond the reach of a typical Elizabethan company, especially if
additional soldiers are required to play the
'Captain' and others which editors add at
174–5 (see note to 175–6).

212 **looks . . . anger** An expression Hall
claims was characteristic (see Appendix
A). 'The big laugh on the king's desire to
escape his approaching wife's fury . . .
is easy to get, but for Margaret this is
an important moment. . . . She's always
known [Henry] was capable of doing
something like this, but now he's done it.
York has many sons, but she has only one
. . . and somehow she believes that York
was responsible for [her lover] Suffolk's
death [in *2 Henry VI*]. Whatever the
nature of her relationship with Henry,
the fact is that the child is everything'
(Penny Downie on playing Margaret,
Players 3, pp. 128–9).

bewray reveal, declare

MARGARET

Who can be patient in such extremes?
Ah wretched man, would I had died a maid
And never seen thee, never borne thee son,
Seeing thou hast proved so unnatural a father.
Hath he deserved to lose his birthright thus?   220
Hadst thou but loved him half so well as I,
Or felt that pain which I did for him once,
Or nourished him as I did with my blood,
Thou wouldst have left thy dearest heart-blood there,
Rather than have made that savage Duke thine heir   225
And disinherited thine only son.

PRINCE EDWARD

Father, you cannot disinherit me;
If you be king, why should not I succeed?

HENRY

Pardon me Margaret, pardon me sweet son,
The Earl of Warwick and the Duke enforced me.   230

MARGARET

Enforced thee? Art thou king and wilt be forced?
I shame to hear thee speak. Ah timorous wretch,
Thou hast undone thyself, thy son, and me,
And given unto the house of York such head
As thou shalt reign but by their sufferance.   235
To entail him and his heirs unto the crown,
What is it but to make thy sepulchre

216 **patient** Three syllables.
  extremes adverse conditions, acute straits
217–26 **Ah . . . son** Reminiscent of Videna's complaints about Gorboduc's decision to give half of Ferrex's 'birthright and heritage' to his younger brother Porrex, *Gorboduc* 1.1.22–9.
222 **pain** i.e. of labour and childbirth
223 **nourished . . . blood** The image could apply to breast-feeding as well as foetal development, since early modern physiology believed a mother's milk was converted from her blood. See Dorothy McLaren, 'Marital Fertility and Lactation 1570–1720', *Women in English Society 1500–1800*, ed. Mary Prior (London and New York, 1985), pp. 22–53.
224 **heart-blood** blood shed in death
  there Margaret may gesture to the stage throne, or, in terms of the dramatic fic-

tion which imagines time having passed and Parliament already having ratified the new articles of succession, to the Parliament house.
231 **Enforced thee?** Editors often mark this with an exclamation. But it may be spoken quietly, to intense effect, as in the 1988 RSC production. This passage was later recalled by Thomas Heywood's *2 King Edward IV*. See Introduction, p. 73.
232 **shame** am ashamed
233 **undone** ruined
234 **head** freedom; chief command; powerful incentive for insurrection
235 **sufferance** leave; express permission
237–8 **What . . . time?** 'The Queen's reproach is founded on a position long received among politicians, that the loss of a King's power is soon followed by loss of life' (Johnson).

And creep into it far before thy time?
Warwick is Chancellor and the lord of Calais,
Stern Falconbridge commands the Narrow Seas,   240
The Duke is made Protector of the realm,
And yet shalt thou be safe? Such safety finds
The trembling lamb environèd with wolves.
Had I been there, which am a silly woman,
The soldiers should have tossed me on their pikes   245
Before I would have granted to that act.
But thou preferr'st thy life before thine honour,
And seeing thou dost, I here divorce myself
Both from thy table, Henry, and thy bed,
Until that act of Parliament be repealed   250
Whereby my son is disinherited.
The northern lords that have forsworn thy colours
Will follow mine, if once they see them spread,
And spread they shall be to thy foul disgrace
And utter ruin of the house of York.   255
Thus do I leave thee. Come son let's away,
Our army is ready; come, we'll after them.

HENRY
Stay gentle Margaret and hear me speak.

---

240 Falconbridge] F, O; Montague OXFORD *conj.*   254 thy] F; the KEIGHTLEY *conj.*

239 **Chancellor** Warwick's father was in fact appointed Chancellor in 1455. See Appendix A.
240 **Stern** fierce; cruel; brave, resolute. See Introduction, pp. 73–4.
  Falconbridge . . . Seas See note to l. 210.
  Narrow Seas English Channel
244 **silly** defenceless, conventionally applied to sheep (*OED* 1c)
245 **tossed** flung in the air; carried
  pikes lances ending in a sharp metal point, the main weapon of foot-soldiers
246 **granted** consented
246, 250 **act** See note to l. 181.
249 **table . . . bed** Legal formula (*a mensa et toro*) for divorce (O. Hood Phillips, *Shakespeare and the Lawyers* (1972), p. 133). In the 1994 RSC production, Margaret conspicuously removed her wedding ring and placed it on a central

table (anticipating Clarence's change in loyalties at 5.1.81).
251 **my son** '[Prince] Edward has become *Margaret's* son here, and he not only stays in her company for most of the rest of the play, but echoes her warlike words and manner' (Howard and Rackin, p. 85).
252 **northern lords** i.e. Westmorland, Northumberland, and Clifford, although Westmorland does not appear again. See Appendix A, 1.2.49–51 and 1.2.49–51.
  forsworn repudiated irreversibly
256–7 **Come . . . come** While Margaret's strength and support eventually 'empower the young prince to claim the patriarchal legacy his father has betrayed' (Howard and Rackin, p. 85), her repetition suggests Prince Edward hesitates and is being coerced, torn momentarily between his parents, before deciding at ll. 262–3.

MARGARET

Thou hast spoke too much already; get thee gone.

HENRY

Gentle son Edward, thou wilt stay me?   260

MARGARET

Ay, to be murdered by his enemies.

PRINCE EDWARD

When I return with victory from the field
I'll see your grace, till then I'll follow her.

MARGARET

Come son away, we may not linger thus.

Exeunt Margaret and Prince Edward

HENRY

Poor queen, how love to me and to her son   265
Hath made her break out into terms of rage.
Revenged may she be on that hateful Duke,
Whose haughty spirit, wingèd with desire,
Will cost my crown, and like an empty eagle
Tire on the flesh of me and of my son.   270
The loss of those three lords torments my heart;
I'll write unto them and entreat them fair.
Come cousin, you shall be the messenger.

EXETER

And I, I hope, shall reconcile them all.   *Exeunt*

260 stay] F1; stay with F2, 0, *and editors*   262 from] F2, 0; to F1   264.1 *Exeunt . . . Edward*]
ROWE (*subs.*); *not in* F   269 cost] F; coast WARBURTON; souse DYCE 1864–7 *conj.*; 'cost HATT-
AWAY (*conj.* Theobald)   274 *Exeunt*] POPE; *Exit* F

260 **stay** stay for (*OED v.*[1] 19); support,
    strengthen (*OED v.*[2] 1). Also see note to l.
    171 above. Emendation to 'stay with' is
    unnecessary.
263 **see** call upon, visit
264 **may** must (Abbott ¶310)
265 **love to me** Perhaps a surprising reaction.
    It may demonstrate Henry's naïvety, or
    his need to believe that Margaret still loves
    him, because of his abiding love for her.
    See 2.1.123 and 2.5.138–9. Performers
    sometimes suggest that their emotional
    relationship, despite outward estrange-
    ment, continues at some deeper level.
267 **may** Can express a possibility, a certain-
    ty (like l. 264), or Henry's wish (Abbott
    ¶313).
268 **wingèd** soaring
    desire longing (for supremacy, power)

269 **cost** cost me, rob me of (Wilson). Peter
    Seary points out (privately) that F's
    spelling could also represent an aphetic
    form of 'accost' (= 'cost), meaning attack
    or assail, as Theobald suggested in a letter
    to Warburton dated 24 January 1730.
    Warburton's alternative, 'coast', means
    the same thing.
    empty hungry
270 **Tire** feed greedily upon; literally to tear
    and pull at the flesh of prey with the beak.
271 **three lords** See l. 252.
272 **entreat them fair** persuade them by gen-
    tle pleading; negotiate with them civilly;
    beseech them kindly
273 **cousin** Familiar, perhaps intimate, term
    of address.
274 *Exeunt* Wilson and later editors reposi-
    tion 1.2's *Flourish* before this *Exeunt*,

1.2   *Flourish. Enter Edward, Richard, and Montague*

RICHARD

Brother, though I be youngest, give me leave.

EDWARD

No, I can better play the orator.

MONTAGUE

But I have reasons strong and forcible.
        Enter the Duke of York

YORK

Why, how now sons and brother, at a strife?
What is your quarrel? How began it first?   5

1.2] CAPELL; *not in* F   0.1 *Flourish*] F; *omitted by* ROWE; *before 'Exeunt' at* 1.1.274 WILSON;
after 'Exeunt' PELICAN

---

moving it from F's succeeding entry direction. It may have been misplaced by the
compositor reading it as a marginal annotation in the manuscript, or as the Oxford
editors suggest, a routine insertion in F.
In performance the repositioning may be
irrelevant, since the exit and entry occur
virtually simultaneously. The 'state exit'
conjectured by Wilson seems inappropri-
ate for the end of 1.1, which closes quietly
in private conversation. Given that F's
musical directions are numerous and
otherwise accurately placed (*pace* Oxford's
reference to 4.7.70.1 which represents a
case of possible duplication but not mis-
placement), there is little reason to emend
F.

1.2 Historically York went to Sandal in late
1460 to gather his forces, 'well knowing,
that the Queen would spurn and impugn
the conclusions agreed and taken in this
parliament' (Hall Ggii^v, Holinshed
Qqqiv^r). As Wilson observes, however,
Shakespeare has York seeming 'to
go home happy with the settlement at
Westminster' (p. 133). Shakespeare may
have followed Holinshed in making this
change, with York's subsequent reversal
on the advice of Richard, to show York
perjuring himself: 'Many deemed that
[York's] miserable end chanced . . . as a
due punishment for breaking his oath of
allegiance unto his sovereign' (Qqqiv^r).
But the moral situation is complicated by
the arrival of the news, prior in narrative
time, of Margaret's armed opposition
immediately after York's private deci-

sion. Both sides perjure themselves
independently.

0.1 *Flourish* A different fanfare from the one
announcing Henry's arrival at 1.1.49.1.
On the Elizabethan stage the music would
have contained a leitmotif personally
identifying York (compare F *Lear*
2.2.355–6: 'CORNWALL What trumpet's
that? . . . REGAN I know't, my
sister's').

1–3 **Brother . . . forcible** In F if Montague is
'really' Salisbury, Edward and Richard
may be in agreement *against* him (see
l. 4). '[S]light contention' (l. 6) sounds
like an understatement, indicating a disagreement between the brothers and
Montague / Salisbury, and thus a new vs.
old generational division that anticipates
York's reluctance and perhaps explains
why Montague remains silent during the
scene until York changes his mind. In O,
by contrast, all three seem to argue over
who will raise the matter with York.

1 **youngest** Richard was in fact only eight in
1560 and is not mentioned by the chronicles until Edward IV's reign.
  leave (to speak)

2 **orator** spokesman, advocate. 'Play the
orator' was proverbial (Dent O74.1).

3 **forcible** compelling. Montague may have
contrary arguments.

3.1 **Enter . . . York** Historically, York prepared
for further fighting. See n. to 1.2 above.

4 **brother** See note to 1.1.14.
  strife difference in opinion (*OED* 2b, citing
this passage). In certain productions such
as the 1983 BBC, the quarrel is genuinely
heated, and York is cross as he enters. The

EDWARD

No quarrel but a slight contention.

YORK About what?

RICHARD

About that which concerns your grace and us,
The crown of England, father, which is yours.

YORK

Mine, boy? Not till King Henry be dead.   10

RICHARD

Your right depends not on his life or death.

EDWARD

Now you are heir, therefore enjoy it now.
By giving the house of Lancaster leave to breathe,
It will outrun you, father, in the end.

YORK

I took an oath that he should quietly reign.   15

EDWARD

But for a kingdom any oath may be broken;
I would break a thousand oaths to reign one year.

RICHARD

No, God forbid your grace should be forsworn.

YORK

I shall be if I claim by open war.

RICHARD

I'll prove the contrary, if you'll hear me speak.   20

1963–4 Hall–Barton and 1992 Ashland performances, on the other hand, sentimentalized the moment: the York brothers, including Rutland, wrestled playfully, each trying on a paper crown as they vied to speak.

6 **contention** verbal disagreement. A word with special resonance for Shakespeare's early audiences, since the first published version of *2 Henry VI* in 1594 was entitled *The First Part of the Contention Betwixt the Two Famous Houses of York and Lancaster*.

10 **Not . . . dead** In the 1952–3 Birmingham Rep production, York's scruples were belied by the chain mail, armour, and breastplate he was wearing underneath a full cloak.

11 **right** entitlement

13 **leave to breathe** an opportunity to recover their strength

14 **outrun** elude

16 **kingdom . . . broken** Proverbial idea: 'For a kingdom any law may be broken' (Dent K90). It occurs in the most famous Elizabethan play about civil war, *Gorboduc* (1561–2), which Shakespeare knew well: 'Know ye that lust [= desire] of kingdoms hath no law' (2.1.143). Faye L. Kelly discusses the 'broken oaths, broken vows, and perjury' that recur throughout *3 Henry VI* and define its vision of social chaos, in 'Oaths in Shakespeare's *Henry VI Plays*', *SQ* 24 (1973), 365–71; p. 366. The broken metre of this line may comment on Edward's ambitions.

17 **I would** Probably pronounced 'I'd'.

18 **forsworn** guilty of perjury

19 **claim** assert my right

YORK

Thou canst not son, it is impossible.

RICHARD

An oath is of no moment being not took
Before a true and lawful magistrate
That hath authority over him that swears.
Henry had none, but did usurp the place.   25
Then seeing 'twas he that made you to depose,
Your oath my lord is vain and frivolous.
Therefore to arms! And father do but think
How sweet a thing it is to wear a crown,
Within whose circuit is Elysium   30
And all that poets feign of bliss and joy.
Why do we linger thus? I cannot rest
Until the white rose that I wear be dyed
Even in the lukewarm blood of Henry's heart.

YORK

Richard enough, I will be king or die.   35

22–34 **An . . . heart** Commentators often describe Richard's argument as 'Machiavellian'. But this may be reading too much back from Richard's later speeches. If F revises O (Introduction, pp. 113–23), Shakespeare may have wished to defer clear Machiavellian resonances until Richard's revelations in 3.2, in order to heighten their dramatic impact. Here, Richard echoes Edward's proverbial assumption (l. 16) and simply argues away the oath on a specious technicality. Theatrically, his predecessors are Vice figures such as Dickon in *Gammer Gurton's Needle* and Ambidexter in *Cambises*. But their legacy of burlesque trickery is plainer in O, where 'Dick's' device is to show York 'the waie to saue your oath, | And dispossesse king *Henrie* from the crowne'. He does so, and then—comically?—contradicts himself (1.2.25+).

22 **moment . . . took** importance . . . taken

24 **authority** power to enforce obedience

25 **place** position (as king and thus chief magistrate)

26 **depose** swear under oath

27 **frivolous** valueless

29–31 **How . . . joy** Hart first observed that these lines echo Marlowe's 1 *Tamburlaine*: 'The thirst of reign and sweetness of a crown | . . . | Wills us to wear ourselves and never rest, | Until we reach the ripest fruit of all, | That perfect bliss and sole felicity, | The sweet fruition of an earthly crown' (2.7.12, 26–9). E. Pearlman sees the shift in poetic style as evidence that Shakespeare experimented with Richard's role at this stage in his composition (pp. 412–14). In the 1983 BBC production Richard speaks this passage softly in York's ear, using the difference in tone for a changed dramatic situation.

30 **circuit** circumference (*OED* 1, quoting this passage)
    Elysium Blissful part of the underworld for the spirits of classical heroes.

31 **feign** invent; represent in fiction; allege. Compare *As You Like It* 3.3.16–17: 'the truest poetry is the most feigning'. Given Richard's echoes of the morality Vice, an audience might also hear more negative meanings: pretend, deceive, dissemble.

33 **white rose** Emblem of the house of York. O calls explicitly for roses to be worn. See collation note for 1.1.0.4.

34 **lukewarm blood** having little warmth and thus lacking enthusiasm, passion. Another reference to Henry's 'coldness'. See above, 1.1.185 and note.

(*To Montague*) Brother, thou shalt to London presently
And whet on Warwick to this enterprise.
Thou Richard shalt to the Duke of Norfolk
And tell him privily of our intent.
You Edward shall unto my lord Cobham,   40
With whom the Kentishmen will willingly rise;
In them I trust, for they are soldiers
Witty, courteous, liberal, full of spirit.
While you are thus employed, what resteth more
But that I seek occasion how to rise,   45
And yet the King not privy to my drift,
Nor any of the house of Lancaster.

    Enter a Messenger

But stay, what news? Why com'st thou in such post?
MESSENGER
   The Queen with all the northern earls and lords
Intend here to besiege you in your castle.
She is hard by with twenty thousand men,   50
And therefore fortify your hold, my lord.

---

36 (*To Montague*)] OXFORD *following* RANN; *not in* F   40 unto my lord Cobham] F (*subs.*); to Edmund Brooke Lord Cobham O   44–5 more‸ | . . . rise,] ROWE (*subs.*); more? | . . . rise, F   47 Lancaster.] F (*subs.*); Lancaster? JOHNSON   47.1 a *Messenger*] O, THEOBALD (*subs.*); Gabriel F   49 MESSENGER] O (*Mes.*), HANMER; Gabriel F

36–8 **Brother . . . Norfolk** Warwick, Norfolk, and others were left in London by York 'to govern the king in his absence' (Hall Ggiii^v–iv^r, Holinshed Qqqiv^r–v; see ll. 56–9).
37 **whet** spur, urge
39 **privily** secretly
40 **Cobham** Edward Brooke, one of York's 'especial friends' who fought at Northampton. See Appendix A. Recent editors follow Cairncross in assuming F's name-change reflects 'an instance of late censorship' (*Textual Companion*, p. 201), partly on the observation that this line is unmetrical. Yet it has ten syllables and five main beats with a trochee in the final foot, just like l. 38 (see Wright, pp. 178–9, 197). And it seems likely that F corrects O's error. See Introduction, pp. 109–10.
41 **Kentishmen . . . rise** Because they had fought with Cobham at Northampton. See Appendix A, 1.2.40.
   rise take up arms

43 **Witty . . . spirit** In *2 Henry VI* Lord Say cites Julius Caesar's *Commentaries* describing Kent as 'the civil'st place of all this isle; | Sweet is the country, because full of riches; | The people liberal, valiant, active, wealthy' (4.7.60–2).
   Witty wise, discerning, sensible; intelligent, ingenious; skilful
   liberal generous, open-hearted; gentlemanly
44 **resteth more** else remains
45 **rise** (to power)
46 **drift** design, scheme; aim, intention
47.1 *Messenger* F's '*Enter Gabriel*' indicates that Shakespeare had in mind a specific actor, probably Gabriel Spencer: see Introduction, pp. 98–9.
48 **post** haste
49–51 **Queen . . . men** Shakespeare seems to have split the difference between the chroniclers' alternative figures. See Appendix A. In most productions York's sons greet this news jubilantly.
52 **hold** stronghold

YORK

Ay, with my sword. What, think'st thou that we fear
  them?
Edward and Richard, you shall stay with me,
My brother Montague shall post to London.   55
Let noble Warwick, Cobham, and the rest
Whom we have left protectors of the King,
With powerful policy strengthen themselves,
And trust not simple Henry nor his oaths.

MONTAGUE

Brother, I go. I'll win them, fear it not,   60
And thus most humbly I do take my leave.

                                          Exit Montague

       Enter Sir John Mortimer, and his brother Sir Hugh
       Mortimer

YORK

Sir John and Sir Hugh Mortimer, mine uncles,
You are come to Sandal in a happy hour.
The army of the Queen mean to besiege us.

SIR JOHN

She shall not need, we'll meet her in the field.   65

YORK

What, with five thousand men?

RICHARD

Ay, with five hundred, father, for a need.

61.2 *Sir John*] O, ROWE; *not in* F   61.2–3 *Sir Hugh Mortimer*] O, ROWE; *not in* F

53, 57 **we** York could be slipping into the royal plural here, as well as speaking collectively.

54 **Edward . . . me** Edward was supposed to follow York north after the Parliament in London, evidently to gather forces in the Marches and Wales on the way (see 2.1. 140). But before he arrived, York went against the advice of his counsellors and precipitously left his castle to engage the Queen's army. Edward learnt of York's death at Gloucester. See note to 2.1.45 below.

55 **brother . . . London** York repeats his command to Montague made at l. 36 while reversing his decision in regards to Edward and Richard. Shakespeare emphasizes that Montague does not par-

ticipate at Wakefield—thereby 'separating' him from his historical persona Salisbury, who did fight there—but goes to London to join Warwick, with whom he will reappear in the new persona of Marquis Montague in 2.1. The point is made again by Montague's leave-taking at ll. 60–1 (F only).

55 **post** hasten

58 **policy** prudence, discernment; expedience, cunning

59 **simple** weak, feeble; half-witted

60 **them** Presumably Norfolk, 'Warwick, Cobham, and the rest' since York has cancelled his first orders to Richard and Edward.
     fear doubt

63 **Sandal** York's castle near Wakefield.

67 **for a need** if need be

A woman's general, what should we fear?
> *A march afar off*

EDWARD

I hear their drums. Let's set our men in order
And issue forth and bid them battle straight.   70

YORK

Five men to twenty: though the odds be great,
I doubt not, uncle, of our victory.
Many a battle have I won in France
Whenas the enemy hath been ten to one;
Why should I not now have the like success?   75

> *Alarum. Exeunt*

1.3   *Enter the Earl of Rutland and his Tutor*

RUTLAND

Ah, whither shall I fly to escape their hands?
> *Enter Clifford and Soldiers*

Ah tutor, look where bloody Clifford comes.

CLIFFORD

Chaplain away, thy priesthood saves thy life.
As for the brat of this accursèd Duke

---

72 uncle] F; uncles DYCE *conj.*   75.1 *Exeunt*] THEOBALD; *Exit* F
   1.3] CAPELL; *not in* F   0.1 *the Earl of Rutland*] O (*the yong Earle of Rutland*); *Rutland* F   1.1
Enter Clifford] This edition; *after l. 2 in* F, O   *and Soldiers*] THEOBALD; *not in* F

---

68 **woman's** F's 'womans' could indicate
(a) woman is (b) womanish. 'If I have
not kept myself within walls for fear of a
great and strong prince, . . . wouldest
thou that I [would] for dread of a scolding
woman, whose weapon is only her
tongue, and her nayles' (Hall reporting
York's words, Ggii^v).
68.1 **afar off** i.e. played on drums off stage,
sounding as if in the distance
69–70 **Let's . . . straight** See Appendix A.
70 **issue forth** sally out (*OED v.* 1a, citing this
line)
   straight immediately
71 **Five . . . twenty** Actors speak this convey-
ing various degrees of doubt. The BBC's
Bernard Hill glanced at the camera,
acknowledging a kind of fatal inevit-
ability.
73 **France** Where York was regent. See *1
Henry VI* 4.1.162–3 and Appendix A.
74 **Whenas** when

1.3 Based on an account in Hall containing
first-person dialogue, which Holinshed
reports in shortened form. See Appendix
A. In the 1963–4 Hall–Barton and
other productions, Rutland wore the
paper crown introduced in the previous
scene, its suggestions of children's games
and playful innocence now terribly
vulnerable. The 1994 RSC production
made use of off-stage sounds to convey
this shift in mood, opening the scene
with morning birdsong. This was
shattered by a steely clash at Clifford's
entry, and the scene ended with galloping
and stamping horses, wolves and
hounds.
4 **this** F's word, contrasting with O's more
conventional 'that', indicates the degree
to which Clifford identifies York's presence in his son, and perhaps indicates
the intensity of the actor's gaze at this
moment. See l. 18.

Whose father slew my father, he shall die.   5

TUTOR

And I, my lord, will bear him company.

CLIFFORD

Soldiers, away with him.

TUTOR

Ah Clifford, murder not this innocent child,
Lest thou be hated both of God and man.

Exit dragged off by Soldiers

CLIFFORD

How now, is he dead already?   10
Or is it fear that makes him close his eyes?
I'll open them.

RUTLAND

So looks the pent-up lion o'er the wretch
That trembles under his devouring paws,
And so he walks, insulting o'er his prey,   15
And so he comes to rend his limbs asunder.
Ah gentle Clifford, kill me with thy sword
And not with such a cruel threatening look.
Sweet Clifford, hear me speak before I die:
I am too mean a subject for thy wrath;   20
Be thou revenged on men, and let me live.

9.1 *dragged . . . Soldiers*] THEOBALD (*subs.*); *not in* F

6 **I . . . company** The Tutor may kneel with Rutland, or make some other gesture of solidarity. In the 1952–3 Birmingham Rep production, he was kept alive and held to watch the murder.

9 **of** by

10 **How . . . already?** The chronicles report that Rutland knelt, holding up his hands and unable to speak for fear. Lines 36–7 may be an alternative point for him to adopt this posture ('So looks . . . o'er' at l. 13 need not be taken literally, or may refer to a difference in height between adult and boy actors). Modern productions have had Rutland standing tensely with arms at his sides, or crouching with hands joined in prayer, or lying in foetal position facing the audience. Clifford may open his eyes with his hands, or by touching his head with his dagger.

13–18 **So . . . look** 'In this act the Lord Clifford was accounted a tyrant, and no gen-

tleman, for the property of the lion, which is a furious and an unreasonable beast, is to be cruel to them that withstand him, and gentle to such as prostrate or humiliate themselves before him' (Hall Ggiii[v]). Shakespeare reverses this proverbial lore.

13 **pent-up** i.e. confined and starved

15 **insulting** in scornful triumph

16 **rend . . . asunder** tear . . . apart

20 **mean** unworthy

21, 27 **revenged . . . revenge** Immediately before the passage recounting Rutland's death, both Hall and Holinshed observe that the heirs and kin of those killed at Wakefield 'revenged their deaths within four months' (Hall Ggiii[r], Holinshed Qqqiv[r]). See Appendix A.

21 **men** Although both chroniclers state he was 12, Rutland was actually York's second son, born in 1443, aged 17 at this time.

CLIFFORD

In vain thou speak'st, poor boy: my father's blood
Hath stopped the passage where thy words should enter.

RUTLAND

Then let my father's blood open it again:
He is a man, and Clifford cope with him.   25

CLIFFORD

Had I thy brethren here, their lives and thine
Were not revenge sufficient for me;
No, if I digged up thy forefathers' graves
And hung their rotten coffins up in chains,
It could not slake mine ire nor ease my heart.   30
The sight of any of the house of York
Is as a fury to torment my soul,
And till I root out their accursèd line
And leave not one alive, I live in hell.
Therefore—   35

        He lifts his hand

RUTLAND

O let me pray before I take my death!
To thee I pray: sweet Clifford pity me.

CLIFFORD

Such pity as my rapier's point affords.

RUTLAND

I never did thee harm, why wilt thou slay me?

CLIFFORD

Thy father hath.

35.1 *He lifts his hand*] JOHNSON (*subs.*); *not in* F   37 To] F; ⌈*Kneeling*⌉ To OXFORD (*conj.* Walker)

22–3 **my . . . enter** See *Macbeth* 1.5.42–3,
  'Make thick my blood, | Stop up th'access
  and passage to remorse'.
25 **and** 'to give emphasis and call attention to
  an additional circumstance' (Abbott ¶95);
  thus, 'and so should'.
  cope fight
26 ff. **Had . . . Clifford** himself often kneels or
  crouches, speaking face to face with Rutland, their intimacy intensified.
27 **sufficient** Pronounced as four syllables.
32 **fury** Alluding to the classical Furies, the
  gods' agents of vengeance, who sometimes included Nemesis.
38 **rapier** The word was used loosely in the
  sixteenth century to describe a wide vari-

ety of blades of different shapes and sizes,
but in England it often denoted 'a long
sword which, though designed both for
cutting and thrusting, placed emphasis
on the use of the point rather than the
edge' (Sydney Anglo, *The Martial Arts of
Renaissance Europe* (New Haven and London, 2000), p. 99). Hall and Holinshed
report that Clifford used a dagger.
40 **Thy . . . born** (a) Clifford may imply that
York has determined Rutland's fate
because he killed Old Clifford in 1455 at
St Albans. Strictly, Rutland's plea is
anachronistic; see note to l. 21; (b) Old
Clifford's death occurred in the conflicts
of the preceding play, before Rutland was

175

RUTLAND   But 'twas ere I was born.   40

Thou hast one son: for his sake pity me,

Lest in revenge thereof, sith God is just,

He be as miserably slain as I.

Ah, let me live in prison all my days,

And when I give occasion of offence,   45

Then let me die, for now thou hast no cause.

CLIFFORD

No cause? Thy father slew my father, therefore die.

He stabs him

RUTLAND

Dii faciant laudis summa sit ista tuae.   *He dies*

CLIFFORD

Plantagenet, I come Plantagenet,

And this thy son's blood cleaving to my blade   50

Shall rust upon my weapon till thy blood,

Congealed with this, do make me wipe off both.

Exit with Rutland's body

1.4   *Alarum. Enter Richard, Duke of York*

YORK

The army of the Queen hath got the field,

My uncles both are slain in rescuing me,

And all my followers to the eager foe

Turn back and fly, like ships before the wind

Or lambs pursued by hunger-starvèd wolves.   5

47.1 *He stabs him*] ROWE (*subs.*); *not in* F   48 *Dii*] F; *Di* DYCE *and some editors   He dies*]
THEOBALD (*subs.*); *not in* F   52.1 *with . . . body*] OXFORD (*adding* '[*and soldiers*]'); *not in* F
1.4] CAPELL; *not in* F

'born' dramatically; (c) Clifford ignores
Rutland's question and responds to the
idea of Yorkist injury, which loosely
might be said to predate Rutland's
birth.

42 **sith** since
48 *Dii . . . tuae* 'May the gods grant that this
be your crowning praise,' exclaims Phyllis
after Demophoon has seduced her and
failed to keep his promise of marriage
(Ovid, *Heroides*, ii. 66).
49 **Plantagenet** i.e. York
I come In the 1983 BBC production, Clifford, speaking to the camera in close-up,
streaks his face with his bloody sword

over his eye, visually reiterating his
revenge obsession ('an eye for an eye
. . .').
1.4.1–29 In modern performances, York
usually enters wounded and exhausted,
and collapses on an open stage. The 1987
ESC production added to the sense of
doom by having him wrench out the
empty bullet cartridge of his rifle.
1 **got** won
3 **eager** hungry (term from falconry; *OED*
7); fierce; angry; full of keen desire or
appetite
4 **back** their backs
5 **starved** famished; emaciated from lack of
food

My sons God knows what hath bechancèd them,
But this I know, they have demeaned themselves
Like men born to renown by life or death.
Three times did Richard make a lane to me
And thrice cried 'Courage father, fight it out!'   10
And full as oft came Edward to my side
With purple falchion painted to the hilt
In blood of those that had encountered him;
And when the hardiest warriors did retire,
Richard cried 'Charge and give no foot of ground!'   15
And Edward cried 'A crown, or else a glorious tomb,
A sceptre, or an earthly sepulchre!'
With this we charged again, but out alas,
We botched again, as I have seen a swan
With bootless labour swim against the tide   20
And spend her strength with over-matching waves.
    A short alarum within
Ah hark, the fatal followers do pursue,
And I am faint, and cannot fly their fury,
And were I strong, I would not shun their fury.
The sands are numbered that makes up my life;   25

8 born] ROWE; borne F   16 And Edward] OXFORD (*conj*. Taylor); And F; Ned COLLIER 1853; Edward CAIRNCROSS (*conj*. Lettsom); He KINNEAR *conj*.; *preceded by a lost line referring to Edward* CAMBRIDGE *conj*.   19 botched] This edition *following* COLLIER *conj*.; bodg'd F; budg'd WILSON (*conj*. Johnson)

6 **sons** Historically only Rutland was present at the Battle of Wakefield. Edward was in the Marches (1.2.54–5 and note); Richard and George were still young boys.
7 **demeaned** conducted, employed (not in a negative sense)
8 **born to renown** destined from birth to become famous. F's spelling 'borne' could also mean 'carried to high distinction'.
9 **make a lane** i.e. battle his way straight through the enemy
12 **purple . . . painted** bloody
falchion Poetically, any kind of sword; strictly, curved with a single outside edge.
14 **hardiest** most courageous, daring
retire retreat
16 **Edward** Probably inadvertently omitted in F, and meant to complete the symmetry of York's report of Richard and Edward in ll. 9–12. If not, the words elaborate on Richard's thoughts at

1.2.29–30, and hint at his ambitions (Hattaway).
18 **out alas** Expression of anger and contempt.
19 **botched** F's 'bodg'd' is a variant of 'botched' = bungled. While *OED* does not cite examples of intransitive uses of either verb, the sense of blundering wearily is clear from the swan metaphor. Many editors have preferred *OED*'s secondary entry listing 'bodge' as a variant spelling of 'budge', which meant 'stir' or 'flinch'.
20 **bootless** futile
21 **spend . . . with over-matching** exhaust . . . against overpowering
25 **sands** As in an hour-glass. The implied image of heaping sand creates an association with a small mound ('butt', l. 29) and York's molehill, l. 67.
makes make. The combination of singular verb and plural noun is normal Elizabethan grammar.

Here must I stay, and here my life must end.
> *Enter Queen Margaret, Clifford, Northumberland, the*
> *young Prince Edward and Soldiers*
Come bloody Clifford, rough Northumberland,
I dare your quenchless fury to more rage:
I am your butt, and I abide your shot.

NORTHUMBERLAND

Yield to our mercy, proud Plantagenet.   30

CLIFFORD

Ay, to such mercy as his ruthless arm
With downright payment showed unto my father.
Now Phaethon hath tumbled from his car
And made an evening at the noontide prick.

YORK

My ashes, as the Phoenix', may bring forth   35
A bird that will revenge upon you all,
And in that hope, I throw mine eyes to heaven
Scorning whate'er you can afflict me with.
Why come you not? What, multitudes, and fear?

CLIFFORD

So cowards fight when they can fly no further,   40
So doves do peck the falcon's piercing talons,
So desperate thieves, all hopeless of their lives,
Breathe out invectives 'gainst the officers.

26.1 *Queen Margaret*] MALONE; *the Queene* F   26.2 *Prince Edward*] RIVERSIDE; *Prince* F; *omit-*
ted in O

29 **butt** mark for archery practice; strictly,
the mound on which the target is
set.
abide await; submit to endure, suffer
32 **downright payment** sheer vindictiveness
(recalling the sense of a vertical stroke at
1.1.12)
33 **Phaethon** Son of Apollo or Phoebus, the
sun god. When he lost control of his
father's chariot he was destroyed by Zeus
for fear of setting the world on fire. See
Ovid, *Metamorphoses*, i. 944–ii. 415. A
conventional emblem of rash aspiration,
especially apt here because the sun was
also a heraldic badge of York. See
2.1.39–40 and 2.6.10–12.
car chariot
34 **made an evening** i.e. fallen into darkness;
declined into the closing period of one's
life

34 **noontide prick** mark on a sundial indicating noon (*OED*, *prick*, *sb.* 2b, citing this
passage). 'Prick' could mean the apex or
highest point, or the bull's-eye of a target
(see l. 29).
35 **Phoenix** Mythical Arabian bird said to be
able to resurrect itself after spontaneously
combusting. Depicted rising from the
flames of a pyre in Geoffrey Whitney's *A
Choice of Emblems* (1586, p. 177), which
Shakespeare knew.
36 **bird** i.e. son. See also 5.6.15.
37 **I . . . heaven** Compare Psalm 123: 1: 'Unto
thee lift I up mine eyes, O thou that
dwellest in the heavens' (*BCP*).
throw cast
40–2 Proverbial: 'Despair makes cowards
courageous' (Dent D216).
43 **Breathe out** speak passionately
officers executioners; jailers

YORK

O Clifford, but bethink thee once again
And in thy thought o'errun my former time,   45
And if thou canst for blushing, view this face
And bite thy tongue that slanders him with cowardice,
Whose frown hath made thee faint and fly ere this.

CLIFFORD

I will not bandy with thee word for word,
But buckler with thee blows twice two for one.   50
He draws his sword

MARGARET

Hold, valiant Clifford, for a thousand causes
I would prolong a while the traitor's life.
Wrath makes him deaf. Speak thou, Northumberland.

NORTHUMBERLAND

Hold, Clifford, do not honour him so much
To prick thy finger, though to wound his heart.   55
What valour were it when a cur doth grin
For one to thrust his hand between his teeth,
When he might spurn him with his foot away?
It is war's prize to take all vantages,

46 And∧ ... blushing,] RIVERSIDE; and∧ ... canst, ... blushing, F; and, ... canst∧ ... blushing, THEOBALD   50.1 *He draws his sword*] JOHNSON (*subs.*); *not in* F   51 MARGARET] This edition; *Queene* F (*and subs. throughout this scene*)

44 **bethink thee** reflect in your own mind
45 **o'errun** go over
46 **And if** if indeed (Abbott ¶105)
   canst for blushing can undeterred by shame
48 **faint** take fright
49 **bandy** give and take; argue obstinately, wrangle (*OED v.* 6c, citing this passage)
50 **buckler** Citing only this passage *OED v.* 2 defines: 'ward [off] or catch blows'. But this seems too defensive for the sense here, which is nearer to O's 'buckle' meaning 'grapple, fight closely'.
51 **causes** reasons
52 **I ... life** In the 1983 BBC production after entering, Margaret stood smiling at York, drinking in the prospect of having him at her mercy, and panting in anticipation.
53 **Wrath ... deaf** Clifford is still itching to fight, and may be restrained by Northumberland and others. The phrase is a translation of Erasmus's *fervore surdus*

describing 'a barbarously cruel schoolmaster' who like a 'butcher' flogged a boy mercilessly (Jones, p. 184 n. 1).
54–60 Northumberland appeals to Clifford's chivalric pride—fighting against 'unequal' odds is dishonourable—but then undercuts himself by claiming that war permits expediency.
55 **prick ... heart** Literalizes and reverses the proverb 'The pricking of thy finger is the piercing of thy heart' (Dent P571.1). 'Prick thy finger' = make even as much as a trifling effort.
56 **were it** would it be
   cur ... grin dog ... bare its teeth (in anger)
57 **thrust ... teeth** i.e. to attempt to choke or throttle it; 'his . . . his' = one's . . . its. Compare *2 Henry IV* 2.4.125–6: 'I'll thrust my knife in your mouldy chaps'.
59 **prize** privilege (*OED sb.*[1] 3b, citing this passage)
   vantages advantages; opportunities

And ten to one is no impeach of valour.   60
  They lay hands on York, who struggles

CLIFFORD
Ay, ay, so strives the woodcock with the gin.

NORTHUMBERLAND
So doth the coney struggle in the net.
  York is overpowered

YORK
So triumph thieves upon their conquered booty,
So true men yield with robbers, so o'er-matched.

NORTHUMBERLAND
What would your grace have done unto him now?   65

MARGARET
Brave warriors, Clifford and Northumberland,
Come make him stand upon this molehill here,
That raught at mountains with outstretchèd arms

60.1 *They . . . struggles*] JOHNSON; *not in* F; Fight and take him o, PELICAN   62.1 *York is over-powered*] CHAMBERS; *not in* F; *In the Struggle* York *is taken Prisoner* THEOBALD; *falls* [*i.e. drops*] *his Sword* CAPELL, *after l.* 65

60 **ten to one** for ten to attack one
  impeach calling into question, discredit to (*OED sb.* 3, citing this passage)
60.1 *They lay hands* In many productions the soldiers approach by taunting the surrounded York with pikes and mocking his vulnerable position. As Hattaway observes (note to l. 60), a director may wish to make the action of this moment match the Messenger's description at 2.1.50 ff.; so one of the soldiers may be identified as the person who later becomes the Messenger, as the 1977 RSC production signalled by having a soldier linger at the end of the scene.
61 **with the gin** against the snare or trap
62 **coney** rabbit. Like the woodcock, proverbially easy to catch. F leaves the kind of struggle here undetermined. O's '*Fight*' indicates a more open clash. The trapped-animal metaphors, however, suggest the exhausted York is subdued quickly and relatively easily (but perhaps also brutally).
63 **triumph** rejoice, 'insult upon an advantage gained (J[ohnson].)' (*OED v.* 4).
64 **true** principled; virtuous, honourable; real
67 ff. **molehill . . .** Derives from Holinshed's account of Whethamsted's alternative version of York's death, which recalls

Christ's passion and Calvary: 'Some write that the duke was taken alive and in derision caused to stand upon a molehill, on whose head they put a garland instead of a crown, which they had fashioned and made of sedges or bulrushes; and having so crowned him with that garland, they kneeled down afore him (as the Jews did unto Christ) in scorn, saying to him: "Hail king without rule, hail king without heritage, hail duke and prince without people or possessions" (Qqqiv^r). Molehills could symbolize noble humility (Dent K55) or contempt for misguided ambition. If the molehill is not imaginary, as it often is in modern productions, it may be represented by a small mound, platform, or low stool. York's raised position may also affect the dynamic of his exchange with Margaret, since she must speak up to him, and on film this may be reinforced by alternating camera angles. The 1966 Ashland production added a bundle of faggots to the molehill to suggest martyrdom.
68 **raught** reached out, grasped; strove (for)
  mountains high places; i.e. supreme offices, positions, contrasting with the triviality of molehills (cf. 'making a mountain out of a molehill' (Tilley M1035)).

Yet parted but the shadow with his hand.
What, was it you that would be England's king?   70
Was't you that revelled in our parliament
And made a preachment of your high descent?
Where are your mess of sons to back you now,
The wanton Edward and the lusty George?
And where's that valiant crookback prodigy,   75
Dicky your boy, that with his grumbling voice
Was wont to cheer his dad in mutinies?
Or with the rest, where is your darling, Rutland?
Look York, I stained this napkin with the blood
That valiant Clifford with his rapier's point   80
Made issue from the bosom of the boy;
And if thine eyes can water for his death,
I give thee this to dry thy cheeks withal.

78 darling,] F; darling‚ O   83 withal.] F; withal. | *Throwing it to him* COLLIER 1853 (*subs.*)

68 **outstretchèd arms** In the 1977 Ashland production, Clifford and Northumberland lashed York's arms lengthwise to a wooden pole or small beam, and in the 1963–4 Hall–Barton version he was chained to crossed poles in the form of an X, in both cases heightening the scene's crucifixion associations.

69 **parted** took for his gain
shadow semblance; fleeting appearance (as opposed to substance); actor's representation

71 **revelled** made merry like masquers or actors, like a lord of misrule or playerking. Sandra Billington discusses the relationship between traditional festive mockery and this scene's 'vicious king game' in *Mock Kings in Medieval Society and Renaissance Drama* (Oxford, 1991), pp. 145–6.

72 **preachment** preachy discourse, tiresome exhortation. Recalling York's 1460 oration to Parliament rehearsing his lineal claim to the throne, reported in Holinshed.

73 **mess** party of four persons (originally at a banquet; *OED sb.* 5, citing this passage)

74 **wanton** Holinshed's chapter on Edward IV quotes More's *History of Richard III* that Edward 'was of youth greatly given to fleshly wantonness' (Uvvviᴿ). See also 3.2 and 3.3.
lusty cheerful; handsome; youthfully vigorous (spoken ironically); lustful

75 **crookback** hunchback

75 **prodigy** freak of nature; ominous monster

76 **Dicky** See note to 5.5.35.
grumbling faintly growling; murmuring discontentedly; uttering dull inarticulate sounds. Perhaps 'a hint to the actor' (Wilson).

77 **cheer . . . mutinies** delight; encourage, incite (to) . . . disputes, quarrels; rebellions

79 **stained** discoloured; defiled; soiled. In the 1996 Washington Shakespeare Theatre production, Margaret had wiped the blood off Clifford's bayonet during her preceding lines.
napkin handkerchief. For Elizabethan playgoers it would recall Hieronimo's bloodstained cloth in Kyd's *The Spanish Tragedy*, in which it becomes a memory-token of his murdered son. For its development as a stage property see Marion Lomax, *Stage images and traditions: Shakespeare to Ford* (Cambridge, 1987), pp. 34–7.

81 **issue** In the context of the crucifixion imagery surrounding York's death, a word associated with the blood and water that came forth from Christ's pierced body (John 19: 34).

83 **give thee this** Margaret may toss the napkin over York's neck or shoulder, or throw it in his face, as in the 1952–3 Birmingham Rep and 1963–4 Hall–Barton productions.
withal with

Alas poor York, but that I hate thee deadly,
I should lament thy miserable state.   85
I prithee grieve to make me merry, York.
What, hath thy fiery heart so parched thine entrails
That not a tear can fall for Rutland's death?
Why art thou patient, man? Thou shouldst be mad,
And I to make thee mad, do mock thee thus.   90
Stamp, rave, and fret, that I may sing and dance.
Thou wouldst be feed, I see, to make me sport.
York cannot speak unless he wear a crown.
A crown for York; and lords bow low to him.
Hold you his hands whilst I do set it on.   95
        She puts a paper crown on his head
Ay, marry sir, now looks he like a king.

95.1 *She puts . . . head*] ROWE (*subs.*); *not in* F

84 **but . . . deadly** Recalls Kyd's Perseda as
she vows revenge: 'A kiss I grant thee,
though I hate thee deadly', *Solimon and
Perseda* 5.4.67 (Hattaway).
  but were it not (Abbott ¶127)

86 **I . . . York** '[Peggy Ashcroft as Margaret's]
portrayal of weakness in cruelty, helpless-
ness in victory . . . [made] other barbarous
episodes [seem] trivial and shocking in
contrast. The cruel humour of the lines
was played close to hysteria: "I prithee
grieve to make me merry" was an almost
necessary request to excuse Margaret's
impulse towards helpless laughter, a
physical and emotional relief and a breakdown of control' (John Russell Brown,
'Three Kinds of Shakespeare', *Shakespeare
Survey* 18 (1965), 147–55, p. 152).
  grieve . . . merry With 'sport' below (l. 92)
recalls the Elizabethan 'sport' of bear-
baiting.

87 **entrails** internal parts 'regarded as the
seat of the emotions' (*OED sb.*[1] 4, citing
this passage)

89 **Why . . . patient** In the 1963–4 Hall–
Barton and 1987 ESC productions, York
was shocked speechless after receiving
the napkin, and stared transfixed with
grief. Only gradually could he regain an
awareness of his own situation. Bernard
Hill's stillness in the 1983 BBC version,
on the other hand, was a conscious effort
of will: he knew the reaction Margaret
wanted and was grimly determined not to
give her satisfaction.

89 **mad** furious

92 **feed** paid (like a performer). Penny
Downie in the 1988 RSC production conveyed a clear impression of having to
improvise lines in the face of York's
non-reaction.
  make me provide me with

93 **cannot speak** A Passion detail: Christ is
conspicuously silent.

94 **bow low** '. . . and [they] bowed the knee
before him, and mocked him, saying,
Hail, King of the Jews!' (Matthew 27: 29,
Bishops' Bible). In the 1983 BBC production the soldiers murmur 'Hail, hail' as
they kneel. Margaret may also curtsy. See
next note.

95.1 *paper crown* In both Holinshed and
Hall, York is crowned with paper after he
has been beheaded. Shakespeare substitutes this detail for the 'garland' Holinshed mentions (see note to ll. 67 ff.) when
York is being mocked as Christ was
(Matthew 27: 27–31): 'Lord Clifford . . .
caused [York's] head to be stricken off,
and set on it a crown of paper, fixed it on a
pole, and presented it to the Queen'
(Holinshed Qqqiv[r], Hall Ggiii[v]). Richard
recalls this moment in *Richard III* 1.3.172.
Margaret usually gets the paper from one
of the soldiers. It may be preformed as a
crown, or she may tear it into shape, as in
the 1987 ESC production.

96 **marry** indeed (spoken ironically); an
oath, originally standing for 'by the Virgin Mary'.

Ay, this is he that took King Henry's chair,
And this is he was his adopted heir.
But how is it that great Plantagenet
Is crowned so soon and broke his solemn oath? 100
As I bethink me, you should not be king
Till our King Henry had shook hands with death.
And will you pale your head in Henry's glory
And rob his temples of the diadem
Now in his life, against your holy oath? 105
O 'tis a fault too too unpardonable.
Off with the crown, and with the crown his head,
And whilst we breathe, take time to do him dead.

CLIFFORD
That is my office, for my father's sake.

MARGARET
Nay stay, let's hear the orisons he makes. 110

YORK
She-wolf of France, but worse than wolves of France,
Whose tongue more poisons than the adder's tooth,
How ill-beseeming is it in thy sex
To triumph like an Amazonian trull

---

97 **chair** i.e. of state. See 1.1.51.
99–100 Holinshed records that some observers linked York's death to his broken oath: 'Many deemed that this miserable end chanced to the Duke of York, as a due punishment for breaking his oath of allegiance unto his sovereign lord King Henry: but others held him discharged thereof, because he obtained a dispensation from the pope' (Holinshed Qqqiv^f).
101 **bethink me** recall
102 **shook hands with** greeted. Proverbial (Dent SS6).
103 **pale** encircle
105 **life** lifetime
107 **Off with the crown** Margaret may knock the paper crown off York's head, as in the BBC version. Alternatively see l. 164.
108 **breathe** rest, relax
   do him dead put him to death (*OED*, *do, v.* 22)
109 **office** particular duty
110 **orisons** prayers
111–42 **She-wolf . . . remorseless** 'a formal rhetorical invective on Margaret's parentage, personal appearance, character, conduct, and nationality' (Cairncross).
111 **She-wolf . . . wolves** Cairncross suggests that York's comparison may rest on an underlying meaning of the Latin word for wolf, *lupa*, meaning 'prostitute', as defined by Cooper's *Thesaurus* (*c*.1580). See 'trull', l. 114 and note.
112 **tongue . . . tooth** Compare Psalm 140: 3: 'They have sharpened their tongues like a serpent: Adders' poison is under their lips'.
114 **triumph** rejoice at another's defeat or distress
   Amazonian trull female warrior prostitute. The Amazons, a mythical race of women warriors believed to live in Scythia, sometimes were regarded as wondrously admirable, but more often as abominably freakish for inverting 'natural' masculine dominance over women. Joan La Pucelle is characterized in both ways in *1 Henry VI*, while the Countess of Auvergne vows to emulate a classical exemplar, Tomyris, triumphing over Cyrus (1.3.83, 2.3.6).

Upon their woes, whom fortune captivates.   115
But that thy face is vizard-like, unchanging,
Made impudent with use of evil deeds,
I would essay, proud queen, to make thee blush.
To tell thee whence thou cam'st, of whom derived,
Were shame enough to shame thee, wert thou not
    shameless.   120
Thy father bears the type of King of Naples,
Of both the Sicils, and Jerusalem,
Yet not so wealthy as an English yeoman.
Hath that poor monarch taught thee to insult?
It needs not nor it boots thee not, proud queen,   125
Unless the adage must be verified,
That beggars mounted run their horse to death.
'Tis beauty that doth oft make women proud,
But God he knows thy share thereof is small.
'Tis virtue that doth make them most admired,   130
The contrary doth make thee wondered at.
'Tis government that makes them seem divine,

122 Sicils,] F; *Sissiles*ₐ O *and most editors*

115 **their woes** the woes of them (Abbott
¶219)
   fortune Fortuna, goddess of chance; accidental mishap, disaster
   captivates subjugates; takes prisoner;
enchants, enthralls
116 **vizard-like** mask-like, impassive; like a
prostitute (who wore masks in public
(*OED* 5)); like certain figures in stage
plays (e.g. the Vice; see Dekker, *Old Fortu-
natus*, 1.3). With 'unchanging', it may
cue the actor's reaction to York: the faces
of both the BBC's and the ESC's Margaret
did not flinch during his agony—a coun-
terfoil to York's initial reaction to her (see
note to l. 89 above). Peggy Ashcroft in
1963, on the other hand, laughed and
fleered, gesturing with her hands 'come
on, give me more!', until 'life-blood of the
child' (l. 138), when she became shaken
and driven nearly to weeping, seeming to
have a premonition of being in the same
situation.
117 **impudent** shameless, unblushing; inso-
lently disrespectful
   use habitual practice
118 **essay . . . blush** venture . . . feel some
guilt for offending propriety, decency

119 **derived** descended
121 **type** distinguishing title (*OED sb.*[1] 3, citing this passage); type = highest dignity
(*OED sb.*[1] 2) (possibly spoken ironically)
   Naples (which included southern Italy)
122 **both the Sicils** (King of) Sardinia and
Sicily
123 **not so wealthy** One objection against
Margaret marrying King Henry in *2
Henry VI* was her lack of a dowry: 'King
René, whose large style | Agrees not with
the leanness of his purse' (1.1.108–9).
   yeoman Farmer owning his own small
estate, just below the rank of gentleman.
See Appendix A.
124 **insult** exult scornfully, abusively; triumph contemptuously
125 **boots** serves
126 **adage . . . verified** proverbial wisdom
. . . exemplified; proved true
127 **beggars . . . death** 'Set a beggar on horse-
back and he will ride gallop' (Dent B238).
York charges Margaret with overreaching
and self-destructive social ambition.
131 **wondered at** a notorious object of
astonishment
132 **government** self-discipline; ethical conduct, decency, discretion

The want thereof makes thee abominable.
Thou art as opposite to every good
As the Antipodes are unto us,   135
Or as the south to the Septentrion.
O tiger's heart wrapped in a woman's hide,
How couldst thou drain the life-blood of the child
To bid the father wipe his eyes withal,
And yet be seen to bear a woman's face?   140
Women are soft, mild, pitiful, and flexible;
Thou stern, obdurate, flinty, rough, remorseless.
Bidst thou me rage? Why now thou hast thy wish.
Wouldst have me weep? Why now thou hast thy will,
For raging wind blows up incessant showers,   145
And when the rage allays, the rain begins.
These tears are my sweet Rutland's obsequies,
And every drop cries vengeance for his death
'Gainst thee fell Clifford, and thee false Frenchwoman.

NORTHUMBERLAND
Beshrew me, but his passions moves me so   150

137 tiger's] ROWE (*subs.*); Tygres F; tygress' CAPELL   150 passions moves] F1; passions move
F2; passion moves CAMBRIDGE

132 **divine** i.e. because such personal conduct reflects the cosmic order guided by
   the divine attribute of reason

133 **abominable** Believed by early modern
   commentators to derive from Latin *ab
   homine*, 'away from man[kind], inhuman, beastly' (*OED*).
135 **Antipodes** dwellers on the opposite side
   of the globe
136 **Septentrion** north. Literally, the seven
   stars of the Plough or Big Dipper.
137 **O . . . hide** The first Shakespearian line to
   be misquoted and parodied, by Robert
   Greene in his 1592 deathbed attack on
   Shakespeare. See Introduction, pp. 124–5.
138 **life-blood . . . child** York may glance or
   gesture to Prince Edward to threaten
   Margaret personally.
139 **withal** with that
141 **Women . . . flexible** Echoes John Knox's
   opinion that a woman is a 'tender creature, flexible, soft and pitiful' (*The First
   Blast of the Trumpet Against the Monstrous Regiment of Women* (Geneva,
   1558; facsimile reprint New York, 1972),
   sig. D1ᵛ).

141 **pitiful** full of pity; compassionate, merci-
   ful, tender
   flexible accommodating, adaptable;
   amenable to persuasion; not rigid
142 **obdurate** Accented on the second syllable; hard-hearted, deaf to pleading,
   unbending (*OED* 1b, citing this passage);
   stubbornly wicked.
   flinty hard, impenetrable; unfeeling
   rough violent; overbearing, uncivil; harsh
145 Proverbial: 'After wind comes rain'
   (Tilley T275).
146 Proverbial: 'Small rain lays [allays =
   abates] great winds' (Tilley R16).
   rage violent storm; extreme sorrow, pain
147 **obsequies** funeral rites; memorial service
149 **fell** cruel
150 **Beshrew me** may I be blamed, cursed.
   If Margaret has momentarily softened
   towards York, Northumberland's sympathy may rekindle her ferocity. Or if she
   has remained impassive, it may steel her
   anger.
   but unless
   passions sufferings; passionate speech or
   emotional outburst. Most editors emend
   to 'passion' on the grounds that Shake-

That hardly can I check my eyes from tears.

YORK

That face of his the hungry cannibals
Would not have touched, would not have stained with
    blood,
But you are more inhuman, more inexorable,
O ten times more than tigers of Hyrcania.   155
See, ruthless queen, a hapless father's tears.
This cloth thou dipped'st in blood of my sweet boy,
And I with tears do wash the blood away.
Keep thou the napkin and go boast of this,
And if thou tell'st the heavy story right,   160
Upon my soul the hearers will shed tears,
Yea, even my foes will shed fast-falling tears
And say 'Alas it was a piteous deed!'
There, take the crown, and with the crown my curse,
And in thy need such comfort come to thee   165
As now I reap at thy too cruel hand.

153 with] F1; the roses just with F2   159 this,] F; this: | *He gives back the handkerchief* JOHNSON
(*after l.* 163)   164 curse,] F; curse, | *Giving back the paper crown* DYCE

speare does not use the plural form elsewhere for the singular thought (*Textual
Companion*, p. 201). But this ignores Q2
Hamlet 2.1.106–7 ('As oft as any passions
under heaven | That does afflict our
natures'), as well as the fact that Shakespeare does not use the word in the same
sense anywhere else. Grammatically, the
plural noun with singular verb combination 'is extremely common in the Folio'
(Abbott ¶333). Moreover the plural form
as a collective singular is attested by
numerous *OED* citations, and the editors
of F2–4, while modernizing the grammatical agreement, did not reject the
plural form. Nor can F be a compositorial
error, since O also reads 'passions' and
this is not an area where editors have
theorized Q3 contamination of F.

150 **moves** move

151 **check** stop

152 **cannibals** Referring originally to the supposedly human-eating Caribs of the West
Indies and later applied, as the New World
was explored, to any native Americans
alleged to do so.

155 **Hyrcania** Region on the south Caspian
Sea (Latin *Hyrcanum*) conventionally

associated with fierce tigers. Dido accuses
the departing Aeneas of behaving like
one, *Aeneid*, iv. 525.

156 **hapless** unfortunate

159 **Keep . . . napkin** If York's hands are free,
he may give back the handkerchief, perhaps presenting it to Margaret. Or he may
offer it to Northumberland to motivate his
weeping at l. 170, or to Prince Edward as a
curse.

160 **if . . . right** York may glance at
Northumberland to prove the truth of his
prediction.
    heavy sorrowful, distressing; hard to bear

164 **There, take** York may drop or toss down
the paper crown. Or if Margaret has
already knocked it off his head (see l.
107), he may gesture to it on the ground.
York may direct his words to Prince
Edward as well as Margaret.

164–6 **curse . . . hand** Following Clifford's
beheading of York, 'great rejoicing was
showed: but they laughed then that
shortly after lamented, and were glad
then of other men's deaths that knew not
their own to be so near at hand' (Holinshed Qqqiv'). To which Hall alone adds 'as
the Queen herself, and her son' (Ggiii'),
a foreshadowing and symmetry Shake-

Hard-hearted Clifford, take me from the world,
My soul to heaven, my blood upon your heads.

NORTHUMBERLAND

Had he been slaughterman to all my kin,
I should not, for my life, but weep with him,   170
To see how inly sorrow gripes his soul.

MARGARET

What, weeping ripe, my lord Northumberland?
Think but upon the wrong he did us all
And that will quickly dry thy melting tears.

CLIFFORD

Here's for my oath, here's for my father's death.   175
        Stabbing him

MARGARET

And here's to right our gentle-hearted king.
        Stabbing him

YORK

Open thy gate of mercy, gracious God,
My soul flies through these wounds to seek out thee.

                                            He dies

MARGARET

Off with his head and set it on York gates,

---

172 weeping ripe] F, O; weeping-ripe THEOBALD   175.1 *Stabbing him*] POPE; *not in* F   176.1
Stabbing him] ROWE; *not in* F   178.1 *He dies*] ROWE (*subs.*); *not in* F

speare takes up when Margaret's lament in 5.5 over the murdered Prince Edward echoes York's words here.

168 **my . . . heads** you will be held accountable for shedding my blood. 'A common biblical expression' (Shaheen).

170 **should not . . . but** could only (Abbott ¶127)
for my life though my life were at stake (*OED*, *life*, *sb.* 3c)

171 **inly** inward, heartfelt, profound (*adj.*); inwardly, deeply (*adv.*)
gripes afflicts, grieves (*OED v.*[1] 7, citing this passage); seizes; seeks to grasp

172 **ripe** plentifully, heart and soul. A hyphen is possibly implied in F, as Theobald and many editors have inferred, in which case the meaning is 'ready to weep'.

174 **melting tears** tears of sympathy, pity;

tears that soften the heart, induce compassion

175.1, 176.1 ***Stabbing him*** Modern stage productions have been remarkably consistent about what this means: Clifford stabs York in the back, and, when he is arched in pain on his knees, Margaret runs him through from the front. In the 1992 Ashland production, Margaret forced Prince Edward to hold her sword as she thrust it in, in a ritual blooding of her son.

176 **right** avenge, vindicate

177 **Open . . . God** Compare 'The Lamentation of a Sinner', a song appended to Sternhold and Hopkins's popular metrical Psalms: 'O Lord turn not away thy face . . . before thy mercy gate. Which gate thou openest wide to those, that do lament their sin' (Shaheen, p. 65).

So York may overlook the town of York.   180
                    Flourish. Exeunt with the body

2.1   *A march. Enter Edward, Richard, and their power*

EDWARD

I wonder how our princely father scaped,
Or whether he be scaped away or no
From Clifford's and Northumberland's pursuit?
Had he been ta'en, we should have heard the news,
Had he been slain, we should have heard the news,   5
Or had he scaped, methinks we should have heard
The happy tidings of his good escape.
How fares my brother? Why is he so sad?

RICHARD

I cannot joy until I be resolved
Where our right valiant father is become.   10
I saw him in the battle range about,
And watched him how he singled Clifford forth.
Methought he bore him in the thickest troop
As doth a lion in a herd of neat,
Or as a bear encompassed round with dogs,   15
Who having pinched a few and made them cry,

180.1 *Exeunt*] F2, 0 (*Exeunt omnes*); *Exit* F1   *with the body*] OXFORD (*subs.*); *not in* F
2.1] ROWE; *not in* F

179–80 York's head is often mounted on an
  upstage gallery where it remains in view
  (see 2.2.2.–3) until replaced by Clifford's
  head in 2.6. But some productions leave
  this action implied. See Appendix A.
2.1 Shakespeare invents the continuing
  action of Edward and Richard participating at Wakefield but being unaware of
  their father's death. Edward was actually
  in Gloucester when he received the news,
  while Richard was with his mother in
  Flanders. Act 2 initially magnifies Lancastrian successes and Yorkist losses to create
  a sharper reversal at Towton in 2.3–6
  (Cairncross). See Appendix A.
0.1 **march** Played on drums either on or off
  stage, sometimes accompanied by fifes, to
  distinctive rhythms that spectators with
  military experience would recognize. See
  Shirley, p. 67.
    power soldiers, possibly also drum and
  colours

1 **I . . . scaped** escaped. This echoes the opening question of the play, drawing attention to fluctuating political fortunes.
4–7 **Had . . . escape** The repetitions suggest
  Edward's anxiety. The 1987 ESC production conveyed this as insomnia, Edward
  lying awake with his brothers in an army
  camp.
9 **resolved** informed; freed from doubt, perplexity
10 **is become** has gone
12 **singled . . . forth** picked out and hunted
13–20 **Methought . . . son** The BBC's Ron
  Cook spoke these poetic comparisons
  abstractedly, as if preparing himself for
  York's death and already mythologizing
  his memory.
13 **him** himself
14 **neat** cattle
16 **pinched** snapped at, bit with his teeth
  (*OED v.* 4, citing this line)
    cry yelp (like hounds; *OED v.* 11b)

The rest stand all aloof and bark at him;
So fared our father with his enemies,
So fled his enemies my warlike father.
Methinks 'tis prize enough to be his son.   20
See how the morning opes her golden gates
And takes her farewell of the glorious sun.
How well resembles it the prime of youth,
Trimmed like a younker, prancing to his love.

EDWARD

Dazzle mine eyes, or do I see three suns?   25

RICHARD

Three glorious suns, each one a perfect sun,
Not separated with the racking clouds
But severed in a pale clear-shining sky.
See, see, they join, embrace, and seem to kiss
As if they vowed some league inviolable.   30
Now are they but one lamp, one light, one sun;
In this the heaven figures some event.

---

20 son.] F (*subs.*); sonne. | Three sunnes appeare in the aire. o *and some editors*

---

17 **aloof** at a distance
20 **prize** reward (hinting at consolation?); privilege
21-4 **See . . . love** Compare Psalm 19: 5: 'the Lord made for the sun, a place of great renown: Who like a bridegroom ready trimmed, doth from his chamber come' (Sternhold and Hopkins, in Shaheen, p. 66), and *The Faerie Queene*, I. v. 2.1–4: 'At last the golden Orientall gate | Of greatest heaven gan to open faire, | And *Phoebus* fresh, as bridegrome to his mate, | Came daunting forth'.
21 **morning opes** i.e. Aurora, goddess of dawn, opens
22 **takes . . . of . . . sun** i.e. bids . . . to . . . Apollo
23 **prime** Literally the first hour of the day; hence, early manhood, age of greatest vigour.
24 **Trimmed** dressed up
    younker fashionable young man
25 **Dazzle mine eyes** is my sight distorted by brightness
    three suns May be notional, like other atmospheric conditions in Shakespeare: the brothers may 'see' them by looking up or out into the audience. Or Edward

may be hallucinating, and Richard humours him, pretending to see three suns too. Hall and Holinshed report this event with a certain scepticism, although modern meteorology confirms the phenomenon does occur. See Appendix A. O's direction 'in the air' suggests that in that version of the play the suns were represented by physical properties displayed from the gallery or lowered from the 'heavens' through a door in the ceiling (see Walter Hodges's conjectural illustration in Hattaway, p. 20). Modern productions often dramatize the moment by means of golden 'dawn' lighting and sound effects such as morning birdcalls.
27 **racking** wind-driven and cumulating
30 **league** alliance. A word with topical resonance in the early 1590s: the Catholic League was a political pact between the French house of Guise and Spain to prevent the Protestant Henry of Navarre, whom England assisted militarily during this period, from succeeding to the French throne.
    inviolable incapable of being broken
32 **figures** reveals; foreshadows

EDWARD

'Tis wondrous strange, the like yet never heard of.
I think it cites us, brother, to the field,
That we the sons of brave Plantagenet,   35
Each one already blazing by our meeds,
Should notwithstanding join our lights together
And overshine the earth as this the world.
Whate'er it bodes, henceforward will I bear
Upon my target three fair-shining suns.   40

RICHARD

Nay, bear three daughters; by your leave I speak it,
You love the breeder better than the male.

Enter a Messenger, blowing ⌐a horn⌐

But what art thou whose heavy looks foretell
Some dreadful story hanging on thy tongue?

MESSENGER

Ah, one that was a woeful looker-on   45
Whenas the noble Duke of York was slain,
Your princely father and my loving lord.

EDWARD

O speak no more, for I have heard too much.

42.1 *a Messenger*] ROWE; *one* F ⌐*a horn*⌐] WILSON; *not in* F; *in haste* COLLIER 1853

34 **cites** calls
36 **by our meeds** because of our (individual) achievements, merits
38 **overshine** illumine (*OED* I, citing this line)
    this this light
40 **target** small shield
40–2 **suns . . . male** Richard puns on 'sons'. In terms of future heirs to the throne, daughters 'would be easier to remove' than sons (Hattaway). His joke (or barb—Edward may take his words as a sly jest even though he speaks seriously) hints at the sexual and political rivalry that will emerge fully in 3.2. 'For Edward [the vision of the three suns] suggests that "the sons of brave Plantagenet" should "over-shine the earth" . . . for Richard it might imply "this could mean royal possibilities for me" . . . but it does not really find its expression until it emerges that Edward is about to get married and the avenues are therefore closing' (Anton Lesser on playing Richard, *Players* 3, pp. 145–6).

42 **love the breeder** 'King Edward . . . loved well both to look [Holinshed = "behold"] and to feel fair damsels' (Hall Hhvi^v, Holinshed Rrrii^v).
42.1 ⌐*a horn*⌐ To announce an urgent arrival (as at 3.3.160.1). Alternatively, F's '*blowing*' could mean the person enters breathing hard, puffing. See Appendix A and next note.
45 **looker-on** May be notional, but if not, it implies an eyewitness. The Messenger's line 'Your princely father and my loving lord' (47), suggests that the 'woeful looker-on' was either a Yorkist who entered silently at some point to watch the scene, or a former Lancastrian who has switched sides and is now covering up his defection. This might explain why he is not initially recognized as a messenger by Richard (compare 3.3.162) and identified simply as '*one*'. See also Appendix C, 2.1.45.
46 **Whenas** when
48 **O . . . much** The chronicles suggest Edward was temporarily overwhelmed

RICHARD

Say how he died, for I will hear it all.

MESSENGER

Environèd he was with many foes, 50
And stood against them as the hope of Troy
Against the Greeks that would have entered Troy.
But Hercules himself must yield to odds,
And many strokes, though with a little axe,
Hews down and fells the hardest-timbered oak. 55
By many hands your father was subdued,
But only slaughtered by the ireful arm
Of unrelenting Clifford, and the Queen,
Who crowned the gracious Duke in high despite,
Laughed in his face; and when with grief he wept, 60
The ruthless Queen gave him to dry his cheeks
A napkin steepèd in the harmless blood
Of sweet young Rutland, by rough Clifford slain.
And after many scorns, many foul taunts,
They took his head and on the gates of York 65
They set the same, and there it doth remain,
The saddest spectacle that e'er I viewed.

EDWARD

Sweet Duke of York, our prop to lean upon,
Now thou art gone we have no staff, no stay.
O Clifford, boist'rous Clifford, thou hast slain 70
The flower of Europe for his chivalry,

---

with grief ('wonderfully amazed', Hall Ggiii^v, Holinshed Qqqiv^r–v).

49 **Say . . . all** Richard's contrasting determination may suggest the depth of his relationship with his father. But in the 1987 ESC production Richard seemed to welcome a legitimizing motive—revenge—that could serve his private ambitions.

50 **Environèd** surrounded, beset. See Appendix A, 1.4.1–29.

51 **hope of Troy** Hector, whose body Achilles dragged behind his chariot around the walls of Troy. The extremity of his suffering confirmed his heroism. Compare Virgil, *Aeneid*, ii. 281: 'spes O fidissima Teucrum' ('O most faithful hope of Troy').

53 Proverbial: 'Hercules himself cannot deal with two' (Dent H436).

54–5 Proverbial: 'Many strokes fell great oaks' (Dent S941).

57 **ireful** angry

59 **high despite** jubilant scorn

62 **steepèd** saturated (*OED v.*[1] 2, citing this line)
harmless innocent

63 **rough** cruel

69 **stay** person for support, to rely on

70 **boistr'ous** savagely violent (*OED* 9, citing this line)

71 **flower . . . chivalry** bravery in war; knightly valour. A description slightly differently applied to Edward: 'this lusty prince and flower of chivalry' (Hall Ggv^r, Holinshed Qqqv^r).

And treacherously hast thou vanquished him,
For hand to hand he would have vanquished thee.
Now my soul's palace is become a prison:
Ah would she break from hence, that this my body   75
Might in the ground be closèd up in rest,
For never henceforth shall I joy again,
Never, O never shall I see more joy.

RICHARD
I cannot weep, for all my body's moisture
Scarce serves to quench my furnace-burning heart,   80
Nor can my tongue unload my heart's great burden,
For selfsame wind that I should speak withal
Is kindling coals that fires all my breast
And burns me up with flames that tears would quench.
To weep is to make less the depth of grief;   85
Tears then for babes, blows and revenge for me.
Richard, I bear thy name, I'll venge thy death,
Or die renownèd by attempting it.

EDWARD
His name that valiant duke hath left with thee,
His dukedom and his chair with me is left.   90

RICHARD
Nay if thou be that princely eagle's bird,
Show thy descent by gazing 'gainst the sun;

---

87 name, . . . death,] F; name; . . . death, COLLIER; name; . . . death‸ PELICAN

---

72 **treacherously** i.e. you must have resorted
to the treachery of unequal odds
74 **soul's . . . prison** Combines two traditional
attitudes towards the body: 'The body is
the temple of the soul' (see *OED, palace,
sb.*[1] 2), and 'The body is the prison of the
soul' (Dent B497).
75 **she** the soul
77 **joy** feel joy
79–84 **weep . . . quench** These baroque
descriptions of raging bodily humours
recall the language of neo-Senecan
revenge heroes. Pearlman (p. 416) suggests they mark Shakespeare's experi-
mentation with Richard's verbal style
before he settles on the 'jaunty mockery
that will eventually become his hallmark'. By speaking these lines intently to
the camera, the BBC's Ron Cook made

them a compelling explanation for his
reaction.
82 **selfsame wind . . . should** the same
breath . . . should use to
87 **venge** revenge
90 **dukedom . . . left** 'The Earl of March, so
commonly called, but after the death of
his father . . . in right very Duke of York'
(Hall Ggiii[v], Holinshed Qqqiv[r]).
chair seat of authority
91 **princely eagle** Regarded as the most noble
of birds, and in traditional lore believed
capable of flying into the sun without
being blinded (Aelian, ii. 26). The eagle
may also allude to another heraldic badge
of York, the falcon (Cairncross). Also
5.2.12.
bird offspring
92 **descent** ancestry

For 'chair and dukedom', 'throne and kingdom' say,
Either that is thine or else thou wert not his.

> *March. Enter Warwick, Marquis Montague,*
> *and their army*

WARWICK

How now fair lords? What fare? What news abroad?   95

RICHARD

Great lord of Warwick, if we should recount
Our baleful news, and at each word's deliverance
Stab poniards in our flesh till all were told,
The words would add more anguish than the wounds.
O valiant lord, the Duke of York is slain.   100

EDWARD

O Warwick, Warwick, that Plantagenet
Which held thee dearly as his soul's redemption
Is by the stern Lord Clifford done to death.

WARWICK

Ten days ago I drowned these news in tears,
And now to add more measure to your woes,   105
I come to tell you things sith then befall'n.
After the bloody fray at Wakefield fought
Where your brave father breathed his latest gasp,
Tidings, as swiftly as the posts could run,
Were brought me of your loss and his depart.   110
I then in London, keeper of the King,
Mustered my soldiers, gathered flocks of friends,

94.2 *and their army*] F; with drum, ancient, and souldiers o

---

94.1 **Marquis** F's title signals Montague's
new persona, that of Warwick's younger
brother. See Appendix B and note to
1.1.0.3.
94.2 **army** soldiers, possibly also drum and
colours
95 **What fare** what's the state of things
(*OED*, *fare*, sb.[1] 7 citing this line)
abroad in the world at large
97 **baleful** sorrowful, painful
deliverance utterance (*OED* 6, citing
line)
98 **poniards** daggers
101–3 **O . . . death** In the 1983 BBC production Edward (and George who was present) wept and fell into Warwick's arms

for comfort, finding in him a surrogate
father. Richard watched his brothers
impassively, taking the measure of their
weakness. Reviewers of the 1952–3
Birmingham Rep production noted that
from this point on, Richard's movements
became independent from his brothers.
102 **redemption** salvation
103 **stern** merciless
105 **more measure to** to the full sum of (see
Matthew 23: 32; *OED* 12d)
106 **sith** since
108 **latest** last
109 **posts** messengers
110 **depart** death
111 **keeper** guardian

And very well appointed as I thought,
Marched toward St Albans to intercept the Queen,
Bearing the King in my behalf along;   115
For by my scouts I was advertisèd
That she was coming with a full intent
To dash our late decree in Parliament
Touching King Henry's oath and your succession.
Short tale to make, we at St Albans met,   120
Our battles joined, and both sides fiercely fought.
But whether 'twas the coldness of the King
Who looked full gently on his warlike queen
That robbed my soldiers of their heated spleen,
Or whether 'twas report of her success,   125
Or more than common fear of Clifford's rigour,
Who thunders to his captives blood and death,
I cannot judge. But to conclude with truth,
Their weapons like to lightning came and went,

---

113 And . . . thought] O; *not in* F   127 captives∧] ROWE; Captiues, F

---

113 **And . . . thought** F omits this line, which is confirmed by a report unique to Hall that Warwick marched towards St Albans 'having the king in their company, as the head and chieftain of the war' (Ggivᵛ). While the sense is not obscured without it, Warwick's speech in O is nearly verbatim except for a few single word variants. The line's omission was therefore probably due to compositorial eye-skip. The apparent duplication at l. 131 suggests the compositor may have misread there too.
appointed equipped; prepared; authoritatively assigned to perform a duty or fill an office (i.e. on behalf of Henry; see l. 116). Elizabethan audiences with experience of military expeditions to the Continent and Ireland would have appreciated Warwick's point. See Introduction, p. 33.

116 **advertisèd** informed

118 **dash . . . decree** 'In 16–17th c. the usual word for the rejection of a bill in Parliament' (*OED*, *dash*, v.¹ 6); referring to the succession agreement in 1.1. See Appendix A, 2.1.116–19.

121 **battles joined** armies met together in conflict

122 **coldness** See note to 1.1.185.

123 **full gently** with deep tenderness, kindness

124 **heated spleen** fiery courage, high spirits

126 **rigour** (policy of) merciless severity

127 **captives . . . death** Clifford has proclaimed no quarter; i.e. all prisoners will be killed rather than ransomed according to normal military customs, which guaranteed captured soldiers clemency. Warwick implies that in the face of virtually suicidal conditions his soldiers' failure of nerve is understandable. For discussion see R. Martin, 'Sins of Omission and Coveted Honour: The Absent Archers in *Henry V*', *Shakespeare in Japan*, Shakespeare Yearbook, vol. 9, ed. Tetsuo Anzai *et al.* (Lewiston, NY, 1999), pp. 306–9.
captives Hattaway suggests 'blood and death' should be read as Clifford's battle-cry, citing O's alternative reading 'captains'. But Warwick's point is Clifford's terrifying treatment of his prisoners. F's punctuation, 'captives, blood and death' may support the idea of direct speech, but in that case the line could be understood as ' "blood" and "death" ' to his captives. O's pointing, 'captains blood and death', does not suggest direct speech, nor does the nearest comparable passage, in *Twelfth Night* 1.5.245, 'With groans that thunder love'.

Our soldiers', like the night-owl's lazy flight   130
Or like an idle thresher with a flail,
Fell gently down as if they struck their friends.
I cheered them up with justice of our cause,
With promise of high pay and great rewards,
But all in vain: they had no heart to fight,   135
And we, in them, no hope to win the day,
So that we fled: the King unto the Queen,
Lord George your brother, Norfolk, and myself
In haste, post-haste, are come to join with you,
For in the Marches here we heard you were   140
Making another head to fight again.

EDWARD

Where is the Duke of Norfolk, gentle Warwick?
And when came George from Burgundy to England?

WARWICK

Some six miles off the Duke is with the soldiers,
And for your brother, he was lately sent   145
From your kind aunt, Duchess of Burgundy,
With aid of soldiers to this needful war.

RICHARD

'Twas odds belike when valiant Warwick fled;
Oft have I heard his praises in pursuit,
But ne'er till now his scandal of retire.   150

WARWICK

Nor now my scandal, Richard, dost thou hear,

---

130 soldiers'] CAPELL; Souldiers F   131 an idle] O, CAPELL; a lazie F

131 **idle** inefficient, inept
132 **Fell** beat, struck
133 **cheered them up** rallied them
139 **post-haste** with all possible speed
140 **Marches** borders (of Wales and England)
141 **making . . . head** gathering another army
142 **gentle** noble
143 **George . . . Burgundy** Historically both George and Richard had fled with their mother for safety to the Netherlands to stay with the Duchess of Burgundy. See next note and Appendix A, 2.1.143–7.
146 **Duchess of Burgundy** At this date refers to Isabella, wife of Philip Duke of Burgundy, daughter of John I of Portugal and Philippa, eldest daughter of John of

Gaunt. She was therefore Edward's second cousin once removed. Shakespeare also merged her with the next duchess, Margaret, who married Charles the Bold of Burgundy in 1468, and who was York's daughter and Edward's sister. While mentioned only briefly, she was a significant supporter of the Yorkists, as the next line and 4.7.5–6 suggest.
148–50 **'Twas . . . retire** The BBC's Ron Cook spoke this as a challenge to Warwick's pride in order to rouse him from the defeatism and weariness of his preceding speech. See also note to 157–65.
148 **'Twas . . . when** the numbers must have been greatly unequal if
150–1 **scandal of retire . . . scandal** notoriety for retreating . . . disrepute, disgrace

For thou shalt know this strong right hand of mine
Can pluck the diadem from faint Henry's head
And wring the awful sceptre from his fist,
Were he as famous and as bold in war   155
As he is famed for mildness, peace, and prayer.

RICHARD

I know it well, Lord Warwick, blame me not,
'Tis love I bear thy glories makes me speak.
But in this troublous time what's to be done?
Shall we go throw away our coats of steel   160
And wrap our bodies in black mourning gowns,
Numbering our Ave-Marys with our beads?
Or shall we on the helmets of our foes
Tell our devotion with revengeful arms?
If for the last, say 'ay', and to it lords.   165

WARWICK

Why therefore Warwick came to seek you out,
And therefore comes my brother Montague.
Attend me lords: the proud insulting Queen,
With Clifford and the haught Northumberland
And of their feather many more proud birds,   170
Have wrought the easy-melting King like wax.

---

158 makes] F2; make F1   162 Marys] *This edition*; Maries F, *editors*

---

153 **faint** weak, half-hearted; cowardly
154 **awful** commanding deep respect
157–65 I . . . **lords** Richard mollified Warwick's anger in the BBC production, and used this speech as a passionate call to arms, as if he was assuming command. But Warwick deflated his incipient ambitions by speaking ll. 166–7 in a sardonically calm, low voice. 'Attend me lords . . .' (168) reasserted his leadership.
158 **love I bear** the devotion I have to
159 **troublous** vexatious, sorrowful; restless; disordered, conflicted. Hall's chapter is titled 'The troublous season of King Henry the sixth' (Oi^r, Ggviii^r), and contrasts with 'The prosperous reign of King Edward the fourth'. Holinshed calls it 'the tragical history of Henry the sixth deprived of his royalty' (Qqqvi^r).
161 **gowns** cloaks (worn at funerals)
162 **Numbering . . . beads** counting over our Hail Marys (Latin = *Ave Maria*, the devotional prayer) with rosary beads. So Margaret describes Henry's disposition, *2 Henry VI* 1.3.58–9.
164 **Tell** proclaim; count over (as in 'tell one's beads')
168 **Attend** Listen to
     insulting scornfully boasting; offensive. See Appendix A, 2.1.168–77.
169 **haught** haughty, presumptuously arrogant
170 **And . . . birds** 'Birds of a feather will flock together' (Dent B393).
171 **wrought . . . wax** Proverbial: 'To work (upon one) like wax' (Dent W138); i.e. easily swayed, malleable. Henry has been re-formed into a 'man of wax'; i.e. the simulacrum of the manly leader they wish him to be (*OED*, *wax*, *sb.*^1 3), and ironically recalling the phrase's alternative meaning, the paragon of a man. Compare *Romeo* 3.3.125–6, 'Thy noble shape is but a form of wax, | Digressing from the valour of a man', and 1.3.77–8, 'A man, young lady . . . he's a man of wax'.

He swore consent to your succession,
His oath enrollèd in the Parliament,
And now to London all the crew are gone
To frustrate both his oath and what beside   175
May make against the house of Lancaster.
Their power I think is thirty thousand strong.
Now if the help of Norfolk and myself
With all the friends that thou, brave Earl of March,
Amongst the loving Welshmen canst procure   180
Will but amount to five-and-twenty thousand,
Why 'via!' to London will we march
And once again bestride our foaming steeds,
And once again cry 'charge' upon our foes,
But never once again turn back and fly.   185

RICHARD

Ay, now methinks I hear great Warwick speak.
Ne'er may he live to see a sunshine day
That cries 'retire', if Warwick bid him stay.

EDWARD

Lord Warwick, on thy shoulder will I lean,
And when thou fail'st—as God forbid the hour—   190
Must Edward fall, which peril heaven forfend.

WARWICK

No longer Earl of March but Duke of York;

---

184 cry 'charge' . . . foes,] This edition; cry∧ Charge . . . Foes, F; cry, *Charge upon our foes!*
JOHNSON *following* ROWE

---

171 **melting** dissolved and refashioned in a
    new image (*OED*, *melt*, *v.*[1] 8b)

173 **enrollèd** legally set down on record
174 **crew** band of soldiers (with an underly-
    ing derogatory sense: mob, rabble)
175 **frustrate** nullify
    what beside anything else whatsoever
176 **make** militate
177–81 **thirty thousand. . . . five-and-twenty
    thousand** These figures in F approximate
    numbers reported at the second Battle
    of St Albans (just described by Warwick),
    whereas O's numbers, fifty and forty-
    eight thousand respectively, are closer to
    chronicle figures for the approaching
    battle at Towton (sixty thousand and
    48,660). See Appendix A.
180 **loving** loyal, devoted

182 The omitted fourth syllable allows for
    emotional emphasis—i.e. is 'replaced' by
    a rhetorical exclamation—and for the
    spoken pause after 'via'. See Wright, pp.
    179–83.
    via onward! come on! (*OED int.* 1, citing
    this line)
183 **foaming** sweating
185 **back and fly** our backs and flee
187 **he . . . sunshine** anyone . . . happy, pros-
    perous
188 **retire . . . stay** retreat . . . stand his ground
190 **fail'st** yield to an enemy (*OED v.* 4);
    disappoint, give no help; fall short; are
    unsuccessful
191 **fall** succumb to attack (*OED v.* 21);
    decline; die
    forfend forbid
192–5 **No . . . along** As in 1.1, Shakespeare

The next degree is England's royal throne,
For King of England shalt thou be proclaimed
In every borough as we pass along,   195
And he that throws not up his cap for joy
Shall for the fault make forfeit of his head.
King Edward, valiant Richard, Montague,
Stay we no longer dreaming of renown,
But sound the trumpets and about our task.   200

RICHARD

Then Clifford, were thy heart as hard as steel
As thou hast shown it flinty by thy deeds,
I come to pierce it or to give thee mine.

EDWARD

Then strike up drums, God and St George for us!
        Enter a Messenger
WARWICK How now? What news?   205

MESSENGER

The Duke of Norfolk sends you word by me
The Queen is coming with a puissant host,
And craves your company for speedy council.

WARWICK

Why then it sorts, brave warriors, let's away.

                        Exeunt omnes

---

206 me$_\wedge$] HANMER; me, F

eliminates Parliament's historical role
and instead locates political change in the
personal actions of the warring families.
See Appendix A.

193–5 **next . . . along** Richard's reaction to
these lines may be telling. An actor must
decide whether, and when, to betray any
hint of the coming into his mind of his
future ambitions before the revelations of
his soliloquy in 3.2.
193 **degree** rank; step in ascent
201–3 **heart . . . mine** Compare *Gorboduc*
4.1.38–40: 'If such hard heart of rock
and stony flint | Lived in thy breast that
nothing else could like | Thy cruel
tyrant's thought but death and blood'.
And see ll. 126–7.
202 **flinty** unfeeling; impenetrable
204 **God . . . us** A conventional battle-cry—St
George is the patron saint of England—
but also reportedly spoken by York before
Wakefield: 'therefore advance my banner,

in the name of God and Saint George'
(Hall only Ggiii^r). Historically, 'Edward IV
aggressively used the image of the saint'
to legitimize the Yorkist government and
to connect royal power with emergent
national identity. See Jonathan Bengtson,
'Saint George and the Formation of English Nationalism', *Journal of Medieval and
Early Modern Studies*, 27 (1997), 317–40,
quotation p. 327.
207 **puissant host** powerful army
208 **company . . . council** As at 1.1.36, F's
spelling 'counsell' could signify 'council'—an assembly of peers—or 'counsel'
—advice, deliberation—in which case the
line may be ironic, or a pun on both
meanings. A comparable instance occurs
in *Antony*: 'Assemble [w]e immediate
counsell' (1.4.76, original spelling),
which editors modernize to 'council'.
209 **it sorts** the world is unfolding as it should
(*OED v.*^{1} 18b, citing this line)

2.2   *Flourish. Enter King Henry, Queen Margaret, Clifford,*
        Northumberland and young Prince Edward, with Drum
        and Trumpets

MARGARET

Welcome my lord to this brave town of York.
Yonder's the head of that arch-enemy
That sought to be encompassed with your crown.
Doth not the object cheer your heart, my lord?

HENRY

Ay, as the rocks cheer them that fear their wrack.   5
To see this sight it irks my very soul.
Withhold revenge, dear God, 'tis not my fault,
Nor wittingly have I infringed my vow.

CLIFFORD

My gracious liege, this too much lenity
And harmful pity must be laid aside.   10
To whom do lions cast their gentle looks?
Not to the beast that would usurp their den.
Whose hand is that the forest bear doth lick?
Not his that spoils her young before her face.
Who scapes the lurking serpent's mortal sting?   15
Not he that sets his foot upon her back.

2.2] CAPELL; *not in* F 0.1 *Flourish*] F; ⌈*York's head is thrust out, above.*⌉ | *Flourish* OXFORD
King Henry] ROWE; *the King* F (*and subs. prefixes throughout this scene*) *Queen Margaret*] HANMER;
the Queene F (*and subs. prefixes throughout this scene*) 0.1–2 *Clifford, Northumberland*] F; *and the
Northerne Earles* O 0.2 *Prince Edward*] O, RIVERSIDE; *Prince* F

2.2.0.3 *Trumpets* Probably played by actors
who mimed sounds produced off stage;
e.g. in the window above the stage roof, as
depicted in the De Witt sketch of the Swan
Theatre. See also Appendix C, 2.2.0.3.

1 **brave** fine

2 **Yonder's** See note to 1.4.179–80.
  head May be imagined, but some productions display a head mounted on the stage
  gallery representing the walls of York, or
  on a pole, as in the 1987 ESC production.
  In the 1983 BBC version the camera pans
  down a row of rotting heads in various
  stages of decomposition.

3 **encompassed** encircled

5 **wrack** shipwreck

8 **wittingly** intentionally
  infringed broken

9 **lenity** show of clemency; mild behaviour.

The ruthless counsellor who favours
crushing political opposition is a stock
figure in early Elizabethan historical
tragedies; e.g. Hermon in *Gorboduc*,
Cador in *The Misfortunes of Arthur* (1587).
Clifford returns to the same theme at
2.6.20–1.

11–18 Clifford's analogies from the natural
  world are early modern commonplaces
  and proverbs, but some also occur in a
  speech recorded by Hall and Holinshed
  in which Warwick justifies his revenge
  after Edward has betrayed his diplomatic
  mission to France. See Appendix A,
  2.2.11 ff.

13 **forest** wild (as opposed to tame) (*OED sb.*
  4b, citing this line)

14 **spoils** steals; harms

15 **scapes** escapes

The smallest worm will turn, being trodden on,
And doves will peck in safeguard of their brood.
Ambitious York did level at thy crown,
Thou smiling while he knit his angry brows. 20
He but a duke would have his son a king
And raise his issue like a loving sire,
Thou being a king blessed with a goodly son
Didst yield consent to disinherit him,
Which argued thee a most unloving father. 25
Unreasonable creatures feed their young,
And though man's face be fearful to their eyes,
Yet in protection of their tender ones,
Who hath not seen them, even with those wings
Which sometime they have used with fearful flight, 30
Make war with him that climbed unto their nest,
Offering their own lives in their young's defence?
For shame, my liege, make them your precedent.
Were it not pity that this goodly boy
Should lose his birthright by his father's fault, 35
And long hereafter say unto his child,
'What my great-grandfather and grandsire got,
My careless father fondly gave away'?
Ah what a shame were this! Look on the boy
And let his manly face, which promiseth 40
Successful fortune, steel thy melting heart
To hold thine own and leave thine own with him.

HENRY
Full well hath Clifford played the orator,
Inferring arguments of mighty force.
But Clifford tell me, didst thou never hear 45

---

17 Proverbial (Dent W909).
18 **in safeguard** in the defence, for the protection
19 **level** aim
22 **raise his issue** advance his child's social rank
25 **argued** proved (*OED v.* 3, citing this line)
26 **Unreasonable** lacking the capacity for reason
29 **them** i.e. the unreasonable creatures
30 **fearful** frightened

35 **fault** neglect
37 **great-grandfather and grandsire got** Henry IV (gained possession of the crown for the house of Lancaster) and Henry V (conquered France)
38 **fondly** foolishly
41 **melting** soft, tender-feeling
43 **orator** advocate, spokesman, with an underlying sense of the formally rhetorical (and therefore possibly duplicitous) qualities of Clifford's speech.
44 **Inferring** citing

That things ill got had ever bad success?
And happy always was it for that son
Whose father for his hoarding went to hell?
I'll leave my son my virtuous deeds behind,
And would my father had left me no more,   50
For all the rest is held at such a rate
As brings a thousandfold more care to keep
Than in possession any jot of pleasure.
Ah cousin York, would thy best friends did know
How it doth grieve me that thy head is here.   55
MARGARET

My lord cheer up your spirits, our foes are nigh,
And this soft courage makes your followers faint.
You promised knighthood to our forward son,
Unsheath your sword and dub him presently.
Edward kneel down.   60
HENRY

Edward Plantagenet, arise a knight,
And learn this lesson: draw thy sword in right.
PRINCE EDWARD

My gracious father, by your kingly leave,
I'll draw it as apparent to the crown,
And in that quarrel use it to the death.   65
CLIFFORD

Why, that is spoken like a toward prince.
        Enter a Messenger
MESSENGER

Royal commanders be in readiness,
For with a band of thirty thousand men

46 Proverbial: 'Evil-gotten goods never prove well' (Tilley G301). Henry may be recalling the troubled legacy of Henry IV's usurpation of the throne, as well as rebuking Clifford.
47–8 Henry disputes the conventional wisdom, 'Happy is the child whose father goes to the devil' (Dent C305); a splendid worldly inheritance does not guarantee contentment.
51 **the rest** i.e. legacy other than virtuous achievements. Henry alludes to England's territorial conquests in France, implying that any material benefits were morally tainted.

51 **rate** cost (material, ethical, personal)
57 **soft courage . . . faint** faint-heartedness . . . lose courage, grow feeble (*OED*, *faint*, *v.* 1, 2)
58 **knighthood** To publicize his status as heir apparent (see l. 64). Historically Edward was eight at the time. See Appendix A.
  forward eager, spirited; precocious
59 **dub** tap ceremonially on each shoulder to bestow a title
  presently immediately
62 **in right** in just causes
65 **quarrel** cause
66 **toward** promising; right-minded
68 **thirty thousand** See note to 2.1.177–81.

Comes Warwick backing of the Duke of York,
And in the towns as they do march along   70
Proclaims him king, and many fly to him.
Deraign your battle, for they are at hand.

CLIFFORD
I would your highness would depart the field,
The Queen hath best success when you are absent.

MARGARET
Ay, good my lord, and leave us to our fortune.   75

HENRY
Why that's my fortune too, therefore I'll stay.

NORTHUMBERLAND
Be it with resolution then to fight.

PRINCE EDWARD
My royal father, cheer these noble lords
And hearten those that fight in your defence.
Unsheath your sword, good father, cry 'St George!'   80
        March. Enter Edward, Warwick, Richard, George,
        Norfolk, Montague, and Soldiers

EDWARD
Now perjured Henry, wilt thou kneel for grace
And set thy diadem upon my head,
Or bide the mortal fortune of the field?

MARGARET
Go rate thy minions, proud insulting boy.
Becomes it thee to be thus bold in terms   85

80.1–2 *Edward . . . Soldiers*] F; the house of *Yorke* 0 0.1 *George*] CAPELL; *Clarence* F (*and subs. prefixes throughout this scene*)

69 **backing of** supporting
   Duke of York i.e. Edward
71 **many . . . him** While the chronicles attest
   to Edward's popular and effective political
   leadership, Shakespeare largely passes
   over these virtues, drawing attention
   instead to his weaknesses. See Appendix
   A and Introduction, pp. 70–1.
72 **Deraign** set in ready order (*OED v.*[1] 4b,
   citing this line)
75–6 **fortune . . . fortune** good fortune; fate
   . . . **success**; future concern
78 **cheer** encourage
80 **St George** See note to 2.1.204.
80.1–2 *Enter . . . Soldiers* If York's head is
   visible, some of the Yorkists may wince at
   the sight. In the 1987 ESC production,

Edward's eyes filled with tears and he
turned momentarily to Warwick for
comfort.
81 **grace** mercy (with a hint of divine fortune
   contrasting with 'mortal fortune' in l.
   83)
83 **bide** confront
   mortal fortune deadly chances
84 **rate** rebuke
   minions favourites (spoken contemptuously), perhaps with a glance at Edward's
   lustfulness ('minion' could mean 'mistress, paramour')
   boy (an insult)
85 **Becomes it** is it proper for
   bold in terms free in words; daring, impudent in language

Before thy sovereign and thy lawful king?

EDWARD

I am his king and he should bow his knee.
I was adopted heir by his consent,
Since when his oath is broke; for as I hear
You that are king, though he do wear the crown,   90
Have caused him by new act of Parliament
To blot out me and put his own son in.

CLIFFORD And reason too:
Who should succeed the father but the son?

RICHARD

Are you there, butcher? O, I cannot speak.   95

CLIFFORD

Ay, crookback, here I stand to answer thee
Or any he, the proudest of thy sort.

RICHARD

'Twas you that killed young Rutland, was it not?

CLIFFORD

Ay, and old York, and yet not satisfied.

89–92 Since . . . in] *continuing as Edward's speech* F2; *Cla⟨rence⟩. Since . . . in* F1; *George.* Since
when he hath broke his oath. | For as we hear you that are king | Though he doe weare the
Crowne, | Haue causde him by new act of Parlement | To blot our brother out, and put his owne
son in o

89–92 **Since . . . in** F's mistaken assignment
of this speech to Clarence has been cited
as evidence that the F compositors were
briefly following O, or specifically Q3,
since it and F seem to agree in some accidentals ('Crowne', 'Parliament', and the
division of the next speech by Clifford into
two lines). In O/Q3, however, this line
lacks the logical symmetry and rhetorical
balance of F, in which Edward compares
the position of sons to fathers. '[H]is own
son' reciprocates (emphatically with the
possessive 'own') the sense of 'Blot me
out' (as son and heir of *my* father). In
O/Q3, by contrast, the point of 'his own'
is lost with 'our brother'. It is also odd
that George uses 'we' and 'our', which
sound like royal plurals, when he
is not apparently speaking on behalf of
himself and Richard. Moreover in O/Q3
Clifford draws dramatic attention to the
identity of the speaker, who appears and
speaks here (earlier than in F) for the first
time: 'And reason *George*'. If the F compositor was following O/Q3, which he
believed to be clearer than Shakespeare's

manuscript, why did he substitute 'And
reason too', if he thought the speech was
really by George? The evidence suggests
F is a revised version, and that cancellation of its prefix may not have been clear
in its copy, since the compositor otherwise routinely altered O's *George* to F's
Clarence.

90 **You . . . crown** Margaret's 'rule' over
Henry is repeatedly emphasized by Hall,
somewhat less so by Holinshed; e.g. 'The
Queen having a wit more than the common sort of women have, and considering the estate of her husband, the
condition of herself, and the peril of her
only son, thought it necessary to pluck
the sword of authority out of their hands'
(Hall Eeiii^(r–v)). See Appendix A.

93 **reason** with reason

95 **butcher** Clifford was nicknamed 'the
Butcher' after his murder of Rutland.

96 **crookback** hunchback (*OED*, citing this
line)

97 **he . . . sort** one . . . lot

99 **old York** Clifford may gesture to York's
head, if it is displayed.

RICHARD

    For God's sake lords give signal to the fight.   100

WARWICK

    What sayst thou Henry, wilt thou yield the crown?

MARGARET

    Why, how now long-tongued Warwick, dare you speak?

    When you and I met at St Albans last

    Your legs did better service than your hands.

WARWICK

    Then 'twas my turn to fly and now 'tis thine.   105

CLIFFORD

    You said so much before and yet you fled.

WARWICK

    'Twas not your valour, Clifford, drove me thence.

NORTHUMBERLAND

    No, nor your manhood that durst make you stay.

RICHARD

    Northumberland, I hold thee reverently.—

    Break off the parley, for scarce I can refrain   110

    The execution of my big-swoll'n heart

    Upon that Clifford, that cruel child-killer.

CLIFFORD

    I slew thy father; call'st thou him a child?

RICHARD

    Ay, like a dastard and a treacherous coward,

    As thou didst kill our tender brother Rutland.   115

    But ere sunset I'll make thee curse the deed.

---

109 reverently.—] This edition; reuerently, F; reverently. POPE   116 sunset] F1; sunne
set 0, F3

102 **long-tongued** chattering (*OED*, citing
    this line)
104 Proverbial: 'One pair of legs is worth two
    pair of hands' (Dent P34).
108 **durst** gave you the courage to
109 **reverently** in profound respect (therefore
    I won't quarrel with you)
110, 112 Both lines have an extra syllable
    before the midline break (112 is
    implied), and 112 has a feminine
    ending (Wright, pp. 160–7). The effect
    is of a packed line expressing urgent
    fury.
110 **refrain** hold back

111 **execution** acting out the passionate
    feelings
    big-swoll'n (with anger)
112 **cruel child-killer** 'Yet this cruel Clifford,
    and deadly bloodsupper [= -sucker], not
    content with this homicide, or child-
    killing, came to the place where the dead
    corpse of the Duke of York lay . . .' (Hall
    Ggiii^v). See Appendix A, 1.3.1–11.
113 **I . . . child?** Clifford deliberately mis-
    understands Richard and twists his words
    to boast of killing *both* father and son.
    Richard ignores his sally.
114 **dastard** contemptible coward

HENRY

Have done with words, my lords, and hear me speak.

MARGARET

Defy them then or else hold close thy lips.

HENRY

I prithee give no limits to my tongue,

I am a king and privileged to speak.   120

CLIFFORD

My liege, the wound that bred this meeting here

Cannot be cured by words, therefore be still.

RICHARD

Then executioner unsheath thy sword;

By him that made us all I am resolved

That Clifford's manhood lies upon his tongue.   125

EDWARD

Say, Henry, shall I have my right or no?

A thousand men have broke their fasts today

That ne'er shall dine unless thou yield the crown.

WARWICK

If thou deny, their blood upon thy head,

For York in justice puts his armour on.   130

PRINCE EDWARD

If that be right which Warwick says is right,

There is no wrong but every thing is right.

RICHARD

Whoever got thee, there thy mother stands,

For well I wot thou hast thy mother's tongue.

133 RICHARD] O, POPE; War⟨wick⟩. F

118 **Defy them** challenge them to combat
122 **still** silent
124 **him . . . all** i.e. God
   resolved convinced
125 **upon his tongue** i.e. rather than his sword. Overactive tongues were gendered feminine and associated with female usurpation of male authority. See ll. 133–4.
127 **broke their fasts** i.e. eaten breakfast (as opposed to fasting prior to mass)
128 **That . . . dine** i.e. but who will die in battle before eating again at dinner-time; their blood will be on Henry's hands
129 **deny** refuse

133 **Whoever . . . mother** Doubts about Prince Edward's paternity allude to Margaret's affair with Suffolk in *2 Henry VI*, as well as rumours that Henry was incapable of fathering children. See also ll. 147–9. 'On the thirteenth day of October [1453] was the Queen delivered at Westminster of a fair son . . . whose mother sustained not a little slander and obloquy of the common people, saying that the King was not able to get a child, and that this was not his son, with many slanderous words to the Queen's dishonour' (Hall Ddvi^v, Holinshed Pppi^r).
   got begot, procreate
134 **wot** know

MARGARET

But thou art neither like thy sire nor dam,   135
But like a foul misshapen stigmatic
Marked by the destinies to be avoided
As venom toads or lizards' dreadful stings.

RICHARD

Iron of Naples hid with English gilt,
Whose father bears the title of a king—   140
As if a channel should be called the sea—
Sham'st thou not, knowing whence thou art extraught,
To let thy tongue detect thy base-born heart?

EDWARD

A wisp of straw were worth a thousand crowns
To make this shameless callet know herself.   145
Helen of Greece was fairer far than thou,
Although thy husband may be Menelaus,
And ne'er was Agamemnon's brother wronged
By that false woman as this king by thee.

---

135 **dam** mother (usually of animals, and thus scornful when applied to humans)
136 **stigmatic** person with physical deformity
137 **Marked** destined; naturally branded
destinies fate. Literally the three classical Fates: Clotho, Lachesis, and Atropos.
138 **venom** poisonous, an erroneous belief going back to classical writers (e.g. Aelian, ix. 11).
lizards' . . . stings Also erroneous, arising from the medieval translation of Latin *anguis* as 'lizard' (Hattaway).
139 **Iron . . . gilt** Alluding to Margaret's impoverished father, René of Naples, and her acceptance as Henry's queen without any dowry (see note to 1.4.123, and ll. 152–3). The literal contrast is between base and precious metals ('gilt'), which in turn relates to several contextual associations: Margaret as a hard, merciless, manly woman; English 'guilt' (shame at having a foreign queen); the classical Iron Age, proverbial for wickedness (perhaps alluding to Margaret's adultery with Suffolk); and the Golden Age, here the memory of lost English conquests under Henry V, with Margaret made a scapegoat (see ll. 150 ff.).
gilt gold or gold plating
141 **channel** gutter; stream. *OED sb.*[1] 3b also

records 'a trough to conduct melted metal to the . . . mould' but gives no citations. Possibly referring to the Sicilian Channel or the Strait of Messina between North Africa and mainland Italy. More familiar is the English Channel, called the 'Narrow Seas' (1.1.240).
142 **Sham'st thou not** are you not ashamed
extraught descended
143 **detect** expose, betray
base-born of low birth; plebeian
144–5 **wisp . . . callet** A callet was a notorious scold. In public shamings or Skimmingtons they could be made to wear a garland of straw (Hart; Nares, *Glossary*) or to rail at a straw figure (*OED, wisp, sb.*[1] 2b, citing this line).
144 **were** would be
146 **Helen** The daughter of Zeus and Leda. She cuckolded her husband Menelaus, King of Sparta and brother of Agamemnon, King of Mycenae, after being abducted to Troy by Paris, which precipitated the Trojan war. Although famed for her beauty ('Was this the face that launched a thousand ships', *Dr Faustus* 5.1.108), she was usually regarded as a whore. See note to l. 133.
148 **wronged** (as much)

His father revelled in the heart of France   150
And tamed the King and made the Dauphin stoop,
And had he matched according to his state
He might have kept that glory to this day.
But when he took a beggar to his bed
And graced thy poor sire with his bridal day,   155
Even then that sunshine brewed a shower for him
That washed his father's fortunes forth of France
And heaped sedition on his crown at home.
For what hath broached this tumult but thy pride?
Hadst thou been meek our title still had slept,   160
And we in pity of the gentle King
Had slipped our claim until another age.

GEORGE

But when we saw our sunshine made thy spring
And that thy summer bred us no increase,
We set the axe to thy usurping root,   165
And though the edge hath something hit ourselves,
Yet know thou since we have begun to strike,
We'll never leave till we have hewn thee down
Or bathed thy growing with our heated bloods.

---

150 **revelled** took his pleasure, rioted (see note to 1.4.71). Compare *Richard III* Add. Pass. J.8: 'To revel in the entrails of my lambs'. Another meaning from early modern physiology was to draw out blood from a part of the body.

151 **Dauphin stoop** See n. to 1.1.109.

152 **he matched** Henry married
state rank; great worth

155 **graced** honoured

156 **brewed** brought about (*OED v.* 4c, citing this line)

157 **washed . . . forth** carried away; blotted out, obliterated
fortunes . . . of possessions, spoils . . . from

159 **broached** instigated (literally, set flowing)

160 **title still** claim to the throne quietly; now as formerly. The phrases 'titles should sleep' and 'titles still to sleep' occur in the chapter censuring York in *Mirror* (Cairncross).

161 **pity of** compassion for; dutiful respect for
gentle King In the 1963–4 Hall–Barton production Edward directed this sarcastically towards Margaret. But other actors

such as the 1983 BBC's Brian Protheroe spoke in earnest here and at l. 172. See Introduction, p. 72.

162 **slipped** deferred

163–5 **But . . . root** Compare Luke 3: 9: 'Now also is the axe laid unto the root of the trees: therefore every tree which bringeth not forth good fruit, shall be hewn down' (Geneva Bible).

163 **sunshine . . . spring** favour made you flourish. Another reference to the sun, a Yorkist emblem (see 2.3.7).

164 **summer . . . increase** prosperity yielded us no harvest, advancement in honour or influence

165 **usurping** The Yorkist view of Henry and his predecessors. See note to 1.1.134.

166 **something** somewhat

167 **strike** hit or cut with blows (*OED v.* 25, 32)

168 **leave** (off); stop

169 **bathed . . . bloods** 'Bathed' suggests 'immersed', in order to drown, wash out, or destroy (see above, l. 167). While *OED* does not specifically mention these effects,

EDWARD

And in this resolution I defy thee,   170

Not willing any longer conference,

Since thou denied'st the gentle King to speak.

Sound trumpets, let our bloody colours wave,

And either victory or else a grave.

MARGARET Stay, Edward.   175

EDWARD

No, wrangling woman, we'll no longer stay.

These words will cost ten thousand lives this day.

Exeunt omnes

2.3   *Alarum. Excursions. Enter Warwick*

WARWICK

Forspent with toil as runners with a race,

I lay me down a little while to breathe;

For strokes received and many blows repaid

Have robbed my strong-knit sinews of their strength,

And spite of spite, needs must I rest awhile.   5

Enter Edward running

EDWARD

Smile, gentle heaven, or strike, ungentle death,

For this world frowns, and Edward's sun is clouded.

---

172 denied'st] F; deniest O, WARBURTON (*subs.*) *and some editors*
    2.3] CAPELL; *not in* F

---

it records 'to bathe in blood', which includes this sense and is used 'to express the great quantity of blood shed' (*OED*, *bathe*, *v.* 3). Alternatively, 'blood' may represent fertilizer (cf. *Richard II* 4.1.128, 'The blood of English shall manure the ground'), in which case the line means 'Or else die in the attempt and feed the growth of your family tree' (Christine Buckley, pers. comm.).

170 **resolution** answer to a question, explanation; conviction; determination
171 **Not willing . . . conference** refusing to have . . . discussion
172 **denied'st** forbade
173 **bloody** foreshadowing bloodshed
    colours flags, ensigns (*OED sb.* 7, citing this line)

177 **These words** this stubborn, provoking talk
2.3.0.1 *Excursions* Entries and exits of attacking soldiers accompanied by sounds of warfare off stage, meant to represent a part of the main battle. 'This deadly battle and bloody conflict continued ten hours in doubtful victory. The one part some time flowing, and sometime ebbing . . .' (Hall Ggvii^r, Holinshed '. . . victory, uncertainly heaving and setting on both sides', Rrri^r). See also 2.5.5–11.
1 **Forspent** worn out
2 **breathe** rest
5 **spite of spite** come what may (Dent SS18)
5.1 *running* George's account of events (ll. 9–10) suggests that Edward's haste signifies alarm or panic.

WARWICK

How now my lord, what hap? What hope of good?
        Enter George

GEORGE

Our hap is loss, our hope but sad despair,
Our ranks are broke, and ruin follows us.   10
What counsel give you? Whither shall we fly?

EDWARD

Bootless is flight, they follow us with wings,
And weak we are and cannot shun pursuit.
        Enter Richard

RICHARD

Ah Warwick, why hast thou withdrawn thyself?
Thy brother's blood the thirsty earth hath drunk,   15
Broached with the steely point of Clifford's lance,
And in the very pangs of death he cried,
Like to a dismal clangor heard from far,
'Warwick revenge, brother revenge my death!'
So underneath the belly of their steeds   20
That stained their fetlocks in his smoking blood,
The noble gentleman gave up the ghost.

8.1 *George*] CAPELL; *Clarence* F; *George, ⌈running⌉* OXFORD   13.1 *Richard*] F; *Richard* running O, OXFORD

8 **what hap . . . good** how have events turned out . . . good fortune
9 **Our hap** George hears Warwick's question as he enters; 'hap' = fate.
   hope . . . despair Probably because no quarter (= taking of prisoners) had been declared. See Appendix A.
12 **Bootless** useless
13 **shun** avoid
15 **Thy . . . drunk** Compare Genesis 4: 10–11: 'thy brother's blood crieth unto me out of the ground. And now art thou cursed from off the earth, which hath opened her mouth to receive thy brother's blood' (Bishops' Bible).
   brother Not Montague, but another brother, Thomas Neville, 'the bastard [son] of Salisbury', killed (but not by Clifford, *pace* l. 16) at Ferrybridge, a skirmish prior to Towton. Another brother or cousin, Sir John Neville, is listed among

the dead at Towton, to which Hall adds the marginal note 'A great slaughter of Englishmen' (Hall Ggvii^r, Holinshed Rrri^r). French and Wilson believed Shakespeare's lines referred to a third brother, Sir Thomas Neville, killed at Wakefield (Hall Ggiii^r, Holinshed Qqqiv^r). Both chronicles thus record that within a year Warwick lost three brothers at Wakefield, Ferrybridge, and Towton respectively (none of whose deaths is associated with Clifford). In *True Tragedy* Richard reports the death of Warwick's father, the Earl of Salisbury. See Appendix B, p. 358.
16 **Broached** pierced to drain
18 **dismal** cheerless; boding disaster
   clangor 'long resonant ringing sound' (*OED*, citing this line)
21 **fetlocks** tufts of hair above a horse's hooves
   smoking steaming

WARWICK
    Then let the earth be drunken with our blood.
    I'll kill my horse because I will not fly.
    Why stand we like soft-hearted women here,   25
    Wailing our losses whiles the foe doth rage,
    And look upon as if the tragedy
    Were played in jest by counterfeiting actors?
    Here on my knee I vow to God above
    I'll never pause again, never stand still,   30
    Till either death hath closed these eyes of mine
    Or fortune given me measure of revenge.

EDWARD
    O Warwick, I do bend my knee with thine
    And in this vow do chain my soul to thine;
    And ere my knee rise from the earth's cold face,   35
    I throw my hands, mine eyes, my heart to thee
    Thou setter-up and plucker-down of kings,
    Beseeching thee, if with thy will it stands
    That to my foes this body must be prey,
    Yet that thy brazen gates of heaven may ope   40
    And give sweet passage to my sinful soul.
    Now lords take leave until we meet again,
    Where'er it be, in heaven or in earth.

---

38 if . . . stands₍ DYCE; (if . . . stands) F

---

23 **earth . . . blood** 'A common biblical expression' (Shaheen).

24 **I'll . . . fly** Warwick slaughtered his horse in fury upon hearing the news of his brother's death, vowing to revenge him. See Appendix A.
    because in order that

25–8 **Why . . . actors** Warwick's shock at the news of his brother's death momentarily defamiliarizes his present situation, so that his inertia feels alienated from the 'proper' masculine response. Anne Righter discusses the metadramatic associations of this passage in *Shakespeare and the Idea of the Play* (1962), pp. 92–3.

26 **Wailing** lamenting, crying over

27 **look upon** watch like spectators (*OED*, *look*, *v*. 46, citing this line)

28 **jest . . . counterfeiting** stage performance . . . impersonating

29, 33 **knee . . . knee** For a discussion of gestures of kneeling signifying allegiance see Kelly, 'Oaths in Shakespeare's *Henry VI Plays*', pp. 365–71.

32 **measure** satisfaction (*OED sb.* 10, citing this line); equal proportion. See 2.6.54.

37 Paraphrases two biblical passages: 'God is the judge; he putteth down one, and setteth up another' (Psalm 75: 8, *BCP*); 'he taketh away kings: he setteth up kings' (Daniel 2: 21, Geneva Bible). At 3.3.157 and 5.1.26 the phrase is applied to Warwick.

38 **stands** agrees

40 **brazen . . . ope** strong (as brass) . . . open. Kyd, *Spanish Tragedy* 3.7.9, has 'And broken through the brazen gates of hell', which is the more usual attribute.

RICHARD

> Brother give me thy hand, and gentle Warwick
> Let me embrace thee in my weary arms.
> I that did never weep now melt with woe,   45
> That winter should cut off our springtime so.

WARWICK

> Away, away. Once more sweet lords farewell.

GEORGE

> Yet let us all together to our troops
> And give them leave to fly that will not stay,   50
> And call them pillars that will stand to us,
> And if we thrive, promise them such rewards
> As victors wear at the Olympian games.
> This may plant courage in their quailing breasts,
> For yet is hope of life and victory.   55
> Forslow no longer, make we hence amain.   *Exeunt*

2.4   *Excursions. Enter Richard and Clifford*

RICHARD

> Now Clifford I have singled thee alone.
> Suppose this arm is for the Duke of York
> And this for Rutland, both bound to revenge,
> Wert thou environed with a brazen wall.

49 all together] ROWE; altogether F
  2.4] CAPELL; *not in* F   0.1 Richard and Clifford] F; *Richard at one dore and Clifford at the
other* O

46–8 **I . . . away** If Warwick is sceptical
of Richard's sentiment, 'Away, away'
may signal his dismissal as well as his
departure.
47 **winter . . . springtime** death, misfortune
. . . flourishing hopes
49 **Yet** now as before
   let us (go)
50 **stay** stand firm (*OED v.*[1] 7b, citing this
line)
51 **pillars . . . stand to** vital supporters . . .
support
52 **rewards** awards; in classical times,
wreaths of olive or bay leaves. See Appendix A, 2.3.49–53.
53 **Olympian games** In ancient Greece took
place over five days every four years at
Olympia, in honour of Zeus.
54 **quailing** dejected

55 **yet is** there is still
56 **Forslow** delay
   make . . . amain advance . . . at full
   speed, with full force
2.4.1 **singled thee alone** separated you from
the others (*OED, single, v.*[1] 3 citing this
line)
2–3, 6–7 **this arm . . . this . . . This is the hand
. . . this** May imply both hands carry
weapons, and that Richard and
Clifford fight using sword and dagger
rather than sword and shield.
4 **Wert thou** even if you were
  environed surrounded. The Messenger's
  term at 2.1.50 reporting York's death,
  deriving from the chronicle account. See
  Appendix A, 1.4.1–29.
  brazen impregnable like brass (*OED a.* 1b,
  citing this line)

CLIFFORD

Now Richard, I am with thee here alone,   5
This is the hand that stabbed thy father York
And this the hand that slew thy brother Rutland,
And here's the heart that triumphs in their death
And cheers these hands that slew thy sire and brother
To execute the like upon thyself;   10
And so have at thee.

> *They fight. Warwick comes and joins Richard.*
> *Clifford flees*

RICHARD

Nay Warwick, single out some other chase,
For I myself will hunt this wolf to death.   *Exeunt*

2.5   *Alarum. Enter King Henry alone*

HENRY

This battle fares like to the morning's war
When dying clouds contend with growing light,
What time the shepherd, blowing of his nails,
Can neither call it perfect day nor night.
Now sways it this way like a mighty sea   5
Forced by the tide to combat with the wind,
Now sways it that way like the selfsame sea
Forced to retire by fury of the wind.

11.1 *and ... Richard*] CAPELL (*subs.*); *not in* F; *and rescues Richard,* & *then exeunt omnes* O (*omitting ll.* 12–13)   11.2 *flees*] This edition: *flies* F
    2.5] CAPELL; *not in* F   0.1 *Alarum ... alone*] F; *Alarmes still, and then Enter Henry solus* O

---

8 **triumphs** exults
10 **execute** perform
11.1 **and joins** F leaves the nature of the fight and of Warwick's entry undetermined, except that Clifford flees. The dialogue makes it clear, however, that Richard and Clifford are eager to fight in single combat (as anticipated by *2 Henry VI* 5.1.211–14). But Warwick's arrival unbalances the odds and prompts Richard to assert his 'prior claim' on Clifford. In *True Tragedy*, by contrast, Richard is endangered and there is no further dialogue.
12 **chase** prey to hunt
2.5.3 **What time** when (*OED, time, sb.* 13)
    blowing ... nails Normally interpreted as

signs of idleness or leisure (*OED, blow, v.*[1] 4b), but more naturalistically, in this early morning context, the action of warming one's fingers (compare *L.L.L.* 5.2.898).
3 **of** on (Abbott ¶178)
5–8 **sways ... wind** The metaphor of the ebb and flow of battle derives from the chronicles' description of Towton. See note to 2.3.0.1. The prominent sea, wind, and tide imagery of Part Three which characterizes civil war in terms of powerfully conflicting elemental forces was a significant aspect of Shakespeare's revision of *True Tragedy*. See Kernan, *passim*, and Introduction, pp. 41–3.

Sometime the flood prevails and then the wind,
Now one the better then another best,   10
Both tugging to be victors, breast to breast,
Yet neither conqueror nor conquerèd.
So is the equal poise of this fell war.
Here on this molehill will I sit me down.
To whom God will, there be the victory,   15
For Margaret my queen and Clifford too
Have chid me from the battle, swearing both
They prosper best of all when I am thence.
Would I were dead, if God's good will were so,
For what is in this world but grief and woe?   20
O God, methinks it were a happy life
To be no better than a homely swain,
To sit upon a hill as I do now,
To carve out dials quaintly, point by point,
Thereby to see the minutes how they run: 25
How many makes the hour full complete,
How many hours brings about the day,

---

21 God,] HATTAWAY; God! F   26 makes] F; make HANMER *and some editors*   27 brings] F1;
bring F2 *and some editors*

9 **flood** flowing of the tide
13 **equal 'poise** equally weighted scales on
both sides of a balance. An image from
both classical epic, in which the gods
weigh the fates of opposing heroes (e.g.
Hector and Achilles in the *Iliad*), and the
Bible, signifying moral judgement (e.g.
Daniel 5: 27, or traditional depictions of
the archangel Michael weighing souls in
Day of Judgement scenes).
fell cruel
14 **molehill** Modern productions sometimes
'return' to the molehill on which York
was killed in 1.4 (see note to 67 ff.). The
scene's stillness may be emphasized by
having Henry spotlit in the centre of a
darkened stage or the gallery, or illumi-
nated in close-up, in either case heightening the sense of an intense personal vision
of war.
17 **chid** driven me away with angry words
21–54 **happy life . . . him** The ideal ruler
as shepherd is a classical and biblical
commonplace (e.g. Plato, *Republic*, i.
345, Jeremiah 23 (Hattaway)), while the
measured tranquillity of rural versus
court life, and escape from political

intrigue and ambition, are core themes of
pastoral poetry (e.g. Virgil, *Eclogues*). A
related historical reference occurs in the
chronicles' report of Clifford's son
Thomas, whom Rutland mentions at
1.3.41. After his father was killed at Dintingdale (see note to 2.6.0.1), he 'was
brought up with a shepherd in poor habit,
and dissimul[at]ed behaviour ever in fear
["ever in fear to be known" = Holinshed]
to publish his lineage or degree, till King
Henry VII obtained the crown' (Hall
Ggvi^v, Holinshed Qqqvi^v).
22 **swain** shepherd
24 **dials** sundials (*OED sb.*[1] 1, citing this line)
quaintly artfully (*OED* 2, citing this line),
skilfully
26–40 **How many . . . grave** '[Henry] is not
aware when he starts the speech that his
imagination will lead him to contemplate
the regular, ordered life of a shepherd,
minute by minute, hour by hour. So each
line is a new thought—or rather a
thought developed' (Ralph Fiennes on
playing Henry VI, *Players* 3, p. 110).
26 **hour** Two syllables (Cercignani, p. 228).
27 **brings about** complete

How many days will finish up the year,
How many years a mortal man may live.
When this is known, then to divide the times: 30
So many hours must I tend my flock,
So many hours must I take my rest,
So many hours must I contemplate,
So many hours must I sport myself,
So many days my ewes have been with young,   35
So many weeks ere the poor fools will ean,
So many years ere I shall shear the fleece,
So minutes, hours, days, months, and years
Passed over to the end they were created,
Would bring white hairs unto a quiet grave.   40
Ah what a life were this! How sweet, how lovely.
Gives not the hawthorn bush a sweeter shade
To shepherds looking on their silly sheep
Than doth a rich embroidered canopy
To kings that fear their subjects' treachery?   45
O yes it doth, a thousandfold it doth.
And to conclude, the shepherd's homely curds,
His cold thin drink out of his leather bottle,
His wonted sleep under a fresh tree's shade,
All which secure and sweetly he enjoys,   50
Is far beyond a prince's delicates—
His viands sparkling in a golden cup,
His body couchèd in a curious bed—

---

33 **contemplate** meditate (contrasting with the active life of public affairs)

34 **sport** divert, refresh

36 **weeks** W. S. Walker conjectured that a line referring to 'months' to agree with the summary at l. 38 was lost due to compositorial eye-skip. This is possible given other omissions in this act, but against it is the absence of either 'months' or 'weeks' in the preceding passage 25–9, and *OED*'s definition of 'weeks' used loosely to refer to 'a duration which is felt as long' (*week, sb.* 2d).
   poor fools Term of endearment, affection.
   ean give birth

39 **Passed . . . end** spent to achieve the purpose for which

40 **white hairs** i.e. of old age

41 **Ah . . . lovely** In the 1987 ESC production Henry became radiantly happy imagining this alternative life, perhaps for the only time in the play. Other actors have conveyed a bitter-sweet tone, since the vision is so opposite to his own reality.

43 **silly** innocent, simple

44 **canopy** i.e. over a throne (see note to 1.1.0.4, *chair of state*) or bed, or carried in procession over the monarch

47 **curds** Curd cheese not needing to be matured—conventional shepherd's fare.

48 **thin** weak

49 **wonted** accustomed

50 **secure** free from care, anxiety, distrust, danger

51 **delicates** luxuries, delicacies

52 **viands** foods

53 **curious** elaborately decorated; fretful

When care, mistrust, and treason waits on him.
Alarum. Enter a Son that hath killed his father at one
door with his father's body, and a Father that hath
killed his son at another door, bearing his son's body
SON

Ill blows the wind that profits nobody.   55
This man whom hand to hand I slew in fight
May be possessèd with some store of crowns,
And I that haply take them from him now

54.1 *Son*] F; souldier O   54.2 *with . . . body*] This edition; *not in* F; *with a dead man in his armes* O; *dragging in the Body* CAPELL   54.3 *bearing . . . body*] This edition *transferred from duplicate direction in* F (*bearing of his Sonne*), *after l.* 78

54 **waits on** attend on (like a servant); lie in wait for (*OED v.*[1] 14j, b)
54.1–3 *Son . . . son* Hall's analysis of Towton sums up the theme of this part of the scene: 'This conflict was in manner unnatural, for in it the son fought against the father, the brother against the brother, the nephew against the uncle, and the tenant against his lord' (Ggvii[r]). D. J. Womersley has traced this *topos* of civil war back to Tacitus' *Historiae*, III, xxv, translated by Sir Henry Savile in 1591, the same year the play was written ('3 *Henry VI*: Shakespeare, Tacitus, and parricide', *N&Q* 230 (1985), 468–73). It also appears in the Tudor government's *Homily Against Disobedience and Wilful Rebellion* (1547; repr. 1587, sig. Nn5[v]), as well as *Gorboduc* 5.2.213–14. In most productions the Son takes a position on one side of Henry, and the Father on the other, creating a balanced tableau.
54.1–2 *Son . . . Father* F prefers grouped directions, while O separates these entries (see note to 1.1.210.1–2). As the Oxford editors explain, this suggests different theatrical conceptions: a symmetrical tableau, versus more narrative-style action. It also suggests revision. F repeats the direction for the *Father . . . son* at 78.1 below, which may be a duplication. The assumption is that Shakespeare wrote the group entry, afterwards decided on a sequential one, and then failed to rewrite the original direction. But the wording of the second Folio direction, '*Enter Father*' seems to assume a familiarity with who the character is that its first, '*a Father*', does not. If the second were merely a duplication, one would expect '*a Father*', just like 'a soldier' in O. Perhaps the sec-

ond entry for the Father is deliberate and what is missing—not uncommon in F, see 113.1 below—is an exit before he re-enters, '*bearing of his Son*'. This would mean he first enters with the Son, observes him, and exits some time before Henry's speech, leaving him time to be ready to carry on his son. The Son may even provide the Father with the idea for his own actions, and hint at the implicit action, at 58–60, lines which appear in F only. If the Father left at this point, before the Son discovers that he has killed his own father, it would also explain why he repeats the Son's error.
54.2 *with . . . father's body* Cairncross and other editors conflate F and O directions, with the result that the Son, who presumably was played by a boy or young man, has to carry on a fully grown adult. O avoids this difficulty by substituting 'soldier' for 'Son', while F leaves open the way in which they enter. Capell's addition '*dragging in the Body*' suggests one possibility. Another could be that the Father enters wounded and collapses on stage, since F does not state that he is a 'dead man', and '*hath killed*' could be anticipatory.
55 Proverbial: 'It is an ill wind that blows no man good' (Dent W421).
56–60 **This . . . me** Compare *Gorboduc* 5.2.204–7: 'All right and law shall cease, and he that had | Nothing today tomorrow shall enjoy | Great heaps of gold, and he that flowed in wealth, | Lo, he shall be bereft of life and all'. If the Father does not enter until later at l. 79 (see note), this self-awareness of war's repetitive instability becomes prophetic too.
58 **haply** by chance

May yet ere night yield both my life and them
To some man else, as this dead man doth me.   60
Who's this? O God, it is my father's face,
Whom in this conflict I unwares have killed.
O heavy times, begetting such events.
From London by the King was I pressed forth.
My father, being the Earl of Warwick's man,   65
Came on the part of York, pressed by his master;
And I who at his hands received my life,
Have by my hands of life bereavèd him.
Pardon me God, I knew not what I did,
And pardon father, for I knew not thee.   70
My tears shall wipe away these bloody marks;
And no more words till they have flowed their fill.

HENRY
⁀O piteous spectacle, O bloody times!
Whiles lions war and battle for their dens,
Poor harmless lambs abide their enmity.   75
Weep wretched man, I'll aid thee tear for tear,
And let our hearts and eyes, like civil war,
Be blind with tears and break o'ercharged with grief.

FATHER
Thou that so stoutly hast resisted me,

61 God,] HATTAWAY; God! F   79 Thou] F; Enter an other souldier, with a dead man | 2. *Soul.*
Lie there thou . . . o   hast] F3; hath F1

59 **ere** before
61, 82 These lines suggest that the faces are
    obscured either by blood or by some form
    of covering such as a helmet.
62 **unwares** unknowingly (*OED adv.* 2,
    citing this line)
63 **heavy** sorrowful, sad
64 **pressed forth** forced to enlist. An issue of
    life and death for many Elizabethan spec-
    tators; government recruitment to fight
    in France, the Netherlands, and Ireland
    intensified throughout the 1590s, but was
    increasingly unpopular and evaded. See
    Introduction, pp. 31–7.
65–6 **father . . . master** Social obligations of
    feudal hierarchy become personal entrap-
    ment.
65 **man** liegeman, retainer
66 **part** side
68 **bereavèd** deprived
69 **Pardon . . . did** An echo of Jesus' dying
    words in Luke 23: 34 ('Father, forgive

them; for they know not what they do').
Also Henry at 5.6.60 and *2 Henry VI*
4.4.37.
71 **tears . . . marks** Echoes York at 1.4.158.
73–8 **O piteous spectacle . . . grief** Henry acts
    partly as a chorus figure, or like the pre-
    senter of a civic pageant, elucidating the
    action's moral. For discussion see Martin,
    Pageantry, pp. 249–51. In the 1965 televi-
    sion version of the Hall–Barton produc-
    tion, Henry turned his face in close-up to
    one side, and the Son–Father actions took
    place 'floating' in the black half of the
    screen, as if imagined in Henry's mind.
75 **abide** suffer
77–8 Chiasmic structure (ab/ba): hearts . . .
    eyes / blind . . . break.
77 **like . . . war** i.e. self-destructively
79 **FATHER** Some productions and editions
    have the Father enter at this point, rather
    than earlier at 54.2–3.
    stoutly vigorously, firmly; stubbornly

Give me thy gold, if thou hast any gold,   80
For I have bought it with an hundred blows.
But let me see, is this our foeman's face?
Ah, no, no, no, it is mine only son.
Ah boy, if any life be left in thee,
Throw up thine eye. See, see, what showers arise,   85
Blown with the windy tempest of my heart,
Upon thy wounds that kills mine eye and heart.
O pity God this miserable age!
What stratagems, how fell, how butcherly,
Erroneous, mutinous, and unnatural   90
This deadly quarrel daily doth beget.
O boy, thy father gave thee life too soon,
And hath bereft thee of thy life too late.

HENRY

Woe above woe, grief more than common grief.
O that my death would stay these ruthful deeds,   95
O pity, pity, gentle heaven pity.
The red rose and the white are on his face,
The fatal colours of our striving houses,
The one his purple blood right well resembles,
The other his pale cheeks, methinks, presenteth.   100
Wither one rose and let the other flourish,
If you contend, a thousand lives must wither.

---

87 kills] F; kill ROWE 1709 *and some editors*   89 stratagems] F3; Stragems F1   100 cheeks] F;
Cheek ROWE 1709 *and some editors*

82 **foeman's** enemy's
85 **Throw** lift
85–6 **showers . . . heart** See 1.4.145–6 and
   notes.
89 **stratagems** bloody deeds
90 **Erroneous** immoral, criminal (*OED* 2, citing this line)
92–3 **life . . . life** state of life after death . . .
   mortal life (*OED* 12b)
93 **late** recently
94 **above** on top of
95 **stay** end
   ruthful lamentable, 'Demanding pity on
   account of cruelty' (Hart).
97–8 **red . . . houses** English Petrarchan
   poetry conventionally described healthy
   facial complexions as a mingling of red
   and white (damask) roses. But here the
   colours represent a struggle between life

and death, and are emblematic of the
warring houses of Lancaster and York, a
conflict which begins dramatically with
the Temple Garden quarrel in *1 Henry VI*
2.4. See note to ll. 101–2.
99 **purple blood** i.e. like crimson-blue blood
   in veins
100 **cheeks** Rowe's emendation assumes the
   appearance of blood on one cheek and
   paleness on the other. But the contrast
   could be between pale cheeks and blood-
   stains or wounds.
   presenteth represents
101–2 **rose . . . wither** Perhaps echoes York's
   prophecy in *1 Henry VI* 2.4.124–7, 'this
   brawl today . . . Shall send, between the
   red rose and the white, | A thousand
   souls to death and deadly night'.
102 **contend** struggle; fight in war

SON

How will my mother for a father's death
Take on with me and ne'er be satisfied?

FATHER

How will my wife for slaughter of my son   105
Shed seas of tears and ne'er be satisfied?

HENRY

How will the country for these woeful chances
Misthink the King and not be satisfied?

SON

Was ever son, so rued a father's death?

FATHER

Was ever father, so bemoaned his son?   110

HENRY

Was ever king, so grieved for subjects' woe?
Much is your sorrow, mine ten times so much.

SON

I'll bear thee hence where I may weep my fill.

Exit with the body

FATHER

These arms of mine shall be thy winding-sheet,
My heart, sweet boy, shall be thy sepulchre,   115
For from my heart thine image ne'er shall go.

113.1 *Exit . . . body*] CAPELL (*subs.*) *following* THEOBALD; *not in* F

103–22 **How . . . kill** The structured sequence of exclamatory questions modulates into a formal lament.

103–8 **How . . . satisfied?** Rhetorically, the verbal repetition at the beginning and end of each speech is an instance of *symploche*, or 'the figure of reply' (George Puttenham, *The Arte of English Poesie* (1589), ed. G. D. Willcock and Alice Walker (Cambridge, 1936), pp. 199–200).

104 **Take on** cry out, rage against

104, 106, 108 **satisfied** appeased, consoled, reconciled

107 **chances** unfortunate events

108 **Misthink** think harshly of (*OED v.* 3, citing this line)

109 **rued** repented, sorrowed over

113.1, 122.1 *Exit . . . body* Theobald, following O, first provided a separate direction for the Son that seems to be missing in F. Whereas the sequential exits in O

are separated by only two lines, so that in stage time the action virtually flows together, in F the Father speaks for nine lines. Thus, if F's single direction was meant to cover both figures, the Son would have to pause. While this staging is possible, and Henry's address to 'Sad-hearted men' could imply that both leave together, the Son's 'I'll bear thee hence . . .' sounds like an exit line and antici-pates the Father's identical words before his own marked exit.

114–15 **arms . . . sepulchre** Compare Marlowe, *Jew of Malta*: 'What sight is this? My Lodowick slain! | These arms of mine shall be thy sepulchre' (3.2.10–11); Dyce, *Notes*, p. 101.

114 **winding-sheet** burial shroud (*OED* 1b, citing this line)

116–17 **heart . . . image . . . breast** Compare Videna grieving the death of her son Fer-

My sighing breast shall be thy funeral bell,
And so obsequious will thy father be,
E'en for the loss of thee having no more,
As Priam was for all his valiant sons.   120
I'll bear thee hence, and let them fight that will,
For I have murdered where I should not kill.

Exit with the body

HENRY

Sad-hearted men much overgone with care,
Here sits a king more woeful than you are.

*Alarums. Excursions. Enter Queen Margaret, Prince
Edward, and Exeter*

EDWARD

Fly father fly, for all your friends are fled,   125
And Warwick rages like a chafèd bull.
Away, for death doth hold us in pursuit.

MARGARET

Mount you my lord, towards Berwick post amain.
Edward and Richard, like a brace of greyhounds
Having the fearful flying hare in sight,   130
With fiery eyes sparkling for very wrath

---

119 E'en] This edition (*conj.* Dyce, *Notes*); Men F1; Man, F4; Even CAPELL; Meet SISSON NR (*conj.*); Mean HULME *conj.*   122.1 *Exit . . . body*] CAPELL; *Exit* F   124.1 *Queen Margaret*] HANMER; *the Queen* F (*and subs. prefix*)   124.1–2 *Prince Edward*] RIVERSIDE (*subs.*); *the Prince* F (*and subs. prefix*)

rex: 'So should not now | This living
breast remain the ruthful tomb | Where-
in my heart yielden to death is graved'
(*Gorboduc* 4.1.18–20).
118 **obsequious** dutiful in observing your
funeral rites, preserving your memory
119 **E'en** (even) expressly. Dyce's proposed
emendation (*Notes*, p. 101), first adopted
by Collier, seems the most persuasive,
though, as the Oxford editors note, the
graphical error it presumes (E/M, e/m) is
unlikely. Perhaps it was not a graphical
error but eye-skip from the 'M' two lines
before ('My sighing . . .'); or possibly the
compositor mistakenly selected M for E,
since M lay directly below E in the early
modern type-case (Christine Buckley,
pers. comm.)
   no more i.e. sons
120 **Priam . . . sons** King of Troy, father of
fifty sons, of whom Hector was his most

deeply felt loss, according to Homer (*Iliad*,
xxiv. 217ff.). Priam came to emblematize
an extreme change in fortunes.
123 **overgone** oppressed
124.1–2 *Enter . . . Exeter* See Introduction, p.
111.
125 **friends are fled** Implies that Henry
has been deserted, while the chronicles
speak of the 'loss' of his supporters. See
Appendix A.
126 **chafèd** enraged
128 **Berwick** Berwick-on-Tweed, on the
Scottish border
   post amain hurry at full speed
129–33 **greyhounds . . . backs** Modern productions often aurally reinforce the poetic
images of predatory violence, which
recur throughout the *Henry VI* plays,
through recorded sounds of dogs, wolves,
etc.
131 **very pure**

And bloody steel grasped in their ireful hands,
Are at our backs, and therefore hence amain.

EXETER

Away, for vengeance comes along with them.
Nay stay not to expostulate, make speed   135
Or else come after. I'll away before.

HENRY

Nay take me with thee, good sweet Exeter;
Not that I fear to stay, but love to go
Whither the Queen intends. Forward, away.   *Exeunt*

2.6   *A loud alarum. Enter Clifford wounded*

CLIFFORD

Here burns my candle out; ay, here it dies,
Which whiles it lasted gave King Henry light.
O Lancaster I fear thy overthrow
More than my body's parting with my soul.
My love and fear glued many friends to thee,   5
And now I fall, thy tough commixtures melts,

2.6] CAPELL; *not in* F   0.1 *wounded*] F; wounded, with an arrow in his necke O   6 fall, thy]
ROWE; fall. Thy F   commixtures melts] F1; Commixtures melt F2; commixtures melts O

132 **steel** i.e. swords
    ireful angry
134–6 **Away . . . after** Henry's apparent
    slowness to react or move is often con-
    veyed as distraction, as the reality of
    war re-intrudes, accompanied by battle
    sounds, and sometimes by regular stage
    lighting representing daylight. In 1987,
    for example, the ESC's Henry was dazed
    and emotionally wrung out by his oppos-
    ing visions of pastoral bliss and civil war.
    The exhortations by Prince Edward,
    Margaret, and Exeter suggest repeated
    attempts to rouse him. In the 1963–4
    Hall–Barton production, Exeter lightly
    slapped his face.
135 **expostulate** discuss, complain (*OED* 3,
    citing this line). This suggests Henry has
    tried to express something about what he
    has just experienced.
137–9 **Nay . . . intends** Henry's remarks have
    struck commentators as odd, but they
    may have been suggested by Holinshed's
    report after the second Battle of
    St Albans, when Northumberland and
    others 'brought the Queen and her son
    Prince Edward unto [King Henry's] pres-
    ence, whom he joyfully received, embra-

cing and kissing them in most loving
wise' (Qqqiv^v).
139 **intends** purposes to go, proceeds
2.6.0.1 **wounded** F does not identify Clifford's
    wounds, and neither do most modern pro-
    ductions. O's call for 'an arrow in his
    neck', which also appears in *Mirror*, spec-
    ifies the injury but also changes the visual
    image, making it perhaps faintly ludicrous
    (and not exactly the same as the chroni-
    cles, which say Clifford was shot in the
    throat—see Appendix A), perhaps closer
    to sensationalized stage deaths such as
    that of Cambises: 'Enter the King, with-
    out a gown, a sword thrust up into his
    side, bleeding' (sc. xi). F's omission of the
    arrow may be a recognition of this, and l.
    27 'seems against it' (Wilson), as do ll. 60
    ff. On the other hand the BBC's Clifford got
    round some of the difficulty by snapping
    the arrow off before the Yorkists entered.
1–2 **candle . . . light** Proverbial: 'candle of
    life' (Dent CC1).
5 **fear** capacity for inspiring terror (*OED sb.*
    5c, first citation *Caesar* 2.1.190)
6 **fall** (dead); die out
    tough strongly cohesive; adhesive, glu-
    tinous; vigorously stubborn

Impairing Henry, strength'ning misproud York.
And whither fly the gnats but to the sun?
And who shines now but Henry's enemies?
O Phoebus, hadst thou never given consent   10
That Phaethon should check thy fiery steeds,
Thy burning car never had scorched the earth.
And Henry, hadst thou swayed as kings should do
Or as thy father and his father did,
Giving no ground unto the house of York,   15
They never then had sprung like summer flies,
I and ten thousand in this luckless realm
Had left no mourning widows for our death,
And thou this day hadst kept thy chair in peace.
For what doth cherish weeds but gentle air?   20
And what makes robbers bold but too much lenity?

7–8 York. | And] F; *Yorke,* | The common people swarme like summer flies, | And 0, THEOBALD,
and some editors

---

6 **commixtures** compound (*OED* 2, citing
this line); union (of those supporting
Lancaster)

7 **misproud** traitorously proud (*OED*, citing
this line)

8 **And . . . sun** Many editors have agreed
with Theobald that preceding this with a
line in 0 'is a necessary Introduction to
That which follows'. This is plausible if
'summer flies' and 'gnats' are regarded as
synonymous. But elsewhere Shakespeare
distinguishes between them. He associ-
ates 'summer flies' with heat, speedy
breeding, and 'flyblown' corruption
(*L.L.L.* 5.2.408; *Henry V* 5.2.305, *Othello*
4.2.68). Gnats on the other hand are
attracted to the sun primarily as a source
of light (e.g. 'When the sun shines, let
foolish gnats make sport, | But creep in
crannies when he hides his beams' (*Errors*
2.2.30–1; see also *Titus* 4.4.82). O can be
defended as a cumulative image, but significantly it drops the line about 'summer
flies' where it occurs at l. 16 in F. At l. 8 in
F, as Vaughan argued, there is a logical
connection between 'gnats', 'sun', and
'the York Coat of Arms, which was a Sun'
(mentioned by Edward at 2.1.40 and elsewhere), whereas at l. 16 'summer flies' is
appropriate to the idea of 'Henry's enemies' multiplying rapidly as enthusi-

asm for his rule wanes and for York's
increases. Whether or not O is deemed to
transpose F's l. 17, conflating the two texts
obscures the feasibility of each and creates a lame repetition benefiting neither.

10–12 **Phoebus . . . earth** See note to
1.4.33.

11 **check** have the reins, control, of (*OED v.*[1]
14b, citing this line)

12 **car** chariot

13 **swayed** ruled

16 **sprung** bred
    summer flies Perhaps with a Shake-
spearian sense of being generated by
corruption. See note to l. 8.

18 **mourning widows** The transposed adjec-
tive emphasizes the action of mourning
(Abbott ¶419).

19 **chair** i.e. of state, throne; old age

20 **cherish** foster
    weeds . . . air Compare *Antony* 1.2.102–
3: 'O, then we bring forth weeds | When
our quick winds lie still'. In a letter,
Theobald wondered whether this was a
typographical error for 'words' (Peter
Seary, pers. comm.). Presumably he had
in mind 'Words are but wind' (Dent
W833); the closest alternative is 'An ill
weed grows apace' (Dent W238). But
because all the early texts read 'weeds', he
did not emend.

21 **bold . . . lenity** confident . . . lenience

Bootless are plaints and cureless are my wounds.
No way to fly nor strength to hold out flight.
The foe is merciless and will not pity,
For at their hands I have deserved no pity.   25
The air hath got into my deadly wounds,
And much effuse of blood doth make me faint.
Come York and Richard, Warwick and the rest,
I stabbed your fathers' bosoms, split my breast.

>   *He faints.*
>   *Alarum and retreat. Enter Edward, Warwick, Richard,*
>   *and Soldiers, Montague and George*

EDWARD

Now breathe we, lords, good fortune bids us pause   30
And smooth the frowns of war with peaceful looks.
Some troops pursue the bloody-minded Queen
That led calm Henry, though he were a king,
As doth a sail filled with a fretting gust
Command an argosy to stem the waves.   35

---

23 flight] F, O; fight JOHNSON *conj.*   29.1 He faints] ROWE; *not in* F   29.3 George] CAPELL;
Clarence F (*and subs. prefixes throughout this scene*)

22 **Bootless . . . cureless** pointless . . . beyond
remedy, fatal
23 **hold out** keep up
26 Proverbial: 'Fresh air is ill for the
wounded man' (Tilley A93), because
the body was thought to be vulnerable to
airborne infection.
27 **effuse** pouring out (*OED sb.*, citing this
line)
29.2 **retreat** Trumpet or drum call to retreat,
perhaps distinctive to an individual army.
Here it also marks the end of the off-stage
battle (see Shirley, pp. 54, 58–9).
29.3 **Montague and George** The unusual
placement of proper names after '*Soldiers*'
suggests entry through a different door, as
from another part of the battlefield. This
may reflect chronicle reports that the
Yorkist battalions at Towton were divided,
with the forward army led by Lord Falconbridge and the rearward by Edward (Hall
Ggvi^v, Holinshed Qqqvi^v-Rrri^r; Shakespeare may have originally confused Falconbridge with Montague. See note to
1.1.210 and Appendix B). In terms of the
copy underlying F, the position of these
names in the direction may represent a

later addition, and/or a marginal note.
Greg (*First Folio*, pp. 112, 195) and some
editors have believed Montague is a ghost
and should be deleted, since he does not
speak and has no implied presence in the
scene. But the fact that his name comes
before George (F *Clarence*), who does
speak, suggests the addition was deliberate. Montague usually enters accompanying his brother Warwick, as at 2.1.94.1
(for first time as '*Marquis Montague*'),
another scene in which he does not speak.
30 **breathe** rest
31 **smooth . . . looks** Compare *Richard III*
1.1.9: 'Grim-visaged war hath smoothed
his wrinkled front'.
33 **were** be (Abbott ¶301)
34 **fretting** ruffling, squalling; discontented,
impatient, vexatious
35 **argosy** Normally refers to the largest size
of merchant vessel (e.g. *Merchant* 1.1.9),
but here the sense is that of a great war-
ship, perhaps with heroic associations of
the legendary *Argo* in which Jason sought
the Golden Fleece (*Merchant* 3.2.240).
stem cut headlong through (*OED v.*³ 1,
citing this line)

But think you lords that Clifford fled with them?

WARWICK

No, 'tis impossible he should escape,
For though before his face I speak the words,
Your brother Richard marked him for the grave.
And wheresoe'er he is, he's surely dead.   40

> *Clifford groans*

RICHARD

Whose soul is that which takes her heavy leave?
A deadly groan, like life and death's departing.
See who it is.

EDWARD   And now the battle's ended,
If friend or foe, let him be gently used.

RICHARD

Revoke that doom of mercy, for 'tis Clifford,   45

---

38 For . . . words,] This edition; (For . . . words) F; For, . . . words CAPELL *and editors*   40.1
groans] F; grones and then dies O   43 See . . . is] *continuing as Richard's speech in* F; *assigned to*
Edward in O

---

38 **For . . . words** The Folio punctuation suggests that 'For though' is combined for
emphasis to mark the whole line parenthetically (see Abbott ¶151), whereas
assigning each one a separate grammatical function—'For' connecting ll. 38 and
40, and 'though' marking the parenthetical thought—seems like a modernization
of early usage. F's punctuation is not
definitive, however, and Capell's alternative, with its slightly different emphasis, is
possible. But in light of similar lines such
as 93–6 below, F should probably be kept.
though . . . speak Even if I were to speak
the words to his face (Abbott ¶368); ironic
with the body of Clifford lying nearby but
as yet unnoticed. Alternatively 'his' may
refer to Richard (Hattaway).

39 **marked** destined, with a related sense
(*OED v.* 5) of being marked with a sign of
the cross (†), a conventional symbol for a
Christian who has died.

40.1 **Clifford groans** Many editors follow O's
addition '*and then dies*'. But 'the exact
moment of Clifford's death is not indicated' (Hattaway), and the dramatic tension during the verbal (and possibly
physical) abuse which follows arises from
an audience's awareness that he may
remain barely alive until some point
before l. 85.

41 **heavy** doleful; wearisome

42 **departing** separation (*OED vbl. sb.* 2, citing this line)

43 **See . . . is** O assigns this part-line to
Edward to precede 'And now . . .', and
some editors since Capell have followed.
But there is little reason for doing so
other than dramatic preference, and
Oxford's suggestion that this may represent authorial revision could run the
other way. Hattaway argues that Edward
asks a question, to which Richard
responds at ll. 45 ff. But there Richard's
lines in F are equally a rejection of
Edward's—characteristically belated—
impulse of clemency. By giving 'See who
it is' to Richard, F subtly changes the
dynamic of command during this
exchange: in O 'Edward is the senior of
the brothers, takes the lead throughout,
and gives instructions' (Sisson, *NR*, ii. 84);
in F Richard seems to be as much in
charge as Edward, perhaps hinting at his
emerging leadership or future ambitions.

43–4 **And . . . used** Edward (unhistorically)
reverses his order that all prisoners
should be killed. See Appendix A, 2.3.9.
Conscience is always an afterthought for
Edward. See 4.1.101–2 and 5.5.43.

44 **gently used** treated respectfully

45 **doom** sentence

Who not contented that he lopped the branch
In hewing Rutland when his leaves put forth,
But set his murd'ring knife unto the root
From whence that tender spray did sweetly spring,
I mean our princely father, Duke of York.   50

WARWICK

From off the gates of York fetch down the head,
Your father's head, which Clifford placèd there;
Instead whereof let this supply the room.
Measure for measure must be answerèd.

EDWARD

Bring forth that fatal screech-owl to our house,   55
That nothing sung but death to us and ours;
        Clifford is dragged forward
Now death shall stop his dismal threat'ning sound,
And his ill-boding tongue no more shall speak.

WARWICK

I think his understanding is bereft:
Speak Clifford, dost thou know who speaks to thee?   60
Dark cloudy death o'ershades his beams of life,
And he nor sees nor hears us what we say.

RICHARD

O would he did, and so perhaps he doth:
'Tis but his policy to counterfeit
Because he would avoid such bitter taunts   65
Which in the time of death he gave our father.

56.1 *Clifford . . . forward*] OXFORD *following* CAPELL; *not in* F   59 his] F2, O; is F1

46–9 **Who . . . spring** Recalls George's image of the family tree at 2.2.165–9. In the 1963–4 Hall–Barton production, Richard's descriptions of Clifford's violence inflamed the York brothers to rush forward and hack his body repeatedly with their daggers, only gradually letting up when there was no reaction.

46–8 **not . . . But** not merely . . . but also

49 **spray** slender shoot

53 **room** place. See Appendix A.

54 Proverbial, deriving from Mark 4: 24: 'With what measure ye mete [portion out], it shall be measured unto you' (Dent M800). But the sense of balancing scores

changes in the next verse, commenting on the unstable nature of revenge: 'For he that hath, to him shall be given; and he that hath not, from him shall be taken even that which he hath' (25). Warwick ignores what goes against his own interests. See 2.3.32.

55–8 Proverbial: 'The screeching owl (raven) bodes death' (Dent R33).

57 **dismal** bringing disaster (*OED* 2, citing this line)

59 **understanding is bereft** ability to understand has left him

61 **beams** glimmers

64 **policy . . . counterfeit** device, stratagem . . . deceive

GEORGE

  If so thou think'st, vex him with eager words.

RICHARD

  Clifford, ask mercy and obtain no grace.

EDWARD

  Clifford, repent in bootless penitence.

WARWICK

  Clifford, devise excuses for thy faults.   70

GEORGE

  While we devise fell tortures for thy faults.

RICHARD

  Thou didst love York, and I am son to York.

EDWARD

  Thou pitied'st Rutland, I will pity thee.

GEORGE

  Where's Captain Margaret to fence you now?

WARWICK

  They mock thee Clifford, swear as thou wast wont.   75

RICHARD

  What, not an oath? Nay then the world goes hard
  When Clifford cannot spare his friends an oath;
  I know by that he's dead, and by my soul
  If this right hand would buy two hours' life
  That I in all despite might rail at him,   80
  This hand should chop it off and with the issuing blood
  Stifle the villain, whose unstanchèd thirst
  York and young Rutland could not satisfy.

WARWICK

  Ay, but he's dead. Off with the traitor's head
  And rear it in the place your father's stands.   85

---

67 **vex . . . eager** torment . . . biting (*OED*, *eager, v.* 1c, citing this line)

69 **bootless** hopeless
penitence i.e. in expectation of expiating or making amends for sins

71 **fell** savage

74 **Captain Margaret** Echoes Holinshed's marginal note to a passage contrasting Henry's pacifism with Margaret's military preparations before the Battle of Northampton: 'The Queen the better captain' (Pppiii^v). See Appendix A.

74 **fence** protect

76 **What . . . oath?** In the 1983 BBC production the Yorkists nearly go wild with frustration at being denied a reaction to their torment.
goes hard is an unfeeling, harsh place

80 **all despite** utter scorn

81 **This hand . . . it** the left hand . . . the right

82 **Stifle** 'to choke by pouring [blood] down the throat' (*OED v.*^{1} 3)
unstanchèd insatiable

85 **rear** raise

And now to London with triumphant march
There to be crownèd England's royal king,
From whence shall Warwick cut the sea to France
And ask the Lady Bona for thy queen;
So shalt thou sinew both these lands together,   90
And having France thy friend, thou shalt not dread
The scattered foe that hopes to rise again.
For though they cannot greatly sting to hurt,
Yet look to have them buzz to offend thine ears.
First will I see the coronation,   95
And then to Brittany I'll cross the sea
To effect this marriage, so it please my lord.

EDWARD

Even as thou wilt, sweet Warwick, let it be,
For in thy shoulder do I build my seat,
And never will I undertake the thing   100
Wherein thy counsel and consent is wanting.
Richard, I will create thee Duke of Gloucester,
And George of Clarence; Warwick as ourself
Shall do and undo as him pleaseth best.

RICHARD

Let me be Duke of Clarence, George of Gloucester,   105
For Gloucester's dukedom is too ominous.

86–7 **London . . . king** See Appendix A.

88 **cut** cross straight over

89 **ask . . . for** request . . . to be given (in marriage)
Lady Bona . . . queen This may come as a surprise to Edward, as in the 1994 RSC production: he gestured to object but was overruled by Warwick. See Appendix A.

90 **sinew** bind fast

91 **France** the king; the country and people

92 **scattered foe** united forces, dispersed (English territorial) conquests in France
rise rebel

94 **buzz** flutter annoyingly; murmur, whisper in meddlesome talk

99 **shoulder** load-bearing part of the body; hence, strength, power (*OED sb.* 3c, citing this line) (perhaps recalling the traditional emblem of St Christopher as a giant bearing Christ as a boy on his shoulder). See 2.1.189.
seat throne

102–3 **create . . . Clarence** Historically this occurred after Edward was confirmed king by Parliament (Hall Hhi[r], Holinshed Rrri[r]). Edward may 'rehearse' the ceremony by 'dubbing' Richard and George.

103 **ourself** Edward uses the royal plural.

106 **ominous** inauspicious, unpromising (because of the fates of previous dukes: Humphrey of Gloucester was murdered by his court rivals (see *2 Henry VI* and 1.1.112 n. above), as was Thomas of Woodstock (see *Richard II*). Hugh Despenser, favourite of Edward II, was executed. 'It seemeth to many men, that the name and title of Gloucester, hath been unfortunate and unlucky to divers . . . as Hugh Spencer, Thomas of Woodstock . . . this Duke Humphrey . . . and after King Richard III also Duke of Gloucester' (Hall Bbiii[v]).

WARWICK

Tut, that's a foolish observation.
Richard be Duke of Gloucester. Now to London
To see these honours in possession.

Exeunt with the body

3.1   *Enter two Gamekeepers with cross-bows in their hands*
FIRST GAMEKEEPER

Under this thick-grown brake we'll shroud ourselves,
For through this laund anon the deer will come,
And in this covert will we make our stand,
Culling the principal of all the deer.

109.1 *with the body*] This edition; *not in* F; *Omnes* O
    3.1] ROWE; *not in* F   0.1 *two Gamekeepers*] This edition; *Sinklo, and Humfrey* F; *two keepers*
O *and editors   cross-bows . . . hands*] F; *bow and arrowes* O   1 FIRST GAMEKEEPER] This edition;
Sink⟨lo⟩. F *(and subs. throughout this scene)*

---

107 **Tut . . . observation** Usually spoken as an
authoritative, sometimes contemptuous,
dismissal, perhaps meant to put Richard
in his place (see above, 2.1.166–7 and note
to 2.1.157–65). Alternatively the humour-
less Warwick may also miss, or ignore,
what Richard intends as a small joke.
observation remark (*OED* 8, citing this
line)

109 **in   possession**   actually   bestowed.
Scanned as four syllables. In the 1963–4
Hall-Barton production, the imperious
Brewster Mason made a 'business-like
survey of the field at the end of . . . Tow-
ton' (*Plays and Players* (1964)), prior
to the interval and the beginning of
Edward's reign.

3.1.0.1 **Gamekeepers** F's 'Sinklo, and Humfrey' are presumed to refer to two actors.
John Sincklo or Sincler, named in the cast
of *2 Seven Deadly Sins* (1590), the Induction of *Shrew*, and *2 Henry IV* (Q 1600),
was a member of Pembroke's Men and
seems often to have been cast for his
physical slightness (Gurr, *Companies*, pp.
72–3). Humphrey Jeffes was a minor
member of Pembroke's Men in 1593
and later of Alleyn's Lord Admiral's
Men (Gurr, *Companies*, p. 273). Willem
Schrickx discovered he was born in 1576
and speculates he may have been abroad
around 1592 ('English Actors at the

Courts of Wolfenbüttel, Brussels and
Graz', *Shakespeare Survey* 33 (1980),
153–68). See Introduction, p. 130.

0.1 **cross-bows** Weapons that define the
quality of the gamekeepers' hunting. In
The Book named the Governor (1531), Sir
Thomas Elyot notes that 'killing of deer
with bows . . . serveth well for the pot . . .
and therefore it must of necessity be
sometime used. But it containeth therein
no commendable solace or exercise, in
comparison to the other form of hunting',
which 'is the very imitation of battle, for
not only it doth show the courage and
strength . . . also it increaseth . . . agility
and quickness' ('The Ancient Hunting',
bk I, ch. 18, fols. 69ᵛ–73ʳ). The gamekeepers may also be poaching. See note to ll.
22–3. While on tour in Bath from June to
August 1592, Pembroke's Men, who are
presumed to have performed the play
underlying *True Tragedy*, ' "Received . . .
for A bowe that was broken by them", 2s'
(Gurr, *Companies*, p. 276).

1 **brake . . . shroud** thicket . . . screen
2 **laund** clearing (*OED*, citing this line)
3 **covert** hiding-place
  make our stand take up a position under
  cover (*OED*, *stand*, *sb.*¹ 3, citing this
  line)

4 **principal** best animals (as if being
  bequeathed by custom, *OED sb.* 6)

SECOND GAMEKEEPER

  I'll stay above the hill, so both may shoot.   5

FIRST GAMEKEEPER

  That cannot be: the noise of thy cross-bow

  Will scare the herd, and so my shoot is lost.

  Here stand we both and aim we at the best;

  And for the time shall not seem tedious,

  I'll tell thee what befell me on a day   10

  In this self-place where now we mean to stand.

SECOND GAMEKEEPER

  Here comes a man, let's stay till he be past.

    Enter King Henry with a prayer book

HENRY

  From Scotland am I stol'n ev'n of pure love

  To greet mine own land with my wishful sight.

  No Harry, Harry 'tis no land of thine,   15

  Thy place is filled, thy sceptre wrung from thee,

  Thy balm washed off wherewith thou wast anointed.

  No bending knee will call thee Caesar now,

  No humble suitors press to speak for right,

  No, not a man comes for redress of thee,   20

  For how can I help them and not myself?

FIRST GAMEKEEPER

  Ay, here's a deer whose skin's a keeper's fee.

---

5 SECOND GAMEKEEPER] This edition; *Hum⟨frey⟩*. F (*and throughout this scene*) 12.1 *King Henry*] O, ROWE; *the King* F *with . . . book*] F; *disguisde* O 13 ev'n] POPE; *euen* F 17 wast] F3; *was* F1

7 **shoot** shot
9 **for** so that (Abbott ¶154)
12 **stay** wait
12.1 *prayer book* In a fifteenth-century context, likely a Book of Hours. F dramatizes Holinshed's accounts of Henry's 'boldness' in longing to return home, but removes chronicle reports of him travelling in disguise, which O refers to in both the direction and the dialogue, instead of the prayer book. The latter suggests Henry's anti-worldly reasoning and 'wise folly', each of which the chronicles proffer as possible motives for his running away. See Appendix A.
13 **am I stol'n** have I removed myself secretly, quietly; left my lair like a hunted animal unperceived by my pursuers (*OED, steal, v.*[1] 9c)

13 **ev'n** wholly out
14 **wishful** yearning, full of desire (*OED* 2, citing this line)
16 **place** i.e. throne
17 **balm** Aromatic oil used in the coronation ceremony to anoint the king, to which his traditional healing powers were often attributed (Hattaway).
18 **knee will call** Shakespeare merges physical action with speech-act.
   Caesar Figuratively, any absolute monarch (*OED* 2, citing this line).
19 **press to speak** importune, beg to plead
   right justice
20 **redress of** remedy, relief for some trouble from
21 **and** if
22–3 **here's . . . him** Edward Berry observes that Shakespeare often mildly satirized

228

This is the quondam king; let's seize upon him.

HENRY

Let me embrace the sour adversities,

For wise men say it is the wisest course.   25

SECOND GAMEKEEPER

Why linger we? Let us lay hands upon him.

FIRST GAMEKEEPER

Forbear awhile, we'll hear a little more.

HENRY

My queen and son are gone to France for aid,

And as I hear the great commanding Warwick

Is thither gone to crave the French King's sister   30

To wife for Edward. If this news be true,

Poor queen and son, your labour is but lost,

For Warwick is a subtle orator

And Lewis a prince soon won with moving words.

By this account then Margaret may win him,   35

For she's a woman to be pitied much:

Her sighs will make a batt'ry in his breast,

Her tears will pierce into a marble heart,

The tiger will be mild whiles she doth mourn,

---

24 the sour adversities] This edition; the sower Aduersaries F; these sour adversities POPE; thee, sour Adversity SINGER 1856, DYCE, *Remarks (conj.)*; thee, sour adversities SISSON, *NR (conj.)* 30 Is] F2; I: F1

the mean self-interest or easy corruptibility of gamekeepers or foresters. Here they 'show sympathy neither to the deer they pursue nor to the king they capture' ('Shakespeare and the Hunt', forthcoming).

22 **fee** Besides a sum of money, a keeper customarily received the deer's head and skin (Wilson).

23 **quondam** (Latin) former

24–5 **Let . . . course** Proverbial: 'Adversity makes men wise' (Tilley A42), and 'He is wise that can be patient in adversity' (Dent A42.1).

24 **adversities** The accent on the second syllable in F's 'Adversaries' suggests a misreading. While unusual variations in stress are fairly common even in early Shakespeare, and the total number of syllables (10 or 11 depending on 'sour') is regular (A. C. Partridge, *Orthography in Shakespeare and Elizabethan Drama* (1964),

ch. 11, pp. 94–104), there are nonetheless good contextual reasons for emendation. Most editors revise to 'Adversity' because the proverb underpinning these lines, which Shakespeare alludes to in *Romeo* 3.3.55 and *As You Like It* 2.1.12, reads 'adversity'. They also assume F's preceding 'the' represents 'thee'. Yet Pope's 'adversities' is more persuasive on orthographic grounds since it is closer to F than 'adversitie' (Sisson, *NR*, ii. 84). And if this is the case, F's 'the', which occurs in an uncrowded line, may stand.

30, 51 **sister** sister-in-law. See note to 2.6.89.

31 **To** as a (Abbott ¶189)

34 **Lewis** Louis XI of France

35 **By this account** (yet) for this reason

37 **batt'ry** bombardment; drumming beat

38 'Tears . . . though marble wear with raining' (*Lucrece* 560) and proverbial (see note to 3.2.50).

39 **tiger** See 1.4.137.

And Nero will be tainted with remorse   40
To hear and see her plaints, her brinish tears.
Ay, but she's come to beg, Warwick to give:
She on his left side craving aid for Henry,
He on his right asking a wife for Edward.
She weeps and says her Henry is deposed,   45
He smiles and says his Edward is installed,
That she, poor wretch, for grief can speak no more,
Whiles Warwick tells his title, smooths the wrong,
Inferreth arguments of great strength,
And in conclusion wins the King from her   50
With promise of his sister and what else
To strengthen and support King Edward's place.
O Margaret thus 'twill be, and thou poor soul
Art then forsaken as thou went'st forlorn.

SECOND GAMEKEEPER
Say what art thou talk'st of kings and queens?   55

HENRY
More than I seem and less than I was born to:
A man at least, for less I should not be,
And men may talk of kings, and why not I?

SECOND GAMEKEEPER
Ay, but thou talk'st as if thou wert a king.

HENRY
Why so I am in mind, and that's enough.   60

55 Say∧ . . . thou] This edition; Say, . . . thou F; Say, . . . thou that ROWE

40 **Nero** Roman emperor (AD 54–68) proverbial for his sadistic cruelty.
   tainted touched (*OED v.* C1, citing this line)
41 **plaints** sorrowful complaints
   brinish salty
43–8 **She . . . wrong** The symmetrical action
   recalls the traditional schematic designs
   of civic pageants, and thus comments on
   Henry's conventionalized—and ultimately mistaken—grasp of the underlying political situation. See Martin,
   Pageantry, pp. 246–51.
47 **That** so that (Abbott ¶283)
48 **his title** about Edward's claims to the
   throne
   smooths the wrong makes plausible
   Edward's wrongs; glosses over, diminishes Margaret's wrongs

49 **Inferreth** cites
51 **what else** anything else (*OED, what*, C4d,
   citing this line)
52 **place** merited high position
54 **forlorn** abandoned; in a miserable condition; doomed to destrution
55 **Say . . . queens** Rowe's widely adopted
   emendation of F, suggested by O, is
   unnecessary because both lines purposely
   begin with strong stresses to convey
   an abrupt or energetic tone (Wright, p.
   175). The missing weak beat (both F and
   O contain only nine syllables) cues the
   Second Gamekeeper's sudden interrup-
   tion of Henry's speech. The same occurs
   below at l. 96, and at l. 80, an eleven-
   syllable line.

SECOND GAMEKEEPER

But if thou be a king, where is thy crown?

HENRY

My crown is in my heart, not on my head,
Not decked with diamonds and Indian stones,
Nor to be seen: my crown is called content,
A crown it is that seldom kings enjoy.   65

SECOND GAMEKEEPER

Well if you be a king crowned with content,
Your crown content and you must be contented
To go along with us. For as we think,
You are the king King Edward hath deposed,
And we his subjects, sworn in all allegiance,   70
Will apprehend you as his enemy.

HENRY

But did you never swear and break an oath?

SECOND GAMEKEEPER

No never such an oath, nor will not now.

HENRY

Where did you dwell when I was king of England?

SECOND GAMEKEEPER

Here in this country where we now remain.   75

HENRY

I was anointed king at nine months old,
My father and my grandfather were kings,
And you were sworn true subjects unto me;
And tell me then, have you not broke your oaths?

FIRST GAMEKEEPER

No, for we were subjects but while you were king.   80

HENRY

Why, am I dead? Do I not breathe a man?

61–2 **But . . . head** Proverbial: 'A mind content is a crown' (Tilley C623). Compare
Edward at 4.3.43–7.
61 **king . . . crown?** In the 1963–4 Hall–
Barton production, Henry was dressed
like a rough beggar, with close-cropped
hair, chewing bread.
63 **Indian stones** precious stones. Perhaps
pearls in the light of Shakespeare's
association in *Troilus* 1.1.100 and *Othello*

5.2.356.
73 **such** i.e. of allegiance
75 **country** region
76 **anointed . . . old** In fact proclaimed at
nine months (1421) and not crowned
(and thus anointed) until 1429. See *1
Henry VI* 4.1.
81 **breathe** live, exist (*OED v.* 4b, citing this
line)

Ah simple men you know not what you swear.
Look as I blow this feather from my face
And as the air blows it to me again,
Obeying with my wind when I do blow   85
And yielding to another when it blows,
Commanded always by the greater gust:
Such is the lightness of you, common men.
But do not break your oaths, for of that sin
My mild entreaty shall not make you guilty.   90
Go where you will, the King shall be commanded,
And be you kings, command and I'll obey.

FIRST GAMEKEEPER
We are true subjects to the King, King Edward.

HENRY
So would you be again to Henry
If he were seated as King Edward is.   95

FIRST GAMEKEEPER
We charge you in God's name and the King's
To go with us unto the officers.

---

82 swear] F; sware CAIRNCROSS (*conj.* Delius)   88 you,] F1; you‸ F3, ROWE   96 and the] F;
and in the ROWE

---

82 **simple** foolish, ignorant
  swear Cairncross emends to 'sware' on
  the grounds that Henry is referring to the
  Gamekeepers' past oaths of allegiance
  to him, 'not to oaths in general'. That
  depends on whether one regards Henry
  continuing the discussion of past succession oaths or setting up the general image
  of shifting popular opinion (whose import
  extends into the present) which immediately follows. F's colon after *swear* suggests this but is not definitive.
83–8 **Look . . . men** Henry's illustration of
  men easily swayed by ambitions for
  worldly power was the thematic core of
  the 1977 Ashland production, according
  to Alan Dessen (*SQ* 29 (1978), p. 284).
83 **Look as** just as (*OED, look, v.* 4b)
  feather Compare *2 Henry VI* 4.7.210–11:
  'Was ever feather so lightly blown to and
  fro as this multitude?' Henry may get his
  feather from a bird in the Gamekeeper's
  belt or pocket.
85 **Obeying with** being obedient to (Abbott
  ¶193)

88 **lightness** fickleness. 'As wavering as
  feathers in the wind' (Dent F162).
  you, Rowe's omission of F's comma may
  make Henry sound more conciliatory, but
  obscures F's dramatic alternative: that
  Henry may be growing somewhat heated
  at the Gamekeeper's failure to see his
  point of view, in which case his change
  in direction ('But . . . My mild entreaty',
  89–90) may represent a reining-in of his
  momentary anger.
92 **And . . . obey** 'The scene shows once
  again the ambiguity of Henry, on the one
  hand a man finding great contentment in
  having lost his crown, but on the other
  asserting, the moment he is challenged,
  his belief in himself as king . . . not the
  wanton assertion of "I am king and
  therefore superior to you"; it is the belief
  that he has been put on this earth by
  God to lead his people spiritually' (Ralph
  Fiennes on playing Henry VI, *Players* 3,
  pp. 110–12).
97 **officers** i.e. of the peace, constables

HENRY

In God's name lead, your king's name be obeyed,
And what God will, that let your king perform,
And what he will, I humbly yield unto.   *Exeunt*   100

3.2   *Enter King Edward, Richard, Duke of Gloucester,*
          George, Duke of Clarence, and Elizabeth, Lady Grey

EDWARD

Brother of Gloucester, at St Albans field
This lady's husband, Sir Richard Grey, was slain,
His land then seized on by the conqueror.
Her suit is now to repossess those lands,
Which we in justice cannot well deny   5
Because in quarrel of the house of York
The worthy gentleman did lose his life.

GLOUCESTER

Your highness shall do well to grant her suit.
It were dishonour to deny it her.

EDWARD

It were no less, but yet I'll make a pause.   10

3.2] POPE; *not in* F   0.1–2 *Richard, Duke of Gloucester, George, Duke of Clarence, and Elizabeth,
Lady Grey*] F (*Gloster, Clarence, Lady Gray*)   3 conqueror.] O, ROWE (*subs.*); Conqueror, F

3.2 Shakespeare chooses not to dramatize King Edward's coronation. Nonetheless, many productions turn this opening into a ritual enthronement, especially if it follows the interval, with sumptuous costumes, ceremonial banners, and festive music. The 1963–4 Hall–Barton and 1988 RSC productions emblematized the occasion with a large sun-in-splendour placed over the central throne, picking up on Edward's vow at 2.1.39–40. Alternatively, the atmosphere may begin relaxed and convivial, except for Lady Grey.

0.2 **Lady Grey** Many productions have Lady Grey enter alone after everybody else, giving Edward an opportunity to take notice of her, sometimes to eye her lewdly as she approaches the throne, which informs the 'pause' at l. 10. She may also be dressed conspicuously as a widow, in black and/or veiled. See Appendix A, 3.2.1–7.

3 **land . . . conqueror** Most editors emend to O's 'lands' to be consistent with the next

line and F's usage elsewhere in the scene. But inconsistency is not error, and perhaps Edward distinguishes between Sir Richard Grey's 'lands' as owned property (*OED sb.* 4), and 'land' as realm, domain, and territory (*OED* 3). The latter definition suits Edward's implied idea of Yorkist conquest. A later Shakespearian instance, however, supports O's reading: '[Fortinbras] Did forfeit . . . all those his lands | Which he stood seized on to the conqueror' (*Hamlet* 1.1.87–3).

4 **repossess** regain possession of. Presumably at issue is Lady Grey's jointure, the legacy of lands and/or money arranged at the time of her marriage to provide for her widowhood, as well as the ownership of her lands.

6 **quarrel** the cause

10 **pause** At this point Clarence and Gloucester usually move away, but within hearing distance, perhaps to a table downstage or in the foreground, as in the 1963–4 Hall–Barton and 1983 BBC productions.

GLOUCESTER Yea, is it so?

⌜*Aside to Clarence*⌝ I see the lady hath a thing to grant

Before the King will grant her humble suit.

CLARENCE ⌜*aside to Gloucester*⌝

He knows the game; how true he keeps the wind.

GLOUCESTER ⌜*aside to Clarence*⌝ Silence.   15

EDWARD

Widow we will consider of your suit,

And come some other time to know our mind.

LADY GREY

Right gracious lord I cannot brook delay.

May it please your highness to resolve me now,

And what your pleasure is, shall satisfy me.   20

GLOUCESTER ⌜*aside to Clarence*⌝

Ay widow? Then I'll warrant you all your lands,

And if what pleases him shall pleasure you.

Fight closer, or good faith you'll catch a blow.

CLARENCE ⌜*aside to Gloucester*⌝

I fear her not unless she chance to fall.

---

12 ⌜*Aside to Clarence*⌝] JOHNSON (*subs. at l.* 11); *not in* F   14 ⌜*aside to Gloucester*⌝] CAPELL (*subs.*);
not in F   15 ⌜*aside to Clarence*⌝] CAPELL (*subs.*); *not in* F   18 LADY GREY] MALONE (*subs.*) *following*
ROWE; Wid⟨ow⟩. F (*and throughout this scene*)   21 ⌜*aside to Clarence*⌝] JOHNSON (*subs.*); *not in* F
24 ⌜*aside to Gloucester*⌝] JOHNSON (*subs.*); *not in* F

---

12 **thing** A sexual pun: 'vagina' (Williams).

14 **game** object of the chase, animal being
hunted; quarry of sexual conquest
(Williams)

true . . . wind persistently he stays down-
wind (to avoid being scented by his prey)

16 **of** the implications of (Abbott ¶173)

18 **brook** endure

19 **resolve** answer

20 **pleasure . . . satisfy** Can refer in a double
sense to sexual pleasure, though Lady
Grey may not intend this meaning. Actors
must decide on the moment when she recognizes Edward's ulterior motives, and
when she does, what attitude to take. In
the 1963–4 Hall–Barton production, Lady
Grey, unveiling herself wearing a low
decolleté, spoke these lines with a slightly
coming-on disposition. From the beginning her game was sexual manipulation
of a nearly out-of-control Edward. In the
1983 BBC production, on the other hand,

Lady Grey was dignified and businesslike.
She became alarmed when she realized
what Edward was after (at 'service', l. 44),
and then increasingly defiant and angry
at being sexually blackmailed.

21–3 **Ay . . . blow** Usually spoken aside to
Clarence. But in the 1988 and 1994 RSC
productions Richard spoke directly to a
bemused Lady Grey, as if giving her
advice.

21 **warrant you** assure you (that you will
regain title to)

23 **Fight** grapple; settle (your suit) by contending (*OED v.* 8)

closer more guardedly, less openly

blow hit; sexual thrust (Williams)

24 **fear her not** do not fear for her

fall yield in fighting; fall prostrate;
surrender her chastity (compare *Romeo*
1.3.44–5: 'Thou wilt fall backward when
thou hast more wit, | Wilt thou not,
Jule?')

GLOUCESTER ⌜*aside to Clarence*⌝

  God forbid that, for he'll take vantages.   25

EDWARD

  How many children hast thou widow, tell me?

CLARENCE ⌜*aside to Gloucester*⌝

  I think he means to beg a child of her.

GLOUCESTER ⌜*aside to Clarence*⌝

  Nay then whip me, he'll rather give her two.

LADY GREY

  Three, my most gracious lord.

GLOUCESTER ⌜*aside*⌝

  You shall have four if you'll be ruled by him.   30

EDWARD

  'Twere pity they should lose their father's lands.

LADY GREY

  Be pitiful, dread lord, and grant it then.

EDWARD (*to Gloucester and Clarence*)

  Lords give us leave, I'll try this widow's wit.

GLOUCESTER

  Ay, good leave have you, ⌜*aside*⌝ for you will have leave

  Till youth take leave and leave you to the crutch.   35

    Gloucester and Clarence move further away

EDWARD

  Now tell me madam, do you love your children?

---

25 ⌜*aside to Clarence*⌝] JOHNSON (*subs.*); *not in* F   27 ⌜*aside to Gloucester*⌝] JOHNSON (*subs.*); *not in* F   28 ⌜*aside to Clarence*⌝] JOHNSON (*subs.*); *not in* F   30 ⌜*aside*⌝] JOHNSON; *not in* F   33 (*to . . . Clarence*)] CAPELL (*subs.*); *not in* F   34 ⌜*aside*⌝] This edition; *not in* F; *at the beginning of line* CAPELL (*subs.*)   35.1 *Gloucester . . . away*] JOHNSON (*subs.*); *not in* F

25 **take vantages** seize upon any opportunities, opening

27 **beg . . . her** invite her to bear his child (i.e. demand sexual favours from her); obtain legal custody of one of her children as ward, who 'could be exploited by the guardian for his own profit' (Hattaway).

28 **whip me** astound me (literally, beat me as a minor outlaw—a mild oath expressing amazement)

30 **ruled** directed; curbed (in your sexual appetites—meaning, ironically, the opposite); laid down judicially (and sexually)

32 **it** my suit

33 **give us leave** retire so we may speak in private (Dent L167.1). See Appendix A, 3.2.26–33.

33 **try** test

34 **good leave have you** gladly, by all means **have leave** have allowance; take liberties; be indulged

35 **take leave . . . leave** forsakes you . . . bequeaths
crutch old age; crippled with the venereal disease (with a pun on 'crotch', an alternative early modern spelling)

36 ff. The 1987 ESC production staged this scene as an elegant cocktail party, with jazz piano playing in the background. Edward and Lady Grey had been bantering pleasantly across their glasses, when

LADY GREY

Ay, full as dearly as I love myself.

EDWARD

And would you not do much to do them good?

LADY GREY

To do them good I would sustain some harm.

EDWARD

Then get your husband's lands to do them good.   40

LADY GREY

Therefore I came unto your majesty.

EDWARD

I'll tell you how these lands are to be got.

LADY GREY

So shall you bind me to your highness' service.

EDWARD

What service wilt thou do me, if I give them?

LADY GREY

What you command that rests in me to do.   45

EDWARD

But you will take exceptions to my boon.

LADY GREY

No, gracious lord, except I cannot do it.

EDWARD

Ay, but thou canst do what I mean to ask.

LADY GREY

Why then I will do what your grace commands.

GLOUCESTER (*aside to Clarence*)

He plies her hard, and much rain wears the marble.   50

50 (*aside to Clarence*)] CAPELL (*subs.*); *not in* F

at this point they started to dance slowly, both smiling superficially. The obvious formality of the occasion led Lady Grey to believe Edward was merely flattering her rather than speaking seriously, even after he began to proposition her directly.

39 **harm** injury, trouble; physical mistreatment (which can be understood in a sexual sense, like many words in this dialogue)

43, 44 **service** Sexual pun, although again Lady Grey may not intend this meaning.

45 **rests in me** lies in my power (*OED*, *rest*, *v.*[1] 6d, citing this line)

45, 47, 48, 49 **do** Sexual pun: copulate with (Williams).

46 **boon** request; (sexual) favour

47 **except** unless

47–8 **do . . . do** physically perform; (sexually) undertake

50 **plies** assails (with talk); works sexually (Williams)

much . . . marble Proverbial: 'Constant dropping [of something causing friction] will wear the stone' (Dent D618), perhaps parodying Thomas Watson's *Hecatompathia* (1582), sonnet 47: 'In time the marble wears with weakest showers: | More fierce is my sweet love, more hard

CLARENCE (*aside to Gloucester*)
  As red as fire! Nay then her wax must melt.
LADY GREY
  Why stops my lord? Shall I not hear my task?
EDWARD
  An easy task, 'tis but to love a king.
LADY GREY
  That's soon performed because I am a subject.
EDWARD
  Why then thy husband's lands I freely give thee.   55
LADY GREY
  I take my leave with many thousand thanks.
    Lady Grey starts to go
GLOUCESTER (*aside to Clarence*)
  The match is made, she seals it with a curtsy.
EDWARD
  But stay thee, 'tis the fruits of love I mean.
LADY GREY
  The fruits of love I mean, my loving liege.
EDWARD
  Ay, but I fear me in another sense.   60
  What love think'st thou I sue so much to get?

---

51 (*aside to Gloucester*)] CAPELL (*subs.*); *not in* F   fire!] ROWE; *fire?* F   57 (*aside to Clarence*)]
CAPELL (*subs.*); *not in* F   56.1 *Lady . . . go*] HATTAWAY (*subs., after l.* 57); *not in* F

---

withal, | Than beast or bird, than tree or stony wall'. See also 3.1.38.

51 **red as fire** Refers to (a) Edward's ardent looks and determined gestures ('fire' = sexual heat; see Appendix A); (b) Lady Grey's blushing, either from Edward's closer attentions and/or from her increasing anger.
  wax . . . melt Proverbial: 'To melt like wax against the fire' (Dent W137.1). Another sexual pun, since 'melt' means 'have an orgasm', though it usually refers to male ejaculation (Williams).
52, 53 **task** Like 'service', ll. 43–44 above.
53 **love** i.e. dutifully and sexually
57 **match is made** Gloucester assumes (too hastily) that Lady Grey has yielded to Edward's desires. 'Match' means 'copulation' (Williams), and 'made' signifies 'arranged to take place' (*OED, make, v.*[1] 12b).

57 **seals** concludes; consents to
58 **stay thee** don't go yet
  fruits emotional experience; sexual enjoyment (associated with generating the 'fruits of the womb')
59 **fruits** immaterial benefits (such as estimation, reputation); restored revenues resulting from my new allegiance as a dutiful subject (recalling her husband's support for the Lancastrians); (the good of my own living) offspring. Or perhaps Lady Grey attempts to shift the dynamic when she realizes what Edward is after, as in the 1996 Washington Shakespeare Theatre production, where for several lines she teased Edward with her scarf until he brutally grabbed her.
  mean have in mind. See Appendix A.
61 **sue** seek to obtain; chase, pursue; plead for (as a claimant); woo (as a suitor)
  get pun on 'beget' meaning 'obtain through copulation' (Williams)

LADY GREY
  My love till death, my humble thanks, my prayers,
  That love which virtue begs and virtue grants.

EDWARD
  No by my troth, I did not mean such love.

LADY GREY
  Why then you mean not as I thought you did.   65

EDWARD
  But now you partly may perceive my mind.

LADY GREY
  My mind will never grant what I perceive
  Your highness aims at, if I aim aright.

EDWARD
  To tell thee plain, I aim to lie with thee.

LADY GREY
  To tell you plain, I had rather lie in prison.   70

EDWARD
  Why then thou shalt not have thy husband's lands.

LADY GREY
  Why then mine honesty shall be my dower,
  For by that loss I will not purchase them.

EDWARD
  Therein thou wrong'st thy children mightily.

LADY GREY
  Herein your highness wrongs both them and me.   75
  But mighty lord this merry inclination
  Accords not with the sadness of my suit.
  Please you dismiss me either with ay or no.

EDWARD
  Ay if thou wilt say ay to my request,
  No if thou dost say no to my demand.   80

LADY GREY
  Then no, my lord, my suit is at an end.

---

62 **death** Secondary sense of orgasm, probably not intended by Lady Grey.
64 **troth** faith
68 **aims at ... aim** seeks to gain ... guess
72 **honesty** integrity; chastity
   dower widow's share of my husband's

estate; dowry ('which I would bring in marriage to a future husband')
73 **that loss** i.e. lying with Edward
   purchase get possession of
76 **merry** amusing, mirthful; facetious
77 **sadness** seriousness, gravity

GLOUCESTER (*aside to Clarence*)
  The widow likes him not, she knits her brows.
CLARENCE (*aside to Gloucester*)
  He is the bluntest wooer in Christendom.
EDWARD (*to himself*)
  Her looks do argue her replete with modesty,
  Her words do show her wit incomparable,   85
  All her perfections challenge sovereignty:
  One way or other she is for a king,
  And she shall be my love or else my queen.
  (*To Lady Grey*) Say that King Edward take thee for his
        queen?
LADY GREY
  'Tis better said than done, my gracious lord.   90
  I am a subject fit to jest withal,
  But far unfit to be a sovereign.
EDWARD
  Sweet widow, by my state I swear to thee
  I speak no more than what my soul intends,
  And that is to enjoy thee for my love.   95
LADY GREY
  And that is more than I will yield unto.
  I know I am too mean to be your queen,
  And yet too good to be your concubine.
EDWARD
  You cavil widow, I did mean my queen.
LADY GREY
  'Twill grieve your grace my sons should call you father.   100

---

82 (*aside to Clarence*)] CAPELL (*subs.*); *not in* F   83 (*aside to Gloucester*)] CAPELL (*subs.*); *not in* F
84 (*to himself*)] JOHNSON (*Aside.*); *not in* F   do] F2; doth F1   89 (*To . . . Grey*)] OXFORD *following*
JOHNSON; *not in* F

---

83 **bluntest** roughest, coarsest; most abrupt-
ly spoken. Edward's bluntness may also
be physical: he may have touched Lady
Grey's hair or breasts during their conversation.
84 **looks do** Emendation seems justified
because in all other instances in Shakespeare 'looks' is plural.
  argue prove
86 **challenge** lay rightful claim to, venture
worthily for
  sovereignty recognition as pre-eminent;

supreme, royal authority. See Appendix
A.
89 **Say . . . queen** If the scene includes a
throne, Edward may seat Lady Grey in it.
91 **subject** topic; citizen
  jest withal trifle, play-act with
93 **state** royal dignity
95 **enjoy** have (sexual) possession of
97 **mean** of humble estate. See Appendix A.
99 **cavil** raise frivolous objections. See
Appendix A.
100 **grieve** anger, offend

EDWARD

No more than when my daughters call thee mother.
Thou art a widow and thou hast some children,
And by God's mother I, being but a bachelor,
Have other some. Why, 'tis a happy thing
To be the father unto many sons.   105
Answer no more, for thou shalt be my queen.

GLOUCESTER (*aside to Clarence*)

The ghostly father now hath done his shrift.

CLARENCE (*aside to Gloucester*)

When he was made a shriver, 'twas for shift.

EDWARD

Brothers, you muse what chat we two have had.

GLOUCESTER

The widow likes it not, for she looks very sad.   110

EDWARD

You'd think it strange if I should marry her.

CLARENCE

To who my lord?

EDWARD   Why Clarence, to myself.

GLOUCESTER

That would be ten days' wonder at the least.

---

107 (*aside to Clarence*)] CAPELL (*subs.*); *not in* F   108 (*aside to Gloucester*)] CAPELL (*subs.*); *not in*
F   110 very sad] F1; sad F2; vexed CAIRNCROSS (*conj.* Vaughan)

---

103 **God's mother** The Virgin Mary—another kind of single parent.
104 **some** i.e. by his various sexual liaisons.
See note to 2.1.42.
104–5 **Why . . . sons** The boasting implication is that both of them are fertile. See
Appendix A, 3.2.104.
107 **ghostly** spiritual (i.e. priestly)
done his shrift finished confessing his subject; imposed his penance (with sexual
innuendo, 'of copulation' (Williams, citing this line))
108 **shriver** confessor
shift a jest; a trick; the sake of (getting
access to) her smock (compare *1 Henry VI*
1.3.98, 'he shrives this woman to her
smock'); a change of mistresses
109 **muse . . . chat** wonder, marvel . . .
familiar talk. See Appendix A.
110 **very sad** Vaughan's conjectured emendation 'vexed', adopted by Cairncross and

others, lacks authority and is unnecessary on the grounds that it 'spoils the
metre'. The line is a regular hexameter,
common in Shakespeare (Wright, p. 143),
although earlier editors often tried to
reduce hexameters to pentameters. F2's
elimination of 'very' is an instance of this
kind of regularization.
110 **sad** serious
111 **strange . . . marry** Clarence assumes
Edward is referring to himself as match-
maker in the aristocratic marriage market, a traditional royal prerogative. See
4.1.53 and note.
112 **who** whom (Abbott ¶274)
113–14 Referring to the proverbial expression 'a nine days' wonder' (Tilley W728).
In the 1963–4 Hall–Barton and 1983 BBC
productions, Clarence was angrily morti-
fied at Edward's action, while Richard
remained quietly disapproving.

CLARENCE

That's a day longer than a wonder lasts.

GLOUCESTER

By so much is the wonder in extremes.   115

EDWARD

Well, jest on brothers, I can tell you both
Her suit is granted for her husband's lands.
          Enter a Nobleman

NOBLEMAN

My gracious lord, Henry your foe is taken
And brought your prisoner to your palace gate.

EDWARD

See that he be conveyed unto the Tower;   120
And go we brothers to the man that took him,
To question of his apprehension.
Widow go you along. Lords use her honourably.
          Exeunt all but Gloucester

GLOUCESTER

Ay, Edward will use women honourably.
Would he were wasted, marrow, bones, and all,   125
That from his loins no hopeful branch may spring
To cross me from the golden time I look for.
And yet between my soul's desire and me—
The lustful Edward's title burièd—
Is Clarence, Henry, and his son young Edward,   130
And all the unlooked-for issue of their bodies

---

119 your] F; as O, CAPELL   123 honourably] F2, O; honourable F1   123.1 *all . . . Gloucester*]
CAMBRIDGE, DYCE 1864–7; *Manet Richard* F (at 123.2); *Omnes.* | *Manet Gloster* and speakes O

118–19 **your . . . your . . . your** The second of
these may be a mistaken anticipation or
carry-over, and O's 'as' may be right. See
Appendix A, 3.1.12.1.
120 **Tower** i.e. of London. See Appendix A.
123 **use** treat
  honourably F's 'honourable' is probably a
  printing error for 'honourably' (O, F2),
  although in Elizabethan usage 'adjectives
  were freely used as adverbs without the
  termination *ly*' (Abbott ¶23).
124 **use** employ sexually (Williams)
125 **wasted** i.e. with (venereal) disease; cf.
  'lustful Edward', l. 129.
  marrow semen (Williams), and regarded
  as the seat of animal vitality and (especially, masculine) strength. Also prover-

bial: 'In 16th–17th c. love was often said
to "burn" or "melt" the marrow' (*OED
sb.*[1] 1b).
126 **loins . . . branch** An iconographic allusion to the traditional Tree of Jesse, in
which the biblical house of David is
depicted rising in a family tree from a
reclining Jesse. The topmost branch is
Christ.
127 **cross** thwart, debar (*OED v.* 14b, citing
this line)
  golden time kingship, golden crown.
  Richard may gesture to the throne, or
  touch his head.
  look for hope for; seek. See Appendix A.
129 **title** i.e. as king
131 **unlooked-for** unforeseeable; undesired

To take their rooms ere I can place myself.
A cold premeditation for my purpose.
Why then I do but dream on sovereignty
Like one that stands upon a promontory   135
And spies a far-off shore where he would tread,
Wishing his foot were equal with his eye,
And chides the sea that sunders him from thence,
Saying he'll lade it dry to have his way.
So do I wish the crown, being so far off,   140
And so I chide the means that keeps me from it,
And so I say I'll cut the causes off,
Flattering me with impossibilities.
My eye's too quick, my heart o'erweens too much,
Unless my hand and strength could equal them.   145
Well, say there is no kingdom then for Richard:
What other pleasure can the world afford?
I'll make my heaven in a lady's lap
And deck my body in gay ornaments,
And witch sweet ladies with my words and looks.   150

---

132 **rooms** places (in the order of royal succession)

133 **cold premeditation** cheerless prospect (Hattaway)

134 **dream** In the negative sense of 'fantasize idly'.

135–9 **Like . . . way** The image recalls Leander gazing yearningly for Hero over the Hellespont in Marlowe's *Hero and Leander* (1593 or earlier, published 1598): 'And then he got him to a rock aloft, | Where having spied her tower, long star'd he on't, | And prayed the narrow toiling Hellespont | To part in twain, that he might come and go' (ii. 148–51).

136 **tread** Besides the ordinary sense of 'walk, step', the word has several underlying meanings: trample, dominate, conquer ('tread on kings', *1 Henry IV* 5.2.85; *1 Tamburlaine* 4.2.64–5); act ('treading the stage/boards'); copulate.

137 **eye** 'look, gaze', and thus 'desires, goals'

139 **lade** empty by bailing (*OED v.* 6, citing this line)

have his way 'to follow or enforce on others the course of action on which one is resolved' (*OED sb.*[1] 12c, citing this line); take (sexual) possession

140 **wish** desire

141 **means** obstacle (*OED sb.*[2] 6, citing this line)

142 **cut . . . off** murder the persons who stand in my way

143 **me** myself

144 **quick** swiftly, keenly perceptive; vitally alive, impatient (with hopes, ambitions, desires)
o'erweens presumes, expects (*OED* 1, citing this line)

145 **My . . . them** i.e. tangible results could fulfil their promptings

147 **What . . . afford** In the 1983 BBC production Richard gestured in the direction of Lady Grey's exit, emphasizing 'pleasure', which he had inflected suggestively at l. 22.

148 **lap** private parts; hence 'I'll devote myself to womanizing'.

149 **deck . . . ornaments** adorn . . . attire

150 **witch . . . looks** In the 1988 RSC production Richard turned this into a conversation by murmuring 'hmm? hmm?', pausing a moment to allow the absurdity to sink in, and then voiced the audience's conclusions with a final negative 'mmm'. In 1987 the ESC's Richard raised his eye-

O miserable thought, and more unlikely
Than to accomplish twenty golden crowns.
Why, love forswore me in my mother's womb,
And for I should not deal in her soft laws,
She did corrupt frail nature with some bribe   155
To shrink mine arm up like a withered shrub,
To make an envious mountain on my back
Where sits deformity to mock my body,
To shape my legs of an unequal size,
To disproportion me in every part   160
Like to a chaos, or an unlicked bear-whelp
That carries no impression like the dam.
And am I then a man to be beloved?
O monstrous fault, to harbour such a thought.
Then since this earth affords no joy to me   165
But to command, to check, to o'erbear such
As are of better person than myself,
I'll make my heaven to dream upon the crown,
And whiles I live t'account this world but hell
Until my misshaped trunk that bears this head   170

---

170 Until . . . head] F1 (*subs.*); Until this misshaped . . . head F3; Until the head this mis-shap'd trunk doth bear HANMER; Until this head my misshaped trunk doth bear HATTAWAY

---

brows in disbelief to evoke a laugh, having spoken the preceding lines in a mocking sing-song.

150 **witch** bewitch, enchant

152 **accomplish** achieve

153–5 **forswore . . . corrupt** Richard sees love as both the negative and positive agent—betraying and vengefully destructive—of his deformity.

154 **for** to ensure that (Abbott ¶154)
  soft laws Because having to do with emotions and feelings (1.4.141: 'Women are soft, mild, pitiful, and flexible'); hence, effeminizing, emasculating.

155 **corrupt** spoil, infect; bribe, pervert, debauch; violate

157 **envious** hateful, spiteful

161 **chaos** disjointed mass (of body parts); amorphous lump (*OED* 4, citing this line and referring to Ovid's definition in *Metamorphoses*, i. 7–9: 'a huge rude heap and nothing else but even | A heavy lump and

clottered clod of seeds . . . | Of things at strife among themselves for want of order due'). See Appendix A and note to 5.6.51.

161 **unlicked bear-whelp** Bear-cubs were believed to be born underformed and without distinguishing marks (= 'carries no impression') but then licked into natural shape by their mothers (= dam); e.g. Ovid's *Metamorphoses*, xv. 416–19: 'The bearwhelp . . . newly littered, is no whelp immediately. | But like an evil-favoured lump of flesh alive doth lie. | The dam by licking shapeth out his members orderly'. Also compare 5.6.51: 'an indigested and deformèd lump'.

164 **monstrous** unnatural, abnormally formed; absurd
  fault error; deficiency

166 **check** rebuke; reproach; repress

167 **better person** higher social rank; more attractive in appearance

170–1 **misshaped . . . crown** Some editors have been bothered by the shift from the

Be round impalèd with a glorious crown.
And yet I know not how to get the crown,
For many lives stand between me and home,
And I, like one lost in a thorny wood
That rends the thorns and is rent with the thorns,   175
Seeking a way and straying from the way,
Not knowing how to find the open air
But toiling desperately to find it out,
Torment myself to catch the English crown;
And from that torment I will free myself   180
Or hew my way out with a bloody axe.
Why, I can smile and murder whiles I smile,
And cry 'content' to that which grieves my heart,
And wet my cheeks with artificial tears,
And frame my face to all occasions.   185
I'll drown more sailors than the mermaid shall,
I'll slay more gazers than the basilisk,
I'll play the orator as well as Nestor,

main to the subordinate clause to complete the thought. Abbott observes, however, that 'that' is often used to introduce
the essential characteristic of the main
antecedent (¶259–60). The general sense
is clear, especially when spoken, even if
the grammatical construction seems odd.

171 **impalèd** encircled, and by association set
apart
173 **home** goal, destiny; my natural condition; self-control, -possession. Proverbial
(Dent H533.1). In the 1983 BBC production Richard gestured to the throne.
175 **rends . . . is rent** tears away . . . is
snagged
179 **Torment myself** During this 'thorny
wood' section, many performers who
begin Richard's speech coolly and/or
casually become agitated and aggressive,
and end this line panting slightly with
exertion. In the 1996 Washington production, Richard's confinement was suggested by a spotlit circle in which he stood
'trapped'.
   catch get possession of (as in a race; *OED
v.* 6, citing this line)
182–93 **Why . . . school** Roger Warren observes that Richard does not suggest a possible course of action in order to mock it,
as earlier (reversals which give his speech
the colloquial force of somebody wrestling

with a problem), but finally identifies the
real talent he has to gain the crown
('"Contrarieties agree"': An Aspect of
Dramatic Technique in *Henry VI*', *Shakespeare Survey 37* (1984), pp. 81–2). In
dramatic terms, Richard turns from
achieving political power by force of heroic will—the conventional route taken by
'aspiring minds' such as Fergus in *Gorboduc*, Mordred in *The Misfortunes of Arthur*,
Tamburlaine, and his father York—to
winning it by playing roles, a quintessen-
tially Shakespearian connection.
184 **artificial** counterfeit though physically
real (*OED* 1b, citing this line)
185 **frame** shape, express to suit (*OED v.* 5b,
citing this line). See Appendix A,
3.2.182–5.
   occasions. Four syllables.
186 **mermaid** Or classical siren, depicted as
half-bird, half-woman, whose deceptively
enchanting songs lured sailors to destruction on the rocks (*Odyssey*, xii. 39–54).
187 **basilisk** Mythical serpent whose mere
look or breath killed those who gazed on it
(Aelian, ii. 5). Named after the crown-like
mark on its head (diminutive form of Grk
basileus = king).
188 **orator** See note to 2.2.43. Here strongly
coloured by the sense of assuming a
theatrical role in order to persuade and
deceive.

Deceive more slyly than Ulysses could,
And like a Sinon take another Troy.   190
I can add colours to the chameleon,
Change shapes with Proteus for advantages,
And set the murd'rous Machiavel to school.
Can I do this and cannot get a crown?
Tut, were it farther off, I'll pluck it down.   *Exit*   195

3.3   *Flourish. Enter Lewis the French King, his sister Lady
Bona, his Admiral called Lord Bourbon, Prince
Edward, Queen Margaret, and the Earl of Oxford.
Lewis sits, and riseth up again*

LEWIS

Fair Queen of England, worthy Margaret,
Sit down with us. It ill befits thy state
And birth that thou shouldst stand while Lewis doth sit.

193 murd'rous] JOHNSON *following* POPE; murtherous F; aspiring O   Machiavel] F (*Macheuill*);
Catalin O
    3.3] CAPELL; *not in* F   0.1–2 *Lady Bona . . . Lord Bourbon*] F (*Bona . . . Bourbon*)

188 **Nestor** Greek leader during the Trojan
Wars reputed for eloquence. He had lived
more than two generations, yet remained
mentally and physically vigorous.

189 **Ulysses** Greek hero of the Odyssey and
eloquently duplicitous leader at Troy (cf.
Troilus). He is twice called 'sly Ulysses' in
Golding's translation of Ovid's *Metamorphoses* (xiii. 68, 115).

190 **Sinon** Pretended Greek deserter who
persuaded the Trojans to take within their
walls the wooden horse, from which
Greek soldiers came forth to sack the city
(Virgil, *Aeneid*, ii. 57–194).

191 **colours** hues; outward shows serving to
conceal; ornaments of rhetoric
    chameleon Reptile proverbial for its ability
to change its colour to camouflage itself;
figuratively, a tricky person (Dent C222).

192 **shapes** guises, assumed appearances;
impersonated characters
    Proteus Sea-god with the power to take on
all kinds of shapes to evade being questioned (Ovid, *Metamorphoses*, viii. 916 ff.).
    for advantages i.e. win supremacy over
Proteus in a contest of changing shapes

193 **set . . . school** become Machiavel's
schoolmaster. Niccolò Machiavelli's *The
Prince* (1513) was popularly believed to

advocate separating morals from the
exercise of power. A 'Machiavel' became
a label for any ruthlessly ambitious
politician (compare *1 Henry VI* 5.6.74:
'Alençon, that notorious Machiavel'),
and in drama this profile became assimilated with the double-dealing figure of the
morality play Vice. See Introduction, pp.
59–61.

194 **Can . . . crown?** In the 1963–4 Hall–
Barton production, Ian Holm preceded
this line by going into a brief fit of weeping distress. He then suddenly looked up
and grinned to indicate it was just an act,
demonstrating how easy it was to join
'this' and the 'crown'.

195 **I'll** I'd

3.3 **Productions** sometimes signal the
change of court and nationality by using
different colours and motifs (e.g. traditional royal blue and fleurs-de-lis) in
decorative hangings and costumes. The
1952–3 Birmingham Rep production also
displayed objects suggesting international
negotiations and diplomacy, such as
maps, large books, a globe, quill pens, etc.

0.1 *sister* i.e. sister-in-law

0.4 *sits . . . again* Probably in his chair of
state.

2 **state** rank

MARGARET

No, mighty King of France, now Margaret
Must strike her sail and learn awhile to serve   5
Where kings command. I was, I must confess,
Great Albion's queen in former golden days,
But now mischance hath trod my title down
And with dishonour laid me on the ground,
Where I must take like seat unto my fortune,   10
And to my humble seat conform myself.

LEWIS

Why say, fair Queen, whence springs this deep despair?

MARGARET

From such a cause as fills mine eyes with tears
And stops my tongue while heart is drowned in cares.

LEWIS

Whate'er it be, be thou still like thyself,   15
And sit thee by our side.

    Seats her by him

                Yield not thy neck
To Fortune's yoke, but let thy dauntless mind
Still ride in triumph over all mischance.
Be plain, Queen Margaret, and tell thy grief;
It shall be eased if France can yield relief.   20

---

11 seat] F; state DYCE 1864–7 (*conj.* Walker)

5 **strike her sail** humble herself; literally
lower a sail in deference to a superior vessel (Dent S24.3). See Margaret's speech in
5.4 for full development of this nautical
imagery.

7 **Albion's** England's

8, 18 **mischance** misfortune. See Appendix
A. 'Margaret . . . seeking help from the
King of France . . . is an odd scene. In one
sense she is returning home, but there is
no feeling of her belonging there either'
(Penny Downie on playing Margaret,
Players 3, p. 132). Historically, the duchy
of Anjou remained independent until the
death of Margaret's father, René, in 1481,
when it came under the control of the
king of France.

9–12 **ground . . . seat . . . despair** Sitting on
the ground is a traditional posture of grief
and despair. *Richard II* 3.2.151–2: 'For
God's sake, let us sit upon the ground, |
And tell sad stories of the death of kings'.

Most modern performers do not act this
out literally, and 'ground' could be relative, referring to Margaret sitting beneath
Lewis's elevated chair on a stool (e.g. *Sir
Thomas More* 4.4.1–3 calling for '*Low
stools*'). See Appendix A.

15 **still** always
thyself i.e. a queen

16–18 **neck . . . yoke . . . triumph** An
image deriving from Petrarch's *Trionfi*
(*Triumphs*), in which allegorical figures
such as Fame are depicted in proces-
sional chariots treading captives beneath
their wheels. See *Lord Morley's Tryumphes
of Fraunces Petrarcke* (*ca.* 1553–56), ed.
D. D. Carnicelli (Cambridge, Mass.,
1971).

17 **dauntless** unsubdued, not cast down
(*OED*, citing this line). '[R]efers, not to
her present condition, but to Margaret's
famous character' (Hart).

20 **France** i.e. the king of France

MARGARET

Those gracious words revive my drooping thoughts
And give my tongue-tied sorrows leave to speak.
Now therefore be it known to noble Lewis
That Henry, sole possessor of my love,
Is, of a king, become a banished man   25
And forced to live in Scotland a forlorn,
While proud ambitious Edward, Duke of York,
Usurps the regal title and the seat
Of England's true anointed lawful king.
This is the cause that I poor Margaret,   30
With this my son Prince Edward, Henry's heir,
Am come to crave thy just and lawful aid,
And if thou fail us, all our hope is done.
Scotland hath will to help but cannot help,
Our people and our peers are both misled,   35
Our treasure seized, our soldiers put to flight,
And as thou seest, ourselves in heavy plight.

LEWIS

Renownèd Queen, with patience calm the storm
While we bethink a means to break it off.

MARGARET

The more we stay the stronger grows our foe.   40

LEWIS

The more I stay the more I'll succour thee.

MARGARET

O, but impatience waiteth on true sorrow.
        Enter Warwick
And see where comes the breeder of my sorrow.

---

26 a forlorn] F; all forlorn COLLIER 1853   42.1 *Enter Warwick] after l. 43 in* F

24 **sole . . . love** A defensive allusion to Margaret's adulterous affair with Suffolk in *2 Henry VI*.
25 **of** from being (Abbott ¶166)
26 **forlorn** forsaken, ruined, hopeless man (*OED sb.* B.1, citing this line)
32 **aid** Historically, France provided a refuge for the defeated Lancastrians. See Appendix A.
33 **And if** if indeed (Abbott ¶105)

33, 58 **done** ended
36 **treasure** treasury
37 **heavy** distressful
38 **storm** i.e. of your vexations
39 **bethink** think of
   break it off cut it short
40 **stay** delay
41 **stay** serve (your needs); support
42 **waiteth on** attends on; awaits
43 **breeder** source

LEWIS

What's he approacheth boldly to our presence?

MARGARET

Our Earl of Warwick, Edward's greatest friend.   45

LEWIS

Welcome brave Warwick, what brings thee to France?
> *He descends. She ariseth*

MARGARET

Ay, now begins a second storm to rise,
For this is he that moves both wind and tide.

WARWICK

From worthy Edward, King of Albion,
My lord and sovereign and thy vowèd friend,   50
I come in kindness and unfeignèd love,
First to do greetings to thy royal person,
And then to crave a league of amity,
And lastly to confirm that amity
With nuptial knot, if thou vouchsafe to grant   55
That virtuous Lady Bona, thy fair sister,
To England's king in lawful marriage.

MARGARET

If that go forward, Henry's hope is done.

WARWICK (*speaking to Bona*)

And gracious madam in our king's behalf
I am commanded, with your leave and favour,   60
Humbly to kiss your hand, and with my tongue
To tell the passion of my sovereign's heart,
Where fame, late ent'ring at his heedful ears,
Hath placed thy beauty's image and thy virtue.

MARGARET

King Lewis and Lady Bona hear me speak   65

47 Ay] F (I); [*Aside*] Ay WILSON (*subs.*)   58 If] F; [*Aside*] If CAPELL (*subs.*)   59 (*speaking to Bona*)] CAMBRIDGE (*subs.*); *after 'Madame' in divided line* 59 F

44 **What's** who's
   boldly without ceremony or salutation.
   See Appendix A.
46.1 **descends** from the elevated throne
   ariseth By standing, Margaret keeps
   attention from being too diverted from the
   action of Lewis greeting Warwick.
47–8, 58 Possibly delivered wholly or partly
   to herself, or to Prince Edward.

51 **I . . . love** Compare 'In kindness, in
   the Holy Ghost, in love unfeigned'
   (*BCP*, Epistle, First Sunday in Lent,
   from 2 Corinthians 6: 6 (Shaheen,
   p. 69)).
57 **marriage** Three syllables.
61 **Humbly** Warwick may kneel.
63 **fame, late** reputation, recently

Before you answer Warwick. His demand
Springs not from Edward's well-meant honest love
But from deceit bred by necessity;
For how can tyrants safely govern home
Unless abroad they purchase great alliance? 70
To prove him tyrant this reason may suffice:
That Henry liveth still. But were he dead
Yet here Prince Edward stands, King Henry's son.
Look therefore Lewis, that by this league and marriage
Thou draw not on thy danger and dishonour, 75
For though usurpers sway the rule a while,
Yet heavens are just, and time suppresseth wrongs.

WARWICK

Injurious Margaret.

PRINCE EDWARD   And why not 'Queen'?

WARWICK

Because thy father Henry did usurp,
And thou no more art prince than she is queen. 80

OXFORD

Then Warwick disannuls great John of Gaunt
Which did subdue the greatest part of Spain,
And after John of Gaunt, Henry the Fourth,
Whose wisdom was a mirror to the wisest,
And after that wise prince, Henry the Fifth, 85
Who by his prowess conquerèd all France;
From these our Henry lineally descends.

WARWICK

Oxford, how haps it in this smooth discourse
You told not how Henry the Sixth hath lost
All that which Henry the Fifth had gotten; 90
Methinks these peers of France should smile at that.

69, 71 **tyrants** usurpers (*OED* 1, citing l. 71)
70 **purchase** procure
   great alliance powerful dynastic alliances through marriage
74 **Look** take care
75 **draw . . . thy** bring on yourself
76 **sway the rule** wield power
77 **suppresseth** defeats
78 **Injurious** insulting; wrongful
   Queen i.e. 'Queen Margaret'
81 **disannuls** cancels the title of
81–2 **John of Gaunt . . . Spain** Duke of Lan-

caster and great-grandfather of Henry VI. The claim that he conquered Spain owes more to popular dramatic tradition and post-Armada embellishment than history, since Gaunt, although King of Castile by marriage, achieved modest success abroad. See *Spanish Tragedy* 1.4.164–7, and *Henslowe's Diary*, p. 168.

82 **Which** who
84 **mirror** model of excellence
88 **haps it** does it happen
   smooth speciously plausible

But for the rest, you tell a pedigree
Of threescore and two years, a silly time
To make prescription for a kingdom's worth.

OXFORD

Why Warwick, canst thou speak against thy liege   95
Whom thou obeyed'st thirty and six years
And not bewray thy treason with a blush?

WARWICK

Can Oxford, that did ever fence the right,
Now buckler falsehood with a pedigree?
For shame, leave Henry and call Edward king.   100

OXFORD

Call him my king, by whose injurious doom
My elder brother the Lord Aubrey Vere
Was done to death? And more than so, my father,
Even in the downfall of his mellowed years
When nature brought him to the door of death?   105
No Warwick no, while life upholds this arm,
This arm upholds the house of Lancaster.

WARWICK

And I the house of York.

LEWIS

Queen Margaret, Prince Edward, and Oxford,
Vouchsafe at our request to stand aside   110
While I use further conference with Warwick.

            They stand apart

---

109 Oxford] F; Lord Oxford HANMER   111.1 *apart*] This edition; *aloofe* F

92 **tell** recount; trace
93 **silly** scanty, meagre (*OED adj.* 2d, citing this line)
94 **prescription** a claim based on long custom or use
96 **thirty and six** Corresponds with Warwick's age rather than his oath of allegiance, since he was born in 1428 and led the French marriage negotiations in 1463–4, but supported York's claim to the throne in 1455 (see *2 Henry VI* 5.1.145 ff.).
97 **bewray** betray
98 **fence** stand up for
99 **buckler** defend (*OED v.* 1, citing this line)
101–7 **Call . . . Lancaster** In the first Par-liament of Edward's reign, 'the Earl of Oxford, far stricken in age, and the Lord Aubrey Vere, his son and heir . . . were attainted and put to execution, which caused John Earl of Oxford ever after to rebel' (Hall Hhi[r], Holinshed Rrri[r]). His speeches indicate that personal grievance and revenge continue to be passed down to a younger generation as motives for war.
101 **injurious doom** wrongful sentence
103 **more than so** what is more
104 **downfall . . . years** decline into ripe old age
110 **Vouchsafe** kindly grant
111 **use . . . conference** have . . . conversation

MARGARET

Heavens grant that Warwick's words bewitch him not.

LEWIS

Now Warwick tell me even upon thy conscience,
Is Edward your true king? For I were loath
To link with him that were not lawful chosen.   115

WARWICK

Thereon I pawn my credit and mine honour.

LEWIS

But is he gracious in the people's eye?

WARWICK

The more that Henry was unfortunate.

LEWIS

Then further, all dissembling set aside,
Tell me for truth the measure of his love   120
Unto our sister Bona.

WARWICK   Such it seems
As may beseem a monarch like himself.
Myself have often heard him say and swear
That this his love was an external plant,
Whereof the root was fixed in virtue's ground,   125
The leaves and fruit maintained with beauty's sun,

---

112 Heavens] F; [*Aside*] Heavens COLLIER MS   124 external] F; eternall o, WARBURTON

112 **bewitch** beguile

114 **were** would be

115 **link** i.e. by marriage (*OED v.*[1] 2, citing this line)
  lawful lawfully; i.e. by right of legitimate descent

116 **pawn my credit** stake my reputation. See Appendix A.

117 **gracious** popular, accepted

118 **unfortunate** plagued by bad fortune

119 **dissembling** concealment, pretended appearances

122 **may beseem** befits; suits the role of
  monarch like himself a truly kingly monarch like Edward

124–5 **love ... ground** external = visible. The contrast is between outwardly visible signs (*OED, external, adj.* 2) and expressions of love and their unseen source in immaterial motives and metaphysical grace ('virtue's ground'). But 'virtue' can also refer to moral excellence and sexual chastity, qualities ironically associated

with Edward.

124 **external** Editors have been misled by Warburton's emendation, following o, 'eternal': Alluding to the plants of *Paradise*'. Warwick's images allude to neoplatonic emblem literature and deploy the language of English Petrarchanism, not biblical discourse. A parallel passage in *1 Henry VI*, in which the King responds to Suffolk's account (and, like Warwick, proxy wooing) of Margaret, illuminates the meaning here: 'Her virtues gracèd with external gifts | Do breed love's settled passions in my heart' (5.7.3–4).

126 **maintained** nourished
  beauty's sun Bona as the radiant paragon of earthly beauty, the incarnation of metaphysical Beauty. Warwick continues to speak the language of neoplatonically influenced English Petrarchanism. In the 1994 RSC and other productions, his intonation and hesitations suggested he was improvising this unfamiliar language.

Exempt from envy but not from disdain,
Unless the Lady Bona quit his pain.

LEWIS

Now sister let us hear your firm resolve.

BONA

Your grant or your denial shall be mine.　　　　　130
(*Speaks to Warwick*) Yet I confess that often ere this day
When I have heard your king's desert recounted,
Mine ear hath tempted judgement to desire.

LEWIS

Then Warwick, thus: our sister shall be Edward's.
And now forthwith shall articles be drawn　　　　135
Touching the jointure that your king must make,
Which with her dowry shall be counterpoised.
Draw near, Queen Margaret, and be a witness
That Bona shall be wife to the English king.

PRINCE EDWARD

To Edward but not to the English king.　　　　　140

MARGARET

Deceitful Warwick, it was thy device
By this alliance to make void my suit;
Before thy coming Lewis was Henry's friend.

LEWIS

And still is friend to him and Margaret.
But if your title to the crown be weak,　　　　　145
As may appear by Edward's good success,
Then 'tis but reason that I be released
From giving aid which late I promisèd.
Yet shall you have all kindness at my hand

---

131 (*Speaks to Warwick*)] *subs. after 'day' in* F　133 tempted] F; tempered CAIRNCROSS (*conj.*
Vaughan)

---

127 **envy . . . disdain** malice, ill will . . .
    loathing, aversion
128 **quit his pain** reciprocate his aching pas-
    sion with her love
129 **resolve** decision
130 **grant** consent
133 **tempted judgement** put my rational
    powers of critical judgement to the test
    with amorous wishes. Cairncross argues
    'No question of "temptation" arises
    here', which is true in the sense of allure-

ment. But temptation can also mean 'put
to the test' (*OED*, *tempt*, 1), which suits
this context.
135 **articles** terms of marriage
136 **Touching** concerning
    jointure husband's willed provision of
    money and lands for his wife in the event
    of his death
137 **counterpoised** equally matched
141 **device** contrivance; purpose
146 **success** fortune

That your estate requires and mine can yield.   150

WARWICK

Henry now lives in Scotland at his ease,
Where having nothing, nothing can he lose.
And as for you yourself our quondam queen,
You have a father able to maintain you,
And better 'twere you troubled him than France.   155

MARGARET

Peace, impudent and shameless Warwick,
Proud setter-up and puller-down of kings,
I will not hence till with my talk and tears,
Both full of truth, I make King Lewis behold
Thy sly conveyance and thy lord's false love,   160
    Post blowing a horn within
For both of you are birds of selfsame feather.

LEWIS

Warwick, this is some post to us or thee.
    Enter the Post

POST (*speaks to Warwick*)

My lord ambassador, these letters are for you,
Sent from your brother Marquis Montague.
(*To Lewis*) These from our king unto your majesty.   165
(*To Margaret*) And madam these for you, from whom I
    know not.
    They all read their letters

OXFORD

I like it well that our fair Queen and mistress
Smiles at her news, while Warwick frowns at his.

PRINCE EDWARD

Nay mark how Lewis stamps as he were nettled.

---

156 Warwick,] F1; Warwicke, peace, F2 *and most editors* 160.1 *Post . . . within*] F; Sound for
a post within o 163 (*speaks to Warwick*)] subs. *after 'you' in* F 165 (*To Lewis*)] CAMBRIDGE;
after 'Maiesty' in F 166 (*To Margaret*)] CAMBRIDGE; *after 'you' in* F

150 **estate** social rank
151 **at his ease** in comfort; at leisure (spoken
   ironically)
152 Proverbial: 'They that have nothing
   need fear to lose nothing' (Dent N331),
   ultimately deriving from St Paul.
153 **quondam** (Latin) former
154 **father . . . you** See note to 2.2.139, also
   Appendix A.

157 **setter-up . . . kings** See note to 2.3.37,
   also Appendix A.
160 **conveyance** underhanded dealing
160.1 *Post* express courier
167 **mistress** female governor
169 **stamps** i.e. (his foot) in anger. The gesture may appear less stagey if Lewis steps
   down from his throne as he does so.
   as as if

I hope all's for the best.

LEWIS

Warwick what are thy news? And yours, fair Queen?

MARGARET

Mine such as fill my heart with unhoped joys.

WARWICK

Mine full of sorrow and heart's discontent.

LEWIS

What, has your king married the Lady Grey?
And now to soothe your forgery and his,   175
Sends me a paper to persuade me patience?
Is this th'alliance that he seeks with France?
Dare he presume to scorn us in this manner?

MARGARET

I told your majesty as much before.
This proveth Edward's love and Warwick's honesty.   180

WARWICK

King Lewis I here protest in sight of heaven
And by the hope I have of heavenly bliss,
That I am clear from this misdeed of Edward's—
No more my king, for he dishonours me,
But most himself if he could see his shame.   185
Did I forget that by the house of York
My father came untimely to his death?
Did I let pass th'abuse done to my niece?
Did I impale him with the regal crown?

172 **unhoped** unexpected
175 **soothe** smooth over (*OED* 6, citing this line)
  forgery deception, fraud (*OED* 2, citing this line)
176 **persuade me** persuade me to have (Abbott ¶382)
181 **protest** solemnly affirm. See Appendix A.
184, 190–7, 212 See Appendix A.
185 **shame** (own) morally disgraceful behaviour
186–90 **Did I** Repetition of the first element in these lines constitutes *anaphora*, or the figure of report (George Puttenham, *The Art of English Poesy*, p. 198), a common rhetorical ornament.
186, 213 **by** by means of (*OED prep.* 34)
187 **untimely** prematurely, before his natural time, because Warwick's father the Earl

of Salisbury was executed after being captured at Wakefield fighting for the Yorkists.
188 **abuse . . . niece** *OED, abuse, sb.* 5 cites this line under the definitions 'ill-usage, injury', but definition 6, 'violation, defilement' is closer to history. Both chronicles report that, besides betraying Warwick's embassy, 'Edward did attempt a thing once in the earl's house which was much against the earl's honesty (whether he would have deflowered his daughter or his niece, the certainty was not for both their honours openly known), for surely such a thing was attempted by King Edward' (Hall Hhvi^v, Holinshed Rrrii^v). This line is routinely cut in modern productions.
189 **impale** encircle (his head), invest

Did I put Henry from his native right?   190
And am I guerdoned at the last with shame?
Shame on himself, for my desert is honour;
And to repair my honour lost for him,
I here renounce him and return to Henry.
My noble queen let former grudges pass,   195
And henceforth I am thy true servitor.
I will revenge his wrong to Lady Bona
And replant Henry in his former state.

MARGARET

Warwick, these words have turned my hate to love,
And I forgive and quite forget old faults,   200
And joy that thou becom'st King Henry's friend.

WARWICK

So much his friend—ay, his unfeignèd friend—
That if King Lewis vouchsafe to furnish us
With some few bands of chosen soldiers,
I'll undertake to land them on our coast   205
And force the tyrant from his seat by war.
'Tis not his new-made bride shall succour him,
And as for Clarence, as my letters tell me,
He's very likely now to fall from him
For matching more for wanton lust than honour,   210
Or than for strength and safety of our country.

202 friend—ay,] This edition *following* ROWE; Friend, I, F

190 **native** natural entitlement (to the crown) by birth
191 **guerdoned** rewarded
192 **desert** proper due
194 **renounce . . . Henry** Historically this did not happen openly until 1470, before which Warwick concealed his sense of grievance. If Warwick is wearing a white rose, he may pull it off, and/or he may kneel to Margaret. The abruptness of Warwick's change often elicits laughter from theatre audiences, and some actors make Warwick conscious of the moment's irony. In the 1963–4 Hall–Barton and 1987 ESC productions, however, Warwick was seriously vexed and switched sides angrily.
196 **servitor** servant; soldier
198 **state** royal office
199 **Warwick . . . love** Another ironic and

potentially comical moment. In the 1983 BBC production, Julia Foster stood open-mouthed, needing a moment to quell her astonishment and find new words before responding. In 1963–4 Peggy Ashcroft paused for several seconds, frowning over Brewster Mason's (clearly reluctant) offer. She then stretched out her arm to one side, forcing Warwick to kneel and kiss her hand. The obvious suspicion on both sides—Warwick glanced up sceptically at 'love'—indicated this was purely a pact of convenience. See Introduction, p. 80.
202 **unfeignèd** authentic
203 **vouchsafe** will be pleased
206 **tyrant . . . seat** usurper . . . throne
209 **fall from** desert; revolt against. See Appendix A.
210 **matching** marrying
   wanton uncontrolled. See Appendix A.

BONA

    Dear brother how shall Bona be revenged
    But by thy help to this distressèd queen?

MARGARET

    Renownèd prince how shall poor Henry live
    Unless thou rescue him from foul despair?   215

BONA

    My quarrel and this English queen's are one.

WARWICK

    And mine, fair Lady Bona, joins with yours.

LEWIS

    And mine with hers and thine and Margaret's.
    Therefore at last I firmly am resolved
    You shall have aid.   220

MARGARET

    Let me give humble thanks for all at once.

LEWIS

    Then, England's messenger, return in post
    And tell false Edward thy supposèd king
    That Lewis of France is sending over masquers
    To revel it with him and his new bride.   225
    Thou seest what's passed; go fear thy king withal.

BONA

    Tell him, in hope he'll prove a widower shortly,
    I wear the willow garland for his sake.

MARGARET

    Tell him my mourning weeds are laid aside

---

226 passed] WILSON; past F   228 I wear] F; Ile O, CAPELL

214 **live** have life which is worthy of his royal position; survive
216 **quarrel** cause for complaint
222 **in post** with speed
224 **masquers** performers masked as allegorical or fanciful characters in entertainments with dancing (= 'revels'), popular at court and noble weddings. Lewis uses this ironic description of soldiers to ridicule Edward's marriage pretences as well as his reputation for pleasure-seeking.
226 **fear** make fearful
    withal with this (news)
228 **wear** Since Capell all editions except Riverside have followed O's reading, pre-ferring to accept the wording of the Post's account of this line at 4.1.100 rather than F's at this point. But the Post's speech in 4.1, while a highly accurate report, is not verbatim; e.g. see Margaret's next line, 3.3.229, and 4.1.104. And as Munro remarks, 'There is some force in Bona pretending to go into mourning for Edward in anticipation, and some additional mockery' (note to l. 228, p. 311).
228 **willow garland** Proverbial symbol of the forsaken woman (Dent W403). See *Othello* 4.3.38 ff.
229 **weeds** garments. Margaret is often dressed soberly, perhaps hooded, as if in mourning.

And I am ready to put armour on.   230
WARWICK
Tell him from me that he hath done me wrong
And therefore I'll uncrown him ere't be long.
⌜*Giving money*⌝ There's thy reward, be gone.

                                     Exit Post

LEWIS But Warwick,
Thou and Oxford with five thousand men   235
Shall cross the seas and bid false Edward battle,
And as occasion serves, this noble queen
And prince shall follow with a fresh supply.
Yet ere thou go, but answer me one doubt:
What pledge have we of thy firm loyalty?   240
WARWICK
This shall assure my constant loyalty:
That if our queen and this young prince agree,
I'll join mine eldest daughter, and my joy,
To him forthwith in holy wedlock bands.
MARGARET
Yes I agree, and thank you for your motion.   245
Son Edward, she is fair and virtuous,
Therefore delay not, give thy hand to Warwick,
And with thy hand thy faith irrevocable,
That only Warwick's daughter shall be thine.
PRINCE EDWARD
Yes I accept her, for she well deserves it,   250
And here to pledge my vow I give my hand.
    He gives his hand to Warwick

233 ⌜*Giving money*⌝] OXFORD; *not in* F; *Giving a purse* DYCE 1864–7

230 **armour** 'Margaret is again the successor of Joan of Arc [in *1 Henry VI*]'
(Cairncross). See Introduction, pp. 94–5.
For a discussion of the ambivalent impact
made by Queen Elizabeth's appearances
in masculine dress, such as her address
to her troops at Tilbury in 1588 in battle-
armour, see Leah S. Marcus, *Puzzling
Shakespeare: Local Reading and its Discontents* (Berkeley, 1988), ch. 2, pp. 51–
105.
231–2 **Tell . . . long** See Appendix A.
233 **reward** payment
238 **supply** reinforcements. See Appendix
A.

239 **but** only (Abbott ¶128)
243 **eldest daughter** Historically Anne
Neville, Warwick's younger daughter.
She and Prince Edward were betrothed,
but his death at Tewkesbury in 1471
occurred before they could be married.
Both chroniclers report that the eldest
daughter married Clarence, and Hall
remarks on the competition this created
between Clarence and Prince Edward for
their father-in-law's favour. See Appendix
A, 3.3.243–9.
245 **motion** proposal
249 **only** 'Margaret is thinking of Edward's
betrayal of the Lady Bona' (Hattaway).

LEWIS

Why stay we now? These soldiers shall be levied,
And thou Lord Bourbon, our High Admiral,
Shall waft them over with our royal fleet.
I long till Edward fall by war's mischance,   255
For mocking marriage with a dame of France.

                              Exeunt all but Warwick

WARWICK

I came from Edward as ambassador,
But I return his sworn and mortal foe.
Matter of marriage was the charge he gave me,
But dreadful war shall answer his demand.   260
Had he none else to make a stale but me?
Then none but I shall turn his jest to sorrow.
I was the chief that raised him to the crown,
And I'll be chief to bring him down again,
Not that I pity Henry's misery,   265
But seek revenge on Edward's mockery.   *Exit*

4.1   *Enter Gloucester, Clarence, the Duke of Somerset, and*
       Montague

GLOUCESTER

Now tell me brother Clarence, what think you

---

254 Shall] F1; Shalt F2 *and some editors*   256.1 all but] CAPELL (*subs.*); *Manet* F   264 chief
... again] F; chief again to ... down CAIRNCROSS *conj.*

4.1] ROWE; *not in* F   0.1 Gloucester] ROWE; *Richard* F   the Duke of Somerset] OXFORD; *Somer-*
set F   1 GLOUCESTER] ROWE; *Rich.* F (*and throughout this scene*)

---

252 **stay** delay
254 **waft** carry over by water (*OED v.*[1] 2, citing this line). See Appendix A, 3.3.253.
255 **long** earnestly desire; am impatient (for)
256 **mocking** pretending to propose (*OED*,
mock, v. 4b, citing this line); making a
mockery of. See Appendix A.
dame woman of high rank
260 **demand** request
261 **stale** screen for deception; laughing
stock (normally applied to a lover or mistress whose loyalty is ridiculed). Holinshed explains: 'for it might be judged he
came rather like an espial, to move a thing
never minded and to treat a marriage
determined before not to take effect. Surely he thought himself evil used, that
when he had brought the matter to his
purposed intent and wished conclusion,

then to have it quail on his part, so as all
men might think at the least wise that his
prince made small account of him, to
send him on such a sleeveless [i.e. futile]
errand' (Rrii[v]).
265–6 **pity . . . mockery** i.e. Warwick's
motive is not justice, as it arguably was
in supporting the house of York, but
personal opportunism and wounded feelings. This is the last time in the play the
word 'revenge' is spoken as a vow or
threat.
4.1 Modern productions sometimes stage the
opening of this scene as a return from
wedding celebrations ('new marriage', l.
2; 'bride', l. 7) and/or the Queen's coronation. The symmetrical groupings called
for by 6.1–3 imply an element of social
formality.

Of this new marriage with the Lady Grey?
Hath not our brother made a worthy choice?

CLARENCE

Alas, you know 'tis far from hence to France;
How could he stay till Warwick made return? 5

SOMERSET

My lords, forbear this talk, here comes the King.

Flourish. Enter King Edward, Queen Elizabeth, the
Earl of Pembroke, Lord Stafford, Lord Hastings. Four
stand on one side, and four on the other

GLOUCESTER

And his well-chosen bride.

CLARENCE

I mind to tell him plainly what I think.

EDWARD

Now brother of Clarence, how like you our choice
That you stand pensive as half malcontent? 10

CLARENCE

As well as Lewis of France or the Earl of Warwick,
Which are so weak of courage and in judgement
That they'll take no offence at our abuse.

EDWARD

Suppose they take offence without a cause,
They are but Lewis and Warwick, I am Edward, 15
Your king and Warwick's, and must have my will.

6.1 *Queen Elizabeth*] RIVERSIDE (*subs.*); *Lady Grey* F (*and prefix in this scene*) 6.1–2 *the Earl of*
Pembroke, Lord Stafford, Lord Hastings] OXFORD (*subs.*); *Penbrooke, Stafford, Hastings* F 13 our]
F; your OXFORD *conj.*

3–5 **worthy choice . . . return** Clarence
usually returns Richard's ironic mockery,
but sometimes with bitter indignation.

3 **worthy** (spoken sarcastically)

5 **stay** delay

6 **forbear** leave off

6.2 *Pembroke* Hall notes that he was elevated
despite his low social status (Iivi^r), which
may explain his minor silent role in this
scene. He may also have been included
because he was the ancestor of Shakespeare's patron, the Earl of Pembroke,
whose company originally performed *The*
True Tragedy of Richard Duke of York.

6.2–3 **Four . . . and four on the other** Implies
each group stands on either side of the
seated King Edward.

8 **mind** intend

10 **pensive** gloomy; meditating on future
plans. Clarence may stand apart to
indicate displeasure. In the 1983 BBC
production, everyone except him
applauded the entry of Edward and
Elizabeth.

13 **abuse** ill-usage, wrong-doing. '[O]ur'
indicates that Clarence feels implicated by
Edward's behaviour.

16 **will** wish; sexual desire

GLOUCESTER

And shall have your will because our king;
Yet hasty marriage seldom proveth well.

EDWARD

Yea brother Richard, are you offended too?

GLOUCESTER   Not I, no,   20
God forbid that I should wish them severed
Whom God hath joined together;
Ay, and 'twere pity to sunder them
That yoke so well together.

EDWARD

Setting your scorns and your mislike aside,   25
Tell me some reason why the Lady Grey
Should not become my wife and England's queen?
And you too, Somerset and Montague,
Speak freely what you think.

CLARENCE

Then this is mine opinion: that King Lewis   30
Becomes your enemy for mocking him
About the marriage of the Lady Bona.

GLOUCESTER

And Warwick, doing what you gave in charge,
Is now dishonoured by this new marriage.

EDWARD

What if both Lewis and Warwick be appeased   35
By such invention as I can devise?

MONTAGUE

Yet to have joined with France in such alliance

17 shall ... king;] This edition; shall ... King: F; you shall ... king? ROWE   30 mine] F1; my
0, F3

17 **And . . . king** The short line beginning
with 'And' may indicate the swiftness of
Richard's rejoinder.
18 **hasty ... well** Proverbial: 'Marry in haste
and repent at leisure' (Dent H196). See
Appendix A.
21–4 **God . . . together** The patterned
irregularity of Richard's verse form is
potentially very effective burlesque, as
much part of his mockery as his sardonic
content. His words echo the *BCP* marriage
service: 'Those whom God hath joined
together, let no man put asunder' (from
Matthew 19: 6), and he may mimic the

priest joining the couple's hands together.
Editors since Capell have tried various
ways of reducing F's four lines (or in the
case of Pope and others, five lines including l. 20) to three, but not succeeded in
gaining greater metrical regularity.
23 **sunder** separate; dissolve (in marriage)
24 **yoke** couple (with a sexual pun on bearing a burden) (Partridge)
25 **mislike** objections; disaffection
32 **About** concerning
33 **gave in charge** entrusted him to perform
36 **invention** solution (but with an underlying negative sense of 'fabrication')

Would more have strengthened this our commonwealth
'Gainst foreign storms than any home-bred marriage.

HASTINGS

Why, knows not Montague that of itself   40
England is safe if true within itself?

MONTAGUE

But the safer when 'tis backed with France.

HASTINGS

'Tis better using France than trusting France.
Let us be backed with God and with the seas
Which he hath giv'n for fence impregnable,   45
And with their helps only defend ourselves;
In them and in ourselves our safety lies.

CLARENCE

For this one speech Lord Hastings well deserves
To have the heir of the Lord Hungerford.

EDWARD

Ay, what of that? It was my will and grant,   50
And for this once my will shall stand for law.

GLOUCESTER

And yet methinks your grace hath not done well
To give the heir and daughter of Lord Scales
Unto the brother of your loving bride;
She better would have fitted me or Clarence,   55
But in your bride you bury brotherhood.

---

43 using] F; losing VAUGHAN *conj.*   than] F4, ROWE; then FI

---

39 **storms** attack. For 1590s audiences this would have recalled the attempted Spanish invasion in 1588.

41 **England . . . itself** Patriotic sentiment widely echoed in the post-Armada period; e.g. *K. John* 5.7.112–14, 117–18.

45 **fence** a defence

46 **only** alone

48–9 **Hastings . . . Hungerford** It was historically his son, the 2nd Lord Hastings, who married Mary, daughter of Thomas Lord Hungerford, but Shakespeare follows Hall. See Appendix A, 4.1.53–5.

50–1 **will . . . law** 'What the king wills, that the law wills' (Dent K72), a traditional but controversial notion by the end of the sixteenth century, as the monarchy's

prerogatives became increasingly challenged. Edward himself recognizes this reality: 'for this once' (l. 51).

53 **To give** Through the feudal Court of Wards, the king was the legal guardian of the country's great heiresses, whose income he could control and profit from while they remained under age. He could also marry them off to his favourites and advisers.

53–5 **heir . . . Clarence** Elizabeth, rich heiress of Thomas Lord Scales (who appears in *2 Henry VI* 4.5), married Anthony Woodville, later Earl Rivers (see 4.4). See Appendix A.

56 **bury** abandon, forget (*OED* 2b, citing this line). See Appendix A.

CLARENCE

 Or else you would not have bestowed the heir
 Of the Lord Bonville on your new wife's son,
 And leave your brothers to go speed elsewhere.

EDWARD

 Alas poor Clarence, is it for a wife   60
 That thou art malcontent? I will provide thee.

CLARENCE

 In choosing for yourself you showed your judgement,
 Which being shallow, you shall give me leave
 To play the broker in mine own behalf,
 And to that end I shortly mind to leave you.   65

EDWARD

 Leave me or tarry, Edward will be king
 And not be tied unto his brothers' will.

ELIZABETH

 My lords, before it pleased his majesty
 To raise my state to title of a queen,
 Do me but right and you must all confess   70
 That I was not ignoble of descent,
 And meaner than myself have had like fortune.
 But as this title honours me and mine,
 So your dislikes, to whom I would be pleasing,
 Doth cloud my joys with danger and with sorrow. 75

EDWARD

 My love forbear to fawn upon their frowns.
 What danger or what sorrow can befall thee
 So long as Edward is thy constant friend

---

67 brothers'] This edition *following* HATTAWAY *conj.*; Brothers F; Brother's ROWE

57–8 **heir . . . son** Cicely, heir to William Lord Harrington and Bonville, was married to Thomas Grey, son of Sir John Grey, the Queen's first husband. Thomas was created first Marquis Dorset by Edward. See Appendix A.
59 **go speed** seek (marital) success
64 **broker** match-maker
65 **mind** intend
67 **tied** bound, obliged
69 **state** social rank
70 **Do me but right** be only fair to me
71 **not ignoble** Elizabeth was the first commoner to become Queen of England, but was of noble descent on her mother's side, being the daughter of Jacquetta of Luxembourg, widow of John Duke of Bedford. See J. R. Lander, 'Marriage and Politics: the Nevilles and Wydvilles', *Bulletin of the Institute of Historical Research*, 36 (1963), 19–52.
72 **meaner** persons of lower social standing
74 **dislikes** disapproval
 whom Referring to the implied antecedent 'you' in 'your dislikes'.
76 **fawn upon** take notice of
78 **friend** patron; ally; lover

And their true sovereign whom they must obey?
Nay, whom they shall obey, and love thee too,   80
Unless they seek for hatred at my hands,
Which if they do yet will I keep thee safe,
And they shall feel the vengeance of my wrath.

GLOUCESTER (*aside*)

I hear, yet say not much, but think the more.
    Enter a Post

EDWARD

Now messenger, what letters or what news from France?   85

POST

My sovereign liege, no letters and few words,
But such as I, without your special pardon,
Dare not relate.

EDWARD

Go to, we pardon thee, therefore in brief
Tell me their words as near as thou canst guess them.   90
What answer makes King Lewis unto our letters?

POST

At my depart these were his very words:
'Go tell false Edward, the supposèd king,
That Lewis of France is sending over masquers
To revel it with him and his new bride.'   95

EDWARD

Is Lewis so brave? Belike he thinks me Henry.
But what said Lady Bona to my marriage?

POST

These were her words, uttered with mild disdain:
'Tell him in hope he'll prove a widower shortly,
I'll wear the willow garland for his sake.'   100

---

84 (*aside*)] JOHNSON; *not in* F   93 the] F; thy O, ROWE

---

84 Proverbial: 'Though he said little he thought the more' (Dent L367).
84.1 *Enter a Post* The lack of any entrance signal or notice may suggest the Post (sent from France in 3.3) comes in quietly or warily.
89 **Go to** Exclamation expressing dismissive impatience.

90 **guess** remember. Shakespeare's association of the word with memory is attested by *Merchant* 1.3.52 but not by *OED*.
92 **depart** departure
96 **brave** bold, boastful (recorded by *OED* only as a verb in these senses)
    Belike perhaps
98 **mild** less severe (compared to Lewis)

EDWARD

   I blame not her, she could say little less,

   She had the wrong. But what said Henry's queen?

   For I have heard that she was there in place.

POST

   'Tell him', quoth she, 'my mourning weeds are done

   And I am ready to put armour on.'   105

EDWARD

   Belike she minds to play the Amazon.

   But what said Warwick to these injuries?

POST

   He, more incensed against your majesty

   Than all the rest, discharged me with these words:

   'Tell him from me that he hath done me wrong   110

   And therefore I'll uncrown him ere't be long.'

EDWARD

   Ha. Durst the traitor breathe out so proud words?

   Well, I will arm me, being thus forewarned.

   They shall have wars, and pay for their presumption.

   But say, is Warwick friends with Margaret?   115

POST

   Ay, gracious sovereign, they are so linked in friendship

   That young Prince Edward marries Warwick's

      daughter.

CLARENCE

   Belike th'elder, Clarence will have the younger.

---

112 Ha.] This edition; Ha? F; Ha! THEOBALD

101–2 **blame . . . wrong** Edward's twinge of
conscience may have been suggested
by Hall's brief opinion inserted in a passage related to 3.3.257 ff.: 'The French
king and his queen were not a little discontent (as I cannot blame them) . . . to
have their sister first demanded, and then
granted, and in conclusion rejected'
(Hhvi^r).

103 **in place** present in person (Fr. *en place*)

104 **weeds are done** apparel has been laid
aside

106 **Amazon** See note to 1.4.114. In some but
not all modern productions Margaret participates in the battles (e.g. 1952–3 Birmingham Repertory and 1992 Ashland
productions); Alan Armstrong discusses
her combatant role in the latter in 'Ore-

gon Shakespeare Festival', *Shakespeare
Bulletin* (Fall, 1992), p. 26.

109 **discharged** dismissed

112 **Ha** Spoken by actors in a variety of ways
to signify incredulity, indignation, contempt, etc. In the 1983 BBC production,
Edward was a little unnerved by Warwick's threats.

   breathe utter vehemently (*OED* 12b)

   so such

113, 127 Proverbial: 'Forewarned is fore-
armed' (Dent H54).

118–22 **Belike . . . yourself** Clarence may
speak these lines partly to himself, or
entirely openly, since the chronicles
observe that his and Warwick's plans
were plainly known. See note to 3.3.243
and Appendix A.

Now brother king farewell, and sit you fast,
For I will hence to Warwick's other daughter,   120
That though I want a kingdom, yet in marriage
I may not prove inferior to yourself.
You that love me and Warwick follow me.

> *Exit Clarence, and Somerset follows*

GLOUCESTER (*aside*)

Not I, my thoughts aim at a further matter:
I stay not for the love of Edward but the crown.   125

EDWARD

Clarence and Somerset both gone to Warwick?
Yet am I armed against the worst can happen,
And haste is needful in this desperate case.
Pembroke and Stafford, you in our behalf
Go levy men and make prepare for war;   130
They are already or quickly will be landed,
Myself in person will straight follow you.

> *Exeunt Pembroke and Stafford*

But ere I go, Hastings and Montague
Resolve my doubt: you twain of all the rest
Are near to Warwick by blood and by alliance;   135
Tell me if you love Warwick more than me.
If it be so then both depart to him:

---

124 (*aside*)] ROWE (*after* 'crown', *l.* 125); *not in* F; *after* 'Not I' OXFORD   135 near] F (neere);
neerest O, CAIRNCROSS; near'st OXFORD

---

119 **sit you fast** i.e. mind your throne (a veiled reference to Clarence's being next in the line of succession)
121 **want** lack
123.1 *Somerset follows* This fictional action allows Shakespeare to link the historical 3rd and 4th Dukes of Somerset dramatically, as the latter always supported the Lancastrians. See note to 4.6.0.2.
126 **Clarence . . . Warwick** Like l. 112, the tone of this line depends on Edward's reaction and attitude. In the 1987 ESC production, he was deeply dismayed by Clarence's desertion, but in others such as the BBC he reacted more philosophically and confidently. See Appendix A, 4.1.123, 126–7.
128 **haste . . . case** Proverbial. See Appendix A, 4.1.128–32.

130 **prepare** preparation (Abbott ¶451)
131 **They** i.e. Warwick and his allies
134 **Resolve** dispel, clear away (*OED v.* 12, citing this line). See Appendix A, 4.1.133–41.
   twain two persons
135 **near** Cairncross and other editors follow O in emending F to 'nearest' or 'near'st'. Whereas F has twelve potential syllables with 'near', O 'needs' the extra syllable in 'nearest' to complete ten syllables: 'You of all the rest are neerest allied'. The metrical contexts are therefore different. It is likely that 'Warwick by' and 'alliance' (if it is not a feminine ending) were elided to emphasize the main beats, a conventional practice in Elizabethan prosody (Partridge, *Orthography*, pp. 84–5, 91–2; Wright, pp. 170–3).

I rather wish you foes than hollow friends.
But if you mind to hold your true obedience,
Give me assurance with some friendly vow   140
That I may never have you in suspect.

MONTAGUE

So God help Montague as he proves true.

HASTINGS

And Hastings as he favours Edward's cause.

EDWARD

Now brother Richard, will you stand by us?

GLOUCESTER

Ay, in despite of all that shall withstand you.   145

EDWARD

Why so, then am I sure of victory.
Now therefore let us hence and lose no hour
Till we meet Warwick with his foreign power.   *Exeunt*

4.2   *Enter Warwick and Oxford in England, with French*
        Soldiers

WARWICK

Trust me my lord, all hitherto goes well,
The common people by numbers swarm to us.
        Enter Clarence and Somerset
But see where Somerset and Clarence comes.

4.2] CAPELL; *not in* F   2 people] F, 0; *sort* OXFORD; *men* HATTAWAY

138 Proverbial: 'It is better to have an open
foe than a dissembling friend' (Dent
F410).
139 **mind** intend
141 **suspect** suspicion
145 **despite** spite
148 **power** army
4.2.0.1–2 *Warwick ... England ... French*
Soldiers The home locale and foreign
allies point historically to the fact that
Warwick publicly revealed his change in
allegiance to the Lancastrians only in
1470, several years after his futile marriage negotiations on behalf of Edward,
and after he had secured aid from King
Louis XI (announced towards the end of
3.3).
2 **people** The line is not unquestionably
hypermetrical as many editors since
Pope have assumed (see note to 4.1.135).

In this case there is an extra unstressed
midline syllable, which in words such
as 'people' with strong first syllables
could be all but dropped or merged
with the next syllable: 'peo*ple by* numbers'. See Wright, pp. 192–3. Emendation
is therefore unnecessary. The phrase
'common people' occurs in Hall (Kki^v and
Appendix A, 4.2.2, 1.1.67–8, 2.6.8,
4.1.18).
2 **by** in (great). Following the Lancastrian
victory over Welsh Yorkists at Edgecote
near Banbury in 1469, both chroniclers
report that 'the Northern men resorted
toward Warwick, where the earl had
gathered a great multitude of people'
(Hall Kki^{r–v}, Holinshed Rrrv^r).
3 **comes** The two proper nouns are treated
as a single subject (Abbott ¶336). See
Appendix A.

Speak suddenly my lords, are we all friends?

CLARENCE

Fear not that, my lord.   5

WARWICK

Then, gentle Clarence, welcome unto Warwick,
And welcome Somerset. I hold it cowardice
To rest mistrustful where a noble heart
Hath pawned an open hand in sign of love,
Else might I think that Clarence, Edward's brother,   10
Were but a feignèd friend to our proceedings.
But welcome, sweet Clarence, my daughter shall be
          thine.
And now what rests but in night's coverture,
Thy brother being carelessly encamped,
His soldiers lurking in the town about,   15

12 welcome, sweet] F (*subs.*), O; come, sweet CAIRNCROSS; welcome, CAPELL   15 town] F;
towns THEOBALD (*conj.* Thirlby) *following* 4.3.13

4 **suddenly** directly
6 **gentle** noble
6–12 **welcome . . . welcome** The first welcome seems provisional, as Warwick
voices his suspicion about Clarence's loyalty, which serves as a warning and to
dispel his own doubts, before his second
definitive welcome. In the 1983 BBC
production, Warwick did not accept
Clarence's hand when he initially extended it. Only after his veiled warning ('Else
might I think . . . feignèd friend') did Warwick shake it.
7 **hold it** regard it as
8 **rest** remain
9 **pawned** pledged
12 **But . . . thine** Regarded as a corrupt line
for which various emendations have been
proposed, yet none has been satisfactory.
The line contains twelve syllables and six
main stresses, therefore in theory is a
hexameter. The 'irregularity', as Pope
recognized, lies in 'sweet Clarence',
'Clarence' being a trochaic foot (Pope
emended to 'But welcome friend, my . . .').
Trochaic disruptions in metre, as Wright
observes (p. 186) were 'galling to Augus-
tans' but not unusual in Shakespeare,
especially when they come at midline
after punctuation (Wright, pp. 195–6,
312, and ch. 13 *passim*). R. B. McKerrow
argued that the Folio compositor consulted a copy of O or Q3 here and at ll. 2 and

15 (see Introduction, p. 122). But his discussion is impressionistic, and pertains
largely to *2 Henry VI* rather than Part
Three. The Oxford editors observe that
'sweet' is used elsewhere to describe
Clarence (5.5.73). Since O and F agree
here in a speech by Warwick, whose relia-
bility overall suggests he may have been
one of the main reporters of O, the line
is probably authentic, and 'welcome'
unlikely to be a compositorial interpolation from ll. 6–8.
13 **rests** remains to be done
    coverture concealing shade; disguise
14 **carelessly** without concern, apprehensiveness. See Appendix A.
15 **lurking** having retired; idling
    town 'at a place called Wolney four mile[s]
from [the town of] Warwick, [Edward]
was taken prisoner, and brought to the
castle of Warwick' (Hall Kki^v, Holinshed
Rrrv^r). Warwick's information, not surprisingly in view of the chronicles' reports
of his military reconnaissance, is more
accurate than the Third Watchman's
(4.3.13, 'towns'), making Theobald's
emendation in favour of the latter unnecessary. See also next note.
    about around nearby (*OED prep.* B.2), a
preposition that follows the noun; thus,
'lurking close to the town'. Compare
Pericles Sc. 10.2: 'No din but snores the
house about'.

And but attended by a simple guard,
We may surprise and take him at our pleasure?
Our scouts have found th'adventure very easy:
That as Ulysses and stout Diomede
With sleight and manhood stole to Rhesus' tents   20
And brought from thence the Thracian fatal steeds,
So we, well covered with the night's black mantle,
At unawares may beat down Edward's guard
And seize himself—I say not slaughter him,
For I intend but only to surprise him.   25
You that will follow me to this attempt,
Applaud the name of Henry, with your leader.
        They all cry, 'Henry!'
Why then let's on our way in silent sort,
For Warwick and his friends, God and St George.

                                                        Exeunt

4.3   *Enter three Watchmen to guard King Edward's tent*
FIRST WATCHMAN
    Come on my masters, each man take his stand,

4.3] CAPELL; *not in* F   0.1 *King Edward's*] PELICAN; *the Kings* F

16 **but attended** he (Edward) attended only
    simple small, weak; dull-witted, imperceptive
18 **scouts . . . easy** 'All the king's doings were by espials declared to the Earl of Warwick [Holinshed "upon secret knowledge had"], which like a wise and politic captain intending not to lose so great an advantage . . . in the dead of the night, with an elect company of men of war as secretly as was possible, set on the king's field, killing them that kept the watch, and ere the king were ware' (Hall Kki^v, Holinshed more briefly Rrrv^r).
    adventure attempting the operation
19 **That as** in the same way that
    Ulysses See note to 3.2.189.
    stout valiant
    Diomede Greek commander at Troy celebrated in Homer's *Iliad* for his boldness in action and wise counsel.
20 **sleight and manhood** Referring respectively to Ulysses and Diomede.
    sleight trickery
20–1 **stole . . . steeds** In *The Iliad*, x. 471–579,

Ulysses and Diomede steal by night into the camp of the Thracian prince Rhesus, who had come to aid the Trojans. They kill him and capture his white horses, preventing them from drinking at the river Xanthus, which an oracle prophesied the horses had to do in order to preserve Troy. Ovid, *Metamorphoses*, xiii. 295–310, Virgil *Aeneid*, i. 469–73, or Marlowe's *Dido Queen of Carthage*, 1.1.70–3, are Shakespeare's possible sources.
21 **fatal** fated by destiny; leading to destruction
22 **mantle** cloak (*OED sb.* 2a, citing this line). 'Night's black mantle' is commonplace (Dent MM7).
23 **At unawares** without warning
25 **surprise** capture unprepared
27 **Applaud** praise in any lively manner (*OED* 1)
27.1–28 **cry . . . silent sort** In the 1983 BBC production the cry was whispered in stealth.
28 **sort** manner
4.3 Hart suggests Shakespeare may have taken a hint for the staging and dialogue

The King by this is set him down to sleep.

SECOND WATCHMAN

What, will he not to bed?

FIRST WATCHMAN

Why no, for he hath made a solemn vow
Never to lie and take his natural rest   5
Till Warwick or himself be quite suppressed.

SECOND WATCHMAN

Tomorrow then belike shall be the day,
If Warwick be so near as men report.

THIRD WATCHMAN

But say, I pray, what nobleman is that
That with the King here resteth in his tent?   10

FIRST WATCHMAN

'Tis the Lord Hastings, the King's chiefest friend.

THIRD WATCHMAN

O, is it so? But why commands the King
That his chief followers lodge in towns about him
While he himself keeps in the cold field?

SECOND WATCHMAN

'Tis the more honour because more dangerous.   15

---

9 nobleman] F4, ROWE; Noble man F1 14 keeps] F (keepes); keeps still *conj.* This edition;
keepeth THEOBALD; keeps here HANMER; keeps state OXFORD *conj.*

---

of this episode from *The Spanish Tragedy*,
3.3.17–45. The event itself is reported by
the chronicles (see note to 4.2.18 and
Appendix A).

0.1 **tent** The tent is not integral to this scene
and may be imagined (for discussion see
Dessen, *Recovering*, pp. 141–4). Or it could
be suggested figuratively by hangings on
the tiring-house wall, or use of a cur-
tained stage-space.

1 **stand** position, station

2 **this** this time
is . . . down has settled himself in a chair
(which anticipates Edward's entrance
'*sitting in a chair*' at 27.6)

6 **suppressed** vanquished

7 **belike** it seems likely

13 **lodge** station themselves, encamp

14 **While . . . field?** A nine-syllable line
apparently missing a beat after 'keeps',
which becomes a monosyllabic foot.

Wright calculates that lines missing a
sixth syllable, as here, are the most frequent metrical irregularities in Shakespeare, though they appear more often in
lines divided between two speakers (pp.
179–84). 'Keeps' may be heavily stressed
to balance the succeeding series of weak
and strong beats, 'in the cold field'. I
prefer not to emend, on the grounds that
Shakespeare's metrical practice was more
flexible, even in this relatively early play,
than previous editors have recognized,
and that in performance the spoken text
negotiates such 'irregularity' easily. If
emendation is considered necessary, I
suggest 'keeps still'. Compare *Macbeth*
5.4.8–9: 'We learn no other but the confi-
dent tyrant | Keeps still in Dunsinane'.

14 **keeps** remains. See Appendix A, 4.2.14.

15 Proverbial: 'The more danger the more
honour' (Dent D35). Edward expresses this
sentiment at 5.1.70.

THIRD WATCHMAN

    Ay, but give me worship and quietness,

    I like it better than a dangerous honour.

    If Warwick knew in what estate he stands,

    'Tis to be doubted he would waken him.

FIRST WATCHMAN

    Unless our halberds did shut up his passage.   20

SECOND WATCHMAN

    Ay, wherefore else guard we his royal tent

    But to defend his person from night-foes?

        Enter Warwick, Clarence, Oxford, Somerset, and

        French Soldiers, silent all

WARWICK

    This is his tent, and see where stand his guard.

    Courage my masters, honour now or never;

    But follow me, and Edward shall be ours.   25

FIRST WATCHMAN   Who goes there?

SECOND WATCHMAN   Stay, or thou diest.

        Warwick and the rest cry all, 'Warwick, Warwick!' and

        set upon the guard, who flee and exit crying 'Arm,

        arm!', Warwick and the rest following them.

        The drum playing and trumpet sounding. Enter

        Warwick, Somerset, Clarence, Oxford, and the

        French Soldiers, bringing King Edward out in his

        ⌈*night-*⌉*gown, sitting in a chair. Gloucester and*

        Hastings flee over the stage

27.2 *flee and exit*] This edition; *flye* F   27.3 *them.* | *The . . .*] F; OXFORD *begins a new scene* (4.4)
27.5 *Clarence, Oxford*] This edition; *not in* F   27.6 *French Soldiers*] This edition; *rest* F   27.6
King Edward] RIVERSIDE; *the King* F   27.7 ⌈*night-*⌉] This edition; *not in* F   27.7 *Gloucester*]
ROWE; *Richard* F   27.8 *flee*] This edition; *flyes* F

16 **worship** respect, esteem. With 'quietness' Wilson parallels the Latin tag *otium cum dignitate* (peace with reputation). The Third Watchman's independent views anticipate Bates's remarks to Henry on the eve of Agincourt (*Henry V* 4.1).

18 **estate** state, condition
    he i.e. Edward

19 **doubted he** feared Warwick

20 **halberds** battle-axes with sharp-pointed tops mounted on long spears. Stage soldiers are depicted carrying them in the Peacham drawing of a performance of *Titus Andronicus* (see Oxford edn, ed. Eugene M. Waith (1984), p. 21).

27.1–3 **Warwick . . . them** See Appendix A.

27.6 **gown** May be a night- or dressing-gown, as editors regularly assume. Modern performances sometimes give this a ribald interpretation. In the 1963–4 Hall–Barton production, a mattress was flung out, with Edward and his 'whore' thrust in naked afterwards. Alternatively, given what the Watchmen say about Edward refusing to take his 'natural rest', it may be a day-gown, a long-sleeved

SOMERSET

What are they that fly there?

WARWICK

Richard and Hastings, let them go, here is the Duke.

EDWARD

The 'Duke'? Why, Warwick, when we parted   30
Thou called'st me king.

WARWICK   Ay, but the case is altered.
When you disgraced me in my embassade
Then I degraded you from being king,
And come now to create you Duke of York.
Alas, how should you govern any kingdom   35
That know not how to use ambassadors,
Nor how to be contented with one wife,
Nor how to use your brothers brotherly,
Nor how to study for the people's welfare,
Nor how to shroud yourself from enemies?   40

EDWARD

Yea, brother of Clarence, art thou here too?
Nay then I see that Edward needs must down.
Yet Warwick, in despite of all mischance,
Of thee thyself and all thy complices,

loose-flowing garment worn with a belt or girdle (of a kind Henry is reported to be wearing when released from the Tower; see Appendix A, 4.6.5). In this case it represents Edward in civilian as opposed to military dress and signals his unpreparedness for attack (see l. 40 and next note).

27.6–7 *sitting in a chair* Suggests Edward's vulnerability and unreadiness. In the 1983 BBC production Edward was brought on stage bound to the chair. The property also ironically recalls the throne as symbol of disputed royal authority which appears several times throughout the play (see Dessen, *Recovering*, p. 116).

27.7 *Gloucester . . . stage* Probably entering at one stage door, running across the stage, and exiting through the other door. *Pace* Hattaway, it is doubtful they would have left the stage through the yard and standing spectators.

28 **fly** flee

29 **Richard . . . Duke** A hexameter with six main beats.

31 **case is altered** Proverbial (Tilley C111).

32 **embassade** diplomatic mission. See Appendix A.

33 **degraded** deposed to a lower rank

34 **create** i.e. re-create

35 **should you** can you possibly (Abbott ¶325)

37 **contented . . . wife** Another reference to Edward's sexual promiscuity.
   wife woman (in a general sense)

39 **study for** be attentive to. Edward was in fact an effective and popular ruler, as Warwick acknowledged earlier at 3.3.117–18. See Appendix A.

40 **shroud** conceal from attack. See Appendix A, 4.4.

41 **Clarence . . . too?** In many productions Edward's recognition that Clarence has actively betrayed him provides the catalyst for the change in tone and attitude in this and his next speech.

42 **needs must down** must inevitably fall (in fortune)

43 **despite** defiance

44 **complices** confederates

Edward will always bear himself as king;   45
Though Fortune's malice overthrow my state,
My mind exceeds the compass of her wheel.

WARWICK

Then for his mind be Edward England's king,
      Takes off his crown
But Henry now shall wear the English crown
And be true king indeed, thou but the shadow.   50
My lord of Somerset, at my request
See that forthwith Duke Edward be conveyed
Unto my brother, Archbishop of York:
When I have fought with Pembroke and his fellows,
I'll follow you and tell what answer   55
Lewis and the Lady Bona send to him.
Now for a while farewell, good Duke of York.
      *Somerset and several Soldiers begin to lead him out
      forcibly*

EDWARD

What Fates impose, that men must needs abide;
It boots not to resist both wind and tide.   *Exeunt*

OXFORD
                                                                  60
What now remains my lords for us to do,
But march to London with our soldiers?

WARWICK

Ay, that's the first thing that we have to do,
To free King Henry from imprisonment
And see him seated in the regal throne.   *Exeunt*

57.1 *Somerset and several Soldiers*] This edition *following* CAPELL; *They* F   *begin to*] OXFORD;   *not
in* F   64 *Exeunt*] ROWE *following* O (~ *Omnes*); *exit* F

---

47 **compass . . . wheel** Fortune is conventionally depicted as a woman turning a wheel
on which the status or prosperity of
princes rises or falls.
  compass circumference (thus figuratively the boundaries of Fortune's
power)
48 **his** i.e. Edward's, continuing to refer to
him in the third person
50 **shadow** semblance; reflection; actor playing a role
52 **Duke Edward** A familiar form of address,
here used contemptuously.

52–3 **conveyed . . . York** George Neville,
fourth son of Richard Neville, Earl of
Salisbury. See Appendix A.
54 **fought . . . fellows** Historically at Edgecote
field, where Pembroke was captured and
afterwards executed (Hall Kki[r], Holinshed
Rrrv[r]).
58 Proverbial: 'It is impossible to avoid
(undo) Fate' (Dent F83).
  abide submit to; suffer
59 Proverbial: 'To sail against wind and tide'
(Dent W435.1).
  boots helps, benefits

4.4   *Enter Earl Rivers and Queen Elizabeth*

RIVERS

    Madam, what makes you in this sudden change?

ELIZABETH

    Why, brother Rivers, are you yet to learn

    What late misfortune is befall'n King Edward?

RIVERS

    What, loss of some pitched battle against Warwick?

ELIZABETH

    No, but the loss of his own royal person.   5

RIVERS

    Then is my sovereign slain?

ELIZABETH

    Ay, almost slain, for he is taken prisoner,

    Either betrayed by falsehood of his guard

    Or by his foe surprised at unawares,

    And as I further have to understand,   10

    Is new committed to the Bishop of York,

    Fell Warwick's brother, and by that our foe.

RIVERS

    These news I must confess are full of grief.

    Yet gracious madam bear it as you may,

    Warwick may lose that now hath won the day.   15

4.4] CAPELL; *not in* F   0.1 *Earl Rivers*] OXFORD; *Riuers* F   *Queen Elizabeth*] HANMER (*subs.*);
Lady Gray (*and subs. prefixes throughout this scene*) F   1 you in] F; in you COLLIER 1853   4
What,] F2, CAPELL; What_∧ F1; What? F3, O; What! ROWE   7 Ay,] ROWE; I_∧ F

4.4 Shakespeare's inspiration for this scene
was an aside by Abraham Fleming following Holinshed's report that, after Edward
had fled to the Netherlands in 1470,
Queen Elizabeth took sanctuary after she
had given birth to Prince Edward (see
below, l. 31). See Appendix A. F's version
differs from O's and departs from the
chronicles' depiction of Elizabeth. See
Introduction, pp. 89–90.

1 **makes you in** is the cause in you of (*OED,*
make, v.[1] 9b)
  change in mood and/or in circumstances.
In the 1987 ESC and 1988 RSC productions, a pregnant Elizabeth packed
her bags and trunk, preparing to leave
the court. She had also changed her

clothes to a simple gown and outdoor
cloak.
2 **are** have
3 **late** recent
5 **loss** ruin by separation
  royal person i.e. his 'body politic', the perpetual legal authority of the Crown
8 **falsehood** deceitfulness
9 **surprised at unawares** captured without
warning
10 **have** am given
11 **committed** sent in custody
12 **Fell** ruthless, terrible
  by that therefore. But see also note to
4.5.6–8.
13 **grief** suffering, pain
14 **may** can

ELIZABETH

Till then fair hope must hinder life's decay:
And I the rather wean me from despair
For love of Edward's offspring in my womb.
This is it that makes me bridle passion
And bear with mildness my misfortune's cross;   20
Ay, ay, for this I draw in many a tear
And stop the rising of blood-sucking sighs,
Lest with my sighs or tears I blast or drown
King Edward's fruit, true heir to th'English crown.

RIVERS

But madam, where is Warwick then become?   25

ELIZABETH

I am informèd that he comes towards London
To set the crown once more on Henry's head.
Guess thou the rest: King Edward's friends must down.
But to prevent the tyrant's violence—
For trust not him that hath once broken faith—   30
I'll hence forthwith unto the sanctuary
To save at least the heir of Edward's right;
There shall I rest secure from force and fraud.
Come therefore let us fly, while we may fly;
If Warwick take us we are sure to die.   *Exeunt*   35

---

17 wean] ROWE; waine F   26 informèd] THEOBALD; inform'd F

---

17 **wean me** distance myself (*OED v.* 2c, citing this line)
19 **passion** suffering; impulse to despair, overpowering emotion. See Appendix A, 4.4.17–19.
20 **cross** affliction
21 **draw in** hold back
21–2 **tear … blood-sucking sighs** Sighs were popularly believed to draw drops of blood from the heart, and Shakespeare often pairs them with tears to suggest the same physical effect; e.g. 'Thy due from me | Is tears and heavy sorrows of the blood' (*2 Henry IV* 4.3.168–9).
23 **blast** blight, destroy. Compare Glouces-

ter's image at 5.7.21.
25 **become** gone
28 **down** fall (from power)
29 **prevent** avoid
   tyrant's i.e. Warwick's. Tyrant = anyone exercising oppressive, cruel authority.
30 Proverbial: 'He that once deceives is ever suspected' (Tilley D180).
31 **sanctuary** Church refuge (in this case Westminster, according to Hall and Holinshed) where one was immune from arrest.
32 **right** title to the throne
33 **force** physical violence
34 **fly … fly** flee … flee

4.5   *Enter Gloucester, Lord Hastings, and Sir William*
          Stanley with Soldiers

GLOUCESTER

Now my lord Hastings and Sir William Stanley,
Leave off to wonder why I drew you hither
Into this chiefest thicket of the park.
Thus stands the case: you know our king, my brother,
Is prisoner to the bishop here, at whose hands   5
He hath good usage and great liberty,
And often but attended with weak guard,
Comes hunting this way to disport himself.
I have advertised him by secret means
That if about this hour he make this way   10
Under the colour of his usual game,
He shall here find his friends with horse and men
To set him free from his captivity.

            Enter King Edward and a Huntsman with him

HUNTSMAN

This way my lord, for this way lies the game.

EDWARD

Nay this way man, see where the huntsmen stand.   15

4.5] CAPELL; *not in* F   0.1 *Gloucester*] ROWE; *Richard* F (*and subs. prefixes throughout this scene*)
0.2 *with Soldiers*] OXFORD; *and Others* CAPELL; *not in* F   4 stands] F2; stand F1   8 Comes]
F2; Come F1

4.5.0.1 *Lord Hastings* The more prominent
non-historical presence of Hastings in *3
Henry VI* may reflect Shakespeare's revision of *True Tragedy* after writing *Richard
III*, in which Hastings appears as
Stanley's friend and ally (see *Richard III*
3.1.167, 3.2.74).
0.2 *Stanley* In the chronicle accounts, the
chief agent of Edward's escape in September 1469 from the Archbishop of York,
but Shakespeare gives this priority to
Gloucester. See Appendix A. Stanley's
presence in this scene may also have topical resonances, since the Stanleys of Lan-
cashire were patrons of Strange's Men
and Derby's Men, both of which acted
Shakespeare plays such as *1 Henry VI* and
Titus Andronicus (see Introduction, pp.
10–11).
2 **Leave off** cease
3 **park** private hunting grounds

4, 18 **case** situation
6–8 **good . . . himself** Both chronicles imply
that York's leniency was owing to his earlier appointment as Archbishop by
Edward: '[In 1464] King Edward, more
for the Marquis Montague's love, than for
any favour he bare to the Earl of Warwick, promoted George Neville their
brother to the Archbishopric of York'
(Hall Ii.iii^r, Holinshed Rrriii^r). This
personal connection may resonate in
Edward's pun on himself as the 'bishop's
deer (dear)' at l. 17 below, if the phrase is
not simply ironic. See also 4.6.86.
8 **disport** recreate (*OED v.* 2, citing this line)
9 **advertised** notified. Accented on the
second syllable.
11 **colour . . . game** pretext . . . sport of hunting (*OED, game, sb.* 9, citing this line). See
Appendix A.
14 **game** chase; quarry

Now brother of Gloucester, Lord Hastings, and the rest,
Stand you thus close to steal the bishop's deer?

GLOUCESTER

Brother, the time and case requireth haste,
Your horse stands ready at the park corner.

EDWARD

But whither shall we then?   20

HASTINGS

To Lynn, my lord.

STANLEY   And shipped from thence to Flanders?

GLOUCESTER

Well guessed, believe me, for that was my meaning.

EDWARD

Stanley, I will requite thy forwardness.

GLOUCESTER

But wherefore stay we? 'Tis no time to talk.

EDWARD

Huntsman, what sayst thou? Wilt thou go along?   25

HUNTSMAN

Better do so than tarry and be hanged.

---

16 Lord Hastings] F; Hastings CAIRNCROSS *following* COLLIER MS   21 STANLEY] This edition;
not in F; *King Edward* WILSON (*conj.* Cartwright)   And] F (*as here, on a new line*); [*To Gloucester.*]
And RIVERSIDE   Flanders?] WILSON (*conj.* Cartwright, Riverside); Flanders. F   22 Well . . .
me,] F ; ⌐aside⌐ Well . . . me— OXFORD

---

16 **Now . . . rest** Metrically a rough line, but
close to 4.7.1 and probably not an error:
'-ther' of Glou-' and 'and the rest' are
probably meant to be elided into two syllables, while strong beats in 'Lord Hastings'
intensify the midline caesura (Wright, pp.
165, 170–3). 'The rest' implies that Soldiers (two or more) accompany Gloucester
and Hastings from the beginning of the
scene. But *pace* Hattaway, Gloucester's
references to 'horse and men' (l. 12), and
'Your horse stands ready at the park corner' (l. 19) do not imply that additional
men and horses are needed on stage.

17 **close** hidden

21 **Lynn** King's Lynn, Norfolk. See Appendix
A.

21–3 **STANLEY . . . forwardness** In F 'And
. . . Flanders' is also assigned to Hastings
on a new line after the latter's 'To Lynn
my lord'. This leaves Edward's singling

out of Stanley for thanks at l. 23 under-
motivated. Edward could be praising
Stanley simply for being part of the rescue
party, as in O; but there both Stanley and
Hastings are mute throughout the scene
and neither is addressed by Edward until
after Gloucester's explanations: 'Come
then, Hastings, and Stanley, I will |
Requite your loves'. Unlike 'loves', 'forwardness' (= eagerness, zeal) suggests
an immediate proactive gesture, such as
cleverly guessing a likely course of action
(signalled dramatically by his completion
of Hastings's line). It also seems anomalous that Stanley would not already
know of Richard's plans.

21 **Flanders** Historically this occurred
nearly a year later in September 1470.

23 **requite** reward

24 **stay** delay

25 **go along** accompany us

GLOUCESTER

Come then away, let's have no more ado.

EDWARD

Bishop farewell, shield thee from Warwick's frown,
And pray that I may repossess the crown.   *Exeunt*

4.6   *Flourish. Enter King Henry the Sixth, Clarence,*
           Warwick, Somerset, young Henry, Earl of Richmond,
           Oxford, Montague, and Lieutenant of the Tower

HENRY

Master Lieutenant, now that God and friends
Have shaken Edward from the regal seat
And turned my captive state to liberty,
My fear to hope, my sorrows unto joys,
At our enlargement what are thy due fees?   5

LIEUTENANT

Subjects may challenge nothing of their sovereigns,
But if an humble prayer may prevail,
I then crave pardon of your majesty.

4.6] CAPELL; *not in* F   0.1–3 *Flourish . . . Lieutenant*] F (*subs.*); Enter *Warwike* and *Clarence*, with the Crowne, and then king *Henry*, and *Oxford*, and *Summerset*, and the yong Earle of *Richmond* 0   0.3 *of the Tower*] ROWE; *not in* F

---

28 **thee** yourself

4.6.0.2 *Somerset* When Edward was driven out of the country in 1470, Edmund Beaufort, 4th Duke, returned from exile in France with the Lancastrians.

0.3 *Montague* He has switched sides to support his brother Warwick. The chronicles suggest that Montague's motives for only temporarily supporting Edward were a mix of personal loyalty and opportunism. See Appendix A, 4.6.0.3 and 4.1.133–41.

0.3 *Lieutenant* Second commanding officer of the Tower of London, below the Constable. His main dramatic importance was likely as a representative figure who signals the locale by carrying jailer's keys in his hands, and who conventionally attends a prisoner being released (see Alan C. Dessen, *Elizabethan Stage Conventions and Modern Interpreters* (Cambridge, 1984), p. 96).

1–18 The action of Henry talking with the Lieutenant as he is being released from the Tower appeared in the last scene of an earlier play, *2 Seven Deadly Sins*, a plot of which was made for Strange's Men around 1590: 'Henry speaks to . . . Lieutenant, Pursuivant, and Warders . . . to them Warwick' (W. W. Greg, *Dramatic Documents from the Elizabethan Playhouses*, 2 vols. (Oxford, 1931), vol. ii).

3 **captive . . . liberty** Some stage productions convey a sense of release by having Henry emerge squinting into strong light, as if from the darkness of the Tower, or by dressing him differently.

5 **enlargement** release from confinement. See Appendix A.

due fees It was customary for comfortably treated prisoners to pay for food and service provided by keepers during their imprisonment.

6 **challenge** demand

7 **prayer** (two syllables) entreaty

HENRY

  For what, Lieutenant? For well using me?

  Nay, be thou sure, I'll well requite thy kindness,   10

  For that it made my imprisonment a pleasure,

  Ay, such a pleasure as encagèd birds

  Conceive, when after many moody thoughts,

  At last by notes of household harmony

  They quite forget their loss of liberty.   15

  But Warwick, after God, thou set'st me free,

  And chiefly therefore I thank God and thee;

  He was the author, thou the instrument.

  Therefore, that I may conquer fortune's spite

  By living low where fortune cannot hurt me,   20

  And that the people of this blessèd land

  May not be punished with my thwarting stars,

  Warwick, although my head still wear the crown,

  I here resign my government to thee,

  For thou art fortunate in all thy deeds.   25

WARWICK

  Your grace hath still been famed for virtuous,

  And now may seem as wise as virtuous

  By spying and avoiding fortune's malice,

  For few men rightly temper with the stars.

---

11 imprisonment] F; prisonment HUDSON 1880–1 (*conj.* Lettsom)

---

10 **requite** reward

11 **For that** because (Abbott ¶287)
  my imprisonment The first two syllables are probably elided (Wright, pp. 154–8).

13 **Conceive** become accustomed to
  moody dejected, disconsolate

14 **notes . . . harmony** 'filling the house with song' (Cairncross quoting Brooke). The metaphor is Shakespeare's, but both chronicles mention that when Henry was released from the Tower and installed in the Bishop of London's palace, he 'there kept his household like a king' (Hall Lliiiᵣ, Holinshed Sssiᵣ).

16 **after** i.e. in terms of causality

18 **author . . . instrument** originator . . . agent

19 **spite** hostility

20 **low** humbly (and safe from downturns on fortune's wheel)

22 **thwarting stars** adverse fortunes (*OED, thwarting, ppl. a.* 2, citing this line), draw-

ing on the astrological belief that the particular position of planets or stars at one's birth determines one's destiny. See ll. 29, 33 below.

24 **government** authority to govern (*OED* 3, citing this line)

26 **still . . . famed for** always . . . reputed as (*OED, fame, v.* 2, citing this line)

27 **wise as virtuous** Hall regards Henry as unwise because he subordinated worldly power to godly ambition, whereas Shakespeare makes Henry's resignation of temporal authority the reasoned outcome of deepening self-knowledge about his moral and political responsibilities to himself and others. See Appendix A and Introduction, p. 37 ff.

28 **spying** discerning

29 **temper . . . stars** accept being 'moulded and managed by their allotted fortunes' (Cairncross quoting Vaughan)
  temper regulate, adapt; harmonize, attune

Yet in this one thing let me blame your grace, 30
For choosing me when Clarence is in place.

CLARENCE

No Warwick, thou art worthy of the sway,
To whom the heavens in thy nativity
Adjudged an olive branch and laurel crown,
As likely to be blessed in peace and war, 35
And therefore I yield thee my free consent.

WARWICK

And I choose Clarence only for Protector.

HENRY

Warwick and Clarence, give me both your hands:
Now join your hands, and with your hands your hearts,
That no dissension hinder government. 40
I make you both Protectors of this land,
While I myself will lead a private life
And in devotion spend my latter days
To sin's rebuke and my creator's praise.

WARWICK

What answers Clarence to his sovereign's will? 45

CLARENCE

That he consents if Warwick yield consent,
For on thy fortune I repose myself.

WARWICK

Why then, though loath, yet must I be content.
We'll yoke together like a double shadow
To Henry's body, and supply his place— 50
I mean in bearing weight of government—

31 **in place** present
32 **sway** rule
33 **in thy nativity** at your birth (astrologically, in terms of planetary disposition)
34 **Adjudged** allotted (*OED v.* 6, although the association of judicial sentence, present in Shakespeare's other uses of the word, is absent here)
37, 41 **Protector** regent during the king's retirement from power. 'The crowns of the realms of England and France, was [*sic*] . . . entailed to George Duke of Clarence . . . to be next heir to his father, Richard Duke of York. . . . Beside this, the Earl of Warwick . . . was made ruler, Governor of the realm, with whom as fellow

and companion was associated George Duke of Clarence his son-in-law. So that by these means the whole estate, both of the realm and the public wealth of the same, were newly altered' (Hall Lliii^v^–iv^r^, Holinshed Sssi^v^, and notes to ll. 56, 57).
40 **government** the business of governing
43 **latter** last
47 **repose myself** place my confidence; put my trust
51 **I . . . government** In the 1983 BBC production, Warwick's remark about 'Henry's body' and supplying his 'place' triggered an awareness that he could be referring inadvertently to Henry's marital

While he enjoys the honour and his ease.
And Clarence, now then it is more than needful
Forthwith that Edward be pronounced a traitor
And all his lands and goods be confiscate.   55

CLARENCE

What else? And that succession be determinèd.

WARWICK

Ay, therein Clarence shall not want his part.

HENRY

But with the first of all your chief affairs,
Let me entreat—for I command no more—
That Margaret your queen and my son Edward   60
Be sent for, to return from France with speed,
For till I see them here, by doubtful fear
My joy of liberty is half eclipsed.

CLARENCE

It shall be done, my sovereign, with all speed.

---

55 be confiscate] MALONE; confiscate F1; confiscated F2   56 determinèd] F (determined); determin'd POPE

'place'; hence this clarification. (His choice of words, 'bearing weight', often a sexual pun in Shakespeare, momentarily betrays what comes into his mind.) In the 1963–4 Hall–Barton and 1987 ESC productions, when Clarence glanced questioningly at 'supply his place', Warwick's explanation was meant to distinguish Henry's position in government from that as king, to avoid any hint of usurpation. See ll. 56–7 below.

53–4 **Clarence . . . traitor** If Warwick felt under scrutiny immediately before, this may imply a further test of Clarence's loyalty.

54–5 **Forthwith . . . confiscate** Again the chronicles but not Shakespeare report that Parliament enacted these matters. See Appendix A.

55 **be confiscate** '-ed' was often omitted after 't' in participles (Abbott ¶342). Oxford citing McKerrow points out that 'confiscate' occurs twice in Shakespeare where the accent theoretically falls on the second syllable (*Errors* 1.1.20, *Cymbeline* 5.6.325, 'And let it be confiscate all so soon'). The latter instance, however, draws attention

to the fact that 'be' or 'are confiscate' was otherwise Shakespeare's preferred form. He used it three more times, but never 'confiscated'. Malone's emendation therefore seems justified.

56 **What else?** Of course—Clarence is not wondering. F's punctuation could represent an exclamation rather than a question.

57 **want** lack
    his part Could refer to Clarence's position as next in line to the throne before the birth of Edward and Elizabeth's son, assuming Henry could put aside his own claim—which his next words about Margaret and Prince Edward remind us (and perhaps himself) is unlikely.

59 **for . . . more** '[Henry] has, I think, a very ironic view of what has happened to him (he almost laughs at himself being used as a puppet) and is ambivalent in his gratitude to Warwick for giving him his "freedom"' (Ralph Fiennes on playing Henry VI, *Players* 3, p. 112).

60–1 **Margaret . . . for** Historically Margaret took this initiative herself. See Appendix A.

62 **doubtful** apprehensive

HENRY

My lord of Somerset, what youth is that   65
Of whom you seem to have so tender care?

SOMERSET

My liege it is young Henry, Earl of Richmond.

HENRY

Come hither England's hope.

  Lays his hand on Richmond's head

                                        If secret powers
Suggest but truth to my divining thoughts,
This pretty lad will prove our country's bliss.   70
His looks are full of peaceful majesty,
His head by nature framed to wear a crown,
His hand to wield a sceptre, and himself
Likely in time to bless a regal throne.
Make much of him, my lords, for this is he   75
Must help you more than you are hurt by me.

  Enter a Post

WARWICK

What news my friend?

POST

That Edward is escapèd from your brother
And fled, as he hears since, to Burgundy.

WARWICK

Unsavoury news. But how made he escape?   80

---

68 *Richmond's*] OXFORD; *his* F

---

68 **England's hope** It was through his cousin
Edmund Beaufort, 4th Duke of Somerset,
that Henry Tudor laid his (circuitous)
claim to the throne. Henry's father
Edmund had married Margaret, daughter
of John Beaufort, 1st Duke, and the
family traced its line back to John of
Gaunt, Edward III's fourth son. See
Appendix A.

68 *Lays . . . head* A traditional gesture of
blessing and prophecy. See also note to l.
69.
secret inwardly discerned by the
heart, soul; beyond ordinary human
intelligence

69 **but** only
divining prophetic; supernaturally
inspired; sanctifying. 'The Earl of Pem-

broke took this child . . . to London to
King Henry the Sixth, whom when the
king had a good while beheld, he said
to such princes as were with him: "Lo,
surely this is he to whom both we and our
adversaries . . . shall hereafter give room
and place". So this holy man showed . . .
that this Earl Henry . . . should in time to
come . . . have and enjoy . . . this realm of
England.' Abraham Fleming in Holinshed
continues: 'So that it might seem proba-
ble . . . that for the time [King Henry] was
endued with a prophetical spirit' (Holinshed Sssi, Hall Lliv^{r-v}).

76.1 *Post* express courier

79 **he** Warwick's brother, Archbishop of
York.

80 **Unsavoury** disagreeable

POST

He was conveyed by Richard, Duke of Gloucester
And the Lord Hastings, who attended him
In secret ambush on the forest side
And from the bishop's huntsmen rescued him,
For hunting was his daily exercise.　　　　　　　　85

WARWICK

My brother was too careless of his charge.
But let us hence, my sovereign, to provide
A salve for any sore that may betide.
　　　　　　Exeunt all but Somerset, Richmond, and Oxford

SOMERSET

My lord I like not of this flight of Edward's,
For doubtless Burgundy will yield him help　　　　　90
And we shall have more wars before't be long.
As Henry's late-presaging prophecy
Did glad my heart with hope of this young Richmond,
So doth my heart misgive me in these conflicts
What may befall him, to his harm and ours.　　　　　95
Therefore, Lord Oxford, to prevent the worst,
Forthwith we'll send him hence to Brittany
Till storms be past of civil enmity.

OXFORD

Ay, for if Edward repossess the crown,
'Tis like that Richmond with the rest shall down.　　　100

SOMERSET

It shall be so, he shall to Brittany.
Come therefore, let's about it speedily.　　　　　*Exeunt*

88.1 *all but*] CAMBRIDGE; *Manet* F (*beginning a new line*)

81 **conveyed** carried secretly; stolen away
82 **attended** watched for
83 **ambush** waiting concealment (*OED sb.* 3, not 'to surprise an enemy')
　　side edge
88 Proverbial: 'There is a salve for every sore' (De... S84,).
　　betide develop
89 **like not of** am not pleased by; do not approve of (Abbott ¶177)

92 **late-presaging** latest foreshadowing
93 **glad** gladden
96 **prevent** avoid
97 **Forthwith . . . Brittany** Historically the Earl of Pembroke fled with Richmond after the Battle of Tewkesbury (Hall Nniii^v, Holinshed Tttiii^r).
100 **like** likely
　　down (be) put down (although *OED* does not record the reflexive use of the verb)

4.7   *Flourish. Enter Edward, Gloucester, Hastings, and*
        Soldiers

EDWARD

Now brother Richard, Lord Hastings, and the rest,
Yet thus far Fortune maketh us amends
And says that once more I shall interchange
My wanèd state for Henry's regal crown.
Well have we passed and now repassed the seas,   5
And brought desirèd help from Burgundy.
What then remains, we being thus arrived
From Ravenspur haven before the gates of York,
But that we enter as into our dukedom?
        Hastings knocks at the gates

GLOUCESTER

The gates made fast? Brother I like not this,   10
For many men that stumble at the threshold
Are well foretold that danger lurks within.

EDWARD

Tush man, abodements must not now affright us.

4.7] CAPELL; *not in* F   0.1 *Gloucester*] ROWE; *Richard* F (*and subs. prefixes throughout this scene*)   0.1–2 *and Soldiers*] F; *with a troope of Hollanders* O   1 *Lord*] F; *omitted by* POPE *and some editors*   9.1 *Hastings . . . gates*] OXFORD (*subs.*); *not in* F

4.7.0.2 **Soldiers** Unidentified in F, but called 'Hollanders' in O, which may reflect Elizabethan playhouse costuming identifying particular nationalities. O's description also agrees with 4.8.1–3 and the chronicle accounts. See Appendix A, 4.7.5–6.

2 **Yet thus far** now as before

3 **interchange** exchange (*OED* v. 2, citing this line). Abraham Fleming remarks in Holinshed on Henry's restoration as king: 'Thus was the principality posted over sometimes to Henry, sometimes to Edward, according to the sway of the party prevailing . . . whereby the heat of hatred gathered the greater force to the consumption of the peers and the destruction of the people. In the mean time neither part could securely possess the regality, when they obtained it' (Sssi^r).

4 **wanèd state** diminished status, condition; lower degree (*OED, waned*, citing this line)

5–6 **passed . . . Burgundy** i.e. from the Netherlands, then in the possession of

the Duke of Burgundy. The Duchess, Margaret, was Edward's sister.

5 **seas** the English Channel

8 **Ravenspur haven** Harbour, at the mouth of the River Humber on the Yorkshire coast, where, as Holinshed observes, Henry Bolingbroke landed to challenge Richard II (Sssii^r). See Appendix A. Ravenspur = today's Spurn Head.

9 **as** as though

9.1 **gates** Stage doors of the tiring house were probably used. This staging recreates details from the chronicles. See Appendix A, 4.7.8–9.1.

10 **made fast** securely shut

11–12 **stumble . . . within** Proverbial (Dent T259). The doomed Hastings reflects on ignoring such warnings in *Richard III*: 'Three times today my foot-cloth horse did stumble, | . . . when he looked upon the Tower, | As loath to bear me to the slaughterhouse' (3.4.84–6).

12 **foretold** forewarned

13 **Tush** Expression of impatient dismissal.
   abodements forebodings, evil omens (*OED*, citing this line)

By fair or foul means we must enter in,
For hither will our friends repair to us.   15

HASTINGS
My liege, I'll knock once more to summon them.
> *He knocks. Enter on the walls the Mayor of York and*
> *his brethren the Aldermen*

MAYOR
My lords we were forewarnèd of your coming
And shut the gates for safety of ourselves,
For now we owe allegiance unto Henry.

EDWARD
But Master Mayor, if Henry be your king,   20
Yet Edward at the least is Duke of York.

MAYOR
True, my good lord, I know you for no less.

EDWARD
Why, and I challenge nothing but my dukedom,
As being well content with that alone.

GLOUCESTER (*aside*)
But when the fox hath once got in his nose,   25
He'll soon find means to make the body follow.

HASTINGS
Why Master Mayor, why stand you in a doubt?
Open the gates, we are King Henry's friends.

MAYOR
Ay, say you so? The gates shall then be opened.
> *He descends with the Aldermen*

16.1 *He knocks*] OXFORD; *not in* F   16.2 *the Aldermen*] DYCE (*subs.*); *not in* F   25 (*aside*)] ROWE
1709 (*after* 'follow', *l.* 26)   29.1 *with the Aldermen*] DYCE (*subs.*); *not in* F

---

15 **repair** return again
16.1 **on the walls** i.e. above the stage, prob-
    ably the tiring-house gallery, which fic-
    tionally represents the walls of the city.
    For Shakespeare's use of vertical staging
    and its associations with hierarchical
    authority and political reversals, see
    David Bevington, *Action Is Eloquence*
    (Cambridge, Mass., 1984), pp. 101–6.
    Here, however, the assault is on civic
    authorities by an opportunistic aristoc-
    racy. Also see Appendix A.
16.2 **brethren** brothers, i.e. fellow Aldermen
23 **challenge** lay claim to. Holinshed reports
    that after he landed, Edward, 'perceiving

how the people were bent, noised abroad
that he came to make none other challenge but to his inheritance' (Sssii^r^). See
also Appendix A.
25 *aside* Richard may speak to himself (and
    us) standing somewhat physically apart
    at this moment, or may address Edward
    and/or Hastings.
    fox . . . follow Proverbial: 'When the fox
    has got in his nose, he will soon make the
    body follow' (Dent F655).
27 **doubt** state of uncertainty, indecision
29 **Ay . . . opened** 'It was almost incredible to
    see what effect this new imagination [i.e.
    Edward's appeal] (all though it were but

GLOUCESTER

A wise stout captain, and soon persuaded.   30

HASTINGS

The good old man would fain that all were well,
So 'twere not long of him; but being entered,
I doubt not I, but we shall soon persuade
Both him and all his brothers unto reason.

*Enter the Mayor with keys to the city and two
Aldermen*

EDWARD

So, Master Mayor, these gates must not be shut   35
But in the night or in the time of war.
What, fear not man, but yield me up the keys,

Takes his keys

For Edward will defend the town and thee
And all those friends that deign to follow me.

*March. Enter Sir John Montgomery with Drum and
Soldiers*

GLOUCESTER

Brother, this is Sir John Montgomery   40
Our trusty friend, unless I be deceived.

34.1 *with . . . city*] This edition *following l.* 37.1 *and* 0 (opens the dore, and brings the keies in his hand); *not in* F   39.1 *Sir John*] CAIRNCROSS *following l.* 40 *and* 0 (sir Iohn Mountgommery); *not in* F

---

feigned) . . . took immediately upon the first opening . . . when it was blown abroad that King Edward's desire was farther from nothing than from the coveting or desire of the kingdom' (Hall Mmi^r, Holinshed Sssii^r, but without Hall's parenthetical opinion). Also *Mirror*: 'Unlooked for [Edward] came to England strait, | And got to York, and took the town by sleight' (Warwick, 55–6, p. 207).

30 **stout** valiant (spoken ironically)
captain, Probably an implied stressed beat on the sixth syllable (the commonest place for this kind of metrical variant (Wright, p. 179)). The actor may use the pause to heighten the humorous effect of his mocking compliment.

31–2 **The . . . him** 'The mayor is willing we should enter so he may not be blamed' (Johnson).

31 **fain** be glad (with a possible secondary sense of 'feign' = pretend, put on a show)

32 **long of him** too long in involving him; because of him (*OED a.*²)

33 **not I** The repeated 'I' is emphatic.

34.1 *keys* This detail, inferred from l. 37, is a common stage property identifying a traditional symbol of office, but is also attributable to Holinshed's account of an earlier meeting between Edward and the Mayor of Exeter. See Appendix A.

37 **fear . . . keys** Suggests the Mayor hesitates, and is coerced into surrendering the keys. The fact that he is not referred to and does not say anything for the remainder of the scene may imply passive resistance. See Introduction, p. 78.

39 **deign** think themselves worthy, think it fit (*OED* 1, citing this line)

EDWARD

    Welcome, Sir John. But why come you in arms?

MONTGOMERY

    To help King Edward in his time of storm,

    As every loyal subject ought to do.

EDWARD

    Thanks, good Montgomery. But we now forget   45

    Our title to the crown and only claim

    Our dukedom till God please to send the rest.

MONTGOMERY

    Then fare you well, for I will hence again.

    I came to serve a king and not a duke.

    Drummer strike up, and let us march away.   50

        The Drum begins to march

EDWARD

    Nay stay, Sir John, awhile, and we'll debate

    By what safe means the crown may be recovered.

MONTGOMERY

    What talk you of debating? In few words,

    If you'll not here proclaim yourself our king,

    I'll leave you to your fortune and be gone   55

    To keep them back that come to succour you.

    Why shall we fight if you pretend no title?

GLOUCESTER

    Why brother, wherefore stand you on nice points?

EDWARD

    When we grow stronger, then we'll make our claim,

    Till then 'tis wisdom to conceal our meaning.   60

HASTINGS

    Away with scrupulous wit, now arms must rule.

GLOUCESTER

    And fearless minds climb soonest unto crowns.

    Brother, we will proclaim you out of hand,

    The bruit thereof will bring you many friends.

---

43 **storm** strife

50.1 *Drum* drummer

51 **debate** discuss (and perhaps with the underlying sense, intended in a friendly mollifying way, of 'debate, contest')

57 **pretend** lay claim to

58 **stand . . . points** raise difficulties about trivial, fussy concerns

60 **meaning** intentions

61 **scrupulous wit** over-subtle, fastidious argument

62 **fearless . . . crowns** Reminiscent of the Machiavellian Fergus in *Gorboduc* or Tamburlaine, as well as being self-referential.

63 **out of hand** right away

64 **bruit** report. See Appendix A.

EDWARD

Then be it as you will, for 'tis my right   65
And Henry but usurps the diadem.

MONTGOMERY

Ay, now my sovereign speaketh like himself,
And now will I be Edward's champion.

HASTINGS

Sound trumpet, Edward shall be here proclaimed.
Come fellow soldier, make thou proclamation.   70
    Flourish. Sound

SOLDIER Edward the Fourth, by the grace of God, King of
England and France, and Lord of Ireland, etc.

MONTGOMERY

And whosoe'er gainsays King Edward's right,
By this I challenge him to single fight.
    Throws down his gauntlet

ALL

Long live Edward the Fourth!   75

EDWARD

Thanks brave Montgomery, and thanks unto you all.
If fortune serve me, I'll requite this kindness.

---

70 proclamation.] F; proclamation. | *giving him a Paper* CAPELL   70.1 *Flourish. Sound*] F;
Trumpet sounds CAPELL   71 SOLDIER] F (*Soul.*); [MONTGOMERY] OXFORD; *in* O *the speech continues
from the previous one assigned to Montgomery*   Edward] F; *reads.* Edward CAPELL

---

66 **diadem** crown
68 **champion** Ceremonial defender of the
sovereign's claim to the throne who
publicly challenges anyone denying his
legitimacy (see 74.1, *Throws . . . gauntlet*).
See Appendix A, 4.7.39.1.
70.1 *Flourish. Sound* This could be a duplicate direction, with either notation written in the margin of the manuscript copy
for F and added by the compositor. Or it
could indicate separate musical flourishes
before and after the proclamation
(Hattaway).
71 **SOLDIER** Assigned with ll. 73–4 to Montgomery in O and by Oxford. Only F
contains l. 70, however, which is not an
obvious error and makes its sequence
intelligible, as is O without the line. Only
if one ignores F's speech prefix does the
designation 'fellow soldier', as Hattaway
observes, become ambiguous, referring
either to Montgomery ('comrade in

arms') or to a common soldier. Oxford
assumes (a) the prefix for Montgomery
was omitted, and (b) that the compositor
inserted the prefix 'Soul.' after reading l.
70 and assuming 'fellow soldier' referred
to a person other than Montgomery. This
is over-complicated and seems less likely
than that O and F are each right as different versions.
71–2 **the Fourth . . . Ireland** F prints this formal list of an English king's titles in italics, possibly indicating that the Soldier is
reading from a paper, although as
Wilson observes, it 'is not required for
this well-known formula'. This is the
only prose in the play.
72 **etc.** May indicate that a full text of the
conventional proclamation is read out, as
explicitly called for in *2 Henry VI* at 1.4.
23.2. Or the speech may be interrupted.
73 **gainsays** denies
77 **serve** favour

Now for this night let's harbour here in York,
And when the morning sun shall raise his car
Above the border of this horizon,   80
We'll forward towards Warwick and his mates,
For well I wot that Henry is no soldier.
Ah froward Clarence, how evil it beseems thee
To flatter Henry and forsake thy brother!
Yet as we may, we'll meet both thee and Warwick.   85
Come on brave soldiers, doubt not of the day,
And once gotten, doubt not of large pay.   *Exeunt*

4.8   *Flourish. Enter King Henry, Warwick, Montague,*
       Clarence, Oxford, and Somerset

WARWICK
   What counsel, lords? Edward from Belgia
   With hasty Germans and blunt Hollanders
   Hath passed in safety through the Narrow Seas,
   And with his troops doth march amain to London,
   And many giddy people flock to him.   5

4.8] CAPELL; *not in* F   0.1 *King Henry*] ROWE; *the King* F   0.2 *Somerset*] F; *Exeter* CAPELL *and editors*

78 **harbour** make our quarters
79 **car** chariot (of Apollo the sun god)
80 **horizon** Accented on the first and third syllables (Cercignani, p. 40).
81 **mates** fellows (spoken contemptuously)
82 **wot** know (i.e. Henry is not the real obstacle)
83 **froward** perverse, unnatural
    evil . . . thee ill it becomes you
86 **doubt . . . day** fear . . . winning the coming battle. See Appendix A.
4.8.0.2 **Somerset** Editors since Capell have substituted Exeter for F's 'Somerset', assuming error because the latter does not speak in this scene and is not mentioned with the other lords, and because F does not provide for Exeter's appearance below at l. 37. Somerset's quiet presence is explained by the fact that, historically, this may represent the third Duke who joined Margaret's forces in 1464 at the Battle of Hexham (not dramatized by Shakespeare) and was killed there; he is different from the fourth Duke who appears in the next scene (see note to 5.1.73). Moreover, Exeter's entry at 32.2,

and not before, signals a notional shift of location and time, even though Henry remains. This situation bothered Wilson and other editors, who believed ll. 33 ff. constituted a separate scene because Henry discusses his forces 'which are not yet . . . in existence,' and that when Edward enters at l. 51.1, Warwick is already 'at' Coventry (l. 58). Yet such compression of dramatic time is common in the histories and untroubling in performance. As Sisson observes (*NR*, ii. 85), creating a new scene is also a 'radical emendation' which requires Henry to exit and re-enter immediately—a situation Wilson admitted was 'most unusual'.

1 **Belgia** the Netherlands
2 **hasty** excitable, rash; quick-tempered
   blunt coarse, uncivilized; rough; stupid
3 **Narrow Seas** the English Channel
4 **amain** at full speed
5 **giddy** inconstant, changeable; unreliable. 'Giddy people' or 'commons' are political clichés of the period; e.g. 'So giddy are the common people's minds, | So glad of

HENRY

   Let's levy men and beat him back again.

CLARENCE

   A little fire is quickly trodden out,

   Which being suffered, rivers cannot quench.

WARWICK

   In Warwickshire I have true-hearted friends,

   Not mutinous in peace yet bold in war.   10

   Those will I muster up, and thou son Clarence

   Shalt stir up in Suffolk, Norfolk, and in Kent

   The knights and gentlemen to come with thee.

   Thou brother Montague in Buckingham,

   Northampton, and in Leicestershire shalt find   15

   Men well inclined to hear what thou command'st.

   And thou brave Oxford, wondrous well beloved,

   In Oxfordshire shalt muster up thy friends.

   My sovereign with the loving citizens,

   Like to his island girt in with the ocean,   20

   Or modest Dian circled with her nymphs,

   Shall rest in London till we come to him.

   Fair lords take leave and stand not to reply.

   Farewell my sovereign.

HENRY

   Farewell my Hector and my Troy's true hope.   25

---

12 up] F; *omitted by* POPE   17–18 beloved, | . . . Oxfordshire$_\wedge$] F (*subs.*); beloved$_\wedge$ | . . . Oxfordshire, HART

change, more wavering than the sea'
(*Gorboduc* 5.1.72–3). See Appendix A.

6 **Let's . . . again** An uncharacteristic
sentiment from Henry, perhaps even
ironical.

7 Inversion of the proverb: 'Of a little spark
a great fire' (Dent S714).

7–8 Proverbial: 'Do not blow the fire thou
wouldst quench' (Dent F251).

8 **suffered** tolerated, unchecked

11 **son** i.e. son-in-law

12 **Shalt stir up** Pope and some recent
editors omit 'up' to make this line conventionally iambic. But it is actually a
'headless' hexameter (i.e. begins on a
stressed syllable), which continues the
rhythm set up in the previous line by 'and
thou son Clarence' and its final weak

beat. Pope and others were obliged to
insert a comma (not in F) after 'Clarence'
to end-stop l. 11, thereby disrupting the
flow of F's enjambment. For a similar
instance see 1.2.42–3.

12–17 **Suffolk . . . Oxford** Only Suffolk and
Norfolk correspond with Holinshed's list
of places where forces were mustered
against Edward. The Earl of Oxford is also
mentioned (Sssii^v).

20 **girt in** encircled (*OED, gird, v.*[1] 6b, citing
this line. 'Girt' is a separate but related
form of 'gird'.)

21 **Dian** Diana, wood-goddess of women
and chastity; so 'modest' means chaste,
decorous.

25 **Hector** Greatest of the Trojan heroes.
   Troy's And London's, since according
to national legend London was founded

CLARENCE

In sign of truth, I kiss your highness' hand.

HENRY

Well-minded Clarence, be thou fortunate.

MONTAGUE

Comfort, my lord, and so I take my leave.

OXFORD

And thus I seal my truth and bid adieu.

    Kissing Henry's hand

HENRY

Sweet Oxford and my loving Montague   30

And all at once, once more a happy farewell.

WARWICK

Farewell sweet lords, let's meet at Coventry.

                        Exeunt all but Henry

    Enter Exeter

HENRY

Here at the palace will I rest a while.

Cousin of Exeter, what thinks your lordship?

29.1 *Kissing . . . hand*] JOHNSON (*at beginning of l.* 29), OXFORD (*subs., also after ll.* 26, 28); *not in*
F   32.1 *all . . . Henry*] This edition; *not in* F; *all . . . Henry and Exeter* CAMBRIDGE *following* CAPELL
32.2 *Enter Exeter*] This edition; *not in* F   33 HENRY] *as here* F; WILSON, OXFORD *begin a new scene*
('4.9 *Flourish. Enter the King . . .*')

---

by Brutus, grandson of the Trojan hero
Aeneas. London was sometimes referred
to as 'New Troy' or 'Troynovant', just as
'Britain' was believed to derive from
'Brut-ain'. See *The Faerie Queene*, III. ix.
44–6.

25 **true hope** Recalls the Messenger's phrase
at 2.1.51 (see note) echoing Virgil's
Aeneid.

26, 29 **truth** loyalty

27 **Well-minded** virtuously disposed (Hattaway). Wilson notes that Hall applies
this phrase originally to Montague—aptly
ironic because like Clarence he too
switches loyalties.

28–29.1 MONTAGUE . . . *hand* Oxford and Hattaway insert a direction to have Montague kiss Henry's hand as well, but
nothing in his line suggests it, unlike
Oxford's 'seal' (see note). Montague may

depart with an alternative gesture such as
a bow.

28 **Comfort** take courage

29–29.1 **seal . . . hand** The connection between 'seal' and 'kissing' is typically
Shakespearian (seven other instances
including 5.7.29 below).

31 **at once** as one

32–32.1 **Farewell . . . Exeunt** Warwick and
the other lords leave through separate
stage doors.

33 **palace** The action is continuous, but
dramatically the scene shifts to the Bishop
of London's palace, where Henry was
captured on 11 April 1471. At that time
the palace stood in the north-west corner
of St Paul's precinct. See Appendix A,
4.8.32.1–33 and 52–57.2.

34 **Cousin** Familiar term of address by a king
to a nobleman, not necessarily implying
kinship (*OED sb.* 5a, citing this line).

Methinks the power that Edward hath in field 35
Should not be able to encounter mine.

EXETER

The doubt is that he will seduce the rest.

HENRY

That's not my fear, my meed hath got me fame.
I have not stopped mine ears to their demands,
Nor posted off their suits with slow delays, 40
My pity hath been balm to heal their wounds,
My mildness hath allayed their swelling griefs,
My mercy dried their water-flowing tears.
I have not been desirous of their wealth
Nor much oppressed them with great subsidies, 45
Nor forward of revenge, though they much erred.
Then why should they love Edward more than me?
No Exeter, these graces challenge grace,
And when the lion fawns upon the lamb,
The lamb will never cease to follow him. 50
        Shout within, 'A Lancaster, A Lancaster!'

EXETER

Hark, hark, my lord, what shouts are these?
        *Enter Edward and his Soldiers with Gloucester
        and others*

50.1 *A Lancaster, A Lancaster*] F; *A York! A York!* DYCE (*conj.* Johnson)   51.1–2 *with . . . others*] HANMER (*subs.*); *not in* F

35 **power** army
36 **encounter** defeat
37 **doubt** fear
   seduce persuade to desert one's allegiance
38 **meed** merit, virtue (*OED sb.* 3, citing this line)
   fame good reputation; honour, renown
39 **their** i.e. the people's
40 **posted** fobbed
42 **swelling** full to overflowing
43 **water-flowing** abundant
44 **desirous** greedy for
45 **subsidies** Parliamentary grants of revenue to the crown, raised through property taxes.
46 **forward of** eager for; inclined to
   erred went astray morally, from their allegiance
47 **love Edward** A rare allusion to Edward

IV's historical popularity. See Introduction, pp. 70–1.
48 **challenge grace** deserve to be privileged, favoured
49–50 **lion . . . him** Isaiah 11: 6: 'The wolf also shall dwell with the lamb, and the leopard shall lie down with the kid; and the calf and the lion . . . together'. An image of transcendent world peace in the well-known chapter describing the line of Jesse, traditionally read as foretelling the coming of the Messiah.
50.1 **within** i.e. in the tiring house, backstage
   A Lancaster While many editors follow Johnson's conjectural emendation, this cry seems more likely to be a Yorkist ruse, 'a misleading cry to gain admittance', or the guards' alarm after having recognized Edward's party (Hattaway). Either alternative is confirmed by 5.1.19–20.

EDWARD

Seize on the shamefaced Henry, bear him hence,
And once again proclaim us king of England.
You are the fount that makes small brooks to flow;
Now stops thy spring, my sea shall suck them dry   55
And swell so much the higher by their ebb.
Hence with him to the Tower, let him not speak.

> *Exeunt several Soldiers with King Henry*
> *and Exeter*

And lords towards Coventry bend we our course,
Where peremptory Warwick now remains.
The sun shines hot, and if we use delay,   60
Cold biting winter mars our hoped-for hay.

GLOUCESTER

Away betimes before his forces join,
And take the great-grown traitor unawares.
Brave warriors, march amain towards Coventry.

> *Exeunt*

5.1   *Enter Warwick, the Mayor of Coventry, two*
Messengers, and others upon the walls

WARWICK

Where is the post that came from valiant Oxford?
How far hence is thy lord, mine honest fellow?

57.1 *Exeunt several Soldiers*] MALONE (*subs.*); *Exit* F   57.2 *and Exeter*] PELICAN; *not in* F   62
GLOUCESTER] ROWE (*subs.*); *Rich.* F
  5.1] ROWE; *not in* F

52–57.2 **Seize . . . Exeter** Nothing else is said
of Exeter and only Holinshed mentions
unnamed others captured with Henry:
Edward, 'being seized his [Henry's] person, and diverse other his adversaries
. . .' (Holinshed Sssiv^r). See Appendix A. In
the 1983 BBC production the soldiers haul
him from the table at which he and Henry
have been sitting, out of camera angle,
and when they exit his body is seen on the
floor, presumably dead.
52 **shamefaced** A misderived variant of
'shamefast' (*OED*, *shamefaced*) meaning
'bashful, shy'. Hall applies the word to
Henry.
54 **fount** spring; i.e. Henry as the source of
power
55 **them** Henry's 'brooks'; i.e. his supporters

59 **peremptory** stubbornly wilful; dictatorial;
destructive
   remains dwells
60–1 Variation of the proverb: 'Make hay
while the sun shines' (Dent H235).
60 **use** make
61 **mars** destroys
62 **betimes** quickly
64 **amain** at full speed
5.1 Holinshed reports two confrontations
between Edward and Warwick at Coventry, first on 29 March 1471: 'And thus
[Edward] being more strongly accompanied than before . . . came before the
walls of the city of Coventry' (Holinshed
Sssiii^r). Unable to draw Warwick into battle, Edward retired to the town of Warwick
where he persuaded Clarence to return to

FIRST MESSENGER
By this at Dunsmore, marching hitherward.
WARWICK
How far off is our brother Montague?
Where is the post that came from Montague?   5
SECOND MESSENGER
By this at Daintry with a puissant troop.
        ⌜*Exeunt Messengers*⌝
 Enter Somerville
WARWICK
Say Somerville, what says my loving son?
And by thy guess how nigh is Clarence now?
SOMERVILLE
At Southam I did leave him with his forces
And do expect him here some two hours hence.   10
 A drum sounds
WARWICK
Then Clarence is at hand, I hear his drum.

6.1 *Exeunt Messengers*] This edition; *not in* F 6.2 *Somerville*] F (*Someruile*); *Sir* John Somervile CAPELL; [Sir Thomas] Somerville HATTAWAY (*conj.* Thomson) 10.1 *A drum sounds*] HATTAWAY *following* CAPELL; *A march afar off* OXFORD; *not in* F

him. He then went back to Coventry on 4 April 1471 where Warwick had been waiting for Clarence's army but was again unable to draw Warwick 'into the fields' (Sssiii'). Hall's report of their movements is different. See Appendix A.
0.2 *upon the walls* See note to 4.7.16.1.

1–15 Shakespeare's invention, although Holinshed mentions that Edward passed through 'Daintry' (Daventry, Northamptonshire, l. 6) on his way from Coventry to London (Sssiii'). The unusual cluster of local references reflects Shakespeare's personal knowledge of Warwickshire geography. See Introduction, p. 75.
1, 5 **post** messenger
3 **this** this time
3, 6 **Dunsmore . . . Daintry** Both lie southeast of Coventry, respectively closer to and further from it.
4 **our** Warwick as Protector has adopted the royal plural. His more imperious tone heightens the contrast with his lack of firm support and certain knowledge.
6 **puissant** powerful

6.1 ***Exeunt Messengers*** The Messengers play no other role 'on the walls', and the actors would most likely be needed later to double the numerous supporting roles as drummers, flag-bearers, and soldiers in this very full scene. See also Appendix C, 5.1.57.1.
6.2 ***Somerville*** Traditionally called Sir John after Capell, though this person lived too early to represent the figure here. Thomson (p. 275) identifies him as Sir Thomas (d. 1500) of Aston Somerville, Gloucestershire, though this too is conjectural and unlikely. See Introduction, pp. 75–6.
7 **son** i.e. son-in-law
9 **Southam** Ten miles south-east of Coventry. Thomson observes that a journey to Southam from Aston Somerville, south of Evesham, would pass close to Stratford-upon-Avon and avoid the town of Warwick (p. 275).
11–13 **Clarence . . . Warwick** Shakespeare imagines the personal effect of Clarence's professed support: 'hearing now that his brother King Edward was landed . . . [Clarence] gathered his people, outwardly

SOMERVILLE

It is not his, my lord, here Southam lies.
The drum your honour hears marcheth from Warwick.

WARWICK

Who should that be? Belike unlooked-for friends.

SOMERVILLE

They are at hand, and you shall quickly know.   15

> *March. Flourish. Enter King Edward, Gloucester,*
> *Trumpeter and Soldiers*

EDWARD

Go, trumpet, to the walls, and sound a parley.

> *The Trumpeter sounds*

GLOUCESTER

See how the surly Warwick mans the wall.

WARWICK

O unbid spite, is sportful Edward come?
Where slept our scouts, or how are they seduced
That we could hear no news of his repair?   20

EDWARD

Now Warwick, wilt thou ope the city gates,
Speak gentle words and humbly bend thy knee?
Call Edward king, and at his hands beg mercy,
And he shall pardon thee these outrages.

WARWICK

Nay, rather wilt thou draw thy forces hence,   25

15.1 *King*] ROWE; *not in* F *Gloucester*] ROWE; *Richard* F (*and subs. prefixes throughout this scene*)
15.2 *Trumpeter*] This edition; *not in* F *and Soldiers*] ROWE; *not in* F; *and his power* O   16.1 *The Trumpeter sounds*] This edition *following* OXFORD; *not in* F   22–4 knee? | . . . mercy, | . . . outrages.] STEEVENS (*subs.*); knee, | . . . mercy? | . . . outrages. POPE; knee. | . . . mercy, | . . . outrages. PELICAN; Knee, | . . . Mercy, | . . . Outrages? F

pretending to pass with them to the aid of the Earl of Warwick . . . although inwardly he meant the contrary. . . . King Edward being then at Warwick, and understanding that his brother of Clarence approached . . . issued forth of that town' (Sssiii^r).

11, 13 **drum . . . drum** Distinctive rhythms were commonly used to differentiate armies. Edward's 'signature tune' might be recognizable to spectators from earlier scenes before he appears here, although Warwick, and perhaps Somerville, seem unable to identify it. As Shirley observes, such distinctions would be clearer in

encounters with foreign armies. But in civil war 'there could be confusion if newly opposed [or aligned] forces moved to their accustomed notes' (pp. 68–9).

14 **Belike** perhaps
16 **trumpet . . . parley** trumpeter . . . call for a meeting to discuss a dispute
18 **unbid spite** unwelcome annoyance
   sportful lustful, lascivious
19 **seduced** beguiled; led astray
20 **repair** approach
24 **outrages** insolent, violent actions. See Appendix A.
25 **draw** withdraw

Confess who set thee up and plucked thee down,
Call Warwick patron and be penitent,
And thou shalt still remain the Duke of York.

GLOUCESTER

I thought at least he would have said 'the King',
Or did he make the jest against his will?   30

WARWICK

Is not a dukedom, sir, a goodly gift?

GLOUCESTER

Ay by my faith, for a poor earl to give;
I'll do thee service for so good a gift.

WARWICK

'Twas I that gave the kingdom to thy brother.

EDWARD

Why then 'tis mine, if but by Warwick's gift.   35

WARWICK

Thou art no Atlas for so great a weight,
And, weakling, Warwick takes his gift again,
And Henry is my king, Warwick his subject.

EDWARD

But Warwick's king is Edward's prisoner;
And gallant Warwick do but answer this: 40
What is the body when the head is off?

GLOUCESTER

Alas, that Warwick had no more forecast,
But whiles he thought to steal the single ten,
The king was slyly fingered from the deck.
You left poor Henry at the Bishop's palace,   45
And ten to one you'll meet him in the Tower.

---

26 **set . . . down** i.e. from the throne. See
3.3.157 and 2.3.37.
27 **patron** lord, master
30 **jest** jeer, taunt
31 **sir** Spoken in mock respect, like 'gallant'
at l. 40.
32 **poor earl** Warwick was in fact very
rich, but an earl is below a duke in
rank.
33 **service . . . gift** i.e. as a grateful feudal tenant to his lord (spoken ironically)
36 **Atlas** The classical Titan conventionally
portrayed holding up the sky or bearing

the earth on his shoulders (e.g. Ovid,
Metamorphoses, ii. 377–8).
41 Proverbial: 'If the head is off, no beast can
live' (Dent H257.1).
42 **that . . . forecast** *that* possibility Warwick
had no more contemplated. Or, if 'fore-
cast' is a noun, 'would that Warwick had
no more designs, schemes'.
43 **the single ten** A single-suit ten, the highest non-royal card in a pack or deck.
44 **fingered** stolen, pinched (*OED v.* 4, citing
this line)
45 **Bishop's palace** See 4.8.33.

EDWARD

'Tis even so. Yet you are Warwick still.

GLOUCESTER

Come Warwick, take the time, kneel down, kneel down.
Nay, when? Strike now or else the iron cools.

WARWICK

I had rather chop this hand off at a blow,   50
And with the other fling it at thy face,
Than bear so low a sail to strike to thee.

EDWARD

Sail how thou canst, have wind and tide thy friend,
This hand, fast wound about thy coal-black hair,
Shall, whiles thy head is warm and new cut off,   55
Write in the dust this sentence with thy blood:
'Wind-changing Warwick now can change no more.'
    Enter Oxford with Drum and Soldier bearing colours

WARWICK

O cheerful colours, see where Oxford comes!

OXFORD

Oxford, Oxford, for Lancaster!
    He and his forces enter the city gates

GLOUCESTER

The gates are open, let us enter too.   60

57.1 *Soldier bearing colours*] OXFORD (*subs.* (*soldiers*)); *Colours* F; *souldiers & al crie*, O   59.1 *He . . . gates*] MALONE (*subs.*) *following* CAPELL; *not in* F

---

47 **Yet . . . still** i.e. yet even knowing this won't change your bad nature in the slightest

48 **take the time** seize the opportunity (to show you are sorry). Proverbial: 'Take time when time comes' (Dent T312). Gloucester may speak these lines sarcastically, and/or pause for a moment in mock patience after 'kneel down'.

49 **when**? why are you waiting!
Strike . . . cools Proverbial (Tilley I94); 'strike' also means 'yield' and anticipates l. 52.

52 **bear . . . strike** Refers to lowering a ship's topsail as a sign of surrender or respect; 'than stoop so low as to submit to your demands'.

53 **wind . . . friend** Proverbial: 'Sail with the wind and tide' (Dent W429). And see 3.3.48.

54–6 **This . . . blood** The vigorous fury of this image conveys the loathing Edward feels towards Warwick's betrayal.

54 **coal-black hair** A striking personal detail. In the quarto of *The First Part of the Contention* (Q1594) Cade is also described as having 'coal-black . . . curled locks' (Malone Society Reprint (1985), l. 2022). Possibly the same actor played both roles.

57 **Wind-changing** continually reversing; controlled by the wind
change switch allegiances

57.1 *Enter . . . colours* Presumably they entered through one stage door, processed across or around the stage, and exited through the door on the other side of the stage. See also Appendix C, 5.1.57.1.
colours an ensign, flag

59.1 *city gates* i.e. the open stage door(s) of the tiring house. See Appendix A and 4.7.9.1.

EDWARD

So other foes may set upon our backs.
Stand we in good array, for they no doubt
Will issue out again and bid us battle.
If not, the city being but of small defence,
We'll quickly rouse the traitors in the same.   65

Oxford appears upon the walls

WARWICK

O welcome Oxford, for we want thy help.

Enter Montague with Drum and Soldier bearing colours

MONTAGUE

Montague, Montague, for Lancaster!

He and his forces enter the city gates

GLOUCESTER

Thou and thy brother both shall buy this treason
Even with the dearest blood your bodies bear.

EDWARD

The harder matched, the greater victory,   70
My mind presageth happy gain and conquest.

Enter Somerset with Drum and Soldier bearing colours

SOMERSET

Somerset, Somerset, for Lancaster!

He and his forces enter the city gates

GLOUCESTER

Two of thy name, both dukes of Somerset,
Have sold their lives unto the house of York,
And thou shalt be the third, if this sword hold.   75

65.1 *Oxford . . . walls*] This edition; *Oxford appears aloft* HATTAWAY; *not in* F   66.1 *Soldier bearing*] OXFORD (*subs.* (*soldiers*)); *not in* F   67.1 *He . . . gates*] MALONE (*subs.*) *following* CAPELL; *not in* F   71.1 *Soldier bearing*] OXFORD (*subs.* (*soldiers*)); *not in* F   72.1 *He . . . gates*] MALONE (*subs.*) *following* CAPELL; *not in* F

---

61 **So** then (Abbott ¶66)
62 **array** battle order
64 **small** weak
65 **rouse** force (an animal) to come out from cover
66 **for . . . help** Possibly spoken aside to Oxford, as an admission of weakness.
   want need; lack
68 **buy** pay for

70 **harder . . . victory** See note to 4.3.15 and Appendix A, 5.3.0.1.
71 **presageth** forms an expectation of
73 **Two . . . Somerset** i.e. the different historical figures represented by 1.1.16, and 4.1–4.8. The Somerset who enters here is the 4th Duke, who fought for the Lancastrians at Barnet and Tewkesbury (see Persons of the Play note).
74 **sold** paid a heavy price with

Enter Clarence with Drum and Soldier bearing colours

WARWICK

And lo, where George of Clarence sweeps along,
Of force enough to bid his brother battle,
With whom an upright zeal to right prevails
More than the nature of a brother's love.
Come Clarence, come; thou wilt if Warwick call.   80

CLARENCE

Father of Warwick, know you what this means?
          He shows a red rose
Look here, I throw my infamy at thee.
I will not ruinate my father's house,
Who gave his blood to lime the stones together,

75.1 *Soldier bearing*] OXFORD (*subs.* (*soldiers*)); *not in* F   78 an] F2; *in* F1   81.1 *He . . . rose*] This
edition; *not in* F; Sound a Parlie, and *Richard* and *Clarence* whispers togither, and then Clarence
takes his red Rose out of his hat, and throwes it at *Warwike* 0 (*after l.* 79)

---

76 **sweeps** moves strongly and evenly; in a
    stately, majestic manner; proudly (as a
    peacock—*1 Henry VI* 3.7.6)
77 **Of . . . enough** with an army powerful
    enough (on its own)
78–9 **With . . . love** Warwick may be boasting
    about his son-in-law whom he regards as
    deferential despite his rank, or trying to
    quell his own doubts.
78 **to right** for justice, moral virtue
79 **nature** natural kinship; familial bonds
80–2 **Come . . . thee** Shakespeare heightens
    the irony of Warwick's misplaced confi-
    dence as well as the surprise of Clarence's
    reversal by omitting to mention that
    George and Edward had been secretly
    reconciled through the mediation of the
    Duchess of Clarence and an envoy of
    the Duchess of Burgundy (Hall Kkvi^r,
    Mmii^v–iii^r, Holinshed Rrrvi^r, Sssiii^r) . See
    Appendix A and Introduction, pp.
    119–21.
81 **Father . . . means?** There is no break in
    the action, the audience is given no fore-
    warning of Clarence's change of mind,
    and so his reversal becomes a *coup de
    théâtre*.
    Father i.e. father-in-law (with underly-
    ing senses of a venerable man, and
    somebody to whom paternal deference is
    due)
81.1 **red rose** Emblem of the house of Lan-
    caster. F is open about how Clarence

throws his rose (if indeed the stage property *is* a rose; without any direction,
F actually leaves 'this' undefined); his
'throw' could be a contemptuous flick,
after he shows it for a moment ('Look
here'). O's direction, by contrast, is explicit and detailed—hence its attraction
for editors and readers. But theatrically it
is also more limiting. Edward's accusa-
tion, 'Et tu Brute, wilt thou stab *Caesar*
too?', leads an audience to expect a
betrayal, so that, in theory, Clarence's
volte-face will have greater dramatic
impact. But its energy may be diverted by
the break in the action. O's direction shifts
the moment's agency to Richard—his
whisperings are stock business deriving
from the Vice tradition of the Tudor
morality drama. O also calls for Clarence
to take the rose 'out of his hat' *before*
Warwick says 'Come Clarence come, thou
wilt if Warwick call'. Warwick therefore
reacts to Clarence's silent gesture, while
the latter's 'I throw my infamy at thee'
becomes an explanation and a defiant
response. In F Warwick's comments
about Clarence's loyalties build up expectations in ll. 78–80, and make him sound
over-confident.
83 **ruinate** lay to ruins (*OED v.* 1b, citing this
    line)
84 **lime** 'cement . . . Lime makes mortar'
    (Johnson).

And set up Lancaster. Why, trowest thou Warwick   85
That Clarence is so harsh, so blunt unnatural,
To bend the fatal instruments of war
Against his brother and his lawful king?
Perhaps thou wilt object my holy oath:
To keep that oath were more impiety   90
Than Jephthah when he sacrificed his daughter.
I am so sorry for my trespass made
That, to deserve well at my brother's hands,
I here proclaim myself thy mortal foe,
With resolution, wheresoe'er I meet thee—   95
As I will meet thee if thou stir abroad—
To plague thee for thy foul misleading me.
And so proud-hearted Warwick, I defy thee,
And to my brother turn my blushing cheeks.
Pardon me Edward, I will make amends,   100
And Richard do not frown upon my faults,

---

91 Jephthah] F (*Iephah*); *Jepthah's* ROWE 1714   94 foe,] CAMBRIDGE; foe: F; foe_∧ HATTAWAY
99 brother] F; brothers O

---

85 **set up** raise to the throne (*OED* 154j)
trowest thou do you believe
86 **blunt unnatural** stupidly 'insensible of paternal fondness' (Johnson). 'Blunt' also means 'unfeeling' (*OED* 4b, citing this line).
87 **bend** direct
89 **object** point out as a contrary reason
holy oath i.e. of allegiance to Henry. See Appendix A.
90–1 Proverbial: 'An unlawful oath is better broken than kept' (Dent O7). In Judges 11: 11–40 Jephthah vows to sacrifice the first person to come out of his house if Israel defeats the Ammonites. After they do and he returns home, his only daughter emerges and he is forced to fulfil his vow, thereby setting his bargain for victory above the life of his daughter. Editors often adopt Rowe's modernization 'Jephthah's'. But as the Oxford editors observe, citing McKerrow, the possessive is unnecessary because Elizabethan grammar allowed such elliptical constructions without it. See Abbott ¶¶382, 415, and Görlach 5.2.2. An explicit possessive also erases a second sense of comparing different actions, as well as oaths: '*keeping* that

oath' and 'Jephthah *sacrificing* his daughter'. See also next note.
91 **sacrificed** See the sermon against swearing and perjury in the Tudor government's *Book of Homilies*: 'And Jephthah . . . promised, of a foolish devotion unto God, to offer for a sacrifice unto him that person of his own house should first meet with him after his return home . . .' (1547; repr. 1587, sig. F8^{r–v}). Also *Hamlet* 2.2.403–12.
92 **trespass made** sin committed
95 **resolution** unyielding determination
96 **stir abroad** emerge from within (the city walls)
97 **plague** afflict, punish (with connotations of biblical plagues and divine wrath)
foul wicked
99 **brother** F's singular noun preserves a more formal, slightly depersonalized tone appropriate to Clarence's solemn vow (absent in O, along with the Jephthah allusion), and to the biblical echoes touching on kinship laws, affinity, and moral duty in this and Edward's following speech. F also seems closer to Holinshed's account, whereas O follows Hall. See Appendix A.
101 **faults** moral failings; offences

For I will henceforth be no more unconstant.

EDWARD

Now welcome more, and ten times more beloved,

Than if thou never hadst deserved our hate.

GLOUCESTER

Welcome good Clarence, this is brother-like.   105

WARWICK

O passing traitor, perjured and unjust.

EDWARD

What, Warwick, wilt thou leave the town and fight?

Or shall we beat the stones about thine ears?

WARWICK

Alas, I am not cooped here for defence.

I will away towards Barnet presently   110

And bid thee battle, Edward, if thou dar'st.

EDWARD

Yes Warwick, Edward dares and leads the way.

Lords to the field. St George and victory!

> *Exeunt King Edward and his company. March.*
> *Warwick and his company exeunt above, re-enter*
> *below, and follow King Edward*

113.1–3 *Exeunt . . . and*] PELICAN (*subs.*); *Exeunt.* | *March. Warwicke and his companie* F   113.3
follow King Edward] PELICAN; *followes* F

102 **unconstant** inconstant. See Appendix
  A.
103–4 **Now . . . hate** Echoes the parables of
  the lost sheep and the prodigal son in Luke
  15: 'It was meet that we should make
  merry, and be glad: for this thy brother
  was dead, but he is alive again; and he
  was lost, but he is found' (15: 31, Geneva
  Bible). One of Shakespeare's favourite
  texts; e.g. *1 Henry IV* 4.2.34, *Merchant*
  2.6.14–19, *All's Well* 1.1.129.
105 **brother-like** May be spoken ironically,
  perhaps with a sly glance to the audience.
106 **passing** unsurpassed. See Appendix A.
108 Proverbial for being showered with
  attacking objects (Dent EE3, *OED*, *ear*, *sb.*
  1c).
109–10 **I . . . presently** Historically, Warwick
  remained within the city and met Edward
  only later after his forces had increased. Shakespeare makes the action
  continuous.
109 **Alas** Ironically expressing the opposite of
  concern, regret (i.e. defiance).

109 **cooped** confined, as in a poultry coop
  (*OED v.*[1] 2).
110 **Barnet** In Hertfordshire, about ten miles
  north of London, location of the third of
  the play's four main represented battles.
  Warwick's geographically odd proposal to
  meet at Barnet—far away from Coventry—is the result of Shakespeare's
  compression of historical events. After
  Edward's party had left Coventry for London to recapture Henry, Warwick 'saw
  that all cavillations of necessity were
  now brought to this end, that they must
  be committed to the hazard and chance
  of one battle'. (Hall Mmiv[r], Holinshed
  Sssiv[r–v]).
  presently immediately
113.1–2 *company* troop of soldiers, host. If
  Montague and Somerset have not joined
  Oxford in the tiring-house gallery with
  Warwick (65.1), they may join them
  when the latter two descend to re-enter
  the main stage and together make a pro-
  cessional exit. See Appendix C, 5.1.57.1.

5.2   *Alarum and excursions. Enter King Edward bringing
           forth Warwick wounded*

EDWARD

So, lie thou there. Die thou, and die our fear,
For Warwick was a bug that feared us all.
Now Montague sit fast, I seek for thee
That Warwick's bones may keep thine company.   *Exit*

WARWICK

Ah, who is nigh? Come to me, friend or foe,   5
And tell me who is victor, York or Warwick?
Why ask I that? My mangled body shows,
My blood, my want of strength, my sick heart shows
That I must yield my body to the earth,
And by my fall, the conquest to my foe.   10
Thus yields the cedar to the axe's edge,
Whose arms gave shelter to the princely eagle,
Under whose shade the ramping lion slept,

5.2] CAPELL; *not in* F 0.1 *King*] ROWE; *not in* F 7 that? . . . shows,] F, O; that‸ . . .
shows?— CAIRNCROSS (*conj.* Vaughan)

5.2.0.1–2 *bringing forth* driving or dragging
him in. Hall and Holinshed report several
accounts of Warwick's death in battle.
One common to both could have supplied
F's idea of a single combat: 'Some write
that this battle was so driven to the utter-
most point, that King Edward was constrained to fight in his own person, and
that the Earl of Warwick, which was wont
ever to ride on horse[back] from place to
place, and from rank to rank, comforting
his men, was now advised by the marquis
his brother, to leave his horse, and to try
to the extremity by hand strokes' (Holinshed Sssvʳ, Hall Mmvʳ).

0.2 *wounded* i.e. unable to defend himself,
and perhaps unarmed

2 bug object of terror (bugbear)
  feared frightened

3 sit fast secure yourself

5–7 who is nigh? . . . that? Warwick's
questions create the impression he has
been separated from the main fighting,
which corresponds with the chronicle
accounts of his death. See Appendix A
and note to 5.2.0.1. 'Who is victor' at first
seems odd, given that he has just been left
for dead by Edward. This suggests the
questions rhetorically signal his physical

exhaustion, inability to see properly,
and/or disorientation, as he clings to life.
This was conveyed in the 1965 televised
version of Hall–Barton's *Wars of the Roses*
by having Warwick's face appear in close-
up, distorted by the camera and with one
eye blinded by blood from his forehead.
See also 33 ff.

7–8 shows . . . shows The repetition again
hints at Warwick's physical distress, in
this case shortness of breath.

11–13 cedar . . . eagle . . . lion 'Elizabethan
types of supremacy, or primates' in their
classes of evergreens, birds, and animals
(Cairncross). From Ezekiel 31: 3–6:
'Behold, [the Assyrian] was like a cedar in
Lebanon with fair branches, and with
thick shadowing boughs, and shot up
very high, and his top was among the
thick boughs . . . Therefore his height was
exalted above all the trees of the field, and
his boughs were multiplied, and his
branches were long. . . . All the fowls of
the heaven made their nests in his
boughs, and under his branches did all
the beasts of the field bring forth their
young' (Geneva Bible).

12 arms branches

13 ramping rearing fiercely

Whose top-branch overpeered Jove's spreading tree
And kept low shrubs from winter's powerful wind.   15
These eyes, that now are dimmed with death's black
    veil,
Have been as piercing as the midday sun
To search the secret treasons of the world.
The wrinkles in my brows, now filled with blood,
Were likened oft to kingly sepulchres,   20
For who lived king but I could dig his grave?
And who durst smile when Warwick bent his brow?
Lo, now my glory smeared in dust and blood,
My parks, my walks, my manors that I had
Even now forsake me, and of all my lands   25
Is nothing left me but my body's length.
Why, what is pomp, rule, reign, but earth and dust?
And live we how we can, yet die we must.
    Enter Oxford and Somerset

SOMERSET

Ah Warwick, Warwick, wert thou as we are,
We might recover all our loss again.   30
The Queen from France hath brought a puissant power.
Even now we heard the news. Ah, couldst thou fly.

WARWICK

Why then I would not fly. Ah Montague,

---

23 blood,] O, ROWE; blood. F

14 **overpeered** towered over
  Jove's . . . tree The oak, supreme amongst deciduous trees. Ovid, *Metamorphoses*, i. 121 'the acorns dropped . . . from Jove's broad tree in field'.
15 **kept** sheltered
18 **search** seek out
22 **bent his brow** scowled
23–8 **Lo . . . must** Seems to echo the chapter 'How filthy and loathsome the body is after it is dead: And of the burying of it in the grave', in Luis de Granada's *Of Prayer, and Meditation* (1582, fols. 201ᵛ–205ʳ, Cc1ᵛ–5ʳ). Shakespeare later recalled this chapter in the Gravedigger's scene (5.1) of *Hamlet*. See Harold Jenkins's Arden edition (London and New York, 1982), pp. 550–1, on 5.1.74–110.
24 **parks** private hunting grounds
  walks garden paths

25–6 **all . . . length** Proverbial: 'Six feet of earth make all men equal' (Dent F582).
27 **pomp** ostentatious display; vainglory
28 **live . . . must** Proverbial: 'All men must die' (Dent M505). See Appendix A.
31 **Queen . . . power** Margaret's forces landed on the same day as the Battle of Barnet, 14 April 1471. See Appendix A.
  puissant power mighty army
32, 48 **fly** hasten away
33–9 **Ah Montague . . . dead** The imagery and tone of this emotional speech anticipate the sentimentalized deaths of York and Suffolk in *Henry V* 4.6.7–34, discussed by R. H. Wells in '*Henry V* and the Chivalric Revival', *Shakespeare and History*, Shakespeare Yearbook, vol. 6 (Lewiston, NY, 1996), 119–49, p. 139. See Appendix A.

If thou be there, sweet brother, take my hand
And with thy lips keep in my soul awhile. 35
Thou lov'st me not, for brother if thou didst,
Thy tears would wash this cold congealèd blood
That glues my lips and will not let me speak.
Come quickly Montague, or I am dead.

SOMERSET

Ah Warwick, Montague hath breathed his last, 40
And to the latest gasp cried out for Warwick,
And said, 'Commend me to my valiant brother.'
And more he would have said, and more he spoke,
Which sounded like a cannon in a vault
That mought not be distinguished, but at last 45
I well might hear, delivered with a groan,
'O farewell Warwick.'

WARWICK

Sweet rest his soul. Fly lords, and save yourselves,
For Warwick bids you all farewell, to meet in heaven.

He dies

OXFORD

Away, away, to meet the Queen's great power. 50

Here they bear away his body. Exeunt

---

44 cannon] F; canon OXFORD (*conj.* McKerrow); clamor O, WARBURTON   49.1 *He dies*] ROWE
(*subs.*), O; *not in* F   50.1 *Exeunt*] F; *Ex. ambo.* O

---

35 **lips . . . soul** seal my lips with a kiss.
Souls of the dying were conventionally
thought to depart the body at the
mouth.

41 **latest** final

44 **sounded . . . vault** Like artillery heard
echoing in a vaulted building, as opposed
to distinct blasts or words. *Pace* Oxford,
most modern editors since Hart have
accepted F's 'cannon'. McKerrow's con-
jecture 'canon', adopted by Oxford and
Hattaway, assumes that the reverbera-
tions Somerset has in mind are musical
rather than military, an image which
seems strained in this context (e.g. Hatt-

away's gloss 'part song' for 'canon').
As Sisson remarked, 'There is no justifica-
tion for this emendation. . . . The sound of
cannon . . . is surely entirely appropriate
here, reverberating with a deep hollow
noise, confused, echoing' (*NR*, ii. 86). O's
alternative 'clamour' has merit as an
image in the context of this passage, but
can only be substituted if it is assumed
that F is unquestionably corrupt.

45–6 **mought . . . might** could . . . was able
to (Abbott ¶312)

49 **For . . . heaven** This alexandrine is appropriate to the moment of a dying man
drawing out his last breath.

5.3   *Flourish. Enter King Edward in triumph, with*
           Gloucester, Clarence, and Soldiers

EDWARD

Thus far our fortune keeps an upward course,
And we are graced with wreaths of victory.
But in the midst of this bright-shining day
I spy a black suspicious threat'ning cloud
That will encounter with our glorious sun   5
Ere he attain his easeful western bed:
I mean, my lords, those powers that the Queen
Hath raised in Gallia have arrived our coast,
And, as we hear, march on to fight with us.

CLARENCE

A little gale will soon disperse that cloud   10
And blow it to the source from whence it came.
Thy very beams will dry those vapours up,
For every cloud engenders not a storm.

GLOUCESTER

The Queen is valued thirty thousand strong,
And Somerset with Oxford fled to her;   15
If she have time to breathe, be well assured
Her faction will be full as strong as ours.

EDWARD

We are advertised by our loving friends
That they do hold their course toward Tewkesbury.

5.3] CAPELL; *not in* F   0.2 *Gloucester*] ROWE; *Richard* F (*and 'Rich.' at l.* 14)   *Soldiers*] OXFORD
(*subs.*), O; *the rest* F

5.3.0.1 *in triumph* Like a laurel-bound conquering hero in his chariot. See Appendix
A.

0.2 *Soldiers* F's '*in triumph . . . and the rest*'
may imply more than the usual minimum
of two soldiers: perhaps Hastings, who is
named in O, as well as a flag-carrier.

2 **And . . . victory** The same line occurs
in Marlowe's *Massacre at Paris*, sc. 17, l. 2.
See also note to 5.7.14.

5 **encounter** meet in battle
sun Yorkist heraldic emblem. See 2.2.163
and note. The 1994 RSC production
used the same bright morning lighting
which appeared at 2.1.21 ff. to illustrate
Edward's metaphors.

7 **powers** forces

8 **Gallia** (pronounced as two syllables)
France

10 **little gale** fresh breeze

12 **very beams** mere rays (of the sun, l. 5)
vapours mists

13 Proverbial: 'All clouds bring not rain'
(Dent C443).

14 **valued** estimated (in number) at
thirty thousand Not in Hall or Holinshed.

16 **breathe** pause to gather further strength

18 **advertised** notified (*OED* 4d, citing this
line)

19 **Tewkesbury** Town in Gloucestershire
where the rivers Avon and Severn meet,
scene of the last of the play's four main
battles. After Barnet, Edward ascertained
Margaret's movements and pursued her

We having now the best at Barnet field   20
Will thither straight, for willingness rids way,
And as we march our strength will be augmented.
In every county as we go along
Strike up the drum, cry 'Courage!' and away.

March. Exeunt

5.4   *Flourish. March. Enter Queen Margaret, young Prince*
           Edward, Somerset, Oxford, and Soldiers

MARGARET

Great lords, wise men ne'er sit and wail their loss
But cheerly seek how to redress their harms.

22–3 augmented. | . . . along‸] This edition; augmented: | . . . along, F; augmented, | . . .
along: ROWE   24.1 *March*] WILSON (*subs.*); *not in* F
   5.4] CAPELL; *not in* F   0.1 *Queen Margaret*] HANMER; *the Queene* F   *Prince*] ROWE (*subs.*), 0;
not in F

---

there (Hall Nniᵛ, Holinshed Sssviʳ), where
she was trying to cross the river to join
Jasper Tudor.

20 **best** victory
21 **straight** immediately
   willingness rids way eagerness covers dis-
   tances (removing obstacles in the way)
   quickly
22 **march** march along
22–3 **augmented. | . . . along** All editors
   since Rowe have changed F's punctuation
   in ll. 20–4 to follow O, which reverses
   ll. 22–3 ('And in euerie countie as we
   passe along, | Our strengthes shall be
   augmented'), omits F's l. 24, and ends
   with three lines of its own. O likewise separates 'as we pass along' from its own
   'Come lets go' by putting the latter in a
   new sentence on the next line. O's punctuation works well for its wording but not
   for F's, which makes good sense in itself. F
   also avoids the slight redundancy of having 'as we march' and 'as we go along' in
   the same sentence.
22 **augmented** i.e. by those inspired by the
   sight to join us
24 **Strike . . . drum** i.e. to advertise our cam-
   paign and attract recruits. See Appendix
   A.
5.4.1–38 **Great . . . loss . . . fear** Shakespeare
   virtually ignores the chronicles' accounts
   of Margaret's abject grief after the Lan-

castrian débâcle at Barnet, instead connecting the action to Tewkesbury, by
which time she had recovered her determination and managed to rally her troops
(see Appendix A, 5.4 and 5.4.2). The 1987
ESC's June Watson and 1994 RSC's Ruth
Mitchell performed the scene in this heroic manner. Other actors, however, have
played Margaret struggling in bleak
desperation. In 1963–4 Peggy Ashcroft
addressed her huddled troops muffled in a
cloak against howling winds, snow, and
darkness. In the 1983 BBC version, after
Warwick's corpse is carried past, a
demoralized Julia Foster steels herself to
cheer her lame and exhausted soldiers.
Wilson first observed that the imagery of
her speech is based closely on a passage
from Arthur Brooke's *The Tragical History
of Romeus and Juliet* (1562), 1359–80. See
Appendix D.
1–2 **wise . . . harms** Compare Carlisle,
   Richard II: 'My lord, wise men ne'er wail
   their present woes, | But presently pre-
   vent the ways to wail' (3.2.174–5).
2 **cheerly** cheerfully (and associated
   with 'a cry of encouragement among
   sailors', meaning 'heartily' (*OED adv.*
   1b))
   harms injuries. Also a proverbial sentiment: 'One must not bemoan a mischief
   but find out a remedy for it' (Dent
   M999a).

305

What though the mast be now blown overboard,
The cable broke, the holding-anchor lost,
And half our sailors swallowed in the flood?   5
Yet lives our pilot still. Is't meet that he
Should leave the helm and, like a fearful lad,
With tearful eyes add water to the sea,
And give more strength to that which hath too much,
Whiles in his moan the ship splits on the rock   10
Which industry and courage might have saved?
Ah what a shame, ah what a fault were this.
Say Warwick was our anchor, what of that?
And Montague our topmast, what of him?
Our slaughtered friends the tackles, what of these?   15
Why, is not Oxford here another anchor?
And Somerset another goodly mast?
The friends of France our shrouds and tacklings?
And though unskilful, why not Ned and I
For once allowed the skilful pilot's charge?   20
We will not from the helm to sit and weep,
But keep our course, though the rough wind say no,

---

4 holding-anchor] F; holding anchor JOHNSON

3–32 **mast . . . death** The ship-of-state metaphor derives ultimately from Horace, *Odes*, i. 14 ff. and/or Plutarch, *Precepts of Statecraft* (in *Moralia*, trans. H. N. Fowler, Loeb edn, 14 vols. (London and Cambridge, Mass., 1949), x. 158–299). See also next note.

4 **holding-anchor** Shakespeare's coinage formed from 'anchor' and the verbal noun indicating its function deriving from 'to hold' (see citations under *OED*, *anchor*, *sb.*[1]). It apparently refers to a sheet-anchor, the largest and heaviest anchor held in reserve for times of greatest danger. Plutarch's *Precepts of Statecraft* mentions it (pp. 228–9, where it is called in Greek a 'sacred' anchor). Lucian also refers to it in *The Runaways* (*Fugitivi*) and *Zeus Rants* (trans. A. M. Harmon, Loeb edn, 8 vols. (London and Cambridge, Mass., 1955), v. 68–9 and ii. 164–7, respectively).

6 **pilot** i.e. King Henry

7 **lad** ship's boy. Compare *2 Henry IV*

3.1.18–19: 'Wilt thou upon the high and giddy mast | Seal up the ship-boy's eyes . . . ?'

8 **add . . . sea** Proverbial image of wasteful redundancy: 'To cast water into the sea' (Dent W106).

10 **in his moan** during the pilot's state of grief, lamentation (Abbott, 'In' ¶161)

11 **industry** application of skill, ingenuity; diligent exertion

12 **fault** dereliction of duty

15 **tackles** rigging

18 **shrouds** paired riggings running from the top of a mast to the ship's sides. *K. John* 5.7.52–4: 'The tackle of my heart is cracked and burnt, | And all the shrouds wherewith my life should sail | Are turnèd to one thread'.
   tacklings arms, weapons; rigging

19 **unskilful** not expert
   Ned Prince Edward

20 **charge** turn of duty

21 **from** i.e. leave

From shelves and rocks that threaten us with wrack.
As good to chide the waves, as speak them fair;
And what is Edward but a ruthless sea?   25
What Clarence but a quicksand of deceit?
And Richard but a ragged fatal rock—
All these the enemies to our poor barque?
Say you can swim: alas 'tis but a while.
Tread on the sand: why there you quickly sink;   30
Bestride the rock: the tide will wash you off
Or else you famish—that's a threefold death.
This speak I, lords, to let you understand,
In case some one of you would fly from us,
That there's no hoped-for mercy with the brothers   35
More than with ruthless waves, with sands, and rocks.
Why, courage then, what cannot be avoided
'Twere childish weakness to lament or fear.

PRINCE EDWARD

Methinks a woman of this valiant spirit
Should, if a coward heard her speak these words,   40
Infuse his breast with magnanimity
And make him, naked, foil a man-at-arms.
I speak not this as doubting any here,
For did I but suspect a fearful man
He should have leave to go away betimes,   45
Lest in our need he might infect another
And make him of like spirit to himself.
If any such be here, as God forbid,
Let him depart before we need his help.

---

24 fair;] JOHNSON; fair. F   27 ragged] ROWE; raged F

---

23 **shelves . . . rocks** Compare Whitney, p. 203, *Auxilio divino*: 'in storms and tempest's force, | By ragged rocks, by shelves, and sands, this Knight did keep his course. | By gaping gulfs he passed . . . And through them all, in spite of all, his shaken ship did guide.'
shelves submerged ledges of rock; sandbanks
wrack shipwreck
24 **As good** it were as good (*OED* 21)
speak . . . fair speak to them kindly
27 **ragged** jagged
28 **barque** ship

29 **a while** for a short time
34 **In case** if it should happen
fly from desert
35 **brothers** Edward, Clarence, Richard
41 **magnanimity** steadfast courage
42 **naked** unarmed
foil . . . arms defeat a fully armed soldier (or knight) (*OED*, *arm*, *sb.*[1] 3, citing this line)
44–9 **For . . . help** See Appendix A, 2.3. 49–53.
44 **suspect** believe I had detected
fearful timid
45 **betimes** immediately

OXFORD

    Women and children of so high a courage,   50
    And warriors faint? Why, 'twere a perpetual shame.
    O brave young prince, thy famous grandfather
    Doth live again in thee. Long mayst thou live
    To bear his image and renew his glories.

SOMERSET

    And he that will not fight for such a hope,   55
    Go home to bed, and like the owl by day,
    If he arise, be mocked and wondered at.

MARGARET

    Thanks gentle Somerset, sweet Oxford thanks.

PRINCE EDWARD

    And take his thanks, that yet hath nothing else.
        Enter a Messenger

MESSENGER

    Prepare you lords, for Edward is at hand   60
    Ready to fight. Therefore be resolute.

OXFORD

    I thought no less. It is his policy
    To haste thus fast to find us unprovided.

SOMERSET

    But he's deceived, we are in readiness.

MARGARET

    This cheers my heart to see your forwardness.   65

OXFORD

    Here pitch our battle; hence we will not budge.
        Flourish and march. Enter Edward, Gloucester,
        Clarence, and Soldiers

EDWARD

    Brave followers, yonder stands the thorny wood

66.1 *Gloucester*] ROWE; *Richard* F; *Glo. Hast⟨ings⟩.* O

<table>
<tr><td>51 faint faint-hearted</td><td>63 unprovided unprepared; unfurnished</td></tr>
<tr><td>52 grandfather i.e. Henry V</td><td>with arms, men</td></tr>
<tr><td>54 image likeness</td><td>65 forwardness eagerness, zeal</td></tr>
<tr><td>56–7 owl . . . at Because the owl is nocturnal;</td><td>66 pitch our battle position our line of troops</td></tr>
<tr><td>proverbial 'To be like an owl to wonder at'</td><td>in battle array. They may form notional</td></tr>
<tr><td>(Dent O94.1).</td><td>camps on either side of the stage with the</td></tr>
<tr><td>59 his . . . that the thanks of one who</td><td>Yorkists.</td></tr>
<tr><td>yet . . . nothing else thus far . . . (to offer)</td><td>67–72 Brave followers . . . lords Edward may</td></tr>
<tr><td>62 policy strategy</td><td>address the audience from above Mar-</td></tr>
</table>

Which by the heavens' assistance and your strength
Must by the roots be hewn up yet ere night.
I need not add more fuel to your fire, 70
For well I wot ye blaze to burn them out.
Give signal to the fight, and to it lords!

MARGARET

Lords, knights, and gentlemen, what I should say,
My tears gainsay: for every word I speak
Ye see I drink the water of my eye. 75
Therefore no more but this: Henry your sovereign
Is prisoner to the foe, his state usurped,
His realm a slaughterhouse, his subjects slain,
His statutes cancelled, and his treasure spent,
And yonder is the wolf that makes this spoil. 80
You fight in justice; then in God's name, lords,
Be valiant, and give signal to the fight!

Alarum, retreat, excursions. Exeunt

---

68 heavens'] CAPELL; Heauens F; Heaven's ROWE   82.1–5.5.0.1 *Alarum . . . Enter*] F;
Alarmes to the battell, *Yorke* flies, then the chambers be discharged. Then enter the king, *Cla. &
Glo.* & the rest, & make a great shout, and crie, for *Yorke*, for *Yorke*, and then the *Queene* is taken,
& the prince, & *Oxf. & Sum.* and then sound and enter all againe. o

garet in the gallery, if not from the
other side of the stage. In the 1983 BBC
production Edward speaks off stage in
an audibly confident tone. During his
speech, the camera focuses on Margaret,
who weeps in frustration (anticipating
her lines 74–5 below).

67–9 **thorny . . . up** Richard's metaphor at
3.2.174–81 and George's at 2.2.165–9.
Whereas Hall mentions only the Lancastrians pitching their battle in a generic
'fair park' next to the town, Holinshed's
topographical detail matches Edward's
brief description. See Appendix A.

70 **add . . . fire** Proverbial (Dent F785). Also
Spanish Tragedy 3.10.74.

71 **wot** know

74 **gainsay** contradict

74–5 **for . . . eye** Psalm 80: 5 'Thou hast fed
them with the bread of tears, and hast
given them plenteousness of tears to
drink' (*BCP*).

77 **state** kingship

80 **spoil** plunder

82.1 ***Alarum, retreat*** Both chronicles record
that the Yorkists made a tactical retreat to
draw out and entrap the Lancastrians,
who were initially successful: 'the Duke of
Gloucester for a very politic purpose, with
all his men recoiled back' (Hall Nnii[r],
Holinshed Sssvi[r]). Somerset pursued out
of the woods, thinking he was being supported from behind by Lord Wenlock's
forces. But Wenlock may have been colluding with the Yorkists and failed to follow, leaving Somerset exposed to attack.
O's direction indicates how this action
was dramatized: 'Alarms to the battle,
York flies, then the chambers be discharged'. This might have been represented by Edward's being chased through
one stage door and re-entering another to
surprise or overpower the Lancastrians
who remain on stage. Also see Appendix
A.

5.5   *Flourish. Enter Edward, Gloucester, Clarence, and*
          Soldiers, with Queen Margaret, Oxford, and Somerset
          prisoners

EDWARD

Now here a period of tumultuous broils.
Away with Oxford to Ham's Castle straight.
For Somerset, off with his guilty head.
Go bear them hence, I will not hear them speak.

OXFORD

For my part, I'll not trouble thee with words.   5

SOMERSET

Nor I, but stoop with patience to my fortune.
                Exeunt Oxford and Somerset guarded by Soldiers

MARGARET

So part we sadly in this troublous world
To meet with joy in sweet Jerusalem.

EDWARD

Is proclamation made that who finds Edward
Shall have a high reward and he his life?   10

GLOUCESTER

It is. And lo where youthful Edward comes.
                Enter Soldiers guarding Prince Edward

5.5] CAPELL; *not in* F   0.1 *Gloucester*] ROWE; *Richard* F *(and subs. directions and prefixes throughout this scene)*   0.1–2 *and . . . with*] CAPELL *(subs.)*; *not in* F   0.2 *Margaret*] HANMER; *not in* F
0.2–3 *and . . . prisoners*] ROWE; *Somerset* F   6.1 *Oxford . . . guarded*] CAPELL; *not in* F   *by Soldiers*]
This edition; *not in* F   11.1 *Soldiers guarding*] This edition; *not in* F   *Prince Edward*] MALONE;
the Prince F

5.5.1 period end
    broils quarrels
  2 **Ham's castle** Ham, a town in Picardy on
    the Somme in the territory joined to
    the English.
    'John Earl of Oxford, which after Barnet
    field . . . yielded himself to King Edward
    (his life only saved). . . . But to be out of all
    doubtful imaginations, King Edward sent
    him over the sea, to the castle of Hams,
    where by the space of twelve years he was
    in strong prison miserably kept' (Hall
    Nnv^r, Holinshed Tttiii^r).
    straight immediately
  3 **For** as for
    Somerset 'And on the Monday [6 April
    1571, Holinshed says Tuesday 7] next
    ensuing was Edmund Duke of Somerset
    [*et al.*] . . . beheaded in the market place
    at Tewkesbury' (Hall Nnii^v, Holinshed

Sssvi^v).
  6 **stoop** humble myself
7–8 **So . . . Jerusalem** These lines have struck
    many commentators as out of character.
    Perhaps like Henry IV dying in the
    Jerusalem chamber at the end of *2 Henry
    IV*, Margaret uncannily fuses worldly and
    spiritual longings. 'Jerusalem' refers sym-
    bolically to heaven, but there is also a per-
    sonal association, since Margaret's father
    was nominally King of Jerusalem. Fur-
    ther, Holinshed reports that after Mar-
    garet fled the battlefield at Tewkesbury,
    she 'was found in a poor house of reli-
    gion, not far from thence, into the which
    she was withdrawn for safeguard of her-
    self' (Sssvi^v). This was Little Malvern
    Priory, about ten miles north-west of
    Tewkesbury.
 10 **he** Prince Edward. See Appendix A.

EDWARD

Bring forth the gallant, let us hear him speak.

Prince Edward struggles

What, can so young a thorn begin to prick?
Edward, what satisfaction canst thou make
For bearing arms, for stirring up my subjects,   15
And all the trouble thou hast turned me to?

PRINCE EDWARD

Speak like a subject, proud ambitious York.
Suppose that I am now my father's mouth:
Resign thy chair, and where I stand, kneel thou
Whilst I propose the selfsame words to thee   20
Which, traitor, thou wouldst have me answer to.

MARGARET

Ah, that thy father had been so resolved.

GLOUCESTER

That you might still have worn the petticoat,
And ne'er have stol'n the breech from Lancaster.

PRINCE EDWARD

Let Aesop fable in a winter's night,   25

12.1 *Prince . . . struggles*] This edition *following* HATTAWAY; *not in* F

12 **gallant** fine gentleman (spoken sarcastically)
12.1 **struggles** Alternatively, in the 1983 BBC production Prince Edward remains standing before the seated Edward and is pushed to his knees by Richard after l. 13. He rises before l. 19.
13 **thorn . . . prick** Proverbial: 'It early pricks that will be a thorn' (Dent T232).
14 **satisfaction** reparation, amends
15 **bearing . . . subjects** 'King Edward . . . demanded of [Prince Edward] how he durst so presumptuously enter into his realm with banner displayed' (Holinshed Sssvi[v], Hall Nnii[r–v]).
stirring up inciting to rebellion
16 **turned** driven
17–21 **Speak . . . to** 'The prince, being bold of stomach and of good courage, answered saying, "to recover my father's kingdom and inheritance, from his father and grandfather to him, and from him, after him, to me lineally divoluted"' (Hall Nnii[v], Holinshed Sssvi[v]).

18 **now . . . mouth** speaking with the supreme authority of my father
19 **chair** throne (probably notional, although productions often have Edward sitting on a stool or bench)
20 **propose** present
23 **That** so that (Abbott ¶283)
still always
23–4 **petticoat . . . breech** 'She wears the breeches' (Dent B645), proverbial for female unruliness and gender inversion.
25 **Aesop** Sixth-century BC Greek writer of fables used to illustrate moral truths. He was a slave and later sometimes reputed to be hunch-backed, owing to confusion with Aesopus, first-century BC tragic actor and contemporary of Roscius (J. A. K. Thomson, *Shakespeare and the Classics* (1952), pp. 95–6); see 5.6.10). Prince Edward taunts Gloucester's misshapenness.
fable tell fictitious tales; talk idly (*OED v.* 2, citing this line)
in . . . night i.e. when there are long hours to pass

His currish riddles sorts not with this place.
GLOUCESTER
By heaven, brat, I'll plague ye for that word.
MARGARET
Ay, thou wast born to be a plague to men.
GLOUCESTER
For God's sake, take away this captive scold.
PRINCE EDWARD
Nay, take away this scolding crookback rather.   30
EDWARD
Peace, wilful boy, or I will charm your tongue.
CLARENCE
Untutored lad, thou art too malapert.
PRINCE EDWARD
I know my duty, you are all undutiful.
Lascivious Edward, and thou perjured George,
And thou misshapen Dick, I tell ye all   35
I am your better, traitors as ye are,
And thou usurp'st my father's right and mine.
EDWARD
Take that, the likeness of this railer here.
          Stabs him

---

26 sorts] F, O; sort ROWE *and some editors*

---

26 **currish** contemptible (referring to Aesop's hunchback and slave status); satirical or cynical (which like 'cur' means 'dog-like'); because in Aesop's fables beasts allegorize particular attitudes or behaviours. See also 5.6.77.
riddles sorts not enigmatic tales do not suit
27 **plague** punish
28 **born . . . men** Alluding anachronistically to the Tudor theory that Gloucester, future Richard III, was sent by God as England's final bloody scourge for unlawfully deposing Richard II.
30 **crookback** hunchback
31 **Peace . . . charm** silence . . . silence (*OED*, charm, *v.*[1] 4 *obs.*)
32 **Untutored** ill-bred, unmannerly (*OED*, citing this line)
malapert presumptuous, impudent

35 **Dick** Contemptuous diminutive for Richard (and the term Margaret uses at 1.4.76—Prince Edward has learnt his mother's language). Can also refer to any ordinary or low fellow; Dickon, the bedlam Vice in Mr S's *Gammer Gurton's Needle* (and *Richard III* 5.6.35). During this speech, the York brothers may exchange glances, silently colluding about answering Prince Edward's insults, or may look away and/or betray no response before reacting.
37 **right** i.e. to reign
38, 39 **Take that** The action is usually swift and explosive. But in the 1987 ESC production, Edward moved calmly and impersonally, afterwards passing his bayonet to Gloucester for his turn. See Appendix A.
38 **this railer** one who speaks abusively, i.e. Margaret

GLOUCESTER

Sprawl'st thou? Take that to end thy agony.

Gloucester stabs him

CLARENCE

And there's for twitting me with perjury.   40

Clarence stabs him

MARGARET O, kill me too.

GLOUCESTER Marry, and shall.

Offers to kill her

EDWARD

Hold, Richard, hold, for we have done too much.

GLOUCESTER

Why should she live to fill the world with words?

Margaret faints

EDWARD

What, doth she swoon? Use means for her recovery.   45

Some begin to revive her

GLOUCESTER

Clarence, excuse me to the King my brother:

I'll hence to London on a serious matter,

Ere ye come there, be sure to hear some news.

CLARENCE What? What?

GLOUCESTER Tower, the Tower.   *Exit*   50

44.1 *Margaret faints*] OXFORD (*subs.*); *not in* F   45.1 *Some . . . her*] This edition; *not in* F   50
Tower, the Tower] F; The Tower man, the Tower, Ile root them out O *and some editors*; The
Tower, the tower CAPELL *and some editors*

39 **Sprawl'st** i.e. in writhing convulsions. In
the 1963–4 Hall–Barton production, consistent with its tendency to exaggerate
physical violence, Gloucester stabbed
Prince Edward in the groin (perhaps
recalling 3.2.126–7).
  to . . . agony Probably meant sarcastically
and ironically.
40 **twitting** reproaching. Usually only in a
mildly annoying way; compare Proteus in
Two Gentlemen 4.2.8: 'She twits me with
my falsehood to my friend'. The lack of
gravity thus becomes incongruous with
Clarence's extreme and deliberate violence. He is the last to strike, and in
some productions does so with slight
hesitation, as if feeling pressure to prove
his loyalty to his brothers.
42 **Marry, and shall** indeed I will
43 **Hold . . . much** Spoken after he has

watched Gloucester and Clarence act out
his own violence. In the 1983 BBC and
other productions, consciousness of what
they have done hits Edward suddenly, and
he moves to contain further violence.
44 **live . . . words** Richard prophesies Margaret's role as nemesis in *Richard III*.
45 **means . . . recovery** Traditionally by
wringing the nose (see *Venus* 475, and *2
Henry VI* 3.2.34, where Henry faints). But
modern productions usually employ some
alternative gesture, such as fanning, or
splashing water in Margaret's face, perhaps aggressively.
48 **be . . . to** rest assured you will
49–50 **What . . . Tower** Could be meant to be
spoken interchangeably by Gloucester
and Clarence: 'What? Tower. What? The
Tower', with 'The *Tower*' being spoken
more emphatically and tellingly.

MARGARET

O Ned, sweet Ned, speak to thy mother, boy.
Canst thou not speak? O traitors, murderers!
They that stabbed Caesar shed no blood at all,
Did not offend, nor were not worthy blame,
If this foul deed were by to equal it.   55
He was a man; this, in respect, a child,
And men ne'er spend their fury on a child.
What's worse than murderer that I may name it?
No, no, my heart will burst and if I speak.
And I will speak, that so my heart may burst.   60
Butchers and villains, bloody cannibals,
How sweet a plant have you untimely cropped.
You have no children, butchers; if you had,
The thought of them would have stirred up remorse.
But if you ever chance to have a child,   65
Look in his youth to have him so cut off
As, deathsmen, you have rid this sweet young prince.

EDWARD

Away with her, go bear her hence perforce.

MARGARET

Nay, never bear me hence, dispatch me here.
Here sheath thy sword, I'll pardon thee my death.   70
What, wilt thou not? Then Clarence do it thou.

CLARENCE

By heaven I will not do thee so much ease.

MARGARET

Good Clarence do, sweet Clarence do thou do it.

---

53 **Caesar** Besides the reference at 3.1.18,
and in O 5.1, allusions to Caesar's assas-
sination as the exemplar of political murder and personal betrayal were common
in Elizabethan drama and turn up sporadically in the chronicles.
55 **equal** compare to; match
56 **in respect** by comparison
57 **spend** use up, exhaust; expend
59 **and if** if indeed (Abbott ¶105)
61 **cannibals** bloodthirsty savages (*OED* 1b,
citing this line). See 1.4.152 and note.
62 **sweet . . . cropped** Perhaps echoes
Hieronimo's words upon discovering the
corpse of his murdered son: 'Sweet lovely

rose, ill-plucked before thy time' (*Spanish
Tragedy* 2.5.46).
63 **no children** Untrue, as we know from
Edward at 3.2.101–4.
64 **remorse** compassion
65–7 **But . . . prince** A curse reminiscent of
York's on Margaret (and by implication
Prince Edward) at 1.4.164–6, and thus
ironic here.
67 **deathsmen** executioners
rid killed
68 **perforce** forcibly
69 **dispatch** kill
70 **Here** i.e. in my body
72 **ease** pleasure; comfort

CLARENCE
Didst thou not hear me swear I would not do it?
MARGARET
Ay, but thou usest to forswear thyself.   75
'Twas sin before, but now 'tis charity.
What, wilt thou not? Where is that devil's butcher
    Richard?
Hard-favoured Richard? Richard, where art thou?
Thou art not here, murder is thy alms-deed;
Petitioners for blood thou ne'er putt'st back.   80
EDWARD
Away I say, (*to Soldiers*) I charge ye bear her hence.
MARGARET
So come to you and yours as to this prince.
                    Exit Margaret guarded by several Soldiers. Other
                    Soldiers carry off Prince Edward's body
EDWARD Where's Richard gone?
CLARENCE
To London all in post, and as I guess,
To make a bloody supper in the Tower.   85
EDWARD
He's sudden if a thing comes in his head.

---

81 (*to Soldiers*)] This edition; *not in* F   82.1 *Margaret . . . Soldiers*] OXFORD (*subs.*); *led out forcibly* CAPELL; *Queene* F   82.1–2 *Other Soldiers . . . body*] HATTAWAY (*subs.*); *not in* F   84 and] F; ⌈*aside*⌉ and OXFORD

75 **usest . . . thyself** are a habitual breaker of oaths
77 **What . . . Richard?** A twelve-syllable line, with an omitted weak beat supplying the emotional pause at the midline break.
    devil's butcher 'a butcher set on by the devil' (Johnson)
78 **Hard-favoured** ugly: 'Richard Duke of Gloucester . . . was little of stature, evil featured of limbs, crook-backed . . . hard favoured of visage . . .' (Hall AAiᵛ and Holinshed Uvvviᵛ, following Sir Thomas More).
79 **alms-deed** practice of charity (*OED* 2, citing this line)
80 **putt'st back** turned down
82 **come** befall
84 **all in post** at full speed
85 **make** prepare (a meal); become (*OED, make, v.*¹ 49)

85 **bloody supper** There may be a secondary sense of 'one who sups' (*OED, supper, sb.*²) and thus of 'bloody supper' (or 'bloodsucker'), an epithet Hall applies to Clifford's murder of Rutland: 'Yet this cruel Clifford, and deadly bloodsupper' (Ggiiiᵛ).
86 **He's . . . head** Commentators observe that Edward seems blind to, or refuses to see, Richard's intentions. Modern actors, however, often suggest that Edward pretends not to understand but actually knows what is going on, and/or speaks this line as a laconic understatement. In the 1987 ESC production, for example, this was a fatuous remark meant to repress articulating the aim of murder. Compare 2 *Henry VI*, 'Now, sirs, have you dispatched this thing?' (3.2.6), and *Richard III* 1.3.339.

Now march we hence, discharge the common sort
With pay and thanks, and let's away to London
And see our gentle queen how well she fares.
By this I hope she hath a son for me.   *Exeunt*   90

5.6   *Enter Henry the Sixth, ⸢reading,⸣ and Gloucester, with
the Lieutenant of the Tower on the walls*

GLOUCESTER

Good day my lord. What, at your book so hard?

HENRY

Ay my good lord—'my lord' I should say rather,
'Tis sin to flatter; 'good' was little better.
'Good Gloucester' and 'good devil' were alike
And both preposterous; therefore not 'good lord'.   5

90 *Exeunt*] ROWE; *Exit* F
   5.6] CAPELL; *not in* F   0.1 ⸢*reading*⸣] OXFORD *(subs.)*; *not in* F   0.1 *Gloucester*] ROWE; *Richard*
F *(and subs. prefixes throughout this scene)*   0.2 *of the Tower*] ROWE *(subs.)*; *not in* F   0.2 *on . . .
walls*] F; *A Room in the Tower* CAPELL *following* 0

86 **sudden** impetuous

87 **sort** soldiers

90 **this** this time
   son for me Historically, Edward's son was
born before Tewkesbury. See Appendix A.
In the 1963–4 Hall–Barton production,
Edward was unnerved at the sight of the
pale bloodied face of Prince Edward,
which the 1965 televised version held in
close-up as the scene ended. In the 1988
RSC production, Edward stumbled over
the body as he turned to leave.

5.6.0.2 *Lieutenant . . . on the walls* The
wording and syntax of F's direction suggest that the Lieutenant, an emblem of
the royal fortress's integrity and security,
appears alone in the stage gallery, and
that Henry and Gloucester enter to the
main stage below. Having signalled the
scene's location by his conventional dress
and accoutrements (see 4.6.0.3 n.), he
may watch Richard enter to Henry,
before being dismissed at l. 6. His
detached observation reinforces the ominous feeling of Richard stalking Henry.

1 **book** Often a Bible or prayer book (see
3.1.12.1). Most modern productions have
Henry reading at a table, perhaps with a
crucifix on it. His meditative self-

possession suggests acceptance of his
inevitable death, and explains why he
risks provoking Gloucester.

2–5 **Ay . . . lord** Traditional wisdom: 'I will
not now . . . give titles to man. For I may
not give titles, lest my maker should take
me away suddenly' (Job 32: 21–2, Geneva
Bible). See also Daniel 11: 32.

3 **little better** (than flattery)

4 **Good . . . alike** 'Henry's death in the
Tower . . . is the meeting of Good and Evil,
and has strong archetypal resonances:
the Good Angel and Bad Angel; Cain and
Abel; Arthur and Mordred. . . . [There is]
a powerful understanding between Henry
and Richard, an understanding deriving
paradoxically from their utterly opposed
sets of values. Because of this they can
talk to each other quite easily. There is
. . . an almost conversational start to the
scene which builds into Henry's frighten-
ing prophecy and condemnation of
Richard' (Ralph Fiennes on playing
Henry VI, *Players* 3, p. 113).
   were would be

5 **preposterous** absurd; reversing the
natural order of things; literally, back to
front. See Patricia Parker, *Shakespeare
from the Margins* (Chicago and London,
1996), pp. 36–9.

GLOUCESTER (*to the Lieutenant*)
Sirrah, leave us to ourselves, we must confer.

Exit Lieutenant

HENRY

So flies the reckless shepherd from the wolf,
So first the harmless sheep doth yield his fleece
And next his throat unto the butcher's knife.
What scene of death hath Roscius now to act?   10

GLOUCESTER

Suspicion always haunts the guilty mind;
The thief doth fear each bush an officer.

HENRY

The bird that hath been limèd in a bush,
With trembling wings misdoubteth every bush,
And I the hapless male to one sweet bird,   15
Have now the fatal object in my eye
Where my poor young was limed, was caught and killed.

---

6 (*to . . . Lieutenant*)] OXFORD; *not in* F   6.1 *Exit Lieutenant*] ROWE; *not in* F   13 bush,] F;
bush∧ CAIRNCROSS   15 male] F, O; mate MASON *conj.*; make OXFORD *conj.*

---

6 **Sirrah** Address to a social inferior.
7 **flies . . . wolf** Compare John 10: 12: 'But
   an hireling [shepherd] . . . seeth the wolf
   coming, and he leaveth the sheep, and
   fleeth' (Geneva Bible).
   reckless careless; unheedful
9 **throat . . . knife** 'But whosoever was the
   manqueller [murderer] of this holy man
   [Henry VI], it shall appear . . . had
   condign and not undeserved punishment
   for their bloody stroke and butcherly act'
   (Hall only, Nniv^r).
10 **Roscius** Celebrated first-century BC
   Roman actor, most famous for comedy
   but also a tragedian. The Elizabethan
   actor Richard Burbage, who likely joined
   Pembroke's Men at the same time as
   Shakespeare (Gurr, *Companies*, pp.
   261–2) and may have played York, was
   often compared to him.
11 Proverbial: 'Who is guilty suspects everybody' (Tilley F117).
   Suspicion anticipation of future evil or
   wrongdoing
12 Proverbial (Tilley T112).
   officer constable (*OED sb.* 3, citing this
   line)

13–14 Proverbial: 'Birds once limed fear all
   bushes' (Dent B394); 'limèd' refers to
   bird-lime, a sticky paste applied to trees to
   catch small birds.
14 **misdoubteth** fears; is wary of
15 **hapless** unfortunate
   male father. The reading is the same
   throughout Qq and Ff, and the former's
   spelling 'maile', according to *OED*,
   was current during the sixteenth and
   seventeenth centuries. I find Cairncross's parallel of *2 Henry IV* 3.2.127–9
   satisfactory to explain this usage: '[Fal-
   staff to Shadow] Thy mother's son! Like
   enough, and thy father's shadow. So the
   son of the female is the shadow of the
   male'.
   bird offspring
16 **object . . . eye** scene . . . mind's eye
17 **Where** in which action
   young child
   caught and killed Henry's knowledge of
   Prince Edward's death suggests a deepened gift for prophecy (see 4.6), since
   Richard's hasty departure for the Tower
   in the previous scene suggests no more
   than natural time has elapsed.

GLOUCESTER

Why what a peevish fool was that of Crete
That taught his son the office of a fowl,
And yet for all his wings the fool was drowned.   20

HENRY

I Daedalus, my poor boy Icarus,
Thy father Minos that denied our course,
The sun that seared the wings of my sweet boy
Thy brother Edward, and thyself the sea
Whose envious gulf did swallow up his life.   25
Ah kill me with thy weapon, not with words,
My breast can better brook thy dagger's point
Than can my ears that tragic history.
But wherefore dost thou come? Is't for my life?

GLOUCESTER

Think'st thou I am an executioner?   30

HENRY

A persecutor I am sure thou art.

20 fool] F; Fowle o, SINGER 1842–3

18 **peevish** senseless; wretched
18–20 **fool . . . drowned** Daedalus, legendary inventor and artist, who when imprisoned with his son Icarus by King Minos made two pairs of artificial wings to escape. He flew safely to Sicily but Icarus went too close to the sun, whereupon his wings melted and he drowned in the sea. Thomson (*Shakespeare and the Classics* (1952), p. 95) suggests this passage was influenced by Ovid's *Ars Amatoria*, ii. 21–200 rather than *Metamorphoses*, viii. 245–344.
19 **office** function
19–20 **fool . . . fool** Originally close in pronunciation, and therefore puns (Cercignani, p. 198, and Weston Babcock, 'Fools, Fowls, and Perttaunt-like in *Love's Labour's Lost*', *SQ* 2 (1951), 211–19, p. 212).
20 **for all** despite
21–9 **I . . . life?** Henry's extension of Gloucester's allusion to Daedalus and Icarus may be his way of playing for time in order to deal with the emotional tension of the moment, or to master his own apprehensiveness. On the other hand in 1988 Ralph Fiennes was neither quietly resigned nor fearful, but spoke

aggressively and competitively: the classical allusion was his way of outdoing Gloucester, just as his prophecy (see below) became a full-volume curse.
22 **denied** thwarted, blocked
course order of succession; ordinary development
23–4 **sun . . . Edward** (the Yorkist emblem)
25 **envious** malicious, spiteful; envious of another's good fortune
gulf voracious depth; whirlpool
27 **brook** endure
dagger's The chronicles' reported weapon, though Gloucester calls it a 'sword' at l. 63. See note to ll. 29–30.
28 **history** story
29–30 **wherefore . . . executioner** 'Poor King Henry the Sixth, a little before deprived of his realm . . . was now in the Tower of London spoiled of his life, and all worldly felicity, by Richard Duke of Gloucester (as the constant fame ran), which, to the intent that King Edward his brother should be clear out of all secret suspicion of sudden invasion [Holinshed = "might reign in more surety"], murdered the said king with a dagger' (Hall Nniv[r], Holinshed Ttti[v]). See 5.7.13–14.

If murdering innocents be executing,
Why then thou art an executioner.
GLOUCESTER
Thy son I killed for his presumption.
HENRY
Hadst thou been killed when first thou didst presume,   35
Thou hadst not lived to kill a son of mine;
And thus I prophesy: that many a thousand
Which now mistrust no parcel of my fear,
And many an old man's sigh and many a widow's,
And many an orphan's water-standing eye,   40
Men for their sons, wives for their husbands,
Orphans for their parents' timeless death,
Shall rue the hour that ever thou wast born.
The owl shrieked at thy birth, an evil sign,
The night-crow cried, aboding luckless time,   45
Dogs howled and hideous tempest shook down trees,
The raven rooked her on the chimney's top,
And chatt'ring pies in dismal discords sung;
Thy mother felt more than a mother's pain,

41 sons] F (Sonnes); sons' KNIGHT   husbands] F; husbands' STEEVENS   46 tempest] F; tempests O *and some editors*

37 **prophesy** Henry may indicate a different mode of speech and authority of insight at this point, such as reading from the book before him. In the 1977 Ashland production this speech became 'a string of insults to goad Richard into the murder' (Alan C. Dessen, 'Oregon Shakespeare Festival', *SQ* 29 (1978), p. 285).
38 **Which . . . fear** 'who suspect no part of what my fears presage' (Johnson)
40 **water-standing** filled (but not flowing) with tears
42 **timeless** premature
43 **rue** wish had never taken place (*OED*, *v.*[1] 7b, citing this line)
    wast born At this point in the 1987 ESC production, Gloucester, who had been listening impassively, flicked his switchblade at Henry, who paused but went on despite the intimidation, knowing he had to speak the truth.
45 **night-crow** Literary creature known for its night-time croaking, regarded as an evil omen.
    aboding forewarning of

47 **rooked her** huddled herself, cowered (variant of the verb 'to ruck'); i.e. even the raven—usually fearless in warning of approaching evil—was terrified. Wilson cites Ovid, *Metamorphoses*, vi. 552–3: 'And on the house did ruck | A cursèd owl the messenger of ill success and luck'.
48 **pies** magpies, more proverbially unlucky birds (Hart)
    dismal foretelling disaster; cheerless
49–54 **mother . . . world** 'He was malicious, wrathful, and envious, and as it is reported, his mother the duchess had much ado in her travail that she could not be delivered of him uncut, and that he came into the world the feet forward, as men be borne outward [at their deaths], and as the fame ran, not untoothed: whether that men of hatred reported above the truth, or that nature changed his course in his beginning, which in his life many things unnaturally committed' [Hall adds 'this I leave to God his judgement'] (Hall AAi^v and Holinshed Uvvvi^v, following Sir Thomas More).

And yet brought forth less than a mother's hope,   50
To wit, an indigested and deformèd lump,
Not like the fruit of such a goodly tree.
Teeth hadst thou in thy head when thou wast born
To signify thou cam'st to bite the world.
And if the rest be true which I have heard,   55
Thou cam'st—

GLOUCESTER

I'll hear no more. Die, prophet, in thy speech,
  Stabs him
For this amongst the rest was I ordained.

HENRY

Ay, and for much more slaughter after this.
O God forgive my sins, and pardon thee.   *Dies*   60

GLOUCESTER

What, will the aspiring blood of Lancaster
Sink in the ground? I thought it would have mounted.
See how my sword weeps for the poor king's death.
O may such purple tears be alway shed
From those that wish the downfall of our house.   65
If any spark of life be yet remaining,
Down, down to hell, and say I sent thee thither,
  Stabs him again

67–8 thither, | . . . fear.] ROWE; thither. | . . . feare, F

51 **indigested** shapeless, chaotic. Cairncross compares Ovid's description of chaos at the beginning of *Metamorphoses*, '*rudis indigestaque moles*' (i. 7–8; 'a huge rude heap, and nothing else but even | A heavy lump'). Also 'indigested lump', *2 Henry VI* 5.1.155. The line itself is 'mis-shaped' by stretching to six beats instead of the usual five.

52 **fruit . . . tree** Compare Matthew 7: 17–18: 'So every good tree bringeth forth good fruit . . . A good tree cannot bring forth evil fruit' (Geneva Bible).

57 **I'll . . . more** If Richard appears visibly provoked by Henry, he may lash out, as in the 1983 BBC production with four sticking jabs. Or he may act more cold-bloodedly. In 1963–4 Ian Holm showed no reaction, but simply stopped Henry's mouth with his fingers, caressed it slight-ly as he took his hand away, and said soft-ly 'I'll hear no more'. He drew his sword, studied it for a moment, and calmly ran through a fearless David Warner while speaking the rest of this line.

58 **ordained** destined as both agent and victim (Cairncross). The word usually implies a primary divine purpose.

60 **God . . . thee** Recalls Christ's dying words: 'Then said Jesus, Father, forgive them; for they know not what they do' (Luke 23: 34). At this point in the 1963–4 Hall–Barton production, David Warner embraced and kissed Gloucester's head.

61 **aspiring** ambitious, lofty reaching (an ironic projection of Richard's own desires)

63 **See . . . death** Gloucester often displays his sword, reverting briefly to the blackly comic show-and-tell mode of the play's opening moments.

64 **purple tears** blood-red drops

66 **spark . . . remaining** Compare *Spanish Tragedy* 2.5.17: 'O speak if any spark of life remain'.

I that have neither pity, love, nor fear.
Indeed 'tis true that Henry told me of,
For I have often heard my mother say   70
I came into the world with my legs forward.
Had I not reason, think ye, to make haste
And seek their ruin that usurped our right?
The midwife wondered and the women cried
'O Jesus bless us, he is born with teeth!'   75
And so I was, which plainly signified
That I should snarl and bite and play the dog.
Then since the heavens have shaped my body so,
Let hell make crook'd my mind to answer it.
I have no brother, I am like no brother,   80
And this word 'love' which greybeards call divine,
Be resident in men like one another
And not in me: I am myself alone.
Clarence beware, thou keep'st me from the light,
But I will sort a pitchy day for thee,   85
For I will buzz abroad such prophecies
That Edward shall be fearful of his life,
And then to purge his fear, I'll be thy death.

84 keep'st] F3; keept'st F1; keptst O

73 **right** claim to the throne
74 **wondered** was struck with amazement
75 **born with teeth** An ominous sign. Compare the proverb when a prince was born with teeth: 'The thorn comes forth with his point forwards' (Tilley T234). Gloucester often sends up this line with a falsetto voice.
77 **play the dog** play the wag, joker (humorous self-congratulation); act the cynic (see note to 5.5.26); be a man. Also perhaps alluding to the proverbial 'Every dog has his day' (i.e. moment of glory), power (Dent D464 and *Hamlet* 5.1.289).
79 **crook'd** devious, perverse
   answer correspond to
80-1 **brother . . . divine** 'Brother' represents both universal and family bonds. 'Beloved, let us love one another: for love cometh of God . . . And this commandment have we of him, that he which loveth God, should love his brother also' (1 John 4: 7, 21, Geneva Bible). Whereas the destruction of father and son relations was a main theme in the first half of the

play, the second half 'constructs a pattern of fraternal loyalty that is then eloquently refuted by [Shakespeare's] fully metamorphosed villain' (Pearlman, p. 427). This development perhaps explains F's dropping of 'I had no father, I am like no father' in the line preceding in O. In the 1963-4 Hall-Barton production at this point, Gloucester was momentarily touched with emotion as he recalled his family; but continuing the speech was a way of finally extinguishing his memory of them.
82 **like** who are the same as
84 **light** (realizing my own) interests, ambitions; sun (Yorkist emblem, implying family headship)
85 **sort** ordain; allot
   pitchy intensely black. Gloucester varies the proverb, 'It will be a black day to somebody' (Tilley D88), which he uses again in *Richard III* (5.6.10).
86 **buzz** rumour publicly
   prophecies portents
88 **purge** 'cure by lancing' (Wilson)

King Henry and the prince his son are gone,
Clarence thy turn is next, and then the rest,   90
Counting myself but bad till I be best.
I'll throw thy body in another room,
And triumph Henry in thy day of doom.

Exit with the body

5.7   *Flourish. Enter King Edward, Queen Elizabeth,
Clarence, Gloucester, Hastings, Nurse with the infant
prince, and Attendants. A chair of state*

EDWARD

Once more we sit in England's royal throne

89–90 King . . . rest] F (*subs.*); *Henry and his sonne are gone, thou Clarence next,* | *And by one and one I will dispatch the rest*, o; King *Henry*, *and the Prince his sonne are gone*, | *And Clarence thou art next must follow them,* | *So by one and one dispatching all the rest*, Q3   93.1 *with the body*] CAPELL; *not in* F

5.7] CAPELL; *not in* F   0.1 *Edward*] O, ROWE; *not in* F   0.1 *Elizabeth*] O, MALONE; *not in* F   0.2 *Gloucester*] ROWE; *Richard* F (*and subs. prefixes throughout this scene*)   0.2–3 *with . . . prince*] CAPELL (*subs.*); *not in* F   0.3 *A chair of state*] This edition; *not in* F

89–91 **King . . . Counting** F, O, and Q3 all differ. Q3 has three lines, F and O two. Because Q3 preceded F and their wording is similar, Oxford proposes that Q3 expanded O, and F in turn consulted Q3. This assumes (a) Q3's lines are padding, the result of problems casting off O as copy for Q3; (b) F's copy was defective and the compositor looked to Q3 and/or O for guidance; (c) O represents a reading closer to F's supposedly illegible manuscript. But if O is a report, and/or an earlier version of F, it is at least one stage removed from F's manuscript, or may not be like it at all. *Pace* Hattaway, O is not metrically superior to F, which is regular pentameter, with first syllable trochees (the most common position) on 'Clarence' and 'Counting'. While O's second line is regular, its first is not. O and Q3's second and third lines respectively sound like a passage in *2 Henry VI* in which Suffolk tells Margaret how their enemies will be entrapped or eliminated: 'So one by one we'll weed them all at last'. Significantly, moreover, O and Q3 use the more archaic phrase 'by one and one' (*OED* 16b), not found elsewhere in Shakespeare. (Perhaps tellingly, Cairncross unconsciously modernized O in his collation note to 'And one by one'. But in the

end, like many other editors, he decided there was not enough certainty about either O or Q3 to displace F.) To assume that F's compositor read and adopted Q3's first line but then conflated its next two 'to provide himself with the single verse line ending in "rest"' (*Textual Companion*, p. 206) which F theoretically required, puts a great deal of faith in his literary discernment. The nature of Q3's putative influence on F in this passage is problematic and uncertain, providing no secure grounds for emendation or substitution from O.

89–91 **King . . . best** 'He slew in the Tower King Henry the Sixth, saying: now is there no heir male of King Edward the third but we of the house of York' (Hall only, AAi[v]).

91 **Counting . . . best** Reversing the proverb: 'Bad is the best' (Dent B316).
   bad contemptible

93 **in . . . doom** on the day you face your god's judgement

5.7.0.2–3 *Nurse . . . prince* 'Nurse' may mean 'wetnurse'. Modern productions sometimes stage the scene as a christening celebration, with clerical attendants and bells ringing. In the 1987 ESC and 1996 New York Public Theatre performances it became a modern photo oppor-

Repurchased with the blood of enemies.
What valiant foemen, like to autumn's corn,
Have we mowed down in tops of all their pride:
Three dukes of Somerset, threefold renowned   5
For hardy and undoubted champions,
Two Cliffords, as the father and the son,
And two Northumberlands, two braver men
Ne'er spurred their coursers at the trumpet's sound;
With them the two brave bears Warwick and Montague,   10
That in their chains fettered the kingly lion
And made the forest tremble when they roared.
Thus have we swept suspicion from our seat
And made our footstool of security.
Come hither Bess, and let me kiss my boy.   15
Young Ned, for thee, thine uncles and myself

5 renowned] O (*renowmd*); Renowme F

tunity, with the media filming and flash-
ing pictures, and at the Washington
Shakespeare Theatre in 1996, the 'royal
family' waved from a balcony at the back
of the stage. Alternatively, the scene
may be staged more traditionally as a
re-enthronement ceremony, with fanfares and a military procession, or as a
return to the *mise-en-scène* of the play's
opening. The 1977 Ashland production
ended as it began, with an empty throne
(Dessen, 'Oregon Shakespeare Festival',
285).

0.3 **chair of state** In the 1988 RSC production a large sunburst emblem appeared
over the throne, redisplaying Edward's
Yorkist emblem, but this time with conspicuous saw-like edges.

2 **Repurchased** 'acquired or obtained again;
a legal term for acquisition [of property]
otherwise than by inheritance or descent'
(Cairncross)

3–14 **What . . . security** Recalls the form of
epic roll-call, in which chivalrous tribute
is paid to the dead on both sides, usually
in a tone of nominal humility (compare *Henry V* 4.8.74–112, *Edward III*
3.5.94–9). But Edward's speech is brag-
ging and triumphalist, and the 'victory'
hollow.

3 **foemen** adversaries
  corn wheat

4 **in tops** in the highest growth; at the
  peak
  pride fortune, exalted state (*OED sb.*[1] 8),
  as well as self-esteem

6 **undoubted** unquestionable (*OED ppl. a.* 2,
  citing this line)

7 **as** namely

9 **coursers** large powerful horses

10 **two . . . Montague** The second 'brave
  bear' refers to Warwick's father, Salisbury, not to his brother Montague. See
  Appendix B.

10–11 **bears . . . chains** A bear chained to a
  ragged staff was the heraldic emblem of
  the Earls of Warwick and of Robert
  Dudley, Earl of Leicester. *2 Henry VI*
  5.1.200–8 describes the image as a
  heraldic device. It appears on the fron-
  tispiece and title-page to Part Two of
  Geoffrey Whitney's *A Choice of Emblems*
  (1586), dedicated to Leicester.

13 **swept** driven away (*OED, sweep, v.* 4, citing this line)
  suspicion . . . seat uneasiness,
  worry . . . throne. See note to 5.6.
  29–30.

14 **And . . . security** Very similar to Marlowe's *Massacre at Paris*, sc. 15, l. 41: 'And
  makes his footstool on security'. The fact
  that the lines in F and O are identical here
  indicates that *Massacre* (*c.*1592–3) is the
  borrower.

15 **Bess** Familiar diminutive of Elizabeth.

Have in our armours watched the winter's night,
Went all afoot in summer's scalding heat,
That thou mightst repossess the crown in peace,
And of our labours thou shalt reap the gain.   20

GLOUCESTER (*aside*)

I'll blast his harvest, if your head were laid,
For yet I am not looked on in the world.
This shoulder was ordained so thick to heave,
And heave it shall some weight or break my back,
Work thou the way, and that shalt execute.   25

EDWARD

Clarence and Gloucester, love my lovely queen,
And kiss your princely nephew, brothers both.

CLARENCE

The duty that I owe unto your majesty
I seal upon the lips of this sweet babe.

ELIZABETH

Thanks noble Clarence, worthy brother thanks.   30

GLOUCESTER

And that I love the tree from whence thou sprang'st,
Witness the loving kiss I give the fruit.
(*Aside*) To say the truth, so Judas kissed his master
And cried 'All hail', whenas he meant all harm.

---

21 (*aside*)] ROWE; *not in* F   30 ELIZABETH] O (*Queen*), THEOBALD; *Cla.* F1; *King* F3   Thanks] O,
F2; Thanke F1   33 (*Aside*)] ROWE; *not in* F

17 **armours** Given Edward's sexual reputation, possibly with a pun on 'arms' (*OED*
3b) and 'amour' (*1 Henry VI* 2.1.24: 'She
[Joan] carry armour as she hath begun').
watched stood on guard; kept ourselves
awake during
18 **afoot** on foot
20 **labours . . . gain** 'One soweth, and
another reapeth . . . other men laboured,
and ye are entered into their labours'
(John 4: 37–8, Geneva Bible).
21 *aside* May include speaking directly to the
audience or the camera.
blast his blight the infant prince's
head were laid wheat-tops are cut to the
ground; heads can be struck off
22 **looked on** given my due regard,
respected
23 **ordained** destined. See note to 5.6.58.
heave mount; rise up above the ordinary
level; strive, struggle; move things

25 **Work . . . execute** Dr Johnson, perhaps
recalling eighteenth-century stagings,
observed: 'Richard laying his hand on his
forehead says, "Work . . . way" then
bringing down his hand and beholding it,
"and . . . execute" . . . , the arm being
included in the shoulder'. Alternatively
Gloucester may reach down to touch
his sword, or may make no physical
gesture.
Work devise, contrive, direct, aim
execute carry it into effect
29 **seal** attest; mark in token
30 **brother** i.e. brother-in-law
31 **tree** forebears; i.e. his own stock
(Cairncross)
33–4 **Judas . . . harm** Compare Matthew 26:
49: 'When he [Judas] came to Jesus, he
said, Hail Master, and kissed him'
(Bishops' Bible). The exact phrase 'All
hail' evidently derives from the mystery

EDWARD

Now am I seated as my soul delights,   35
Having my country's peace and brothers' loves.

CLARENCE

What will your grace have done with Margaret?
René her father, to the King of France
Hath pawned the Sicils and Jerusalem,
And hither have they sent it for her ransom.   40

EDWARD

Away with her and waft her hence to France.
And now what rests but that we spend the time
With stately triumphs, mirthful comic shows,
Such as befits the pleasure of the court?
Sound drums and trumpets, farewell sour annoy,   45
For here I hope begins our lasting joy.

Flourish. Exeunt omnes

---

46 here$_\wedge$ I hope$_\wedge$] F, O; here, I hope, THEOBALD *and some editors*   46.1 *Flourish*] CAPELL; *not in*
F   *Exeunt omnes*] F (*Exeunt omnes* | FINIS.)

---

cycles, such as York's *The Agony and the Betrayal* (*York Plays*, ed. Lucy Toulmin Smith (New York, 1963), l. 243). Shakespeare repeats Judas' greeting in *Richard II* 4.1.160–1. The chronicles also provided a hint for this identification: '[Richard] was close and secret, a deep dissimuler . . . outwardly familiar [Holinshed and More "companiable"] where he inwardly hated, not letting to kiss whom he thought to kill' (Hall AAi^v and Holinshed Uvvvi^v, following Sir Thomas More).

34 **whenas** while on the contrary

39 **the Sicils** Sicily and Sardinia
40 **it** the levied money
41 **waft** transport by water. See Appendix A.
42 **rests** remains to do
43 **triumphs** public celebrations. Some productions end the scene with music and dance—the traditional form of closure in comedy. When people began dancing in

the 1977 RSC production, they did so awkwardly, as if discovering a new social activity, and Gloucester was left out.
44–6 **pleasure . . . joy** Compare Whitney, p. 165, *Post amara dulcia*: 'When griefs be gone, then joy doth make us sing. | When storms be past, the varying weather clears. | So after pains, our pleasures make us glad, | But without sour, the sweet is hardly had'.
45 **annoy** painful vexation
46 **I hope** If spoken emphatically or parenthetically may express slight doubt about the 'lasting joy', but the BBC's Edward lowers his tone in an earnest wish, with the irony to be inferred by the viewer.
46.1 *Exeunt* In modern productions, Gloucester is often the last to leave, or exits conspicuously, in a way which anticipates the action of *Richard III*. See Introduction, pp. 47–8.

COMMENTARY ON HISTORICAL SOURCES

THIS section supplies additional or alternative documentation, beyond that offered in the main commentary, of Shakespeare's interpretive use of his two historical sources, Edward Hall's *Union of the Two Noble and Illustre Families of Lancaster and York* (1548), and the editorial compilation we know as Raphael Holinshed's *Chronicles of England, Scotland, and Ireland*, second edition (1587), vol. iii. Shakespeare often remembered, and/or selected amongst, variant chronicle reports, explanations, nuances of expression, marginal notes, and headings. I have tried to isolate preferences for Hall or Holinshed whenever they diverge in fact or wording. This involves differentiating historical from non-historical speeches and details, while bearing in mind that the distinction is not always clear-cut, since Shakespeare routinely fuses factual and invented material. In places where Hall and Holinshed describe an event using identical language, or where Shakespeare does not make a discernible choice, I have cited the earliest source—Hall—but supplied additional references to Holinshed. These notes also identify additional variant Folio and Octavo passages that can be related to alternative chronicle accounts, beyond those cited in the textual discussion of *True Tragedy* and *3 Henry VI* as earlier and later versions of the play (pp. 117–23). When such differences serve to particularize Shakespeare's dramatic representations of events or figures, I reproduce passages or phrases from both texts to allow them to be compared.

My notes cite the original early editions of each chronicle in modernized spelling, rather than extracts from reprints such as W. G. Boswell-Stone (*Shakespeare's Holinshed*, 1896) or Geoffrey Bullough (*Narrative and Dramatic Sources of Shakespeare*, vol. iii (1960)). Neither of these editions is completely reliable in reproducing the original texts, and their elisions or alterations have sometimes led to mistaken claims about which chronicle version Shakespeare used.

1.1 After the Battle of Northampton in May 1460, Hall and Holinshed report that Henry 'left alone disconsolate, was taken and apprehended as a man born and predestinate to trouble, misery, and calamity. . . . The next day with great solemnity and small comfort, [the Yorkists] set forward the King and by easy journeys brought him to London the sixteenth day of July, where he was faintly received and feebly welcomed' (Hall Ffiv^v–v^r, Holinshed Pppiii^v). A Parliament was called in October. Sitting in the 'throne royal', York declared his lineal claims to the crown in an oration and was made heir apparent (Hall Ffiv^v–Ggii^r, Holinshed Qqqii^r–iii^r).

Shakespeare merged this sequence with the concluding action of *2 Henry VI*, representing the Yorkist victory at the first Battle of St Albans in May 1455. According to Holinshed, Henry was captured and brought to London 'with all honour and due reverence' (Pppii^v). This battle was followed by a Parliament in which York was made Protector, Warwick Governor of Calais, and Salisbury Chancellor (Hall Eeii^v, Ggii^r, Holinshed Qqqii^r, Pppii^v–iii^r). The king's 'escape' in the opening moments of Part Three is therefore invented, as is much of the rest of this scene, namely the show of bloody swords and Somerset's head, the armed intimidation of Henry, and Margaret's repudiation of her husband's disinheritance of Prince Edward.

1.1.1–3 **escaped . . . men** Suggested by Holinshed's report that towards the end of St Albans '[Henry] perceiving his men thus fled from him, withdrew into a poor man's house to save himself from the shot of arrows' (Pppii^r).

1.1.2 **horsemen . . . north** Both Holinshed and Hall report that prior to St Albans, 'The King . . . meaning to meet with the Duke [of York], rather in the north parts than about London, where it was thought he had too many friends . . . departed from Westminster'. He was intercepted at St Albans (Holinshed Pppi^v, Hall Eeii^r).

1.1.4–9 **Northumberland . . . Clifford . . . Stafford . . . slain** 'For there died [at the first Battle of St Albans] . . . Henry the second of that name Earl of Northumberland, Humphrey Earl of Stafford son to the Duke of Buckingham, John Lord Clifford' (Holinshed Pppii^r, Hall Eeii^r). Holinshed reports that it was 'Somerset with the other lords, [who came] to the succours of their companions that were put to the worse, did what they could to beat back the enemies; but the Duke of York sent ever fresh men to succour the weary . . . whereby the King's army was finally brought low, and all the chieftains of the field slain and beaten down', whereas Hall states that Somerset and the other lords 'fought a sore and a cruel battle, in the which many a tall man lost his life' and that only York 'sent ever fresh men to succour the weary . . . by which only policy the King's army was profligate and dispersed'.

1.1.10–14 **Buckingham . . . dangerous . . . Wiltshire's blood** 'Humphrey Duke of Buckingham, being wounded, and James Butler Earl of Ormond and Wiltshire . . . seeing fortune thus against them, left the King alone, and with a number fled away' (Holinshed Pppii^r, Hall Eeii^r). Buckingham was later killed at the Battle of Northampton in 1460 (Holinshed Pppiii^v, Hall Ffiv^v), which Shakespeare here conflates with St Albans in 1455: 'the King's army was profligate and dispersed, and all the chieftains of the field almost slain and brought to confusion' (Hall Eeii^r).

1.1.16 Richard's participation at this point is fictitious because he was only born in 1452. He is not mentioned by the chronicles until Edward IV's reign, after the Battle of Towton.

1.1.25–6 **palace . . . regal seat** In both chronicles York makes a long ora-tion rehearsing his claim to the throne. Only Holinshed records the variant account that 'John Whethamsted the abbot of Saint Albans, who lived in those days and by all likelihood was there present . . . maketh no further recital of any words which the Duke should utter at that time' (Qqqiv[r]). Shakespeare seems to have taken up this option and passed to the debates which resulted ultimately in York being declared regent and heir apparent.

1.1.26–32.1 **possess it York . . . *They go up*** Holinshed reports Hall's account and adds that when York entered the Parliament, he 'stepped up unto the throne royal, and there laying his hand upon the cloth of estate, seemed as if he meant to take possession of that which was his right (for he held his hand so upon that cloth a good pretty while)' (Qqqii[r]), but did not sit down before leaving the upper house.

1.1.29 **hither . . . force** Holinshed alone reports that York 'went to the most principal lodging that the King had within all his palace, breaking up the locks and doors, and so lodged himself therein, more like to a king than a duke', meaning 'to thrust himself in possession of the crown' (Qqqii[r], see l. 34).

1.1.44 See note to 26–32.1 above.

1.1.55–7 **revenge . . . revenged** Hall repeatedly cites revenge for the deaths of fathers and sons as a driving force behind the conflicts in the years between St Albans and Towton (see Eeii[r], Eev[r], Eev[v], Ffi[r], Ggiii[r]): 'whose children shortly revenged their fathers' quarrel, both to the Queen's extreme perdition and the utter undoing of her husband and son' (Ggiii[v]). Holinshed, by contrast, cites revenge less frequently as a motive.

1.1.59 **WESTMORLAND** Several commentators and editors claim that Robert Fabian (whose *New Chronicles of England and France* (1516) were a main source for later Tudor historians and known to Shakespeare) and after-wards Hall mistook the Earl of Westmorland (who did not participate in the Wars of the Roses) for his brother John Neville, who fought for the Lan-castrians and was killed at Towton in 1461. Hall there reports 'the Earl of Westmorland's brother and all his company almost were there slain' (Ggvi[v]), whereas Holinshed says 'the Earls of Northumberland and West-morland' 'in these two days were slain' (Rrri[r]). Hall is correct, but Shake-speare has followed Holinshed in F and O.

1.1.67–8 **city . . . beck** Both chroniclers report that 'The Duke of York . . . with no small company . . . came to the city of London, which he entered . . . with a sword borne naked before him'. But Holinshed adds 'with trumpets also sounding, and accompanied with a great train of men of arms, and other of his friends and servants' (Holinshed Qqqii[r], Hall Ffv[r]). See also 1.1.2 above. Hall alone then continues that York 'took his lodging in the King's own palace . . . the common people babbled that he should be king, and that King Henry should no longer reign'.

Alternatively, Wilson (p. 130) and Cairncross (p. 7) cite an earlier passage in Hall relating to Queen Margaret, who avoided encountering York in London 'because she well perceived [him] to be had in more estimation among the citizens and commonality than the King her husband or her own person' (Eeiv^v).

1.1.105–31 **What . . . his** O's characterization of Henry through this passage, in which he appears more insecure and pleading, differs from F's. This may relate to Hall's and Holinshed's divergent accounts of Henry's response to York prior to the first Battle of St Albans. In Hall's brief report, Henry, 'more desirous of peace than of war', sends messengers to York 'commanding him, as an obedient subject, to keep the peace and not as an enemy to his natural country to murder and slay his own countrymen' (Eeii^r). Holinshed records Hall's account as well as two much longer ones by John Whethamsted (fifteenth-century abbot of St Albans and writer) and Abraham Fleming (antiquary and contributor to the 1587 edition of Holinshed's *Chronicles*). In the first, York demands Somerset's arrest for losing Normandy and Gascony (he later repeats this argument in his 1460 oration to Parliament, adding references to the loss of Anjou, Maine, the Ile-de-France, and Paris—see ll. 110–1, glancing back to *2 Henry VI*). To which 'The king advertised of this answer, more wilful than tolerable, appointed him rather to try battle than deliver the Duke of Somerset to his enemies' (Pppii^r). Fleming quotes letters exchanged between York and Henry. The King warns him and his followers not to

be so hardy to make resistance against me in *my own realm*. For I shall know what *traitor* dare be so bold to raise any *people* in mine own land, wherethrough I am in *great disease and heaviness*. By the faith I owe unto St Edward and unto the *crown of England*, I shall destroy them every mother's son, and eke they to be hanged, drawn, and quartered, that may be taken afterward of them, in example to make all such *traitors* to beware for to make any rising of *people* within mine own land, and so *traitorously* to abide their *king* and governor. And for a conclusion, rather than they shall have any lord that here is with me at this time, I shall this day for their sake in this quarrel *myself live and die*. (Pppi^v, my italics)

F's considerably more defiant Henry seems closer to Holinshed's report based on Fleming and Whethamsted, especially in lines 105 and 125–30, where the wording and ideas match closely.

1.1.172–6 Parliament concluded in 1460 that Henry 'should enjoy the name and title of king, and have possession of the realm during his life natural; and if he either died or resigned or forfeited the same . . . then the said Crown . . . should immediately be devoluted to the Duke of York, if he then lived, or else to the next heir of his line' (Hall Ggii^r, Holinshed Qqqiii^r).

1.1.181–202 Shakespeare follows Holinshed's full-text version of the articles (Qqqiv[r]). *Pace* Cairncross, they are also reported more briefly by Hall, who records the provision that 'if the king did closely or apertly study or go about to break or alter this agreement, or to compass or imagine the death or destruction of the said Duke or his blood, then he to forfeit the crown and the Duke of York to take it' (Ggii[r]).

1.1.197 oath York's terms in Holinshed are flagged by the marginal note, 'The oath of Richard Duke of York', and begin 'Item, the said Richard Duke of York shall promise and bind him by his solemn oath the manner and form as followeth. . . . I . . . promise and swear by the faith and truth that I owe to almighty God, that I shall never consent, procure, or stir, directly or indirectly, in privy or apert, neither (as much as in me is) shall suffer to be done, consented, procured, or stirred, any thing that may sound to the abridgement of the natural life of King Henry the Sixth or to the hurt or diminishing of his reign' (Qqqiii[v]).

1.1.212 looks . . . anger Prior to the Battle of Northampton, Hall alone states, 'a great number was assembled, many for the love they bore to the King, but more for the fear that they had of the Queen, whose countenance was so fearful and whose look was so terrible that to all men, against whom she took a small displeasure, her frowning was their undoing, and her indignation was their death' (Ffii[r]). After the articles of agreement were passed, York sent for Queen Margaret but she refused to come, instead journeying north to muster forces.

1.1.239 Warwick . . . Calais According to both Hall and Holinshed, in 1455 Warwick was 'elected to the office of the captainship of Calais' whereas his father 'the Earl of Salisbury was appointed to be Lord Chancellor' (Holinshed Pppii[v], Hall Eeii[v]). Shakespeare seems to have made this change to diminish Salisbury's role after *2 Henry VI* (perhaps in anticipation of his death and/or the re-creation of Salisbury as Montague; see Appendix B).

1.2.22–34 An . . . heart Holinshed's continuing account may have partly suggested Richard's argument: 'but others held [York] discharged [of his oath], because he obtained a dispensation from the Pope, by such suggestion as his procurators made unto him, whereby the same oath was adjudged void, as that which was received unadvisedly, to the prejudice of himself and disinheriting of all his posterity' (Qqqiv[r]).

1.2.40 Cobham After landing at Sandwich before the Battle of Northampton the Yorkists passed 'through Kent, [where] there came to them the Lord Cobham . . . and many other gentlemen . . . the fame of their landing once known, gentlemen repaired . . . out of all the South-parts' (Ffiv[r], Pppiii[v]). Both chroniclers name Cobham again in the preparations for Northampton (Ffiv[v], Pppiii[v]) as well as earlier (e.g. 'Edward Brooke, Lord Cobham, a man of great wit and much experience' (Hall Ddii[v])), and they call him one of York's 'especial friends' with Salisbury and Warwick (Eeii^r, Pppi^v).

1.2.49–51 **Queen . . . men** 'The queen . . . determined to couple with [York] while his power was small . . . so having in her company . . . in effect all the Lords of the North part, with eighteen thousand men [or as some write, twenty and two thousand], marched from York to Wakefield and bade base [i.e. bases, a running game of opposing 'homes'] to the Duke even before his castle, he having with him not fully five thousand persons' (Hall Ggii^v, Holinshed Qqqiv^r).

1.2.69–70 **Let's . . . straight** 'The Earl of Salisbury and other his friends . . . ordered their men and set them forth in warlike fashion. . . . The Duke of York with his people descended down the hill in good order and array' (Hall Ggiii^r). '[York] having with him not fully five thousand persons . . . would needs issue forth to fight with his enemies' (Holinshed Qqqiv^r).

1.2.73 **France** O's 'Normandy' is closer to Hall than F: 'when I was Regent in Normandy . . .' (Ggii^v).

1.2.74–5 **Whenas . . . success?** 'Their great number shall not appal my spirits but encourage them, for surely I think that I have there as many friends as enemies, which at joining, will either fly or take my part . . . I will fight with them though I should fight alone' (Hall Ggiii^r).

1.3.1–11, 35–6, 47 'While this battle was in fighting, a priest called Sir Robert Aspall, chaplain and school master to the young Earl of Rutland . . . (scarce of the age of twelve years, a fair gentleman, and a maidenlike person), perceiving that flight was more safeguard than tarrying . . . secretly conveyed the Earl out of the field . . . but ere he could enter into a house, he was by the said Lord Clifford espied, followed, and taken, and by reason of his apparel, demanded what he was. The young gentleman, dismayed, had not a word to speak, but kneeled on his knees imploring mercy and desiring grace, both with holding up his hands and making dolorous countenance, for his speech was gone for fear. "Save him," said his chaplain, "for he is a prince's son and peradventure may do you good hereafter." With that word, the Lord Clifford marked him and said, "By God's blood, thy father slew mine, and so will I do thee and all thy kin"; and with that word, struck the Earl to the heart with his dagger, and bade his chaplain bear the Earl's mother and brother word what he had done and said' (Hall Ggiii$^{r–v}$).

1.3.21, 27 **revenged . . . revenge** Likewise prior to Ferrybridge (a minor encounter before Towton) the chronicles report that King Henry and Queen Margaret 'committed the governance of the army to the Duke of Somerset, the Earl of Northumberland, and the Lord Clifford, as men desiring to revenge the death of their parents slain at the first Battle of St Albans' (Hall Ggvi^r, and earlier Eev^v, Holinshed Qqqvi^r).

1.4.1–29 Most of the details in York's speech are invented. Holinshed's first of two accounts of his death runs thus: 'when he was in the plain field [Hall = "ground"] between his castle and the town of Wakefield, he was environed on every side like fish in a net, [Hall adds "or a deer in a buck-stall"] so that though he fought manfully, yet was he within half an hour slain and dead, and his whole army discomfited' (Holinshed Qqqiv^r, Hall Ggiii^r). O's first line is closer to the chronicle passage ('Ah York, post to thy castle, save thy life'), whereas F typically offers a more delocalized representation of events. The end of the speech also differs slightly in each version. In F the emphasis is on York's physical exhaustion and spent will to resist. O seems closer to Hall, who stresses his immobility: 'No way to fly: | No way to save my life? And here I stay: | And here my life must end'. As a result York seems more passively resigned in O.

1.4.30–2 Yield . . . father See note to 1.3.21, 27.

1.4.99–100 how . . . oath 'Many deemed that this miserable end chanced to the Duke of York as a due punishment for breaking his oath of allegiance unto his sovereign lord King Henry. But others held him discharged thereof, because he obtained a dispensation from the Pope' (Holinshed Qqqiv^r).

1.4.123 yeoman '. . . old Duke René of Anjou [Margaret's father], writing himself King of Naples, Sicily, and Jerusalem, having as much profits of the letters of his glorious style as rents and revenues out of the said large and rich realms and dominions' (Hall Hhv^r). See also n. to 3.3.154.

1.4.179–80 Off . . . York 'And at length having thus scorned him with these and diverse other the like despiteful words, they struck off his head. . . . After this victory by the Queen . . . all the prisoners' . . . heads (together with the Duke of York's head) were conveyed to York, and there set on poles over the gate of the city, in despite of them and their lineage' (Holinshed Qqqiv^r, Hall Ggiii^v).

2.1 Shakespeare selects a few particular details from the crowded sequence of battles after Wakefield—Mortimer's Cross (2 February 1461), second St Albans (17 February 1461), Ferrybridge and Dintingdale (after 12 March 1461), and Towton (29 March 1461)—for this and the next five scenes. The virtual omission of Mortimer's Cross (a Yorkist victory against Lancastrian Welsh forces), Warwick's substantial report of the Yorkist collapse at Wakefield, the magnifying of the minor Yorkist loss at Ferrybridge, and the combining of Clifford's death at Dintingdale with the decisive Lancastrian defeat at Towton, 'gives the impression of a run of Lancastrian victories followed by an unexpected and definitive reversal in favour of the Yorkists at Towton' (Cairncross, p. 33, and see Shakespeare's apparent inflation of Lancastrian odds in note to ll. 177–81 below).

2.1.25, 39–40 three suns Before the battle of Mortimer's Cross, 'on

Candlemas day [2 February] in the morning, at which time the sun (as some write) appeared to the Earl of March like three suns, and suddenly joined all together in one, and that upon the sight thereof he took such courage that he fiercely set on his enemies and them shortly discomfited; for which cause men imagined that he gave the sun in his full brightness for his cognizance or badge' (Hall Ggiii^v–iv^r, Holinshed Qqqiv^v).

2.1.42.1 **Enter . . . blowing** Compare: 'When the Earl of Warwick was informed of this feat [the death of his brother Thomas Neville "the bastard of Salisbury"], he like a man desperate, mounted on his hackney and came blowing [Holinshed = "puffing and blowing"] to King Edward . . .' (Hall Ggvi^r, Holinshed Qqqvi^v).

2.1.116–19 **For . . . succession** 'The Queen, still came forward with her Northern people, intending to subvert and defeat all conclusions and agreements, enacted and assented to [Holinshed = "to undo all that had been ordained"] in the last Parliament' (Hall Ggiv^r, Holinshed Qqqiv^v).

2.1.122–8 **But . . . judge** According to Hall and Holinshed: 'Happy was the Queen in her two battles, but unfortunate was the King in all his enterprises, for where his person was present, there victory fled ever from him to the other part' (Ggiv^r, Qqqiv^v). See also 2.2.73–6.

2.1.143–7 **George . . . war** 'The Duchess of York, seeing her husband and son slain . . . sent her two younger sons, George and Richard, over the sea to the city of Utrecht in Almaine, where they were of Philip, Duke of Burgundy, well received and feasted, and so there they remained till their brother Edward had obtained the realm' (Hall Ggiv^v, Holinshed Qqqv^r).

2.1.168–77 **Queen . . . strong** 'During this season, the Queen was greatly encouraged with the victory obtained late at Wakefield, ["partly because the Duke of York her utter enemy was rid out of the world, and partly because she perceived the lords of the North country to adhere and cleave to her part and faction" = Hall only] wherefore with a great multitude of Northern people, she marched toward London' (Hall Ggiv^r, Holinshed Qqqiv^v). Followed by the passage quoted in note 116–19 above.

2.1.177–81 **thirty thousand . . . five-and-twenty** Prior to Mortimer's Cross, 'The people on the Marches of Wales, which above measure favoured the lineage of the Lord Mortimer, more gladly offered [Edward] their aid and assistance than he it either instantly required or heartily desired, so that he had a puissant army to the number of 23,000 ready to go against the Queen' (Hall Ggiii^v, Holinshed Qqqiv^v). Holinshed alone also reports the Lancastrian numbers at 20,000 for the second Battle of St Albans (Qqqiv^v). Shakespeare in F seems to have kept to the numbers in this range (see also 2.2.68) rather than in that for Towton, which were 60,000 for the Lancastrians and 48,660 for the Yorkists (Hall Ggvi^v, Holinshed Qqqvi^v; the latter also records Whethamsted's variant opinion that 'Henry's power exceeded in number King Edward's by twenty thousand men'). O's numbers, however, are closer to those for Towton: 50,000 for Lancaster and 48,000 for York. A related issue may be that each chronicle reports Towton in different places. Hall's account (with the figures discussed above) occurs sooner, at the end of his chapter on Henry VI's reign, where it follows information about Mortimer's Cross and second St Albans fairly closely. Holinshed does not report the details of Towton until his new chapter on Edward IV. His account is separated from the previous two battles by a long section at the end of his chapter on Henry VI discussing non-political persons and events. Thus it seems that O, with its figures linked to Towton, followed Hall whereas F followed Holinshed.

2.1.192–95 **No . . . along** In the chronicles, 'incontinent[ly], Edward Earl of March, son and heir to Richard Duke of York, was by the lords in the said council assembled [called by Edward to restate the Yorkist claim], named, elected, and admitted for king' (Hall, Ggv^r; Holinshed Qqqv^r). The suggestion for Edward's 'proclamation' perhaps comes from the passage which follows: 'the Lord Falconbridge . . . wisely declared to the multitude [of Warwick's people and substantial citizens gathered in St John's field] the offences and breaches of the late agreement done and perpetrated by King Henry the Sixth, and demanded of the people whether they would have the said King Henry to rule . . . to whom they, with a whole voice, answered "Nay, nay". Then he asked them, if they would serve, love, and obey the Earl of March. . . . To which question they answered, "Yea, yea", crying, "King Edward", with many great shouts and clapping of hands' (Ggv$^{r–v}$, Qqqv^r).

2.2.11 ff. Several of Clifford's images derive from a later formal oration (note Henry's 'orator', l. 43) in which Warwick defends his family honour and publicly vows revenge against Edward after being betrayed by Edward in the marriage negotiations with Lady Bona: 'What worm is touched, and will not once turn again? What beast is struck, that will not roar or sound? What innocent child is hurt that will not cry? If the poor and unreasonable beasts, if the silly babes that lack discretion, groan against harm to them proffered, how ought an honest man to be angry when things that touch his honesty be daily against him attempted? But if a mean person in that case be angry, how much more ought a nobleman to fume and stir coals' (Hall Iiiv^r, Holinshed Rrriv^r).

2.2.58 **knighthood** Following second St Albans 'When Queen Margaret had thus well sped, first she caused the King to dub Prince Edward his [Holinshed = "her"] son, knight' (Hall Ggiv^r, Holinshed Qqqiv^v). O reads 'your princely son'.

2.2.71 **Proclaims . . . to him** 'this King Edward the Fourth which was so beloved and favoured of the people that no man was spoken of, no person was remembered, but only he . . . for his liberality, clemency, integrity, and courage, that above all other he was extolled and praised to the very heaven. By reason whereof men of all ages and of all degrees to him daily repaired, some offering themselves and their men to jeopard their lives with him, and other plenteously gave him money to support his charges and maintain his war' (Hall only, Ggv^v–vi^r). F diminishes this positive account, which seems closer to O. See Introduction, pp. 70–3.

2.2.73–6 **I . . . stay** 'Fortune that day [second St Albans] so favoured the Queen that her part prevailed' (Hall only, Ggiv^r). And then: 'Thus was the Queen fortunate [Hall = "happy"] in her two battles, but unfortunate was the King in all his enterprises; for where his person was present, the victory still fled from him to the contrary ["other" = Hall] part' (Holinshed Qqqiv^v, Hall Ggiv^r). Followed by the passage in n. to 58 above. See also n. to 2.1.122–8 above.

2.2.90 **You . . . crown** 'Queen Margaret, whose breath ruled, and whose word was obeyed above the King and his council, within this realm of England . . .' (Hall Eeiv^v, Holinshed Pppiii^r). 'These true tales [of Yorkist recovery after second St Albans] turned the Queen's purpose . . . in so much that she little trusting Essex, and less Kent, but London least of all, with her husband and son departed from St Albans into the North country, where the root and foundation of her aid and refuge only consisted' (Hall Ggiv^v). '[Before Northampton] the Queen perceiving her puissance to be able to match in fight with the adversaries, took upon her to encourage her friends and well-willers; for the King studied of nothing but of peace, quietness, and solitary life' (Holinshed Pppiii^v, and see note to 2.6.74; Hall Ffiv^v). '[T]he Lord Bonville, and Sir Thomas Kiriell of Kent . . . at the Queen's departing from [second] Saint Albans, they were both beheaded, though contrary to the mind and promise of her husband' (Holinshed Qqqiv^v, Hall Ggiv^v).

2.3.9 **hope . . . despair** 'And first of all [before Towton, Edward] made proclamation that no prisoner should be taken' (Holinshed Qqqvi^v and marginal note 'An heavy proclamation'). Later, 'this battle was sore fought, for hope of life was set on side on every part and taking of prisoners was proclaimed as a great offence, by reason whereof every man determined either to conquer or to die in the field' (Hall Ggvii^r, Holinshed Qqqvi^v–Rrri^r and marginal note, 'The obstinate minds of both parts').

2.3.24 **I'll . . . fly** Warwick in an act of furious blood-sacrifice vowed to revenge his brother. See the chronicle account in note to 2.1.42.1, which continues, 'because I see no succours of the world, I remit the vengeance and punishment to God . . . and with that [he] lighted down and slew his horse with his sword, saying, "Let him flee that will, for surely I will tarry with him that will tarry with me", and kissed the cross of his sword' (Hall Ggvi^r, Holinshed Qqqvi^v).

2.3.49–53 **Yet . . . games** 'The lusty King Edward perceiving the courage of his trusty friend the Earl of Warwick, made proclamation that all men which were afraid to fight should depart, and to all men that tarried the battle he promised great rewards with this addition, that if any soldier, which voluntarily would abide, and in, or before the conflict fly or turn his back, that then he that could kill him should have a great remuneration and double wages' (Hall Ggvi^{r-v}). This was the version followed by O, which reads

> Then let us haste to cheer the soldiers' hearts,
> And call them pillars that will stand to us
> And highly promise to remunerate
> Their trusty service, in these dangerous wars.

Holinshed, on the other hand replaces 'remuneration' with 'reward', which is F's term, probably because it suits the traditionally non-monetary awards of laurels to Olympian champions.

2.5.125 **friends are fled** '[King Henry] hearing of the irrecuperable loss of his friends [Holinshed = "irrecoverable loss of his army"], departed incontinent with his wife and son to the town of Berwick, and leaving the Duke of Somerset there, came to the King's court of Scotland' (Hall Ggvii^v, Holinshed Rrri^r). In O's version of this moment, Margaret refers to 'our friends are murdered', while Prince Edward says 'O father fly, our men have left the field', a line slightly closer to Holinshed's wording, and which supplies exact information about Henry's army not given in F.

2.6.0.1 *wounded* At Dintingdale after Ferrybridge 'the Lord Clifford, either for heat or pain, putting off his gorget, suddenly with an arrow (as some say) without an head was stricken into the throat and incontinent rendered his spirit. . . . This end had he which slew the young Earl of Rutland, kneeling on his knees' (Hall Ggvi^v, Holinshed Qqqvi^v).
2.6.8 **And . . . sun** A badge of York and perhaps suggested by a later passage in which Warwick has switched sides to the Lancastrians: 'because that the absence of the Earl of Warwick made the common people daily more and more to long and be desirous to have the sight of him, and presently to behold his personage. For they judged that the sun was clearly taken from the world, when he was absent' (Hall Kkiv^r).
2.6.53 **room** 'After this great victory [at Towton], King Edward rode to York . . . and first he caused the heads of his father, the Earl of Salisbury, and other his friends to be taken from the gates and to be buried with their bodies. And there he caused the Earl of Devonshire and three other to be beheaded and set their heads in the same place' (Hall Ggvii^{r-v}, Holinshed Rrri^r). See also ll. 84–5.

2.6.74 **Where's . . . now** Later in a section focusing on Margaret's preparations for the Battle of Barnet, the chronicles repeat this epithet: 'And of
[Somerset's] own free will, if she would take upon her the name of captain
against her enemies, as she before that often times had enterprised, he
offered a great power' (Hall Mmvi^v).

2.6.86–7 **London . . . king** 'Prosperous fortune and glorious victory . . . in
the mortal battle fought at Towton . . . he being encouraged and set up
. . . began to draw to him and to take his part after the fashion and manner
of a triumphant conqueror and victorious champion, with great pomp
returned to London' (Hall Hhi^r, Holinshed Rrri^r).

2.6.89 **Lady Bona . . . queen** In 1463 Warwick 'came to King Louis the
Eleventh . . . and with great honour was there received . . . of whom, for
King Edward his master, he demanded to have in marriage the Lady Bona
. . . sister to the Lady Charlotte, then French queen. . . . This marriage
seemed politicly devised . . . that by this marriage Queen Margaret . . .
should have no aid, succour, nor any comfort of the French king. . . .
Wherefore Queen Charlotte much desirous to advance her blood and prog-
eny, and especially to so great a prince as King Edward was, obtained both
the good will of the King her husband, and also of her sister' (Hall Hhv^{r-v}).
See also 3.3.55–7. Holinshed offers a much shorter version of Warwick's
mission, omitting the perspective of French female self-interest, although
it still reports that Queen Charlotte negotiated on behalf, and secured the
assent, of King Louis and Bona (Rrrii^r).

3.1.12.1 *prayer book* 'When King Henry was somewhat settled in the
realm of Scotland, he sent his wife and his son into France to King René
her father. . . . But whether it were his destiny or his folly, he so impru-
dently demeaned himself that within short space he came into the hands
of his mortal enemies' (Hall Ggvii^v); 'for he himself, whether he was past
all fear, or that he was not well established in his wits and perfect mind, or
for that he could not long keep himself secret, in disguised attire [Hall =
"apparel"] boldly entered into England. He was no sooner entered but he
was known and taken of one Cantlow and brought toward the King'
(Holinshed Rrrii^r, Hall Hhiii^v).

3.2.1–7 **St Albans . . . life** Grey was in fact a Lancastrian, but the chronicle accounts are unclear about the side on which he was killed: 'In this
battle were slain 23,000 men . . . of whom no nobleman is remembered,
save Sir John Grey, which the same day was made knight' (Hall Ggiv^r,
Holinshed Qqqiv^v). Shakespeare may have mistakenly called him Richard
because that was the name of Lady Grey's father: 'the King being on hunting in the forest of Wychwood beside Stony Stratford . . . where the
Duchess of Bedford sojourned, then wife to Sir Richard Woodville, Lord

Rivers, on whom then was attending a daughter of hers, called Dame Elizabeth Grey, widow of Sir John Grey' (Hall Hhv^v, Holinshed Rrrii^v). '[W]hen that King Edward was king . . . this poor lady made suit to the King to be restored to such small lands as her husband had given her in jointure' (Hall CCvi^r, Holinshed Bbbbi^v, based on Sir Thomas More's *History of Richard III*. Holinshed records a much briefer account). For 'conqueror' see note to 2.6.86–7.

3.2.26–33 **How . . . give us leave** '[W]hen the King beheld and heard her speak, as she was both fair and of good favour, moderate of stature, well made and very wise, he not alonely pitied her, but also waxed enamoured on her, and taking her secretly aside began to enter into talking more familiarly' (Hall CCvi^r, Holinshed Bbbbi^v). Compare Hall's account, which Shakespeare seems also to have followed in certain phrases and details: 'This widow having a suit to the King . . . found such grace in the King's eyes that he not only favoured her suit but much more fantasied her person, for she was a woman more of formal countenance than of excellent beauty, but yet of such beauty and favour that with her sober demeanour, lovely looking, and feminine smiling (neither too wanton nor too humble), beside her tongue so eloquent and her wit so pregnant . . .' (Hhv^v).

3.2.51 **red as fire** '[W]here he was a little before heated with the dart of Cupido, he was now set all on a hot burning fire' (Hall Hhv^v).

3.2.59 **mean** '[W]hose appetite when she perceived, she virtuously denied him, but that she did so wisely and that with so good manner and words so well set that she rather kindled his desire than quenched it' (Hall CCvi^r, Holinshed Bbbbi^r).

3.2.86 **sovereignty** '[S]he was able to ravish the mind of a mean person when she allured and made subject to her the heart of so great a king' (Hall Hhv^v). (Compare O's version of l. 84, 'Her looks are all replete with majesty'.) 'After that King Edward had well considered all the lineaments of her body and the wise and womanly demeanour that he saw in her, he determined first to attempt if he might provoke her to be his sovereign lady' (Hall Hhv^v). Also 'he finally resolved with himself to marry her' (Holinshed Rrrii^v; Hall and More's word is 'determined').

3.2.97 **mean** 'And finally . . . she well espied the King his affection toward her so greatly increased. . . . And in conclusion she showed him plain that as she wist herself too simple to be his wife, so thought she herself too good to be his concubine. The King much marvelling of her constancy, as she that had not been wont elsewhere so straitly said nay [*sic*], so much esteemed her continency and chastity that he set her virtue in stead of possession and richesse; and thus taking counsel of his own desire, determined in haste to marry her' (Hall CCvi^{r-v}, based on More).

3.2.99 **cavil . . . queen** '[He] affirming farther that if she would thereunto condescend, she might so fortune of his paramour and concubine to be changed to his wife and lawful bedfellow' (Hall Hhv^v).

3.2.104 **some** Edward's mother objected strongly to the match and was not easily convinced. Edward wrote to persuade her: 'That she is a widow and hath already children, by God his Blessed Lady, I am a bachelor and have some too, and so each of us hath a proof that neither of us is like to be barren' (Hall DDi^r, based on More).

3.2.109 **muse what chat** 'And after that he was thus appointed and had between them twain ensured her, then asked he counsel of his secret friends, and that in such manner that they might easily perceive that it booted not to say nay' (Hall CCvi^v, based on More).

3.2.120 **Tower** See n. to ll. 3.1.12.1 above. After being apprehended by Cantlow, Henry was by 'the Earl of Warwick met on the way . . . and brought him through London, to the Tower, and there he was laid in sure hold' (Hall Hhiii^v, Holinshed Rrrii^r).

3.2.127 **cross . . . look for** 'Friend and foe was much what indifferent where his advantage grew, he spared no man's death whose life withstood his purpose. . . . And they that thus deem, think that he long time in Kings [*sic*] Edward's life forethought to be king, in case that the King his brother (whose life he looked that evil diet should shorten) should happen to decease . . . while his children were young' (Holinshed Uvvvi^v, quoting More's *History of Richard III*; Hall offers an abridged version).

3.2.161 **chaos** 'Richard . . . was in wit and courage equal with the other [brothers], but in beauty and lineaments of nature far underneath both, for he was little of stature, evil-featured of limbs, crook backed, the left shoulder much higher than the right, hard favoured of visage, such as in estates is called a warlike visage . . . He was malicious, wrathful, and envious, and as it is reported, his mother the Duchess had much ado in her travail that she could not be delivered of him uncut' (Hall AAi^v, based on More).

3.2.182–5 **Why . . . occasions** 'He was close and secret, a deep dissimuler, lowly of countenance, arrogant of heart, outwardly familiar where he inwardly hated, not letting [refraining] to kiss whom he thought to kill' (Hall AAi^v, based on More). See also 5.7.32–4.

3.3.1–14 **Margaret . . . cares** 'Queen Margaret his wife, hearing of the captivity of her husband, mistrusting the chance of her son, all desolate and comfortless, departed out of Scotland, and sailed into France' (Hall Hhiii^v, Holinshed Rrrii^r). While the image of fallen fortune (also ll. 16–18) is conventional, it seems to have been suggested by Hall's later remarks, which expand on Margaret's grief when she learns of the Yorkist victory at Barnet and Edward's reclaiming of the crown: 'Such an unstable and blind goddess is Fortune, for when he that sitteth highest on the wheel falleth to the ground, all that be underneath fall also and can neither have aid nor help of her, nor yet of themselves' (Hhiv^r).

3.3.9–12 **ground . . . seat . . . despair** 'When she heard all these miserable chances and misfortunes so suddenly one in another's neck, . . . she like a woman all dismayed for fear fell to the ground, her heart was pierced with sorrow, her speech was in manner passed, all her spirits were tormented with melancholy. The calamity and misery of her time she detested and abhorred, her unstable and contrariant fortune she steadfastly blamed and accused, her painful labour, her care of mind, turned into infelicity she much lamented and bewailed . . . her senses were so vexed . . . that she preferred death before life, rather desiring sooner to die than longer to live' (Hall Mmv^v–vi^r).

3.3.32, 148 **aid** In 1461 'Queen Margaret thus being in France did obtain and impetrate of the young French king that all fautors [= supporters] and lovers of her husband and the Lancastrial band might safely and surely have resort into any part of the realm . . . prohibiting all other of the contrary faction' (Hall Ggvii^v, Holinshed Rrri^r).

3.3.44 **boldly** In 1463 Warwick 'came to King Louis the Eleventh . . . lying at Tours, and with great honour was there received . . . of whom, for King Edward his master, he demanded to have in marriage the Lady Bona, daughter to Louis Duke of Savoy' (Hall Hhv^r, Holinshed Rrrii^r).

3.3.55–7 **nuptial . . . marriage** See note to 2.6.89.

3.3.116 **pawn my credit** After hearing news of Edward's marriage to Lady Grey in 1465, '[Warwick] was not a little troubled in his mind, for that he took it his credence thereby was greatly minished and his honour much stained' (Holinshed Rrrii^v. Both he and Hall expand this reaction later in Warwick's oration publicly declaring his opposition to Edward, Ii.iv^r).

3.3.154 **father . . . you** When Warwick was negotiating on behalf of Edward in 1463, 'Queen Margaret . . . and Prince Edward . . . were then sojourning at Angiers with old Duke René of Anjou her father, writing himself King of Naples, Sicily, and Jerusalem, having as much profits of the letters of his glorious style, as rents and revenues out of the said large and rich realms' (Hall Hhv^r, Holinshed Rrrii^r mentions only that she 'remained [in France] with her father Duke René').

3.3.157 **setter-up . . . kings** Warwick's oration against Edward ends: 'I will surely spend my life, land, and goods in setting up that just and good man King Henry the Sixth and in deposing this untrue, unfaithful, and unkind prince, by our only means called King Edward the Fourth' (Hall Ii.iv^v, Holinshed Rrriv^r).

3.3.181 **protest** 'But when the Earl of Warwick had perfect knowledge by the letters of his trusty friends that King Edward had gotten him a new wife, and that all that he had done with King Louis in his embassade for the conjoining of this new affinity was both frustrated and vain, he was earnestly moved and sore chafed' (Hall Hhvi^{r-v}, Holinshed Rrrii^v, omitting 'and that . . . vain').

3.3.184, 190–7, 212 Wording and details again deriving from Warwick's oration: 'consider that our name, chief title, and principal authority, was to us given by King Henry the Sixth and not by him. But if every man will remember who first took part with [Edward's] father when he claimed the crown. . . . All this brethren you know to be true; the dishonour of one is the dishonour of us all. . . . Wherefore rather than I will live unrevenged or suffer him to reign, which hath sought my decay and dishonour, I will surely . . . (Hall Ii.iv^{r-v}). (Passage continues in note to l. 157.)

3.3.209 **fall from** 'The Earl of Warwick . . . [who] either perceived by other or had perfect knowledge of himself that the Duke of Clarence bare not the best will to King Edward his brother . . . thought first . . . to open to him (if he saw him flexible to his purpose) the secret imaginations of his stomach, thinking that if he might by policy or promise allure the Duke to his party, that King Edward should be destitute' (Hall Ii.iv^v, Holinshed (in a briefer version) Rrriv^r).

3.3.210 **wanton** 'But though the Earl of Warwick was earnestly inflamed against the King, for that he . . . having regard only to the satisfying of his wanton appetite more than to his honour or surety of his estate' (Holinshed only, Rrrii^v).

3.3.231–2 **Tell . . . long** Continuing the passage quoted in note to l. 181: '[Warwick] thought it necessary that King Edward should be deposed from his crown and royal dignity, as an inconstant prince, not worthy of such a kingly office' (Hall Hhvi^v only).

3.3.238 **supply** '[T]he Earl . . . not a little regarding such an offer . . . determined with the Duke [of Clarence] and the Earls of Oxford and Pembroke (because Queen Margaret and her son were not fully yet furnished for such a journey) to go before with part of the navy and part of the army . . . then should Queen Margaret and her son with the residue of the navy and people follow into England' (Hall Kkvi^v, Holinshed Rrrvi^r, omitting 'not . . . offer' and 'then . . . England').

3.3.243–9 **I'll . . . thine** King Louis' aid followed a league concluded by this marriage: 'for the more sure foundation of the new amity, Edward Prince of Wales wedded Anne second daughter to the Earl of Warwick' (Hall Kkv^v, Holinshed Rrrv^v).

3.3.253 **Lord Bourbon** In 1470 'the French king lent both ships, men, and money unto Queen Margaret and to her partakers, and ["that they might the surer sail into England" = Hall only] he appointed the Bastard of Bourbon, Admiral of France, with a great navy to defend them against the navy of the Duke of Burgundy' (Holinshed Rrrvi^r, Hall Kkvi^{r-v}, which reads 'Burgundy' in error for 'Bourbon', and 'them' for 'unto . . . partakers').

3.3.256, 266 **mocking . . . mockery** 'The French king and his queen were not a little discontent . . . to have their sister first demanded and then granted and in conclusion rejected, and apparently mocked without any cause reasonable' (Hall only, Hhvi^r). See also 4.1.31.

4.1.18 hasty . . . well 'When this marriage was once blown abroad . . . noblemen detested and disdained it, the common people grudged and murmured at it, and all with one voice said that [Edward's] unadvised wooing, hasty loving, and too speedy marriage were neither meet for him being a king, nor consonant to the honour of so high an estate' (Hall only, Hhvi^r).

4.1.37–9 Yet . . . marriage 'This marriage seemeth politicly devised. . . . King Edward therefore thought it necessary, to have affinity in France, and especially by the [French] Queen's sister' (Hall Hhv^r, Holinshed Rrrii^r).

4.1.53–5 heir . . . Clarence In 1465 at her coronation, Queen Elizabeth's 'brother Lord Anthony, was married to the sole heir of Thomas Lord Scales, and by her he was Lord Scales' (Hall Hhvi^r, Holinshed Rrrii^v). Clarence continues: ' "This you know well enough, that the heir of the Lord Scales he hath married to his wife's brother, the heir also of the Lord Bonville and Harrington he hath given to his wife's son, and the heir of the Lord Hungerford he hath granted to the Lord Hastings—three marriages more meeter for his two brethren and kin than for such new foundlings . . . I swear, if my brother of Gloucester would join with me, we would make him know that we were all three one man's sons, of one mother and one lineage descended, which should be more preferred and promoted than strangers of his wife's blood" ' (Hall only, Ii.iv^v).

4.1.56 bury brotherhood When Warwick perceived Clarence's discontent (see note to 3.3.209), he 'began to complain to the Duke' of Edward's duplicity. Clarence 'in a great fury answered, "Why my lord, think you to have him kind to you that is unkind, yea, and unnatural to me being his own brother . . . ? Think you that he will exalt and promote his cousin or ally, which little careth for the fall or confusion of his own line and lineage?" ' (Hall only, Ii.iv^v).

4.1.57–8 heir . . . wife's son 'Sir Thomas Grey, son to Sir John Grey the Queen's first husband, was created Marquis Dorset and married to Cecily, heir to the Lord Bonville' (Hall Hhvi^r, Holinshed Rrrii^v).

4.1.118–22 Belike . . . yourself '[T]o win the Duke's heart the Earl . . . offered him his eldest daughter (being of ripe age and elegant stature) in marriage, with the whole half-deal of his wife's inheritance . . . [and for whom] . . . the Duke of Clarence, being in amours, had no small affection' (Hall Ii.v^r; Holinshed Rrriv^r, varies the last phrase '. . . (being in love with her person) had great desire').

4.1.123–7 You . . . happen 'When King Edward (to whom all the doings of the Earl of Warwick, and the Duke his brother were manifest and overt, and were come to that point that he expected and looked for) was by diverse letters sent to him certified that the great army of the Northern men were with all speed coming toward London . . .' (Hall Ii.vi^r). Holinshed's variant wording lays less stress on the openness of Warwick's and Clarence's plans: 'King Edward having perfect knowledge of all the doings of the Earl . . .' (Rrriv^v).

4.1.128–32 **haste . . . you** Both chroniclers continue: 'Therefore in great haste he sent to William Lord Herbert . . . Earl of Pembroke that he should without delay encounter with the Northern men with the extremity of all his power. . . . And to assist and furnish him with archers, was appointed Humphrey Lord Stafford' (Hall Ii.vi^r, Holinshed Rrriv^v).

4.1.133–41 **Montague . . . suspect** '[T]he Lord Marquis could by no means be reduced to take any part against King Edward till the Earl [of Warwick] had both promised him great rewards and high promotions, and also assured him of the aid and power of the greatest princes of the realm. Even as [he] unwillingly, and in manner coacted, gave his consent to this unhappy conjuration . . . so with a faint heart and less courage he always showed himself enemy to King Edward, except in his last day' (Hall Ii.iv^v, Holinshed Rrriii^v). In Holinshed this passage comes before Warwick's complaint about Edward's mistreatment rather than after. Later when both chroniclers report Montague acting on behalf of the King in efficiently putting down a small rebellion in York stirred up by Warwick, they consider his motives: 'Some say he did it to the intent that he would seem faultless and innocent of all his brother's doings. . . . But other affirm and say that he, for all his promise made to his brother, was then deliberately determined to take part with King Edward, with whom . . . he in small space entered into great grace and high favour' (Ii.v^v, Rrriv^v). In a different context, Holinshed also mentions that Edward's appointment of Montague's brother George Neville to the Archbishopric of York was 'more for the love of the Marquis Montague than for any favour he bare to the Earl of Warwick' (Holinshed Rrriii^r).

4.2.2 **by numbers** Edward likewise assembled a 'great army', but only Hall adds that 'ever as he went forward his company increased, because he commanded it to be noised and published to the common people that his only intent was to destroy . . . such pernicious persons as would disturb and bring in thraldom the quiet commons and peaceable people' (Kki^v).

4.2.3 **Clarence comes** 'The Earl of Warwick . . . sent in all haste possible to the Duke of Clarence (which was not far from him with a great power) requiring him that both their hosts might join in one. . . . The Duke hearing these news, in good order of battle came and encamped himself with the Earl's host' (Hall Kki^v, Holinshed more briefly Rrrv^r). Neither chronicler mentions Somerset at this point.

4.2.14 **carelessly** Each chronicle gives a different reason for Edward's carelessness, however. Hall states that after a mutual exchange of letters 'declaring their griefs' and using friends as go-betweens 'to common of peace', 'the King conceiving a certain hope of peace in his own imagination, took both less heed to himself and also less feared the outward attempts of his enemies, thinking and trusting truly that all things were at a good point and should be well pacified' (Kki^v). Holinshed explains that 'the King (because they [he and Warwick's party] were entered into terms by way of communication to have a peace) took small heed to himself, nothing doubting any outward attempt of his enemies' (Rrrv^r).

4.3 'The capture of the king [Edward] here depicted took place in July, 1469, before Warwick's reconciliation with King Henry and without the aid of French soldiers. In March, 1470, Edward suddenly regained his power, and Warwick was obliged to flee to France. Here he united with the Lancastrians, and in September (1470) he landed at Dartmouth, accompanied by French troops. Edward then found himself deserted by his followers and fled to Holland' (Brooke, note to 4.3.22.1). See also note to 4.5.21.

4.3.4–6 for . . . suppressed Possibly suggested by 'The King likewise sore thrusting to recover his loss late sustained [after Edgecote field], and desirous to be revenged of the deaths and murders of his lords and friends' (Hall only, Kki^v, preceding the passage quoted in note to 4.2.2).

4.3.27.1–3 *Warwick . . . them* This stage action apparently derives from the turning point of the Battle of Edgecote field, when one of Warwick's captains, John Clapham, gathered a local force from Northampton and surrounding villages, 'having borne before them the standard of the Earl with the White Bear, crying "a Warwick a Warwick". The [Yorkist] Welshmen thinking that the Earl of Warwick had come on them with all his puissance, suddenly as men amazed fled' (Hall Kki^r, Holinshed Rrriv^v–v^r).

4.3.32 embassade While Warwick's list of charges relate to previously staged or reported events, his speech also recalls his oration declaring his public support for the Lancastrians: ' "Let these [previous charges] overpass, and speak of the ungentle, untrue, and unprincely handling of me in the last embassade, being sent to the French king" ' (Hall Ii.iv^r, Holinshed Rrriv^r).

4.3.39 study . . . welfare Contradicts reports by both chroniclers that Edward IV governed well, but agrees with Warwick's oration against him: ' "King Edward . . . is a man contumelious, opprobrious, and an injurious person . . . now detesting to take any pain for the preferment or maintenance of the public wealth of this realm, but all given to pastime, pleasure, and dalliance" ' (Hall Ii.iii^v, Holinshed Rrriv^r).

4.3.52–3 conveyed . . . York '[T]o the intent that the King's friends might not know where he was . . . [Warwick] caused him by secret journeys in the night to be conveyed to Middleham Castle in Yorkshire, and there to be kept under the custody of the Archbishop of York' (Hall Kki^v, Holinshed Rrrv^r).

4.4 'But what might be the heaviness of this lady's heart (think we) upon consideration of so many counterblasts of unhappiness inwardly conceived? Her husband had taken flight, his adherents and her friends sought to shroud themselves under the covert of a new protector, she driven in distress forsook not that simple refuge which her hard hap forced upon her; and (a king's wife) wanted in her necessity such things as mean men's wives had in superfluity, and (a corrosive to a noble mind) a prince of renowned parentage was by constraint of unkind fortune not vouchsafed the solemnity of Christendom due and decent for so honourable a personage [referring to her son's christening "with small pomp like a poor man's child"]' (Holinshed only, Sssi^r).

4.4.17–19 wean . . . passion By contrast with F's stoical and more politically discerning Elizabeth, O's is 'passionate', despairing, and grief-stricken. Rivers is also the stronger presence in O, and his remark, 'King Edward's noble mind his honours doth display', echoes Holinshed in the passage previously quoted. On the other hand three of his later lines seem to follow Hall's account:

> Yet comfort yourself, for Edward hath more friends
> Than Lancaster at this time must perceive,
> That some will set him in his throne again.
> *Queen.* God grant they may . . .

'But all King Edward's trusty friends went to diverse sanctuaries, daily looking and hourly hearkening to hear of his health and prosperous return, who afterward served him manfully and truly. Amongst other, Queen Elizabeth his wife, almost desperate of all comfort, took sanctuary at Westminster' (Llii^v–iii^r).

4.5.0.1 Stanley 'King Edward being thus in captivity spake ever fair to the Archbishop and to the other keepers; but whether he corrupted them with money or fair promises, he had liberty diverse days to go on hunting, and one day on a plain, there met with him Sir William Stanley, Sir Thomas of Borough, and diverse other of his friends with such a great band of men that neither his keepers would, nor once durst, move him to return to prison again' (Hall Kki^v–ii^r, Holinshed Rrrv^r).

4.5.11 colour . . . game In Hall the remark about Edward possibly bribing his keepers relates to gaining his freedom to hunt. Holinshed, however, repositions this remark to follow the description of Edward's escape, thereby suggesting that while his liberty was owing to the Archbishop's clemency, his rescue was the result of the keepers' complicity with Stanley. Holinshed alone also remarks, 'and therefore [because of money or promises given, the keepers] suffered him thus to scape out of danger' (Rrrv^r). In Shakespeare, however, the keeper is innocent of Edward and Gloucester's plan.

4.5.21 **Lynn** Edward actually progressed to London and was met there by Warwick, where the parties failed to settle their differences. In March 1470, following a Yorkist victory at Lose-coat Field, Warwick and Clarence departed for France. They returned to England on 13 September with troops supplied by the French king (preparations for which Shakespeare represents as the upshot of Warwick's abortive mission to Lady Bona in 3.3). Edward fled the country because popular support for Warwick had grown and he was unable to raise an army: 'King Edward being in this perplexity . . . wherefore his near friends advised and admonished him to fly over the sea to the Duke of Burgundy, his brother-in-law. . . . [With] all haste possible [he] passed the washes (in greater jeopardy than it beseemed a prince to be in) and came to the town of Lynn, where he found an English ship and two hulks of Holland ready (as fortune would) to make sail' (Hall Lli^v, Holinshed Rrrvi^r).

4.6.0.3 *Montague* The chronicles mention several times Montague's switching back and forth between Warwick and Edward, first when Warwick publicly declares himself against the Yorkists and manages to persuade the Archbishop of York and Clarence: 'But the Lord Marquis could by no means be reduced to take any part against King Edward till the Earl had both promised him great rewards and high promotions, and also assured him of the aid and power of the greatest princes of the realm. Even as the Marquis unwillingly, and in manner coacted, gave his consent . . . so with a faint heart and less courage he always showed himself enemy to King Edward, except in his last day' (Hall Ii.iv^v, Holinshed Rrriii^v). Later in 1470 following Edward's victory at Lose-cote Field, Montague surrendered himself, obtained a pardon, and was 'courteously received' (Holinshed Rrrv^v, Hall Kkv^v). Then after Warwick reinstated Henry as king (see next note), 'To this Parliament came the Lord Marquis Montague, excusing himself that only for fear of death he declined to King Edward's part, which excuse was so accepted, [Hall alone continues] that he obtained his pardon, which after was the destruction of him and his brother; for if he had manfully and apertly taken King Edward's part, surely he being an open enemy had much less hurted than being a feigned, false, and a coloured friend' (Hall Lliv^r, Holinshed Sssi^v). When Edward later returned from Flanders to England, Montague lent him passive support by allowing him to pass unmolested, against Warwick's orders (Hall Mmi^r, Holinshed Sssii$^{r–v}$).

4.6.5 enlargement 'Upon the twelfth day of October [1470, Warwick] rode to the Tower of London [Hall adds "which was to him without resistance delivered"] and there took King Henry the Sixth out of the ward. . . . And the twenty-fifth day . . . the Duke of Clarence accompanied with the Earls of Warwick, Shrewsbury, and the Lord Stanley, and other lords and gentlemen, some for fear and some for love, and some only to gaze at the wavering world, resorted with a great company to the Tower of London, and [Hall adds "with great pomp"] brought King Henry the Sixth apparelled in a long gown of blue velvet, through [Hall "the high streets of"] London to the cathedral church of St Paul' (Hall Lliii^r, Holinshed Sssi^r). O's staging follows Hall's version of this event.

4.6.14 notes . . . harmony The metaphor is Shakespeare's, but both chronicles mention that when Henry was released from the Tower and installed in the Bishop of London's palace, he 'there kept his household like a king' (Hall Lliii^r, Holinshed Sssi^r).

4.6.27 wise as virtuous A passage that immediately follows in Hall assesses Henry's character and his imminent return to 'accustomed captivity and usual misery. This ill chance and misfortune by many men's opinions happened to him because he was man of no great wit, such as men commonly call an innocent man, neither a fool, neither very wise, whose study always was more to excel other in godly living and virtuous example than in worldly regiment or temporal dominion, in so much that in comparison to the study and delectation that he had to virtue and godliness he little regarded, but in manner despised, all worldly power and temporal authority' (Lliii^r).

4.6.54–5 Edward . . . confiscate 'When King Henry had thus obtained again the possession and dominion of the realm, he called his high court of Parliament . . . in the which King Edward was declared a traitor to his country . . . and all his goods were confiscate' (Hall Lliii^v, Holinshed Sssi^r–v).

4.6.60–1 Margaret . . . for 'Queen Margaret . . . when she knew by her husband's letters [Edward's overthrow] to be obtained, she with Prince Edward her son and her train entered their ships to take their voyage into England; but the winter was so sore, the weather so stormy . . . that she was fain to take land again and defer her journey till another season' (Hall Lliv^r, Holinshed Sssi^v).

4.6.68 England's hope 'About the same season, Jasper [Tudor, Richmond's uncle] Earl of Pembroke went into Wales . . . where he found Lord Henry son to his brother Edmund Earl of Richmond, having not full ten years of age, he being kept in manner like a captive, but honourably brought up by the Lady Herbert' (Holinshed Sssi^v, Hall Lliv^r). Hall adds 'This Lord Henry was he that . . . obtained the crown and regality of this realm, whom we ought to believe to be sent from God and of him only to be provided a king, for to extinguish both the factions and parts of King Henry the Sixth and of King Edward the Fourth' (Lliv^r).

4.7.5–6 passed . . . Burgundy When Edward sought the Duchess of Burgundy's aid, her husband 'to blind withal the French king . . . declared openly that he would in no wise minister any succours to King Edward, straitly charging . . . that no man should once pass the sea with him . . . notwithstanding when the Duke saw that King Edward, upon the hope of his friends, would needs repair into England again . . . [he] caused privily to be delivered to him fifty thousand florins . . . and further caused four great ships to be appointed for him' (Hall Llvi^{r–v}, Holinshed Sssi^v–ii^r). The phrase 'pass the seas' occurs twice in the passage from Holinshed that Shakespeare seems to have consulted for the part played by the Mayor in this scene; see note to l. 34.1 below.

4.7.8–9.1 haven . . . *gates* 'King Edward being thus furnished . . . sailed into England and came on the coast of Yorkshire to a place called Ravenspur' (Hall Llvi^v). Hearing of this, Warwick 'wrote to all the towns of Yorkshire and to the city also, commanding all men . . . to shut their gates against the King's enemies' (Hall Mmi^r, Holinshed Sssii^{r–v}).

4.7.16.1 *on the walls* 'King Edward, without any words spoken to him, came peaceably near to York, of whose coming when the citizens were certified, without delay they armed themself and came to defend the gates, sending to him two of the chiefest aldermen of the city, which earnestly admonished him on their behalf to come not one foot nearer . . .' (Hall Mmi^r). Shakespeare has added the Mayor's role from an earlier passage in Holinshed describing a similar confrontation between Edward and the citizens of Exeter. See note to l. 34.1 below.

4.7.23 challenge 'King Edward . . . was not a little troubled and unquieted [at being rebuffed] . . . but with lowly words and gentle entreatings . . . [declared] that he came neither to demand the realm of England . . . but only the duchy of York his old inheritance' (Hall Mmi^{r–v}).

4.7.34.1 *keys* Prior to Holinshed's report of Edward's journey for aid to the Duchess of Burgundy, Abraham Fleming includes John Hooker's account of the Yorkists' twelve-day siege, led by Sir William Courtney, who 'did send his messenger to the mayor and required the gates to be opened and to give him entrance. . . . The mayor and his brethren . . . did so order and handle the matter as that by good speeches and courteous usages' a treaty was negotiated and the Yorkists allowed to enter on 3 April 1470. King Edward with a force of 40,000, accompanied among others by the Duke of Norfolk, the Earl of Wiltshire, the Duke of Buckingham, Lord Hastings, and Lord Stanley, followed on 14 April. 'Who when [they were] come, the mayor did his most humble obeisance . . . congratulating his coming to the city . . . [and] delivered unto the King the keys of the gates and the maces of his office. . . . The keys and the maces [Edward] delivered back to the mayor, and then the mayor took the mace and did bear it through the city bare-headed before the King' (Holinshed Rrrvi^v). The last sentence, indicating the mayor led Edward in procession, is called for by O: 'We thank you all. Lord Mayor lead on the way.'

4.7.39.1 *John* After leaving York on his way to London, Edward passed through Nottingham, 'where came to him . . . Sir Thomas Montgomery and diverse other of his assured friends . . . which caused him at the [Holinshed "their"] first coming to make proclamation in his own name, King Edward the Fourth boldly saying [Holinshed "affirming"] to him, that they would serve no man but a king' (Hall Mmii^r, Holinshed Sssii^v).

4.7.64 **bruit** When it became known that Montgomery *et al.* had joined Edward and that Montague had allowed him to march south unimpeded past Pontefract, 'princes and noblemen on all sides began to fall to him, firmly believing that either the Marquis Montague, bearing favour to King Edward, would not once with him encounter, or that he was afraid' (Hall Mmii^r; Holinshed Sssii^v alternatively attributes Montague's lack of action either to his belief that Edward had come only to claim his dukedom, or to fear).

4.7.86, 4.8.9–18 **doubt . . . day . . . In . . . friends** Edward proceeded from Nottingham towards Warwick, whom he knew 'to be come into Warwickshire, where and in the countries adjoining he was busied in levying an army with the which he purposed to distress him' (Holinshed only, Sssiii^r).

4.8.5 **giddy** Holinshed reports of Warwick's return from France to aid Henry: 'It is almost not to be believed how many thousands men of war . . . resorted unto him . . . and the great repair of people that came flocking in unto him . . .' (Rrrvi^r).

4.8.32.1–33 *Exeunt . . .* **palace** In the chronicle accounts Edward confronts Warwick at Coventry but is unable to draw him out to battle. Instead he persuades Clarence to rejoin his side (represented by 5.1) and departs with a large force towards London. There 'When the Duke of Somerset and other of King Henry's friends, saw the world thus suddenly changed, every man fled . . . leaving King Henry alone, as an host that should be sacrificed, in the Bishop's palace of London' (Hall Mmiii^v). In Holinshed, Somerset and other Lancastrians leave London to meet Queen Margaret's forces arriving from France, and it is the Archbishop of York, perceiving the Londoners 'were now bent in favour of King Edward', who hands over Henry to Edward when he enters the City (Sssiii^v–iv^r).

4.8.52–57.1 **Seize . . .** *Exeter* As Henry 'went from Paul's to Westminster' (Holinshed Sssiv^r). While Holinshed mentions unnamed others being captured with Henry, Hall reports that at the Bishop's palace he 'was by King

Edward taken and again committed to prison and captivity' (Mmiii^v). Both chronicles state that Exeter remained at this time with Warwick, but Hall's report of the latter's reaction to Clarence's betrayal (prior to Henry's seizure in the chronicles, but represented afterwards by Shakespeare) may have been suggestive: 'Lord, how he detested and accursed [Clarence], crying out on him that . . . had shamefully turned his face from his confederates' (Mmiii^r).

5.1 In Hall Edward goes first to the town of Warwick, which the Earl of Warwick has left for Coventry. Edward follows him there, where Warwick awaits reinforcements from Clarence. Edward meets the latter en route and persuades him to switch sides (see below) and together they march towards London. Hall omits a second confrontation with Warwick at Coventry (Mmii^v–iii^r).

5.1.11–13 Clarence . . . Warwick '[H]earing now that his brother King Edward was landed . . . [Clarence] gathered his people, outwardly pretending to pass with them to the aid of the Earl of Warwick . . . although inwardly he meant the contrary. . . . King Edward being then at Warwick, and understanding that his brother of Clarence approached, in an afternoon issued forth of that town' (Holinshed Sssiii^r).

5.1.24 outrages United with his two brothers at Warwick, Edward 'offered large conditions: as a free pardon of life to the Earl and all his people. . . . But the Earl would not accept any offers, except he might have compounded so as it pleased himself' (Holinshed only, Sssiii^r).

5.1.59.1 city gates 'There came to the Earl of Warwick, whilst he lay thus at Coventry (besides the Earl of Oxford), the Duke of Exeter, and the Lord Marquis Montague, by whose coming that side was greatly strengthened' (Holinshed Sssiii^v). Somerset's participation is invented.

5.1.80–2 Come . . . thee Hall and Holinshed offer different reasons for, and action leading to, Clarence's change of loyalties, alternatives reflected in the Folio and Octavo texts. Both chronicles initially report in early 1470 that 'there landed at Calais a damsel, belonging to the Duchess of Clarence . . . [who] persuaded the Duke of Clarence that it was neither natural nor honourable to him either to condescend or take part against the House of York (of which he was lineally descended) and to set up again the House of Lancaster. . . . These reasons . . . so sank in the Duke's stomach that he promised at his return not to be so an extreme enemy to his brother as he was taken for. . . . With this answer the damsel departed into England, the Earl of Warwick thereof being clearly ignorant' (Hall Kkvi^r). Holinshed, however, says this unnamed woman 'persuaded [Clarence] so much to leave off the pursuit of his conceived displeasure towards his brother King Edward', and includes the marginal note 'The promise of the Duke of Clarence' (Rrrvi^r). Later in April Hall reports that when Edward's army met Warwick at Coventry and Clarence approached, 'Richard Duke of Gloucester, brother to them both, as though he had been made arbiter between them, first rode to the Duke and with him communed very secretly; from him he came to King Edward and with like secretness so used him that in conclusion no unnatural war but a fraternal amity was concluded and proclaimed, and . . . both the brethren lovingly embraced, and familiarly communed together'. This corresponds to O's version of events:

> Edward. Et tu Brute, wilt thou stab Caesar too?
> A parley, sirrah, to George of Clarence.
>
> Sound a parley, and Richard and Clarence whispers together, and then Clarence takes his red rose out of his hat, and throws it at Warwick. (E2^r)

Hall then reminds the reader, however, that this was the expected result because of the earlier efforts of the Duchess of Clarence's envoy (Mmii^v–iii^r). He thus asserts that the effect of Richard's actions remains partly or largely determined by the prior agency of the 'damsel'. O transfers this authority entirely to Gloucester.

Holinshed by contrast makes Clarence more inwardly and collectively motivated. He states in a lengthy passage that while Edward was gathering support in Flanders, 'the Duke of Clarence began to weigh with himself the great inconvenience into the which as well his brother King Edward, as himself and his younger brother the Duke of Gloucester were fallen through the dissension betwixt them (which had been compassed and brought to pass by the politic working of the Earl of Warwick)'. He is also counselled by 'right wise and circumspect persons', but 'most specially the Duchess of Burgundy their sister also'. Clarence is persuaded to a reconciliation, but marches to Coventry publicly as Warwick's ally. Holinshed's marginal note at this point states 'The dissimulation of the Duke of Clarence'. When he encounters Edward's army, Clarence meets the King, 'his brother of Gloucester, the Lord Rivers, the Lord Hastings, and a few other . . . and so they met betwixt both the hosts, with so sweet salutations, loving demeanour, and good countenances, as better might not be devised'. Holinshed underscores the fraternal bonds re-established by this 'joyful meeting', recording in the margin 'The brethren meet lovingly together' (Sssiii^{r-v}).

5.1.89 **holy oath** 'After this, King Edward caused to be proclaimed that the Duke and all that came with him should be taken as his true friends. . . . But this notwithstanding, it seemeth that God did neither forgive nor forget to punish the Duke . . . for violating and breaking his oath solemnly and advisedly taken and made to the Earl of Warwick' (Hall only, Mmiii^r).

5.1.99 **brother** Holinshed's emphasis on the reconciliation between Edward and Clarence corresponds with F's singular 'brother' at l. 99, whereas O's 'brothers' reflects Hall's focus on Richard's intervention in reuniting all three: 'the King withal brought the Duke unto his army, whom he saluting in most courteous wise, welcomed them into the land; and they humbly thanking him, did to him such reverence as appertained to the honour of such a worthy personage. . . . And either part showing themselves glad thus to meet as friends with the other, they went lovingly together' (Holinshed Sssiii^v).

5.1.102 **unconstant** Prior to this reconciliation, Hall reports that Edward hoped to persuade Clarence, 'knowing that the Duke was in nothing constant, nor in one mind long permanent' (Mmii^v).

5.1.106 **O . . . unjust** 'But to the Duke's messengers [sent by Edward to entreat a peace, Warwick] gave none other answer but this, that he had liefer be always like himself than like a false and a perjured duke' (Hall Mmiii^r, Holinshed Sssiii^v).

5.1.110 **Barnet** After Edward's party had left Coventry for London to recapture Henry, Warwick 'saw that all cavillations of necessity were now brought to this end, that they must be committed to the hazard and chance of one battle. . . . [He] determined clearly to spend all his riches, yea, and all that he could imagine upon the chance of this battle' (Hall Mmiv^r, Holinshed Sssiv^r). See also 5.2.24–6.

5.2.0.1 *bringing forth* Alternatively, Holinshed also reports that Warwick 'was not slain in the heat of the conflict', but 'coming into a wood where was no passage, one of King Edward's men came to him, killed him, and spoiled him to the naked skin' (Sssv^r).

5.2.28 **live . . . must** 'This end had Richard Neville Earl of Warwick, whose stout stomach . . . after so many strange fortunes . . . caused death before he came . . . to take from him all worldly and mundane affections; but death did one thing that life could not do, for by death he had rest, peace, quietness, and tranquillity, which his life ever abhorred' (Hall only, Mmv^r).

5.2.31 **Queen . . . power** After hearing of Edward's ascendancy and Henry's recapture, Margaret 'gathered together no small company . . . with Prince Edward her son' and crossed the Channel, having to land at Weymouth because of bad weather (Hall Mmv^v, Holinshed Sssv^r). In O, Oxford at this point reports that 'Our warlike Queen with troops is come from France, | And at Southampton landed all her train'. This detail derives from Holinshed: 'The Countess of Warwick, having a ship of advantage, arrived before the other [i.e. Margaret's ships] at Portsmouth, and from thence she went to Southampton, meaning to have gone to Weymouth, where she understood that the Queen was landed; but here had she knowledge of the loss of Barnet field, and that her husband was there slain. Whereupon she went no further . . . but . . . took sanctuary' (Sssv^r).

5.2.33–49 Ah Montague . . . heaven 'The Marquis Montague, thinking to succour his brother [at Barnet], which he saw was in great jeopardy . . . was likewise overthrown and slain' (Hall Mmv^r, Holinshed Sssv^r). Shakespeare's proleptically mournful linking of Warwick's and Montague's deaths may derive from the report after the battle: 'The dead bodies of the Earl and Marquis were brought to London in a coffin, and before they were buried, by the space of three days lay open visaged in the cathedral church of St Paul, to the intent that all men might easily perceive that they unfeignedly were dead. The common bruit ran that the King was not so joyous of the Earl's death as sorrowful for the loss of the Marquis, whom he full well knew . . . to be his faithful friend and well-willer' (Holinshed Sssv^r, Hall Mmv^v). Warwick's speech in O, however, emphasizes his heroic exhaustion rather than F's fraternal devotion, and it combines a line from the messenger's report of York's death, F 2.1.54, and Warwick's lines at F 2.3.3–5, with 'rest awhile' altered to 'yield to death'.

5.3.0.1 in triumph 'King Edward after this victory . . . was greatly rejoiced and comforted after the manner of a victorious conqueror, leading with him King Henry like a captive in most triumphant manner' (Hall Mmv^v, which adds that 'King Edward had gotten again the garland'; Holinshed Sssv^r).

5.3.24 Strike . . . drum Holinshed gives a geographically detailed account, expanding considerably on Hall, of how 'every man being bent to battle' in support of Margaret, 'gathered his power by himself' in virtually every county and major city west of London (Holinshed Sssv^v).

5.4 Shakespeare alludes only briefly by way of negative example to Hall's account of Margaret's initial reaction to Barnet: 'When she heard all these miserable chances and misfortunes . . . she like a woman all dismayed for fear, fell to the ground, her heart was pierced with sorrow. . . . The calamity and misery of her time she detested and abhorred . . . her painful labour, her care of mind, turned into infelicity she much lamented, and bewailed the evil fate and destiny of her husband' (Mmv^v–vi^r).

5.4.2 But cheerly Prior to Tewkesbury, 'the Queen and her son Prince Edward rode about the field, encouraging their soldiers, promising to them (if they did show themselves valiant against their enemies) great rewards and high promotions, innumerable gain of the spoil and booty of their adversaries, and above all other fame and renown through the whole realm' (Hall only, Nnii^r).

5.4.52–4 O . . . glories See note to 5.5.18.

5.4.67–9 thorny . . . up Whereas Hall mentions only the Lancastrians pitching their battle in a generic 'fair park' next to the town, Holinshed's topographical detail matches Edward's brief description: 'Hereupon [the

Lancastrians] pight their field in a close, even hard at the town's end . . . and upon each side of them they were defended with cumbersome lanes, deep ditches, and many hedges . . . Herewith [Edward] approached the enemy's camp, which was right hard to be assailed by reason of the deep ditches, hedges, trees, bushes, and cumbersome lanes, wherewith the same was fenced' (Sssvi[r]).

5.4.82.1 *Alarum, retreat* Holinshed continues: 'The King or (as other have) the Duke of Gloucester, taking the advantage that he adventured for, turned again face to face unto the Duke of Somerset his battle . . . and with great violence put him and his people up towards the hill from whence they were descended'. Somerset was also attacked by a secondary force of 200 spear-carriers 'in so violent wise upon the sudden, that where they had before enough to do with those with whom they were first matched, now with this new charge given . . . straightway they took them to flight' (Holinshed Sssvi[v]). Again O dramatizes this in stage terms: 'Then enter the king, Clarence and Gloucester and the rest, and make a great shout and cry, "For York, for York", and then the Queen is taken, and the Prince, and Oxford and Somerset'.

5.5.2 Away . . . straight See Commentary, 5.5.2.

5.5.10 **he** O follows Hall's account by having Margaret and Prince Edward captured in the field with the other Lancastrians ('the Prince was apprehended and kept close by Sir Richard Crofts') (Hall Nnii[r]). F, however, follows Holinshed's report of his separate capture 'as he fled towards the town'; 'After the field was ended, proclamation was made that whosoever could bring forth Prince Edward alive or dead should have an annuity of a hundred pounds during his life, and the Prince's life to be saved, if he were brought forth alive. Sir Richard Crofts . . . brought forth his prisoner Prince Edward, being a fair and well proportioned [Hall = "goodly feminine and well featured"] young gentleman' (Holinshed Sssvi[v], Hall Nnii[r]).

5.5.15 **stirring up** 'King Edward . . . demanded of [Prince Edward] how he durst so presumptuously enter into his realm with banner displayed' (Holinshed Sssvi[v], Hall Nnii[r–v]).

5.5.18 **now . . . mouth** 'The Prince, being bold of stomach and of good courage, answered saying, "To recover my father's kingdom and inheritage, from his father and grandfather to him, and from him after him to me lineally divoluted"' (Hall Nnii[v], Holinshed Sssvi[v]).

5.5.38–40.1 **Take that . . . him** 'At which words [of Prince Edward] King Edward said nothing, but with his hand thrust him from him (or as some say, struck him with his gauntlet). Whom incontinent, they that stood about, which were George Duke of Clarence, Richard Duke of Gloucester, Thomas Marquis Dorset, and William Lord Hastings, suddenly murdered and piteously manquelled [murdered]' (Hall Nnii[v],

Holinshed Sssvi^v). In O, only Edward speaks and strikes, despite 'we' at l. 43 and 5.6.34.

5.5.90 **son for me** Holinshed reports the birth of Edward's son when Edward re-enters London from Flanders: 'he went to the Queen to comfort her . . . and in the mean season was delivered of a young prince, whom she now presented unto him, to his great heart's rejoicing and comfort' (Holinshed Sssiv^r).

5.7.41 **waft** 'Queen Margaret like a prisoner was brought to London, where she remained till King René her father ransomed her with money' (Hall Nnii^v, Holinshed Sssvi^v–Ttti^r). Hall adds 'After the ransom paid, she was conveyed into France with small honour . . . and in her very extreme age she passed her days in France, more like a death than a life'.

MONTAGUE

THE Folio text's Montague seems to personify two different figures: (1) Warwick's father and York's brother-in-law, Richard Neville, in Scenes 1.1–2; (2) Warwick's brother, John Neville, Lord and later Marquis of Montague, who appears from 2.1 onwards.

In 1.1 Montague calls York his 'brother' at ll. 14 and 117–18 in both O and F. In 1.2 he is Richard's and York's 'cosen' at ll. 1, 38, 56 in O, but still York's 'brother' at ll. 4, 36, 55, and 60 in F.

O's opening direction lists '*Richard* Duke of Yorke, The Earle of *Warwicke*, The Duke of Norffolke, *Marquis Montague, Edward Earle of March* . . .' Later at 2.1.94.1–2, O reads 'Enter the Earle of *Warwike, Montague*', and throughout the text he continues to play this role. Both Edward's and York's use of 'cousin' in O 1.2 is correct in referring to Montague as the John Neville who was Warwick's brother. But 'Marquis Montague' as York's 'brother' in 1.1 is anomalous.

F's opening direction, which follows the usual (but not invariable) practice of listing nobles in order of rank, places '*Mountague*' after '*Plantagenet, Edward, Richard, Norfolke*' but before '*Warwicke, and Souldiers*'. Montague, again without title, is named after Richard and Edward in the opening direction of 1.2. When he next enters at 2.1.95.1, however, the direction reads '*Enter Warwicke, Marquesse Mountacute, and their Army*'. Here he follows Warwick and for the first time is called marquis. When he is named in subsequent directions in F, he always follows Warwick. Warwick also seems to introduce him in 2.1 as a 'new' figure by explicitly drawing attention to their relationship: 'And therefore comes my brother Montague' (168). F's use of the title 'Marquis' in 2.1 and its change in precedence apparently announces a different character under an existing role (something Shakespeare does elsewhere; e.g. 'Somerset' in Part Three represents three historical dukes). F is closer to history in styling Montague marquis in the same scene (2.1) where Warwick names Edward king and Edward vows to create his brothers Clarence and Gloucester, since Edward elevated John Neville and made his brothers dukes when he succeeded to the throne in 1463. John Neville is not mentioned by either chronicler before Towton. When he was made marquis, Montague was technically higher in rank than his brother or father, yet as the chronicles observe, the Earldom of Warwick was more ancient and distinguished: '[Edward IV] preferred Sir John Neville, to the style of Marquis Montacute, and so by that means, he was in estate and degree higher, than the earl of Warwick his elder brother, but in power, policy, and possessions, far baser and lower

[Holinshed = "far meaner"]' (Hall Hhiii[v], Holinshed Rrrii[r]). In terms of dramatic importance and historical standing, Shakespeare seems to clarify their relationship in F.

If Shakespeare had in mind two historical Montagues in F, as he seems to have done, York's 'brother' in 1.1–2 most likely refers to his brother-in-law, the Earl of Salisbury, Warwick's father. 'Old Salisbury' appears in *2 Henry VI*, where in the final scene following the first Battle of St Albans he anticipates his coming death:

> God knows how long it is I have to live,
> And it hath pleased him that three times today
> You have defended me from imminent death.
> (5.5.22–4)

The Contention conveys the same idea in different words:

> And thou braue bud of Yorkes encreasing house [= Edward],
> The small remainder of my weary life,
> I hold for thee . . .
> (H3[v])

As Shakespeare knew from Hall and Holinshed (Ggiii[v], Qqqiv[r]), Salisbury died at Pontefract in 1461 after being captured by the Queen's forces at Wakefield. O reports his death in 2.3:

> *Rich.* Thy noble father in the thickest thronges,
> Cride full for *Warwike* his thrise valiant son,
> Vntill with thousand swords he was beset,
> And manie wounds made in his aged brest,
> And as he tottering sate vpon his steede,
> He waft his hand to me and cride aloud:
> *Richard*, commend me to my valiant sonne,
> And still he cride *Warwike* reuenge my death,
> And with those words he tumbled off his horse,
> And so the noble Salsbury gaue vp the ghost.
> (C1[v])[1]

Given the testimony of Part Two and the chronicles, O's version is unlikely to originate with reporting players alone, and must be authorial. Like F, O distinguishes Warwick's father from his brother Montague, but in a different way, by reporting his death, and by giving Montague one consistent persona throughout the play—except for York's references to Montague as his 'brother' in 1.1.

In Part Three's final scene, York refers to

---

[1] In F, Richard reports the death of another of Warwick's brothers, Thomas Neville, 'the bastard [son] of Salisbury', killed at the skirmish of Ferrybridge (2.3.15–22).

> two brave bears Warwick and Montague,
> That in their chains fettered the kingly lion
> And made the forest tremble when they roared.
>
> (5.7.10–12)

While this description is apt for Warwick, it hardly corresponds to his brother's minor role. The other 'brave bear' must refer to Salisbury, as *2 Henry VI* recalls when collectively the Yorkists and Lancastrians confront each other for the first time:

> YORK
>
> . . . I am thy king, and thou a false-hearted traitor.
> Call hither to the stake my two brave bears,
> That with the very shaking of their chains,
> They may astonish these fell-lurking curs.
> (*To an attendant*)
> Bid Salisbury and Warwick come to me.
>
> *Exit attendant*
> *Enter the Earls of Warwick and Salisbury* . . .
>
> (5.1.141–145.2)

Warwick also later states: 'Now by my father's badge, old Neville's crest, | The rampant bear chained to the ragged staff' (200–1), and Cairncross notes that this visual device appears on pp. 105–7 and the frontispiece of Geoffrey Whitney's *Choice of Emblems* (1586), which Shakespeare knew, besides knowing it from living in Warwickshire and London.

Shakespeare's reasons for changing the character's name from Salisbury to Montague between Parts Two and Three and equating him with Warwick's father before 2.1 are not obvious, but they may lie partly in his reconsideration of the chronicle accounts, which is observable from revisions made elsewhere between O and F. Richard Neville gained his alternative name when he 'was espoused to Lady Alice, the only child and sole heir of Thomas Montacute Earl of Salisbury, slain at the siege of Orleans . . . of which woman he engendered Richard [= Earl of Warwick], John [= Lord and later Marquess Montague], and George [= Archbishop of York]' (Hall Eei[v], Holinshed Pppi[r–v]). Warwick's father therefore inherited his title through marriage, not through his own family. (Likewise, the chronicles tell us immediately after that Warwick inherited his earldom and title from his wife Lady Anne, sister and heir of Henry Beauchamp, first and only Duke of Warwick, 1425–25.) In *2 Henry VI* Shakespeare seems to anticipate including a scene, or at least a report, of Salisbury's death in the sequel play. This stage of composition is preserved by O, but does not explain York's two references to his 'brother' Montague in 1.1. In F, however, Shakespeare eliminated an account of Salisbury's death (just as he later disappoints expectations for the return of Falstaff raised in the Epilogue to *2 Henry IV*).

In O 1.2.38+ York asks Montague to go 'to *Norffolke* straight, | And bid the Duke to muster vppe his souldiers', whereas it is Richard who 'to *London* strait shalt post, | And bid *Richard Neuill* Earle of *Warwike* | To leaue the cittie'. Historically, Norfolk was in London (see Commentary, 1.2.36–8). After the Messenger's arrival with news of Margaret's approaching army, York reiterates his order to Montague, 'Cosen *Montague* post you hence'. He is therefore absent from the Battle of Wakefield.

In F 1.2 York initially sends 'Brother' Montague to London to 'whet on *Warwick* to this Enterprise' while Richard is sent to Norfolk. But after the Messenger's news York changes his mind and tells Richard and Edward to stay with him, while 'My Brother *Mountague* shall poste to London' (55). Montague takes his leave at ll. 60–1, promising to 'winne them'. His departure is therefore more conspicuous in F, and dramatically seems to accomplish two tasks: to allow Salisbury as Montague to die away from Wakefield, and to enable the 'new' marquis to arrive with his brother in 2.1 after Wakefield.

CASTING ANALYSIS OF 'TRUE TRAGEDY'
AND '3 HENRY VI'

THE following tables revise studies of the playing personnel and role-distribution in the Octavo and Folio texts by David Bradley, *From text to performance in the Elizabethan Theatre: Preparing the play for the stage*, and T. J. King, *Casting Shakespeare's plays: London actors and their roles, 1590–1642*.[1] In one small but important respect Bradley and King misrepresent conventional Elizabethan practices of doubling. They assume that older boys who played major female roles (e.g. Margaret) or male adolescents (e.g. Prince Edward) could not occasionally double in non-speaking male roles such as drummers, flag-carriers, or soldiers. The assignment of these parts is crucial in plays such as *True Tragedy* and *3 Henry VI*, which contain multiple battle scenes and a large number of roles overall (more than fifty in *3 Henry VI*). Evidence supplied by contemporary theatrical documents, discussed below, indicates that older boys did routinely double in these kinds of roles, which are discussed briefly in the section which follows.

Boys were taken on as apprentices to train under adult players at about the age of ten. Their training was extensive, and included fencing, dancing, and tumbling to instil physical control and ease of movement.[2] Such training would also presumably include marching and drumming, as well as singing. Boys would begin to play minor female parts at eleven to thirteen and graduate to major roles at about fifteen.[3] By this age they could be called upon to portray a wide range of emotional states using expansive gestures. Even after their voices broke, boys were able to preserve their 'female' singing voices until about sixteen, and their acting voices until nineteen or twenty.[4] Presumably the reverse also holds true: in minor male roles they could use their 'new' deeper adult voices. And at these ages, boys could look like young adult men.[5] Younger boys often played pages, while young men, who at this age would generally be physically the

---

[1] Respectively, Cambridge, 1992 and Cambridge, 1992. See also Arthur Colby Sprague, *The Doubling of Parts in Shakespeare's Plays* (1966), William A. Ringler Jr, 'The Number of Actors in Shakespeare's Early Plays', in *The Seventeenth-Century Stage*, ed. G. E. Bentley (Chicago, 1968), pp. 110–34.

[2] W. Robertson Davies, *Shakespeare's Boy Actors* (1939), pp. 27–8.

[3] T. W. Baldwin, *The Organisation and Personnel of the Shakespearean Company* (New York, 1927), pp. 33–5.

[4] Davies, pp. 34–7; J. B. Streett, 'The Durability of Boy Actors', *Notes and Queries*, n.s. xx (1973), 461–5.

[5] As opposed to boys of thirteen, the age Bradley has in mind (p. 19).

same size as adults, doubled as both female attendants and male figures such as prologues, choruses, and attendants.[6]

W. W. Greg observed that the evidence from stage plots and actors' parts for casting boys is slim.[7] Often major female roles were not specifically assigned, while minor ones were. This implied division of labour did not strike Greg as unusual because, as he put it, 'one hardly expects to find a leading lady doing hack work [i.e. doubling in minor roles] on the stage'. But the evidence from Elizabethan documents about doubling by boys or young men does not bear out Greg's anachronistic assumptions about "ladies"' roles. In the plot of *The Battle of Alcazar* the older boy Richard Jubie performed two scenes in the female role of Abdula Rais as well as three scenes as Christophero de Tavora, a young man and soldier who participates in the play's culminating battle in 5.1.[8] Jubie may also have doubled the allegorical role of Weapons (who appears with War, Death, and Blood) in the Induction to Act 4.[9] Another boy, Thomas Parsons, played the first Fury (Megaera) with two other male Furies. Since the latter also play soldiers and guards in the climactic battle scene, it is likely, as Greg allows, that Parsons would have joined them as a soldier, as would the other older boys.[10] Another piece of evidence occurs in Act 3 Scene 4 which calls for the Portuguese army, drum, and colours. It is a very full scene in which every other named character is present and only two adult actors are spare (one sharer, one hired man). Greg notes that attendants are also needed to move a chariot across the stage.[11] It therefore seems certain that some of these parts had to be taken by older boys, probably Dab, Harry, and/or James Bristow, who doubles in the major female role of Rubin. In the plot of *Orlando Furioso*, there are two boys named, Sanders Cooke and Robin Gough. Cooke played Soldan, Orgalio (a page), Medor (rival lover of Orlando) and an adult Peer. Gough took the main female role of Angelica as well as Rossillion (a count and soldier), Melissa (an old witch who speaks a Latin incantation), and a Peer. Such doubling confirms Davies's observation that mature boy actors had to possess considerable versatility in their performance skills. The evidence of both plots—especially *Alcazar*, which resembles *True Tragedy* and *3 Henry VI* in being a play of battles and massed action that makes heavy demands on its players—makes it certain that older boys or young men would have had no difficulty impersonating soldiers and doubling as drummers and flag-carriers.

Taking these factors into consideration, I have reassessed the casting of O and F by tabulating role and doubling assignments in terms of general

---

[6] Shen Lin, 'How old were the Children of Paul's?', *Theatre Notebook*, 45 (1991), 121–31.

[7] *Dramatic Documents from the Elizabethan Playhouses*, 2 vols. (Oxford, 1931), i. 66–9.

[8] W. W. Greg, *Two Elizabethan Stage Abridgements* (Oxford, 1922), pp. 66–7, 75, 84.

[9] *Abridgements*, p. 62 and cast list facing p. 68.

[10] *Abridgements*, p. 67.   [11] *Abridgements*, p. 62.

scene clearances, as well as time on and off stage within scenes, linked to precise exit and entrance lines.[12] My figures share the basic assumption established by previous investigators: that when stage directions call for multiple unspecified numbers (e.g. '*soldiers*'), a minimum of two should be assumed. The results show that while *True Tragedy* and *3 Henry VI* vary in roles and numbers within particular scenes or sequences, most notably Act 4, the moment of 'immediate juxtaposition'[13] where numbers of departing and entering characters is highest, occurs between 2.1 and 2.2 in *True Tragedy*. It requires nineteen players at this point, while *3 Henry VI* calls for seventeen. In both cases this includes four boys. Since every other scene in O requires no more than seventeen players, the extra two needed as soldiers for 2.1–2 may have been hired walk-ons. In *3 Henry VI* the highest demand occurs in 4.7, where an extra soldier is needed, and 5.1, where two 'others' silently attend the Mayor of Coventry. The two extra players were also probably hired walk-ons, in which case the personnel requirements for O and F are everywhere else the same. Even if readers judge the proposed doubling assignments to be burdensome (though in view of what surviving documents about Elizabeth staging suggest, I trust this possibility is remote[14]), potential readjustments would not lead to any significant difference between O and F in acting personnel.

Entry and exit lines in O are keyed to lineation in the Oxford facsimile reprint of the 1595 edition (Oxford, 1958), and in F to this edition. Figures in parentheses are inferred from the closest marked line number.

Notes relating to casting and role assignments

1.1.167.1 O Enter Souldiers In O, these Soldiers and the ones already on stage leave after 174 ('*King.* Conuey the soldiers hence, and then I will. | *War.* Captaine conduct them into *Tuthill* fieldes'), whereas in F they remain in view. The reason for this exit may be because O requires two more players than F prior to this point (Rutland and Drummer, reaching 17 players). This exit gives the two boys playing Queen Margaret and Prince Edward time for a costume change before they re-enter at O 209.1.

2.1.45 F looker on The Messenger has either notionally witnessed York's death, or he could have been one of the Soldiers who enter with the other Lancastrians at 1.4.26.2, in which case he watches the action and then switches sides to report York's death. I have therefore cast him as the same

[12] This kind of specificity is routinely followed by modern stage companies when assigning roles and personnel, but has not been consistently observed in academic studies. I am grateful to Ms Linda McNutt for providing me with information about this methodology and for constructing the casting tables.

[13] McMillin and MacLean, p. 99.

[14] McMillin and MacLean calculate that an actor might normally 'be assigned between four and eight roles' in a demanding play (p. 99).

actor. The fact that no Yorkist soldiers are present in 1.4 is absolute in O's opening direction, 'Enter the Duke of *Yorke solus*', while F has '*Enter Richard, Duke of Yorke*'.

2.2.0.2 O **Northerne Earles** Does not include Westmorland, as it did in 1.1.

2.2.0.3 F *Trumpettes* The practice of actors miming musical sounds produced off stage is attested by the plot of *Tamar Cam Part One* (Greg, *Dramatic Documents*) in which a trumpet part in 2.5 is taken by one of the boy actors, Dick Jubie.

2.2.80.1 O **Enter the house of** *Yorke* Presumably this means Edward, Richard, George, Warwick, Montague, and Norfolk (who dies at the Battle of Towton).

2.3.0.1 F *Warwicke* His 'immediate' re-entry, like others in this and later battle sequences, is allowed by the intervening '*Alarums*' and continuous stage action.

3.2.0.1–2 O *Montague, Hastings* They do not speak in this scene, nor are they referred to, and at the end of Edward's interview with Lady Grey he refers only to his brothers. They may therefore be ghosts. If the direction is followed, however, they could be played by actors 4 and 8, who exit at line 33 ('Lords giue vs leaue').

5.1.15.2 *Trumpeter* (inferred from F) May exit before the end of the scene and be available for doubling.

5.1.57.1 F *Enter Oxford . . . Colours* They enter the 'city' in both F and O, but only in F is it certain that Oxford re-appears aloft with Warwick ('Oh welcome Oxford, for we want thy help', l. 65). Montague and Somerset presumably also re-enter aloft to join them because the scene's closing direction calls for '*Warwicke and his companie*' (F 113.1) to exit. It seems reasonable to suppose that '*company*' refers to more than just the Mayor and Somerville. (The corollary is that the two Messengers who enter at the beginning of the scene leave when Somerville enters, or when the Yorkists do, and therefore are available to double as Drummers, Colours, or Soldiers. O makes this seems particularly likely because it identifies the first Messenger as '*Oxf. post*'. He might reasonably re-enter with Oxford later in the scene.) If Oxford's Drum and Colours do join him aloft (which modern productions sometimes stage), they are available to double for Somerset's entry, but not Montague's, which leaves too little time. Montague's Drum and Colours could likewise possibly double to accompany Clarence. For Oxford, Somerset, Montague, and their respective Drums and Soldiers, individual exits are specified in O for each party, which explicitly permits doubling.

5.3.0.1–2 F *in triumph . . . and the rest* May imply more than the usual minimum of two soldiers, perhaps a flag-carrier, as well as Hastings, who is named in the next scene in O at Edward's entrance, 66.1.

5.5.0.2 *Soldiers* (inferred from F) They enter guarding Oxford and Somerset and escort them off at 6.1; they are left with five lines before bringing in Prince Edward at 11.1. This may allow for doubling. O by contrast has Prince Edward enter guarded with the others at the beginning of the scene, which may require an extra Soldier (one each to lead off Oxford and Somerset at 5.1 and 6.1, one to lead away Queen Margaret at 82, and two to carry off Prince Edward's body—unless it is taken away by Clarence and Edward).

TRUE TRAGEDY

Casting Analysis

Octavo/Scene	Actor	Cast/Role	Enter	Exit
1.1	Mr 1	Duke of York	0.1	206.1
	Mr 2	Earl of Warwick	0.1	207
	Mr 3	Norfolk	0.2	208
	Mr 4	Montague	0.2	209
	Mr 5	Edward	0.2	206.1
	Mr 6	Richard	0.3	206.1
	b15	Rutland	0.3–4	206.1
	b16	Drum (1)	0.4	175
	Mr 12, 17	Soldiers (2)	0.4	175
	Mr 7	King Henry	49.1	274
	Mr 8	Exeter	49.1	274
	Mr 9	Northumberland	49.2	186
	Mr 10	Westmorland	49.2	180
	Mr 11	Clifford	49.3	188
	b13, 14	Soldiers (2)	167.1	175
	b13	Queen Margaret	209.1	260
	b14	Prince Edward	209.1	262
1.2	Mr 5	Edward	0.1	69
	Mr 6	Richard	0.1	69
	Mr 4	Montague	0.1	69
	Mr 1	Duke of York	3.1	69
	Mr 12	Messenger	48	69
	Mr 3	Sir John Mortimer	50.1	69
	Mr 17	Sir Hugh Mortimer	50.1	69
1.3	b 15	Rutland	0.1–2	52 (d)
	Mr 10	Tutor	0.2	7
	Mr 11	Clifford	2.1	52
	Mr 8, 12	Soldiers (2)	2.1	7

Octavo/Scene	Actor	Cast/Role	Enter	Exit
1.4	Mr 1	Duke of York	0.1	180.1 (d)
	b 13	Queen Margaret	26.1	180.1
	Mr 11	Clifford	26.1	180.1
	Mr 9	Northumberland	26.1	180.1
	Mr 8, 12	Soldiers (2)	26.2	180.1
2.1	Mr 5	Edward	0.1	209.1
	Mr 6	Richard	0.1	209.1
	Mr 3	Drum (1)	0.1	209.1
	Mr 17, 18	Soldiers (2)	0.2	209.1
	Mr 10	Messenger	45	67
	Mr 2	Warwick	94.1	209.1
	Mr 4	Montague	94.1	209.1
	b 15	Drum (1)	94.2	209.1
	b 16	Ancient	94.2	209.1
	Mr 12, b 16	Soldiers (2)	94.2	209.1
	Mr 1	Messenger	200.1	209.1
2.2	Mr 7	King Henry	0.1	177.1
	b 13	Queen Margaret	0.1	177.1
	b 14	Prince Edward 'Northerne Earles'	0.1	177.1
	Mr 11	Clifford	0.2	177.1
	Mr 9	Northumberland	0.2	177.1
	Mr 8	Drum (1)	0.2	177.1
	Mr 10, 19	Soldiers (2)	0.3	177.1
	Mr 1	Messenger 'house of *Yorke*'	66.1	177.1
	Mr 5	Edward	80.1	177.1
	Mr 6	Richard	80.1	177.1
	Mr 12	George	80.1	177.1
	Mr 2	Warwick	80.1	177.1
	Mr 4	Montague	80.1	177.1
	Mr 3	Norfolk	80.1	177.1
2.3	Mr 2	Warwick	0.1	48.1
	Mr 5	Edward	5.1	48.1
	Mr 12	George	(8.1)	48.1
	Mr 6	Richard	(13.1)	48.1
2.4	Mr 6	Richard	0.1	11.2
	Mr 11	Clifford	0.2	11.2
	Mr 2	Warwick	11.1	11.2

Octavo/Scene	Actor	Cast/Role	Enter	Exit
2.5	Mr 7	King Henry	0.1	137
	Mr 4, 10	Soldier with Dead Man	21.1	114.1
	Mr 9, 17	Soldier with Dead Man	70.1	122.1
	b 13	Queen Margaret	124.1	137
	b 14	Prince Edward	133.1	137
	Mr 8	Exeter	128.1	137
2.6	Mr 11	Clifford	0.1	110.1 (d)
	Mr 5	Edward	30.1	110.1
	Mr 6	Richard	30.1	110.1
	Mr 2	Warwick	30.1	110.1
	Mr 12	George	30.1	110.1
	Mr 9, 10	Soldiers (2)	30.2	110.1
3.1	Mr 8, 17	Keepers (2)	0.1	101.1
	Mr 7	King Henry	12.1	101.1
3.2	Mr 5	King Edward	0.1	123
	Mr 12	Clarence	0.1	123
	Mr 6	Gloucester	0.1	195
	Mr 4	Montague	0.1	33
	Mr 8	Hastings	0.2	33
	b 16	Lady Grey	0.2	123
	Mr 9	Messenger	117.1	123
3.3	Mr 11	King Lewis	0.1	255
	b 15	Lady Bona	0.1	255
	b 13	Queen Margaret	0.1–2	255
	b 14	Prince Edward	0.2	255
	Mr 1	Oxford	0.2	255
	Mr 9	'Attendant'	0.3	255
	Mr 10	Lord Bourbon	0.3	255
	Mr 2	Warwick	(43.1)	265
	Mr 17	Post	155.1	255
4.1	Mr 5	King Edward	0.1	148.1
	b 16	Queen Elizabeth	0.1	148.1
	Mr 12	Clarence	0.1	123
	Mr 9	Somerset	0.1	123
	Mr 6	Gloucester	0.2	148.1
	Mr 4	Montague	0.2	148.1

Octavo/Scene	Actor	Cast/Role	Enter	Exit
	Mr 8	Hastings	0.2	148.1
	Mr 3	Pembroke	0.3	148.1
	Mr 4, 17	Soldiers (2)	0.3	148.1
	Mr 10	Messenger	85.1	148.1
4.2 (continuous to 4.3)	Mr 2	Warwick	0.1	—
	Mr 1	Oxford	0.1	—
	Mr 11, 17	Soldiers (2)	0.1	—
	Mr 12	Clarence	3	—
	Mr 9	Somerset	3	—
4.3	Mr 2	Warwick	—	(66.1)
	Mr 10	Tent Guard (1)	(23)	26.1
	Mr 11, 17	Soldiers (2)	—	57.1
	Mr 6	Gloucester	(26.1)	(26.1)
	Mr 8	Hastings	(26.1)	(26.1)
	Mr 1	Oxford	—	(66.1)
	Mr 5	Edward	26	57.1
	Mr 12	Clarence	—	(66.1)
	Mr 9	Somerset	—	(66.1)
4.5	Mr 6	Gloucester	0.1	27.1
	Mr 8	Hastings	0.1	27.1
	Mr 3	Stanley	0.1	27.1
	Mr 5	Edward	(13.1)	27.1
	Mr 4	Huntsman	(13.1)	27.1
4.4	b 16	Queen Elizabeth	0.1	24
	Mr 1	Lord Rivers	0.1	24
4.7	Mr 5	Edward	0.1	83.1
	Mr 6	Gloucester	0.1	83.1
	Mr 8	Hastings	0.1	83.1
	Mr 10, b 13	Hollanders (2)	0.2	83.1
	Mr 11	Mayor of York	16.1	29.1
			30.1	83.1
	Mr 3	Sir John Montgomery	38.1	83.1
	b 15	Drum (1)	38.2	83.1
	b 14, 16	Soldiers (2)	38.2	83.1
4.6 (continuous to 4.8)	Mr 2	Warwick	0.1	—
	Mr 12	Clarence	0.1	—
	Mr 7	King Henry	0.2	—

Octavo/Scene	Actor	Cast/Role	Enter	Exit
	Mr 1	Oxford	0.2	—
	Mr 9	Somerset	0.2	—
b 15	Earl of Richmond	0.3	—
	Mr 4	Montague	0.3	—
4.8	Mr 17	'one with letter'	0.1	(33)
	Mr 2	Warwick	—	(33)
	Mr 12	Clarence	—	(33)
	Mr 7	King Henry	—	59.1
	Mr 1	Oxford	—	(33)
	Mr 9	Somerset	—	(33)
	b 15	Earl of Richmond	—	(33)
	Mr 4	Montague	—	(33)
	Mr 5	Edward	33.1	59.1
	Mr 3, 10	'his train' (2)	33.1	59.1
5.1	Mr 2	Warwick	0.1	113.1
	Mr 7	Oxford Post	0.1	11
	Mr 12	Montague Post	0.1	11
	Mr 8	Summerfield	0.1	113.1
	Mr 5	Edward	11.1	113.1
	b 13, 14	'his power' (2)	11.1	113.1
	Mr 6	Gloucester	11.1	113.1
	Mr 1	Oxford	58.1	59
	b 15	Drum (1)	58.1	59
	Mr 10, b 16	Soldiers (2)	58.1	59
	Mr 9	Somerset	(62.1)	63
	Mr 11	Drum (1)	(62.1)	63
	Mr 3, 17	Soldiers (2)	(62.1)	63
	Mr 4	Montague	(66.1)	67
	b 15	Drum (1)	(66.1)	67
	Mr 10, b 16	Soldiers (2)	(66.1)	67
	Mr 12	Clarence	(69)	113.1
	Mr 11	Drum (1)	(69)	113.1
	Mr 3, 17	Soldiers (2)	(69)	113.1
5.2	Mr 2	Warwick	0.1	(51) (d)
	Mr 1	Oxford	26.1	(51)
	Mr 9	Somerset	26.1	(51)
5.3	Mr 5	Edward	0.1	(25)
	Mr 12	Clarence	0.1	(25)

Octavo/Scene	Actor	Cast/Role	Enter	Exit
	Mr 6	Gloucester	0.1	(25)
	Mr 3, 4	Soldiers (2)	0.1	(25)
5.4 (continuous to 5.5)	b 13	Queen Margaret	0.1	—
	b 14	Prince Edward	0.1	—
	Mr 1	Oxford	0.1	—
	Mr 9	Somerset	0.1–2	—
	b 16	Drum (1)	0.2	—
	Mr 11, 3	Soldiers (2)	0.2	—
	Mr 10	Messenger	57.1	82.1
	Mr 5	King Edward	66.1	82.1
			82.2	—
	Mr 12	Clarence	66.1	82.1
			82.2	—
	Mr 6	Gloucester	66.1	82.1
			82.2	—
	Mr 8	Hastings	66.1	82.1
			82.2	—
	Mr 2, 4	Soldiers (2)	66.1	82.1
			82.2	—
5.5	Mr 5	King Edward	—	90.1
	Mr 1	Oxford	—	5.1
	Mr 9	Somerset	—	6.1
	b 16	Drum	—	6.1
	Mr 11, 3	Soldiers (2)	—	5.1, 6.1
	b 13	Queen Margaret	—	82
	b 14	Prince Edward	—	90.1 (d)
	Mr 6	Gloucester	—	50.1
	Mr 2, 4	Soldiers (2)	—	82
	Mr 12	Clarence	—	90.1
	Mr 8	Hastings	—	90.1
5.6	Mr 6	Gloucester	0.1	93.1
	Mr 7	Henry	0.1	93.1 (d)
5.7	Mr 5	King Edward	0.1	46.1
	b 16	Queen Elizabeth	0.1	46.1
	b 15	Nurse	0.1	46.1
	Mr 12	Clarence	0.2	46.1
	Mr 8	Hastings	0.3	46.1
	b 13, 14	'Attendants' (2)	0.3	46.1
	Mr 6	Gloucester	0.3	46.1

Summary

Octavo	Mr 1	York, Oxford, Rivers, Messenger, Soldier
	Mr 2	Warwick, Soldier
	Mr 3	Norfolk, Sir John Mortimer, Pembroke, Stanley, Montgomery, Drum, Soldier, Train
	Mr 4	Montague, Sir Hugh Mortimer, Soldier with dead man, Huntsman, Soldier
	Mr 5	Edward
	Mr 6	Richard/Gloucester
	Mr 7	King Henry, Oxford Post
	Mr 8	Exeter, Keeper, Hastings, Summerfield, Drum, Soldier
	Mr 9	Northumberland, Soldier with dead man, Attendant, Soldier, Messenger, Somerset
	Mr 10	Westmorland, Tutor, Messenger, Dead Man, Soldier, Lord Bourbon, Tent Guard, Hollander, Train
	Mr 11	Clifford, King Lewis, Mayor of York, Drum, Soldier
	Mr 12	George/Clarence, Soldier, Messenger, Montague Post
	b 13	Queen Margaret, Soldier, Hollander, Power, Attendant
	b 14	Prince Edward, Soldier, Power, Attendant
	b 15	Rutland, Lady Bona, Richmond, Drum, Nurse
	b 16	Lady Grey/Queen Elizabeth, Drum, Ancient, Soldier
	Mr 17	Soldier, Sir Hugh Mortimer, Dead Man, Keeper, Post, One with letter
	Mr 18	Soldier (2.1 only)
	Mr 19	Soldier (2.2 only)

3 HENRY VI

Casting Analysis

Folio/Scene	Actor	Cast/Role	Enter	Exit
1.1	Mr 1	York	0.1	210.1
	Mr 2	Edward	0.2	210.1
	Mr 3	Richard	0.2	210.1
	Mr 4	Norfolk	0.3	210.2
	Mr 5	Montague	0.3	210.2
	Mr 6	Warwick	0.3	210.1
	Mr 12, 17	Soldiers (2)	0.4	210.1
	Mr 7	King Henry	49.1	274.1
	Mr 8	Clifford	49.1	189.1
	Mr 9	Northumberland	49.1–2	189.1

Folio/Scene	Actor	Cast/Role	Enter	Exit
	Mr 10	Westmorland	49.2	189.1
	Mr 11	Exeter	49.2–3	274
	b 13, 14	'the rest' (2 Soldiers)	49.3	189.2
	b 15, 16	Soldiers (2 'show')	170.1	210.1
	b 13	Queen Margaret	211.1	264.1
	b 14	Prince Edward	211.1	264.1
1.2	Mr 3	Richard	0.1	75.1
	Mr 2	Edward	0.1	75.1
	Mr 5	Montague	0.1	61.1
	Mr 1	York	3.1	75.1
	Mr 12	Messenger	47.1	75.1
	Mr 4	John Mortimer	61.2	75.1
	Mr 9	Hugh Mortimer	61.2–3	75.1
1.3	b 15	Rutland	0.1	52.1 (d)
	Mr 10	Tutor	0.1	9.1
	Mr 8	Clifford	1.1	52.1
	Mr 12, 17	Soldiers (2)	1.1	9.1
1.4	Mr 1	York	0.1	180.1 (d)
	b 13	Queen Margaret	26.1	180.1
	Mr 8	Clifford	26.1	180.1
	Mr 9	Northumberland	26.1	180.1
	b 14	Prince Edward	26.2	180.1
	Mr 10, 12	Soldiers (2)	26.2	180.1
2.1	Mr 2	Edward	0.1	209.1
	Mr 3	Richard	0.1	209.1
	Mr 11, 12	'their power' (2)	0.1	209.1
	Mr 10	Messenger	42.1	209.1
	Mr 6	Warwick	94.1	209.1
	Mr 5	Montague	94.1	209.1
	Mr 1, b 16	'army' (2)	94.2	209.1
	Mr 4	Messenger	204.1	209.1
2.2	Mr 7	King Henry	0.1	177.1
	b 13	Queen Margaret	0.1	177.1
	Mr 8	Clifford	0.1	177.1
	Mr 9	Northumberland	0.2	177.1
	b 14	Prince Edward	0.2	177.1
	b 15	Drum	0.2	177.1
	Mr 11, 17	Trumpets (2)	0.3	177.1

Folio/Scene	Actor	Cast/Role	Enter	Exit
	Mr 10	Messenger	66.1	177.1
	Mr 2	Edward	80.1	177.1
	Mr 6	Warwick	80.1	177.1
	Mr 3	Richard	80.1	177.1
	Mr 12	George	80.1	177.1
	Mr 4	Norfolk	80.2	177.1
	Mr 5	Montague	80.2	177.1
	Mr 1, b 16	Soldiers (2)	80.2	177.1
2.3	Mr 6	Warwick	0.1	56
	Mr 2	Edward	5.1	56
	Mr 12	George	8.1	56
	Mr 3	Richard	13.1	56
2.4	Mr 3	Richard	0.1	13
	Mr 8	Clifford	0.1	11.2
	Mr 6	Warwick	11.1	13
2.5	Mr 7	King Henry	0.1	139
	Mr 10, 5	Son with father	54.1–2	113.1
	Mr 9, b 15	Father with son	54.2–3	122.1
	b 13	Queen Margaret	124.1	139
	b 14	Prince Edward	124.1–2	139
	Mr 11	Exeter	124.2	139
2.6	Mr 8	Clifford	0.1	109.1 (d)
	Mr 2	Edward	29.2	109.1
	Mr 6	Warwick	29.2	109.1
	Mr 3	Richard	29.2	109.1
	Mr 9, 10	Soldiers (2)	29.3	109.1
	Mr 5	Montague	29.3	109.1
	Mr 12	George	29.3	109.1
3.1	Mr 11	1 Gamekeeper	0.1	100
	Mr 5	2 Gamekeeper	0.1	100
	Mr 7	King Henry	12.1	100
3.2	Mr 2	King Edward	0.1	123.1
	Mr 3	Gloucester	0.1	195
	Mr 12	Clarence	0.2	123.1
	b 16	Lady Grey	0.2	123.1
	Mr 11	Nobleman	117.1	123.1

Folio/Scene	Actor	Cast/Role	Enter	Exit
3.3	Mr 8	King Lewis	0.1	256.1
	b 15	Lady Bona	0.1–2	256.1
	Mr 10	Admiral Bourbon	0.2	256.1
	b 14	Prince Edward	0.2–3	256.1
	b 13	Queen Margaret	0.3	256.1
	Mr 1	Oxford	0.3	256.1
	Mr 6	Warwick	42.1	266
	Mr 17	Post	162.1	233.1
4.1	Mr 3	Gloucester	0.1	148
	Mr 12	Clarence	0.1	123.1
	Mr 9	Somerset	0.1	123.1
	Mr 5	Montague	0.2	148
	Mr 2	King Edward	6.1	148
	b 16	Queen Elizabeth	6.1	148
	Mr 4	Pembroke	6.2	132.1
	Mr 10	Stafford	6.2	132.1
	Mr 11	Hastings	6.2	148
	Mr 17	Post	84.1	148
4.2	Mr 6	Warwick	0.1	29.1
	Mr 1	Oxford	0.1	29.1
	Mr 8, 10	Soldiers (2)	0.1–2	29.1
	Mr 12	Clarence	2.1	29.1
	Mr 9	Somerset	2.1	29.1
4.3	b 13, 14, 15	3 Watchmen	0.1	27.2
	Mr 6	Warwick	22.1	27.3
			27.4	64
	Mr 12	Clarence	22.1	27.3
			27.5	64
	Mr 1	Oxford	22.1	27.3
			27.5	64
	Mr 9	Somerset	22.1	27.3
			27.5	59
	Mr 5, 8	Soldiers (2)	22.2	27.3
			27.5	59
	Mr 2	King Edward	27.6	59
	Mr 3	Gloucester	27.7	27.7
	Mr 11	Hastings	27.7	27.7

Folio/Scene	Actor	Cast/Role	Enter	Exit
4.4	Mr 10	Rivers	0.1	35
	b 16	Queen Elizabeth	0.1	35
4.5	Mr 3	Gloucester	0.1	29
	Mr 11	Hastings	0.1	29
	Mr 4	Stanley	0.1–2	29
	b 13, 14	Soldiers (2)	0.2	29
	Mr 2	King Edward	13.1	29
	Mr 8	Huntsman	13.1	29
4.6	Mr 7	King Henry	0.1	88.1
	Mr 12	Clarence	0.1	88.1
	Mr 6	Warwick	0.2	88.1
	Mr 9	Somerset	0.2	102
	b 15	Richmond	0.2	102
	Mr 1	Oxford	0.3	102
	Mr 5	Montague	0.3	88.1
	Mr 10	Lieutenant	0.3	88.1
	b 16	Post	76.1	88.1
4.7	Mr 2	King Edward	0.1	87
	Mr 3	Gloucester	0.1	87
	Mr 11	Hastings	0.1	87
	Mr 18, b 13	Soldiers (2)	0.2	87
	Mr 8	Mayor of York	16.1	29.1
			34.1	87
	Mr 10, 17	Aldermen (2)	16.2	29.1
			34.2	87
	Mr 4	Montgomery	39.1	87
	b 15	Drum	39.1	87
	b 14, 16	Soldiers (2)	39.2	87
4.8	Mr 7	King Henry	0.1	57.1
	Mr 6	Warwick	0.1	32.1
	Mr 5	Montague	0.1	32.1
	Mr 12	Clarence	0.2	32.1
	Mr 1	Oxford	0.2	32.1
	Mr 9	Somerset	0.2	32.1
	Mr 11	Exeter	32.2	57.2
	Mr 2	King Edward	51.1	64.1
	Mr 4, 10	Soldiers (2)	51.1	57.1
	Mr 3	Gloucester	51.1	64.1
	b 13, 14	'others' (2)	51.2	64.1

Folio/Scene	Actor	Cast/Role	Enter	Exit
5.1	Mr 6	Warwick	0.1	113.2
			113.2	113.3
	Mr 10	Mayor of Coventry	0.1	113.2
			113.2	113.3
	Mr 7, 8	Messengers (2)	0.1–2	6.1
	Mr 18, 19	'others' (2)	0.2	113.2
	Mr 4	Somerville	6.2	113.3
	Mr 2	King Edward	15.1	113.1
	Mr 3	Gloucester	15.1	113.1
	Mr 17	Trumpeter	15.2	57.1
	b 13, 14	Soldiers (2)	15.2	113.1
	Mr 1	Oxford	57.1	59.1
			65.1	113.3
	Mr 8	Drum	57.1	59.1
			65.1	113.3
	Mr 7	Colours	57.1	59.1
			65.1	113.3
	Mr 5	Montague	66.1	113.3
	b 15	Drum	66.1	67.1
	b 16	Colours	66.1	67.1
	Mr 9	Somerset	71.1	113.3
	Mr 17	Drum	71.1	72.1
	Mr 11	Colours	71.1	72.1
	Mr 12	Clarence	75.1	113.1
	b 15	Drum	75.1	113.1
	b 16	Colours	75.1	113.1
5.2	Mr 2	King Edward	0.1	4
	Mr 6	Warwick	0.2	50.1 (d)
	Mr 1	Oxford	28.1	50.1
	Mr 9	Somerset	28.1	50.1
5.3	Mr 2	King Edward	0.1	24.1
	Mr 3	Gloucester	0.2	24.1
	Mr 12	Clarence	0.2	24.1
	Mr 4, 5	Soldiers (2)	0.2	24.1
5.4	b 13	Queen Margaret	0.1	82.1
	b 14	Prince Edward	0.1–2	82.1
	Mr 9	Somerset	0.2	82.1
	Mr 1	Oxford	0.2	82.1
	Mr 4, 8	Soldiers (2)	0.2	82.1

Folio/Scene	Actor	Cast/Role	Enter	Exit
	Mr 10	Messenger	59.1	82.1
	Mr 2	Edward	66.1	82.1
	Mr 3	Gloucester	66.1	82.1
	Mr 12	Clarence	66.2	82.1
	Mr 5, 6	Soldiers (2)	66.2	82.1
5.5	Mr 2	King Edward	0.1	90
	Mr 3	Gloucester	0.1	50
	Mr 12	Clarence	0.1	90
	Mr 4, 8	Soldiers (2)	0.2	6.1
			11.1	82.2
	Mr 5, 6	Soldiers (2)	0.1	82.1
	b 13	Queen Margaret	0.2	82.1
	Mr 1	Oxford	0.2	6.1
	Mr 9	Somerset	0.2	6.1
	b 14	Prince Edward	11.1	82.2 (d)
5.6	Mr 7	King Henry	0.1	93.1 (d)
	Mr 3	Gloucester	0.1	93.1
	Mr 1	Lieutenant	0.2	6.1
5.7	Mr 2	King Edward	0.1	46.1
	b 16	Queen Elizabeth	0.1	46.1
	Mr 12	Clarence	0.2	46.1
	Mr 3	Gloucester	0.2	46.1
	Mr 11	Hastings	0.2	46.1
	b 15	Nurse	0.2	46.1
	b 13, 14	Attendants	0.3	46.1

Summary

Folio		
	Mr 1	York, Army, Oxford, Lieutenant
	Mr 2	Edward
	Mr 3	Richard/Gloucester
	Mr 4	Norfolk, John Mortimer, Messenger, Pembroke, Stanley, Soldier, Montgomery, Somerville
	Mr 5	Montague, Gamekeeper, Soldier, Son's father
	Mr 6	Warwick, Soldier
	Mr 7	Henry, Messenger
	Mr 8	Clifford, King Lewis, Huntsman, Mayor of York, Messenger, Trumpeter, Soldier

Mr 9	Northumberland, Hugh Mortimer, Father, Somerset, Soldier
Mr 10	Westmorland, Tutor, Son, Bourbon, Stafford, Rivers, Lieutenant, Alderman, Mayor of Coventry, Messenger, Drum, Soldier
Mr 11	Exeter, Hastings, Trumpet, Messenger, Gamekeeper, Nobleman, Power, Other, Colours
Mr 12	George/Clarence, Messenger, Soldier, Power
b 13	Queen Margaret, Watchman, Soldier, Other, Rest, Attendant
b 14	Prince Edward, Watchman, Soldier, Other, Rest, Attendant
b 15	Rutland, Father's son, Lady Bona, Watchman, Richmond, Drum, Soldier, Nurse
b 16	Lady Grey/Queen Elizabeth, Post, Drum, Power, Army, Colours, Soldier
Mr 17	Colours, Soldier, Trumpeter, Post, Alderman, Drum, Soldier
Mr 18	Soldier (4.7), Other (5.1)
Mr 19	Other (5.1 only)

QUEEN MARGARET'S TEWKESBURY ORATION

THE Folio version of Margaret's speech at 5.4.1–38 is based on Arthur
Brooke's *The Tragical History of Romeus and Juliet* (1562, Evi^v–vii^r, reproduced in a slightly different and unmodernized version in Geoffrey Bullough's *Narrative and Dramatic Sources of Shakespeare*, vol. i (1957), p. 321,
ll. 1359–80).

A wise man in the midst of troubles and distress
Still stands not wailing present harm, but seeks his harm's redress,
As when the winter flaws with dreadful noise arise
And heave the foamy swelling waves up to the starry skies,
So that the bruisèd barque, in cruel seas betossed,   5
Despaireth of the happy haven in danger to be lost.
The pilot bold at helm cries, 'Mates, strike now your sail',
And turns her stem into the waves that strongly her assail.
Then, driven hard upon the bare and wrackful shore,
In greater danger to be wrecked than he had been before,   10
He seeth his ship full right against the rock to run,
But yet he doth what lieth in him the perilous rock to shun.
Sometimes the beaten boat, by cunning government—
The anchors lost, the cables broke, and all the tackle spent,
The rudder smitten off, and overboard the mast—   15
Doth win the long desirèd port, the stormy danger past.
But if the master, dread and over-pressed with woe,
Begin to wring his hands and lets the guiding rudder go,
The ship rents on the rock or sinketh in the deep,
And eke the coward drenchèd is. So, if thou still beweep   20
And seek not how to help the changes that do chance,
Thy cause of sorrow shall increase, thou cause of thy mischance.

ALTERATIONS TO LINEATION

THE following list records this edition's changes to the Folio's printing of verse lines, as well as emendations adopted by previous editors but rejected by this edition in favour of the Folio's arrangement. It does not cite every attempt at reordering the play's verse, or instances of short lines shared by two speakers that editors combine as single verse-lines (since the Folio never follows the modern practice of indenting the second half of a divided line to indicate this). All Folio entries appear in original spelling.

1.1.76–7	I . . . thine] F; *as one verse-line* WRIGHT, *Works*
114	You . . . lose] POPE; now,/ F
117	Good . . . arms] POPE; Brother,/ F
156	Thou . . . power] POPE; deceiu'd:/ F
212	Here . . . anger] POPE; Queene,/ F
265	Poor . . . son] POPE; Queene,/ F
1.2.49	The . . . lords] POPE; Queene,/ F
53	Ay . . . them] POPE; Sword./ F
69	I . . . order] POPE; Drummes:/ F
1.3.10–12	How . . . them] F; *as two lines* (fear$_\wedge$/) POPE
22–3	In . . . enter] POPE; *as three lines* (Boy:/ passage$_\wedge$/) F
47	No . . . die] F; *as two lines* (cause!/) POPE
1.4.111	She-wolf . . . France] POPE; France,/ F
120	Were . . . shameless] POPE; thee,/ F
152–3	That . . . blood] WARBURTON; *as three lines* (his,/ toucht,/) F
2.1.33	'Tis . . . of] POPE; strange,/ F
41	Nay . . . it] POPE; Daughters:/ F
2.2.101	What . . . crown] POPE; *Henry,*/ F
2.3.44	Brother . . . Warwick] POPE; Brother,/ F
48	Away . . . farewell] POPE; away:/ F
2.6.67	If . . . words] POPE; think'st,/ F
75	They . . . wont] POPE; *Clifford,*/ F
3.1.80	No . . . king] F; *as two lines* (No;/) STEEVENS–REED
93	We . . . Edward] POPE; king,/ F
3.3.16–18	And . . . mischance] THEOBALD; *as four lines* (side./ yoake,/ triumph,/) F
21	Those . . . thoughts] ROWE; words$_\wedge$/ F
38	Renownèd . . . storm] ROWE; Queene,/ F
59	And . . . behalf] POPE; Madame,/ F

134 Then . . . Edward's] POPE; thus:/ F
163 My . . . you] POPE; Ambassador,/ F
166 And . . . not] HANMER; you:/ F
171 Warwick . . . Queen] POPE; Newes?/ F
199 Warwick . . . love] POPE; Warwicke,/ F
233–4 There's . . . Warwick] F; *as one verse-line* WRIGHT, *Works*
234–5 But . . . men] F; *as one line* OXFORD
4.1.9 Now . . . choice] POPE; Clarence,/ F
11 As . . . Warwick] POPE; France,/ F
20–4 Not . . . together] F; *as three lines* (wish∧/ together./ well./)
POPE; *as four lines* (I:/ sever'd,/ pity,/) CAPELL
30–2 Then . . . Bona] POPE; *as four lines* (opinion:/ Enemie,/
Marriage∧/) F
62 In . . . judgement] POPE; selfe,/ F
85 Now . . . France] F; news,/ CAPELL
89–90 Go . . . them] CAPELL; *as three lines* (thee:/ words,/) F
104 'Tell . . . done] POPE; she)/ F
116 Ay . . . friendship] POPE; Soueraigne,/ F
118 Belike . . . younger] POPE; elder;/ F
124–5 Not . . . crown] POPE; *as three lines* (I:/ I∧/) CAPELL; (I:/
matter:)/ F
4.3.30 The . . . parted] POPE; Duke?/ F
41 Yea . . . too] POPE (*subs.*); Clarence,/ F
4.4.4 What . . . Warwick] POPE; battell∧/ F
25 But . . . become] POPE; Madam,/ F
4.5.14 This . . . game] POPE; Lord,/ F
15 Nay . . . stand] POPE; man,/ F
20–1 But . . . lord] F; *as one verse-line* WRIGHT, *Works*
21 To . . . Flanders] CAPELL (*as one verse-line, assigned all to
Hastings*); Lord,/ F
25 Huntsman . . . along] POPE; thou?/ F
28 Bishop . . . frown] POPE; farwell,/ F
4.6.68–9 Come . . . thoughts] POPE; *as three lines* (Hope:/ truth∧/)
F
4.7.10 The . . . this] POPE; fast?/ F
17 My . . . coming] POPE; Lords,/ F
45–7 Thanks . . . rest] POPE; *as four lines* (*Mountgomerie:*/ Crowne,/
Dukedome,/) F
59 When . . . claim] POPE; stronger,/ F
76 Thanks . . . all] POPE; *Mountgomery,*/ F
5.1.48 Come . . . down] POPE; *Warwicke,*/ F
53 Sail . . . friend] POPE; canst,/ F
107 What . . . fight] POPE; *Warwicke,*/ F

5.2.47–8 O . . . soul] *as one verse-line* POPE, CAIRNCROSS

      48–9 Sweet . . . heaven] CAPELL; *as three lines* (soul!/ bids∧/) POPE;
            Soule:/ selues,/ F

5.5.41–2 O . . . shall] F; *as one verse-line* CAIRNCROSS

    5.6.57 I'll . . . speech] POPE; more:/ F

INDEX

THIS is a selective index to words and expressions explained in the Commentary, and to names and original works mentioned throughout the edition. It excludes biblical quotations, proverbs, and classical allusions. A group entry, 'productions', is subheaded according to director, place or company, and date (e.g. Hands, RSC (1977)). An asterisk indicates a note that supplements information given in the *Oxford English Dictionary*.

The Oxford World's Classics Website

www.worldsclassics.co.uk

- Information about new titles
- Explore the full range of Oxford World's Classics
- Links to other literary sites and the main OUP webpage
- Imaginative competitions, with bookish prizes
- Peruse *Compass*, the Oxford World's Classics magazine
- Articles by editors
- Extracts from Introductions
- A forum for discussion and feedback on the series
- Special information for teachers and lecturers

www.worldsclassics.co.uk